Disaster at Cane Creek

Disaster at Cane Creek

An Unforgettable Story Especially For Those Who Lived It

Kymberly Mele

Copyright © 2017 Kymberly Mele
All rights reserved.

ISBN: 9780998975207
ISBN: 0998975206

Publisher: Dulcinea Publishing:
Salt Lake City, Utah, 2017.

Library of Congress Control Number: 2017911333
Kymberly Mele, Vernal, Utah

Front Cover Photo: Survivors, Paul McKinney and Blake Hanna, brought to the surface of the mine by two mine rescuers, Frank Markosek and Henry Laviolette, and were helped out of the bucket by rescue workers, August 28, 1963. (Carl Iwasaki/*LIFE Magazine*, 1963/Getty Images)

Dedication

Dedicated to the twenty-five miners at Cane Creek: the eighteen men who lost their lives in the fiery explosion and the loved ones who mourned them; the seven men who lived, their spirit of survival and all who rejoiced in their rescue. And to the mine rescue teams who worked tirelessly with the faith their job would not be in vain while putting their lives in danger going into the depths of the earth to aid another human being, while Grand Providence looked down upon them all.

And a special dedication to my father, Donald Blake Hanna (1936-2017). A survivor at Cane Creek, he was able to read the finished manuscript a month before he passed away.

Contents

Illustrations ix

Part One 1
Chapter 1   Mining, A Hazardous Occupation 3
Chapter 2   "In The Land of Moab" 21
Chapter 3   Point of Eruption 45
Chapter 4   Caught in the Smoke 65
Chapter 5   Chaotic Aftermath 75
Chapter 6   Rescue Preparations Underway 83
Chapter 7   Enduring the Unknown 100
Chapter 8   "A Special Breed" 106

Part Two 127
Chapter 9   Into the Deep Abyss 129
Chapter 10 "A Miracle if Anyone is Alive" 149
Chapter 11 Running out of Time 166
Chapter 12 "Nine Men Alive!" 203

Part Three 217
Chapter 13   "Free at Last". 219
Chapter 14   Rumor Mill and Erroneous Reports 243
Chapter 15   "Canary in the Coal Mine" Moment. 269

Part Four. 295
Chapter 16   Back to "Plan A" 297
Chapter 17   Utter Turmoil of Waiting. 315

Part Five 349
Chapter 18   Charges Hit the Fan. 351
Chapter 19   Behind the Barricade?. 359
Chapter 20   Search of the Entire Mine 364
Chapter 21   Final Announcement. 376
Chapter 22   Tombstone and Moon Lilies 392

Aftermath. 399
Chapter 23   Blowin' in the Wind 401
Chapter 24   Million to One Combination. 425
Chapter 25   Charges and Countercharges 444
Chapter 26   Wheels of Justice?. 479
Chapter 27   Life Goes On. 493
Chapter 28   Epilogue: "Safety, the Responsibility of All". 513

Appendix A Mine Rescue and
Recovery Team Members 519
Selected Bibliography 523
Acknowledgments 529
About the Author. 535
Endnotes. 537

Illustrations

Utah Map and Routes Traveled to the Cane Creek
Potash Mine-Mill Complex 34
Cane Creek Mine-Mill Complex 44
Vertical View of Mine Map and Close-up of Raise Area 74
Mucking Bucket with Crosshead and Guide Ropes,
Shaft Schematic and Hoist Signals. 86
Cane Creek Mine Map with the Victims' Locations 487

"From the lands that stretch three thousand miles behind me, the pioneers of old gave up their safety, their comfort and sometimes their lives to build a new world in the West. They were not captives of their doubts...we stand today on the edge of a New Frontier—the frontier of the 1960's—a frontier of unknown opportunities and perils—a frontier of unfulfilled hopes and threats."

—John F. Kennedy

Part One

Chapter 1

Mining, A Hazardous Occupation

Sheppton, Pennsylvania
August 27, 1963
Tuesday, about 2:00 a.m. (EST)

With his hands fastened above his head and attached to the hoisting cables, everything was now ready. Mine rescue workers hundreds of feet above ground gathered the slack in the wires and prepared to pull, hand over hand. A red all-purpose utility truck,[1] the type used to set poles and string wire, was in position. Its winch was attached to one of two cables. One was for the actual hoisting, the other, a safety line in case the first line[2] snapped or tangled.

In breathless silence, the crowd watched as the rescuers slowly started to pull the cables.

"Keep her going," Henry Throne said, as he rose from the mine. "Keep her going. All right fellows. I'm coming up." Each pull that took him up caused him to turn, and soon he was spinning.[3]

"Boy, what a ride this is!" he shouted. On the surface, the winch's motor whined while coiling the slack in the hoisting line. Up Throne came through the small eighteen-inch borehole, up from the mine's depths, through the earth from 331 feet below.

"I'm gonna lose my gumboot. I don't want it to hit Davey," he hollered into the microphone attached to his collar.[4] From the surface, rescue workers warned David Fellin, another trapped miner below to "get out of the way."

Throne was on his way to safety. Trapped for fourteen days in a cold, damp coal mine near Sheppton, Pennsylvania with two other miners,[5] the lean, dark-haired man worked at the pit for only a short time before a cave-in cut them off from the rest of the world.

Originally, specially made metal capsules,[6] the size a man could fit inside, were to bring the men to the surface but examining the hole revealed ledges left by the drill.[7] Fearing the miners could get stuck, rescuers decided not to use them. As a last-minute replacement, rescues used parachute harnesses sewn to coveralls in their place. One rescue official reported on the revised plan and asked his listeners to say a prayer for the men.[8]

The harnessed coveralls lowered to the miners enabled them to don them in the confines of their underground chamber without the confusion of figuring out how to arrange the harness straps. All they had to do was pull them on, but before Throne started his ride to the surface, he had difficulty, reporting he could not lift his hands above his head. An instructor at the top had him take the coveralls off and start all over, giving him each step until dressed correctly.[9]

The men were also supplied with a pot of grease, football helmets, and a neck brace to protect and support their heads for their trip to the surface. Dressed and ready, the men were instructed to smear the grease all over to prevent friction. Their hands were fastened above their heads as a precaution in the event they passed out, rescuers would still be able to hoist them to the surface.

As Throne continued up, his hoisting cables became tangled from spinning, and the lift was halted at least three times to untangle the lines. Near the top, the extra safety line was cut free from the hoisting and communications lines.[10] Rescuers continued the lift until Throne arrived on the surface. Immediately, a loud cheer erupted from the large crowd. Eight hundred onlookers stood behind police lines to watch this highly-anticipated event. Freed from the cables, Throne did a happy little jig under the glaring floodlights, as teary-eyed rescuers and the crowd watched.

The twenty-eight-year-old miner with a coal-blackened face, dressed in the special coveralls, with an orange football helmet[11] on his head, emerged from the hole in the early morning hours, at 2:10 a.m. (EST).[12] He was hustled to a nearby hospital tent on a stretcher borne by a crew of Navy hospital corpsmen who double-timed the fifteen yards to the shelter. After a five-minute examination, Throne was taken to a Marine Corps helicopter. (Its rotor blades were already warming up before he reached the surface.) Military policemen and state troopers[13] lined the forty foot trail from the tent to the helicopter. Once placed on the chopper, Throne was whisked to the Hazleton State General Hospital nine miles away, where a prepared hospital ward awaited both men. There, they would be reunited with their wives and other family members.

Rescuers prepared the hoisting cables and communications lines to bring David Fellin to the surface. The stocky, fifty-eight-year-old coal miner, part mine owner, and crew boss had started working in the area mines at the age of fifteen.[14] Known for his kind nature, Fellin lived within three miles of Sheppton since birth and mining was all he knew.[15]

Fellin attached the cables to his harness, put the blue football helmet[16] with white stars over his thick, curly gray-brown hair and secured his hands above his head. Giving the signal, he felt the cable lift him up from the depths.

"Keep it up, keep it going," he told rescuers. "This is the best ride I've ever had." Moving up, he concentrated on working the lines so they wouldn't spin him the way they had Throne.[17]

On his way up, Fellin started singing, "She'll Be Coming 'Round the Mountain," and exclaimed again, "This is the best ride I ever, ever had."[18]

Fellin had three brief stops because of tangled lines. After four minutes into his ascent, he shouted, "I can see a little light now," and asked, "Is it a nice day up there?" The rescuers informed him, "Yes, but it's the middle of the night."[19]

Fellin kept thinking about his wife, Anna—about where she was and how she was bearing up.[20] He reached the surface as the crowd, shivering from low temperatures in the 40's, let go with another loud cheer. Fellin reached the top at 2:42 a.m.,[21] about seven minutes faster than Throne. While rescuers removed the lines, he spotted his brother, Joe, who came over and shook hands.[22] Fellin was also rushed to the hospital tent on a stretcher, examined for about fifteen minutes and then taken by a second helicopter to the hospital.

After establishing communications when first found until the moment of liberation, Fellin and Throne kept up an exchange of good-natured banter with their rescuers on the surface. Even in the last agonizing moments of entombment, the two men shouted encouragement, instructions, and wisecracks to the rescue crew.[23] Their mild manner and good sense of humor endeared them to everyone.

The joy at the moment surrounding the rescue operation was tempered by concern for the third trapped miner. While in the tent, Fellin drew a map to show officials where he thought the other miner, forty-two-year-old, Louis Bova, might be located. Fellin was able to furnish only meager information.[24] During the cave-in, Bova became separated from the other two men by what Fellin thought was about twenty-five feet of fallen debris.

A second drill had been unsuccessful after four attempts to drill a small lifeline hole in the search for Bova. Determined rescuers continued their efforts even though a week had passed since the other two miners had last heard from him.

The two coal miner's dramatic rescue was a climactic event after a two-week drama that caught worldwide attention near the small town of Sheppton in the hard coal region in northeastern

Disaster at Cane Creek

Pennsylvania. Patiently, the trapped miners waited in their small chamber as the drills bit into the earth. Never before had a borehole of such great length and small dimensions been instrumental in rescuing trapped miners.[25]

Two weeks earlier, August 13, 1963, started out like any other day at work for the miners at the Fellin Coal Company, Oneida No. 2 slope mine.[26] A small independent "bootleg" coal mine,[27] it was located halfway between the tiny towns of Sheppton and Oneida,[28] Pennsylvania. Independent mines cropped up in the region in the 1950's as the big coal companies shut down operations,[29] and the more modern and safer surface mining operations took hold. The "bootleg miners" would go into abandoned mines left by the big companies and set up operations[30] where many times, unsafe conditions existed. They were freelancers willing to scramble for a small profit. Officially, their hole was classified as a Title One mine, which meant it employed less than eight workers and made them exempt from state and federal safety regulations.

The Fellin Coal Mine had seven employees who worked two shifts: four employees on the day shift, three underground, and a hoisting engineer on the surface. Three other employees worked the graveyard shift.[31] Bova had regularly worked the graveyard but had wanted to spend time with his newborn son. So Fellin told him to report that fateful Tuesday morning[32] for the day shift. About nine in the morning, the miners sent a buggy full of coal to the surface to be dumped. Fellin and Throne were across the tracks from Bova. Bova hit the switch to send the buggy topside, up the mine's steep incline.

Timbers started to creak, as all hell suddenly broke loose and tons of coal and rock came crashing down all around, sending the men scrambling for cover. Separated from Bova, Fellin and Throne found themselves together in a small long slanted 14-by-9-foot chamber ranging in height from six-feet high to eighteen-inches,[33] with no way out. The men worked to shore up the roof and ribs (mining term for walls) the best they could with what they could find as the mine continued to cave around them. By the next day, they were in total darkness when the batteries to their cap-lamps went dead. Fortunately, however, it was not before Fellin found a jug and managed to collect some water from an underground drain in the floor below them. The men survived on the brackish sulfur water and chewed on bark from support timbers while sitting against each other to keep warm in the cold, damp mine.

For days, rescue teams on the surface made repeated attempts to enter the damaged mine down the steep slope, which was the only way in, but they were forced back by continual caving as deadly blackdamp gas gathered from exposed cavities,[34] putting the lives of rescuers in extreme danger. By day four, all hope had dimmed of ever reaching any survivors.[35] Everything looked hopeless, and rescuers were ready to give up.[36]

Backed by local union officials, Joseph Fellin, whose brother was trapped in the mine, proposed to rescue officials to consider drilling a six-inch borehole to probe the depths. Joseph Fellin knew of a 'monkey,' a small chamber off the main shaft,[37] where his brother and the other men may have escaped during the cave-in and could still be alive. He wanted them to at least try and see if they could hit this chamber.

It was a "million-to-one-shot" and would take "a miracle" to hit the small space over three hundred feet below. Pennsylvania's top mining official,[38] directing the rescue operation was willing to try and began to put everything into motion. Rescuers reviewed any available maps, which were mostly outdated, and consulted with employees familiar with the mine. Painstakingly, measurements were taken from the slope, and a wooden stake was hammered in the ground to mark the spot to drill.

They brought in a small, high-speed truck mounted drill.[39] While backing up, the truck experienced mechanical failure about twenty feet from the stake. Since the attempt to reach the men through a borehole bordered on the impossible, and with little recourse and less time to waste, rescuers decided to drill where the truck broke down.[40]

Six days since the cave-in and after many long hours of tedious drilling, the bit broke into a void 331 feet below. Removing the steel from the six-inch borehole, rescuers gathered around. In the hot, sticky midnight darkness, one rescue worker called down into the hole. The difficulty was hearing anything. Rescuers lowered a sound powered phone which proved to be ineffective.[41] Finally, an employee from WMBT Radio connected a microphone to an amplifier[42] on the surface, along with a light, and lowered them down.

"Is anyone there?" A rescuer listened, then thought he heard a faint voice. "Hey, Dave," he hollered again.

"Who's calling?" echoed a faint, high-pitched voice from the darkness below. Utterly shocked, the rescuer nearly fell over, as another rescue worker pushed to the hole, put his mouth to the hole and shouted, "Look for the light!" He placed his head above the borehole opening, cupped his ear and waited. Seconds later, he leaped to his feet, waved his arms wildly and screamed, "They're alive! I hear them! They're alive," as hard hats sailed into the air.[43]

Gene Gibbons, the co-owner with Fellin of the Fellin Coal Company, next yelled down into the mine and asked Fellin if he could see the light they lowered.

"No," responded Fellin.

"Where are you?" Gibbons asked.

"We are blocked in a hole and can't get out," Fellin said.

Following the voice, Fellin worked his way towards the light. Soon, he was clearly heard by the crowd for the first time over the transistor microphone WMBT had lowered[44] into the hole.

Rescuers soon learned they hit a chamber where two of the three miners were alive, David Fellin and Henry Throne. Within hours, other state and federal mine rescue officials along with other mining and drilling experts converged on the scene. Officials now had to determine the best way to bring the men safely to the surface.

The news of finding miners alive became a top news story and quickly gained worldwide coverage. Newspaper and television reporters descended on the mine site. Soon, two television towers loomed over the site, and scaffolding was set up to give reporters a better view. The two courageous miners and their perilous situation stirred the interest and sympathy of people who followed the rescue's day-by-day progress. The special rescue operation was unprecedented in the annals of mining history.

A two-way communications system was set up in the six-inch borehole rescuers dubbed the "miracle hole." They lowered water, food, medicine, lights, a sleeping bag, and other needed items to the trapped miners. The plan was to drill another hole, twelve inches in diameter, into the chamber. Then, after reaming the hole to the size a man could fit inside, they would pull the miners to the surface. A sixty-five-ton massive track drill[45] was brought to the site while the smaller drill was moved over to a nearby location to probe the depths to locate the third missing miner, Louis Bova. The father with the newborn son, he was thought to be on the other side of the slope.

For the next eight days, rescue crews and the trapped miners endured one frustration after another. The first attempt caused the roof to crack as the drill came near. Fearing the chamber would collapse in on the men, rescuers quickly abandoned this strategy. The next attempt missed the intended target. Drill breakdowns throughout the rescue operation were also frequent. On the third attempt, the drill finally hit the chamber, and the delicate reaming process began to enlarge the twelve-inch hole to eighteen inches. The hole's lower part was temporarily filled with a cement plug to prevent debris from falling on the trapped men while every precaution was taken to avoid collapsing the fragile chamber. Like distant thunder, hour by hour the sixty-five-ton maroon and yellow drilling rig spun the 1,350-pound reamer[46] inch by inch through the crumbling coal and shale above the two miner's heads.

Finally, in the early morning hours of August 27, 1963, six hours short of two weeks since the cave-in, David Fellin and Henry Throne were brought safely to the surface. The drilling for Bova halted during the rescue of the two men, but as soon as they were on their way to the hospital, drilling resumed.

At the hospital, the men were able to take a tub bath, clean two weeks of grime off and shave before being reunited with their tearful wives. Although unable to get much rest the remainder of the night, both were doing well. Doctors wanted to keep them at least a week to be sure.

By mid-morning, Pennsylvania state mining officials and James Westfield, the Assistant Director of Health and Safety for the U.S. Bureau of Mines, from Washington, D.C., interviewed both rescued coal miners. Westfield had assisted the state mining officials during the long rescue operation and was near the borehole when the two coal miners were rescued. He was instrumental through his federal connections to bringing in Navy communication experts and their advanced radio equipment that was used during the rescue operation.[47]

While both rescued men were cooperative, Fellin had the most detailed information about the mine. He could talk of nothing but Bova, asserting "I've got to try to help out my buddy."[48] He felt Bova was still alive, although probably injured and in a weakened condition. He drew detailed maps and made extensive notes concerning the physical conditions underground and the extent of mining in the slope. The officials even made a recording of one such interview to assist those at the mine site on the strategy committee.[49]

While Fellin spent considerable time with rescue officials to help locate Bova, Throne felt good enough by early afternoon to meet with anxious journalists who repeatedly requested a news conference with the survivors. Agreeing to a brief meeting, Throne came before the press in a wheelchair dressed in pajamas, a green and yellow dotted bathrobe, and wearing sunglasses. The lights from the camera bulbs bothered him so much he had to shield his eyes. At one point, while speaking about Bova and his ordeal Throne broke down in tears and was wheeled away with blackened palms pressed to his eyes.[50] Weak and near collapse, he was assisted into bed.

For the remainder of the afternoon, Fellin and Throne tried to rest and recover from their ordeal in the Hazleton Hospital, while a drill was driving a borehole down through more than 300 feet of rock and coal trying to locate Louis Bova.

Moab, Utah
August 27, 1963
Tuesday, about 2:00 p.m. (MST)

While rescue crews were drilling in search of Louis Bova in Pennsylvania, hard-rock miners in Moab, Utah, working the afternoon shift, were getting ready to leave for work. Moab, nestled in a long, green valley amid towering vibrant red sandstone cliffs that created a vivid and beautiful juxtaposition of colors, is located in the famous red-rock country in southeastern Utah. An unexpected oasis cradled amid a vast desert wilderness.

Eighteen months earlier, the slim built, twenty-seven-year-old, Blake Hanna moved to Moab with his wife and four small children, from Price, Utah to work at the new Cane Creek Potash Mine west of town. His pretty wife, Myrna, was born in Moab. Her parents moved away when she was young, to a farm near Price, Utah where she grew up with five other siblings, often returning to Moab and the La Sal Mountain homestead to stay with grandparents. Now, Myrna was living back in this beautiful, enchanted valley around extended family members.

Hanna was always a restless soul, with dark blue eyes that craved adventure. For now, he worked hard to support a growing family. At times, he could be quite impatient, especially on the graveyard shift where the noise of small children and the difficultly of sleeping during the day could wake the "sleeping giant" incurring his wrath and making him grumpy. In spite of any flaws, imagined or real, Hanna was a hardworking provider and took pride in taking care of his family.

A faded blue, older model Travelall (precursor to the modern full-size SUV) pulled to the curb in front of Hanna's small, modest home located behind the old brick church building that they used for kindergarten classes on the corner of 100 N. 100 E. The horn honked to pick up the last rider in a carpool. Exiting the home, Hanna jumped into the vehicle and slammed the door shut, which made a hollow, clanging metal sound. The radio played as the Travelall headed towards Main Street and the men settled back and chatted.

The vehicle traveled north out of town, passing the intriguing hilltop mansion perched high on the red cliffs above the highway, built by the colorful uranium millionaire, Charlie Steen, the city's most famous character who put Moab on the map. He gained notoriety during the 50's in a real rags-to-riches story after he located a vein of high-grade ore near Moab, which spawned a boom in the area where the big game in town was uranium.[51] Steen bought the mountain and atop the red-rock cliff built his dream home with a spectacular panoramic million-dollar view of the entire Moab Valley. The money-green, mid-century modern mansion, lavish for Moab,[52] cost $250,000 and was complete with a greenhouse, the largest swimming pool in the state, and a separate cottage for servants.[53] Built in 1955, around the time uranium fever was at its peak. Steen hosted lavish parties at his mansion that were the stuff of legends. He would invite the whole town, and many Hollywood celebrities would attend his parties while they were in the area filming movies.[54]

Moab achieved fame on the big screen for its rugged scenery, attracting filmmakers who were shooting westerns in the surrounding landscape. In 1939, director John Ford filmed *Stagecoach,* his first western in the area south of Moab, starring John Wayne. Looking for a picturesque desert for scenes of another movie, the *Wagon Master*, Ford was back in Moab in 1948 using an area not used before.

Moab was a small town that was originally settled by Mormons.[55] Ford loved the Mormon people, admired their sense of community, and viewed them as a society of outcasts. "[Moab had] the greatest faces in the world," enthused Pat Ford, the son of John Ford. "I'd snap pictures of the people and bring them home and he [would] look at them and say, 'These are what I want. These are the people I want...I want stone-age faces. I want the faces of men who have seen people die of snake-bite, where babies die at childbirth, women die in childbirth, and guys die from being bucked off horses—just the life of a primitive people."[56]

John Ford loved the red-rock vistas and returned the following year (1949) to direct *Rio Grande,* starring John Wayne[57] and Maureen O'Hara. That same year, the Moab Film Commission was formed to promote the town and the region for such purposes, the first such commission in the world.[58] In 1961, Ford was back again filming *The Comancheros,* starring John Wayne. Ford's Westerns were at the very least a kind of mirroring of the "Wild West" forever etched into the American consciousness: dusty trails, ten-gallon hats, rolling tumbleweeds and, perhaps most prominently, the six-shooter pistol. Such iconography was found throughout his work.[59]

When John Wayne was asked, "Why Moab?" He answered because it's "...where God put the West."

"We made *The Alamo* in Texas. To do justice to the story we had to," he explained. "We made *The Comancheros* at Moab for the same reason,"[60] he said. "TV you can make on the backlot, but for the big screen, for the real big-scale outdoor dramas, you have to do it where God put the West...and there is no better example of this than around Moab."[61]

While John Wayne acquired a world-wide image as a Western hero, Director John Ford turned Westerns into film classics. He brought Moab and Monument Valley landscapes to the screen in such forceful images, the region became known in Hollywood as "John Ford Country." From 1938 to 1961, Ford directed nine movies in the area with the superb use of vast desert panoramas. The list of stars and producers who have made this Moab and Monument Valley their temporary homes reads like "Who's Who in Hollywood."[62] New productions coming to the Moab area were highly anticipated and always the talk around town. Even Moab locals snagged roles as extras in many of the films shot in the area throughout the years, including employees from the new Cane Creek Potash Mine and their family members. In May of 1963, when the movie, *The Greatest Story Ever Told*, about the life of Christ, starring a host of stars filmed some scenes near Moab, they needed 400 extras, stand-ins, and bit players. A few potash employees and even family members were among those who snagged a role.[63]

It was always a treat for locals when movies were being filmed in the area. After being out on location all day, celebrities were often seen around town in the evening. Many attended youth sporting events, were theater-goers; and were seen downtown and in local restaurants. John Wayne even gave the Apache Motel its share of notoriety as the place he stayed while on location in Moab.

Moab was a versatile area for filming Westerns. It contained a variety of scenic locations, from spruce and aspen forests in the nearby La Sal Mountains to the east, to the red rocks of Arches National Monument to the north, and the dramatic canyons to the west of town in the recently proposed Canyonlands National Park area. The city of Moab flourished as a support center for film crews by providing catering, lodging, extras, and stock, such as horses, cattle, oxen, and the wagons they pulled.[64]

The previous month, July 1963, Warner Brothers announced they would be back in the Moab area when John Ford would direct the film *Cheyenne Autumn* with a host of top-billed stars.[65] Reportedly, the film company planned to employ over one hundred local people as extras, sixty would be cavalrymen. They were also bringing into the area approximately "sixty Indians as extras."[66]

The Moab miners riding to work chitchatted as the volume increased while talking about current events.

The old Travelall crossed the bridge over the now placid and calm Colorado River. Several large sandbars in the river were visible during months of low water levels. Heading north up Moab Canyon, the road curved past the Atlas Uranium Reduction Mill built by Charlie Steen. In a short distance, the vehicle made a left hand turn off the main highway onto the new river road, named Potash. Upon the canyon wall directly in front of the Travelall, was the recently completed North entrance to the 7,100-foot tunnel of the new railroad spur, built exclusively for the new potash mine.

The road curved sharply in a southeasterly direction, heading back towards the river near the site where the Old Spanish Trail[67] crossed the Colorado River, which was initially called the Grand River, the name given to it by the Spaniards. The Old Spanish Trail, the northern overland route, cut a path through Utah and was a major trade route during the late 18th and early 19th centuries. Often, the impassable canyon country of the Colorado Plateau necessitated a detour far to the north,[68] using the natural river crossing at the northwestern end of Moab Valley.

The trail brought goods from missions in Santa Fe to California. Woolen goods—rugs, blankets, and other woven products—were traded for horses and mules, which were driven back to Santa Fe and sold. Along the route, traders sometimes swapped animals for Paiute slaves or children stole outright from the relatively weak tribes. The slave trade peaked in the 1830's and 1840's, with Chief Wakara's Ute bands playing a significant role in capturing and trading slaves who brought good prices in California.[69] The slave trade was gradually disrupted after the arrival of Mormon pioneers in the late 1840's.

The Potash Road curved west and entered between a pair of 1,000-foot towering, smooth, sandstone cliffs flanking the entrance

Disaster at Cane Creek

to the river canyon dubbed "The Portal." The road hugged the river's northern bank, leaving Moab Valley behind. The harsh afternoon sun drenched the towering red sandstone cliffs in the picturesque canyon country as the Travelall maneuvered the serpentine twists and turns along the river while the men engaged in animated conversations about anything and everything as they bantered as usual. Usually, they talked about hunting, fishing, sports, their families or other current events. The hot topic of conversation today was the dramatic rescue in Pennsylvania of the two coal miners, Fellin and Throne, who had been pulled to the surface through a drilled borehole in the early morning hours. The rescue was a riveting two-week ordeal, and of course, fellow miners followed the dramatic international story intently. Each day, the men talked about the progress of the rescue operation, especially today, when the news dominated the highly anticipated and successful rescue of the two miners.

"They would sure have a heck of a time drilling for us if anything ever happened down there,"[70] Chuck Byrge said as he looked back at his buddies, Matt Rauhala and Kenneth Milton, who were seated in the very back seat. The very back was where Milton always sat. The men clearly understood what Byrge was saying. The Sheppton mine was 331-feet below the surface while the new Cane Creek Potash Mine, where they worked, was 2,789-feet below the surface.[71] Over a half-mile, the underground mine was one of the deepest potash mines in North America.[72] Its depth was nine times deeper than that of the Pennsylvania coal mine and was the equivalent of two Empire State buildings stacked on top of each other.

The driver of the Travelall, Roland Roy, and his brother, Armond, were seated up front and chatted with the others in their distinctive broken English accent. Canadian nationals, the two "Canucks," an affectionate slang term for French Canadians, added their part to the conversation, while "the Americans" or "the Yanks" always took great delight in parroting back to them one of the Canadians most distinctive expressions, "eh?"[73] Pronounced as a long "a," it was usually added to the end of nearly everything the Canucks would say, or so it seemed.

The men swayed a bit as the Travelall rounded the curves in the road that traced the winding path of the Colorado River. The previous month, the new river road was still being surfaced[74] and hadn't always been so smooth to travel. The new road took nearly two and a half years to construct and was a source of angst among the construction crews and miners forced to take longer alternate routes or a boat down the river to get to work. With the price of gas around thirty cents a gallon,[75] Roland charged each rider three dollars a week to carpool.[76] Not bad considering the old beat up Travelall could maneuver and handle the rough, steep terrain of the back roads they were forced to take.

Now, with the river road finished, the drive to work was more placid, much like the river this time of year. The beautiful river canyon was, at times, even magical. An occasional hanging garden of green vegetation could be seen high against the red sheer cliff walls, fed by springs in the rock crevices or occasional rainstorms. These same rains could send temporary waterfalls cascading over the cliff faces as the water drained to the river.

With eyes fixed forward, Hanna tried to keep from getting car sick[77] as the vehicle made its way around the bends in the road. Byrge sat behind the driver in the middle seat next to Hanna. A sociable, friendly type, Byrge could talk to pretty much anyone. He and his wife, Colleen, had six young children and his little ones were his pride and joy and his favorite topic to talk about at work. Thirty-years-old, Byrge worked underground as a miner on Hanna's crew, as did Kenneth Milton.

Forty-three-years-old Milton was a good-hearted man and extremely well liked by those he worked with. His dark hair with a square hairline outlined his ruggedly handsome face, while his eyes portrayed his good nature. A West Virginian, he spoke with a slight mountain twang accent.

Disaster at Cane Creek

Matt Rauhala had eyes that seemed to smile on the outer corners, and his broad grin hinted that he was a bit of a tease. He and his wife, Edith, had three grown children and had moved to Moab from Sunnyside, Utah, a coal camp near Price, northwest of Moab in Carbon County. Forty-seven-years-old Rauhala worked on the surface as the Bucket Dumper and occasionally, helped the Toplander.

Byrge and Milton were fishing buddies,[78] something they enjoyed doing when they weren't working. Crews who work day in, and day out together many times become close, much like a family. These men worked seven days a week with lots of overtime and therefore, spent the majority of their time with their crew. What little time they did have off, they spent with family, did home chores, caught up on much-needed sleep or simply got ready to go back to work.

The Roy brothers, along with other Canadians, came to Moab with Harrison International, Inc., a Canadian contracting company operating out of Miami, Florida in the States. Harrison International specialized in shaft sinking in Canada and other countries. On April 7, 1961, Texas Gulf Sulphur (TGS) awarded Harrison International the multi-million dollar contract to sink their deep mine shaft and develop the underground mine for the new Cane Creek Potash Mine-mill complex west of Moab.

Harrison handpicked a team of workers from Canada, many of them supervisors and foremen who came at the beginning of the project when sinking the shaft started in earnest in June of 1961.[79] Other Canadian employees followed once they completed contract work on previous projects.

After the project was underway and the workload increased, Harrison International hired other miners from surrounding areas, such as Carbon and Emery County northwest of Moab, the large coal mining region of Utah. The market for coal was going through a slump, and some miners found steady work at the new potash mine. Although from different towns, Hanna, Byrge, and Rauhala, all experienced coal miners, came from Carbon County; Milton, also an

19

experienced coal miner, came from West Virginia. Working seven days a week, the men rotated shifts each week on Sunday, which only gave them eight hours off, the equivalent of the difference in the extra time workers picked up between shift changes. The work was grueling, but the pay was good.

There was a hum of tires gripping the road and in the wind was an ocean-like smell from the river, typical of alkaline waterways in Utah deserts. The intoxicating bittersweet aroma from the pinkish and white plumes of the tamarisk, growing in thickets along its bank, wafted in the warm August breeze which blew through the open windows, cooling the men from the heat of the day. The latest country hits such as *I Walk the Line* and *Ring of Fire* by Johnny Cash or *Act Naturally* by Buck Owens blasted on the radio, helping to pass the time for the men on their way to work—if they could get reception in the canyon.

Traveling the new river road were other vehicles with other miners on their way to work as the Colorado River made its way towards the Grand Canyon and then to the sea at the Gulf of California. Like a river, a road is a perfect metaphor for life with its twists and turns. It's always a formidable witness of the journeys rooted in the story and drama of those who travel its expanse, where they come from and are going. This road was central to the flurry of activities over the last three years, culminating in the construction of the new Cane Creek Potash Mine-mill complex that was nearing completion.

Chapter 2

"In The Land of Moab"

The vast expanse over the Colorado Plateau[1] a remnant of the Wild West, spans four western states, Utah, Colorado, New Mexico and Arizona. In 1936, the region on the Plateau surrounding the Colorado River canyons in southeastern Utah was identified as the single largest roadless area in the lower forty-eight states. It centered over "The Confluence," where the Green and Colorado Rivers[2] merge in the red rock canyon country, west of Moab, Utah. In all, twenty million acres in six huge roadless areas on the Plateau[3] were identified and was largely unexplored until 1950[4] when some oil, gas and mineral exploration began to reduce its size. Into the 60's, the area west of Moab remained the largest block of undeveloped land in the West.[5] An arid and unforgiving frontier, there was a poetic grandeur about this vast, expansive area with its breathtaking splendor. Surreal, the beauty of this high desert was altogether compelling and provocative.

Here, in the "Land of Moab," on the edge of this rugged, roadless frontier, amid barren, broken rock, and flaming color, Texas Gulf Sulphur Company found themselves, in the spring of 1960.[6] On April 28th, Texas Gulf Sulphur (TGS), a company from Newgulf, Texas, announced they had acquired Delhi-Taylor Oil Corporation's potash reserves. The high-grade potash deposits were discovered in 1956, at the Cane Creek Anticline, a geological region west of Moab. Owned by oil magnate, Clint Murchison,[7] the Delhi-Taylor Oil Company was based in Dallas, Texas.

With corporate offices located in New York City, Texas Gulf Sulphur (TGS) was investing twenty-five to thirty million dollars of capital and savings in building a new modern potash mine-mill complex to produce the ore commercially. As the world's largest producer of Sulphur,[8] a plant solvent used in fertilizers, the company already had a ready market structure that potash, another component of fertilizer, would complement. This multimillion dollar acquisition was the first major move towards diversification for the company and promised to become a sound investment.

Immediately after making the deal, TGS went to work and began confirmation drilling and coring the first week of May of 1960. This process was necessary to verify the potash reserves value, its thickness, and grade. This "technical evaluation" work was ahead of actually acquiring and commercially mining the potash and TGS had eight months, until January 1, 1961, to make their examination under the option.[9]

Only two dirt roads serviced the Cane Creek Anticline at this time.[10] One was the old river road from Moab; the other one was the longer, more treacherous sixty-mile route over the Shafer Trail, which was accessed by traveling over Big Flat Mesa[11] north of Moab. It continued southwest about twenty miles over the mesa to the head of the Shafer Trail. Here, it dropped off the rim a thousand feet in about the first half-mile via the half-dozen switchbacks and hairpin curves, with precipitous drop-offs to Shafer Canyon, 1,200 feet below. While the narrow dirt road traveled down the steep terrain, above it, the cliffs and sheer red sandstone walls tower ever higher. Continuing through Shafer Canyon, the trail gradually descends past White Rim and heads towards the northeast and to the potash facility on the Colorado River.

Disaster at Cane Creek

The Shafer Trail, north of "The Confluence," where the Green and Colorado Rivers merge, started out as an old Indian trail. In the late 1800s, it was used by horse thieves, cattle rustlers, and outlaws roaming the area. The region's most famous outlaws, Butch Cassidy,[12] the Sundance Kid and the Wild Bunch gang, hid out from the law in the Robbers' Roost area, a maze of practically impregnable canyons west of "The Confluence."[13] Once described as the "king of Roosters, an aristocrat among mere cattle rustlers,"[14] Butch Cassidy was the alias name of Robert LeRoy Parker, born April 13, 1866. The oldest of thirteen children of devout Mormon pioneer parents, he was raised on a ranch near Circleville, Utah, about a hundred miles west of Robbers' Roost. Before moving on to robbing banks and trains,[15] Cassidy began his life of crime as a cattle rustler and horse thief in the canyon country west of Moab. When Moab was a fledgling settlement, Cassidy, along with other rustlers and outlaws, often frequented or passed through Moab when in the area. They used the trails, ravines, and canyons to their advantage to hide horses and cattle taken from ranchers before driving them to market. This frontier area over the Colorado Plateau red canyon country became famous in Wild West lore and was notorious for the Outlaw Trail, stretching from Canada to Mexico.

In the early 1900s, cattle rancher, Frank Shafer hired his brother, John L. Shafer to tend to his cattle out on the range west of Moab. While there, John also worked on improvements to the treacherous trail which would soon become known as Shafer Trail. Over the course of several years, John worked to make the trail safer to move cattle to and from summer rangelands. It was during this time the trail picked up its name.[16] As horse-stealing, cattle rustling and outlaw gangs died out, those going into this rugged backcountry the decade before TGS's investment, were mostly a hand full of ranchers, oil companies who did limited and sporadic drilling, and prospectors and miners with small uranium interests. In 1953, during the uranium boom in the Moab area, Shafer Trail was widened and made into a road using a tractor and a four-wheel-drive truck by uranium miners to transport extracted ore. A few years later, after surveying, the Atomic Energy Commission turned the rugged route into a better road. Still, the remote country west of Moab, the Cane Creek Anticline, remained a challenge to get into; the chief problem was transporting equipment and supplies.[17]

With no dams to control spring runoff from the Rocky Mountain's western slopes, the Colorado River would rise to high levels in May, June and sometimes in July. Therefore, TGS, moving in one step, took three drilling rigs into the Cane Creek Anticline using the river road ahead of high water[18] from spring runoff. With steadily rising river levels, the narrow dirt road would eventually be under water in several different places making passage impossible. Once inaccessible, personnel were forced to travel down the river using charter boats or the longer Shafer Trail[19] route.

Just over a month into the evaluation work and deeply immersed in drilling, TGS had two wells going. They had already completed the third well and were moving the rig to a new location when the river rose to high peak levels and flooded, making the river road impassable. By the next week, the river dropped enough to permit needed repairs, but the river rose again during the weekend, wiping out the road work and forcing traffic back over the Shafer Trail.[20] The company, from the start, recognized the need[21] for a viable access road. On May 20, 1960, TGS officials met with the Utah State Road Commission to review plans for the state to build a two-lane highway down the river to the new potash facility. The road was paved with intentions to service not only the potash site but also oil and scenic interests in the area.[22]

By the end of July, as river levels were subsiding, TGS had a total of six holes drilled. Consultants and experts in shaft designs were called in, and the Colorado School of Mines worked to prepare two studies of various processing plant designs for the actual mining process.[23] For the next month, these experts would make almost daily trips to Moab to study the Cane Creek location. The preliminary reports from these consultants and specialists were due by September 1st.

Also, due at the same time was a decision by the U.S. Department of Interior for the withdrawal of oil and gas leases on the potash reserves consisting of 9,445 acres of public lands[24] owned by the federal government in the Cane Creek area. TGS expected to mine the deposits at depths ranging from 2,500 to 5,000 feet; oil exploration in the area threatened the development, making conditions too dangerous to mine the potash safely. Only by withdrawing all oil and gas leases and plugging all holes drilled to obtain core samples with cement to prevent possible leakage of gas or oil into the mine, was TGS able to move forward with the project.[25]

By this time, seventeen core test holes had been drilled in the Cane Creek area by Delhi-Taylor and TGS; upon completion, however, these holes were cemented in anticipation of future mining to protect the miners. They also determined there were eight oil wells drilled in the area since 1946, which also needed cement plugs.[26] Delays in the decision to withdraw the leases jeopardized the proposed project, and TGS indicated their investment funds were at risk unless a decision came soon. Support came from all four Utah Congressmen and Governor George D. Clyde. With virtually unanimous support within the state,[27] TGS asked the U.S. Secretary of the Interior to expedite the matter favoring the potash interests.[28] On August 30, 1960, Secretary Fred A. Seaton[29] finally announced the decision to withdraw the oil and gas leases in the area for ten years, compensating the oil companies for their withdrawn leases.

By mid-October, the Utah State Road Commission approved a new paved two-lane highway, estimated to take several years to complete.[30] Their first plan included an eight-mile stretch that would leave the river canyon and climb to the top of Big Flat Mesa. It would become the main route to the newly designated,[31] Dead Horse Point State Park. The Road Commission would eventually revise their plan, eliminate this section of road, and opt instead to use the existing county road from the main highway across Big Flat Mesa to Dead Horse Point.[32]

On November 2, 1960,[33] at a board meeting in New York City, TGS's board of directors, satisfied with the evaluation work and results, approved plans to move ahead and exercise the option with Delhi-Taylor to build the multi-million-dollar Cane Creek Mine-mill complex.[34] The Cane Creek Anticline encompassing the area inspired the name for the new complex. TGS made the much-anticipated and hoped-for announcement two months ahead of the January 1st deadline.

A week later, John F. Kennedy won a close election for president, running on the campaign slogans to, "Get America Moving Again," and "To Seek a New Frontier." He had announced his candidacy to run for the Presidency of the United States on January 2, 1960, several months before TGS first announced they were acquiring the potash reserves in Utah. As the 1960 presidential election campaign got underway, Kennedy's promise to, "Get America Moving Again" referred to a downturn in the American economy resulting in a recession,[35] which would peak with an unemployment rate of 7.1 percent.

In light of a distressed economy, the announcement by TGS was especially good news for the state of Utah and the residents of Grand and San Juan County. Coming after the huge uranium boom in the area that appeared to be slowing down, a new construction boom from potash mining loomed large on the horizon. Estimates of 300, possibly 400 workers, were expected to be employed[36] at the new mining facility once developed. Also, once the construction phase for the potash projects started, there would be a gradual increase in workers, eventually peaking at different times to over 600, 1,000 and 2,000, and creating a construction boom for several years in the Moab area.[37]

This massive potash venture involved four major projects: the building of a modern potash processing plant; the mine's shaft sinking along with the underground development; a thirty-six-mile railway

Disaster at Cane Creek

spur built to the site; and a suitable paved access road down the river. For the next few years, this would be a massive undertaking on a scale not seen before in these parts. TGS would coordinate every aspect of the projects with attention to detail and timing. The logistics of this enormous effort was headed by Dr. C. F. Fogarty,[38] Senior Vice President of TGS in New York and a Colorado School of Mines graduate. Frank Tippie,[39] Project and General Manager, along with his team in Moab, would oversee the construction and direct the work.

The mine-mill facility's location that was determined during the exploratory drilling was about twenty miles from Moab on the banks of the Colorado River. By the first of December of 1960, TGS announced Stearns-Roger Manufacturing Company of Denver, Colorado, a principal designer of similar plants in the U.S. and Canada, would be the main contractor over all phases to build the surface facilities.

The New Year began with the inauguration of John F. Kennedy as the 35th President of the United States on January 20, 1961. The charismatic former U.S. senator, his beautiful wife, Jacqueline (Jackie) and their adorable young children, Carolyn and John, were mesmerizing to the American public. They seemed to represent the hope for a better future for the country.

As promised during his campaign, to "Get America Moving Again," President Kennedy soon provided businesses with tax relief by liberalizing the depreciation allowance on new plants and equipment and gave companies a seven percent investment tax credit. Eventually leading to record high corporate profits, the stock market rebounded, and the start of rapid growth in the 1960's began.[40]

Just over a month later, on March 2, 1961, company officials were on hand[41] at the new Cane Creek site for a mid-morning blast, which formed the opening for the eventual mine shaft and the start of the first phase of building the new Cane Creek potash plant. Stearns-Roger would take it down to about eighty feet[42] to construct the shaft collar and a foundation for a massive concrete Headframe they would build over the shaft.

At the end of March 1961, nearly a year after the initial announcement, W.W. Clyde Construction of Springville, Utah, the low bidder, became the contractor on the new river road project. Work began almost immediately. Prompt action was necessary, and red tape was cut to get the project underway before another season of high water from spring run-off prevented the use of the present road.[43] As TGS and W.W. Clyde prepared for the road closing for the year-round construction, the company announced an improved alternate route on the eastern side of the Colorado River over the Hurrah Pass to a point opposite the plant site. There, they would transfer personnel across the river using a cabled barge. The only other viable route, the longer Shafer Trail, was frequently impassable.[44]

At the Cane Creek site, stockpiling of essential material was underway so construction could continue when the road closed. A major item stored was 7,000 sacks of cement needed for the foundation and construction of the 179-foot tall cement Headframe and the shaft collar.[45]

The Hurrah Pass route proved to be unacceptable for workers, so three weeks later Ironworkers of Local 23 halted work, and cement finishers also walked off in sympathy. They objected to using the long, dirt route and demanded travel time to and from the job or furnished transportation.[46] The dirt road over Hurrah Pass went through colorful red rock canyons and switchbacks and took considerable time to travel. For those who took a boat down the river to get to work, a small dock was built while the companies began exploring other options to try and solve the transportation problems.

Towards the end of June, W.W. Clyde Construction began blasting down the sides of cliffs and nudging the river over as work forged ahead on the massive highway project.[47] About this same time, Stearns-Roger's subcontractor, Isbell Construction Company of Reno, Nevada, began transferring equipment to the Cane Creek plant site to begin excavation to level several areas of the rolling hill for the plant facility. Rock extraction and grade work were expected to take about six months to complete.[48]

Disaster at Cane Creek

About this same time, Harrison International, Inc., the Canadian owned contract company, was selected for the shaft sinking project and the mine development underground. Shaft sinking in both Europe and North America during this period was nearly always carried out by contractors, in contrast to South Africa where the mining companies generally sank their own shafts.[49] The shaft sinking construction contractors would finish off a job in one place, work on a shaft excavation in another, and then be on the road again for the next big challenge.

One important event that dramatically affected shaft sinking in Canada was the arrival of Patrick Harrison. Born in Belfast, Ireland around the turn of the century, 'Paddy' Harrison immigrated to Canada in 1921. After working as a miner and shaft sinker, he became a mining contractor in 1934.[50] His first contacts were in Val-d'Or, Quebec, where his company sank a number of shafts in the area.[51]

His company, Patrick Harrison & Co. Ltd., based in Toronto, Quebec, Canada along with his other subsidiary companies, dominated shaft sinking in North America from its inception.[52] They sunk over 500 mining shafts, more than fifty of which were deeper than 3,000 feet. One assignment was a 4,000-foot shaft complex in Canada for International Nickel Company,[53] plus thirty miles of underground 'drifts' (a mining term used for passageways in metal/nonmetal mine). But the work carried out in the unstable ground conditions of Quebec's asbestos mines is what established the company as a dominant force in North American shaft sinking.[54]

'Paddy' Harrison became a legendary construction entrepreneur in Canada who managed a widely scattered business, with projects all over the world.[55] The early sixties were a busy time for the company and 'Paddy' assigned his brother, Norman Harrison, to manage the company's projects in the United States.

Harrison International began work at the Cane Creek site in June 1961. They predicted the project would take seventeen months to complete the contract.[56] But from the start, the job was a rocky

29

road. Even before the company began work, they were plagued by problems. A month before Harrison International was on site, a subcontractor they had hired, Eben Scharf Construction Company of Moab, sparked a wildcat walk-off of Ironworkers employed by Stearns-Roger, the plant contractor. A thirty-six-hour walkout was over the unloading of steel building material by a crew from Scharf Construction, a non-union company.

One hundred and forty men were idled temporarily by the wildcat strike.[57] The cement pouring operation, a continuous twenty-four-hour operation, was about one-fourth complete at the time the walkout occurred. Of the twenty-six Ironworkers who walked out, four returned, but the company replaced the rest with new crews. Due to the rapid resumption of work, the operation resumed. They poured the first eighty feet of the shaft and the foundation for the Headframe. Before long, the work was fifty percent complete.

Scharf Construction remained on the job, with twenty-two men working to build temporary quarters for Harrison International's operation.[58] A man camp had been constructed for their employees about two miles down from the mine site up away from the river. They had a bunkhouse with trailers brought in by Harrison International where the workers could live. The camp had a cook-house, and a woman from Moab was hired to cook meals.[59] The contracting company also built a large metal building west from the Headframe that housed their office, dryhouse (change house), a small warehouse, shop, and the large mine air compressors.[60] Between Harrison International's main building and the Headframe, crews also built three wood hoist houses, each lining up one after the other, and each having temporary hoisting machinery. Part way up the Headframe, temporary equipment and platforms were attached. Through the roofs of the three hoist houses, hoisting cables were strung up to sheave wheels located inside the Headframe where the buckets and the Galloway Stage (a three-level work platform) were attached to the ends of the hoisting cables that hung down inside the shaft.

Disaster at Cane Creek

TGS's construction photos of Headframe and Mine Site, taken between 1961 and 1962. (Intrepid Potash)

Crews also prepared concrete forms[61] to line the round twenty-two-foot diameter shaft where concrete was poured to form a foot-thick liner as work progressed downward in the shaft sinking process. Stearns-Roger had already taken the shaft down eighty feet to construct the Headframe's collar and foundation. Work got underway as Harrison International also assembled the Galloway Stage, a new advanced shaft sinking technology developed in Africa.[62] 'Paddy' Harrison was an innovative entrepreneur and used the latest machinery in shaft sinking to improve on the previous shaft sinking records. He even patented a piece of equipment in 1949, a cage and operating mechanism for shaft shovels.[63]

The Galloway Stage, a movable three-level work platform, allowed crews to do different aspects of work in the shaft sinking process simultaneously. The three-level stage hung suspended in the shaft and was hoisted up or down as needed. On the bottom, the men blasted and mucked out the hole as buckets brought the waste rock to the top. One stage up, the shaft's sides received concrete and another stage up, the concrete forms were stripped as work progressed continually downward.

Transportation remained a problem as the river road was periodically closed for construction and would remain that way until completed. As usual, personnel was transported by boat down the river, across the river by ferry from the Hurrah Pass on the east side or the men traveled down Shafer Trail near the Dead Horse Point Rim.[64]

Don C. Sutherland, Inc., of Denver, Colorado, designed and engineered the railway spur.[65] A massive project in itself, the survey stage was in the works since the beginning of 1961. The company eventually determined the best route the thirty-six-mile rail spur would take to the potash plant through the rugged red-rock country. In order to descend gradually into the Colorado River canyon (specifications of a 1.2 percent grade), the line had to make it possible for a four-unit diesel power train to pull fifty cars carrying seventy tons each at fifty miles per hour.[66]

Grade work began in the spring of 1961 with Corn Construction Company[67] of Grand Junction, Colorado doing work at points along the proposed new spur. Starting the first week of April, bids went out for the primary contractor to construct the rail spur. The railroad tracks from Cisco to Crescent Junction, Utah was also being re-laid by a couple hundred workers, mainly consisting of Navajo Indians[68] from the Four Corners Area. The thirty-nine-mile Cane Creek spur would be the longest ever built on the D&RGW line and would connect with the railroads mainline at Brendel, near Crescent Junction. It would then run through some of the most spectacular, scenic country[69] on its way to the potash complex at the "end of the line."

At the end of July, Morrison-Knudsen Construction Company, Inc.,[70] (M-K) of Boise, Idaho, one of the world's largest construction firms,[71] was awarded the contract to build the new rail spur line. Members of the initial Morrison-Knudsen group expressed pleasure, saying the project appeared to be "a very interesting job all the way through."[72] For years, M-K constructed hundreds of major infrastructure projects such as dams, highways, and other projects throughout the U.S. and the world. They were a principle contractor on the Hoover (Boulder) Dam and the San Francisco—Oakland Bay Bridge, which was just two of their large American infrastructure projects.[73] Innovative, to handle the enormous and formidable task of building the Hoover Dam, Morrison-Knudsen brought together a consortium of six different companies needed to do the work. The start of the new company, Six Companies, Inc., introduced the practice of joint-venture construction.

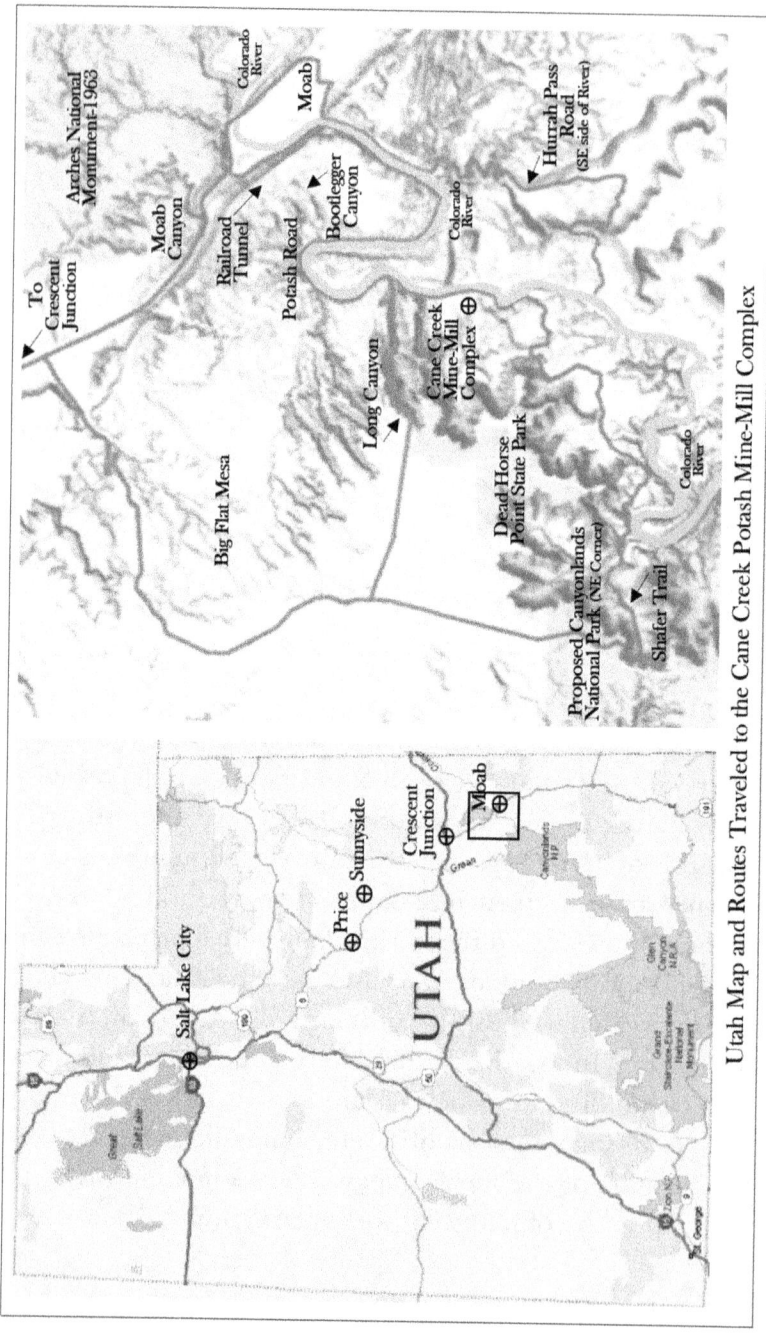

Utah Map and Routes Traveled to the Cane Creek Potash Mine-Mill Complex

Disaster at Cane Creek

On August 14, 1961, officials from the Denver and Rio Grande Western Railway (D&RGW), TGS and several other companies, along with local business dignitaries were on hand for the groundbreaking ceremony for the new railway spur that would service the potash facility. The ceremonial affair was held[74] at the proposed tunnel's north portal, directly west of the uranium plant, high on the bluff above Moab Valley.

Also in August, plans were underway for TGS and Isbell Construction to build a dirt road down through Long Canyon.[75] It was to be an alternate route to alleviate the persistent travel problems and provide better access to the Cane Creek complex for men and equipment during closures during the river road's construction.

Starting from the Dead Horse Point road on Big Flat Mesa, the new road spiraled down off the rim with a series of drops, switchbacks, and narrow chutes with dramatic scenery down through the canyon to the Colorado River. The new road met up with the new river road near the Cane Creek Mine site. The grades reached nineteen percent in places, and straight segments were rare. Initially, the new road was called Shipman's Cutoff, after the route's designer, Oran Shipman, the project manager for Stearns-Roger, but it later took on the name of Long Canyon.[76]

By October, work was well underway on the railway spur. Several of the projects within this massive undertaking was huge. A tunnel, 7,100-feet long and measuring, sixteen by twenty-four feet, was blasted through the canyon wall above the Moab Canyon to the head of Bootlegger Canyon. From there the line curved to follow the Colorado River and the new river road. The major difficulty with the railroad design was the criteria established on grade and curvature. Only a maximum of 1.2 percent grade and five percent curvature was allowed.[77]

The presence of Bootlegger Canyon made the rail spur feasible. The canyon, as its name and antique stills attest, had been useful in

35

the past, but not because of accessibility. Bootleggers used the canyons during the Prohibition era. The remote back canyon country was used to their advantage to hide their moonshine stills.[78]

The "Big Cut,"[79] a part of the rail spur project at the head of Moab Canyon was as large if not bigger than the 7,100-foot tunnel. Using large, heavy machines and blasting, Morrison-Knudsen actually cut a canyon of their own. The giant cut measured 120 feet across, and 120 feet[80] deep which were necessary to maintain the needed grade required by D&RGW Railway. The cut was terraced at its deepest point and at thirty-foot intervals, fifteen-foot benches were cut to stock any falling rocks. The terracing also reduced the size of the passage to thirty feet at the bottom where the line passed through. By December, construction of the tall Headframe at the mine site continued as crews did grade work at the mine-mill complex and sub-grade for the rail road yard.

At the beginning of 1962, three hundred men were working on the rail project, and by June, the light was seen out the other end of the tunnel[81] as crews broke through into Bootlegger Canyon. A month later, finishing touches were made on the "Big Cut."[82] By the fall, the majority of work was completed on the rail spur; it had taken nearly a year to complete. D&RGW Railroad designated the Cane Creek Mine-mill complex, "Potash, Utah, U.S.A." as the name of the termination point for the line.[83]

The contract with Morrison-Knudsen[84] was a massive project, and the construction statistics were unbelievable to those unfamiliar with the rugged terrain over which the track ran. Overall costs ran over $6 million, excavation required three million cubic yards, and a construction overpass over Highway 160 required a huge 120-foot cut to maintain the 1.2 percent grade. Finally, a tunnel had to be hollowed out of solid sandstone. All this, before the tracks could wind the remainder of their way down the river canyon to the TGS plant on the river's edge.

Disaster at Cane Creek

At the end of May 1962, work on the other major projects was proceeding at a fast pace when workers again walked off the job for six days over transportation problems.[85] The alternate routes were all dirt roads through the rugged back-country and, at times, workers had to deal with muddy or washed out places from spring runoff or heavy rainstorms which made passage treacherous from flash floods ripping through the canyons. Because of this, the Long Canyon road was now in rough condition. Travel over new construction on the river road was sporadic, and a bus line carrying the route shut down, sparking the walk-off.[86] For those using a boat to get to work, torrential rains would dump water from all the canyons causing the river to swell making conditions too dangerous to navigate the swift currents.

At this same time, construction crews on the river road were also battling high spring runoff again. The river would recede enough for the road to reopen but would rise causing another closure. Constant efforts were exerted to keep the road open against encroaching waters, creating a daily fight for construction crews.[87] Enormous work was going into making this wilderness frontier area conform. Rugged and untamed, the land was like the wild horses and outlaws who once roamed the area, and nature was not about to yield willingly. Immediately, the company made the needed improvements to the Long Canyon route, and C.S. Thomson of Moab opened a bus service to the site,[88] satisfying the disgruntled workers as work resumed.

By June 1962, all the major buildings and structures at the potash mine-mill complex were under construction, giving a definite shape to the massive operation. The other buildings were still only ten percent complete but proceeding rapidly. The Headframe over the shaft was virtually complete although installation of permanent hoists and other equipment continued.[89] The tallest industrial structure in the state, the rectangular shaped Headframe, stood off-set on the property with a large opening on one end, facing a northwesterly direction.

The mine shaft was at the 1,701-foot level in July when Harrison International's crews ran into the water again. They were far behind schedule due to all the groundwater they kept encountering. Six months earlier, at the 949-foot level in December of 1961,[90] their crews first hit the water. Not a lot. But they spent two days grouting—a process of sealing off water flow in rocks by forcing a thin slurry of cement into the crevices.

A month later, at 980 feet, they again ran into the water and had to grout.[91] By February, at the 1,180 level, a substantial amount of water was encountered. Grouting again sealed the water off but consumed 26 days.[92] While probing down 155 feet, crews found another water zone which meant more grouting. By the middle of June, at 1,434 feet, the halfway point for the shaft, crews ran into another major water problem, delaying work yet again. This time, workers took twenty-eight days to grout, ten of those days they used a chemical grout. There were reports from workers of grout coming up in the river. A young, TGS engineer went looking to see if there might be any truth to the rumors and found grout and water coming out of a natural rock formation below the property's edge on the south side, where the ground had not been graded and leveled.[93] The crews started using every type of quick setting grout to get the shaft sealed.[94] Finally, they were successful in shutting off the water from the fissures permeating throughout the strata at this level.[95]

At the 1,701 level, they were expecting to hit another water zone at 1,800 feet, and grouting would commence again.[96] While the Cane Creek site sits on the banks of the Colorado River, encountering water should have been no surprise,[97] but the amount of groundwater they kept running into was what was so concerning. When they first hit the water in the shaft, the contract between

Harrison International and TGS was broken. They had based their bid on a dry shaft[98] and had to re-negotiate the terms. Besides the delays and the costs, the water made work conditions in the shaft miserable for the men. The crews installed an underground station room to house the pumps at the 1,330-foot level with collecting rings at 600-foot intervals down the shaft to catch groundwater to pump out of the mine.[99]

As Harrison International crews reached the bottom, ninety feet above the predetermined shaft station level, instead of water, they encountered large amounts of crude oil.[100] Crews worked to contain the huge mess and used foam to get it sealed and hung curtains to contain the fumes.[101]

By the end of 1962, the new river road, although still not complete, was opened to traffic using a schedule to move traffic through construction areas during specified times. The delays were maddening at times, and workers complained to the state about the huge dust problem which posed a driving hazard. The state remedied the situation by watering down the road before the scheduled times for traffic.

Also at this time, the TGS office personnel moved from town to the new main administrative office building at the mine site. The building had elements of mid-century design with a stacked rock wall partition in the lobby, floor-to-ceiling windows, and large roomy offices and work areas.

During the cold, snowy months of December and January of 1962-63, the mill complex was nearing completion, and the majority of work left to complete was inside the buildings. By the end of January, Stearns-Roger completed construction on the new mill complex,[102] and by the end of February, Harrison International had reached the shaft bottom. Work now began on the mine's construction. They still had to develop two parallel drifts out to the ore bed, with several crosscuts connecting them and to build raises (small vertical shafts) for underground storage bins before the contract's completion. Once completed, they would then turn the mine over to TGS to start the mining and milling of the potash ore.

At the end of February, TGS completed their new mining/engineering offices and change house building. Located below the main administrative office building, their current employees in the mining and engineering departments promptly moved into the office spaces. The change house had 322 clothing baskets that lined the ceiling, many awaiting the influx of permanent employees who would eventually be employed at the operation once TGS took possession of the mine.[103]

By the first of June, the state was surfacing the new river road.[104] With most of the major projects completed at the mine-mill complex, scaled back work crews continued with the finish work and cleanup.

As July rolled around, the construction of the potash mine-mill complex was in the final phase, and the cost was reported to now be at thirty-five million. With the surface facilities completed, the operation was ready as soon as the underground mine development permitted actual mining. Limited production was estimated to get underway sometime in August, using Harrison International's temporary hoisting and conveyor equipment installed for the construction phase.[105] But that date was pushed into September, and the company hoped crews would get to the potash ore by then.

The delays pushed everything back, even a planned shutdown scheduled for September when Harrison International would scale back crews and do the work to divide the deep shaft with a cement wall. This cement partition would become part of the permanent ventilation system that would be constructed at that time. Huge air compressors would force fresh air down one side of the shaft and into the mine with exhaust air coming up the other side.

Also, during this time, the remainder of permanent hoisting conveyor equipment would also be installed, allowing the miners to use the new hoist equipment at the top of the Headframe. This part of the project was expected to take about three months.[106] But this work couldn't start until Harrison International's crews had the two mine drifts (the passageways) mined out to the ore bed and other aspects of the development work completed for the underground mine.

The new Potash Road turned out to be a beautiful scenic drive meandering through the picturesque river canyon with sheer cliffs in shaded tones of varnished hues of red, orange and purple. Constantly changing, the incandescent light and shadows moved throughout the day, casting an essence of sheer poetic beauty. This red Wonderland was filled with ardent emotion and brilliant intensity. It's no wonder writer Edward Abbey filled books about this red rock paradise: "It's the most weird, wonderful, magical place on earth," he wrote of this incredibly beautiful sculptured desert landscape.[107]

For some of the men working at the Cane Creek Mine, they hardly noticed the beauty anymore. The beautiful, red canyons had become commonplace, mundane, and a part of the everyday humdrum of working and etching out a living for their families—like all too many who get lost in living a life of prosaic ordinariness.

Speeding along, the Travelall navigated the turns of the road, eventually meeting up with the new railroad spur on the right side, the river on the left. After passing an arch running down the side of a cliff, resembling a jug handle, the canyon walls opened, giving a small peek of an open valley in the distance. The upper part of the mine's Headframe jetted above the distant landscape that was still obscuring part of the view. Moving closer, each curve in the road gradually revealed other structures: metal buildings, tanks, conveyor lines, and the broadside of one of the two massive storage sheds. At times, things seemed surprisingly close, a mystical phenomenon where distant objects are magnified by the crystalline air[108] of the Colorado Plateau.

As the Travelall left the narrow river canyon near the complex, on the last leg of the journey, the site came into full view. The large facility, situated in a rugged valley, was surrounded by ancient red sandstone mounds[109] and cliffs. In the rough, desert geography, the mine-mill facility sat on a knoll, once a loaf-like hill chewed down to half its original size by crews who spread, smoothed, compacted, and leveled the earth to build foundations.[110]

At the west end of the property, the large Headframe sat over the deep mine shaft. Some of the structures and buildings, painted in different muted hues of industrial greens, tans, beige, and gray (with one silo painted a brilliant red), were situated near or between the Headframe and the massive storage sheds. The whole complex gradually sloped towards the river. With several large, multi-level areas for the structures, roads slopped to access the different areas. The site had wood stairs scattered around the site for employees to traverse the various levels. Slightly downhill from the gigantic storage sheds, nearest the river, was the train load-out facility which straddled the railroad tracks where potash would soon be loaded into rail cars and sent to market.

Just ahead was the end of the paved road. The pavement of the new river road ended south of the mine-mill property where it turned into a dirt road, a road seemingly without end. This dirt road leads into the rugged, meandering back-country at the ends of the earth, where the county resembles an "other-worldly" landscape, an apt description of the red, spectacular Canyonlands country. It's also where the Shafer Trail traverses a sliver of this vast wilderness area.

Arriving at the facility, the Travelall took a right turn off the paved road, crossed the tracks and headed up the hill to the parking lot at the top end of the facility. Other afternoon employees were also arriving on site. A Chevy Suburban Carryall driven by Ivan James, a Hoistman, pulled in as Paul McKinney and several other men riding with him scrambled out. More vehicles pulled in and parked as the workers made their way over the dusty red dirt, to Harrison International's change house to dress for work. The site bustled with activity as the surface day shift employees were getting last minute tasks done before the shift change.

From the vantage point of the parking lot, looking east across the greenish-blue Colorado River was an impressive view of a large canyon and mountain peaks. Sheer cliffs rose hundreds of feet in varnished shades of reds and purple. In the distance were the smooth, rounded tops of lighter colored pinkish-blush Navajo Sandstone mesas. These domes obscured much of the view of the bluish-gray La Sal Mountain range beyond, with only its peaks visible, silhouetted against a vibrant blue sky filled with billowy white clouds. The lush, forested La Sal Mountains were a sharp contrast from desert red rock country.

This desert country was a place of high drama and wild extremes with its moving light and changing color. Explorer John Wesley Powell's journal describes a "weird grand region of naked rock with cathedral shaped buttes, towering hundreds or thousands of feet, cliffs that cannot be scaled, and canyon walls that shrink the river into insignificance,...and all highly colored."[111]

The whole Cane Creek Mine-mill complex was swallowed up in the expansive grandeur of this ancient land. Nevertheless, the 18-story cement Headframe, over the entrance to the mine, dominated the site as the flag on top blew in the wind. This tall majestic structure stood erect, like a sentinel standing at attention guarding the entire complex. The tall headframe dutifully watched over the whole operation, with a sense of bravado and assured pride. A beacon, broadcasting the hope and promise of a thriving new industry, signaled to all a newfound hope as the new mining facility neared completion. This new industry was a huge deal for the people living in Grand and San Juan Counties and the state of Utah.

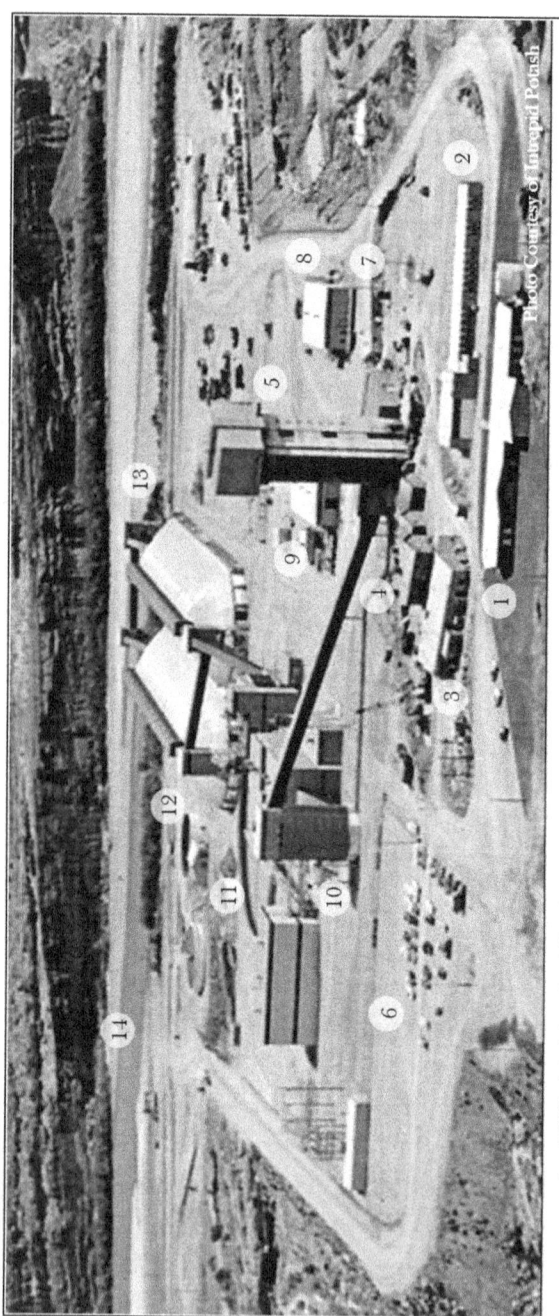

1. TGS's Administrative Office Building
2. TGS's Mine Offices & Change House
3. Harrison's Dry House, Office, Warehouse & Shop
4. Harrison's three Hoist Houses
5. Headframe
6. Designated Employee Parking Lot
7. Lavatory Building and Core House (behind the Lab)
8. Central Warehouse
9. Machine Shop
10. Red Ore Bin with Conveyor Belt
11. Potash Dryer
12. Product Storage Buildings
13. Railroad Loadout Area
14. Colorado River

Cane Creek Mine-Mill Complex

Chapter 3

Point of Eruption

The ceiling of Harrison International's change house was lined with wire baskets hung up high and each accessed by its own chain and pulley system, typical in the mining industry. The men lowered their baskets, retrieved work clothes, and then replaced them with street clothes and shoes, often hanging some items on hooks attached to the bottom of the baskets. The baskets were then raised back up to the ceiling out of the way. At the end of a shift, wet work clothes hung under the baskets to dry in the warmer air which circulated near the ceiling. Often, by the end of the week, work clothes were stiff and crusty from the accumulation of sweat from the men and salt from the mine and could practically stand up by themselves.

Once dressed, the men working underground picked up a small industrial battery pack from a charging rack. The battery was placed inside a leather pocket on their mine belt, with its power cord connected to their cap-lamp, which was then attached to the front of their hard hats.[1] The battery, typically good for up to 12 hours, was recharged after each shift. Mines are very dark places. The battery-operated cap-lamps gave miners the light they needed while leaving their hands free to work.

Ready for work, the men made their way down to their work areas. The afternoon Hoistmen relieved the day shift Hoistmen, located in the first two hoist houses near the Headframe. The other surface workers went to their respective workplaces as the miners headed to the Headframe to catch a bucket to take them underground.

Inside the Headframe, the first group of men jumped into a waiting bucket on the west side, Rene Roy being one of them. When ready, the Toplander signaled the Hoistman to lower the bucket; three bells, a pause, followed by two bells; everyone, either inside the bucket or sitting on the rim, braced themselves for the descent.

Shaft mines use a system of electric-powered Bell Signals to communicate with the Hoistman using a code posted at each station or level in the mine. These bells ring at the different locations and hoist houses. One bell for stop, two bells to lower, and so forth. Following the commands from inside the hoist houses, the Hoistmen operated levers that controlled the hoists to either raise or lower the buckets hanging in the shaft at the end of the metal hoisting cables. At Cane Creek, they also used an intercom system[2] along with the bell setup.

Rene Roy, a Shift Walker (Shift Foreman), generally worked on the previous shift and was known for being tough and assertive. Sometimes called 'Frenchie,' he was a fun-loving French Canadian from Ontario. A seasoned hard-rock miner, he had worked for Harrison International through the years on other shaft construction projects and had been asked specifically by Harrison International to come with others to Moab to get the new shaft and mine started.[3]

Today, Rene agreed to work the afternoon shift for Bert Trenfield[4] so Trenfield could take his wife out to dinner later in the evening for their tenth anniversary. Trenfield, Harrison International's Mine Superintendent, had been filling in for one of his other Shift Walkers, Henry Laviolette, who was the regular Shift Walker but was off for the week. To take the day off, much less a week off, was difficult for the men. They were working seven days a week[5] trying to make up for unanticipated delays mostly from encountering water while sinking the shaft. Harrison International was now eight months over the seventeen months they initially estimated it would take to sink the shaft and develop the mine.[6]

At the collar, the remaining men gathered in small groups and chit-chatted while waiting for the next bucket to surface to take them underground. It was another typical work day with the August temperatures still in the nineties. The conversation soon turned to Rene Roy (filling in as the Shift Walker on their shift) and to the new vehicle he had just purchased earlier in the day from the car dealership in Moab.[7]

"There's the car he bought this morning," one of the guys said, pointing towards the parking area. The men all looked in the direction where a brand new 1963 Chevy Impala[8] was parked. The brown, four-door sedan, sparkled in the afternoon sun and sported the popular long, low, sleek, sexy design with pointed front and rear fenders.[9]

A bucket surfaced as day shift workers jumped out and shuffled towards the change house stirring up red dust with their boots. Time for a quick shower before heading home for the day. The afternoon workers crowded around the metal railing, went through the rail opening and piled into the bucket while a few of them rode the rim. The Toplander belled the Hoistman and the bucket disappeared down into the mine.

At the bottom of the mine on the west side of the shaft station, small knots of workers gathered around, as the bucket came to a stop. The men piled out, then a waiting group of day shift workers climbed in for the trip out. The afternoon shift started at 3:30 p.m. After several trips up and down the shaft to transport men, the shift change was complete.

From the shaft station, two main drifts,[10] the passageways, extend nearly parallel to each other with each on a downward grade in a southwesterly direction toward the potash deposits. The East Drift named 3U was at a higher elevation than the other and was already excavated out from the shaft station 3,170 feet, just over a half-mile. The shorter West Drift, named 2 South, was now out about 2,080 feet from the shaft station. At the end of each drift was the Face. The Face is a mining term for where miners dynamite as they blast their way towards the known potash vein as they advance the passageway.

Dispersing to their designated work areas, the miners walked or hitched a ride in the back of a shuttle car left parked by the day shift crews around the station. Shuttle cars were used to haul muck (the waste rock) to the shaft station to dump into the hopper of the feeder-breaker. The twenty-ton Stamiler feeder-breaker, on steel track wheels, crushed the rock, then with its conveyor arm, modified with a chute, dumped the muck into buckets. Running the feeder-breaker and filling the buckets was orchestrated by the operator called the Skip Loader. Robert Bobo was the Skip Loader on the east side of the shaft, while Jesse Kassler was the Skip Loader on the west side.

Hanna, the Lead Miner of the crew working in the East Drift (called 3U), stood nearby as his men gathered and gradually got on the back of one of the four parked shuttle cars, which would transport them to their working Face over a half-mile away. Hanna became Lead Miner when the drift development work started. Harrison International's bosses from Canada were more experienced in shaft sinking, and when they discovered Hanna had previous experience in running key pieces of mining equipment in the working Face, they made him a Lead Miner.[11]

An experienced miner from the coal fields near Lorado, West Virginia, Shuttle Car Operator (Torkar), Kenneth Milton, got into the seat of his shuttle car, located on the side. Earlier that day, his wife, Ina, wanted him to stay home so he would be there when his sister and her family arrived from West Virginia. They were moving to Utah because Milton had told them how wonderful Moab and the people were. But he didn't stay home. He was never one to miss work.

While waiting for other crew members to gather, Milton put in a wad of 'Baby Chew,' his preferred brand of chewing tobacco.[12] Coal miners typically chew tobacco underground since smoking was strictly forbidden. Smoking could easily start a fire by igniting gas or coal dust that could quickly get out of control since there was an unlimited supply of fuel to burn in the mine. In an exception, many of the hard rock miners could freely smoke underground in those mines not hampered with gas.

One of the crew members, a young, twenty-two-year-old kid named Paul McKinney, was already in the back of the shuttle car and sitting near Milton when Sherman Holbrook, the Shuttle Car Operator from the day shift, walked back to talk to Milton. He told Milton the batteries to his shuttle car were going dead, and he would need to put them on charge the first chance he got. Holbrook also said they were still waiting for the new alternator to fix the problem. Milton assured Holbrook he would charge the battery.[13]

Tom Trueman, another Shuttle Car Operator, headed towards the first crosscut to get over to the East Drift with a couple of crew members in the back. Trueman came to Cane Creek from Canada to work for Harrison. Originally from Ireland where his parents still lived, Trueman had red hair and spoke with an Irish accent.[14] Rene Roy, the Shift Walker, hopped into the back of Milton's shuttle car[15] along with Hanna and the rest of the crew and off they went, following not far behind Trueman.

The West Drift crew and their Lead Miner, Fred Rowley, headed down the West Drift in the other two shuttle cars towards their working Face. The remainder of the men dispersed to other working areas in the mine, a couple of them worked in the raise area and a handful of them worked near the shaft station and shop. There were still other men coming and going into the mine.

The two Lead Miners, Blake Hanna and Fred Rowley, tried to keep careful watch over the well-being of their crews. Safety had become a significant concern, particularly at this mine. Both men, experienced coal miners from Carbon County, were highly trained. They were certified as Facebosses and in the use of flame safety lamps. They took proper gas readings throughout the day and regularly conferred with each other[16] on safety issues as their crews advanced both drifts out towards the ore bed each day.

Several of Hanna's men arrived at the Face of the East Drift (3U) and surveyed the work done by the day shift. Passing Trueman's parked shuttle car at the transformer station, Milton drove past and down near the Face.[17] The remaining crew members jumped out and gathered with the other men.

Everyone knew crews were getting close to the potash. The word was that the day shift had finally reached the ore bed. Rene Roy would have been on the day shift had he not traded, so he came to see for himself. Sure enough, a small portion of potash was exposed on the Face wall above the muck pile. The variegated light to dark pinkish colored ore contrasted against the gray shale still all around.[18] One, possibly two shots, and the crews would be completely into the potash ore bed.[19] Potash was the pay dirt everyone had worked so hard to reach since April of 1961.

The shorter West Drift (called 2 South) was still only about three-fourths of the way to the ore bed. An exciting time, everyone felt like they were finally making progress after a long-fought battle against the will of Mother Nature. Now she was beginning to yield up the prize and the bounties of the earth.

After surveying the work done by the day shift crew, the men assessed what they needed to do and went to work. Rene spoke with Hanna, as they coordinated the work between the two drifts. Rene knew the West Drift crew was getting ready to dynamite the Face and they wouldn't need the extra shuttle cars on their side to clean out the muck for a while. At least one could come and help on the east side.

Crew members dispersed to gather needed materials and to set up equipment. Paul McKinney, 'C.C.' Clark and Pete Sviscsu were getting ready to roof bolt. At the Face, there was about three shuttle car loads of muck still left on the ground from the day shift. The men liked to stand on the muck pile that was just the right height for drilling and rock bolting. Rock bolting is the drilling and gluing of long metal rods into the Back (metal/nonmetal mining term for the roof). Rock bolting the Back gave added support, making it safer for the miners to work beneath.

"Why don't you leave us the muck until we get the roof bolting done, then we'll muck afterward?" McKinney inquired.[20] Rene and Hanna agreed, and the men went to work. Hanna had a great crew of five men: Paul McKinney, Charles Clark, known as 'C.C.,' Pete Sviscsu, Wesley Barber and Kenneth Milton (who was their assigned Shuttle Car Operator).

Twenty-seven-years-old, 'C.C.,' a nice-looking family man with four young children, was a hard-working miner. He had a slender build and kept his dark hair closely cropped. He came to Cane Creek in 1961 from Wyoming where he "roughnecked" for an oil company. Mostly quiet-spoken, he was also known for his humorous side and did a fair bit of kidding around. He was good at telling stories or jokes. A genuine guy, he was well liked by the other men.

Pete Sviscsu, a single, forty-two-year-old, was originally from an eastern European country. He had worked at a uranium mine in Grants, New Mexico before coming to Cane Creek several months before and had only been on Hanna's crew a few weeks. A pleasant sort of person, he was a serious, hardworking man. Because of his thick Slavic accent, many of the other men had a difficult time understanding him, so some of them didn't know too much about him.

Thirty-five-year-old Wesley Barber was a Canadian miner who came from Elliot Lake, Ontario and had only worked at Cane Creek for the past six weeks. He too was a good hand.

While getting his roof bolter set up, McKinney overheard Milton tell Rene his shuttle car's alternator wasn't working and he needed to charge the battery as soon as possible. Rene said okay, but he wanted to leave with him. A few minutes later, the shuttle car left with both men headed up the drift, back towards the shaft station towards the charging station, located next to the shop.[21]

Rene had worked for Harrison International at a previous shaft sinking project at Esterhazy, Canada before coming to Cane Creek. At Esterhazy, Harrison International sunk a 3,300-foot shaft for International Mosaic Company (IMC) at their new potash mine. When crews in Canada hit the potash ore bed, Rene was one of the first two men who rode on top of a muck bucket, hand carrying chunks of potash to the surface to present to officials.[22] Rene also took a souvenir piece of potash home to Ontario. He wrapped it in foil and kept the chuck in the fridge, where unbeknownst to him, his young children would sneak and take licks of the salty tasting ore.

Ideally, the workflow started at the Cane Creek Mine when Harrison International's crew from one drift advanced their Face by shooting it using dynamite, then transporting the fallen rock called muck to the shaft in the shuttle cars, where it would then be taken out of the mine in ore buckets.

In the meantime, the crew in the other drift was usually busy doing roof bolting and advancing the utilities (the large corrugated metal vent air line, the small compressed air line, the water line, electrical lines, etc.), to the Face. Then the crew would drill the Face and pack dynamite into the holes in preparation to blast. Meanwhile, the other drift would advance their utilities. Back and forth the work

Disaster at Cane Creek

continued in the two drifts, and barring any complications, they would create a continuous rhythm of work.

At the surface, on the outside wall of the Headframe, a fixed ladder led to a landing—a catwalk—on about the fourth story level where the Bucket Dumper worked. Once the buckets were filled with muck down in the mine, the filled buckets were hoisted to this landing and dumped into ore bins hanging on the outside of the Headframe. Dump trucks parked under the ore bins. With chutes on the bottom, they opened to load the muck into the trucks. It was then hauled away to a designated area and dumped.

Upon the landing, Matt Rauhala[23] was busy working, dumping buckets. A filled bucket was raised higher than the landing, then with the push of a button, metal doors closed automatically over the shaft. Lowering the bucket to the landing, Rauhala used a hooked rod to snag the large metal ring attached to the bottom. Securing the bucket to the metal railing of landing with a chain, he then slowly lowered the bucket as the top tipped down, pouring the muck onto the chute leading to the ore bins.

Dust was flying everywhere as Clell Johnson made his way up the ladder to the landing. He worked the day shift and was now working overtime. His deep-set hazel eyes were framed within a square face and were inquisitive as he came to see what Rauhala needed.[24] The forty-four-year-old electrician had been employed at Cane Creek for the past six months. Originally from Huntington, Utah, Clell moved his family to Dragerton in 1952 after taking a job near there as an electrician and mechanic at the Kaiser Steel Coal Mine. Dragerton was the same small coal town in Carbon County where Rauhala was from, and both men knew each other well.

Clell had worked in the area coal mines all his life and lost the end of his pointer finger[25] on his right hand and nearly lost his life on several other occasions in previous mining accidents. While working at the coal mine near Hiawatha, Utah, a small coal mining camp southwest of Price, he had been fixing a large mining machine when

53

it pinned him against the Rib. Smashing him, it nearly cut him in half. Not expected to live, Clell lost a kidney and after several surgeries, endured a full body cast for six months. He eventually pulled through. Tess, his wife, had an especially difficult time. They had four small children. Ned, the oldest, and Carolyn, the third child, came down with rheumatic fever during this period. Carolyn also contracted the scarlet fever.[26]

Clell was also electrocuted while working at the Kaiser Steel Mine. He killed the power to a particular cable he was working on, but by the time he got back to where he was working, somebody had switched the power back on. (This happened before the industry enforced any safety lockout mechanisms.) Clell was electrocuted while kneeling with one leg on the ground next to the rail tracks using a pocket knife to strip the insulation off of the power cable. The current went directly into his hand and his bent leg, burning his leg severely. Had he been standing, most likely, the current would have gone throughout his body and killed him.

When the market for coal dropped, many coal miners were laid off in Carbon County. Clell decided to leave before he too lost his job. He first found work at a potash mine near Carlsbad, New Mexico. Too far from home, he was eventually hired closer to home at the Cane Creek Mine, about the time the drift development work started down in the mine. Clell and Tess moved to Moab with their youngest son, Kirt, who was now sixteen and the only one of their children still living at home. They bought a mobile home to live in and rented out their house in Dragerton.[27]

Once emptied, Rauhala, after unhooking the now upright bucket from the railing and opening the metal shaft doors, gave the Bell Signal for the Hoistman to take the bucket back down into the depths of the mine. Rauhala noticed Clell and started to tell him that he needed him to put in some lights on that level.

"You can't even see up here," he proceeded to tell Clell.[28] Even though Rauhala had a cap-lamp on his hard hat, better lighting was needed, especially on the afternoon and graveyard shifts when night came.

Clell told Rauhala he had to go underground but would be back and put the lights up as soon as he could. Rauhala knew how things worked around there and knew they would probably keep him underground doing other things. Insistent, he told Clell to get his lights put in first before he went underground.

Clell reassured Rauhala that when he finished, he would be back to set up his lights. For now, he needed to help fix one of the machines[29] down in the mine, and he wanted to see for himself the potash ore.[30] He had heard the rumor that the day shift in the East Drift had reached the potash bed.

"Damn it Clell," Rauhala scolded, "I need you to get me my lights up and do it now. You know what's gonna happen," Rauhala warned, "you'll go down below, and you'll never get back up."[31] Clell smiled and said he would be back, then started down the ladder disappearing out of sight.

While Harrison International's men were still in the process of developing the new mine, TGS regularly had employees working underground on two shifts, days and swing (or afternoon as many referred to it). They did the engineering and provided the maintenance of some of the equipment. Their employees also did ventilation checks, temperature readings, gas testing, and collection of other needed data.[32]

Forty-seven-year-old, Grant Eslick, who went by the nickname 'Blackie,' was recently hired by Texas Gulf Sulphur (TGS) because of his past mining experience. He was to be one of their Mine Foremen once the actual mining of potash began. An estimated 400 employees would be needed to work the new operation. Harrison International would be finished with the contract work soon, but for now, 'Blackie' was doing mine inspections and assumed the role of a Fire Boss.[33]

A Fire Boss is a person designated to examine the mine for gases, particularly explosive, poisonous or suffocating gases, as well as other dangers. Usually, the Fire Boss is the first person to enter a mine to inspect and verify it is safe before crews enter the mine and who usually make other examinations during the shift.

In the Middle Ages, this was extremely dangerous work, which was generally done by a criminal to atone for his crimes, or by a penitent for the benefit of mankind. The person would wear thick clothes or a hooded cloak, usually soaked in water; and at times, they were called the "Penitent" because of his monk-like appearance. He would go throughout the mine, sometimes crawling low to the ground with a lit candle affixed to the end of a long stick. Held high towards the roof, he pushed the flame ahead, exploding any pockets of gases present in the mine. At times, large pockets of gas would not spare the one on the other end.[34] Eventually, less dangerous methods were developed, such as adequate ventilation where the air was pumped into the mine to dilute the levels of hazardous gases from the explosive ranges, making them harmless while the current of air expelled the gases out of the mine.

At 3:10 p.m., 'Blackie' went underground ahead of the afternoon shift change. After greeting employees at the shaft station, he headed to the underground shop.[35] The shaft station and shop areas were well lit with installed lighting while the rest of the mine was dark, illuminated only by the battery-operated cap-lamps on the miners' hard hats or the headlights on the mobile mine equipment.

The shop, located on the west side, was not far from the shaft station. There, 'Blackie' checked on some equipment undergoing repairs—a loader and a shuttle car.[36] The men working in the shop were getting ready to leave for the day, and while there, 'Blackie' made no gas checks. A TGS employee had already made a gas check at 3:00 p.m., just before 'Blackie' came on shift, but he had found none.[37]

Today, 'Blackie' was assigned a new duty, to observe the work by Hanna's crew at the Face of the East Drift (3U). He also had a new piece of equipment[38] for taking temperature readings he wanted to try out as well. After the afternoon crews headed to their work areas, 'Blackie' walked to the East Drift and spent ten to fifteen minutes taking temperature readings on the way before arriving at the Face.[39] There, the crew was busy drilling rock bolt holes using jackleg drills.[40] With his gas meter, 'Blackie' took readings for methane gas but found none.[41] He then took some temperature readings while part of the crew started to attach a section of chain link fencing to the back with rock bolts.[42] Hanna and a couple of other crew members were working up the drift about a hundred feet from the Face, removing and replacing the flexible vent tubing with the thirty-six-inch steel vent line, the work of advancing it towards the Face.[43]

'Blackie' sat down on a nearby loader to take some more tests and record the data. A quiet, reserved man, he had moved his family to Moab eight years ago and was well-known[44] around town. Originally from Mullin, Idaho, he was an experienced miner and had worked in the uranium mines around the Moab area before being hired on by TGS.[45]

It was a little after 4:00 p.m. when the shuttle car with Milton and Rene Roy went through the first cross cut into the West Drift (2 South). They moved over into a recessed area when they saw Chuck Byrge coming towards them in his shuttle car.

Four diesel-powered shuttle cars (Torkars), worked the mine. Each drift had one assigned to it; Milton worked the East Drift, and Keith Schear worked the west side. The other two shuttle cars, driven by Tom Trueman and Chuck Byrge, went where they were needed between the two drifts.[46]

Byrge stopped to let Milton know he had checked at the surface shop on the alternator for his shuttle car.⁴⁷ He was told the part wasn't in yet—possibly tomorrow. Milton let Byrge know that he was headed to the charging station to put the battery on charge but first he was dropping off Rene to check on the west side crew and their work progress.⁴⁸

Rene chimed in and told Byrge to pick up a six-foot long piece of thirty-six-inch, metal vent pipe that had rolled down the incline further up the drift from them. Afterwards, Byrge needed to head to the other side and help Hanna's crew extend their vent line into the Face.

Byrge proceeded to inform Rene the crew in the West Drift was getting ready to blast, and he was helping them with the primer and powder. Normally Byrge didn't like being in the drift where they were shooting the Face because of the thick black powder smoke. Typically, he headed to the other side until the smoke dissipated.⁴⁹

"You take the pipe and get on over there. Keith can help them, eh," Rene ordered. He was referring to Keith Schear, the young Shuttle Car Operator who had come back to work the previous week after being off for several weeks following a mine accident. Byrge wasn't too happy about going to the other side and tried to get Rene to change his mind.

"I'm sooree, if you don't like it get oot. Get your ass in the bucket and get on oot of here,"⁵⁰ Rene threatened in his thick French Canadian accent. Milton's shuttle car then headed down the drift towards the West Face.

Byrge started the engine and headed to pick up the section of pipe before heading towards the shuttle car lube and service area, located at the outby (mining term relating to nearness to the shaft) entrance of the shop near the shaft station.⁵¹ While picking up some supplies near the shaft area, Byrge saw several guys working over near the station. After getting what he needed, he started to get on his shuttle car when he noticed something in the opposite direction out of the corner of his eye. Over in the shop, the lights were out,

Disaster at Cane Creek

and in the darkness, he saw what looked like a glow on the walls. Puzzled, he went to check things out. He walked around the corner into the shop from the shaft station and found no one was around; he assumed everyone was probably in the West Drift helping to fix the drilling or loading machines.[52]

Byrge found the source of the glow on the walls. There, towards the middle of the shop near the Rib, a flame safety lamp was suspended from the Back by a wire. The lamp, belonging to TGS, was on fire. The flame was burning up through the gaze, (the metal mesh above the wick area of the lamp). Smoking like crazy, the flame was depositing a large circle of soot onto the roof. Chuck shook his head in disbelief. A coal miner from the coal fields in Carbon County, he knew this wasn't good. Flame safety lamps are used in gassy mines to detect the presence of methane gas, but if not used correctly they can cause mine explosions by igniting pockets of gas.[53]

Only a month earlier, TGS and the Utah State Industrial Commission handed out flame safety lamps after a pocket of gas had ignited down in the East Drift. There were some stories about the misuse of the flame safety lamps that was common knowledge among the miners. Unfortunately, many of the men never knew how to use the lamps and were never actually trained in their proper use.[54] Apparently, someone thought occasionally observing a hanging lamp was considered an appropriate gas test. Apparently, someone from the day shift left the lit lamp hanging there unattended.[55]

Typically, gas readings were taken at the beginning of each shift and before and after blasting. Correct readings were done by raising a lighted lamp slowly up towards the ceiling, especially in areas where gas can collect. While observing the small flame, encased in glass, they look for any changes in the size, shape, and color of the flame indicating the presence of gas. Maintenance of the lamps is vital. Each shift, they are supposed to be properly cleaned, serviced and refueled.

Hanging at arm's length, Byrge reached up to turn the wick down to extinguish the flame. Too hot to touch, he tried several times. Frustrated, he finally left thinking the lamp would soon burn the remaining fuel and go out on its own.[56] Cursing under his breath, and mumbling a few choice words, Byrge went back to his shuttle car and left, traveling through the first cross cut to get to the East Drift.

The Cane Creek Mine was not classified as a gassy mine, and the shop seemed an unlikely place to find methane gas. The shop was unlike the working Faces where gas checks were done regularly to detect methane liberated from the strata during the regular mining process. The men believed, if the company were so concerned about methane gas, they should have taken other precautions as well, such as the use of permissible mining equipment, unlike the diesel shuttle cars they used. The experienced coal miners at Cane Creek— Hanna, Byrge, Fred Rowley, and a handful of other men—all tried to tell Harrison International's bosses about the misuse of the flame safety lamps. But, some of the Canadian supervisors wouldn't listen.[57] Many were hard rock miners, and most basically had no experience with gassy mines.

―――――◆―――――

During the day shift, the crew working the shorter West Drift (2 South) was drilling rounds[58] to blast the Face when an air hose on the drilling machine stopped working. They needed a saw blade to cut through the hose to make repairs, but couldn't find one. So the crew halted work at 3:00 p.m. leaving a few holes left to drill by the afternoon shift[59] before the Face could be blasted.

The forty-one-year-old Lead Miner of the west side crew, Fred Rowley,[60] was an experienced coal miner from Carbon County. The guys who worked for him were John Tinall, Jimmy Hollinger, Emile LeBlanc, and one other miner, 'Bill' Huzil, who was filling in for one of the regular workers who was gone that week. And finally, there was Keith Schear, who was running the shuttle car on their side.[61]

Once the crew had the drilling machine repaired, they finished drilling the remaining holes then began charging them with dynamite[62] while one of the men retrieved the shared blasting unit from the other drift.[63] The crew was nearly ready to shoot the Face, something the day shift would have done had they not had problems with the drilling machine. The men strung the blasting cables out from the Face about 450 feet and set up the blasting unit.[64]

One west side crew member walked up the drift about a thousand feet from the Face, where some TGS guys were working. He informed one of them, Morris Worley,[65] the company's Rocks Mechanic Engineer that the crew was getting ready to blast the Face. They would need to leave the area.

Earlier in the day, Worley had gone underground to take the daily measurements at his rock closure station. Once finished, he joined the Mine Surveyor, Bill Smith, who was trying to get ahead of the month-end measuring game.[66] Ed Ziolkowski, another TGS Engineer, was also helping Smith with the survey work.[67] The men set line points for the crew as they mapped the advance in both drifts.[68] It was getting close to quitting time on the day shift, and Bill Smith was more than ready to leave. Unfortunately, they still needed to shoot side shots to mark the Ribs in the drifts.

Smith didn't care to be underground and would get headaches from the diesel fumes from the shuttle cars going back and forth through their area. An irritating nuisance, they typically had to move the tripod to let the shuttle cars by and then set the equipment back up again.[69] After the men had been told they needed to leave, they picked up the theodolite transit and tripod then made their way towards the shaft to an alcove further up the drift where they stored the surveying equipment in the mine.[70]

Ziolkowski went on ahead of Worley and Smith as the two put the survey equipment away. After everything had been stored, the men headed towards the shaft station to bell a lift to go topside. As they passed the inby (closest to the Face) entrance to the shop not far from the storage area, they passed Lawrence Davidson, Harrison International's Master Mechanic, who was repairing a loading machine.[71] He was a young surface employee who had requested permission to go underground earlier in the day to tour the new mine.[72]

At the Face, the crew was nearly ready to blast as they headed up the drift a safe distance. As soon as their area was cleared of workers and the blasting unit was wired, the crew shot the round of dynamite.

Hanna's crew in the East Drift were busy working when they heard the round of dynamite detonate over on the west side. The parallel drifts were close enough that the men could hear popping sounds whenever shots went off on the other side.[73] 'Blackie' was still sitting on the loader tinkering with his equipment and taking gas readings when he heard the shot go off. He looked at his watch and noted the time, 4:20 p.m.[74]

Blasting was nothing out of the ordinary as the men continued to work. The men down at the Face were still roof bolting while standing on the muck pile. McKinney, Sviscsu, and 'C.C.' were running the roof bolt machines while Trueman helped them with the chain link fencing and other tasks. Hanna, Barber, and Byrge were over a hundred feet from the other men, changing out the collapsible fan tubing to the large corrugated metal vent line and advancing it to the Face.[75]

Standing on the catwalk[76] in the Headframe above the shaft collar about four floors up, Rauhala, the Bucket Dumper, braced himself against a safety railing while he unloaded another ore bucket that came up from the mine.[77] Before long the filled buckets stopped coming. The Hoistman belled Rauhala off, and he descended the ladder to assist Ernie Simmons, the Toplander.[78] Ernie was busy loading and unloading material from the buckets and needed Rauhala's help.

At the collar, the two men loaded supplies as other workers came up from the mine and others went down. Some employees on day shift heard that the crew in the East Drift (3U), had reached the potash ore bed earlier in the day. Clell, one of them, wanted to check out the rumors.[79] So he headed down with Myrlen Christensen, Sr., the Master Mechanic on the afternoon shift.

About this time, three scientists from California doing contract work for the U.S. Bureau of Mines came up the shaft. They were doing testing work about half-way down the shaft at the 1,330 foot level at the pump station. Finished for the day, they surfaced and headed towards TGS's change house.[80]

It wasn't long before Rauhala and Ernie were caught up with filling orders from the mine. Ernie decided he wanted to smoke a cigarette but only had his lighter with him. So Rauhala told Ernie to go ahead; he would finish up and listen for the phone and would take care of everything. With a lighter in hand, Ernie went in search of his cigarettes while Rauhala got on a loader to retrieve a 50-gallon drum of oil[81] from the other side of the Headframe. Once Rauhala had the oil, he rolled the drum into an ore bucket and loaded some rope and cable that he fastened to the large heavy ring attached to the bottom of the bucket.

There was soon a lull in the work, so Rauhala decided to wait for telephone requests from the mine in the "Dilly Shack." The Dilly Shack was a temporary enclosure made of plywood with a roof to keep out the dust; it was located inside the Headframe, close to the twenty-two-foot round shaft.[82] Diamond plate metal flooring covered the shaft and had four openings for the buckets to go through as they went up and down the shaft. Each opening had railings and individual doors for closing down over the openings when not in use.[83]

The Dilly Shack, named by the Canadians, was where Harrison International's men kept their lunch buckets. Rauhala knew his wife, Edith, had fixed him a nice lunch that day, so he decided now would be as good a time as any to grab a bite before things got busy again.[84]

―――

Tuesday - August 27, 1963
4:40 p.m. (MST)

The hot afternoon sun was slowly making its westerly descent as a few employees from the day shift were headed towards the parking lot to leave the mine site for the day. A couple of cars were pulling out, heading towards town.

Morris Worley and Bill Smith came from the depths of the mine and realized their car pool had already left for the day. No one was around as they trudged across the yard toward TGS's new mining/engineering office and change house building.[85] They were wondering if someone left them a pickup truck to take home.

Unexpectedly, a huge, violent, destructive concussion erupted out of the shaft with tremendous force. The explosion was quickly followed by a deep, rumbling sound. Everyone instinctively knew this was no ordinary blast. Debris fell around the miners as plywood flew out of the Headframe, some from the Dilly Shack and some from other makeshift enclosures erected by Harrison International men.[86] The blast blew everything to smithereens as the violent concussion shook the massive concrete Headframe. It spread destruction and sent dust and debris out of the openings. The destructive force traveled up the concrete structure and blew out windows as it ripped and tore whatever was in its path.[87]

Chapter 4

Caught in the Smoke

Deep in the mine, a hundred feet from the Face, Hanna, along with Barber and Byrge had taken a section of thirty-six-inch metal vent pipe out of the back of Byrge's shuttle car and were working to attach the end to the metal vent line. Without warning, a tremendous explosion of searing hot air came through the end of the vent line, threw the men to the ground[1] and knocked their hard hats off. It happened so fast yet it felt like everything was in slow motion, suspended in mid-air for a few seconds. The men instinctively put their hands over their ears as unbearable pressure quickly built up. No sound. Only immense pressure. The concussion subsided but soon hit again, reverberating with less pressure.

During an explosion, air is forced violently out of the mine which creates a vacuum. Then the air is sucked back in, filling the void while pulling too much air back in, then back out again until the pressure finally equalizes.[2]

Several other men down near the Face were nearly knocked down by the blast. The men running roof bolt machines at the time held on, bracing themselves.[3] 'Blackie' was sitting on the loader waiting to make a temperature reading with his new gauge when the concussion from the blast nearly knocked him off.[4] One of the other two men working nearby was knocked down.

The explosion created a muffled sound,[5] followed by the tremendous concussion, as pressure continually built, making their heads feel like they were going to burst.[6] The pressure was horrendous, pushing their ear drums together so hard it felt as though they would meet in the middle of their heads. The pressure went in hard, then out like it was going to pull their ear drums out. In real hard again, then gradually tapering down.[7]

The running machines stopped in an instance. A palpable pause, as the typically noisy mining environment became quiet and still. Immediately, after the overpowering shock, the men knew something was terribly wrong. It was no ordinary round going off in the Face of the other drift. No doubt it was a powerful explosion, but where?

Instinctively, 'Blackie' looked at his watch to record the time of this unusual occurrence in the mine. It was 4:40 p.m., and whatever happened was not normal.[8]

Gathering their wits, and a bit stirred up, the four men near the Face headed up the drift, moving fast.[9] 'Blackie' was nearby, about fifty to sixty feet.[10] Everyone knew something was terribly wrong as they all gathered up by Hanna[11] and the other two men working with him.

"We need to get the hell out of here," Hanna said.[12] Stirred up and concerned, all were in agreement as the eight men quickly piled into Byrge's shuttle car. Byrge started the engine, turned on the headlights and raced up the incline towards the shaft station, over a half-mile away.

Byrge had been in two other explosions at other mines. He had no doubts it was an explosion. But no one knew the cause. One thing they all agreed on: "Let's get out of the mine.[13] Fast!"

Through the openings of the Headframe, the blast hurled debris in all directions. Worley and Smith turned around towards the shaft and saw Matt Rauhala, the Ore Dump Operator staggering away from the Headframe, bleeding severely.[14] The force had propelled Matt Rauhala backward through the plywood wall of the Dilly Shack on the ground level, catapulting him out about fifteen feet[15] from the Headframe and smashing him to the ground. Then the roof of the plywood structure landed on top of him.[16]

"What the heck[17] have I done? I better get out of here," Rauhala thought to himself as he crawled out from under the debris. His first instinct was to get up and run before another explosion. He got to his feet, staggered, then tripped over something[18] and fell. He slowly got up again and staggered to a pickup truck parked nearby. Leaning against the front fender with his head bent over, he tried to regain his senses. "What happened?" he thought, feeling dazed and weak. "A box of blasting powder must have gone off."[19]

Blood ran down his face and dripped off his nose from a large, gaping wound on his forehead. Beginning to come around a bit, he soon realized he was trying to write his initials[20] on the fender using the blood dripping off his nose.

Worley and the others rushed towards Rauhala. Bill Smith reached him first and raised his head.[21]

"Oh boy, it's bad," was all Bill said as he raced off to the shaft phone to call for the ambulance.[22]

Ed Ziolkowski witnessed the blast[23] from his office window. He had been underground during the day shift helping with the survey work. After surfacing, and taking a shower, Ziolkowski had just sat down at his desk to make some notes for a company party that was coming up. Through his window facing the Headframe, he saw debris flying everywhere and a cloud of dust spewing from the Headframe as a barrel rolled out into the yard. He raced out of the office as fast as he could run.[24]

Bleeding severely, Rauhala was laid on the ground while someone applied pressure to his forehead to stop the bleeding. They also found a cut on one of his fingers as Worley probed for broken bones.[25] He found none, although, Rauhala complained of back pain.

Badly banged up, Rauhala started coming around and asked about his head. Ziolkowski told him, "It looked like someone took a spoon and scooped some out."

"Shit, if that's all it is, I'm all right," Rauhala responded.[26]

"What do you think happened?" Ziolkowski asked.

"We've had a bad one, a big explosion down there," Rauhala answered.[27] Then Ziolkowski rushed off towards the Headframe.

In confusion, people were scurrying everywhere, some to the Headframe, some gathered around Rauhala asking if he was okay. Everyone was trying to figure out what had just happened. Some thought the blast came from down in the mine; others thought they were transporting dynamite underground that exploded in the Headframe or shaft.

No dynamite was sent down, and Rauhala was sure the blast must have come from the bottom of the mine. He also didn't think anyone could have survived the explosion.[28] Concerned for his buddies, Rauhala asked the others to find out about the men in the mine. Some workers were already calling the phone underground, but they got no response. Several from day shift were aware Clell Johnson and Myrlen Christensen, Sr. had just gone down in a bucket, and it was estimated they were probably at the shaft station at the time the explosion happened.[29]

Whatever the cause, "It sure knocked me for an oozy," Rauhala said as they waited for the company ambulance. "I'm sure lucky I wasn't up in the Headframe dumping buckets. It would have knocked me down the shaft," he added.

It was also too close for comfort for Worley. He thought about how he and Bill Smith had just left the mine when the blast hit. For Worley, the day started as just another routine summer day.[30] He too realized just how close they had come to being underground when the mine exploded. For now, all they could think about were the men down in the mine.

―――――――

Underground, Bob June and Lamar Rushton would have normally been working on the west side, in a connecting drift at the bottom of the raises on the lower level. But today they were assigned to do some special drilling to build a bridge across[31] the larger raise on the upper level.

At the time of the explosion, the concussion knocked both men over and rolled them down the drift. They soon heard a guy screaming down in the large raise for what seemed like a long time.[32] At first, the screaming was further away, then came closer to the bottom of the raise. The man was screaming for help.

June and Rushton weren't quite sure who they heard but one thing they knew: the man was badly hurt from the explosion and needed help. June and Rushton yelled to let him know they were trying to find a rope or something to throw down to him. Desperate, they quickly searched to find something, anything to get to the guy. About this time, they both saw the lights of a shuttle car coming up the incline. They hoped whoever was coming could help.

Once the shuttle car got to the top of the incline, both June and Rushton were waiting near the three-way junction, frantic and upset. They told the other men how they heard a guy down through the raise on the lower level screaming. Agitated, June and Rushton explained how a man was screaming right after the explosion, and they needed help to get to him. The miners piled out of the shuttle car and followed June and Rushton back into the raise area to investigate.[33]

No one had a rope, a chain ladder, or anything they could use to get to the injured man. Nevertheless, all the men ran into the raise area out of instinct to check out the situation for themselves.[34] They crossed over a lagging, which was a long, 3 to 4 inch thick, foot-wide wood plank laid over the first raise to get from one side to the other. The first of the two large raises was eighteen feet across the entire width of the drift. The second was only half-finished and was about halfway across the drift. Both holes were about ten to twelve feet from one side to the other and 105-feet deep.[35] At the bottom of each was the lower level that connects through a crosscut drift to the West Drift (2 South). Back at the 3-way junction where the shuttle car stopped was a smaller Manway raise, measuring six feet by six feet. When completed, it would have a ladder or lift installed to take miners between the two levels in the mine.[36]

The men yelled down into the raise trying to get a response but heard nothing. Even if the guy screaming were still at the bottom, no one would have been able to get to him. Even if they had a rope, chances were it wouldn't have been long enough to reach.[37]

As the men hastily discussed what they should do next, white smoke started coming up from both of the large raises. The mine was starting to re-vacuum, pulling air back down the shaft and pushing smoke deep into the mine's passageways, as the environment strained to become normalized.[38]

As the smoke came up through the raises, it also started coming at the men from the top end through the crosscut[39] from the direction of the shaft station. Almost as quickly, the smoke also began to come around at them from the three-way junction just down the drift. The smoke wasn't moving real fast[40] but was getting thick and coming in from all around, surrounding the men in the raise area.

The thick white smoke boiled in from all directions, surrounding the ten men.[41] "We've gotta get out of here," some of the men yelled. They scrambled to get back over the foot-wide plank, which was about twelve feet across with no railing and smoke coming up out of the raise. One by one they crossed over the lagging. Still able to see enough to get everyone across, the smoke bellowed in on them and quickly became thick.

The men had to go back the way they came, run through the smoke and get ahead of it before it reached the Face.[42]

"Get ahead of the smoke," someone yelled.

"Outrun it," another said.

A large can of water was on the other side of the raise, and everyone grabbed a rag, anything they could find to wet and put over their face.[43] Already, the men were beginning to cough. The smoke became so thick that they couldn't even see their hands in front of their face. Unable to see where they were going, the men started yelling directions to each other.

"Get to good air," came a muffled voice.

"Stay to the left Rib," another yelled.

They tried to keep track of each other as they went. Some were spread out. Others together.

"Keep going, get ahead of the smoke."

They hugged the left Rib to maintain their bearings in the smoke and repeated instructions as they groped their way through the thick smoke, making their way back to the junction, trying to account for everyone along the way.[44]

"Stay to the left. Stay to the left Rib," came muffled instructions through the rags over their faces.

The men knew they had to stay to the left Rib. Ahead, against the right Rib was the small Manway raise at the junction. It was 105-feet deep with no railing and was near the parked shuttle car. The raise area was the worst place in the mine to get caught in smoke. As long as the men stayed to the left, they would be okay, but one wrong step and they could get turned around and fall into one of the raises. Once the men got to the junction, they would have to let go of the Rib and walk across to the other side where they would hit either the left Rib and the large metal vent line next to it or the left front of the shuttle car.

McKinney felt his way along the Rib, when he suddenly hit his shin[45] on the small ventilation fan used in the raise area. He remembered the fan sat about six to eight feet from the corner of the junction. He reached out, touched the fan, then the Rib and aligned himself. Going straight about twenty feet across the junction, he estimated he should hit the vent line or the shuttle car parked just over ten feet down from the corner on the other side. Hesitant, McKinney let go and headed straight ahead, the whole time reaching out, arms flailing about, trying to touch something, anything. Surrounded by thick smoke, he had to keep moving as fast as he could. Fearful, he realized he should have reached the other side by now. He worried he had unknowingly got turned around in the smoke.[46] Terrified this might be the case, he cautiously kept going.

Finally, McKinney hit something but couldn't tell what. Feeling down the side, pointing his cap-lamp, and getting as close as he could, he tried to see through the smoke to determine what he had hit. It was the shuttle car, but not the front left side. He ran into the right corner. The realization hit that he could have easily walked into the Manway raise not far away and fallen a hundred feet below. What McKinney didn't know was that the small ventilation fan he hit his shin on had recently been moved forty feet up into the raise area. Not knowing this, he let go of the left Rib way too soon. Far away from the junction and disoriented in the smoke, he could have easily walked right into the Manway hole.[47]

As the other men groped through the dense smoke, several others hit the right side of the shuttle car as well. 'C.C.' came the closest[48] to falling in the Manway raise. His foot went into the hole and scared him to death; but, he was able to pull his foot out before he lost his balance and plummeted to the bottom.

Coughing, McKinney and the other men nearby felt their way past the shuttle car. Once they got their bearings and lined themselves up with the left Rib, they started down the incline at a dead run. Some of the men were spread out, others together, all were running to get ahead of the smoke. They could hear the coughing as they moved as fast as possible.

About two hundred feet down the incline, the men near McKinney were still running to get out ahead of the smoke. The thick cloud was possibly a mixture of smoke and fog that had formed after the explosion when it stirred up fine salt and shale dust.[49]

Each man had their wet rags against their faces while coughing, as tears streamed down their cheeks. They knew they had to build a barricade[50] as quickly as possible if they were going to survive. When someone had mentioned building a barricade, they all knew that was what they needed to do. Once they got ahead of the smoke, they just needed enough time to get a barrier built before the smoke overtook them again.

'Blackie' knew if a man was going to lose it, it would be in the smoke.[51] Losing one's bearings and becoming disorientated can cause overwhelming panic and fear.

A typical reaction of this type of fear while in smoke was not unlike one miners' experience in the Sunnyside, Utah No. 1 mine explosion in 1945.

"A crew of eight miners was coming out of the mine after their shift when the explosion flattened them to the ground and darkened the mine. They all agreed to hang onto each other so no one would get lost or separated from the rest. Without warning, one of the men went berserk. Screaming and kicking, he broke away from the group. His crew finally located him in the blackness, clutched his hand and started onward once more. Again, the man's frayed nerves gave out. Kicking and yelling, he again dashed off into a side passageway. Once more the crew found him. This time, he was placed in the center of a ring formed by the men and virtually herded out to safety."[52]

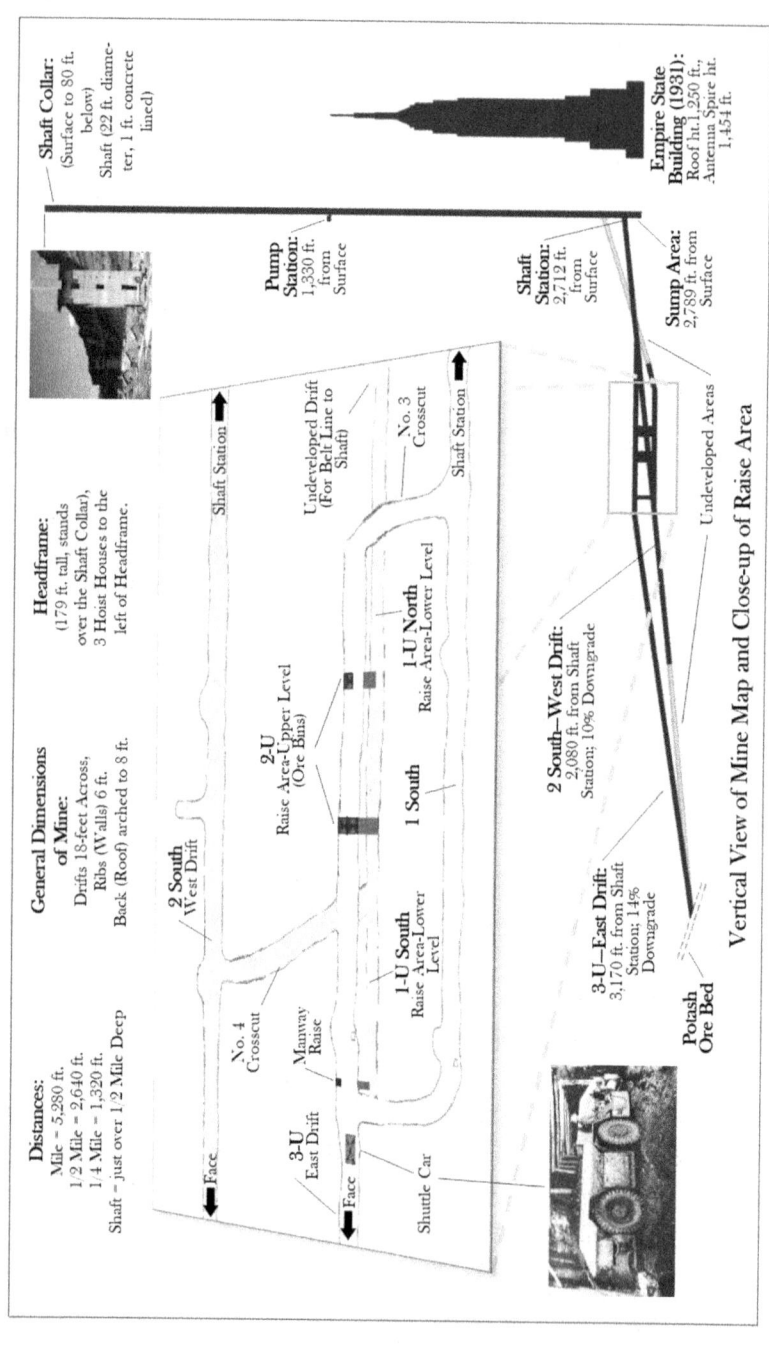

Chapter 5

Chaotic Aftermath

'C.C.' Clark was near Chuck Byrge when they broke ahead of the smoke. Looking back, they saw a billowy white cloud of smoke moving slowly at them. Chuck said they needed to get a barricade built as fast as they could.[1]

Hanna was with the first group of men who reached the transformer station[2] where they grabbed one of the packages of thirty-six-inch collapsible fan line[3] laying on top of the transformer. Quickly, they strung the material from Rib to Rib as 'C.C.' used his pocket knife to cut[4] an eighteen-foot length. They then ripped the cloth open lengthwise, giving them a seventy-two-inch curtain to hang from floor-to-ceiling. Working as fast as they could, some of the men held the curtain in place while others tried to secure the material to the Back the best they could.

Coming down the incline, several more men arrived at the transformer station, with the smoke not far behind. While building the barricade, Hanna ran back up the incline[5] about 400-feet to break open the three-inch compressed air line. This high-pressure line was used to run mining tools, and he hoped the pressurized air blowing out into the drift would act as a dam to hold back the smoke and give them more time to build the barricade. Jumping on top of the large thirty-six-inch corrugated metal vent line, he could easily reach the compressed air line hung on brackets near the Back. At this location, the compressed air line had a three-inch gate valve. After shutting the air off with the valve, he tried to separate the line when several other men ran down the incline ahead of the smoke. One of them was McKinney, who stopped to help him. They muscled the bolts and broke open the line just below the gate value. Turning the valve back on, they discovered it had no air.[6]

Both men quickly jumped down from the vent line and scrambled to catch up with the others further down the smoky drift at the transformer station. The men had the curtain nearly hung across the drift, although somewhat haphazardly. A difficult area to hang a curtain, they couldn't make it airtight. The smoke was now about shoulder high and hovered around the men while they continued to try to get the curtain hung.[7] The Back was elevated in this spot, so the curtain did not completely reach the ground.

At this same time, Hanna was made aware that three men had stayed at the top of the incline. On their way through the smoke in the raise area, 'Blackie' had seen Lamar Rushton break open the large metal vent line near the junction. Rushton cut off the wire band and opened the line between two sections in a desperate attempt to get some fresh air. Several other men had stopped with him. 'Blackie' told Rushton that he better come with them as he headed down the incline. But two of the men stayed with Rushton.

Hanna said he would go after the men thought to still be up at the 3-way junction. But first, he directed the men[8] to go further down the drift and build two more barricades where the Back wasn't as high and where chain link fencing was roof bolted across the top. There they would be able to make the curtains more airtight. He said to grab everything they could find they might need and take with them. Taking a deep breath of good air and holding the air deep down in his diaphragm, Hanna headed up the incline[9] through the smoke at a dead run.

While gathering up materials, the men discovered the first curtain, though haphazardly hung, had stopped the rolling smoke. Only whiffs came around the sides. They grabbed everything they could find and hurried down the drift about four hundred feet to build a second barricade. They took with them scraps of wood like 2 x 4s, 2 x 2s, and short pieces of pipe. And they grabbed the other packages of the collapsible fan line laying on the transformer.

A coal miner before coming to Cane Creek, Chuck Byrge had been in a couple of explosions before, so he knew firsthand what to do along with several of the other miners who had been trained in building barricades. Everyone contributed and worked together as fast as they could.

At the end of the vent line not far from the Face, 'C.C.' could hear the men through the large metal line and hollered at them. He told them to come down to where he and the others were building the barricades. He yelled as loud as he could, letting them know the air was good. But all he could hear was muffled sounds of coughing and talking, though he couldn't make out what the men were saying.

Concerned, 'C.C.' still could not bring himself to go after them. He became disoriented in the smoke and nearly fell into the Manway raise, and was also not able to get enough air into his lungs. He wasn't about to go back into the smoke. Besides, he was sure Hanna would bring them back. Eventually, 'C.C.' and the other men had to seal the end of the vent line when puffs of smoke started coming through, threatening to contaminate the air inside their barricade.[10]

The men hustled as they built a second barrier in the oil shale formation where the roof was only about six feet high and hung the vent cloth to the chain link fencing attached to the Back. After cutting the flexible tubing a bit longer than the width across the drift, they then cut it open lengthwise and fastened the curtain as tight as they could with wire to the fencing. Quickly, they then went another twenty-five feet further down the drift and threw up the third barricade. McKinney looked at his watch. Clocking from the time of the explosion, to getting to the raise area, to coming back down the incline, and then to throwing up the barricades, it had all taken place in a matter of twenty minutes at a dead run.[11] Slowing down their pace just a bit, they worked awhile longer to make the curtains as air tight as possible[12] and waited for Hanna to come back with the other three men.

On the surface, time went slow and seemed like an eternity before the ambulance finally arrived. The men put Rauhala onto a stretcher to transport him to the Moab hospital. By this time, black, sooty clouds of smoke were pouring from the shaft. Evidently, they had a disaster on their hands.[13]

A young kid, about eighteen-years-old, was driving the ambulance.[14] He was a TGS employee who worked in the shop on the surface. Rauhala didn't know who he was. He hardly knew any of the men who worked for TGS, except those such as the engineers who worked closely with Harrison's men.

On the winding river road, Rauhala swayed from side to side in the back of the ambulance. Rauhala finally told the kid to slow down. He was driving like "a bat out of hell."[15]

"Just take it easy, I'm not hurt that bad," he added.

The kid said he had to get him to the hospital. Out of nowhere, a deer darted into the road, and the kid hit the brakes. He swerved to miss it while Rauhala was thrown all over the place. The ambulance hit the deer anyway, which nearly sent them into the river.[16]

"What the hell's happened?"

"I hit a deer," the kid said.

"Well, you just about killed a Finlander," Rauhala scolded him, feeling the pain in his back as they continued on their way. Finally, they arrived at the hospital. As the kid wheeled Rauhala into the emergency entrance, Rauhala told the kid to "take it easy going back." The kid said he would, but was worried he'd get fired for the dent on the front of the ambulance.[17]

As word continued to spread, mine officials and employees from both companies gathered around the Headframe. A few of the day shift employees were still in the change house showering when word came of an explosion. Others were in the parking lot getting ready to leave the mine site. Still others had made the trip into town only to turn around and head back to see if they were needed.

The situation looked extremely grave when dark smoke started billowing out of the shaft. As soon as Rauhala was on his way to the hospital, Worley, certified in mine rescue, raced up the hill to the safety room[18] adjacent to Harrison International's dry house. When he got to the door, he met up with two Harrison International officials, Norman Harrison, the Project Manager,[18] and Bert Trenfield, the Mine Superintendent. Already aware that something had happened, they headed towards the Headframe as Worley continued inside to the safety room to grab a couple of breathing apparatuses.

He grabbed a pair of Chemox self-contained breathing apparatuses, which would allow a safe descent into the shattered mine.[20] Time was of the essence, and it was urgent to get underground as quickly as possible to check if anyone survived the explosion.

Once he was back at the Headframe, Worley and Trenfield checked out the fit of the oxygen masks while someone fetched another machine from the safety room cache[21] for Norman Harrison. Neither company had a trained mine rescue team, and with lives on the line, they would have to improvise. Worley became certified in mine rescue while attending college at the Colorado School of Mines and assumed the two senior Canadians were also trained; they seemed to know how to use the breathing units.[22] In Canada, the Ontario Department of Mines equipped and trained their men in mine rescue and adhered strictly to the standards adopted by the U.S. Bureau of Mines.[23]

Still, amid the chaotic commotion, nothing was heard from the miners working below. Not a single hint that anyone lived through the explosion. The trio, Worley, Harrison, and Trenfield, donned their breathing apparatuses and prepared to man a bucket to enter the smoke-filled shaft for an initial exploration of the damaged mine. They desperately hoped to find men who had survived the blast.

Hanna ran up the smoky drift—a steep fourteen percent incline, and it was just over a quarter of a mile to the top. The smoke was thick and unsettling as he held his breath. Learning from hard rock miners how to breathe while in black powder smoke after blasting, he held his breath down in his diaphragm. With teeth clenched, he could sip air through his teeth using his diaphragm to breathe without taking in air from the environment.[24]

Getting near, Hanna could hear the men talking, mumbling and coughing. Finally, he reached the top—up near the corner of the junction where the men had opened up a seam in one of the sections of the large thirty-six-inch metal vent line. Two of them, Lamar Rushton and Pete Sviscsu, were kneeling with their faces in between the vent line. Wesley Barber was up in the tubing, feet first and facing out, as the two were trying to get him situated. They were arguing with bouts of uncontrollable coughing as tears ran down their faces. Distressed and in great agony, they were groping for air in the dense smoke. Rushton, with slow, slurred speech, was giving directions to Barber.[25]

Hanna asked Rushton, through his clenched teeth, to move enough for him to get in the air as he struggled to hold his breath, his heart pounded in his chest from running up the incline. Rushton told him "there is no air." In the light of Hanna's cap-lamp, he saw the agony they were going through revealed on their faces. Barber was moving around up in the vent line while Rushton argued with him to get further up so that he could breathe better air.

Hanna told the men to come with him. The others were building a barricade where they had better air to breathe.[26] No one paid attention to him. They seemed confused and wouldn't listen. They were probably already suffering from the effects of smoke inhalation and were not able to think clearly.

Hanna had worked with Rushton at different times during the last year and a half. The husky built, thirty-five-year-old, and was one of Harrison International's Lead Miners. And he was known for being an experienced, strong-willed miner.

Barber had worked at Cane Creek for about six weeks, and Sviscsu had been employed at the mine for a couple of months. Both men worked on Hanna's crew, and he felt personally responsible for them, but they just wouldn't listen.[27]

Hanna couldn't hold his breath much longer. Feeling drained, he thought he might not be able to get back to the barricade. He needed some air and had to go. He tried again to convince the men to come with him but to no avail. He turned again to go but agonized over leaving them. He just couldn't leave them there and turned back one more time. But they still wouldn't listen.

"There is no use," Rushton told Hanna.

Not able to handle it any longer, Hanna had to leave. He took off as fast as he could while continually swinging his arm to the side hitting the metal vent line next to the Rib to keep his bearings in the smoke, and praying he would get back to the barricade. A torturous decision. Every part of his being told him not to leave the three men. At the same time, he had to go. Now![28]

"I've got to make it," Hanna thought to himself. His lungs felt like they were going to burst as he tried harder to hold his breath which was getting more difficult. If only he had convinced one of the men, he muttered to himself, maybe the others would have followed. Getting harder to walk, the fear was intense as he pushed himself on through the dense smoke and the eerie surroundings. Doubts set in that he wouldn't get back at all.

Hanna wanted so much to breathe in deeply but resisted the temptation as much as he could, knowing he had nothing but bad air all around him. Sluggish and weak, he continually swung his arm, hitting the vent line. Beginning to stumble and stepping heavily, he continued down the incline and was almost ready to fall or pass out. It was all he could do to hold himself up as the smoke stung his eyes. Hardly able to keep them open, tears flowed down his face. He couldn't go much further.[29]

Chapter 6

Rescue Preparations Underway

It was around 6:00 p.m., nearly an hour and a half after the explosion,[1] when the first bucket was finally lowered into the damaged mine manned by Morris Worley, Norman Harrison, and Bert Trenfield. "Under oxygen," the Chemox apparatuses held about forty-five minutes of air supply. The bucket disappeared, cautiously descending into the smoky shaft. The men manually steadied the bucket by holding onto the bucket's two guide ropes since the blast destroyed the crossheads used to stabilize the buckets.

The middle of the crosshead bar rides just above each bucket on the hoist line, and each end slides up and down its own guide ropes to keep the buckets in their hoisting lane. All four buckets were equipped with two guide ropes each that are stationary inside the shaft while the crossheads prevented the buckets from twirling and swinging from side to side.[2]

Inching slowly down, the rescuers had to steady and realign the bucket continually. They had the bell cord with them and were able to bell hoisting signals to the Hoistman.[3] The three rescuers made damage assessments on the way down towards the bottom. One of the primary concerns was the guide ropes in the shaft. They found all eight cables still intact with only one a little loose.

The ventilation intake air traveled underground from the surface through the large vent line down the side of the shaft, while return air from the underground workings flowed through the open areas of the shaft. Now contaminated with carbon monoxide and gases from the explosion, these conditions required everyone to exercise extreme caution.[4]

The closer the bucket got to the bottom the more destruction and debris the three men found. Descending slowly, they picked their way through the shredded remains of the corrugated vent line and twisted service lines.[5] Some groundwater was falling in the shaft. The men shoved debris out of their way as they went down deeper. In places, the tangled wires were like a mass of spaghetti. Too smoky to see much further than beyond the ends of their hands, the men threaded their way down to just above the shaft station[6] as the downward movement became impossible because of the dense debris. They were only able to examine part of the shaft[7] and assess the damage.

The men beat on the pipes going down the shaft and then listened for a reply from the bottom, hoping for any sign of the missing men. The muffled calls through their masks were met with eerie silence.[8] Only the slow screeching sound of the damaged metal still shifting and moving in the shaft and mine could be heard. Hampered by the smoke and fumes coming up the shaft, they could see little in the darkness as the large empty shaft acted like an echo chamber as they desperately tried to get a response.

Trying to descend, slack developed in the bucket's hoisting line. The men knew from experience this was not good and belled to be hoisted up before the bucket could break lose. About this same time, the bells on their Chemox apparatus started to ring, signaling their air supply was getting low. Reluctantly, they slowly returned to the surface to initiate a rescue operation,[9] sickened by what could be the fate of the missing miners. The fact was not lost on Bert Trenfield that he had traded shifts with Rene Roy. For Norman Harrison, this was personal. His men had worked together at Cane Creek for the past two years, and many of the Canadians had been employed together for years on other projects. Friendships and bonds were strong, and many of their families were close.

Once in the emergency room, Rauhala was examined by the doctor[10] while hospital personnel contacted his wife, Edith. While putting stitches in Rauhala's head, the doctor listened to Rauhala tell about the blast. Rauhala recounted how he was dumping buckets up in the Headframe and was asked to help the Toplander fill orders to send materials down into the mine. After the orders had been filled and the work slowed down, he said he was asked to listen for phone calls from the mine. Rauhala told how he went into the Dilly Shack and sat down to eat his lunch. He unwrapped his cheese and bologna sandwich[11] and took a bite when a huge blast threw him back through the wall and into the air.

"At first, I wondered what my wife put in that sandwich," Rauhala said with a wide grin. Amused, the doctor smiled as Rauhala continued his story. Had he been up in the Headframe dumping buckets, where he generally worked, he would have been thrown down into the mine.[12]

Rauhala's daughter, Sheila was over at a friend's house visiting when her mother called and told her she needed to come home. There had been an emergency, and they needed to go to the hospital. Sheila graduated from high school the year before in Carbon County, and had moved with her parents to Moab, but was to leave soon to attend college in Price on a scholarship.[13]

By the time Edith and Sheila arrived at the hospital, the doctor was still stitching Rauhala's head as blood dripped creating a puddle on the floor. When Edith first walked in and saw her husband, she was alarmed and thought he was going to die because of all the blood.[14]

Shaft Specifications:

- Circumference: 22-feet; 1-foot thick concrete lined
- Depth: Shaft Station 2,712; Stump 2,789-feet
- 4 Mucking Buckets with Crossheads
- Hoist-Counter Balance Wind
- 8 Stationary Guide Ropes (2 for each Bucket)

Cane Creek Mine Hoist Signals

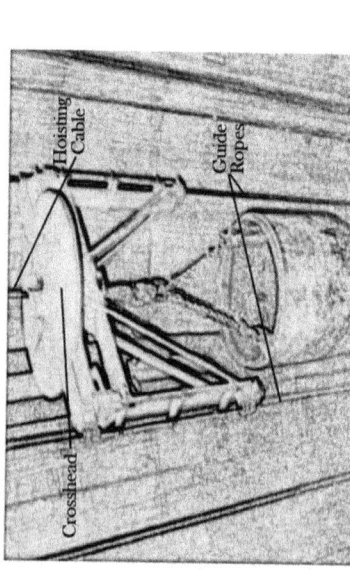

Shaft Schematic
(not to scale)

Mucking Bucket with Crosshead and Guide Ropes, Shaft Schematic and Hoist Signals

"You should know they can't kill a Finlander when you hit him in the head," Rauhala told her, using humor to reassure them both.[15] He started to recount the events of the explosion to his wife and daughter, telling how the ambulance driver hit a deer, and how they nearly went into the river on the way to the hospital.

"If the mine didn't kill me, the ambulance driver would," he said with a smile. Always kidding around, Rauhala was one of those types who found humor in everything.[16]

———◆———

A couple of the miners behind the barricade heard someone running down the drift, coughing and hitting the vent line. Hanna had stumbled his way back, alone. The men helped him through the curtains and the next thing Hanna knew he was sitting against the Rib coughing his lungs out. In poor condition,[17] Hanna had no memory of getting back to the barricade. He sat coughing for the longest time, his lungs trying to dispel the smoke. At first, the other men weren't even sure he would make it.[18] And they were totally distressed over the three guys not coming back with him. Why wouldn't they come? What were they doing? None of them could believe it. June reacted with angry outbursts, yelling and cursing.

The men continued to work on the barricades. They had shoved shirts, rags, or whatever they could find, into the gaps along the Back. They used wood wedges or copper wire to secure the material tightly to the fencing. The pieces of wood and pipe were used to hold the curtain against the left Rib. On the right Rib (when looking up the incline) they secured the curtain around the metal vent line.

Some of the men shoveled salt across the bottom of the curtain, which overhung on the ground. Making the curtain as tight as possible, they hoped the barricades would keep the smoke and deadly gases out. While some worked on the barricades, others searched for and gathered items they thought they might need. The only water they could find was in a large metal igloo water cooler they brought into the area with them. Water was vital and especially because of the high temperatures in the mine. Even with ventilation, the mine was hot, generally around 95 to 100 degrees. With no air coming through the vent line, the temperature could go up to 130 degrees, if it was not already that hot from the heat of the blast.

Scrambling about, each of the men continued to work to secure the curtains to trap the good air and keep the smoke and creeping gas out making each curtain of the barricade as air tight as possible. Overall, they worked for an hour and a half on the curtains, sealing out the smoke.[19] Another large piece of the flexible vent tubing was cut open and spread out on the ground for a place to sit.[20] No one knew how long they had to wait for rescue crews to come.

Seven were alive and safe. Blake Hanna; two of his crew members ('C.C.' Clark and Paul McKinney); two of the roving Shuttle Car Operators (Chuck Byrge and Tom Trueman); Bob June, who had been working in the raise area; and 'Blackie' Eslick, the only TGS employee.

Twenty-two-year-old Paul McKinney was the youngest of the seven men. A big kid, he was always very quiet. A more serious type, he always enjoyed being around the other men who were witty and fun.[21]

Bob June was a fun-loving guy who liked to kid around and joke. The thirty-six-years-old had a talent for sketching, and often drew cartoons, sometimes on the other men's hard hats[22] when asked.

Nearly two hours since the blast, the men started to settle down a bit as they talked about their situation and tried to guess what was happening on the surface. Collectively, from their training or personal experiences, they evaluated their situation. After a short time, they moved their ground cover about halfway down the drift so they would have better air. There, they set up a camp area, away from the barricade curtains and any gases seeping through the curtains.[23]

In these types of situations, air is one of the most important considerations. One of the first things mine rescue teams will do is work to re-establish air into a damaged mine. In anticipation of this happening, the survivors broke the large vent line next to their camp and sealed the end. If any air came through the vent line, they would know immediately. Not confident about the quality of air already inside the barricade, the men also discussed the possibility of running out of oxygen. Afraid they would use up the oxygen in their "camp area," some tried to figure how many cubic feet they had inside their barricade and how long the air would last. The air trapped in the barricade with them was all they had. The best they could figure, they had maybe three days' worth of air.[24] Even before the blast, the ventilation in the mine was never very good, and any gas seeping through the barricade could contaminate and displace the oxygen. Eventually, even normal breathing would use up what oxygen they had as well.

The unbearable heat was also a huge concern. The ten-gallon water cooler the men had was a little more than a quarter full, which they rationed immediately. They also had the one-inch water line used for equipment they could drain if they ran out of the fresh water. They quickly shut off all the hoses connected to the line and stopped any dripping to preserve what water there was.

They also decided to take turns, one or two guys, every two hours, to go up behind the first built barricade, to see how thick and if the smoke was dissipating.[25] As soon as they got everything secured, the men settled down at their "resting place." The air was hot; each one was sweating as they tried to get comfortable. Boots, mine belts, and hard hats came off. Some were already bare-chested as a few slipped off their pants to get cool.

Some had already turned off their cap-lamps, but Hanna felt all the lights should be turned off and used only one at a time, and only when needed so they could conserve the batteries. They had no way of knowing just how long they would be trapped. But one of the men objected. He opted to keep his light on at first and, at the very least, was brave enough to disclose his fear to the other six men.

The jet-black darkness in a mine, where one can see no farther than their eyelids, can be suffocating and can create a claustrophobic feeling of fear and doom. When the lights went out, the men, swallowed up in a dark, black abyss, and sealed off from the outside world, were surrounded and smothered by total darkness, both physically and psychologically. The pitch black areas of the imagination can be terrifying, conjuring up visions of their worst fears and torments. They were now trapped between the world of the living and the dead, suspended a half-mile below ground in a dreadful sort of limbo.

From time to time, a light would come on, giving each man a reprieve from the consuming darkness. Even with the small amount of light from a cap-lamp, they were still enveloped in the unforgiving, creeping shadows of darkness that smothers the soul. Some of the men sat on the ground cover as they talked a bit. Tom Trueman curled up to rest and barely said much. The red-headed thirty-seven-year-old had worked around mining in Canada for about five years, but this was the first time he had been employed underground. He was mostly quiet and seen as somewhat of a loner,[26] except within his small circle of friends outside of work.

As the men talked, Hanna and some of the others worried the shaft might have caved in from the explosion. A cave-in would be a major problem for rescuers trying to get into the mine. Byrge remembered saying the same thing earlier in the day on their way to work as they talked about the Sheppton rescue, which was still so vivid in everyone's mind. They each wondered about rescuers and were sure they would be on their way soon. Several of the survivors believed the explosion came from a dynamite explosion.[27] Maybe someone was transporting some into the mine, and it exploded. No one knew for sure, but whatever happened, things didn't look good.

Disaster at Cane Creek

Despite occasional doubts, the men felt their situation was only temporary. For each miner, the greatest support and reassurance came from his fellow miners and the informal but sacred miners' code. A shared understanding among all miners in case of a mine disaster is that the miners on the surface would work ceaselessly to the last man or until the last body in the mine is found. This pact was carried out regardless of the difficulty or futility of the operation or the danger to the rescuers. Rescue work was viewed as a sacred duty to friends, co-workers, and fellow miners and had become a traditional part of the fabric and responsibility in the mining industry. By virtue of their common occupation and association, all miners knew they might face a similar situation in the future.[28] This unanimity gave each miner the complete assurance his comrades would not stop rescue work even if all hope were abandoned.[29]

The men talked a little, some about their families, and what they might be doing. They wondered if they had heard yet. And then they talked a bit about the other three men who didn't come to the barricade. They wanted to believe the three would be okay and hoped they were able to get to the shaft station and were still alive. No one knew. Miraculous things had happened throughout the long history of mine rescue. The Sheppton miracle was just one example.

It was hard to believe the three men wouldn't come back to the barricade with Hanna, but Rushton was known to be stubborn. He had been a Lead Miner during the sinking of the shaft and now worked to build the raises. An experienced miner, he was a large, thirty-four-years-old, commanding man with a relatively young family. June was close to Rushton, they rode to work each day together and worked side-by-side.

Barber was a young family man with two young daughters. Hanna was extremely fond of him, and it was torturous for him to think about what Barber's fate might be as he tried to put thoughts of the three out of his mind.

Pete Sviscsu had been at Cane Creek for several months but was with Hanna's crew for only a couple of weeks. He was a serious miner and a hell of a hard worker. He always worked hard to get things done. One time, to save time fetching something, he jumped across the undercutter bar on the cutting machine instead of walking around. The cutting bar is like a chain saw bar but was much larger and about ten feet long. The undercutter was used to cut a gap under the Face so the rock, when dynamited, would mostly fall down into the gap instead of exploding out into the drift. Hanna got after Pete for jumping the bar, and everyone told him not to do stuff like that, reminding him that he could get his legs cut off real quick. An extremely nice guy,[30] everyone liked Sviscsu even though he could barely speak English. Some of the men talked with him at times and learned Pete was from some European country like Yugoslavia or Czechoslovakia.[31] He had been a young man during World War II. Years later, he emigrated west and eventually made his way to Moab and started work at the Cane Creek Mine.

Bob June lashed out at times, going off and swearing, damning TGS, and blamed them for the explosion. No one was sure how 'Blackie' was taking what June was saying.[32] 'Blackie' stayed silent. Clearly, June was traumatized by the man he heard screaming right after the explosion but was unable to get to him. And now June's buddy, Lamar Rushton, was one of the three who wouldn't come down to the barricade. No one knew if the three men died there or not. To think about their fate was too horrible.[33]

The majority of the employees of the two companies, TGS and Harrison International, hardly interacted and their employees didn't always know each other, such was the case with 'Blackie.' No one knew for sure what he was doing. 'Blackie' usually worked up around the shop area. But today he was given a last-minute change in assignments,[34] to observe the crew working in the East Drift (3U).

Four weeks earlier, after a gas ignition that burned several men, Texas Gulf Sulphur (TGS) had decided to exercise some surveillance over the contractor.[35] Maybe that was why 'Blackie' was there. Or maybe it was because TGS would soon take over the mine once construction of it was completed. They would then begin to mine the potash. 'Blackie' had been hired by them to be one of their Facebosses. Whatever the reason, 'Blackie' was there trying out a new temperature gauge[36] he had with him. Now he was trapped with Harrison International's men behind a barricade in the deepest reaches of the mine.

After making preliminary appraisals of the damage down in the shaft, the first three rescuers, Norman Harrison, Bert Trenfield, and Morris Worley, arrived back on the surface. The men immediately jumped into the fray with other officials and workers still gathering back at the mine site. Norman Harrison assumed leadership of the initial rescue operation as efforts slowly started to formulate.

Inside the Headframe, Worley checked the two-hour McCaa units, fit-tested the Harrison International miners who were certified to wear them, and manned the telephone at the shaft collar.[37] Worley was also assigned to keep a log of everyone going into and out of the mine.[38]

It seemed everyone was moving at a feverish, almost unbelievable pace.[39] Personnel was trying to contact their key employees needed for a rescue operation: Engineers, Mechanics, Electricians, etc. Other employees from both companies trickled back to the mine site as word spread, and other mining companies in the area started calling to see what they could do to help.

J.G. Pinkerton, the office manager at TGS,[40] and his wife had spent the whole day moving into their newly-built home in Moab. Pinkerton was taking a load of trash to the dump when his wife answered a call just after 5:00 p.m., coming from the mine. Pinkerton called back and learned about the explosion. They needed him to come as soon as possible. He took a quick shower and left for the mine.[41]

Tired, he thought about what had happened and wondered how long the night would last as he headed north out of town. Just past the Atlas Minerals facility, Sheriff Deputies had the river road barricaded. They recognized Pinkerton and pulled aside the barriers and waved him through.

When he arrived at the mine site, some people had gathered at the general mine office, and they all needed something. Pinkerton quickly organized tasks and the people the best he could amid the surrounding chaos as he began work on the notification process to get the word out about the emergency. With lives on the line, every minute was vital.[42]

Throughout the early evening, notifications went out according to the mine's disaster response plans and procedures. With some calls already made, Pinkerton continued down the list as he contacted the different mine agencies and organizations who normally participate or give expert assistance during mine emergencies. Law mandated they notify certain agencies. With law enforcement already contacted, other emergency agencies were also notified. Pinkerton also needed to get in touch with company personnel back in New York at the corporate headquarters for Texas Gulf Sulphur (TGS) and inform them of the events.

Previously notified, the Utah State Industrial Commission[43] in Salt Lake City immediately dispatched their state mining officials to the area. From Carbon County, Steve Hatsis, a state coal mine inspector, and a methane gas expert was sent to Moab while other Commission officials made arrangements to travel to Moab as soon as possible.

Specially trained mine rescue teams,[44] belonging to the Carbon County Disaster Group were also mobilized from the coal fields, northwest of Moab. These highly skilled teams from the Kaiser Steel Company and the U.S. Steel Corporation, assembled their mine team members and gear. Coming from the small mining communities of Dragerton, Columbia, and Sunnyside, they were about two hours away from Moab.

The Sunnyside, Utah No. 1 coal mine explosion[45] on May 9, 1945, near Sunnyside, Utah that killed 23 miners led to the formation of these expert rescue teams[46] as well as Utah's Carbon County Disaster Group.[47]

Various federal mine officials and inspectors at the U.S. Bureau of Mines, at their district office in Utah, the sub-district office in Denver, Colorado, and Washington D.C. offices, were also notified. Their personnel and experts immediately made the necessary arrangements to travel to Moab; some were expected to arrive late in the night.[48]

The presence of the state and federal mine agencies was vital to bring together needed expertise and resources to assist in rescue operations. James Westfield, the Assistant Director of Health and Safety for the U.S. Bureau of Mines, was consequently notified of the Utah mine explosion late in the evening, while still in Sheppton, Pennsylvania. He had been in Sheppton for just over a week[49] assisting with the rescue of the three trapped coal miners. Two had been rescued in the early morning hours and for the third, Louis Bova, rescuers continued their efforts throughout the day. After Westfield had been notified about the Cane Creek Mine explosion, he made plans to travel to Moab early the next morning.

The U.S. Bureau of Mines was founded in 1910 after the deadliest decade in mining history occurred from 1900 to 1909 when a total of 3,660 miners died in 133 mine disasters.[50] December 1907, became known as "Bloody December," and was the deadliest month on record for the U.S. underground mining industry. During that month, 703 miners died in five mine explosions. On December 1st, near Fayette City, Pennsylvania, 34 miners were killed. December 6th, Monongah, West Virginia, 362 were killed (the worst mining disaster in U.S. history). December 16th, Yolande, Alabama, 57 miners were killed. December 19th, Jacobs Creek, Pennsylvania, 239 were killed, and December 31st, Carthage, New Mexico, 11 miners were killed.

In the wake of these tragedies, an Act of Congress established the U.S. Bureau of Mines within the Department of the Interior on July 1, 1910, to deal with a wave of catastrophic mine disasters. The Bureau's primary directive was expressly clear—to reduce fatalities in the mining industry.[51]

Through research, investigations, and training, the U.S. Bureau of Mines was instrumental in reducing the fatalities in the mining industry. Throughout the years, they disseminated vital mining information through circulars, bulletins, reports, and hands-on training. The Bureau believed knowledge was critical to protecting the nation's mining workforce. Knowing how to detect danger and to dictate an appropriate defensive action was imperative to help keep the miners safe. Over the years, knowledge was incorporated into mine safety practices and procedures[52] with the goal to make specific responses to stimuli and the accompanying procedures "automatic" for miners facing a dangerous situation.

Regarding day-to-day activities, miners became better trained in safety procedures designed to meet the threat of the unknown and the dangerous. By providing better training, they were taught basic skills they could use when there was dangers or threats to life.[53] In times of a disaster, each underground worker would know from his past experiences and accumulated knowledge what to do. His miner's skills could be put to good use, and he would know how to handle various dangers. Miners became much better skilled in an environment which they knew intimately.[54]

The Bureau had training programs and circulated all types of up-to-date, much needed information throughout the nation in circulars and brochures. For example, in June of 1946, in response to a number of mine disasters the previous year, the U.S. Bureau of Mines released circular, IC 7353,[55] "A Plan for Training Mine Officials in Rescue Organization and Disaster Prevention." The objective was to help train mining officials on how to organize rescue and recovery activities to avoid panic. The plan dealt with how to prevent chaos, indecisions, delays, bad practices, and lack of organization after a mine disaster. Complete lists were included with details of duties, organization, and equipment used in mine rescue work. This circular and others were available and assimilated throughout the mining industry. The knowledge was critical when lives hung in the balance.

Meanwhile, word of the Cane Creek Mine explosion continued to spread, and other mining experts offered their assistance. The Independent Coal and Coke Company near Kenilworth, Carbon County, Utah and Deseret Coal Mines near Orangeville, Emery County, Utah, each sent two supervisors[56] to Moab. Standard Metals Company, a mining company in the Moab area, assembled rescue crews ready to assist. They also had their airplane warmed up at the Moab Airport willing to take survivors to Salt Lake City if need be.[57]

Stitched up and x-rays taken, Rauhala was lying in a hospital bed, with his wife and daughter nearby, talking about his harrowing experience.[58] The doctor told him they were going to keep him overnight for observation. He had a concussion and was beaten up, but there were no broken bones.[59]

"If it's at all possible, you might as well let me go home," Rauhala said. "If they can get to the men, you're gonna have this hospital full."

The doctor seemed to think things were not all that bad, or the hospital would have heard from the mine by now. That's when a nurse called the doctor to answer a phone call. Rauhala could hear him talking just down the hall but couldn't make out what was said. When the called ended, the doctor left.[60]

It wasn't long before Rauhala heard two nurses talking just outside his door discussing preparations for sixteen extra beds for possible victims from the mine, then they scurried off.[61]

The hospital staff were alerted, and after a while, the doctor came back to Rauhala's room to speak with him. He asked if he thought he would be all right if they sent him home. Rauhala assured him he would.

"It's as bad as I think it is, isn't it?" Rauhala asked.

"Evidently, it's pretty bad," the doctor said.

It was Rauhala's worst fear. Distressed, he again thought about his buddies down in the mine and worried about all the men working underground. He had been employed in mining for the past twenty years and knew the dangers. He saw a lot of things happen but nothing like this. In April, he had decided to make a change, and went to work on the surface as the Toplander and then took over as the Bucket Dumper.[62]

After treatment,[63] hospital authorities released Rauhala, and his wife and daughter took him home to rest. Suffering from a concussion, a forehead laceration, bruises and lower back strain, Rauhala felt like he had been beaten up, but he was grateful he was alive and wasn't hurt worse.

―――――

As the scope of the emergency started to become more evident, Moab's Civil Defense organization was activated, and I.W. Allen Hospital was getting ready for the worst. The entire hospital, with a twenty-bed capacity,[64] was put on emergency alert status. Everyone was busy making every necessary preparation to handle any emergency presented by the explosion.

Doctors and nurses made preparations to go to the mine site along with extra ambulances and supplies. With only four doctors in Moab, additional physicians, nurses, and clergymen were summoned to the scene from surrounding areas in the state. Other hospital personnel were called in or put on standby. Professionals outside the area were alerted in case their services were needed.

The Moab hospital prepared blood supplies to send to the mine site in the event anyone was brought up alive.[65] Extra blood was also ordered to have on hand from Salt Lake City, the nearest blood bank. The Utah Highway Patrol was asked to fly the large supply of blood and other medical supplies to the hospital in Moab.[66] Everyone was gearing up for the worst possible scenario.

Grand County Deputy Sheriff, Dick Wells, acting as Civil Defense Coordinator during the rescue operation, was preparing to move seventy-five cots and the blankets to the mine site for use by rescue personnel. He also notified the women of the Grand County Sheriff's Jeep Posse auxiliary. Their services would soon be needed during the rescue operation to assist by serving sandwiches, coffee, cold drinks and possibly later, hot meals to rescue crews and other rescue personnel.[67]

Chapter 7

Enduring the Unknown

When notifications went out to mine rescue team members in Carbon County, some were working the afternoon shift. The men were brought out of the mines as they and other team members gathered to get their equipment ready to go to Moab. At a Rotary Club meeting in Price, Utah, there was an emergency call at 6:30 p.m., to alert mine rescue experts attending the meeting to help with rescue operations at the Cane Creek Mine. Also at the meeting was Robert 'Bob' Mullins, a Pulitzer Prize-winning newspaper reporter. He was the Price Bureau Chief for the *Deseret News and Salt Lake Telegram*,[1] having worked his way up after twelve years at the paper. Within minutes, the short, stocky, built-like-a-fullback, black haired,[2] thirty-eight-year-old had alerted the newspaper staff in Salt Lake City, of the explosion. He was on his way to Moab, a two-hour drive from Price. Also rushing to the scene from the main office in Salt Lake City was a staff writer, Steve Hale, and a staff photographer, Dave Jirovec, who left immediately by auto.[3]

Five other *Deseret News* staffers were deployed to the scene,[4] several were expected to arrive later that evening, and the others were due to arrive the next morning. They would provide a six-man team coverage, accompanied by two staff photographers. This team would

Disaster at Cane Creek

eventually be backed up by the entire 100-man editorial staff at the paper[5] to bring their readers the latest news of developments and photos using Wirephoto. This technology enabled photos to be transmitted over a standard long-distance telephone line using portable equipment. This same scenario played out throughout other news agencies as the press from places near and far caught wind of the explosion and descended on the small town of Moab.

The notable reporter, Bob Mullins, was born on December 16, 1924, in Scofield, Utah. Serving in the U.S. Army during World War II, he fought in Europe and was decorated with the Bronze Star. Upon his return to the U.S., he enrolled at the University of Utah, where he obtained a B.A. degree in 1950. In 1951, he became a reporter for the *Deseret News and Salt Lake Telegram*.[6]

In May 1962, Mullins won the Pulitzer Prize in the category of "Local Reporting, Against Deadline Pressure," now called Breaking News Reporting, for his work during July 4-10, 1961, covering a murder-kidnapping near Dead Horse Point State Park[7] in Grand County near Moab, Utah. Proud of Mullins' reporting, the *Deseret News* added to its masthead under the name of the paper, "The Mountain West's First Newspaper, And 1962 Pulitzer Prize Winner, Now In Its 114th Year."

His reporting that won the coveted writing prize started when Mullins received a call on July 4th, at his home in Price, about a murder near Moab. Mullins was on his way to Grand County as the FBI, and other law enforcement agencies began an intense manhunt as they scoured the region for the suspect and his kidnapped victim. The intensely dramatic event was the beginning of a weeklong adventure of risk taking, fierce determination, and indefatigable reporting, creative resourcefulness, and a little luck. His tenacity paid off and led to Mullins winning journalism's highest honor, the Pulitzer Prize.[8]

The suspect had killed the mother, wounded her companion, then kidnapped the fifteen-year-old daughter. By July 7th, a suspect was stopped at a roadblock. When an FBI agent tried to question the suspect, he shot himself in the head, dying two hours later. His kidnapped victim was not with him, and an intense search continued but turned up no signs of the missing teenager, now feared dead.[9] The story was sensational with whereabouts of the missing teenager still a mystery. Now Mullins was returning to the same area to report on another story, the explosion at the Cane Creek Mine.

Not to be outdone, *Deseret News'* major competing newspaper in Utah, the *Salt Lake Tribune*, moments after the first telephone reports of the explosion came into their news bureau, made immediate travel arrangements for one of their reporters, Grant Messerly, and two photographers Brandt Gray and Borge Andersen. Before long they were aboard a chartered plane headed to Moab. Once the *Salt Lake Tribune's* portable Wirephoto machine was set up, they would transmit pictures directly to newspapers throughout the world.[10]

Other *Tribune* reporters followed the initial team. George A. Sorensen drove to Moab while Carolyn Habbeshaw later took another charter plane, her first ride in the air. Business Editor, Robert W. Bernick, would provide expert knowledge of the mine. For the last few years, Bernick regularly reported in his feature column "Up and Down the Street," in the business section, writing about the progress of the construction of the Texas Gulf Sulphur Potash Mine-mill complex since the time of the company's first announcement in 1960. Other reporters at the paper were assigned to take calls from the disaster scene and wrap things up. Their staff artist would then apply his magic touch, creating illustrations. The *Tribune's* seasoned personnel were very familiar with hard-to-cover, sad-to-cover news events throughout its far-flung circulation area.[11]

Officials and employees from both companies continuously gathered at the Headframe on the surface, to help the men already making preparations to get other rescuers into the mine. Furiously

Disaster at Cane Creek

they worked, some barked orders for materials, others for assistance. Noisy and chaotic, the hot afternoon sun beat down from the west on the frantic scene.

One of the first things they did was to assess the damage from the explosion. Workers examined the upper part of the shaft,[12] and the hoisting apparatus, which consisted of the metal hoisting cables, the sheave wheels, and guide ropes.

The explosion had tangled or severed the metal hoisting cables to the four muck buckets. The telephone lines, bell signal lines and power cables running down the side of the shaft were also damaged or destroyed. Some of the men worked on the communications system, essential for a rescue operation. Everyone worked as fast as they could, preparing to make another descent down into the deep shaft.

Smoke was still billowing out of the shaft after the explosion and hampered the preparation work.[13] After making the first initial examinations at about 6:00 p.m., mine officials had notified members of the Utah State Industrial Commission of the explosion[14] and began discussions about rescue plans. Preparations for a rescue operation started as Harrison International's Electricians re-rigged two buckets to make sure they were safe. Once ready they made two test runs,[15] sending the buckets down empty. These efforts ran into trouble because of the jumble of wires and cables down in the shaft. After an emergency hoisting system was rigged and was ready to lower men into the mine,[16] the third descent would be manned by the next rescue team. The electricians continued getting everything ready and worked on an alternative communications system because the previous bell system wasn't functioning after the electricity was turned off to the mine.

———

In the darkness of the barricade when the lights went off, the trapped men settled down, resting[17] on the large piece of fan cloth laid on the ground. The salt floor of the drift was hard and lumpy. The men had a difficult time trying to get comfortable. The suffocating heat was unbearable. No one slept other than Tom Trueman, who was curled up, in what seemed to some, a fetal position. Or maybe he was sleepy from the effects of the heat as he had to be awakened to take his ration of water.[18]

The others lay quietly in the dark, passing the time with their own thoughts hoping rescuers would arrive at any movement. It wasn't long when one of the guys rolled over at the upper end of the cloth. The whole drift was on a fourteen-degree incline. McKinney, at the lower end of the ground cover almost immediately felt a little trickle of cool moisture hit his side. Startled, he quickly turned on his light. What he saw was a small stream of sweat from the other men laying up from him that was running down the middle of the cloth and was about the width of a pencil. The sweat rolled off of everyone. It was like being in a hot sauna that you couldn't get out, and the heat was exhausting both physically and mentally.

Getting out his thermometer, 'Blackie' took a temperature reading which read 138 degrees.[19] Usually, the temperatures in the mine with ventilation averaged around 100 degrees.[20] All they knew was that the air was hot as hell. They sweat everywhere. Everything on them sweated, even the tips of their fingers. Without the water they brought into the barricade, they would have died of heat exhaustion. And now, they were quickly running out of that fresh water.

In an attempt to get some relief from the heat, several of the men cut the cuffs off of their shirts to fan themselves. Fashioning makeshift fans, they cut off the sleeves, about six inches above the cuffs, turned them around and fastened the cuffs back onto their wrists. Flopping out from their hands, they fanned themselves. Unfortunately, they were only circulating the hot air.

There wasn't a whole lot of conversation, and it was nothing out of the ordinary. They mostly talked about the rescue. After checking on the smoke outside the barricade, each man took another ration of water and settled back down. They laid there resting in the darkness as they conserved their lights, while some fanned themselves the best they could with their cut-off shirt cuffs.

The same pattern repeated itself throughout the evening. A light would come on for a short time, with periodic moments filled with some conversation, interspersed with rest. Someone would stir for whatever reason; the others would react and become active again. While resting, they were, for the most part, caught up in their inner thoughts—the kind vexing to the soul. Thoughts filled with questions, with no real answers.

They knew something terrible happened. Did dynamite blow up or was there a gas explosion? Did the explosion cause a cave-in somewhere in the mine or shaft? What was going on with the rescue? Why weren't they here yet? What was the fate of their three buddies at the top of the incline? How about the other men working in the mine? What about their families? What were they thinking? Surely their families had heard by now. They even wondered if they would get out alive. Everything was all too surreal, just one horrible nightmare. Trapped, like the men in the Sheppton cave-in, now they were living that reality.

Chapter 8

"A Special Breed"

Surface preparations were underway for a full-scale mine rescue operation as the sun reached the jagged edges of the canyon rim in the west, giving everyone relief from the exhausting desert heat as the shadows slowly enveloped the river canyon.

The Cane Creek officials were busy working out rescue procedures[1] with support from Utah State Industrial Commission personnel by phone while their other mining officials were in route to Moab from various locations in the state. Others from the different U.S. Bureau of Mines offices were also on their way.

Trained rescue teams dispatched[2] earlier from Carbon County, a two-hour drive, were now also on their way to the mine site. It was a race against time, and the primary objective was to get rescuers with oxygen equipment, used to protect them from deadly gases, into the now toxic mine as soon as possible. Workers worked on communications equipment so the rescue teams could be in constant contact with the men on the surface, directing efforts.[3]

Electricians turned the water pumps off in the shaft, for fear of causing electrical shorts or electrocutions[4] to rescue teams. The power was normally turned off after mine explosions to prevent a secondary explosion, which could occur either from additional gas or from carbon monoxide that could rise into an explosive range.

Around the mine's change house and associated offices, little knots of men talked or assembled rescue equipment.[5] Engineers were busy, buried under questions. Some of the men sipped coffee or munched on emergency food supplies stocked for them. Though seemingly disinterested in the refreshments, nevertheless, everything disappeared quickly.[6]

Four hours after the explosion, the entire mine site was engulfed in darkness.[7] The night air was filled with tension while everything seemed to be drawn down to a small circle of activity around the Headframe.[8]

One hundred feet above ground level, dim lights reflected from the base of the Headframe. The glow behind tinted green windows cast no light, but only defined dimly the Headframe outline. A cluster of men steadily hovered at the large opening of the Headframe while others moved in and out of the structure. Some would often peer down into the shaft opening. They always moved, for the most part, it seemed, without purpose. As if a magnet was dictating their movements, they were drawn back to peer into the twenty-two-foot wide circular shaft. Below, 2,712 feet, two passageways drifted out to the potash ore that Texas Gulf Sulphur (TGS) had sought since 1961. But now they were seeking something else during this night.[9]

In the offices of the company, a deluge of long distance calls came from news services, anxious relatives, company officials and the naturally curious. The answer was always the same: "No, we do not have a release to give out at this time. No, we cannot give you any names. No, we are not able to reach him at this time."[10]

News spread throughout the town of Moab practically from the moment the explosion happened. First, by word of mouth by the potash workers who were called to the mine site to help with the rescue, by those associated with the hospital, by those notified through the civil defense network, and sometimes even by law enforcement. The news spread from person to person, friend to friend, neighbor to neighbor, by family members, waitresses, store clerks and gas station attendants.

No one knew much. There were conflicting reports about the number of men involved. No official notifications were ever actually made to families. The only ones who may have known the names of the men were relatives of the miners working the afternoon shift and those now at the mine site furiously working on the rescue. Even these people didn't give a clear indication of who was underground at the time. Since workers went into and out of the mine throughout a shift for various reasons, family and friends called everyone to make sure they were not part of the ill-fated shift.

The local radio station reported any news they could get, which wasn't much at first. They broadcast public bulletins by law enforcement, which let everyone know, that only those helping with the rescue were allowed at the mine site. They requested the public to keep the roads clear for emergency vehicles.

Mine disasters were always big news. Utah knew this all too well. Throughout the state's mining history, it was punctuated with several devastating mine disasters. Two of the largest were the Scofield Mine Explosion and the Castle Gate Explosion. On May 1, 1900, the Scofield Mine Explosion killed 200 miners and was the largest, at that time, in the United States. The Castle Gate Mine Explosion followed twenty-four years later. On March 8, 1924, 171 miners were killed. Both disasters devastated families and communities in the coal-rich region of Carbon County. Although other U.S. mine disasters killed more men in a single event, both the Scofield and the Castle Gate disasters would remain in the top ten worst mine disasters for the nation.

Disaster at Cane Creek

Small bits of information of the Cane Creek explosion came into news bureaus, which were quickly disseminated throughout the media outlets and news organizations who quickly dispatched reporters and photographers to the area. Publishers from weekly newspapers from all over the state of Utah had just attended a three-day convention in Moab over the prior weekend. The highlight for the group had been a boat ride down the Colorado River which had stopped at the new TGS potash plant for a tour of the new facility by company officials.[11] With construction virtually complete on the surface, touring the new mill complex for the past year had become a popular stop for groups or dignitaries visiting the area. News of the explosion for those media folks who had attended the newspaper convention was all too real. They had just been at the site three days before. Now, some of them prepared to return to Moab, or they sent reporters to cover the story.

Late in the evening, the media started to converge on the small community, nestled in the fiery red canyon cliffs. At first, a few reporters trickled in and were permitted to gather at the mine site as long as they didn't get in the way.

Don Robinson, a reporter for the local newspaper, the *Times-Independent*, Moab's weekly paper, was the first reporter on the scene. He knew many of the people who worked at TGS from his reporting on the new potash facility for the past few years of construction. Bob Mullins, the *Deseret News* Pulitzer-Prize-winning reporter from Price, was not far behind him and other reporters and photographers trickled in throughout the evening.

At the same time, the locals and family members started to get word of the explosion. Anxious, they heard through word-of-mouth, TV, and radio. At the mine site, the telephone lines rang busy as families tried desperately to get more information. Some decided to go to the mine site but were turned back at a roadblock. There wasn't a lot of information, which added to the confusion and stress of relatives who knew their husbands worked at the mine. With the names not released or families notified, it only added to the confusion.

Seventeen-year-old Bill Eslick (the son of 'Blackie' Eslick), and a buddy of his were sitting at the lunch counter at Walker Drug on Main Street. They were waiting for their other friend, who worked at the drugstore, to get off work. From where both boys sat—on stools at the end of the counter—they could see out the opened back door across the alley to the town's newspaper office, the *Times-Independent*. Their back door was also open, and they were busy printing this week's edition of the paper.[12]

Walker Drug, a five-and-dime drugstore, opened in Moab in 1958 by Jack Walker, carried all types of merchandise. At the lunch counter in the back of the store, they had a soda fountain where customers could get a cola, root beer float, chocolate malt or milkshake. The smell of burgers, hot dogs and grilled cheese sandwiches cooking on the grill filled the air.

Someone came into the drugstore and reported to everyone about the explosion. Bill was alarmed because his dad was working at the mine on the afternoon shift. Bill, with his friend, immediately drove home to inform his mother; however, when they arrived, his mother was with her friend who had already told her the news. The friend's husband also worked at the mine, and he was now at the mine site helping with the rescue operation.[13]

Sixteen-year-old Jean Davidson was also uptown with friends when she heard the news and rushed home to tell her mother, Opal Davidson. Opal had heard nothing. She had been home all evening with her two youngest children, Jane, twelve-years-old and Marnie, two and a half. Her husband, Lawrence Davidson, was a Master Mechanic working the afternoon shift. Opal tried to call the mine but like the others, couldn't get through. All she got was a busy signal. The radio continually broadcast updates, and asked people to stay home; rescue personnel was on their way to the scene. TV coverage on the evening news wasn't much better.[14]

Disaster at Cane Creek

After hearing about the explosion, thirty-three-year-old Lorraine Rushton was waiting out the ordeal at her home as relatives gathered. Friends also trickled in as news spread throughout the community. They, too, were trying to get any information they could. Her husband, thirty-four-year-old Lamar Rushton, or 'Rush' as he was called by many, was a Lead Miner working for Harrison International underground.[15]

As the evening wore on, reporters, acting on information that Lamar Rushton was one of the missing miners, showed up at the Ruston resident to see if they could speak with family members. Lorraine politely answered questions and told them what she knew.

"Yes, he was working the afternoon shift and is probably trapped with the other miners," she answered.

"It was Sunday," she said. "That's the day they changed the shift. He came off the graveyard shift and went on the afternoon shift," she said with a firm voice.[16]

Rushton moved with his family of three young children: fourteen-year-old Maureen, thirteen-year-old Bonnie, and nine-year-old Randy, from Murray, Utah to Moab several years before to work at the potash mine.

"Yes, he's one of the ones down there," Lorraine said. "They don't know for sure how many are down there, thirty or maybe thirty-one."

"I think Robert June's down there, too. He rode to work with my husband," Lorraine added.

"I work in the morning, and my husband works in the afternoon. I didn't even see him before he went to work." Her voice trembled as friends helped steady the miner's wife.[17] There were no doubts Rushton was in the mine even though an official list of the miners involved had yet to be released.

Eudeene Hollinger, the wife of James Hollinger, was at home with her two children. Late in the evening, a friend, who worked at the mine, came to tell her about the explosion. Since Eudeene didn't have a phone, the friend called her parents for her in Pioche,

Nevada and told them that he didn't have any news but knew Jim was one of the men caught in the mine explosion. Eudeene's mother and father indicated they would drive through the night to get to Moab, as did other family members once they heard. Jim's parents, living in Moab, along with Eudeene endured a long night trying to get any available information. No one knew if any of the men survived the explosion or if they were all dead. The situation did not look good.[18] Still, everyone clung to hope—a vital necessity in this rugged land.

Law enforcement, notified not long after the explosion, set up a road block north of town at the turnoff onto Potash Road, the new highway down the river leading to the mine site. At first, only TGS and Harrison International personnel, as well as those essential to the rescue operation, were permitted through while they turned others away.

Those not let through, formed a long line of cars that soon lined the main highway, all wanting more information about the explosion. Some came out of curiosity, the lookie-loos. Others came to see what they could do to help. Miners getting off work from other mines in the area came to lend assistance, but were also turned away.

As darkness engulfed the small community of Moab, radio stations in the area kept broadcasting news bulletins of the explosion, regularly reporting any new developments. All anyone knew was that an undetermined number of miners were caught in a blast with no contact from anyone in the mine. One employee was hurt on the surface and taken to the I. W. Allen Hospital where he was treated and released.

The whole community seemed caught up in the situation and was glued to their radios and televisions, trying to get any scraps

Disaster at Cane Creek

of information they could. Moab, a small, close-knit community of about 6,000 residents, was a town where most knew each other. As more people around town became aware of the explosion, telephone party lines buzzed with news, rumors, and speculation. Everyone was caught up in the intensity of the moment.

The Grand County sheriff's office reported they had earlier indications of sixteen miners missing.[19] No one knew for sure the exact number. The shift work roster, still being checked, had not been released and official notifications did not go out to the families of the missing miners.

Everyone had their take on the explosion and the fate of the men. Moab policeman, Robert L. Pipkin, said he doubted anyone could survive down there.

"That's 130-degree heat down in that mine," he said, "If they did survive, they'd probably suffocate in the intense heat," Officer Pipkin said to the inquiring reporters.

He also indicated rescue teams dispatched from the nearby communities of Sunnyside and Dragerton were on their way. The highway was closed at the underpass near Green River, Utah while police escorted two five-man rescue teams to the mine site.[20]

Concerning the activities underground, he couldn't say.

"We have no connection with them at present," he said. "There's a telephone at the guardhouse, but it's away from the mine."[21] They were only letting rescuers go through the roadblock and were no longer allowing women or children at the mine site.

Around 9:30 p.m., the crowd gathered near the road block, spotted flashing red lights in the darkness further up the highway in Moab Canyon. Coming closer, everyone saw the police escort. People and barriers were moved out of the way as the convoy of nearly a dozen vehicles of station wagons, trucks, and Travelalls slowed down to make the turn onto Potash Road. And deputies waved them through. The crowd soon figured out these were the rescue teams sent from the coal fields of Carbon County. Another fifteen minutes and the escort traveling the winding river road would arrive at the mine site.

———

Earlier, some of the coal mine and Utah State Industrial Commission officials started to arrive at the mine site, around 9:30 p.m. Arriving about the same time were two Kaiser Steel Rescue Team members, Johnny Schmidt and Louie Villegos, both from Sunnyside, Utah. They drove together in Schmidt's pick-up truck with their team's rescue equipment in the back. Mine officials wanted them to get ready to go down the shaft right away. The two rescuers said they had to wait for the rest of their team to arrive, who weren't far behind.[22]

By 10:00 p.m.,[23] the two rescue teams,[24] escorted to Cane Creek from Carbon County, reached the mine site. One team was from the Kaiser Steel Corporation, the other from the U.S. Steel Company. They joined the handful of trained and certified rescuers working for TGS and Harrison International. If any could, these teams would be able to get down into the mine to any miners who may have survived the explosion.

A sense of urgency hung heavy in the evening air and animated the rescue scene. Through the loud humming of machinery, a deafening sound of dread permeated everyone's conscience. There was only one prevailing thought: get to the men below before it's too late.[25] Clearly, this was a race against time at full speed. Steve Hatsis, the State Coal Mine Inspector, had also arrived and was ready to coordinate and direct the mine rescue team activities. Various officials and workers were assigned specific roles. At the shaft entrance, floodlights that had been erected made the immediate area brighter. A feverish pace within the buildings slackened a bit, replaced by the systematic activity of preparation by rescue crews.

Disaster at Cane Creek

Rescue team members and their support personnel went to work unpacking rescue gear and getting set up. The important process of assembling and servicing breathing apparatuses by Benchmen got underway, as team members dressed and gathered other needed rescue gear each man would need. Mine rescue work is difficult and often dangerous. It requires adequate and essential training with attention to many details.

Since the mining industry is varied, mine rescue operations can be a huge challenge. Rescuers have to adapt to the different extraction processes each mine site institutes as well as the various types of disasters they might encounter.

Usually, miners take up rescue work as a choice; some because they have a liking for it, some because they are encouraged to do so by their employer because of their leadership skills. They were usually men of determination, of sound mind and body. And accustomed to hard and strenuous work. These expertly-trained teams are composed of courageous men who had become known in the mining industry as the "best of the breed." Mine rescuers are willing to give their lives for a fellow miner, and throughout mining history, there have been rescuers who have died tragic deaths while attempting to help trapped miners.

As soon as everyone was ready, rescue officials and Engineers[26] briefed the rescue teams at the Headframe. A large mine map sat on an easel near the opening close to the shaft collar at the large opening of the Headframe. Officials posted a rotation list for the other teams.

Officials told the rescuers that the first descent would consist of a four-man team. They would travel to the bottom of the mine in the larger Nordberg No. 1 ore bucket and ascertain how much fresh air was in the vent tubing near the shaft station.[27] Kaiser Steel's No. 1 Team, was selected to be the first team down the shaft, while U.S. Steel's Columbia Team, was chosen as the backup team, and positioned at the shaft collar. Put on standby was a team made up of the other Kaiser Steel Team members. Teams that generally consisted of five or six were reduced to three or four rescuers because of lack of space in the ore bucket. The knowledgeable, highly-trained Carbon County teams were soon ready to get the rescue underway.

The shaft collar on the surface served as the current fresh air base until one could be established at the bottom of the shaft. The men listened intently to the briefing. Surprisingly patient, they were filled-in on all the vital information. Their faces reflected the urgency of the situation and the typical comment was, "Let's get down there." Anxious to get going, these extensively trained teams operated on the theory that trapped miners "are alive until it's proven otherwise."[28] If there are men still alive, they will be expecting rescue teams to come for them.

From a distance, the scene around the Headframe was one of bobbing white helmets with an occasional glimpse of a solitary, white-clad nurse or the two black-frocked clergymen who paced back and forth from the shaft area to the change house. Their appearance seemed somewhat out of place because of the hard hats they wore,[29] as white or light shirted officials periodically passed into and out of the light and everyone scrambled to get ready.

Kaiser Steel No. 1 Rescue Team would be the first down; the team members were Frank Markosek, the Captain; Clive Peterson (known as 'Blondie') the Co-Captain; and George Ferguson (nicknamed 'Red'), was the Communications Man.[30] The remaining team members, Lloyd Jaramillo, Louis Villegos, and John Palacios (known as 'Johnny Smoke' or 'Smoke') choose the fourth man by drawing straws. Villegos picked the shortest straw making him the fourth man on the team.[31]

Mining has always been a dangerous occupation and one that all miners fully recognized as dangerous and life threatening. The underground miner had become the epitome of "maleness," a hard-won source of pride.[32] Throughout the years, the most prevalent belief and definition of their role was "real men were miners."[33] They shared similar self-conceptions, and core traits of male masculinity with the armed forces, among them were courage, endurance, and toughness[34] as each faced uncertain, unpredictable, and threatening situations.[35]

Many mine rescuers and miners working in the industry at the time were veterans of World War II and the Korean War and had seen and experienced the horrors of war.

For example, George 'Red' Ferguson, thirty-nine, served in the Marine Corps during World War II.

Lloyd Jaramillo also served in the Marine Corp and was stationed in the Pacific. He married a woman from Australia[36] who he later brought back to the States.

Louis Villegos, forty-three, who worked as a Faceboss at the Kaiser mine, served with General Patton's army in North Africa, Italy, France, Germany, and Czechoslovakia. He was most proud of his picture taken with the Pope while in Rome.[37]

'Johnny Smoke' Palacios, thirty-four, served for two years in the 2nd Infantry Division of the U.S. Army in Germany. When the Division returned to the U.S. in 1945, they found out Palacios was only seventeen-years-old and discharged him. During his time in the Army, he trained other recruits. He was in at fifteen and out before he was eighteen. Returning home to Utah, he worked in various mines before going to work at Kaiser Steel in 1954. He was made the Longwall Section Foreman in 1960 and played an instrumental part in the installation of the United States' first Longwall Face at the Kaiser's Sunnyside mine. A "hard-working, energetic" individual, "they called him 'Smoke' because he could show up anywhere in the mine, anytime."[38]

Fifty-two, John Peperakis, the Superintendent of the Kaiser Steel, Sunnyside operation, was also the mayor of Sunnyside. He came to Cane Creek to help supervise the Kaiser Rescue Teams. As a young mining Engineer, Peperakis was a member of the U.S. Army Corps of Engineers, Solid Fuel Unit attached to Supreme Headquarters,

Allied Expeditionary Forces (SHAEF).[39] After World War II, as part of the Marshall Plan, the U.S. government sent Peperakis overseas to help stabilize and rebuild the German coal mines.[40] The European unit was organized from men with mining experience to rehabilitate the mines damaged from bombardment in the Essen mining district of Germany. While in the service, John rose from the rank of 1st Lieutenant to Lieutenant Colonel.[41] "Later, back in the States, U.S. Steel and Kaiser Steel were having issues in their mines with deep cover; the industry was really weak on roof control and had a lot of roof-fall fatalities. Peperakis remembered what he had seen in German mines—using longwall mining as a safe technique for mines under deep cover[42]—and brought the technology to Utah.

These men and many others were a part of the greatest generation who fought in WWII. The miners who did not serve in the military furthered the necessary war effort by working in the nation's mines and producing the much-needed raw material. They were also seasoned miners who were highly trained and very skilled rescue team members and described in the industry as the "best of the breed."

Late in the evening, around 10:00 p.m., the trapped miners underground realized the fresh water they brought into the barricade was now empty. The ten-gallon can of water had only been a quarter full. Enduring suffocating heat, water was their biggest worry.[43] They knew they had water in the water line, but no one knew how much.

They had nothing to eat. All of the lunch buckets were on the surface in the "Dilly Shack." That's where they kept them when they were sinking the shaft and continued to once they started work on the drifts. Going topside gave the men a chance to get out of the hot mine and get some fresh air before they went back to work after eating their lunch.[44]

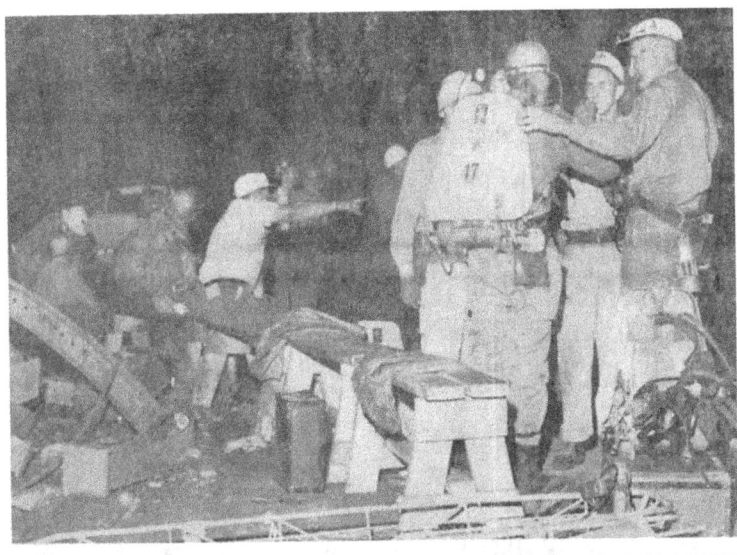

1. Rescue teams equipped with cap lamps, flashlights, and oxygen tanks huddle outside mine before their descent into the shaft. (*Deseret News*) 2. Rescuers polish face masks while waiting for the next trip. (*Daily Sentinel*) 3. Teams gather near the shaft collar. (*Leader Post*)

The men started conserving the fresh water right after the explosion. Rationing helped to preserve their supply to last as long as possible. First, a half a cup to each guy and then a quarter of a cup, and then, it was finally gone.

The men tapped the water line used for mine equipment piped in from the Colorado River. At their camp spot, they broke the line below a shut-off valve and soon had a water faucet at their disposal, netting them an ample supply of 98-degree water, treated but muddy. On this, they could survive.[45]

The men now had hot, gritty water they drained into the bucket. So black, the hot brew looked like black coffee because of the old iron pipes. McKinney thought they were all "gonna die from ptomaine poisoning from that stuff."[46]

They had to gulp quickly to take the sand down with the liquid. After the water had set awhile, it cleared a bit on top. But the water at the top was hotter than the dirty water in the bottom of the bucket. So they waited until the water was pretty thick before dumping the bucket for a refill.[47]

No one thought to ration when they first started drinking the drained water, assuming they could have as much as they could stand. They would drink a cup of it, then swear to themselves, "Boy, I'm not gonna drink anymore of that! That will last me!" Guaranteed, thirty minutes later, they would be back over at the bucket having another cup of the black, hot water. Then thirty minutes later, back again, and continuing on the rest of the night.[48] Because of the heat, the men drank water, sweated, and worried.[49]

Inside the Headframe, the large ore bucket dangled in the shaft opening, its top rim level with the metal floor of the collar. A four-man team,[50] dressed in orange rescue uniforms,[51] stood in the bottom of the bucket nearly ready to make their first descent into the half-mile deep mine. Heavy, thirty-pound breathing apparatus' were strapped to their backs and oxygen masks covered their faces. With their gear, the large ore bucket was cramped. The men shuffled around trying to position themselves, careful not to hit their apparatus' against anything.

Bustling with activity around the shaft collar, a half dozen rescue officials and workers stood on the platform above the bucket, some leaning against, others leaning over, the metal railing. They gave final instructions and made last minute checks as ventilation fans hummed in the background. One worker, speaking into a walkie-talkie did final signaling tests with the communications man in the bucket and the Hoistman. The Hoistman, located in the first of the three temporary hoist houses, was about fifty feet to the west of the Headframe.

The rescue team's Communications Man, George Ferguson, stood down in the bucket and gave an audible grunt sound, "Ruuumph...ruuumph," as he signaled back through his walkie-talkie.[52] The job of the surface communications worker, located at the collar, was to relay commands to and from the rescue team in the bucket and to the Hoistman. Maintaining constant communications at all times between the rescue team and the fresh air base was extremely critical. The face masks worn by rescuers made it difficult to be heard, much less understood; so, all mine rescue teams use a uniform code of signals to communicate and kept talking to a minimum. Teams trained using this code of signals until communicating this way became second nature. They used clear audible sounds by using a horn, bell, whistle, click, hoot or a throaty grunt sound. These signals translate into commands: one signal for "stop," two, meant to move "forward" or "lower" and so forth.

Adrenaline coursed through the rescuer's veins; they were eager to get into the mine and do what they had been trained to do: get to living miners before it's too late. Some had a sense of trepidation concerning the shaft. Coal miners generally enter a coal mine by going in through portals. Not so with the Cane Creek Potash Mine, where ore buckets were used to descend into the deep shaft.

As the team did last minute checks, the Captain noted the time on his watch. Tom McCourt, the team trainer, leaned over the railing and told them to come back up if they didn't feel right about it.[53]

It could be extremely dangerous for rescuers, who couldn't always know the hazards they might encounter. Mining history is full of examples of rescuers who lost their lives trying to get to trapped miners. The men tried not to think about things like that as they concentrated on the team's assignment. The rescue operation's first objective was to establish a fresh air base at the bottom of the mine. But first, the Kaiser Steel Team's assignment this night was to get near the shaft station and test how much fresh air was going through the large vent line at the bottom.[54]

The backup rescue team, U.S. Steel's Columbia-Geneva Team, was nearby; their gear was on, and they were ready to go at a moment's notice should an emergency arise. They would be the second team to enter the mine. The third team in the rotation was on standby as they prepared their equipment. As soon as the first team surfaced, they would become the next backup team. Officials made a rotation schedule with teams consisting of three or four men, and that allowed each man several hours of rest between missions. Being "under oxygen" can be taxing on the body especially with physical exertion, heat, and other taxing stressors.

The team made a final check of each apparatus and recorded the relevant information and the time. Trained in the latest models of breathing apparatuses, they had only a two-hour oxygen supply that needed to be continually monitored.

Positioned in the bucket, the team was finally ready. With cap-lamps turned on, the Captain, Frank Markosek, gave the signal to "go" using two audible sounds as the Map Man recorded the time, 11:00 p.m.[55] Ferguson, the Communications Man, relayed the signal into the walkie-talkie. The command, received by the surface worker, was then relayed to the Hoistman. Only then did the team start moving slowly down into the dark, smoky shaft. Rescue officials and surface rescue workers peered over the railing as they watched the bucket disappear into the darkness and out of sight. Visibility was poor, and the team was only able to see about a foot in front of them as their lights cast eerie shadows in the smoky darkness.

With the bucket crossheads destroyed in the blast, the rescue team soon realized that without these stabilizing features, the bucket moved easily by the slightest shift of weight or movement and twirled and knocked into the other guide ropes in the shaft. The rescuers continually steadied the bucket by grabbing onto the guide ropes to keep it from turning while descending.

Groundwater that seeped into the shaft generally drained into water rings around the perimeter of the shaft and was then taken to the pumps at the 1,330-foot level, where it was pumped out of the mine. Starting at the 500-foot level, there were five of these water collection rings at 600-foot intervals down the length of the shaft. After the explosion had severely damaged the pumps, baffles, and collection rings,[56] the rescue official had the power to the pumps turned off. They feared a secondary explosion from electrical shorts or rescuers getting electrocuted.[57] With the pumps no longer working the water rings overflowed and as the bucket passed under these rings, water flowed into the bucket.[58]

In addition, water fell down the shaft like rain as the bucket continued slowly down, descending deeper into the mine. Drops bounced back and forth off of debris and spewed out into the shaft when it fell or flowed in front of compressed air forced through holes in the torn and battered corrugated metal air vent line.

Almost immediately the water knocked out the walkie-talkie, and the team lost communication with the surface. Heavy droplets of water pounded down on the men's hard hats and flowed off the hat brims in a stream. After repeating the command several times, the bucket eventually came to a stop. The smoke was thick, and the water, heat and moist air coming up the shaft caused the rescuer's oxygen masks to become foggy, making visibility tough. The spit the men rubbed on the lens inside their oxygen masks before putting them on hadn't helped.[59] Down for over twenty minutes, the team made an oxygen check on their apparatuses. The Gas Man also attempted a gas and temperature check, but the water prevented him from getting a good reading.

Seeing over the rim was also difficult in the large, deep bucket, as the men tried to get a sense of the damage around them while steadying the bucket. One rescuer would gently push the bucket back as a man on the other side would reach out and steady it from going too far in the opposite direction to keep it from twirling. By grasping the guide rope and sliding their hand down with the movement of the bucket, they managed to maintain the bucket in the lane.

The bucket was over halfway down the shaft when the rescuers caught glimpses through the smoke of broken and damaged vent lines and service pipes, some hanging from torn brackets. To get by, they had to push some of the debris out of the way. The bucket was filling with water, so Markosek gave the signal to take the bucket up as Ferguson relayed the signal to the surface. But the water was still causing interference with the walkie-talkie. After several attempts, the bucket finally started slowly moving up. While passing the pump station, several of the men thought they heard voices[60] coming from behind the machinery at the back of the hollowed-out room.

The team had only been down forty minutes before the bucket surfaced at the collar at 11:40 p.m.[61] The water that had collected in the bucket was nearly up to the waists of rescuers as workers helped them out of the bucket.[62]

Thoroughly soaked, the rescue team was debriefed and reported they had not been able to get to the bottom to take a reading in the vent line.[63] They reported the damage they observed and about the water falling in the shaft. But more importantly, they told of hearing voices that sounded like they were coming from behind the pump station.

Officials marked any pertinent information on the large mine map as curious workers crowded around wanting to know what the team had found on this trip. Rescue officials at the Command Center conferred with each other to determine the next course of action as support workers emptied the water out of the bucket and cut several lengths of 14 x 14-inch crib blocks to put in the bottom of the bucket for rescuers to stand on.⁶⁴

1. A rescue team getting ready to descent into the deep shaft. Far right, John Peperakis. (*Times-Independent*) 2. Rescue officials and workers peer hopefully down into the shaft as a bucket bearing four rescuers are lowered. The tension mounts while they wait for word of trapped miners. (*Salt Lake Tribune*) 3. A priest, nurse, and rescue workers watch as progress is marked on mine map. (*Daily Sentinel*)

Part Two

Chapter 9

Into the Deep Abyss

In the exhausting heat inside the barricade, the seven survivors sat in the dim light from a cap-lamp. They discussed what they thought the rescuers would do first. They were probably working on establishing air into the mine as fast as they could by any means possible. Since no air was in the large vent line where Rushton had opened the sections, the explosion must have damaged the line. The only hope they had was for rescuers to reestablish air in the small compressed air line used for tools in the mine.

Hanna realized if this happened, the air from the line wouldn't come to the barricade. He, with McKinney's help, opened that line earlier in an attempt to dam up the moving smoke when they built the first barricade, only to discover it had no air. They decided they needed to get up the drift and put the small air line back together.[1]

Trapped and not knowing how long they would be there, all the men felt that if conditions deteriorated inside the barricade, at least the air, if reestablished in the line, would get to them and could save their lives. Assuming the worst, the men had no way of knowing how bad things might get. They had heard many stories about trapped miners. Never did they think they would become

129

the story. Discussing different scenarios was their way of anticipating and creating a contingency plan. They had nothing else to do but try to improve their chances of living the best they could.

They needed to make repairs to the air line. They had air locks between the three barricades, especially the last two to prevent gases from seeping in and contaminating their air. Although safety training stresses to stay behind the barricades, both Hanna and McKinney felt they would be okay to leave.

It was around midnight[2] when both men left. They held wet rags against their nose and mouth to breathe through. If they ran into any problems and felt they couldn't make it back, they would rap on the vent line and the others would know to come and help them get back to the barricade.

The broken air line was 400-feet up the incline. Smoke was all around as Hanna and McKinney stood on the large metal vent line making the needed repairs. One bolt was missing that they were unable to find. Able to get the other bolt on the clamp coupling, they haphazardly hung the line back together. With only one bolt it was a poor connection,[3] but it was the best they could do as they turned the gate valve back on. Still, no air in the line.

Both men were coughing and feeling pretty bad when they got back to the barricade. Moving past the three curtains and resealing them, they made their way to their resting place. Both men were able to recover in a relatively short amount of time once they got back out of the smoke.[4] It had taken roughly twenty minutes before they began to feel well again and the coughing stopped. The smoke wasn't like electrical smoke or powder smoke, which can literally choke a person down.

Once recovered sufficiently, they removed the blow hose from the compressed air line at their camp spot and opened all the valves to relieve undue pressure on the poor connection they made further up the drift. Now, if rescue teams were able to restore the

Disaster at Cane Creek

compressed air pressure[5] in the line, air should get to the men in the barricade.

Around midnight, other state and federal officials arrived[6] at the mine site to assist with the rescue efforts. Also, additional rescue team members from the two coal mining companies, Kaiser Steel and U.S. Steel, were also making their way to the mine site. Many were mine supervisors and foremen and were needed until the shift change around midnight before they could make the two-hour drive to the Cane Creek Mine.

Just after midnight, standing near the Headframe, a rescue official yelled out the names of the next backup and standby teams. Kaiser Steel's suited rescue crew entered the brilliantly lit entrance into the Headframe.[7] Tools hung from their mine belts made clanging sounds as they walked. Their rescue equipment was inspected and secured as they moved into position as the new backup team.

The team ahead of them, U.S. Steel's Columbia Geneva Mine #1 Team was preparing to go underground. Their team Captain gave the order for his men to go "under oxygen" as they donned their masks and made final checks of their own and each other's gear in preparation for their descent.

Briefed and ready to go, the Columbia-Geneva team, boarded the bucket. Dressed in gray team uniforms, they were assigned to investigate the reported sounds at the pump station and evaluate any damage to the machinery.[8] This trip would be the first descent made by a U.S. Steel Team.[9]

Descending cautiously downward, the Hoistman knew exactly where to stop the bucket at the pump station, the 1,330 foot level of the deep shaft. A small platform, several feet long and a couple of feet wide, held flush against the shaft wall, was unlatched and lowered as chains on each side held it perpendicular. The men climbed out onto the platform using the steps formed on the side of the bucket.[10] The team members first checked for survivors back in the hollowed out room. Finding none, they inspected the machinery. After the explosion, the power to the mine was cut off to protect rescuers from being electrocuted. It disabled the pumps and the bell system.

The team determined they couldn't stop the flow of water even if they restored the power. The pumping system in the shaft was severely damaged[11] causing groundwater to cascade down the shaft not long after the explosion.

The rescue crew, back in the bucket, continued down the shaft. The force of the blast ripped the air, power, and communications lines in the shaft and filled the bottom with a tangle of pipe and rubble.[12] Debris and twisted metal were everywhere, and at least seventy-five feet of rubble was stacked up above the shaft station.[13] They saw how the blast damaged or destroyed large sections of the ventilation system, but it appeared, at least, one air hose, the six-inch compressed air line used for tools, remained intact all the way to the bottom.

Nearly out of the air in their apparatuses, the team signaled the surface. With limited oxygen, it was imperative for teams to set up a fresh air base as quickly as possible to eliminate the need to waste an hour of their vital oxygen supply traveling up and down the shaft. In a race against time, rescuers were anxious to get down into the mine to probe the drifts for men who may have survived the explosion.

Don Robinson, a full-time high school teacher, was also a part-time reporter for the Moab newspaper, the *Times-Independent*. He dutifully watched the rescue operation from the main office building as he scrawled copious notes for an article he was writing. Nearby, Bob Mullins, the Pulitzer Prize-winning reporter, was there with several other *Deseret News* press people. Other reporters were there from nearby communities. Reporter Jack Kisling and photographer Bob Grant from the *Daily Sentinel* in Grand Junction, Colorado, about a two-hour drive away, were also covering the story.[14] They too had regularly reported during the construction phase of the new potash mine for the past several years. Other reporters milled around the main office building as more continued to arrive throughout the night. A few wore the stylish fedora hats, with sharp dark business suits and skinny ties. Others wore a more casual business dress with their dress shirt sleeves rolled up. A few exuded an air of sophistication, a somewhat typical behavior in their profession. Others were down-to-earth type guys.

Their "polished metal gear gives them a robot appearance," Robinson wrote about the rescuers wearing their breathing apparatuses. "Yet they moved with a fluidity that belies their cumbersome look. Those waiting resemble an audience so intent, they watch each individual performance or perhaps actors waiting for their cues," he poetically added.[15]

In the darkness of the night, the floodlit rescue operation was well underway in a concentrated area around the Headframe. It was a relatively small area compared to Texas Gulf Sulphur's (TGS) large mine-mill complex.[16] In the air was tension and a sense of foreboding.

By 1:30 a.m. the suited rescue team from Kaiser Steel, the next one in the rotation, stood in the bucket, ready for the next descent into the mine. It would be the third such trip by a Carbon County team. Rescues had still not made it to the bottom of the shaft to begin a search in the mine for survivors, and everyone was restless for results.

The sheave wheel started to turn and creaked as the bucket slowly began its descent down disappearing into the darkness. Rescue workers on the surface went about doing the only thing they could do. Wait.

A single person stood peering down into the hole, as though gazing into a deep abyss,[17] an "enormous gulf, like the jaws of hell itself"[18] from which its "vapors rise from the depths, as if from a "hell-broth, whose reek poison...were being brewed down below. One would think this was where Dante went down and saw the inferno, with all its horror and immitigable [sic] pain."[19]

The person standing at the shaft was very still as if listening.[20] Other workers stood in small groups chatting while a row of men, back-lit, sat immobile facing the shaft. In the darkness, workers came and went[21] across the yard from the other buildings nearby. In the bench area, each rescue team's Benchman, with the help of other rescue workers, stayed busy servicing and inspecting the oxygen breathing apparatuses.

1. This structure atop mine shaft in which 25 miners were trapped. (*Salt Lake Tribune*) 2. Paul Clark (left) and Frank Markosek get rescue gear ready. Members of the rescue team await the order to descend into the mine shaft. Other rescue workers whisper quietly in the background. (*Deseret News*) 3. Tight-lipped, wet, cold and grimy, this unidentified rescue worker reflects the tension of mine rescue operation. (*Salt Lake Tribune*)

Oxygen tanks were filled, the units cleaned and repairs made, then they were tested. A Benchman's job required meticulous attention to every detail. A rescuer's life depended on their apparatuses' proper maintenance and function.

Occasionally, the bright lights from cap-lamps on individual hard hats bobbed in the darkness and pointed in different directions with every turn of the head.[22] Those chatting turned their heads slightly to the side to keep their cap-lamps from shining in the eyes of the ones with whom they were speaking, mostly an unconscious trait among miners. Patiently, rescue workers on the surface continued to wait in the slightly chilly night air for the return of the bucket from the depths of the shaft.

Earlier in the evening, at the administrative office, 300 yards west of the Headframe,[23] Pinkerton, and others initially spent a lot of time making the vital notification calls. As word spread of the explosion, it wasn't long before the switchboard was flooded with incoming or outgoing calls. The mine site had only four lines and those lines were constantly tied up.[24]

Pinkerton needed to sort out the priorities of who could have a telephone line. He had employees with previous experience working the switchboard come to the mine site and help. But after several hours with the help, it wasn't much better. So Pinkerton decided to take over the switchboard himself. The rescue operation needed one line open at all times in the event they had to reach any emergency services or vehicles.

Pinkerton took on the responsibility to prioritize the lines. He started to monitor and sort out the calls. The word soon got out to those working the rescue; they could call him on one of the local office lines and tell him they needed a phone line out and the reason.

Pinkerton would get an open line, call them back and let them know they could go ahead and make their call.

Pinkerton took up his post by the switchboard for the duration of the rescue operation, monitoring communications. Eventually, a cot was brought in and put next to the switchboard so he could rest when not busy. Others took over only briefly when he needed a break or went home to take a shower.

Sometime around 1:30 a.m., Pinkerton received a call from a worker down by the Headframe saying they needed food for the rescue workers. Pinkerton thought about how he would get food out to the mine site, then remembered a friend from Rotary Club, Frank Yama, who owned a grocery store in town. Pinkerton made a late night call to Yama, who told him he would make sandwiches if Pinkerton could get others to help. Pinkerton called his wife, Joan. He then called Dot Crawford, the wife of June Crawford, the Chief Engineer at TGS, to help Frank and his wife, Rosemary. They all went to the store in the middle of the night and made sandwiches. When finished, Pinkerton sent a driver to pick up the food to bring out to the mine site. The rescue operation was slowly getting organized. Food, provisions and other needed supplies continually made it to the mine site while vital mine experts and rescue personnel continued to arrive throughout the night.

It wasn't long before Pinkerton received another call from down by the Headframe. This time, it was from Art Redd, who worked in the purchasing department. Rescue crews now needed a particular type of battery. Pinkerton got on the phone and called Ralph Miller, Jr., who owned Miller's Supermarket out on the south edge of town. Pinkerton gave him the number of the battery and how many they needed.

Miller told him, "Absolutely, I'll get the batteries you need."

Redd was sent to fetch the batteries, and when he arrived, he discovered Miller had phoned other store owners in Moab, who also had the required batteries on hand. Those store owners had gone to their stores in the middle of the night. They brought their supply of batteries to Miller's Supermarket and were standing in the dark in front of the supermarket waiting. They handed over their batteries with an attitude, "if you need one maybe you better take twenty." This type of atmosphere, one of helping and concern from the people of Moab, as well as others in the mining industry, would permeate and prevail throughout the entire rescue operation. The spirit from everyone was: whatever was needed. So many were willing to help in any way they could.

Kaiser Steel's rescue crew was just over halfway down the deep shaft where they were working to remove debris. The larger Nordberg bucket made it difficult for the four-man team to lean over the rim even with the wood crib blocks to stand on. The team did what work they could. Because of air limitations and realizing it was nearly time to surface, the team found they were unable to communicate using the walkie-talkie. The water pouring down knocked it out, leaving them stranded in the shaft as water collected in the bottom of the bucket.[25]

On the surface, anxious officials knew the team should have started up, but still, there was no signal. Making repeated attempts to communicate with the team, officials decided to bring them up. Slowly, the Hoistman engaged the hoist in raising the bucket. It started slowly up as water poured down on the team. It moved past areas where the forced air was blowing from damaged sections in the vent line, as the water poured in on them or was spit at them and trickled down. The water was nearly waist high in the bottom of the bucket.

Moving up slowly, the bucket jerked when the rim suddenly snagged onto a piece of heavy metal debris sticking out in the shaft. The men scrambled to release it as the bucket continued up. Frantically, they yelled over the walkie-talkie, hoping the surface would hear and stop, but it kept going up with no way to signal to the surface.

Up, up, it went. Gradually, the hooked bucket started to slowly tip on bail, shifting the men to one side. As it continued to tip, the metal hoisting cable began to stretch. Desperate, the men, encumbered by rescue gear, were shifted into an awkward position in the small confines of the bucket. They struggled to free it from the debris but to no avail. The bucket kept tipping and stretching the hoisting cable as it started to groan and creak under the tension. The bottom of the bucket rose higher as the water started to pour out.

The bucket, now in a horizontal position, kept tipping as the soaking wet rescuers lay over the top of one another, mashed between apparatuses and against the side of the bucket. Shoulders or arms of some smashed against the rim. Up the bucket went. Horrified, the men held on tight to the bucket, to each other, to the chains, anything they could grab onto as all of the water poured out. Absolutely nothing could be done as the bucket tipped almost completely down while they hung on, fearing the worst. Powerless and gripped with intense terror, they struggled and squirmed as much as they could from side to side to get the bucket free and keep themselves from being dumped out. As the hoist continued to wind, stretching the cable even more, it threatened to break and send the heavy bucket to the very depths of the deep shaft.

Without warning, the bucket jerked loose and slid off the piece of metal. Instantly released, the bottom of the bucket flung down with tremendous force. And from the tension built up in the cable, the bucket wildly jerked up and down, slinging and hurling itself about the shaft. It bounced against guide ropes and tossed itself violently as it whirled and swung. Inside, the helpless rescuers were smashed down on top of each other and then tossed and thrown from one side to the other while it spun out of control. It took what-seemed-like-forever before the bucket's movements slowed and eventually came to a stop.

On the surface, the Hoistman, and others saw the jerks and wild movements of the hoisting cable. Immediately, the hoist brake was applied. They had no idea what had just happened and frantically called over the walkie-talkie trying to get a response. It had to be dire; the Hoistman refused to bring the bucket up until they knew it was safe to do so. Otherwise, the lives of the rescue team could be endangered, if something terrible hadn't already happened.[26]

With no way to communicate with the team, rescue officials quickly evaluated the situation. The team would run out of oxygen soon if they didn't do something quickly. Officials promptly deployed two rescuers from the backup team at the collar, who was ready to go at a moment's notice. They were tasked to go down in a second bucket and find out what had happened. They were to communicate with ropes since the water knocked out the walkie-talkies. The backup team was instructed to assess the situation and make sure the Kaiser Steel Team knew how to give the signals with a rope to get them to the surface. The Hoistman refused to move their stranded bucket without their signal. The two men rehearsed the signals. "Stop" was one shake or wave of the rope, given if the bucket was already in motion. If the bucket was not in motion, "Down" was one shake and "Up" was two shakes.

The two rescuers, Guy Hersh and Willie Poglajen from the U.S. Steel-Horse Canyon Team, quickly went "under oxygen" and made final checks to their gear. Boarding the second bucket they were ready. With adrenaline pumping, the bucket went slowly down into the dark, smoky shaft. As it descended, they watched the light of the round opening of the shaft above them get smaller and smaller as dread and fear seized them not knowing what they might find.

Slowly, Guy and Willie's bucket inched its way down towards the four men in the stranded bucket. Finally, more than halfway down the deep shaft they were barely able to make out a cluster of four dim beams of light from the men's cap-lamps directed towards them shrouded in the smoky haze.[27] As they drew nearer, and from what they could tell in the darkness and unrelenting rain, all the men were accounted for and appeared to be okay.

Not knowing what they would find as they traveled from the surface, their fears, held hostage by their imagination, were finally allayed and replaced by an overpowering sense of relief. As they neared the stranded bucket with the orange suited Kaiser Steel Team, Guy gave one hard shake on the rope to signal to the Hoistman to stop. But the bucket kept moving downward.[28]

Twenty feet below the bucket of the stranded rescuers, it came to an abrupt stop. Guy gave two shakes to take them back up. After a short pause, their bucket slowly moved upwards, back up towards the stranded men peering over the rim of their own bucket. Back alongside the other bucket, Guy gave the stop signal. But up they continued, twenty-five, thirty feet before the bucket came to a stop. Again, Guy gave two shakes on the rope to take them back down. Getting closer he gave one shake to stop, only to pass them again as before. Looking up at the bottom of the other bucket, Guy tried again to get level; back and forth this motion continued until the lower part of their bucket was nearly level with the top rim of the stranded rescuers' bucket, the closest they were able to get thus far.[29]

Willie shouted down at the stranded crew the instructions, the signals they needed to give the Hoistman with their rope. But his face mask muffled his voice and the water falling into the cement echo chamber drowned out the sounds making it nearly impossible for them to hear. Both Willie and Guy shouted, but the men seemed not to understand. Finally, in the smoke and pouring rain, Willie leaned out over the edge of his bucket, while Guy held onto his legs and feet. He squirmed to position his body as far out as he could to get near the bucket in the other hoisting lane. Wiggling out even more and leaning down to get as close as he could to the men just below him, he continued to stretch. The bucket Willie and Guy were in was the smaller, shorter one and could tip more easily.[30]

Petrified, Guy thought to himself, "What if Willie slipped?" He held on as tight as he could, afraid he could lose his grasp, sending Willie toppling down to a certain death. It wasn't a good situation.

Willie yelled through his face mask as loud as he could the instructions the other team needed. Finally, James 'Jim' Harvey, the Captain of the stalled Kaiser Steel Team,[31] was able to understand. After several hair-raising minutes, Willie squirmed back inside to the safety of his bucket as both men breathed a sigh of relief. They watched the once-stranded bucket slowly begin to move upward, moving pass them on their way to the surface. Both men, overcome with relief and "just a little bit emotional," waited while the other bucket reached the surface. Because the hoisting apparatuses suffered damage from the explosion, Harrison International's electricians re-rigged two buckets, but only one could be hoisted at a time.

Guy and Willie settled back, knowing they would be there for a while as the rain poured down on them and collected in their bucket. Reflecting back on the whole event, Guy realized why they were never able to get more level with the other bucket. By the time the signal on the rope traveled the distance up the shaft, over a quarter-mile, it had created a lag time before the Hoistman got it and then acted on the signal. What he should have done, he thought to himself, was give the signal to move, then almost immediately give the signal to stop. Maybe it would have made a difference. It didn't matter now; the stranded team was safe and now on their way out of this dangerous hell hole.[32]

After a while, accounting for the time it would take for the other bucket to reach the surface, Guy gave two shakes on their rope to signal to the Hoistman that it was okay to take them up when they were ready. It wasn't long before the bucket slowly started up and

Guy gave a relieved sigh. He could see the tiny dot of light above growing larger as they came closer to the surface.[33]

Relieved rescue officials and workers greeted the stranded Kaiser Steel Team when the bucket surfaced at the shaft collar. Jubilation was quickly consumed and replaced with worry when they realized the soaking wet men were in bad shape. Rescue workers helped each of them out of the bucket as doctors at the mine site were alerted. Concern grew as the word spread, and a crowd gathered around as workers helped the men out of their face masks and breathing apparatuses.

'Johnny Smoke' watched near the collar, as other Kaiser Steel rescuers crowded around, checking on their teammates. One of them, George Ferguson was intent as he watched. His brother-in-law was the team's Captain, James Harvey. It was evident the men were "sicker than hell."[34] Because of the violent motion experienced by the men in the bucket while "under oxygen" and the intense emotional fear, they were in horrible shape. Moved to gurneys, the doctors and nurses attended to their needs. Making each man as comfortable as possible, the doctors administered tranquilizers to sedate them. Consequently, they were not allowed to go back "under oxygen" for the duration of the rescue operation.[35]

After such a close call, where rescuers nearly died in the shaft, the General Mine Managers of the two Carbon County rescue teams, John Peperakis and Robert 'Bob' von Storch,[36] refused to let any of their men go back into the mine until debris was cleared out of the shaft. Too many rescuers have died in past rescue operations[37] across the nation, and Peperakis and von Storch wanted to make sure nothing happened to their rescuers.

The Command Center debated the best way to move forward. After intense debate, it was finally decided to task the Harrison

Disaster at Cane Creek

International men to help with the work of clearing debris in the shaft. They were the ones most experienced and agile to work down in the shaft.

There was only one problem. Most of Harrison International's men were not certified rescuers or trained to go "under oxygen," so officials decided to get them trained and certified onsite. Time was slipping away; it was going on ten hours since the explosion and rescue teams had still not made it to the bottom of the shaft to get into the mine. Survivors, if there were any, would be counting on them before it was too late.

With the doctors available on site to certify the health of each man, Steve Hatsis, the Utah State Coal Mine Inspector, would see to their training and could legally certify them once instructed in the proper use of the oxygen apparatuses. Other seasoned rescuers also helped with the training of the Harrison International's men.[38]

Training and certification was a serious matter, and mining officials were well aware of the concerns as they signed off on the plan. In a 1944 information circular provided by the U.S. Bureau of Mines, it showed from 1911 to 1949, twenty-six men lost their lives while wearing oxygen breathing apparatus in this country.[39]

Harrison International's men immediately started taking physicals with training to follow. For other rescue teams, it took hours upon hours of training to learn the intricacies of being a mine rescuer and trained in the proper use of the breathing apparatuses. For Harrison International's men, it would take only a short time to get men qualified enough, to at least help clear debris in the shaft.[40]

In town, a reporter stopped by the Grand Country Sheriff's Office to gather what information he could on the explosion. Geneva Narron, the Sheriff's Office dispatcher, tried to answer his questions.

"The explosion blew everything, the communication lines, air lines, electrical lines, and windows out of the Headframe and injured one man above ground," said Ms. Narron.[41]

"Some of the trapped men are from Moab, some are employees of Harrison International from Canada," she said. "Harrison International has Canadian workers down here all the time," she added.[42] The reporter made notes as they chatted.

"There are sixteen men trapped in a drift off the 2,700-foot level," Ms. Narron said.

"That's the definite count,"[43] she said as her voice trailed off with uncertainty.

There were many conflicting reports about the number of men caught in the explosion. Otto A. Wiesley, the Chairman of the Utah State Industrial Commission, was reporting that thirty men were in the blast while the General Manager for TGS, Frank Tippie, said it was only twenty-five men. No one knew what to believe as rumors continued to spread.

As the night wore on, with the rescue operation well underway, rescuers were working to get down into the mine. The fate and the exact number of men missing were still unknown. Conflicting reports continued to circulate while many feared the men were dead. They either didn't survive the blast or died from the deadly carbon monoxide gas generated by the blast from burning debris. One radio station claimed all the men were dead, causing extreme stress to family members who happen to hear the report.[44]

A list of the men working in the mine was still not made available adding to the conflicting information. The contractor never used a tag-in/tag-out board generally used in the mining industry, which made it possible to know at any given moment who was in the mine.

Reporters were not the only ones seeking information at the sheriff's office. Moab was a town not able to sleep as word continued to spread while family and friends sought out information wherever they could find it. It was a long, sleepless night for so many around Moab, who were worried sick about the men trapped down in the mine.

About 3:00 a.m., a white-haired woman entered the sheriff's office and asked Deputy Lane Foot who was on duty at the time, "Do you think there is any chance?"

"Yes," replied the deputy firmly.

Tiredly, the little woman turned and left the office.[45]

Relatives of the trapped miners had been coming in throughout the long night seeking any information they could get about their loved ones who were trapped underground by the fiery explosion.[46] For many, it was a sleepless night filled with tears and anxiety.

In total darkness, the trapped survivors in the barricade waited. In an unnerving way, mines have a way of flirting with the abyss. Even old superstitions of subterranean creatures, like the Tommyknockers (impish, gnome-like men about two feet tall, greenish in color and who often wore a traditional miner's outfit) helped to explain the creaking of the earth as the mine at times would settle. Some mines are far worse for these types of creaking or popping sounds than others. Many miners thought these were sounds of hammering as the Tommyknockers worked.

For now, it was quiet, other than the sound of men breathing and the rocks. They could hear all the little noises in the mine not noticed before, like pebbles falling from the roof and hitting the large metal vent line. It was amazing how many little pebbles fell in a stretch of time not normally heard in the ordinary course of a work day. Sometimes larger rocks would fall. First, one. Maybe two. It caused the men to think rescuers were coming, only to realize it wasn't so.

Periodically, throughout the night, the men would take turns going up behind the third barricade, which had been the first one built. They would go on the other side where the thickest smoke was and check to see if the smoke had cleared some. They did this every few hours or so. At first, they could hardly see their hand in front of their face, then gradually they could see just a little bit further. By 3:30 a.m., the smoke was still thick but had dissipated enough to see the ground just out in front of their feet with their cap-lamps.[47]

Then it was back to waiting. Again, they turned the lights off and rested in total darkness to wait for help they knew would come. Now and then someone would turn on a light to refill the water can and get a drink; the shuffling sounds aroused the others to do the same. Then silence again, a silence borne of isolation, cut off from a living and robust world. This silence was different. Evocative, it resounded of a deathly silence. A silence that was too quiet. It had the ringing sound of inner noise as each retreated into their own, inner world of thoughts.

All through the night, the trapped men waited. They dozed some, talked little. When they did talk, it was mostly about rescuers or about their waiting families and how they must feel.[48]

Twenty-seven-years-old 'C.C.' was a quiet-spoken, young man. He kept thinking, "How will my family cope without me?"[49] What was Adeline, his wife, and his four young children doing? Maybe they hadn't heard about the explosion yet.

Each man had his thoughts and worries, mostly about their wives, their children and about getting out of the mine.

'Blackie' was a quiet, intense man. Although he worked alongside the other men building the barricade during that harrowing time after they were surrounded by smoke, in a way he still felt as though he didn't quite fit in with the Harrison International crew.[50] Crew members often become very close when they work day in and day out with each other, and 'Blackie' hardly knew the other men, nor did they know him.

Reticent, he thought about his family, about his wife, Vivian. He knew by now she must be alarmed. In his long mining career, he had been involved in other minor mining accidents, but he was always prompt to notify his wife of them. By now, she had to know he was in big trouble.

In the stillness, 'Blackie' thought of his children, Trudy, twenty, who was a natural-born horsewoman. Her favorite possession was a big sorrel stallion named Senator Tom. And he thought of his son, Bill, a senior in high school, who rode, skied and soon would need to go to college. He pictured their cozy living room with its red, white and blue drapes to match the wall of red, white and blue trophy ribbons the kids had won at horse shows. A man never sees his home as good as he does in the velvet blackness of a one-way cave,[51] 'Blackie' thought to himself.

———

In the darkness of the early morning hours, while Harrison International's men were getting physicals, fifty-year-old, Steve Hatsis,[52] heading the rescue operation,[53] boarded a bucket with two other rescuers to make a reconnaissance trip down into the shaft.[54] With breathing apparatuses on their backs, the other men with him were forty-year-old Caratat Olsen, known as 'Oly,' and forty-three-year-old Fred Tatton, both from the Kaiser Steel Team. Hatsis needed to know firsthand the difficulties the rescue teams were running into, especially after the bucket caught on debris and nearly dumped the men down the shaft.

The men traveled slowly down into the dark, wet shaft to a point just about a hundred feet from the bottom. There they found debris stacked up and blocking the shaft.[55] Not able to get to the bottom,[56] the rescuers leaned over the sides and worked it down another thirty-five feet, maneuvering it slowly through the debris and rubble. Their cap-lamps on their hard hats illuminated the smoky darkness as the water pounded down on them. They found seventy-five feet of debris near the bottom of the shaft[57] and conditions were as poor as the teams had reported.

Some of the debris consisted of severely damaged sections of the large spiral steel vent tubing that needed to be replaced.[58] The concussion from the explosion ricocheted up the sides of the shaft and badly damaged the corrugated metal vent line in different places. Five lengths were torn loose or crushed from the blast,[59] and other sections were loose or had holes of various shapes and sizes torn in them. High pressured air was blasting across the shaft from the damaged areas of the vent line while some of the tubings were just hanging there. In some places, the men had to push the sections out of the way.[60] Miles of metal hoisting rope from the fouled lines of the hoisting buckets and all the service lines such as electrical wiring, bell cord, etc., were snarled and hanging throughout the debris like spaghetti.

The team was not able to get to the bottom or see into the mine. Taking gas readings, they found carbon monoxide and combustible gas.[61] The air was hot and very moist, making visibility difficult through the face masks protecting them from the carbon monoxide gas.[62] After about an hour and a half in the shaft and carefully examining conditions, the team surfaced. Understanding the situation better, Hatsis directed teams to start clearing the debris blocking the bucket lanes first so teams could get all the way down into the mine and then work on establishing a fresh air base at the bottom.

They also decided to replace six sections of the damaged vent line[63] and made an emergency order for flexible, thirty-inch diameter plastic air tubing from Denver. These replacements, once hooked up, would direct the needed air to the bottom of the mine.[64]

Chapter 10

"A Miracle if Anyone is Alive"

Rescuers lowered into the mine three or four at a time in the two-ton ore bucket, continued to work their way towards the bottom, going as far as they could through the seventy-five feet of debris. Tired and weary, the teams descended one after the other as the hours wore on, in the deep, wet shaft.

At 5:45 a.m., a rescue team surfaced with the disconcerting news. At the bottom of the shaft, the team ran into significant levels of deadly carbon monoxide and methane gas.[1] These gas levels were considerably worse than the ones taken earlier. Rescuers also got a temperature reading of 130 degrees at the bottom.

For some, the news of deadly gases further dimmed already slim hopes that any men would be found alive.[2] The presence of higher levels of gas also posed a serious problem to the rescue teams. Hours after the smoke billowing from the shaft had stopped, there were reports of large quantities of carbon monoxide still flowing from the mine opening, probably from smoldering debris.

Just before 1:00 a.m., several gas tests[3] were made at the shaft collar on the surface, revealing deadly gas was still coming from the mine. Rescue workers not under apparatus were warned to be careful when getting close to the shaft opening. One rescue worker passed out from the fumes, but other workers quickly revived him.[4]

The presence of the methane gas gave further credence to what many already believed: the explosion was probably the result of hitting a pocket of methane gas that ignited. It also meant rescuers had to proceed with extreme caution to prevent another explosion.

Ventilation was always the key in dealing with mine gases, using high volumes of air to dilute and flush out. It was nearly impossible to get more air into the mine until they repaired the damaged vent line.

It was also standard procedure in underground mines, known or suspected of being gassy, to check continually for gas in the course of mining. It was even more critical for mine rescue teams to take gas readings, especially after an explosion as they advanced further into the unknown of a damaged mine.

The intrepid rescuers understood the dangers they faced each time they went down the shaft. The crews continued working throughout the early morning to restore the vent line towards the bottom. The water and intense heat made the work grueling. Meanwhile, teams did what they could while they waited on the 30-inch diameter flexible plastic pipes being brought to the site from Denver to replace the metal vent line shattered by the explosion.[5] Rescuers also needed to string communications lines, so crews would be in contact with the men on the surface directing rescue efforts.[6]

Just after 6:00 a.m., over thirteen hours since the explosion, there were still no signs of rescuers. The trapped men all believed that rescue operations were underway[7] but couldn't understand why they hadn't gotten to them by now. After all, it's a new mine with only two drifts to search. It wasn't like more established mines with miles of honeycombed inter-workings rescuers had to search through.

Hanna felt, at the very least, the rescuers should have restored the compressed air into the mine. Still, no air. Hanna started to believe the shaft was probably inaccessible to him. The worry was intensifying. What if the entrance into the mine had caved in, like at Sheppton, with no way for rescuers to get to them? Even if they could dig or drill for them, it would take too much time, something the men didn't have. They had no food and only enough water for another day or so. They could live without food but not water, especially in the hot, suffocating heat. And soon they would even run out of the good air.

Were they to die a slow agonizing death, Hanna thought to himself? The heat was sapping every bit of energy the men had, and they could easily die of heat exhaustion. They would just go to sleep and never wake up.

What about their families? Hanna knew his family needed him. There would be no way they could get along without him. How could his wife manage with the kids or pay the bills? What was his wife thinking right now or going through, he wondered.

Thoughts kept tumbling through his head as his lungs and ribs ached from coughing and his eyes hurt from the smoke. More than anything, Hanna thought about the three men who refused to come into the barricade. What if they were still alive and they needed help.

Possibly, he understood about being helpless. As a young child growing up on the family farm in Carbon County, while his family worked in the beet field, he tried to jump on the running board of a large, beet truck and fell. The loaded truck ran over his chest and hips smashing him into the dirt. He lay in the field, with broken ribs and pelvis, for what seemed a long time before anyone got to him. In terrible pain and all alone, he was afraid and completely helpless. It took months to heal, and he was in a cast from his neck to his legs, and ultimately, had to learn how to walk again.

All Hanna could think about was wondering what the three men at the top of the incline were going through if they were still alive. He felt agonizing regret; if only he had grabbed one of them, perhaps the others would have come back with him to the barricade. Why hadn't he, he kept asking himself? They were haunting thoughts, even though he barely made it back to the barricade himself. As the Lead Miner, he felt deeply responsible for his men.

After getting a drink of water, Hanna retreated down the drift towards the working Face to be alone. He sat next to the loader with his knees up and arms wrapped around them. His head hung down, in complete and utter despair and feelings of hopelessness engulfed him. Not a particularly religious person, Hanna silently stumbled through a heartfelt prayer.[8] "Lord, help us get through this. Help me to know what to do," he said as he pushed back the tears swelling up in his eyes while pouring out his heart for guidance. After a while, a feeling of calm and serenity washed over him. It was as though he knew what he had to do. As he lifted his head and in the light of his cap-lamp, he clearly saw the large Marine emblem tattooed on his left forearm. It reaffirmed his decision.

Hanna grew up on a farm in Wellington, Utah, not far from Price, Utah. Always a restless soul, he quit school in the eighth grade (much to the consternation of his parents) and worked on a ranch in Colorado for a while. At sixteen, Hanna was able to get a draft card which enabled him to work in the coal mines back in Carbon County even though he wasn't old enough. He worked as a driver of a mule team in the Latuda Coal Mine. Owned by Liberty Fuel Company, the mine was located up Spring Canyon above Helper, Utah.

Before long, Hanna enlisted in the Marine Corps. Underage, his mother hesitantly signed for him. He was only seventeen. Off he went to San Diego, California for basic training and then to survival training in Alaska. He, like other young boys, had grown up through the war years with patriotic images of serving in the military and being a part of a brave and noble cause, but before he finished basic training, the Korean War was coming to an end. And although he never saw combat, he was nonetheless a Marine. He obtained the rank of Sergeant and took pride in being a Marine and their code of honor, codes like 'Semper Fidelis" ('always faithful') and "leave no man behind."

Resolute, Hanna had his mind made up. He was going to leave the barricade and go back after the three guys at the top of the incline, Rushton, Sviscsu, and Barber, and bring them back to the barricade. Hopefully, it wasn't too late. But he knew he had to try, and he would need help from the others.[9]

A deceptive air of calm hung over the Texas Gulf Sulphur (TGS) Potash Plant early Wednesday morning as more reporters made their way to Moab to cover events. Brilliant hues of red, pink and orange illuminated the canyon walls as the sun came up and drenched the plant buildings with a warm glow.

A plane flew over the site with press people working for the *Deseret News and Salt Lake Telegram*, in Salt Lake City. One of their staff writers and a photographer, flew to the area by chartered plane to join their colleagues who came the night before.[10] The paper's news Bureau Chief from Richfield also flew to Moab to set up the News' mobile telephoto transmitter, while several stayed at the main office as rewrite men.[11]

From what the newsmen could tell from their overhead view from the plane, "very little" indicated there had been a major mine explosion. There were some cars parked around the area but few signs of activity on the ground. It is hard to imagine an explosion had struck, there were no external signs of damage. A flag still flew at full-staff atop the tall cement Headframe covering the shaft." The plane circled several times while the photographer adjusted his dark browline eyeglasses and aligned his camera to snap photos of the scene. It was a peaceful August morning with the Colorado River flowing soundlessly in the distance, past the rescue scene[12] as sunlight glittered across the water's surface.

When the story broke, the *Denver Post* deployed two veteran staff members, a reporter, and a photographer to provide on-the-ground coverage of the rescue attempt. The men flew from Denver at 4:30 a.m. and reached the scene shortly after 7:00 a.m. They planned to telephone reports to their news bureau in Denver, but because of limited phone lines at the mine site, they had to travel to Moab to transmit the pictures by Wirephoto.[13]

There was a continuous flow of press people into the area to cover the story. All the local radio stations in the surrounding area were also reporting on the disaster. One young reporter was flown by private plane from Grand Junction, Colorado, to the scene to do direct reporting for a small radio station he worked for, KWSL. He was there to do continuous coverage, determined to do so with speed, accuracy, and professionalism. Strictly a KWSL news coverage effort, thousands listened to his reports.[14]

Disaster at Cane Creek

Graphics of the Texas Gulf Sulphur Cane Creek Potash Mine-Mill Complex that shows the two underground drifts in relationship to the surface facility. (*AP Telephoto*)

In the early morning hours, reporters milling around in offices at the main office building came across some bright red, white and blue signs announcing a company party planned for Thursday evening[15] for the miners, their relatives, and company officials. The party was to commemorate the crews reaching the potash ore bed. Frank Tippie's home in Moab was to be "gaily festooned" for a victory celebration, and some of these painted signs were to direct party goers to available parking.[16]

Yesterday, the afternoon shift was within one or two shots of completely exposing the potash ore bed—the pay dirt, the treasure in the earth that Harrison International's crews were seeking for the past two years. With the dynamite's "bite into the cash load, the potash ore," limited production was scheduled, and TGS promised permanent jobs as soon as Harrison International completed the development work in the mine.[17]

Everyone was waiting for the dynamite's final bite through the hard rock into the potash ore which should have happened on the afternoon shift. To celebrate this accomplishment, the company had planned an ice cream and cake party for the families. Now, many believed it was a dynamite blast that most likely hit a pocket of methane gas instead. When discovered, the brightly colored signs appeared grotesquely out of place. Now, there would be no celebration. Concerns now centered on the fate of the missing men trapped underground and the rescue operation.[18]

Back at the survivor's campsite, Hanna asked for two volunteers to go with him after the three men, Rushton, Barber and Sviscsu. He needed to check on them to see if they were dead or alive. He told the other survivors that if they were still alive, he would need help to bring them back to the barricade.[19]

Paul McKinney volunteered to go with Hanna. He figured he had been part way up the drift already to help Hanna fix the valve on the broken compressed air line during the night and didn't have any major problems, only a little bit of coughing. So, he thought he'd be okay.[20]

Paul McKinney was a quiet, introspective type. Born in Norwood, Colorado, he later graduated from high school in Grand Junction, Colorado, after which he went to work in the minefields (as a construction and production miner) in the Grants, New Mexico area. Wanting to get out of the mining industry, he decided to move to Moab and went back to body and fender work which he had taken up while in high school. After working for Moab Body and Glass for only a few months, the owner decided to sell the company. It was the beginning of 1963 and McKinney, and his brother decided to buy the shop. His brother, married with one child, and McKinney newly married, soon realized there wasn't enough income for two families. That's when McKinney decided to go to work for Harrison International at the new potash mine to supplement his income. And now, his wife Mollie was pregnant with their first child.[21]

There was also some talk about trying to get to the mine shaft to see if they could get a ride topside[22] if the other three had made it out. Not everyone felt it was a good idea to leave.

"No," 'Blackie' said, "better stay here."[23] But Hanna and McKinney had their minds made up. They were leaving.[24] They all knew the risks, and 'Blackie' knew each man needed to make their own decisions in these types of situations.[25] Both were leaving with the same understanding as before: if they ran into problems, the men would beat on the metal vent line, and the guys who stayed would come to help them get back to the barricade.

It was around 7:30 in the morning, when Hanna and McKinney wet rags to put over their faces and then disappeared through the barricade curtains at the left side of the drift. 'Blackie' felt sure he would never see them alive again.[26]

The two men took Tom Trueman's shuttle car parked just on the other side of the first barricade curtain at the transformer station. They would use it to bring the men back. Hanna had his flame safety lamp to take gas readings along the way.

Still smoky, it had stratified a bit with the thickest part of the smoke below the waist. Both men got on the shuttle car; McKinney was driving with Hanna in the back. McKinney tried to start it several times, but the engine wouldn't turn over. Finally, after several attempts, it started. Slowly the shuttle car chugged up towards the top of the incline[27] as whiffs of smoke moved in the air current made by the movement of the shuttle car. The flame safety lamp went out on the way, and Hanna hit the striker a few time to light it again, watching for any changes to the flame while testing for the presence of gas.[28]

In the light of the morning sun, the mine site gradually came alive in the clear air of the red canyon country as the cliffs glowed in an array of rosy morning colors. The men sat in small groups and talked in low tones amongst themselves about the gases found and the 130 to 140 degrees temperatures underground. Women volunteer groups served breakfast to the rescue workers and noticed they wanted mostly milk and water. Other than the hum of the fans, it was quiet around the mine site.[29] Weary rescuers sat in the yard near the Headframe with their faces propped in their hands, fatigued and glum.[30] Some managed to catch a few moments of sleep between their turn in the shaft[31] on cots set up around the Headframe or in nearby buildings,[32] or wherever they could find them. A long, drawn out night, most everyone had a look of total exhaustion on their faces. It was a familiar, tragic picture[33] of a mine rescue operation.

A few curious reporters heard about the hour-long reconnaissance trip made into the mine hours earlier and wanted to know what they found and the chances the missing men were still alive. They directed their questions to the rescuers involved on that trip.

"We couldn't see much, and it's wet down there," 'Oly' Olsen, told them. "We got within seventy-five feet from the bottom of the shaft but couldn't see into the drifts."[34]

"There is a pipe blocking the hole near the bottom," Tatton said.

Asked about the danger of further caving and debris falling, Tatton said he didn't think so. It looked like "the shaft's foot-thick concrete wall was undamaged by the blast."[35]

Steve Hatsis, over the rescue operation, explained about the urgent need for a fresh air base.

"Before rescuers can go any farther, they must establish a fresh air base at the bottom, and this will involve installing new tubing in the bottom to pump in fresh air. Some of the old tubings were destroyed by the explosion," Hatsis said. "We can't get into the drifts until we get air," he added.

The three rescuers told of the dark, smoky shaft, still choked with deadly carbon monoxide gas and large amounts of water pouring down. These conditions made it difficult for rescue workers probing its depths, especially while confined inside a bucket and wearing the cumbersome self-contained air packs[36] on their backs.

Hatsis reported the large quantities of carbon monoxide flowing from the mine meant debris was probably still smoldering in the mine.[37] When asked about the chances of the missing men, Hatsis said he felt the situation was "very, very grave."[38]

"It would be a miracle if anyone is alive," he said.[39] The possibility of men remaining alive in such gas is poor, but then he conceded, "There is a slim hope some men might be sheltered deep in the drifts if air pockets exist."[40]

June Crawford, Chief Engineer at TGS, had expressed the same sentiments earlier to reporters. "Men might be in either of two drifts branching out from the bottom of the hole. If the blast force packed air into the drifts, then there might be a chance of survival," Crawford said.[41]

Officials knew the missing men were working in three groups inside the mine—one in a shop and station area near the base of the shaft and the others in the two horizontal drifts branching out from the shaft.[42]

The mine inspector said rescue workers would not be able to enter the drifts before this afternoon. It could take up to five or six hours to complete the new ventilation system and get on with the search, barring further complications.⁴³ Others felt it might take longer. With so much work to do, some felt it would take a day or two before they would find the missing men.⁴⁴

Hatsis also praised the efforts of the mine rescue teams.

"They're doing a splendid job," he said, as he squinted while looking towards the Headframe. A rescue crew was boarding a bucket for another trip down into the shaft.⁴⁵

"It takes a lot of nerve for those guys to go down into that hole," Hatsis said. "Those guys" he was referring to were veterans of mine rescue. From the Carbon County area, they operate as a sort of "Minuteman" crew, who answer calls for rescue work in mine accidents.⁴⁶ These rescuers continually trained and honed their skills competing in mine rescue competitions held locally and across the nation each year.

The group dispersed as the reporters made their notes and the rescuers went to check on the training process to get Harrison International's men certified in the use of the oxygen apparatuses.

One Harrison International man getting certified was Armond Roy, the brother of Roland Roy. Roland, the owner, and the driver of the Travelall was also helping out with the rescue operation. Several of the missing men rode in his carpool, which made the rescue effort even more disheartening for him.

In the meantime, teams continuously descended every hour or so into the deep shaft to clear debris to set up a base of rescue operations.⁴⁷ Harrison International's men had knowledge of the mine and were tasked to clear the debris out of the shaft and repair the large vent line. An expert rescuer from one of the Carbon County teams would go with the Harrison International team to do regular gas checks and to assist with the apparatus checks. These composite teams would have to be careful, with gas present in the mine; they would use non-sparking tools while they worked to keep from setting off another explosion.

Disaster at Cane Creek

1. Rescue Teams prepare their equipment for their descent down the shaft; Bert Frandsen, (far right) and Henry Laviolette (right-back). (*Denver Post*) 2. A rescue worker helps to strap on oxygen equipment for one of Harrison's men. (*Deseret News*) 3. Rescue teammates adjust equipment before going to the bottom of mine as they work in relays. (*Daily Sentinel*) 4. Geneva Mine Rescue Team don their equipment to enter the mine. (*Deseret News*)

At the top of the incline, the shuttle car Hanna and McKinney used came to a stop on the left side of the drift, parking back about sixty feet from the three-way junction and about thirty feet behind the first shuttle car used just after the explosion. Both men had their wet rags over their faces. Hanna re-lit the flame safety lamp again then jumped off the front end of the shuttle car. He started up the drift while McKinney shut off the engine, walked around the front of it and went towards the back of the other parked shuttle car. From there, McKinney walked between the right side of the shuttle car and the Rib, a space of about six feet and followed the vent line up the drift.[48]

The men could only see a couple of feet in front of them,[49] while the light of their cap-lamps cast eerie shadows in the smoke. They were bare-chested, and sweating profusely from the heat; perspiration beaded across their foreheads while they breathed through their rags.

Hanna walked up the middle of the drift ahead of McKinney, checking for gases with his flame safety lamp as he went. Near the three-way junction, just past the front of the parked shuttle car, he glanced towards the Rib, to the spot where the men broke open the line. Moving closer, through the smoke, Hanna saw Rushton and Sviscsu, kneeling on the ground with their faces in the vent line. He could see the layers of dust that had settled in their hair. Hanna concluded Barber was still inside the vent line, where he had last seen him. Rushton was to the left, slightly over Sviscsu. They were completely still, leading Hanna to believe they were dead. He quickly shined his light on the compressed air line high above the two dead men. It was all right. He then did a gas check.[50]

McKinney, not far behind, was only able to see a couple of feet away through the smoke when he nearly walked into one of the men. A step closer, he saw a completely surreal and startling scene. To the front of the shuttle car, barely discernible through the thick smoke, McKinney saw what looked to be the outline of one of the men. He was sitting up erect facing up the drift several feet out from the vent line. "One's alive," was McKinney's first thought. As he walked slowly around the man, he quickly discovered it was Wesley Barber.[51]

It was a heartbreaking scene. Barber was sitting in a crouched position, his right knee and shin on the ground, and he was sitting back on his haunches on his foot while the other foot was on the ground with the knee bent. His upper body was leaning slightly forward as his forearm rested across his thigh, bracing him upright. He sat frozen in this position. His head was tilted back slightly with his hard hat still on his head, but the light of his cap-lamp had burned out. Barber's face was starting to turn dark red, and nearly black in blotches throughout his face and down his neck, characteristic of carbon monoxide poisoning that causes lividity, where the blood pools and eventually turns dark. It looked like Barber was just sitting there resting.[52]

To the front of Barber, five feet or so away was Rushton and Sviscsu next to each other with their bodies facing the Rib, their faces stuck into the opened sections of the vent line. Lamar was on the left side, with his right shoulder and arm positioned just over the top of Sviscsu. His head was part way in the opening above Sviscsu's head, and both were in a squatting position on their hands and knees, frozen as they died. One hard hat lay on the ground to the left of Rushton, the other to the right of Sviscsu.[53] It was devastating to witness and sad to think of the men dying in such an agonizing manner, a slow, gasping death.

Standing behind the two men, McKinney lingered for a moment looking at them when Hanna turned to him and asked him to check to make sure they were dead. Hanna walked towards the corner that turned into the connecting drift called 1 South, which leads directly up to the shaft station.[54]

McKinney was devastated by what he saw and completely shaken by the haunting scene in front of him. It was evident they were dead. In the back of his mind, he somewhat expected the men to be dead, so he thought he would be prepared for that possibility. But what McKinney saw was so startling, it was something he had not expected. It was a scene that would be imprinted forever in his memory.[55]

Hanna also struggled to put the scene out of his mind, while blaming himself. If only, he thought over and over. If only he had been able to convince the men to come back to the barricade or been more forceful,[56] they could have lived.

Throughout mining history, numerous mining stories exist of horrific scenes of dead miners found by rescue teams. Miners "frozen in time" in positions they were in when death overtook them[57] and when they drew their last breath. No doubt many of these stories reflect bodies in a state of rigor mortis, which generally lasts about eight to twelve hours with environmental conditions also affecting the duration.[58] Following are just a few examples of haunting scenes from the many accounts of mine disasters, describing the types of positions the bodies were in when found.

After the Avondale Mine Disaster, on September 6, 1869, at Plymouth, Pennsylvania, that killed 110 miners, two rescuers pierced the brattice curtain where they encountered, "a view that appalled the stoutest heart among them. Grouped together, in every possible position, laid the dead bodies of sixty-seven men and boys." Many victims appeared merely to be asleep; fathers embraced their sons, men assumed the attitude of prayer, others had their hands clasped to their throats. One was sitting down with his head bent forward upon his breast, with his hands clasped in front of him, while another body was reclining a few feet distant with his face turned to the one sitting, as though he had been engaged in conversation with him a moment previous to drawing his last breath. Still others were found leaning against the gangway walls.[59]

After the Fraterville Explosion, on May 19, 1902, near Coal Creek, Tennessee, 216 miners died. Many of the men survived for hours in side-passages, only to eventually suffocate. One of the rescuers stated, "The first bodies we came to were four. Two of them were on their knees in a praying position, the other two being partly on their side, a few yards away, at the head of the entry. The men were sitting close to each other with their arms on their knees folded and their heads on their arms. In this position, seventeen of them had died."[60]

The Monongah Mine Disaster,[61] on December 7, 1907, Monongah, West Virginia, killed 367 miners, and was the deadliest mine disaster in U.S. history. One account reported how some men died without changing their positions, "One [was] seated upon a bench...his dead body found sitting upright in the same attitude." Another account tells of "One miner, caught in the afterdamp some distance from the shaft bottom, realized the inevitability of his death and kneeled against the Rib to pray, using his finger to draw a cross in the coal dust." Another miner was "sitting with his back against the coal Rib, his lunch bucket between his legs, and a piece of bread in his mouth held by his hand."[62]

Chapter 11

Running out of Time

In the morning light, the only obvious evidence of an explosion was a shattered wooden panel at the top of the 18-story concrete Headframe. There was a little bit of activity inside the Headframe as the hum of the huge fans blowing air into the shaft caused those who talked to raise their voices. Parked nearby were three ambulances with their rear doors open,[1] ready to roll and at least, one or two doctors, along with a couple of nurses, were on site at all times.

Throughout the night and into the morning hours, workers went about vital tasks as teams entered the shaft every hour or so. The rescuer's apparatus had a two-hour supply of oxygen, and teams were required to keep a half-hour in reserve to protect them in the event something unforeseen happened. Using a cautious speed to raise and lower the bucket, it took nearly a half-hour for the bucket to go down the deep shaft and then a half-hour to return to the surface.[2] It left about a half-hour of air to do any rescue work, making the work frustratingly slow. But weary rescuers, battling the water pouring down on them, pressed on doing whatever was needed. Limited oxygen was one of the main reasons it was vital to get a fresh air base established at the bottom of the mine; it eliminated the waste of nearly an hour of oxygen traveling up and down the shaft.

The first teams who descended into the mine made initial assessments of the damage caused by the explosion. It had been a long and perilous night, and by early morning, the work centered on cleaning out debris and clearing the clogged bucket lanes. Clearing the shaft was slow, backbreaking work as crews leaned over the sides of the bucket to cut through the seventy-five feet of debris clogging the way.[3] There were more than 3,000 feet of congested signal cord and wire,[4] much of it the men cut or wired back out of the way. The men also needed to remove some damaged sections of vent line out of the mine, then install new sections down the shaft to restore ventilation to the bottom. The teams still needed to establish better communications between topside and the entrances to the drifts.[5] In the heat and torrential rain, the teams slowly made progress. They were fighting against time.

Hanna and McKinney were supposed to go back to the barricade after checking on the three men. It was the plan they had told the other guys before they left. But Hanna audaciously kept going, up around the corner, he headed up the 1 South drift which ran parallel with the raise area and went directly up to the shaft area. McKinney, still a bit shaken, followed not far behind.[6]

They walked along this flat section, about 800-feet in length. Why they kept going wasn't clear to McKinney. They were now coughing a bit more but were still doing relatively well in the smoke and suffocating heat. McKinney figured he could still go back to the barricade with no major problems. They couldn't see much in the stratified smoke, only a few feet out in front of them. Hanna continued to check the compressed air line, and he also watched his flame safety lamp. The height of the flame indicated the level of deadly gases. It either glowed red, or the flame went out in its presence. Whenever Hanna moved the lamp below his waist, where the smoke was the thickest, it would knock out the flame.[7]

The men went about six hundred feet, just past No. 3XC (crosscut) going into the top end of the raise area. Here, the large metal vent line was bowed out[8] into the drift for about 100-feet, but the compressed air and water lines were still intact.[9] Both men were coughing some but were still doing fairly well as they kept going further.

For another 100 feet, they passed more and more damage to the vent line.[10] The line consisted of twenty-foot long sections of spiral galvanized pipe, coupled together with bands. Each section was made from corrugated steel sheets, spiraled and welded to form a thirty-six-inch diameter pipe. The explosion tore apart coupling bands and broke the welds, tearing open the spirals.[11]

Hanna kept a close watch on the flame safety lamp for any changes in the shape and color of the flame. The flame turned red a couple of times, but they kept going[12] as they quickly moved through the area, holding their wet rags to their faces. Both were coughing a bit more as they tried not to breathe in the toxic smoke-laden air all around them. Lifting the flame safety lamp high to test for gas near the roof, Hanna slowly lowered it but never found methane gas. A few more times the flame went out from lack of oxygen or the presence of other gases, which was most likely carbon monoxide. Each time, Hanna used the striker to relight it.[13]

After traveling 800-feet from the junction,[14] Hanna and McKinney came to the bottom of a shorter incline that was on a ten percent grade. It was about 360 feet to the top[15] near the No. 1XC, the crosscut closest to the shaft station. Both men were now coughing a bit, and their eyes were burning from the carbon monoxide throughout the drift. The destruction was also getting gradually worse. The force of the explosion twisted, stacked and shoved sections of the vent line down the drift. There were pieces of it blown all over the place creating a mess of smashed and tangled steel spirals. The compressed air and water line were knocked off of the wires they were hung with and were now lying on the ground, although still hooked together.[16]

At this point, McKinney decided he wanted to go back to the barricade. Discussing their situation, Hanna felt he had nothing to go back to and wanted to go further.

Coughing more, they were both struggling to breathe. "Listen," Hanna said, as he stood completely still. He thought he could hear air blowing.[17] They both listened in the quiet stillness. McKinney worried they might be hearing things, and the carbon monoxide was making their thinking a bit hazy.

Somewhat convinced it was blowing air they could hear, they both took off up the drift. The men moved sections of vent line and climbed over others as they continued up[18] the incline. It wasn't long before the vent line was completely gone, blown to smithereens. At the top of the incline where the drift flattens out, the air and water lines were still intact.

Passing by the No. 1XC (crosscut), they were now about 150-feet from the shaft station.[19] About thirty to forty feet before the corner leading into the station area, the compressed air line came to an end; it was the same with the water line, both completely blown apart.[20]

The sound of air was getting closer as they continued to the end of the drift and rounded the corner into the shaft area. Feeling weak, they were coughing and their eyes burned. Quickly making their way through the hazy smoke towards the sound of hissing air, they nearly tripped over a couple of high spots in their path not there before the explosion.[21]

As they reached the edge of the shaft, they discovered the source of the air they heard hissing. The compressed air, forced down the shaft through a six-inch line, branched into two three-inch lines,[22] one going to each drift. The explosion had torn the six-inch air line off the brackets that once held it to the side of the shaft, and it was now hanging out towards the middle. Above the station, the pipe branched, and on the side going to the West Drift, it was completely broken off. The pipe going to the East Drift still had[23] two twenty-foot sections connected and reached just past the edge of the east side of the shaft station. The end of this line was about five feet off the ground. The men only had to walk up to the end and put their faces into the current of blowing air. Now, they could finally breathe, and it didn't take long before both men started to feel better from breathing the fresh air.

The only other sound besides the hissing air was the water coming down the shaft like a heavy rainstorm. The water beat down, making different plunking sounds as drops smashed and reverberated against the different surfaces and debris in the shaft and around the station. The drops splattered and pinged against the metal surfaces of various shapes and thicknesses in an almost rhythmic fashion.

"As luck would have it," McKinney thought to himself as he filled his lungs with air.

It was still fairly early when Bob Mullins, the Pulitzer Prize-winning reporter working for the *Deseret News and Salt Lake Telegram*, knocked on the door of Matt Rauhala. Following up on a lead, he had heard that Rauhala was the survivor who was hurt in the explosion on the surface. Mullins hoped to get his story.[24] Still dressed in her floral, cotton housecoat, Edith Rauhala answered the door as Sheila, their daughter, appeared from another room.

Bare-chested with pajama bottoms on, Matt Rauhala was in the living room sitting on the sofa trying to get comfortable. Banged up a bit from his harrowing experience, Rauhala had a bandage over the laceration on his forehead and mostly complained about his back. Other than that, he was in relatively good shape as his wife and daughter looked after him. Rauhala was trying to get an update on the rescue operation at Cane Creek. But the only news on the television at that time on most of the channels was national coverage of a huge civil rights demonstration in Washington D.C. Folk singers had been performing musical numbers during the morning while the huge crowd gathered. At the moment, the popular group, Peter, Paul, and Mary, was just finishing their recent hit, "Blowin' in the Wind."[25] The haunting melody, from an old slave spiritual tune, was riveting. Their hit song was written by Bob Dylan, a twenty-two-year-old, up-and-coming entertainer. Next, Dylan started singing one of his other hits, "When the Ship Comes In," as Joan Baez joined young Dylan at the microphone to sing harmony.[26] There were other popular 60's folkies[27] and gospel singers connected to the civil rights movement, who was also performing at this national event.

Mullins and Rauhala exchanged introductions and pleasantries as Rauhala, a short, stocky man, limped to the small wood console to turn off the black and white television set, then headed back to the sofa. The limp was not from any injury, one of his legs was a few inches shorter than the other from a bone disease he had when he was very young, for which he had spent eighteen months in the hospital in Salt Lake City.[28]

Mullins sat down and adjusted his horn-rimmed glasses as he glanced at his notes. Looking up, he asked Rauhala if he would recount his experience the day before about the explosion. Rauhala talked about the carpool and the men he rode to work with the day before and how three of the men, Blake Hanna, Kenneth Milton and Chuck Byrge, were down in the mine at the time of the explosion.

"What hurts me is that two of those fellows, Chuck [Byrge] and Kenneth [Milton], worked under me all the time we were sinking the shaft. I got really close to them," he said. "We were talking about that Pennsylvania rescue on the way to work yesterday," he said. "Now they are down in the mine..."[29] He paused for a short moment.

"You don't think much about a mine disaster even though you're working down there. Something like the Pennsylvania deal makes you wonder a little, though," he said. He remembered what Byrge

171

had said about them having "a hard time drilling for us if something like that happened where we worked. Cane Creek was a much deeper mine.[30]

"The way the explosion knocked me back, I'm sure it must have come from the bottom of the mine," Rauhala said. "It was so strong, I really don't think anyone in the bottom could have survived. At first, I thought a box of powder went off, but the blast didn't knock me out."[31]

He went through all the details and told Mullins everything he could remember. He recounted how he was usually working up in the Headframe dumping buckets but was fortunately down to the shaft collar and was helping the Toplander fill orders from the mine.

"My first instinct was to get up and run before something else happened. I did even though I was staggering. I tripped on something and fell down. I suffered a bad cut on my forehead, but just how I got it, I'm not sure," Rauhala said pointing to the bandage on his head.[32]

"The first thing I remember was being on the ground with a Texas Gulf Sulphur (TGS) employee leaning over me. He asked me what happened. I told him we've had a big explosion down there," Rauhala said.[33]

"It's fortunate I wasn't high up in the Headframe working; the force of the blast might have toppled me into the shaft," Rauhala said.[34] They talked about his injuries, which weren't too serious and his trip to the hospital.

Mullins took a picture of Rauhala, with his wife and daughter. Once Mullins had all the information he needed for his story, he left for the local telephone office to send it and the photo by Telephoto to the newspaper office in Salt Lake City, where another writer would do rewrites and put his touches to the story before print.[35]

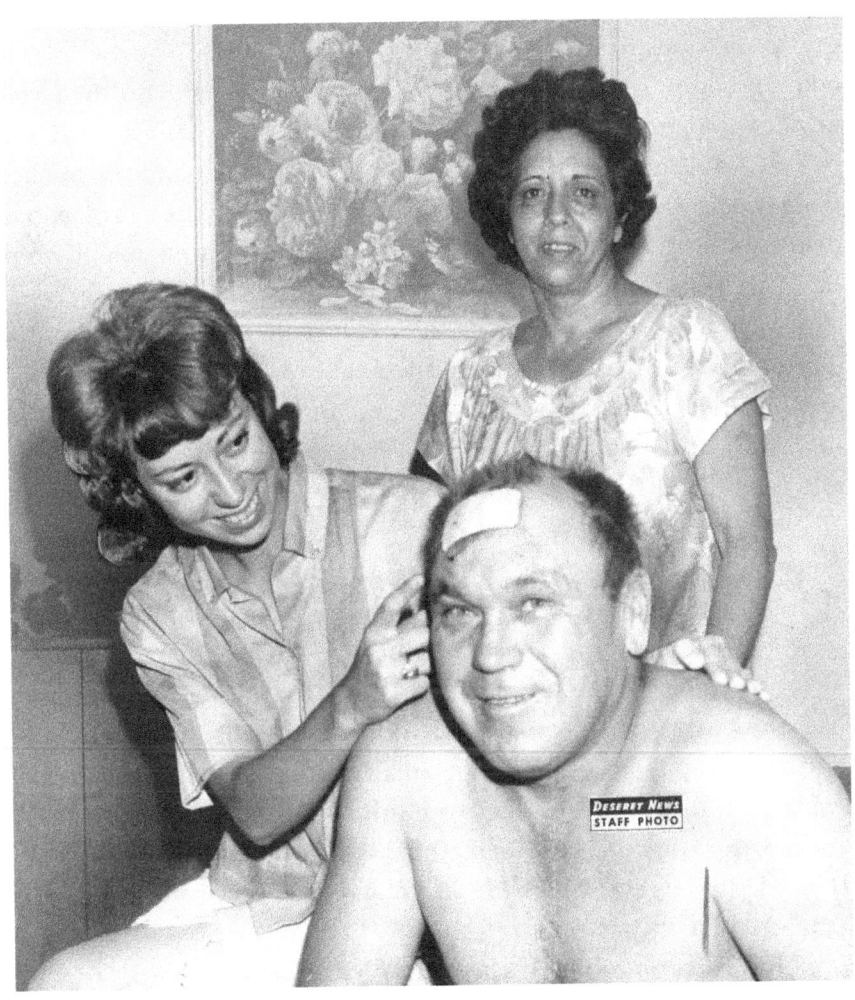

Matt Rauhala, the surface worker who survived the explosion, is treated with some special care by his loving daughter Sheila and wife Edith. (*Deseret News*)

The desert sun drenched the fiery red cliffs and barren landscape. More family members made their way to the mine site. Behind ropes, used to keep the crowd back from the immediate work area, family members and reporters congregated. They stood in small groups anxious to hear any news from below. The Headframe cast a large shadow over the main entrance on the west side of the large cement structure as rescuers moved in and out, getting ready for the next descent as soon as the current team surfaced in the bucket from the depths. A tiny, brown-haired woman[36] in white canvas shoes displayed, with wistful pride, a photo of a young man with curly red hair in a Navy uniform.

"They are pretty close," she said. "They always hunt and fish together." Irene Christensen, only five-foot-two, clad in a blue blouse and black slacks, talked with several rescue workers who were on the other side of the rope barrier. She was from Spring Glen near Price and knew many of the rescuers from Carbon County.[37]

"'I'm not giving up hope yet and I won't until we know about every one of those men down there," she said in low tones. "I really appreciate the families of the other men. Miners' families always seem to stick together," she said as they talked.[38]

Forty-four-year-old Myrlen Christensen, Sr., Irene's husband, had worked in and around coal mines for twenty-five years near Sunnyside and Wattis, another small mining town southwest of Price. Now he was the Master Mechanic at the Cane Creek Mine. He started work in March (1963) when Harrison International crews hoisted the large parts of mining machinery down into the mine and assembled them underground.[39]

The handsome boy in the photo with dark-red hair was their son.[40] He was the oldest of five children, Myrlen Christensen Jr., known as 'Myrley,' served in the Seabees, the construction branch of the Navy.[41] Married in February, 'Myrley' and his wife, Margo, were now expecting their first baby.[42] He was working at the newspaper office in Price when Harrison International hired him at the Cane

Creek Mine. 'Myrley' worked as a mechanic's helper on the surface and took care of the air compressors, the same job his cousin worked on another shift.[43]

The previous evening, Irene was at home with her three children. Her sixteen-year-old son, Gail, was just home from football practice when they first learned of the explosion. They were in the kitchen when the news came over the radio. Irene went to see if Margo, her daughter-in-law, had heard anything. Her son and Margo lived in an adjoining apartment next door.[44]

Margo hadn't heard anything, so they listened to the radio and the TV for additional information. They didn't try to call the mine. The radio broadcast said not to since it would jam the lines. The news also reported no one should come to the mine; officials wanted to keep the highway opened for the emergency vehicles. It was getting late in the night, so Irene stayed at Margo's place as they worried.

When 'Myrley' didn't come home after the afternoon shift, his wife and mother just figured he was at the mine site helping with the rescue effort to get to his father and the other men, and for whatever reason, he wasn't able to call home. As the night wore on, Margo was getting worried and scared. She kept asking Irene about 'Myrley.' Irene was scared too because they hadn't heard from him but told Margo "he wouldn't leave his dad."[45]

When morning came, Irene's brother, LeGrande Prichard, who lived near them in Moab, came and took Irene, Margo and Harriette Rowley, the wife of Fred Rowley, out to the mine site. The Rowley's were also from Spring Glen, and both families knew each other well. Fred started work at Cane Creek as soon as school was out and his family moved with him to Moab at that time. That was also when Irene moved with her children. They lived in a small apartment while her married daughter and son-in-law lived in their house in Spring Glen.[46] The Christensens lived in Moab through the summer, and the kids had just started school in Moab on Monday.

At the mine site, Irene and the others went to TGS's administrative office building. When they asked to see a list of the missing men, Harriett noticed the man who showed it to them had broken out in cold chills. Even though it was still a partial list, this was when Irene and Margo received the devastating news. 'Myrley's name was also on the list with his father's name. 'Myrley' was down in the mine and was now one of the missing men, along with his father. Irene went through utter turmoil over the thought of possibly losing her husband and now, maybe even her son. Her heart was breaking for Margo who was completely devastated. Fred's name was also on the list as was Clell Johnson. Clell was Margo's uncle, a younger brother of her mother, Myrl Johnson Grange.[47]

'Myrley' had never been down in the new mine and yesterday afternoon, he requested to be allowed[48] to go down with Lawrence Davidson, the Master Mechanic, for a tour. They were taking down some needed parts for one of the underground machines.[49] 'Myrley's dad would never take him underground and didn't want him to work in the mines.

The women were all scared and tried hard to lean on their faith.[50] Irene and the others went down near the Headframe near the roped off area to see if they could get any news. There, they were able to talk to some of the rescuers they knew on the Carbon County teams and several rescue workers. The men told them what they knew, which wasn't much. 'Wallie' Christman, on the Kaiser Steel Team, spoke with Irene as did Luther Thomas, one of Harrison International's men helping with the rescue work. Irene's husband first stayed with Luther after he was hired at Cane Creek, before Irene and the children moved to Moab.[51]

"I've got plenty of tears left," Irene reassured those around her. Her eyes were dry,[52] but her anxiety was apparent. Margo, six months pregnant, was quiet. The women were reeling from this devastating blow.

1. Rescuers at work or resting near the entrance to Headframe as family and press gather near the rope-line. (*Deseret News*) 2. Irene Christensen (left) waits with other family members for news on their loved ones. Margo Christensen (2nd from the right). (*Daily Sentinel*) 3. Alice Barber with daughter Linda Lou, (2), waiting at the hospital for news of her trapped husband, Wesley Barber. (*AP Telephoto*)

They went back to town to call family members. Irene's brother, Bert Prichard, headed to Moab from Price as did other family members from Salt Lake City and Carbon and Emery Counties. Margo's family members were also informed and were coming to give her moral support.[53] After informing family, LeGrande and the women headed back to the mine site to wait for any news as their family members headed to Moab.[54]

More and more people were showing up at the mine site, some were assisting with the rescue operations, some were family members of the missing miners, and others were news reporters and photographers. Also, a significant number of telephone calls came into the mine office. The atmosphere at the main office was chaotic as Pinkerton worked to sort out requests while working the switchboard.[55]

The office building located at the top end of the mine property had large glass windows offering a panoramic view of the entire mine-mill complex. It was possible to see some of the action going on with the full-scale rescue operation underway. A tremendous sense of urgency hung in the air as people scrambled to assist those at the forefront of the rescue with whatever they needed. Everyone had so much anxiety over the explosion, and the welfare of miners down in the mine was on everyone's mind.

With television still in its infancy, many radio shows started calling the mine office, and they would invariably get J.G. Pinkerton when he answered the switchboard. Many of them wanted him to describe what he saw out his window on live radio. He decided he wasn't about to do this and resisted placing himself in a circumstance of trying to give out radio interviews. Besides, the office was about 300 yards away from the Headframe. He couldn't know with certainty what was going on, but it didn't stop the radio people from calling.

Pinkerton even answered a couple of strange calls from those claiming to be psychics. One of them told him she knew all the men were alive down in the mine. The other one claimed to know where the men were at in the mine and said she could help the rescuers get to them.

The hardest calls to answer were from family members trying to get any news they could of their loved ones. Pinkerton could hear the fear and despair in their voices. Initially, radio broadcasts discouraged anyone from going to the mine site, and many were turned back at the roadblock. During the night, several families managed to get to the mine site, and by the next morning, more families were arriving. In the early morning hours, Kay Tippie, wife of Frank Tippie, the General Mine Manager, was instrumental in getting the lab building set up to use for the family members. The building was near the Headframe, and Pinkerton and others stayed busy with her requests for items they might need to help the families be as comfortable as possible during such trying times.

Rescuers seemed a little more hopeful today. Men might still be alive if they were in an area far from the explosion. The area of the blast in the mine and the cause were still not known, but some rescuers theorized,[56] that if the blast originated in one of the two drifts, members of the crew in the other drift might still be alive. Another factor figuring into this theory was the continued operation of the high-pressure air line, the smaller line that supplied compressed air for the workers' tools. The blast hadn't knocked out the line going down the shaft and air could be getting to trapped miners, a hopeful sign men might still be alive.

Even some mining officials and experts speculated on the cause of the explosion and the fate of the missing miners, as reporters solicited comments. On scene and helping to coordinate rescue operations, Casper A. Nelson, a member of the Utah State Industrial Commission, blamed methane gas as the cause of the explosion. He told reporters, "No one knows for sure what the cause was, but we have come to the conclusion methane probably caused it. This country is a natural for methane pockets."[57]

Asked if men might still be alive, he responded, "My personal opinion is that these men's chances of survival are not good. However, rescuers returning from the bottom of the shaft reported there were enough pockets of oxygen at the bottom to sustain human life," he said. "Air is the key to the trapped men's chances. Their fate," he said, "depends on whether any of the men survived the blast and the fire that followed."[59]

Officials first hoped to reach the trapped men by noon today. But Nelson said, "It was going to be at least late afternoon. We'll get them out, but it's going to be slow going," he added.[60]

In Salt Lake City, upon hearing about the gases encountered during the night by mine rescuers, Otto A. Wiesley,[61] Chairman of the Utah State Industrial Commission, also speculated, "Methane gas may have caused the explosion."

"There were petroleum "drips" in the shaft which could account for such accumulations of gas," he said.[62]

"If workers were using dynamite to blast, it could have touched off the explosion," he said.

Both Nelson and Wiesley openly tabbed a methane gas pocket as the probable cause.[63] TGS officials had not "officially" labeled deadly methane gas as the trigger of the searing blast, they were trying to keep a tight security clamp on all official statements and wouldn't comment as to the cause, and refused to speculate.

But many of the rescuers, themselves miners, had battled underground gases before and were pretty confident it was a methane gas explosion, probably touched off by a dynamite blast by a work crew.

"It might also have been a natural gas free flow or even an oil pocket," said one rescue worker. Some of the rescuers dropping down into the deep shaft, labeled gas as their biggest hazard. Steve Hatsis, the state coal mine inspector and a methane gas expert, said rescue operations were being carried out in such a way to keep "risks" at a minimum.[64]

"Rescuers have still not been able to get into the mine to explore the drifts and won't until the danger of the deadly gas fumes were reduced," said another rescue official. Getting into the mine was not expected to happen until late that night, or possibly the next day. They also reported there was still no contact with the men since the blast that occurred yesterday afternoon. Rescuers in rotation continued to work hard in the deep shaft making progress to get down into the mine.

Harrison International's men were finally certified and were working down in the shaft to clear debris while rescuers from Carbon County accompanied them to check for carbon monoxide and methane.[65]

1. Harrison International team member, George McCloud, briefs other rescuers on the underground trip. (*Daily Sentinel*)
2. Columbia-Geneva Steel rescuer, Lloyd Miller adjusts face mask in preparation to enter the mine. (*Deseret News*)

Around 9:00 a.m.,[66] a bucket surfaced and a team of Harrison International Rescuers[67] piled out, as workers helped them with their gear. George McCloud yanked his mask down off his face as a worker helped him squirm out of his heavy breathing apparatus. Soaking wet, his boots oozed water, as water dripped from his nose, his clothes and the brim of his hard hat. After debriefing and exchanging a few words with other rescuers, McCloud shuffled wearily from the towering Headframe towards the change house 100 yards away, to shower and to crawl into dry clothing before driving into town with another rescuer to call their families.[68]

Sam Taylor, the editor, and publisher of Moab's weekly newspaper, the *Times-Independent,* was hard at work getting the current issue printed early with coverage of the explosion for their readers. Usually, the paper was published on Wednesday afternoon of each week for Thursday morning distribution. But today Sam wanted the stories on the front page about the explosion to be closed out by twelve noon and the paper printed within an hour. Nevertheless, it would still carry the Thursday publication date.[69] One of his reporters, Don Robinson, was the first reporter on the scene at the mine site the previous night. He turned his story in at the newspaper office about the events the night before while Sam and his wife, Adrien, worked on several other stories. Sam planned to go to the mine site as soon as he had the paper printed and other demanding commitments checked off.[70]

All morning, the newspaper office was swamped with calls from relatives, friends, and just anyone wanting more information about the explosion. But there was little to tell. The medium-built, young editor wore thick black-rimmed glasses, with his hair almost clean shaved. Sam was very popular and always a veritable treasure trove of information and opinion around town. The thirty-year-old was a natural as a small-town newspaper editor,[71] and was always at the center of community life in the small town of Moab where he grew up.

Not only was Sam a well-known figure in Moab, but he was also well known around the state of Utah. He was active in many of the local civic and governmental organizations. Severing as a director of the Utah State Press Association, he was presently on the business committee of the state-wide organization. He was also well known among the press people around the state.

Other news reporters, now in town to cover the story, knew Sam personally. Many dropped by the office seeking more information. Sam took a few minutes to chat and share what little he knew.

"There isn't much to say, we can't find out much," he said as he took a puff of his cigarette. "We think the trapped men were starting out on the afternoon shift,"[72]

A small town of about 6,000 residents, Moab was stunned by news of the explosion.[73] It was mirrored on the faces of residents, a mixture of hope and tragedy.

"People are pretty pessimistic," Sam said. "No one is sure of anything, except it looks bad."[74]

Sam's father, Bish Taylor, became publisher of the *Times-Independent* in 1911 at the age of nineteen. Sam took over the paper from his father in 1956, after returning home from the Army. Later, after he married, Sam was joined at the paper by his wife, Adrien.[75]

In April 1962,[76] Governor George Clyde appointed Sam to fill the vacant State Senate seat, over District 12 (Grand, San Juan, and Emery counties), when Charlie Steen resigned. Steen had become disillusioned with politics and surprised his constituents in March of 1961 when he resigned and moved to Nevada.[77] Sam was just twenty-nine-years-old at the time he was appointed; he was the youngest ever to serve in the Utah Legislature. The young, savvy editor planned to run for the Senate seat in the fall.[78]

After Steen's rags-to-riches story, the flamboyant uranium magnate played a huge role in the state in the development of the uranium industry throughout the 1950s, and Moab became known as the "uranium capital of the world." Many Moabites benefited either directly or indirectly throughout the boom years as the population of Moab[79] (and the unincorporated areas of Moab Valley) grew the decade during the 1950's from 1,903 to 6,332.

An article in *McCalls'* December 1956 issue brought national attention to Moab when it reported, "the world's greatest concentration of millionaires lived in Moab, and the percentage was about fifty times the national average." By some accounts, the town had as many as two dozen millionaires in 1956, although some were mere "paper millionaires" whose wealth evaporated when their stock became worthless after the uranium boom died down a few years later.[80]

During the mid-1950's, the Moab airport was second in the state in traffic and gas sales and ranked second in the nation in ownership of airplanes per capita. The *McCalls* article also claimed Moab did not look like a town of millionaires. Although bustling, it retained a small-town character, somewhat more disheveled than might be expected due to the trailers and tar-paper shacks in which many residents of Moab lived: "Moab's backyard strikes you as one vast trailer camp." Even the truly wealthy lived modestly, with no ostentatious show of wealth. Charlie Steen was the exception, though his house was considered lavish in Moab, it would not be considered pretentious in most areas of wealth.[81]

Steen made many important contributions to building up the community, donating to many worthy causes and gifting land to five churches and the School District.[82] Although Moab ultimately lost its most famous and flamboyant resident, Charlie Steen's mining and milling operations remained.[83]

For the past three years, there was another surge in growth created during construction of the TGS mine-mill complex. It followed on the hills of the uranium boom which had slowed down a bit. While busy building homes, many potash workers and their families lived in hotels, lodges, trailers, or wherever they could until housing became available.

Moab City did a survey at the end of 1960 to determine how many Moab families were living in mobile homes. It showed a total of 781 trailer homes within the city limits as the building of new homes fell behind growth.[84] Infrastructure was also lacking causing growing

Disaster at Cane Creek

pains for the bulging boom town. The town couldn't keep up with the demand for housing and a typical home in Moab sold for 4,000 to 5,000 dollars.[85] Many workers kept their homes where they came from and had temporary housing since they knew the construction phase was temporary. Once the mine construction is completed by contractors, and TGS takes over the operation, workers could then secure permanent employment at the facility and more permanent living arrangements.

"This potash operation has been a big boost to Moab's economy. It's a tragic price to pay for a shot in the arm," Sam said to a reporter. Adding, "Yesterday's violent explosion was probably the worst known."

For many residents, the tragic blast brought back sad memories of a restaurant explosion in the nearby town of Monticello in 1957, which took seventeen lives.[86]

Around town, the mine explosion was on everyone's mind. The Grand County Sheriff, John Stock, showed signs of fatigue from the rescue ordeal and expressed deep shock.

"This is much more tragic than the Monticello thing," Stock said as if he held no hope for survivors.

Kirk Robertson, a service station operator and lifelong resident of Moab, said he hoped for the best but feared the worst.[87] Other townspeople, from service station attendants to waitresses, and regular folks, expressed similar grief over the news of the explosion.

Earlier that morning, Sam received a pressing phone call from one of TGS's supervisors. Sam became friends with many of the men who worked there while covering the construction of the Cane Creek Mine over the last several years. The supervisor complained about how the city press was giving the company a hard time. They were taking things out of context and acting like the company was hiding something.[88]

Sam advised him on how to handle the press. They needed to answer their questions honestly. If they didn't know something, just say "we don't know." If you say, "We can't answer that," it makes it sound like you are hiding something, he told him.[89]

The press, notorious for turning things around, could creatively make something out of nothing just for the sake of a story. And with so many reporters covering the story, it was becoming a media circus. The city press was especially known for being competitive among the daily newspapers. Each wanted to get a jump on a story and outdo their competition.

Coughing, Hanna and McKinney were somewhat weakened from breathing toxic air, which was also making their eyes sting out of their heads.[90] The smoke was beginning to thin out in areas from the compressed air line blowing from two openings on the line: one at the header and one on the east side. The amount of water raining down the shaft was an "awesome sight," Hanna thought to himself, notwithstanding the devastation all around. The carnage and the extent of the damage were extensive. It looked like a bulldozer plowed through and shoved rubble into every nook and cranny with twisted metal and other debris buried in mounds of muck. Everything was scorched, coated with dust, and mixed with a bit of light-colored, reddish dust probably brought down into the mine at the time the blast's concussion was equalizing.

The feeder-breaker on the west side was blown out and wedged in the shaft. Hung up on something, it was positioned out over the sump, which was nearly eighty feet deep.[91] Water was pouring down the shaft and splashing around the sides of the shaft station, and the putrid smell of death from decomposing bodies hung heavy in the air.

McKinney found that he was only able to be away from the fresh air for about five minutes at a time. Sometimes, it would be a bit longer before he would begin to cough and need the air again. Then it would take fifteen to twenty minutes of standing in the fresh air before he felt well enough to leave it again.[92] Hanna seemed to be doing a bit better.

To the side of the feeder-breaker, on their side of the shaft, was a load of twenty-foot lengths of compressed air line pipe brought down into the mine the day before and stored in a shallow alcove. Some of the pipes were damaged, blown around and stacked like pixie sticks. Hanna decided they could find enough sections to repair the compressed air line and get the fresh air to the guys back in the barricade. About a hundred feet of the line was blown out, but they thought they could salvage enough good pieces to use. Hanna had his crescent wrench on his tool belt they could use,[93] so all they needed was to find enough clamps to connect each of the twenty-foot sections together.

Back and forth they went, as they worked on repairing the air line. When either of the men needed good air, they would head back to the air line. Refreshed, they'd move away from it to work some more.

McKinney was in pain from burns on his backside caused when the battery to his cap-lamp leaked acid. He now had third-degree burns with nothing to clean the acid off. The groundwater coming down the shaft was salty, and some thought it was laced with arsenic or sulfuric acid and would only make his burn worse.[94] McKinney spent only a short time away from the fresh air, then he was chased back, coughing and hacking. Hanna, not as much. Conditions were bad, but both men kept working.

Sometimes one of them would scrounge up a section of pipe before needing some air; sometimes they would get it dug out, sometimes they wouldn't. At times, they would find a clamp, sometimes they wouldn't. Sometimes they would drag a section over where it was needed. It was like this all morning long.[95]

Crawling around, they clawed through mounds and piles of rubbish, scrounging for parts, only to discover several of the mounds they came across were dead bodies. They had tripped over the top of a couple of them when they first ran towards the sound of hissing air.[96] The bodies were covered in thick dust and were difficult to see in the smoke, which was thickest near the ground. While digging through debris, finding or salvaging clamps from damaged pipes and connecting them, both men had to be careful and watch where they walked. They soon found another body not far from the other two and Hanna also came across a glove with the hand still inside on top of the feeder-breaker. The body it belonged to was nearby.[97] They were still able to recognize the dead.

They discovered another body at the edge of the shaft, shoved up under the front end of the feeder-breaker. Water coming down the shaft splashed several feet around the edge and washed some of the dust off. It was in bad shape, burned and broken from the fiery explosion and a bit swollen from the heat. The smell all around them was horrendous.[98] It was heartbreaking. These were their buddies and friends. Hanna and McKinney stayed busy trying not to think about them.

Their biggest worry at this point was staying alive while getting the compressed air line back together. The men would find a clamp and attach a section of pipe. After the first twenty-foot section had been attached, the open end of the line lay on the ground. Now, both men had to lay down next to the current to get air. This was when the ninety pounds of air pressure[99] kicked up salt and little rocks into Hanna's eyes causing damage. It was miserable as both men kept working, dragging themselves back to the air when they needed.

———

At the morning news conference, Frank Tippie, the general manager of the TGS Company, had the unenviable position of facing the press. Wearing a khaki work shirt and pants and sporting a crewcut, Tippie addressed the latest rescue developments at the Cane

Creek Mine as he recapped other information for the newly arrived reporters.

"We have established the definite number of men is twenty-five," Tippie said. "The blast knocked out the mine's communications, so we are not certain of the men's location.[100] Twenty-four of them were employed by Harrison International, the construction firm.[101] They were putting finishing touches on the shaft and the underground mine when an explosion of undetermined origin occurred at 4:40 p.m."

One other worker was a TGS employee, an inspector, who entered the mine just before the shift started.[102] Tippie reported there was a shift change at 3:30 p.m. and the men were in the mine just over an hour when the explosion occurred. The missing men were scattered throughout the mine and working mostly in two lateral drifts to the south of the shaft.[103] The blast apparently caught them without warning.[104]

Tippie said the men in the West Drift were using dynamite.[105] Once they drilled the holes under normal procedures, Tippie said, they then tested the drilled holes for any signs of gas. With no evidence of gas, dynamite would have been placed in the holes and exploded. It's assumed the men followed this procedure and the blast detonated a pocket of methane gas. Tippie also emphasized the exact cause of the explosion was still not known and expressed hope the trapped miners would be found alive, but he couldn't say in which drift they would find the miners.

"We have every hope of getting through to the facings and men sometime tonight," Tippie said.[106] "But there are some indications it might be several days,"[107] he added.

He explained how "there was a violent surface disturbance at the time of the explosion and smoke later curled from the shaft but cleared up in about an hour or so."[108]

Tippie continued as he talked about the rescue operation and the three rescue squads sent to the mine from Carbon County.

Rescuers wearing oxygen masks were sent down the shaft three or four at a time, with crews rotating. Currently, about thirty men are directly involved in the rescue attempt.[109]

He told how rescue workers reported high temperatures at the bottom of the shaft, where rescue crews were working in heat up to 130 to 140 degrees, Fahrenheit. Normal temperature in the mine is usually around 107 degrees, he said. The crews were working to complete repairs on the vent line in the shaft so a search of the drift areas could begin.

Tippie said the rescue teams lowered into the shaft had not established contact with the trapped men. They did find debris seventy-five feet from the bottom of the shaft.[110] The rescue work is slow going, with debris and damaged equipment clogging the way.[111] He also said they did not know whether the blast obstructed the drifts.

Tippie expressed doubt there was a major cave-in in the mine, explaining how the "huge salt section" in the mine is very hard."

He was then asked if there is any chance the men are alive.

"I wouldn't even attempt a guess. I think there's a chance," Tippie said.[112]

"Before rescuers can go further," Steve Hatsis, the mine inspector said, "they must establish a new air supply line in the shaft going straight down the distance of nearly ten football fields." He told how this would involve installing new sections of vent tubing to the bottom and pumping in fresh air since the explosion destroyed the old tubing.[113] Then the workers will push efforts to establish the "fresh air station" at the bottom of the mine with the newly installed sections of the vent line. Rescuers won't move into the drifts until they complete the fresh air station, expected later in the afternoon.

The company finally released the official list to the press with the names of twenty-five missing men. While the news of the mine disaster carried the name of TGS as the owner of the mine, calls from relatives came into the office from all over the country, mostly from those related to TGS employees. They wanted to know if their father, son, brother or uncle was in the mine. Pinkerton, the office manager manning the switchboard, didn't have any trouble assuring them their loved one was not in the mine since only one TGS employee was among the missing men.[114]

For various reasons, it proved difficult to get the names of Harrison International's men caught in the explosion; it was like pulling out eye teeth to get a good list.[115] With no official list, newspaper headlines across the nation reported erroneous numbers such as, "16 Buried in Utah Mine,"[116] or "Fiery Blast Traps 16 in Depths of Utah Mine."[117]

It took Harrison International's employees awhile to track down employees to verify information before they felt confident enough to release their list. By late morning, Harrison International finally handed over an accurate list, which including one Texas Gulf employee. The list named twenty-five men working in the mine at the time of the explosion.

The apparent holdup came from trying to verify if one man, William 'Bill' Huzil, was working at the time. According to officials, he was not on the shift list, but he was on the days-off list. Normally, he would have been on one of the other shifts where he worked as a Lead Miner, but he had agreed to work the week on the afternoon shift for a fellow miner who wanted to travel home to Canada and see his family.[118] Once Harrison International was able to verify everyone working on the afternoon shift, they gave the list to TGS personnel.

'Bill' Huzil, from Yorkton, Saskatchewan, Canada, was living in Moab while his wife, Mary, and their four children stayed in Canada. When Mary Huzil heard her husband was one of the missing miners through the media, she waited at her home with family and friends for word of her husband and closely followed the news of the rescue operation.[119]

Once TGS had the list of the missing men, they gave it out to the press.[120]

NAMES OF TRAPPED MINERS:

Wesley Barber, 35; Box 175, Red Rock Lodge, Moab, Utah; Hometown: Elliot Lake, Ontario, Canada.

Robert Bobo, 33; Shady Rest Trailer Court, Moab, Utah.

Charles Byrge, 30; Box 45, Helper, Utah.

Charles Clark, 27; 377 South 3rd East, Moab, Utah.

Myrlen H. Christensen, Jr., 21; 406 Wingate RT#1, Moab, Utah.

Myrlen H. Christensen, Sr., 44; 406 Wingate RT#1, Moab, Utah.

Lawrence Davidson, 45; Box 1158, Moab, Utah.

Grant Eslick, 47; Box 939, Moab, Utah.

Jess Fox, 52; Moab Utah; Hometown: Orangeville, Utah.

Donald Blake Hanna, 27; Moab, Utah.

Jim N. Hollinger, 33; 153 South 4th East, Moab, Utah.

William Huzil, 41; Harrison's Man Camp, Hometown: Yorkton, Saskatchewan, Canada.

Clell Johnson, 44; 14 Holiday Haven, Moab, Utah.

Robert June, 36; Moab, formerly of Kansas.

Jess Kassler, 38; Moab Hotel, Moab, Utah.

Emile LeBlanc, 32; Red Rock Lodge, Moab, Utah; Hometown: Elliot Lake, Ontario, Canada.[121]

Paul McKinney, 22; Box 1183, Moab, Utah.

Kenneth Milton, 43; 423 Ute Circle, Moab, Utah.

Fred Rowley, 41; Route 1, Box 105A, Helper, Utah.

Rene Roy, 40; Harrison's Man Camp; Hometown: 275 Terrace Lawn Drive, North Bay, Ontario., Canada.

Lamar Rushton, 34; U.S. Highway #160, Moab, Utah.

Keith Schear, 22; P&W Trailer Court, Moab, Utah.

Pete Sviscsu, 42; Harrison's Man Camp, Potash Mine, Utah.

Thomas Trueman, 35; Harrison's Man Camp; Hometown: Toronto, Ontario, Canada.

John Tinall, 38; Box 821, Moab, Utah.

Five of the men were Canadians. The Canadian press was closely following the story as they watched events unfold with deep concern. Both countries shared a rich mining heritage. Closely connected in many ways, Americans often referred to Canadians as, "the children of a common mother, our good neighbors to the north."[122]

Sometime during the early morning hours, TGS officials had gathered family members in the company's laboratory building. Kay Tippie, the wife of Frank Tippie, the General Mine Manager, with the help of other TGS wives, had set up the lab as a family center. They worked to make it as comfortable as possible, equipping it with cots and blankets. They made sure refreshments were available and arranged for women organizations in Moab to bring and serve meals. The local doctors, nurses, and clergymen at the mine site were also constantly available to family members[123] during this difficult time.

A leader in the Moab Girl Scout program, Kay Tippie, brought the Cadette[124] and Senior Girl Scouts[125] to the mine site to also help. The girls served coffee, refreshments, and meals and tried to make everyone comfortable under the stressful circumstances. The girls also helped to watch and entertain children. Their smiles and courtesy seemed to help pass the time.[126]

The lab building was about a hundred yards south of the Headframe and rescue officials brought frequent bulletins and updates using a large map as they explained the progress of the rescue operation to the families.[127] It was emotionally difficult for officials to view the heartbreaking anxiety these families were experiencing and they tried to give as much information as they could to answer their questions.

At the family center, the relatives were able to assemble and were kept isolated from the press,[128] who were asked to respect their privacy.[129] And for the most part, the press did so.

The center also served as a place of refuge for the relatives to get out of the searing desert sun. The families were completely engulfed at the moment, swallowed up in the immensity of time and space. They waited breathlessly for any news as the drifting sweltering breeze left the whole soul parched and broken.

Some family members used the cots provided,[130] while others sat or rested in their vehicles parked nearby.[131] Periodically, some of the relatives would move towards the Headframe, getting as close as possible to the roped off area, as if drawn by a magnet.[132] They watched the rescuers, who were continually busy making preparations for the next crew to enter the mine, once the previous team was back on the surface.[133] For a few moments, family members would watch without expression, then move back to the laboratory or their vehicles to wait some more.[134]

It was an all-too-familiar scene, played out time after time at mine disasters throughout the past, as distraught wives and family members gathered at the mine site. Stunned and in shock, they came to get any information they could about their loved ones. Standing silently, anxious men and women, mostly women, reeled under a heavy burden. The strain of not knowing showed on their faces as they waited.

After returning to the mine site, LeGrande Prichard, Irene Christensen's brother, parked his truck in the parking lot so the women could put the tail gate down to sit on it while they watched the rescue effort from a distance. A reporter came near, wanting to talk with the women, but a rescue worker ran him off.[135] Irene's three children stayed home from school and were also at the mine site while other family members were on their way to Moab.

Eudeene Hollinger and her two children were at the mine site along with other family members. Her parents drove from Nevada to

Moab through the night. Jim's parents, Joe and Blanche Hollinger, and his two brothers, Keith and Joseph, also waited with Eudeene for any news. Keith, the youngest brother, had just celebrated his nineteenth birthday the day before and by evening was devastated when he learned his older brother was one of the miners trapped in the mine.[136]

Eudeene was two months pregnant, and the wait was stressful, but she tried to stay optimistic. Her daughter, Madge, six, wasn't completely aware of what was going on, while her twelve-year-old son, Billy, understood the situation[137] a bit more.

As the rays of the mid-morning sun beat down on the rescue operation, Myrna Hanna sat in the back seat of her in-law's car at the mine site waiting for any news of her husband below. The night before, she didn't hear about the explosion until late in the evening. She had taken their four small children to the Hill Top Drive-In in Moab to see the movie, *My Six Loves*, starring Debbie Reynolds. It was a double feature, but since school started the day before, they only stayed for the first movie so Myrna could get the kids home and in bed.[138]

On the way home, Myrna felt a little uneasy for some unknown reason and was a bit sick to her stomach. When she arrived home around 10:30 p.m., she found neighbors standing on her front porch with news of the explosion. While they told her what little they knew, seven-year-old Danny was nearby and overheard. Old enough to understand, he was afraid for his dad while the other children were taken into the house and put to bed, unaware of what was happening.[139]

Myrna's aunt, Dorothy Anderson, was at the house earlier to tell Myrna the news but had to leave to get home to her youngest son and other children. Her two-year-old had fallen and broken his collarbone late in the afternoon. When Dorothy took him to Dr. Munsey's office to have it set, she found out about the mine explosion. The doctor was at the mine site, so she had to take her son to the hospital. Afterward, she took him home to rest, then went to check on Myrna. Myrna wasn't at home, and after waiting for a while, Dorothy finally felt she couldn't stay any longer and left after neighbors showed up. They said they would wait to give Myrna the news once she returned home.[140]

It wasn't long before other family members living in Moab came, as did family members from Price, a two-hour drive away. First Myrna's parents showed up, then Blake's parents, and finally, his younger sister, Carol. Leaving the children in capable hands, Myrna and her parents got into the back seat of her father-in-law's car and headed towards the mine site.

Stopped at the road block, Jack Hanna (Blake's father), in no uncertain terms, told them his son was one of the missing miners and he was going through. A no-nonsense type of man who always said it as it was, worked as a Mine Foreman at the Horse Canyon Coal Mine owned by U.S. Steel in Carbon County (whose rescue team was already at the mine site). Belonging to the Carbon County Sheriff's Posse, Jack knew his way around these types of situations. The deputies pulled aside the barriers and let them through, and the Hannas arrived at the mine site around the time the first rescue team from Carbon County descended into the mine.[141]

They stayed all night in the vehicle until TGS opened the lab building near the Headframe for family members. Eventually, the Hannas were joined by nine other family members, some who arrived in the early morning hours. The Hannas were some of the first family members to show up at the mine site along with reporters, with more people trickling in throughout the night and early morning. During the long hours of waiting, Jack and two of his other sons, Harold and Wayne, would get updates from rescuers, most of whom they knew from Carbon County. Harold also worked at the Cane Creek Mine, so he knew many of the Harrison International men as he helped out with the rescue.[142]

Disaster at Cane Creek

Mostly a sleepless and tearful night, Myrna managed to rest a little sitting in the backseat of the car. It was about 6:00 in the morning when she woke up from what seemed like a dream. She had an overwhelming feeling Blake would be okay, and he would make it through. She didn't know how when so many felt despair and a sense that there was no chance of anyone making it out alive. Myrna thought about the day before when Blake was getting ready for work. He had told her about a premonition. He had a foreboding that he shouldn't go to work that afternoon. But he soon talked himself out of staying home, telling her his men needed him. If only he had listened to his feelings, she thought to herself.[143]

Premonitions, warnings and even dreams have been a large part of the mining culture for centuries, and it's believed by some, they either predicted disaster or prevented trouble.[144] There are numerous stories of miners who had a feeling, a premonition, to move from a particular spot only to have the roof cave-in where they had been moments before. Or they reported having an overpowering feeling not to work that day and were saved from a subsequent mine disaster. Historically, working in mines has always been dangerous, so it's not surprising miners and their families paid very careful attention to these omens.

Dreams were also highly respected for their powers of forecasting disasters. In the early century, some bosses accepted dreams as an excuse for a work absence,[144] though officially condemned, they were informally approved. Today, beliefs brought from the old countries are largely ignored or unknown, although some superstitions currently persist among some miners.

Even the tricks played on coworkers, from the nailing of lunch buckets to the floor, to putting mice in a bucket before a miner takes it home to his wife, (and a myriad of other ways to scare co-workers), seemed to serve the miners somehow. The ones who suffered the most from "miner's humor" were the new employees. It seemed the experienced miners' favorite pastime was to develop increasingly creative ways to terrorize the already frightened apprentices.[145] Initiation rites and rituals embedded in the culture served as an informal and mostly unconscious method of eliminating the psychologically unfit miner. Mining has always been one of the most dangerous professions, and miners had to feel they could depend on each other during times of crisis, such as a cave-in or entombment.[146] Those who couldn't take the jokes and hazing didn't stay, which potentially weeded out those who were unable to handle a crisis.

By early morning, Myrna and her family left for town to check on the children. After they showered and dressed in fresh clothes, they ate breakfast at one of the cafes. They headed back to the mine site to see if there was any news about the missing men. There was none, so they went back to the arduous task of waiting along with the other families.[147]

Reporters were everywhere, milling around and taking notes, scrambling to get the latest updates or attempting to speak with rescuers. Some tried to talk to family members, and if they couldn't, they just listened in on their conversations. Photographers were positioned next to the roped off area or were perched up high on the dirt embankments. One was even on top of a ten-foot ladder near the large opening of the Headframe. With a telephoto lens, they could see inside and were able to get shots of the rescue teams getting into and out of the buckets. It was a beehive of activity around the large Headframe.

About every hour and a half, sometimes less, rescue teams descended into the poisonous, stifling-hot shaft to work, clearing away debris. Wearing cumbersome equipment much like scuba divers, the rescuers in ore buckets clambered through smashed tubing and rubble in the smoke and darkness. The rescue workers all had a look of determination.[149] The air was hot and extremely moist as water fell all around them, making visibility difficult through the face masks the rescuers wore. The hope was that the missing men survived the explosion and fire and were in a pocket of air.[150]

More rescue workers had arrived at the site. The Kaiser Steel Mine at Sunnyside closed down Tuesday night at the end of the afternoon shift; their other rescuers came to the Cane Creek Mine to help with the rescue work. More rescuers from the U. S. Steel Mines also came to the mine site.[151] There were now about twenty-five rescuers from the Kaiser Steel Mine and about twenty-six from the U.S. Steel Mines.[152]

Needed material also arrived at the mine site to replace the damaged sections of the vent line. The emergency materials that were flown from Denver[153] finally helped to improve progress on repairs to the vent line in the shaft. Five lengths of the large diameter pipe were torn loose or crushed in the blast and rescue workers worked to patch the vent line to the bottom of the mine shaft. Some of the damaged sections were brought up out of the shaft and laid in the yard, as the flexible plastic air tubes, thirty inches in diameter, were lowered and hooked up to get air to the bottom as crews below ground worked in miserable conditions.

Above ground, the mine and plant buildings were bustling with rescue operations as the latest bucket emerged at the surface. One rescuer who spoke softly, in almost a whisper, was overheard telling others nearby, "It's hell down there." He then spat and shuffled toward a nearby building for hot coffee.[154] His waterlogged leather mine boots sloshed with each step he took.

Rescuers were working desperately to restore the ventilation and then the communications to the bottom so they could get into the two drifts and search for the twenty-five miners who were trapped.[155] And still, there was no communication with any of them.[156] Time after time, dirty and soaking wet, the rescuers with vacant eyes came up out of the deep hole to rest and then return. Many were veterans of similar disasters.

In the round 22-foot-diameter shaft still choked with carbon monoxide gases, teams took turns throughout the morning, working its depths as they dropped over a half-mile down the shaft time and again. The rescue crews were sent down in teams of three or four at a time, with Harrison International team members among them to help safely maneuver the bucket in the shaft.

Rescuers continually[156] shrugged themselves into apparatuses and wore bulky face masks each time they stepped into the two-ton bucket. The heavy oxygen apparatuses strapped to their backs weighed 30 pounds,[157] and their gear made them appear as though they were men from another world, much like the red canyon country surrounding the mine site. The oxygen protected the rescuers from the deadly carbon monoxide fumes still heavy in the shaft's atmosphere,[158] which only allowed them to work a short time in the mine as crews fought to clear the debris stacked up at the bottom.[159] Their primary mission was to set up a fresh air base at the bottom before they could probe the drifts.[160]

All wore hard hats, some white, others dark, to protect their heads from falling debris. At first, many wore rubber coveralls or slickers to help shield them from the torrent of water falling into the shaft.[161] Some of the hard hats were of the hard rock miners' type, with a wide brim all the way around. These shaft hard hats were useful for directing water away from the miner's faces and necks as they worked. It was backbreaking work; their energy sapped, even more, while "under oxygen" in the hot moist atmosphere.

Many of the rescuers continually described the conditions as working "in a hard rainstorm," as they came out of the potash mine dripping wet. The "rainstorm" from the natural seepage still could not be drawn out of the shaft because of the danger of electrocuting rescuers.[162] Hampered by water spilling at the rate of forty gallons a minute,[163] with no way to stop the flow, it was something they simply had to endure.

"It's worse than a cloudburst," one rescuer was heard to say, as he stepped from the bucket, soaked to the skin.

"The water makes it so dark down there, even with my light I can't see my wristwatch," another one said.

"It's a helluva job," one rescuer exclaimed hoping to catch a wink of sleep, "but we all know it's got to be done, and the sooner, the better. We can all imagine ourselves in the same situation."[164]

One rescuer asserted, "There is plenty of oxygen at the bottom of the shaft, more than enough to sustain life." However, he added, "carbon monoxide is present down there also." There was no evidence of a prolonged fire as reported by other men.[165]

Unsmiling, the red-eyed rescuers worked in the shaft about an hour and then would return to replenish their oxygen supply. They would rest for a while as their tanks were refilled and serviced, then they prepared for another trip down into the shaft.

While clearing debris near the bottom, a rescue team reported seeing one of two feeder-breakers (the loading mechanism used to fill muck into the ore buckets at the shaft station) that had been tipped and wedged out in the shaft.[166] This feeder-breaker was from the west side of the shaft, while the one on the east side was still in place, leading rescuers and officials to believe the blast came from the direction of the West Drift.[167] It was this shorter 2,500-foot-long West Drift where, reportedly, the crew was getting ready to blast the Face.

After getting this news, Casper A. Nelson, Utah State Industrial Commissioner, who helped to coordinate the rescue operations, was led to believe, as well, the explosion occurred in the West Drift.

"I don't hold much hope for those on the explosion side," he added.

He said the men in the West Drift would not only have had to survive the blast after a dynamite detonation apparently ignited methane gas, but would have had to barricade against the smoke and poison gases.

"That's very unlikely," he said.[168]

Texas Gulf Sulphur tasked June Crawford, as the company's spokesman, to pass along word from responsible officials as soon as he obtained it. He would either confirm or refute rumors.

Crawford said crews were preparing a 500-pound dynamite charge in one of the two drifts and believed it was where the destructive explosion occurred just before 5:00 p.m. yesterday. He explained adequate manpower and equipment were available, but time was not.[169] Rescue crews were well aware they were working against time. Officials first hoped to reach the trapped men by noon. Later in the morning, they said, "it is going to be at least late afternoon." So the press and families went back to waiting.[170]

Chapter 12

"Nine Men Alive!"

Hanna and McKinney spent all morning working on the air line. It had been about three hours since they left the barricade and now they had five joints of pipe put back together. They still lacked about eighteen inches to hook the two ends together.[1] As they laid in the air current, Hanna used his hard hat to direct the air into the other end. With a significant amount of air pressure coming out, they hoped some of the air was going into the other end and getting to the barricade. But there was no way of knowing for sure.[2]

Both men had nothing to drink since the time they left the barricade and were weak and dehydrated from the heat. Their eyes were burning and they coughed. All they could think about was staying alive.[3]

At one point, Blake decided to cross over a small cement ledge just over a foot wide that ran alongside the shaft wall, leading to the west side of the station. With the water pouring down, it was wet, and if he slipped, he'd fall into the sump area and into the smoke and darkness below. Harrison International's men used that ledge all the time. But now, Hanna cautiously made his way to the other side because of the water.

Paul had told him some self-rescuers (small portable breathing canisters) had been brought down into the mine the week before. So Hanna went to the other side to check the shop for anything they could use like self-rescuers, water, and first-aid supplies. Not far from the shop entrance, Hanna passed by a body and a shuttle car. Both were badly burned and damaged from the explosion.

Once in the shop, the only thing Hanna found was more destruction. Everything was scattered and blackened from one end to the other.[4] There, he could tell where the explosion had originated near the center of the shop. The debris was scattered in both directions.

Not finding anything of use, Hanna headed back towards the shaft station. Next to the shaft was a fifty-five-gallon oil drum that had been cut in two and was about three feet high. Harrison International's men used it to clean the hammer heads to the drills. The drum was now overflowing with water that collected from the water pouring down the shaft. Hanna sat down next to it and began to splash the water into his eyes and push his eyes with his thumb until numb, then he could see again. The salt in the water caused his eyes to sting, but it also seemed to soothe them a bit.[5]

That's when some metal fell down the shaft[6] in front of him. Apparently, rescue crews were working in the shaft. A couple of times during the morning, Hanna and McKinney had heard stuff coming down. They knew somebody was up there doing something. It gave them hope that rescuers were on their way; although, they had no idea how far up in the shaft they were or what they were trying to do.[7]

Hanna searched around and found a ten-foot long drill steel and reached out and hit the metal lines running down the side of the shaft. He banged out "S." "O." "S.", using Morse code, hitting the steel hard trying to get the attention of whoever was up there.[8] At the same time, he aimed his cap-lamp at the end of the cord hanging around his neck, up into the shaft. He was shaking it up and down trying to signal to anyone who might see the light through the pouring water and smoke.

McKinney came from around the corner from where the air was located on the east side to see what Hanna was doing.[9] He crossed over the ledge to where Hanna was, and they both listened, but there was no reply. It appeared no one heard. Discouraged and weak, Hanna gave up and they headed back to the other side to the air line.

There was hardly any conversation between Hanna and McKinney, other than when needed as they laid by the side of the pipe, breathing the air. Both of their cap-lamps were going dim. They turned them out, knowing it wouldn't be long before they would burn out. They realized their options: keep trying to get the attention of someone from the top or go back to the barricade. They could work their way back by unhooking a couple of sections, move them eighteen inches and hook them up again as they made their way back.[10]

A Harrison International Rescue Team was working in the shaft clearing debris when Henry Laviolette thought he saw a light below moving up and down. The others thought they heard banging on the pipes. The other two men didn't see the light even though Laviolette pointed it out. They thought maybe those on the surface were banging, so the team gave the signal to take them to the surface.[11] No one knew anything about the banging. There were no senior officials around. They were over at the mine offices having lunch. So, the team went back down, but this time, they went to the very bottom. Only able to get about sixty feet above the shaft station because the bucket lane was blocked, the rescuers started yelling and moving their light up and down. If someone was alive, they hoped they would see or hear them.[12]

Weak and in a daze, Hanna and McKinney thought they heard noises, or what might be voices. They went around the corner to the station and looked up where they saw rescuers dangling in a bucket up in the shaft. They could barely see their small lights through the smoke and water.[13]

The rescuers were hollering, but their oxygen masks made it hard to hear what they said as the sound of water coming down the shaft drowned out the sound. Hanna and McKinney tried to make out the rescuers muffled shouts as the hollering went back and forth, each trying to comprehend the other.[14]

Hanna and McKinney figured out why they didn't come down to the station. It was because a section of damaged vent line was out in the middle blocking the bucket lane. They tried to let the rescuers know there were five other guys back behind a barricade, but they weren't sure if they understood. Finally, the bucket started moving slowly up as the rescuers' little lights disappeared.[15] Hanna told McKinney they would be back and they went back to the air to wait.

On the surface at the shaft collar, a rescue worker wearing a Texas Gulf Sulphur (TGS) hard hat was waiting at the top holding a walkie-talkie. Meanwhile, not far from the Headframe, reporters huddled together while comparing notes and discussing rumors. The motor of a ventilator fan roared continuously, making conversation impossible unless one shouted.[16]

Several reporters chatted with Fred Tatton, a rescuer from the Kaiser Steel Team. They were discussing the reconnaissance trip Tatton made earlier in the morning with two other rescuers as he shared what they found. He also explained a few things about mine rescue work.

"We always work on the assumption the miners are alive until we know otherwise," Tatton told them.[17] Soon the men parted, and Tatton headed towards the Headframe.

A few minutes later, Tatton's assumption dramatically played out when the bucket surfaced just after 10:30 a.m. A three-man rescue team made up of Harrison International men, excitedly reported of men alive at the bottom of the mine who were yelling for help.[18]

"There are survivors,"[19] the excited team exclaimed. The whole place erupted in incredible joy as the news spread like fire. The rescue team told what they knew as they climbed out of the bucket. Giving more details, they explained how they made voice contact with survivors,[20] as workers helped them out of their rescue gear. Other workers gathered around each man to hear the details.

The men told how they were working to clear the shaft when they heard banging on the pipes or saw a light. Coming to the surface, they weren't able to find the source of the banging, so the team decided to check things out at the bottom. Getting down as far as they could in the shaft, they began to holler. Moments later, men at the bottom answered back. Two of the rescue team members, Robert Rediger[21] and Benny Cable,[22] said they were told the number of survivors through a shouted conversation.[23]

"Nine men were yelling for help at the bottom," Rediger said.

Word spread fast. Bruce Miller, the newsman for the radio station KALL in Salt Lake City, reported live from the mine site that rescue workers said they heard men shouting. Miller quoted one of the rescue workers as saying, "the men hollered back there were nine survivors."[24]

Before, there was little hope of any of the men surviving the explosion, the fire, and the drifting currents of carbon monoxide gas.[25] Now, hope quickly returned with the report of men alive.[26] In the confusion and excitement, reporters rushed to get the dramatic story into print.

Immediately, Henry Laviolette, the Harrison International Rescuer, and Frank Markosek, a Captain from one of the Kaiser Steel Teams made preparations to go after the survivors. Laviolette, also called 'Big Henry' by his men, was also the normal Shift Walker for this group of miners. He grabbed a fresh oxygen apparatus to change into, and both men quickly went "under oxygen." They had gathered other items they might need: a bunch of the small self-rescuers and a chain ladder. Down the shaft they went, headed to snatch the survivors from the shattered mine.

George McCloud and his buddy, a fellow rescuer, had earlier driven into town. He waited at the telephone office while his buddy nearby made calls to relatives of one of the missing men. McCloud sat slumped in an overstuffed chair staring slightly downward and looking too tired for a young man of only twenty-five years.[27]

"Did you go down in the hole?" he was asked.

He glanced up and nodded yes.

"What does it look like?"

"My crew only got down 1,800 feet," George said in a voice pitched not much higher than a murmur. "We couldn't tell much." He paused then continued his downward gaze. He added slowly, even more softly, "My cousin is down there."[28]

About ten minutes later, George still hadn't stirred himself or his stare, when a man ran in and said there had been a report of men alive in the shaft. The word buzzed through the men and women waiting in the office. Someone looked around to ask McCloud's opinion of the report. He was gone. He and his buddy were out the door headed down the winding road towards the mine to verify the latest report. He would take up his silent vigil at the mine and wait for news from underground, or again be summoned to plunge down into the shaft and continue the rescue work.[29]

Reports of voices at the mine sent Moab's hospital officials scurrying to prepare for treatment of possible survivors at the I.W. Allen Hospital, a new, modern medical facility.

"This community is behind us 100 per cent," Victor Pauls, the hospital administrator said.

"We've had calls from nursing personnel and housewives offering help. If we need them, all we have to do is call,"[30] he said. The hospital had sufficient space to provide for twenty to twenty-five casualties.

"We would have enough beds and cots for 200 if need be," he said, "But space is the problem." Hospital facilities in nearby Monticello and Price are available if necessary.[31]

And doctors in Monticello, Dragerton, Price and Salt Lake City are also ready to converge at a moment's notice by telephone since there are only four local physicians.[32]

In Salt Lake City, Governor Clyde expressed deep shock and sorrow over the Moab mine disaster.

"I have been close to the situation since last night," he told reporters. "The state has been making all efforts possible to lend assistance.

"The State Health Department has been alerted. The facilities of the Utah Highway Patrol have been used in relaying communications," Governor Clyde said.[33]

Members of the Flying Physicians Association of Utah were also alerted for possible calls to Moab should the need arise for emergency medical or surgical procedures of a highly specialized nature in treating rescued victims of the disaster. The Salt Lake orthopedic surgeon,[34] who headed the organization, said he called doctors in the specialties most likely needed to treat injuries involved, or who were also to help Moab physicians.

The Flying Physicians Association, now on standby, was comprised of about twenty-three doctors, all of whom had pilot licenses. It was estimated about fifteen of them owned their planes, and the others made frequent flights in rented planes. Early this summer, the association conducted a practice "fly-in" at Salt Lake Airport, where a practice operation for an emergency would require a quick assemblage of doctors at some spot in the state.[35]

An emergency shipment of blood consisting of eighteen pints of whole blood and four pints of serum albumin was sent to Moab before noon once word came that some of the miners were alive. The shipment from the Intermountain Regional Blood Center, American Red Cross, in Salt Lake City, was flown to Moab in a Highway Patrol plane and was taken to I.W. Allen Hospital.[36]

After the shipment of two large cardboard boxes containing the bottles of blood[37] were flown to Moab from the blood bank, the medical technologist and X-ray technician at the hospital, C. M. McCurdy, had nothing but praise for the Utah Highway Patrol.

"I'll never speed again, or if I do, I won't squawk about getting a ticket," he declared.[38]

Down in the dark, hot mine, it had been nearly an hour since Hanna and McKinney last saw the rescuers. They were lying next to the air line when they heard hollering. Turning on their cap-lamps, they walked around the corner to the shaft. They could barely see the rescuers in a bucket through the smoke out over the shaft. They had come down in a different bucket, the larger Nordberg bucket, and were in a different bucket lane over on the other side of the shaft. The bucket moved slowly down and was twenty feet over the feeder-breaker when it stopped abruptly.

Weak and weary, Hanna and McKinney headed over to the narrow ledge to get to the west side. It was perilous as each one stepped onto the foot-wide ledge, where the water fell all around them. Carefully, they crossed the ledge. McKinney bent his head down to look where he was going when his hard hat unexpectedly fell off his head taking the cap-lamp and cord with it. It echoed in the darkness as it tumbled down into the sump. Hanna had left his hard hat over by the air line, but he still had his cap-lamp at the end of the cord, hung around his neck.³⁹ Using his light to see where they were going, they scooted across the ledge.

Once they were safely on the west side, they had to crawl upon the grungy, industrial yellow feeder-breaker to get closer to the bucket. They had no idea what was holding the feeder-breaker and keeping it from plunging down into the sump area. Hanna went first, hesitantly shifting his weight to see if it would move. He certainly didn't want it tumbling down into the sump carrying him with it.⁴⁰

The bucket wasn't moving down. Impatient, Hanna grabbed the guide rope next to the bucket. In good shape, he shimmied up one of the metal guide ropes,⁴¹ twenty feet towards the bucket. His flame safety lamp hooked to his mine belt fell off and tumbled down, bouncing onto the shaft station. Once he reached the bucket, the two rescuers grabbed him by his arms and pulled him into it as it tipped a bit to the side.

McKinney's turn. In a weakened state, there was no way he could get up the guide rope. The rescuers threw the chain ladder⁴² they had brought with them, over the side for him to climb as 'Big Henry' blocked it in the bottom of the bucket with his foot to hold it tight.

A bigger guy, McKinney hesitated, then slowly started up the ladder towards the bucket. 'Big Henry' struggled to hold the ladder with his feet while McKinney had a difficult time climbing, but once at the top, the others leaned out to help him into the bucket. Safe in the bucket, their rescuers were literally a welcome sight for sore eyes, as tears rolled down their cheeks, partly from being emotional and partly from the carbon monoxide. McKinney was shaking, and Hanna was anxious with brief and specific instructions:

"Let's get the hell out of here."⁴³

The rescuers Markosek, and Laviolette checked to make sure they were okay and got them settled in the bucket. Hanna knew Markosek from Kaiser Steel, where he had previously worked. And both knew Laviolette, or 'Big Henry' as they called him. He was the Shift Walker over Hanna and McKinney's shift.

Both survivors seemed to be okay, but each one was coughing and breathing heavy. Their rescuers had brought down a bunch of little self-rescuers, the W65's and shoved them into their mouths. Hanna and McKinney started sucking through them and immediately had better air to breathe. It wasn't long before the self-rescuers became a bit hot from a chemical reaction inside from the carbon monoxide levels in the air. Heating up, they burned the men a bit around their mouths, but still, it was like heaven, and they were soon breathing more easily. The rescuers handed them a bunch of self-rescuers they brought with them to hold, anticipating more than two survivors. McKinney had five or six of the self-rescuers in his hands, and Blake had about the same. Each self-rescuer was good for about an hour, so both men felt they had it made.[44]

Their eyes were still burning out of our heads, and they could hardly see anything. The groundwater loaded with salt and probably some arsenic, splashed or trickled around them and made their eyes burn even more. Their eyes were so sore they could hardly keep them open. The water especially caused more pain for McKinney because of the burns on his backside.[45]

The two survivors sat down on the wood blocks in the bottom of the bucket where the water was collecting. They watched as 'Big Henry' tried to talk over a walkie-talkie, telling the surface to take them to the top, but the water was drowning him out. Frustrated, he kept hollering over and over the same thing. "Take us oop, take us oop!" Laviolette shouted slowly with his deep voice over and over in a discernible French Canadian accent. Finally, after what seems like forever, the bucket started moving up. It went up about fifteen feet before it suddenly stopped.[46] Deep in the shaft, the air was no longer coming through the vent line. The rescuers and the rescued waited in the stalled bucket for what seemed like a long time.[47] Laviolette kept talking over the walkie-talkie while he took small comfort from his flame safety lamp, which showed no sign of gas. The flame continued to burn, evidence the amount of carbon monoxide in the air had not reached the danger level,[48] which would snuff out the flame. After testing, Laviolette hung his lamp on one of the three heavy chains attached to the rim of the bucket.

It was frustrating to the rescuers and the two survivors. 'Big Henry' kept saying over and over, "Take us oop." At one point, Hanna even became agitated and yelled expletives into the walkie-talkie. None of the men knew why the air was off or why the bucket wasn't being hoisted. "We've gotten into this bucket, now we're stuck and can't even get pulled up," McKinney thought to himself. With the self-rescuers in his hand, he imagined he could go back to the barricade if they would just let him get back out of the bucket. Minutes later, after more water had collected in the bottom of the bucket, the machinery throbbed to life[49] and the bucket started moving up at a slow rate of speed, about 150 feet a minute, as it hoisted the two weary survivors to the surface.

Hanna and McKinney were breathing better with the little self-rescuers in their mouths as the bucket continued slowly moving up. They didn't talk much, but at one point did try to let the rescuers know of the other five men down in East Drift behind a barricade.[50] But they weren't sure the rescuers heard or understood what they told them.

After hours of frantic rescue efforts, the news of rescue teams making contact with nine trapped miners stunned everyone. As the news spread, crowds converged on the scene. With emotional anticipation, family members who spent a tearful night, hung onto every word, any scrap of information they could get on the progress of rescue efforts. Their greatest hope: their loved one would be one of the nine survivors.

The press clamored about taking notes and finding a vantage point to witness the rescue as photographers set up cameras to get the perfect shot. Everyone was anxious, knowing a rescue team was now down in the mine bringing survivors to the surface. Gathered down as close as they could get to the Headframe, everyone was trying to find the best spot outside the roped off the perimeter.[51]

Near the first hoist house, closest to the Headframe, freelance photographer Hikaru "Carl" Iwasaki,[52] from Denver, Colorado, sat high on top of a ten-foot ladder. He was positioned to get photos inside the Headframe over the heads of the rescue workers as they crowded around the shaft area. Carl worked for *LIFE* magazine, America's most widely read pictorial magazine. He was dispatched to Moab by *LIFE* to get photos of the disaster for their next issue. Known for his iconic photos, Carl also did work for *Time* and *Sports Illustrated* and had gained some notoriety for shooting stories about the marginalized and disenfranchised. It was his photos of the civil rights movement, taken since the middle of the 50's, that were some of his most poignant.[53]

The president and chairman of the board of TGS Company, Claude O. Stephens and his wife, Loin, had flown in from New York City and had just arrived at the mine site. At the general mine office, J.G. Pinkerton was still at his post working the switchboard when he was relieved to welcome the company executive and his wife. Pinkerton couldn't help but think how their visit didn't help the chaotic situation swirling all around. They would need to be taken care of, and he would have to be the one to see to their needs on top of everything else he was trying to juggle. People were clamoring back and forth through the reception area of the office anticipating the survivors would be brought to the surface at any moment. Pinkerton greeted the Stephens, and he proceeded to update them on the rescue operation.[54]

The couple hadn't been there long when everyone heard the cranking sound of the hoist. News quickly spread. The survivors are on their way to the surface. People bolted to get down near the Headframe. Caught up in the excitement, Claude and Loin Stephens ran out of the building along with others. Pinkerton watched through the door and the large, floor-to-ceiling windows. He leaned against the rock wall partition in the lobby area as he watched the couple run down the sidewalk towards the Headframe. Then they abruptly stopped.

It seemed like an awkward moment, Pinkerton thought. It seemed as though the Stephens didn't know what to do next. It was like when people want to reach out to others in a desperate moment, but they don't know how. It wasn't that the Stephens didn't care. They did. They were very fine people. But since they were introverted types, it seemed to Pinkerton they weren't comfortable with emotions. It was as though they got caught up in the excitement of the moment, but the moment was one they weren't equipped to handle. The Stephens slowly made their way back to the office to watch from a more comfortable distance with Pinkerton.[55]

Near the Headframe, photographers were getting situated, adjusting their cameras and preparing to get a good shot of the dramatic rescue. Reporters were scribbling notes to document the moment, and trading facts with each other as family members crowded around. The mood was intense as everyone tried to find a spot where they could see inside the large opening of the Headframe. The wait was intense as the hot afternoon sun beat down on the gathering crowd.

Part Three

Chapter 13

"Free at Last"

Unbeknownst to the two rescuers and two survivors, the source of the bucket stalling at the bottom of the shaft came when Laviolette gave the signal to stop. The bucket stopped when the Hoistman punched the hoisting controls causing it to blow a fuse. It took a bit of time to change it out. During this time, the rescuers were not able to get the bucket lowered further, so the two survivors climbed to the bucket.[1]

After the fuse was changed on the surface and they received a signal from the bottom to take the bucket up, the Hoistman again punched it. Just as the bucket moved up, again a fuse blew. The hum of machinery at the hoist house went off, and the fans pumping air down the large metal vent line in the shaft stopped turning.[2]

The crowd gathered around the Headframe and watched with breathless concern. It was a terrible moment as rescue workers worked as fast as they could to restore the power, again. But this time when the power pole next to the first hoist house was climbed to change the fuse, the pole started to fall over. Other rescue workers scurried to hold it upright while an electrician replaced the fuse. Minutes later, power to the hoisting machinery came to life, and everyone could hear the creaking sound of the sheave wheel again as it turned, lifting the bucket from the deepest part of the shaft. The workers continued to hold the pole upright while the bucket made its way slowly to the surface.[3] They planned to secure the pole back in the ground once the survivors were safe on the surface.

Rescue officials and workers crowded around the metal railing, some peering over into the dark shaft, as the bucket slowly moved closer. The anticipation was nerve-racking. One of Harrison International's men, a young Engineer, laid down on the metal diamond plate flooring and stuck his head under the railing for a better look. Deep in the shaft, he spotted two small lights as the sheave wheel, high in the Headframe, creaked as it turned. Aiming a light down into the darkness, he could only make out two men in the bucket. He yelled out what he saw to those gathered around him. His shouts echoed in the cement shaft. Concerned officials and rescue workers expected the bucket to be full of survivors and had anticipated that it could take several trips to bring all nine survivors to the surface.[4]

As the bucket got closer to the shaft collar, it began to swing. Laviolette grabbed the guide rope on his side to try and steady it. Hanna, knowing what to do, jumped up and grabbed the other guide rope on his side to help. That's when the young Engineer, peering into the darkness, saw there was a third person in the bucket and promptly informed the others around him. Just then, he spotted a fourth one as the bucket inched closer to the surface, easing some concern for those on the surface.[5]

The bucket reached the surface at 11:55 a.m.,[6] as a large crowd held their breath. The bucket was hoisted high above the landing while workers closed the metal shaft door. Some in the crowd craned their necks and stood on tiptoes to get a better look. In the bucket, only the top of the men's heads was visible above the rim, but as they stood on the wood blocks at the bottom, the crowd could see what looked like two survivors—soaking wet and bare from the waist up. They didn't appear too seriously injured.[7]

1. The bucket bringing the two survivors is raised above the shaft station as rescue workers close shaft door. (*UPI Telephoto*) 2. Rescuers, Frank Markosek and Henry Laviolette (left), and survivors, Blake Hanna (middle) and Paul McKinney (right) watch from the bucket as rescuer workers crowd around to help. (Carl Iwasaki/*LIFE Magazine*, 1963/Getty Images)

By now, both rescuers, Laviolette and Markosek had taken off their face masks and squirmed out of their apparatuses. Too encumbered with their gear on, they needed to assist the survivors out of the bucket and communicate with other rescue workers on the surface. Laviolette put his hard hat back on while Markosek was bareheaded like the two survivors. This visual eventually led to rumors that three men came up in the first bucket trip.

The silent crowd intently watched as they stretched and maneuvered, trying to see who the survivors were. The suspense was gripping. News photographers snapped away, getting shots as the drama unfolded. Reporters were furiously scribbling notes to document the moment for the next big headline. Television crews taped the event for viewing on later news broadcasts once they flew the tapes back to their studios. Radio announcers made their pronouncements, broadcasting to listeners riveted to their radio.

Dirty and in a daze, the survivors' eyes blinked and streamed tears. They looked haggard and worn from their physical ordeal. McKinney held a self-rescuer in his mouth, a clamp over his nose, and he leaned his head back on one of the heavy metal chains of the bucket. Rescue workers crowded around the large bucket to assist. Dripping wet and dirty, the survivors were very much alive.[8] They had spent a total of nineteen hours imprisoned by the blast.[9]

McKinney handed someone the handful of small self-rescuers he was holding as rescue workers stretched to help him out of the bucket. Another worker reached up and pulled out the self-rescuer he had in his mouth. Instantly, McKinney felt as though he could not breathe. It didn't make sense to him; he knew he was in the good air now, all he had to do was breath, but everything started going fuzzy. He could hear voices as his eyesight started going blurry.[10]

Behind McKinney, rescuers were trying to help Hanna climb out of the bucket when he promptly told them he was "all right." He could do it himself, he informed them, with a determined look on his face.[11]

McKinney tried to walk, then heard one of the workers say, "He's passing out." Rescuers clamored to catch the big guy and put him onto a stretcher. Never losing consciousness, McKinney could still hear sounds and voices although they sounded a bit foggy and off in the distance.[12] Workers finally maneuvered him onto a gurney.

Photographer Carl Iwasaki, who was perched on the ladder, was able to get shots of the two survivors as workers helped them from the bucket. Other photographers also clicked away while rescue workers prepared and loaded the two men into ambulances.

Rescue workers found McKinney's two brothers, Lloyd and Ivan, in the crowd and let them know Paul was one of the two survivors.

The brothers watched intently, grateful their younger brother was alive. They would head to town to let his wife know just as soon as the workers had Paul loaded in the ambulance.[13]

As rescuers put Hanna onto a stretcher, he spotted his younger brother, Wayne, in the crowd and called to him, "I'm okay, I'm okay."[14] He knew his wife Myrna would be nearby, but he could not find her. Rescuers quickly wrapped blankets around[15] each man and put oxygen masks on them. Hanna told them to "get that damn thing off" of him. He didn't need it up to this point, and he didn't need it now.[16]

Each survivor was put into separate ambulances to rush them to the hospital. Hanna was able to talk to officials only briefly[17] but wasn't sure if they heard him. Through the chaos, he tried to tell them that he headed a crew which included McKinney and there were five other men still alive in the East Drift. He tried to tell about the three miners who wouldn't go into the barricade and died, and about the air line. With all the commotion to get them on their way, there was nothing said or asked about any of the other men.[18]

McKinney was still a bit foggy as the two ambulances started up out of the yard. They were at the main gate when the doctor put a cloth saturated with ammonia over his face. He came out from underneath the cloth real fast and started breathing while coming around. Shocked into awareness, he swore that stuff could make the dead breathe.[19]

McKinney also tried to tell those in the ambulance with him of the other five survivors, but no one seemed to pay much attention in all the commotion. He kept trying to tell them someone needed to get down there to get to them or connect the air line. Breathing better—much better, he worried the word didn't get to the right people as the ambulance rushed through the river canyon towards town and to the hospital.[20]

Attendants and personnel at the hospital were alerted and on standby for the survivors who were on their way from the mine site.

"They told us they would bring the men out one at a time, and it would be about thirty minutes between each man," Cecilia Thompson, the hospital business manager, said. Wives and relatives gathered at the hospital for the agonizing wait[21] for ambulances to arrive and hoped their loved ones were among the nine survivors.

While some family members waited at the mine site to watch the rescue efforts for themselves,[22] others waited out the long hours at home. As word spread of the impending rescue, many rushed to the hospital. They sat in the lobby, in autos and on the low stone walls,[23] desperate for any news.

"Do you have any names?"[24]

It was the same question asked over and over as townspeople trickled into the hospital's crowded lobby.[25] On assignment from California, Robert Flick,[26] a reporter for United Press International (UPI), was writing in a small notebook while viewing a scene nearby. "Three young wives sat nestled together, like starlings on a bench, all sobbed," wrote the big, commanding, "burly bear of a guy."[27] Looking up for a brief moment, he went back to his notes. "A tiny blond with her hair up in curlers wiped her eyes with a handkerchief and stopped crying. And then another started. And so it went as the clock ticked on as rumors scurried up and down the quiet corridors as mice through a pantry,"[28] the left-handed reporter scrawled, creatively using simile to describe the tragic scene before him.

"They've found nine more," or, "they've found three more," was the oft-repeated response.

"Oh, my goodness. Do you have any names?" Hopes rose then sank as report after report proved false. The real truth, nobody knew.[29]

Outside the front door, a grizzled hulk of a man stood silently holding hands with his wife, wondering about his brother. His eyes were as tear-filled as those of the three young wives. Some of the families sat knotted together on the grass in front of the flagstone, one-story hospital.[30]

Dorothy LeBlanc, the wife of missing miner Emile LeBlanc, maintained a lone vigil near the concrete ambulance entrance. A small, pretty mother of three small children from Elliot Lake, Ontario, Canada, had arrived with her husband in Moab the previous week.[31]

Dorothy with her three young children was at home when Johnny MacDonnell and his wife Francis, also Canadians, came to the door and told her there was an explosion at the mine. Francis stayed with the three young children, as Johnny took Dorothy to the mine site where she stayed for a while praying for all the men who were trapped.[32]

"Are there any names?" She asked the question[33] repeatedly as she waited. With hope in her gray eyes, she approached a man rumored to have talked to two known survivors.

"Please," she said, "Did they give you any names?"

"No ma'am," the man replied. "I'm sorry."[34]

Dorothy's head bowed as she studied the gravel in the path.[35] She turned and walked slowly back to wait with her friend,[36] Alice Barber, the wife of Wesley Barber, who was also missing.

The Barbers, another Canadian family, also came from Elliot Lake. Dorothy sat down while Alice's two small daughters, Linda, two, and Louise, five, played in the gravel. The little girls giggled not knowing the fate of their father and too young to understand what was going on. The Barbers had moved to Moab only six weeks ago.[37]

Alice stood up when a reporter stopped to speak with her. She told him how the Sheriff came by their home at the Red Rock Lodge late last night and drove them to the building at the mine site reserved for waiting relatives.[38] She reached down to pick up her youngest daughter, Linda, and gave a weary smile as a reporter asked about her family.

"Louise loved the ride in the car but was sorry to miss kindergarten today," she said talking about her five-year-old. "My husband worked in a uranium mine. There he had an accident, and his jaw was broken. He doesn't seem to learn his lesson,"[39] she said lowering her head.

After the reporter had moseyed on, Alice nudged the gravel with her shoe. She looked up to ask a person passing by if the hospital people have mentioned any names yet.[40]

"No," she was told, "they haven't." In frustration, Alice kicked at the blades of grass next to the gravel drive and went back to waiting with her friend.[41]

A young mother left the hospital and tossed a wad of paper forcibly on the ground. She heard only seven miners were known to be alive after the blast.

"Why don't they give us their names?" she cried.[42]

On the lawn standing or sitting were other tearful women, some in hair curlers, a few with the popular bouffant hairstyle. Some wore slacks, some peddle-pusher or stirrup pants, while others were in gingham house dresses. They all tried to console each other.[43]

At times a stranger approached, and they became chatty for a few strange seconds.[44] Children romped across the lawn, seeming not to know that in perhaps twenty-four to forty-eight hours, they would know if they would ever see their fathers again.[45] Time was torture for the wives of the missing men who were somewhere under a half-mile of rough colored rock. Weary and impatient, the women were very frightened. Some of them wept easily, while others did not.

"I can't stand the waiting," said one woman, her face etched by tears. "But I dread the time when this waiting is over. I don't know what they are going to tell me, and maybe I don't want to know."[46]

Across from a grove of cottonwood trees, somebody spotted an ambulance winding along the river road where it horseshoed on the other side of the Colorado River on its way from the potash mine.[47] When the first tiny wail of the ambulance siren reached the ears of sixteen-year-old Martha Milton, daughter of Kenneth Milton, the small attractive blond wearing blue jeans began to sob. She then ran for the emergency entrance[48] along with a dozen other women.[49] Her boyfriend and other family members were not far behind her.

Martha first learned of the explosion the day before from her aunt and her aunt's family who just arrived in Moab at the end of their long trip from West Virginia. They heard news about it on the radio while driving through the subdivision to Martha's home. Once informed, Martha's mother, Ina, tried to find out more but couldn't get any information. It wasn't long before Martha's boyfriend, Mike Dowd, showed up also with news of the blast.[50]

Mike worked for Scharf Construction, the construction company hired by Texas Gulf Sulphur (TGS) to do finish work at the mine-mill complex. The day of the explosion he had worked at the facility all day. After arriving in town after work, a little after 5:00 p.m., he met up with some friends from work. They had learned about the explosion from the radio. Mike figured he was probably still in the parking lot at the mine site when it happened but was unaware it had happened until he got into town.[51]

Mike drove to Martha's house and took her to the mine site to get more information with her mother and other family members heading there as well. Periodically, a TGS official near the Headframe hollered out information to the gathering crowd to let everyone know what was going on and what was known. When the rescue was in the beginning stages, the Milton family stayed in the lab building with a few other families throughout the night, waiting for word from the mine as company officials gave periodic updates.[52] When the rumors spread of miners found alive at the bottom of the shaft and subsequently brought to the surface, no names were released. Families were instead instructed to go to the hospital where hospital officials would announce the survivors' names.

Already at the emergency entrance of the hospital was Dorothy LeBlanc and Alice Barber. Violet June, Opal Davidson and Lynn

Schear[53] and other family members gathered nearby. Violet June, the wife of Bob June, was red-eyed from worry and lack of sleep. She said she had been comforted by neighbors who had been with her all night.[54]

"This is an awful wait," Violet told one reporter. "I can't do anything but sit here and hope. I can't even talk."[55] Bob June worked for a motor car company in Scott City, Kansas before taking the job at the mine last year. The Junes had six children,[56] five still at home, ranging in age from sixteen years old to eighteen months. Their oldest daughter, Julie Bennett, who was married, was in Kansas waiting with other family members there on word of Bob's fate. Violet had gone to the hospital when news came of survivors. She had last seen her husband the day before on her way home from the diner where she worked as a waitress, when she passed Bob and Lamar Rushton headed to work on the afternoon shift.[57]

Opal Davidson, the wife of Lawrence 'Dave' Davidson, had spent the night at home by her telephone.[58]

"It only rang once," she said. "An officer told me my husband was one of the men in the mine."[59] She first learned of the explosion when her sixteen-year-old daughter, Jean, heard about it while out with friends and rushed home to tell her mother. The news broadcasts told everyone not to go to the mine site except those needed for the rescue operation, so Opal stayed home by her phone and the radio.[60]

Lynn Schear had moved to Moab three months ago from Dove Creek, Colorado with her husband, Keith, and their eighteen-month-old son, Garry Lee.[61] Two of Keith's older brothers were already working at the new potash mine when he too was hired. The month before, two other men, along with Keith and his brother, Johnnie, had sustained injuries in a mining accident. Keith had just gone back to work at the mine while his brother was still recuperating in the hospital; his injuries had been more severe than the other men.

Tuesday morning, Keith visited his brother at the hospital just before going to work on the afternoon shift. Later that afternoon,

Carolyn Schear, Johnnie's wife, was at the hospital visiting Johnnie when they heard some commotion in the hallway. Carolyn investigated and learned of the mine explosion, but understood it happened on the day shift. She headed home to tell Lynn, Keith's wife, who was babysitting for her while she was at the hospital. Carolyn and Lynn went to a friend's house who also worked at the mine to see if they could get more information. They discovered that the explosion had not occurred on the day shift, but on the afternoon shift—the shift Keith was working. After being informed of the disaster, some of the other Schear family members, still living in Dove Creek, came to Moab throughout the evening and the early morning and were now waiting at Carolyn's home or the hospital for word of Keith.[62]

The first ambulance, then the second one, rolled up and came to a stop by the emergency room entrance. Everyone strained for a look and any hopeful sign.[63] They huddled in a tight little knot, all on tip-toe, straining for a peek at the first survivor. Out rolled a stretcher from the first of two large black ambulances[64] (which were converted hearses)[65] used to carry the two survivors. A man wearing a hard hat helped to lift the stretcher onto the ground and, with the aides, wheeled it toward the entrance. As it eased by, necks craned and stretched to catch a peek of the face of the man on the stretcher. There seemed to be no woman present there to welcome the survivor. Every eye was fastened on the large man with the reddish complexion laying on the stretcher. There was a tense silence. No one seemed to recognize him. Then someone called out, "That's McKinney!"[66]

"I need something for my eyes and a drink of water," McKinney said as they wheeled him into the hospital.[67]

The second stretcher was fast on the wheels of the first. It was about to enter the emergency room door when Hanna abruptly rose up when he caught sight of Violet June, one of the wives standing near the door and shouted at her.[68]

"Your husband is all right. He's okay! He's okay! I was with him," Hanna said referring to Bob June, who was still in the mine. Violet collapsed backward in a state of semi-shock, then burst into tears, "Oh my, he's all right?" she said to those around her, not able to believe it was true.[69]

The word was there were nine survivors at the bottom of the mine. So, the crowd at the hospital waited for the next scream of another ambulance siren,[70] but it never came. After a while, the crowd eventually learned there were only two survivors pulled from the mine as the remainder of family members still waiting, slowly dispersed.

By 12:15 p.m.,[71] Hanna and McKinney were laying on gurneys in the emergency room as nurses scurried about and doctors examined them. It was clear that both were exhausted, but relieved they were finally out of that hell hole.

Hanna had problems with his lungs, and there was some damage done to his eyes. The gases in the mine and the salt and pebbles kicked up from the high-pressure air line had taken its toll.[72]

Meanwhile, the mother of Paul McKinney arrived from Colorado and went straight to the hospital to see if there was any news of her son. They told her he was one of the two survivors just brought to the hospital. She broke down weeping, relieved and grateful he was alive.[73]

"Oh, thank God, he's here!" McKinney's mother said through the tears of joy.

"He's not badly hurt," she was told by the nurse.

"We've prayed all night and on our way from Colorado that he would be all right," she sobbed as nurses took her to her son's side.[74]

"Thank God! Thank God!" she softly repeated as she stood over her son lying in bed. "I prayed all the time."[75]

After greeting his mother, McKinney's thoughts turned to his wife, Mollie.

"I want to talk to my wife," he said.

"She'll be here right away," promised his mother as the nurse brought water and some eye compresses.

As McKinney's mother leaned over her son trying to comfort him, Hanna lay on a gurney nearby. Brazen, photographers took photos of both men with gauze squares over their eyes as reporters took down every word they could hear.

After the doctor had finished examinations, nurses took both men to different hospital rooms where they could get cleaned up and be reunited with their families.

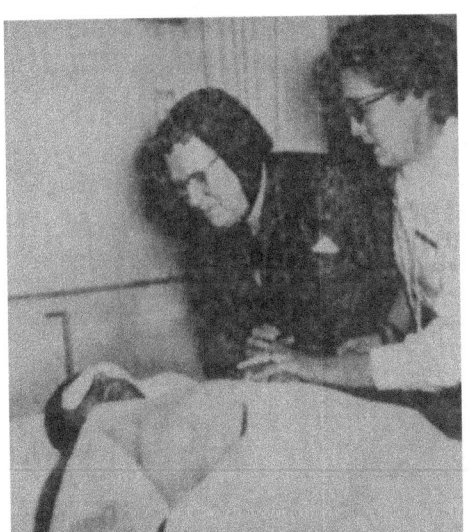 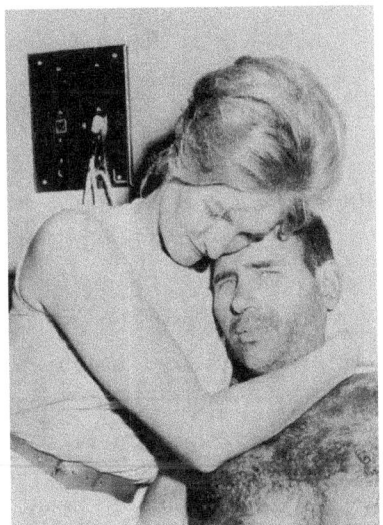

1. As Paul McKinney lies on a hospital gurney, his mother, Mrs. Glen Jacobs, is brought to his side by an attending nurse. (*Deseret News*) 2, Weary from his ordeal, Blake Hanna is reunited with his wife, Myrna.

Weary and weak, Hanna was sitting upright in his hospital bed when Myrna first came through the door. Weeping, she rushed to his side and hugged him around his neck while flashbulbs went off. Lowering his head against his wife, Hanna was blinking from the bright flashes. Several reporters and photographers were already in his room. What should have been a private, tender moment when reunited with his wife, was not. After such a harrowing, life-and-death experience, it was hijacked by the press and was, in a very real sense, very awkward.[76]

The bearded, balding survivor,[77] still grimy and bare from the waist up, seemed near collapse while his weeping wife embraced him.

Reporters asked Myrna how she felt. Shyly, she confessed she was relieved.

"I felt sure he'd be all right. I knew if there were survivors, Blake would be among them. I just had a feeling deep inside," she softly said.

Asked how he felt, Hanna slowly replied with one word: "Hungry!"[78]

A nurse immediately brought a large meal.[79]

"Man, I'm hungry," he exclaimed as he wearily looked at the food set down in front of him.

Myrna sensed her husband needed some privacy and told the press it was time to leave and to let him rest. Hanna's younger brother Wayne brought Myrna from the mine site and was standing near the door. He immediately backed Myrna's request and ushered the throng of reporters out.[80]

Shuffling out, one reporter asked Myrna about the children. She said she kept the news from them.

"I didn't think it would do any good to tell," she said. "Maybe our seven-year-old had an idea about it. But now, I'll go home and tell them everything."[81]

The door closed as Myrna walked back towards the bed and her exhausted husband. Blake had been through a horrible ordeal, and now his prayer was that it wouldn't be long before the other five men would be brought to the surface and join him and McKinney at the hospital. Myrna sensed her husband didn't want to talk about his traumatic experiences, at least not yet. Feeling it wasn't her place to ask, she was confident he would open up when he was ready. Right now, he needed to eat something and get the grime cleaned off.[82]

Hanna's other family members arrived at the hospital and were waiting in the lobby to see him. His mother, Helen Hanna, sobbed, "I've been praying he would be all right, and now he is."[83] When word first came that he was one of the survivors, Helen was overjoyed. She wanted to spread the good news by calling other family members,[84] but she became so frustrated she couldn't remember how to operate the pay telephone. The waiting and stress had taken its toll on everyone.

Weary, McKinney was finally laying in a hospital bed where the air was clean and comfortable. He seemed to be doing well aside from his tender eyes and the third-degree acid burns on his backside from battery acid. He was doing much better after nurses washed his eyes and the burn was cleaned and bandaged.

McKinney was happily reunited with the rest of his family. His wife, Mollie, soon arrived with her sister, who came from Grants, New Mexico to be with her. His two brothers[85] also stood nearby.

Mollie, expecting their first child soon, was kept home after the explosion, as family members tried to shield her from as much stress as possible as they waited for any news throughout the night.[86] It turned out to be a good day for Mollie after a terrible night of anxiety.[87] Quiet, Mollie did say she prayed Paul would be okay. The happy, dark-eyed, expectant mother sat next to her husband who was resting in bed. The other family members gathered around happily smiling, as they talked in low voices.[88]

After nineteen hours trapped underground,[89] both men felt joy at seeing their loved ones. The realization had barely set in. They were now finally safe.[90] Throughout the rest of the afternoon, only family members were allowed into the men's rooms. They were exhausted and needed to rest.

Even while both men were resting quietly, reporters and photographers boldly took every opportunity, dodging hospital personnel, to stroll into Hanna's or McKinney's rooms to ask questions or take photos. They seemed to linger everywhere waiting to talk with the two survivors and get their survival story. They wanted to know everything. But for now, as the press lurked around waiting, they were held at bay.

Examined and treated by doctors, by 1:00 p.m. mst, Hanna and McKinney, were resting comfortably in their hospital beds. They were finally reunited with family members who huddled around their beds. Freed from the horrible conditions they endured while held deep in the mine, they were thankful they were alive. The rescue operation at the mine site started immediate efforts to get to the five miners reported to be alive by Hanna and McKinney.

At the same time that Hanna and McKinney were resting in their hospital beds in Moab, several thousand miles away, near Sheppton, Pennsylvania (at 3:00 p.m., EST), at the other mine rescue operation, the two coal miners rescued the day before were recuperating in their hospital rooms. Both men were beginning to recount the extreme trials and anguish they endured while imprisoned. At the Sheppton mine site, rescue workers continued the search for the third miner still missing.[91]

In Washington D.C., it was also 3:00 p.m., EST. At the "March on Washington," Dr. Martin Luther King, Jr., had just ended his seventeen-minute long speech. The concluding speaker for the day, he followed other prominent Civil Rights Leaders. His notable and stirring speech would later be famously known as the "I Have a Dream" speech.[92]

This monumental event began earlier in the day where more than 250,000 people from across the nation descended on Washington D.C. for a peaceful march ending at the steps of the Lincoln Memorial. While the massive crowds gathered, musical numbers were performed, then were followed by speeches. Throughout the day, this event dominated television and radio coverage across the nation.

These three stories unfolded onto the front pages of the nation's newspapers. Nationwide coverage detailed the Cane Creek explosion and the continuing Sheppton rescue operation, as well as the "March on Washington."

Of these three simultaneous stories, "The March on Washington" event would become memorialized in history. More than 500 reporters applied for credentials to cover the story—far more than any coverage of an inauguration.[93] The Sheppton mine rescue was heavily covered both nationally and internationally for several weeks and would also become another big story of the year. Although there were far fewer reporters covering the Cane Creek Mine explosion in Moab, Utah, nonetheless, it was still front page news right up there with the other two big events.

At the mine site, after Hanna and McKinney were brought to the surface, another rescue team immediately boarded a bucket and started down the shaft to bring up the other men reported earlier to be at the bottom.[94] They were quickly brought back up when officials discovered there were no other survivors at the bottom. Instead, the other survivors reported being alive were behind a barricade over a half-mile away (at the end of the longest drift). And there were only five more survivors, not seven, as previously reported.

Not long after the first two survivors were settled into the hospital, mine officials visited them. They needed more information from them that might help the rescuers.[95] There was still a lot of confusion so Hanna and McKinney, now in separate rooms, told them everything they could, recounting all the events from the time of the explosion, to the smoke they were caught in, to the barricades they built.

They told about the three men who wouldn't come to the barricade, and who, by the next morning, when checked on, were dead. So they passed by them as they headed towards the shaft station.

They told about repairing the compressed air line, working on it for hours, but lacking about eighteen inches. They let the rescuers know that someone needed to connect the two ends so the air would go into the barricade[96] and get to the other trapped miners. They shared everything they could to help the rescuers get to the other five men.

"The others have water," Hanna said. "I'm pretty sure they can hold out for twenty-four hours."[97]

But nobody really knew.

School started for the year at the beginning of the week, and on Tuesday, the big talk in sixth grade, at the Helen M. Knight Elementary School in Moab, was the dramatic rescue of the two men at Sheppton, Pennsylvania—a story to warm the hearts of every miner's son.[98]

Talking with a reporter, eleven-year-old Larry Rauzi said everybody in class was talking about the rescue in Sheppton because the sixth grade has a lot of boys whose fathers[99] go down in the local mines to work. Today, he said, they talked about another mining drama, one that broke the hearts of some of his pals, because their fathers were some of the miners trapped in the potash mine.

"Harry Milton's dad is down there, and Mr. Roy and Chucky Byrge's dad and a lot of other guys. Byrges have got six kids. My mother is over at their house now trying to keep her calm."[100]

"A lot of my friends' dads are miners," Larry added. It was 1:00 a.m. last night when he said a lot of his friends in the neighborhood were still up. Everyone waited for news, but there was very little as people on the streets of this mining town exchanged bits of information and scraps of rumors.[101]

Disaster at Cane Creek

Virginia Patton told of how several students in her high school class were absent from school today, and she knew her friends' fathers were in the mine.[102]

The five June children stayed home from school. Sixteen-year-old Patricia June, the oldest daughter of Bob June, was at a friend's house babysitting at the time she heard news of the explosion and rushed home. When morning came, she was too upset to go to school. At one point during the day, she tried to make a call, but when she picked up the telephone, she heard men talking on the party line about the explosion. Then one of them said, "Careful what you say, little ears are listening." It was distressing to hear them talking about the explosion,[103] not knowing the fate of her father or if she would ever see him again.

Sixteen-year-old Kirt Johnson, the son of Clell Johnson, went to the mine site to wait while the rest of his family stayed at home. A quiet young man, he sat and watched as rescuers worked and he waited for any news about his father. He knew many of the men on the Carbon County mine rescue teams. His aunt, Myrl, his father's older sister, and her daughter were waiting nearby for news as well. Her daughter, Margo, was married to one of the missing miners, 'Myrley' Christensen.

Seventeen-year-old David Kassler had been at the mine site with his girlfriend. Sixteen-year-old Martha Milton was there with her boyfriend and family. All were waiting to hear any news about their fathers.

Extremely anxious when family, nurses, reporters—anyone—came into his room, Hanna would repeatedly ask, "Have they got to them yet, have they got to them yet?" Both men were concerned with the other men still in the mine and wanted to know as soon as rescue teams were able to get to them.[104]

From their hospital beds in different rooms, Hanna and McKinney began to open up and talk a little about their experience with reporters. They told how they had survived an explosion in the deep potash mine and tried to save others.[105] Throughout the rest of the afternoon and into the early evening, both men would share their story.

Both had eyes that constantly smarted, a reminder of deadly gases present in the mine. And both were grateful for the coolness of the hospital beds after enduring the 130-degree heat of the mine.[106]

McKinney was a sight from burns around his eyes,[107] but seemed in good condition as he rested in his hospital bed. A reporter came into his room asking to do a short story. McKinney, mostly a quiet person, spoke a bit but didn't go into much detail. He felt the reporter was asking some really dumb questions,[108] and believed they would never get it right anyway.

"There are some others down there. I don't know how many...," McKinney said, hesitant to share details. He told them how they quickly built barricades to block off the smoke. Haggard, McKinney[109] just wanted to be left alone to get some rest. The reporter soon left realizing he wasn't getting much information.

Hanna, the more voluble of the two,[110] was agreeable to speaking with a few reporters who filtered in, several together, others alone, throughout the afternoon. He told the basics of their ordeal, sometimes adding a little more than before and answering specific inquiries that brought out more detail.

Hanna said how he headed a crew working in one of the underground drifts.[111] He and two other men[112] were putting in some metal vent line (a routine part of their work),[113] not far from the end of the East Drift. Hanna said he heard a dynamite blast in a shorter drift, and then about a half-hour later, he heard a terrible explosion rock the mine workings. "The concussion from the blast knocked us to the ground," he said. "It happened about 4:40 p.m. It knocked me down. There was a lot of smoke and dust getting in my eyes.[114] "I knew we'd had an explosion somewhere, but I didn't know where it was.[115] I'm sure it was a methane gas explosion," he said.[116]

After the men gathered, they started toward the mine shaft where hoists had lowered them earlier for their shift. Halfway along the drift, they hit heavy smoke, then retreated.[117] Some of the smoke poured in behind them. Hanna told the men to flee to the end of the drift.[118] They fell back. "I got my crew and started building bulkheads to curtain off smoke," he said. "We made barricades by tearing nylon vent bags in half," Hanna said. He told how three miners, however, stayed toward the front of the drift and Hanna left to get them. In vain he said he tried to get them to come back with him. "I went back three times to try to persuade the others to come with me and damn near didn't make it back the last time."[119]

"McKinney and I didn't even try to get out for the first twelve hours or so. There were five other guys around us. They're a great crew," he said. Pausing, he then added, "I'm sure they'll get out okay."[120]

"We waited behind the barricades until 7:30 a.m. Finally, I figured we could try to get out. I asked who wanted to go with me. Paul said he would, and we headed out." The reporters soon found out that Hanna's survival story wasn't entirely one of happiness.[121] On the way, they passed the bodies of three dead companions.[122] "From there a lot of wreckage was in the way, and there was still a lot of smoke. We had my flame safety lamp, and it saved our bacon."[123]

They groped forward through the drift. "On the way, we found the broken air line and attempted to repair it, crawling through the debris to find couplings." They were unable to connect the two ends of the pipes but felt the blast of air coming from one end towards the other could possibly reach the other men left behind.[124]

"I think we saved those five guys. I'm pretty sure they are getting air. They've also got water, and I'm pretty sure those guys should be all right,"[125] he said. "I'm pretty sure the explosion came from the west-side drift."[126]

He tried to explain how it was a desperate struggle and how the air pressure kept blowing little rocks into their faces and eyes.

"We lacked about a foot getting a good connection," Mr. Hanna said, "I lay down next to the line for a while trying to get air through it. I'm hopeful we did get air to the others."[127]

"We were near the main shaft, and that's when I saw this lift bucket. It was going back up, but I knew then we'd get out—that they'd come back. I have been mining eleven years—since I was sixteen. I knew they'd be back. It got kinda depressing, waiting. Then I started to bang on a pipe a couple of times. Then the bucket came down. I sure felt relieved. But I sure wanted to get the hell out of there."[128]

"Then when I got into the bucket for the ride to the top, I wanted to get out of that mine. I wanted to get out and walk on my own, too. I didn't want anybody helping me. We kept pushing ourselves. And I'm sure those other five guys are going to make it. That air should be okay. McKinney sure wanted to get out. His wife's about seven months pregnant—it'll be their first baby. I tell you, boy, getting out of that mine was like Christmas when I was a little kid."[129]

Prior to this, some were saying there were five men, others seven. Hanna confirmed it was five. He was brought to a hospital in relatively good condition, except for minor shock and some burns about the eyes.[130]

Undaunted, rescuers were hard at work and now even more determined to get into the mine to the survivors reported to be behind a barricade. The prevailing thought was that if Hanna and McKinney could make their way to the shaft station through all the smoke and gases, rescue teams could do the same to get to the barricade.

Before voice contact was first made, just before noon with both survivors, the hope of finding anyone alive had already dwindled among many involved with the rescue operation. So everyone was astonished when rescuers heard banging and then later, heard Hanna and McKinney's calls for help.[131]

Teams were also buoyed up by the dramatic rescue the day before in Sheppton, Pennsylvania of the two coal miners trapped for fourteen days. Both events further sharpened each rescuer's determination and resolve.[132] Mining has numerous examples of survivors beating the odds when others have given up hope.

Rescue officials brought back more accurate and detailed information after talking with the two survivors at the hospital. At the Command Center, officials had a planning meeting to determine what their next course of action would be since the latest circumstances changed everything. After pouring over maps, making calculations and discussing different scenarios, they finally decided there would be a change in their original plan. Instead of going by the book and first establishing a fresh air base at the bottom of the shaft, they would instead have rescue teams make a run for the barricade[133] and get to the five men reported to be alive as soon as they could.

Before Hanna and McKinney dramatically made their appearance, teams were busy working in the shaft to clear debris and replace damaged sections of vent tubing to establish the fresh air base. Now, teams would no longer work on the vent line, but they would need to clear the bucket lanes of any debris so that teams could get into and out of the mine safety. Teams had still not gotten down into the mine. The closest they had come was twenty feet above the shaft station when Hanna and McKinney were brought up.

Conditions in the shaft and mine had not changed. They were still getting readings of extremely high temperatures and deadly gases lurking, so teams still had to wear their rescue gear. That meant they were still limited in time by the amount of oxygen in their apparatus. But everyone felt confident that they could cover the distance to the barricade and back out and still keep a half-hour reserve of air. This limit in oxygen is what had made the rescue operation so painfully slow.

There was also nothing that could be done to stop the flow of water pouring down the shaft; with the river so close, there was an endless torrent. Other than getting rescuers soaking wet, and making it miserable and difficult to see, the water seemed to pose no other serious problems.[134]

With two men already out, teams wanted to rescue the others, while hopes and momentum were still high.[135] They would go as fast as they could and as far as they could with oxygen tanks.[136]

The desert sun beat down on the mine site as afternoon temperatures soared and determined rescuers and workers on the surface prepared to put the new plan into action. They were determined to get to the five survivors—known to be alive in the barricade before the men ran out of good air or water.[137] The fate of the other missing miners was still unknown, and mine officials were not saying much. There were unofficial reports and rumors of three men who were dead that Hanna and McKinney had seen, but not much else was known.

Chapter 14

Rumor Mill and Erroneous Reports

Reporters at the mine site made repeated requests to mine officials to interview the two rescuers, who had rescued Hanna and McKinney. They were eager for more details of the dramatic rescue, so at 3:00 p.m. a news conference was held at the main office building. Mine officials brought the two rescuers Frank Markosek, and Henry Laviolette, up to the administrative office so reporters could get their story. The two somewhat reluctant rescuers sat in chairs next to each other while reporters asked about the rescue.

Fifty-year-old Frank Markosek was from Sunnyside, Utah and worked at the Kaiser Steel Mine as a Superintendent and was a Team Captain of one of their mine rescue teams. A quiet, modest man he was credited by fellow workmen for his heroism in saving seven lives after an explosion at Utah Fuel Company's coal mine near Sunnyside, Utah, on May 9, 1945. Markosek, thirty-three-years-old[1] at the time, was a foreman and that day he was working near the entry of the mine at the time of the explosion. Without thinking about his safety, he ran to the blast area and found seven men scattered along the way. They were still alive but lying face down and unconscious in the powdered coal dust. He turned each of them over, saving them from certain suffocation. Twelve hours after the blast killed twenty-three miners, he was still in the mine assisting rescue squads. A year later, Markosek received the top award[2] from the Joseph A. Holmes Safety Association, honoring his bravery with a Bronze medal and diploma. (It is given each year to those who save one or more persons in the mining industry.)

The other rescuer, wearing a dark shaft hard hat and speaking with a distinctive French Canadian accent, was forty-two-year-old Henry Laviolette. A tall, brawny man, he was known by those who worked with him as 'Big Henry.' Laviolette had moved to Utah with Harrison International[3] last September, his wife and eight children having just recently joined him, coming from Regina, Saskatchewan, Canada. Laviolette had a second-grade education and already had over fifteen years' of mining experience when he came to Utah.[4]

On Tuesday, he was off shift at the time of the explosion, and he was called to assist with rescue work. Laviolette and his team were working in the shaft clearing debris, when they heard banging on the pipes. After checking it out, they soon discovered men at the bottom, but couldn't get to them. The lane that the bucket was in had a pipe and wire cables blocking the way. When they surfaced, Frank Markosek joined Laviolette as they grabbed items they might need for the survivors and jumped into the other bucket.

The rescuers explained to the throng of reporters how they heard the two men first, then saw them. They were standing about thirty feet from the end of the downward slanting East Drift which branches off from the bottom of the mine shaft.[5]

Disaster at Cane Creek

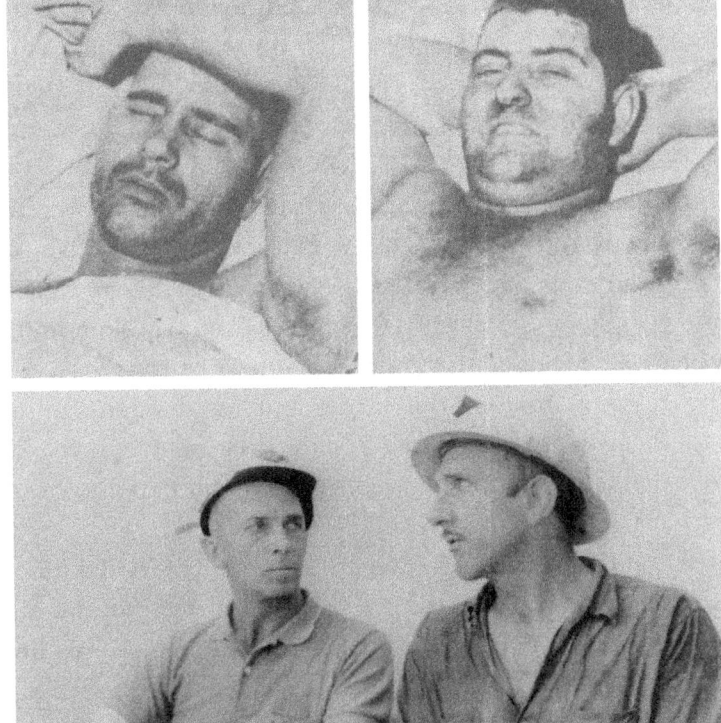

1. Survivor, Blake Hanna rest after his long ordeal. (*Daily Sentinel*) 2. Paul McKinney chats with a reporter. (*Daily Sentinel*) 3. The two miner rescuers, Frank Markosek (left) and Henry Laviolette (right), who brought Blake Hanna and Paul McKinney out of the mine, sit next to each other as they answer reporters' questions. (*Times-Independent*)

"One was crying and very anxious," Laviolette said, "the other shaking."[6]

After climbing the guide rope, Markosek and Laviolette lifted Hanna over the side of the bucket with his arms.[7] Weak from the

245

ordeal, the rescuers said they threw a chain ladder[8] over the side for McKinney, who struggled as he climbed to the top and was pulled into the bucket.

Markosek said Hanna's first words after the men got into the bucket were, "Let's get the hell out of here."[9]

Both men stated that they were "all right" but were suffering from burns around the eyes and McKinney had acid burns on his side. Mine officials added that McKinney's acid burns came from the battery of his miners' lamp which had probably been broken by the explosion. He added that only McKinney's battery was damaged.

The rescuers told of the terrible moment when the bucket stopped[10] near the bottom of the shaft as they waited. Laviolette said he took small comfort in his safety lamp. It continued to burn, evidence that the air had not reached the danger level.[11] They found out later that the bucket stalled when the power shorted. Once workers on the surface restored the power, they hoisted it to the surface.

According to officials, Hanna and McKinney not only brought out the word of others still alive, but also brought out news about the air line they worked on to repair. It was because of their reports that everyone learned there was apparently no serious caving[12] where they had been in the mine.

———

In the excitement and confusion, the first report that there were miners alive multiplied and the word quickly spread that "nine men were yelling for help at the bottom." People soon discovered that only two survivors had been brought out of the mine; five others were behind a barricade still at the bottom of the mine. And the first erroneous report of nine survivors needed to be scaled down to seven survivors.[13]

The rumor of nine survivors gained currency when a short time later it was offered as fact by the official mine spokesman,[14] June Crawford.

This mistaken news of nine men alive at the bottom of the mine was even rushed to press, as newsmen clamored to be the first to get their sensational stories out and the AP and UPI picked it up as well. Many major headlines read, *"Mine Blast Traps 25; Nine Alive, 3 Rescued;"*[15] *"Nine Out of 25 Survive Deep Mine Blast;"*[16] *"Nine Found Alive In Utah Potash Mine;"*[17] or even, *"3 Miners Rescued; Others Are Alive."*[18]

The erroneous numbers made its way not only into print, but also into the town grapevine, and spread to the hospital. The rumors mushroomed and spread like wildfire from word of mouth and were printed in newspapers across the nation before people began to realize the real facts.

Officials started to play it safe after rumors ran amuck. They began to give more vague information—"there are an undetermined number of survivors. We can't say for certain how many."[19]

Hour after endless hour, the men behind the barricade heard sounds up the drift only to realize is was pebbles dropping on the large metal vent line. When help didn't come, they soon forgot about the noises. Often they dozed, only to awaken to take a drink of water. And as usual, they talked little.[20]

As the five remaining men behind the barricade talked less and less and dozed more and more, they sweat continually in the smothering heat. After Hanna and McKinney had left, throughout the day the men listened for footsteps of them returning. They also listened for them to rap on the pipe for help.[21] Finally, the realization sunk in. Hanna and McKinney would probably not return. They either made it or didn't make it.

Hanna could be headstrong and determined and was known as a scrapper, so hopefully, they made it through. 'C.C.' remembered how one day while they were still sinking the shaft, Hanna got into a fight with one of the other men and when they went topside for lunch, both men duked it out in a fistfight behind the Headframe. When lunch time was over, they both jumped into the bucket and went back down to work.[22]

Sometime during the late morning, the men thought there was a small amount of air coming through the compressed air line, but not much. Maybe it was a sign rescue teams were coming. But they couldn't be sure.[23]

There wasn't much air, and the water was horrible. Each would gulp quickly to avoid taking the sand down with the liquid. After the bucket had sat a while, the water cleared a bit on top. But it was hotter on top than the dirty water in the bottom of the bucket, and they waited until it was pretty thick before dumping it for a refill.[24]

At one point, the men began to fear their water supply was running out, so they drank less. After a time, it seemed to taste a little better to some of them. The most difficult part was that time went by so slowly. And still, there were no signs of rescuers. Several times 'Blackie' had to persuade a couple of the men not to leave the barricade whenever the subject came up.[25] They just couldn't take it much longer.

The press created difficulties and concerns when they first started arriving at the mine site not long after the explosion. It kept getting worse as more came the next morning. It was total madness compared to the night. At the company's main administrative office building, reporters would slip around through the offices and pick up a phone and start placing their outgoing calls to do a radio interview that broadcast live. Or they would call to get their story out to their editors or use the line to send telephotos they had taken. Down by the mine, the company personnel there also had a lot of problems with the reporters doing the same things, tying up their offices and phones in the middle of a serious rescue operation.[26]

With only four outside phone lines at the mine-mill complex, Pinkerton tried to get a handle on the situation during the night when he began to monitor calls going through the switchboard. Using a headphone, he could tell if somebody had picked up a phone and in which building it originated. He would listen to the call, and if he discovered it was someone making a call for a newspaper report, he would cut in on the line. It was awkward and difficult at first, but Pinkerton would say, "I'm sorry I can't let you continue to use this line. We need it for emergency purposes." And he'd take the line away from them and thus, gained some measure of control. It was a touchy place for him to be, but it was necessary.[27]

Somewhat sympathetic, the company also felt the press needed some lines to get their stories out and gave them several phone lines to use. They would have liked to have had twenty-five lines. Still, a few reporters persisted in going where they were not supposed to be, and some of their behavior bordered on rude. They shoved microphones at family members who were already under extreme stress at the thought of losing a loved one. They were even brazen enough to stick microphones into the faces of rescue workers who were trying to keep their heads about the dangerous work they were performing.[28] Still other reporters gathering information would quote those not officially in charge, who didn't have all the facts. It resulted in misinformation going to print. They would shout, yell questions, and interrupt. They could be very obnoxious while putting people on the defensive who didn't know how to deal with the press.[29]

The metropolitan press and city reporters were very competitive and could be terribly ruthless. The reporters for the daily newspapers had deadlines to make to get their stories out, while radio and television sometimes had hourly deadlines. TV reporters would even rush film to the airport to get their stories back to their studios for

249

news broadcasts. Some in the press even accused the company of hiding things, especially since they hadn't released the official list of men trapped in the mine. What they didn't know was that Texas Gulf Sulphur (TGS) was having a hard time getting the list from Harrison International's people. It didn't help that when reporters repeatedly asked TGS for the list of the missing miners, they were often told, "I can't tell you that." The reporters were deducting from answers like that that the company was hiding something and was being evasive.[30] Instead, the company should have simply said, "We don't know." It was all in the wording.

During the past three years, while covering the new TGS potash mine-mill operation, Sam Taylor, the editor of Moab's newspaper, had become acquainted with many of the people working at TGS. Some were in his bowling league, some were members of other local clubs, and some were simply involved in other community activities. A couple of the TGS personnel had called Sam on the phone early in the morning at the newspaper office, frustrated over problems they were having with the press. They complained of reporters getting wrong information from different employees and misrepresenting the company. Not trained in public relations, but trying to answer questions, Sam tried to advise them on how to handle the situation a bit better.[31]

He told them to have an official spokesman and to put a muzzle on the other company personnel to keep them from talking to reporters and to keep them from making statements such as, "I've been instructed not to say anything." Comments like this made it sound like the company was hiding something when, in reality, many of the employees didn't always have the right or up-to-minute information, especially since the rescue operation was so fluid and constantly changing.[32]

Sam advised that personnel should direct any questions to the official spokesman. Sam told them they also needed to hold designated press briefings, keep the press in a central location, and tell them what they knew. "If asked something and you don't know, say you don't know. And, he emphasized, don't be evasive. If you don't know, just say so. If grilled by reporters and you don't have an answer to a question, just say, "I'm not trying to hide anything, I'm not evasive, I simply don't know." Most reporters will accept that answer," he told them.[33]

It was the early afternoon by the time Sam finished printing the paper's current weekly issue and had it ready for distribution, so he headed to the mine site. Stopped at a checkpoint at the main entrance of the potash facility, he was waved on through since the deputies recognized him. He mostly came at TGS's request to help them get the situation under control with the press.

The office personnel was busy working on the partial list of names of the missing miners to get out to the media. When Sam looked at it, he recognized some of them from covering their kids who were active in high school sports or other youth activities.[34]

After speaking with Sam that morning, Pinkerton had already put all the press people in a large room located on the west side in the administration office building. June Crawford, Chief Engineer at TGS, took over the handling of the press people and helped with some of the functions as spokesman. He was known to be a tough-minded man when he needed to be, and this was one of those times. Frank Tippie was the official company spokesman and would now conduct all news briefings.[35]

With Sam's help, the company also imposed some press rules that Tippie explained were established for "safety reasons." The press was not happy and dubbed the rules as, "some wall-to-wall security," and turned it into a story that was sent out by the Associated Press (AP). The *Deseret News and Salt Lake Telegram* covered this security calling it "*Strict Rules Set at Mine,*"[36] the article read:

> — Reporters covering the story of the explosion that trapped twenty-five miners near here ran into some wall-to-wall "security" measures early today.

"The ground rules as established by officials at the mine:

1. All reporters must wait in one room of a company building, must not talk to any "unauthorized persons," must not leave the premises without an escort.
2. Reporters who violate these conditions are subject to the loss of "telephone privileges."

The request by reporters to go to the mouth of the shaft was turned down. Instead, they would be taken by car to within 150 feet of it while photographers were permitted to go somewhat closer for long range shots. Everyone was provided with working space and some telephones lines to use. And the only news "officially released" came from Frank Tippie, TGS's General Manager. News reporters felt the tight security measures by officials gave newsmen only limited information."[37]

The company was now doing what the U.S. Bureau of Mines had outlined years earlier in a 1916 circular titled, *"Rescue and Recovery Operations in Mines after Fires and Explosions."* It states, "During the progress of the rescue and recovery work, all entrances should be guarded, and no unauthorized person should be admitted." It goes on to say that, "To protect the many spectators who visit the scene of the disaster and to prevent interference in the work of exploring the mine, the shaft, all entrances should be roped off. Place guards to prevent the curious from gaining admission and crowding the space needed by the rescue workers."[38] These measures and much more were outlined by this early circular and were still standard procedures for rescue operations as the U.S. Bureau of Mines continually built upon their earlier information while updating it as needed throughout the years.

By mid-day, after the officials had implemented their rules, the situation with the press was pretty much under control. Sam stayed near the main administrative office building and never made it down to the area around the Headframe. He didn't even bring a notebook with him to take notes since he didn't have to worry about doing any stories for a while. He had plenty of time before the next issue to write and make sure all his facts were correct.[39]

The Midland Telephone Company, with headquarters at Moab, was also instrumental in helping to improve the situation at the mine site. The day before the explosion was just an ordinary day with the same amount of plant activity and about the same number of calls as any other Tuesday. When the explosion happened, it created a demand for telephone circuits between the mine and the central office in Moab, way beyond any expectations.[40]

Initially, all the circuits to the mine were being used to summon aid in the form of rescue crews and supplies, doctors, ambulances and other emergency equipment. Since it didn't take long after the news of the explosion broke, the area was swarming with reporters from the newspapers, news agencies, and television and radio stations. All had one purpose: Secure the news and get it to the outside world as fast as possible.[41]

Those at the Midland Telephone Company knew there were limited telephone lines at the mine complex and stepped in early in the morning to help remedy the problem as much as was possible. Coordinating with Pinkerton, they made available all of the spare telephone facilities between the mine and Moab to the news people. Also, they placed two mobile radio cars at their disposal. The press would use these mobile units so extensively that the automobile motors got very hot and had to be shut down at intervals to cool. As a further aid to the reporters, several rooms in the telephone company's central office were made available to them in Moab for sending their news of the disaster to the outside world. Even though reporters had to travel into town, they found it was quicker than waiting for one of a few phone lines to become available at the mine site. The Midland Telephone office soon became so busy it was more like the press room of a large paper than a small community phone office.[42]

Because of the demand for up-to-the-minute news on the rescue operation, the telephone company also placed additional operators on the switchboard while their plant men worked around the clock trying to install additional circuits. Mountain States Telephone Company sent mobile radio cars from Salt Lake City on a stand-by basis. Even installation work began on portable television equipment to provide live telecast for one major TV network.[43] A huge effort was put forth by the employees of Moab's independent telephone company[44] who were working extremely hard to meet the needs of the mine, the reporters, the community, and anxious relatives.

On the surface, weary rescuers endured the hot, August heat as they waited their turn to go down into the mine. Some rested on cots or the ground; some read books, others sat or stood in small groups chatting, others played cards. They did anything to stay busy as the afternoon dragged on and the current team worked to make progress in the shaft.

Rescue teams working in the shaft spent the afternoon clearing the debris and making sure the bucket lanes were clear of any obstructions. What little progress they made was painfully slow and laborious as rescue efforts to get to the barricade slowed to a crawl. Besides being plagued by water, gases and communications breakdowns, now they were having mechanical trouble with the bucket hoist.[45] The first indication of problems with the hoist was when they were bringing Hanna and McKinney to the surface, and the power blew.

The sheave wheel creaked as the Hoistman slowly brought the current team to the surface while the backup team prepared their gear for their turn in the shaft. Teams detested the deplorable conditions in the shaft. The incessant deluge raining down was never ending. It was something they had to endure. And now, it was causing numerous short circuits to the hoisting equipment.[46] Rescue workers repeatedly fixed the mechanical problems; and each time, the rescue efforts resumed.

Around 4:00 p.m., four rescuers from the Kaiser Steel Team were lowered down the shaft in the large Nordberg two-ton ore bucket,[47] to continue the exhaustive, backbreaking work. Everyone knew it needed to be done and the sooner the teams were able to get down into the mine, the sooner they would be able to get into the drifts and then to the barricade and the five survivors. Everyone was confident this would happen later that evening.

Once the Kaiser Steel Team had spent the allotted time working in the shaft, they signaled to have the bucket taken up. Nothing happened. Again, water caused mechanical failure to the hoist that lifted the bucket.[48]

For an hour, the team was stalled in the shaft until workers and electricians on the surface could get the hoist running again. Water beat down on the men like a torrential downpour, all the while collecting in the bucket. Higher and higher the bucket filled with water.[49] It filled so high one rescuer, who was short in stature, Howard Kissell,[50] had to be lifted by his teammates by his underarms to keep his head above water so he wouldn't drown.[51]

By the time the team (still wearing their oxygen masks) finally reached the surface, the water had filled the bucket to the rim. Rescue workers helped the team out of the bucket and emptied the water. But this time, workers decided to drill holes in the bucket's bottom. Once again, the next team of rescuers donned their oxygen masks and with their miners' cap-lamps on, were lowered into the shaft.[52]

───◆───

Only twenty-four hours after the explosion,[53] Interior Secretary, Stewart Udall, issued a dispatch from Washington, D.C., blasting the lax safety practices in "some segments of the industry in the Utah mine explosion and the Pennsylvania ordeal." He immediately ordered federal investigations.[54] Underneath the formal message, many knew Udall was essentially saying safety measures were not up to standard in some places and the U.S. Bureau of Mines Inspectors from the Department of Interior should have been in charge.[55] The political posturing and finger pointing had begun.

When the Kennedy Administration hit town, with it came a young, aggressive Secretary of the Interior, Stewart L. Udall, of Arizona. Udall was a classic "New Frontiersman," a term taken from President Kennedy's inaugural address and subsequently used by the press to describe those who served in his administration. The term "New Frontier" was also ascribed to the Kennedy Administration, their aspirations, policies and economic and social programs.[56] What exactly did the term "New Frontier" mean? It was the optimism, progress, science,[57] industry, technology—the progress of the modern world. It was the idea that improvements in the material and cultural status of humanity were available. You fight for it, you can get it. This growing moment of optimism was best expressed in the moon shot at the beginning of January of 1963. Eighty-two percent of the American people even felt that the country was destined to become more powerful in their own situations and more desirable.[58]

Growing up in a small Arizona town founded by his Mormon forebears, Stewart Udall developed a love for the land and a zest for the outdoors. He often went hiking, fishing, camping, and mountain climbing. In many ways, Udall embodied the image of a youthful, athletic, vigorous "New Frontiersman."[59] He was a gunner in World War II, a college basketball player at the University of Arizona, and a self-described "Jack-Mormon," who did not follow his religion's bans on alcohol.

"Initial reports indicate clearly elementary safety precautions would have prevented most of the serious accidents which have occurred this year," Udall said in the dispatch. "In the case of the Utah mine, for example, I am informed the contractors were warned of severe dangers only three weeks ago when methane gas ignited while workmen were drilling rock bolt holes in the drift where yesterday's explosion occurred."[60]

After meeting with President Kennedy, Udall said the President expressed to him his personal concern over such disasters. That afternoon, President Kennedy, busy with events surrounding the "March on Washington," managed to send a congratulatory telegram[61] to the two rescued Sheppton, Pennsylvanian coal miners. Not long after that, Udall had spoken with the President about the mine explosion near Moab. Udall said that President Kennedy told him he believed that a country which has our wealth and scientific resources should be able to perfect safety devices and procedures which would enable us to extract the mineral resources we need without excessive loss of human life.[62] The President was clearly sensitive to the plight of the miners and their families.

In Udall's dispatch, he also said a completed study of coal mine safety practices would be forthcoming. Conducted at President Kennedy's direction,[63] his department would recommend changes to Congress before the end of the week aimed at strengthening coal mine safety laws. He pointed out that two years ago, in response to a recommendation by the Kennedy Administration, Congress authorized a two-year study[64] of safety conditions and practices of nonmetallic mines such as the TGS Mine where the explosion occurred. "They will have the study completed shortly," he said. Adding that "my department will recommend the procedures which will extend the scope and strengthen the enforcement powers of the mine safety division of the U.S. Bureau of Mines."[65] Kennedy also authorized Udall to conduct an intensive review, in other words, an investigation.

"I know you share my concern over these disasters and the deep sympathy," Udall said. "I feel for the families and friends of those who perished. It is imperative we take every necessary step to avoid such accidents in the future," Udall added.

Udall's dispatch did not go over well in Utah. Many felt it was too premature to know if workers were warned of methane gas, since the cause of the explosion had yet to be determined.[66] The dust had not even settled yet from the explosion the night before, and a major mine rescue operation was still ongoing—with the lives of the missing men hanging in the balance.

Udall's criticisms were not lost on Utahns who were well aware of recent fighting that had spanned the last few years between the President's Frontiersman[67] and his proponents against Utah Governor Clyde and his backers. There were heated differences over the terms for the proposed Canyonlands National Park. The vitriol and animosity between the two opposing sides were played out continually in the press as Udall and the Governor became "bitter political enemies."[68]

After flying over those areas "still untouched" in the red rock canyon country of Utah in July of 1961, Udall had set his sights on making this spectacular area into a national park. He was met with opposition over the size and the strict preservation requirements. Those against him, wanted a smaller size and did not want to lock up the State's mineral resources, so they advocated limited commercial use. Back and forth the two sides went, and by the November election of 1962, Canyonlands was the most controversial issue in the State's congressional races. Democratic candidates supported Udall's vision, while Republicans opposed it. Udall was stunned when the Democratic candidates were defeated,[69] giving his opposition the needed power to defend their position.

By December, right after the election, Secretary Udall denied Utah and TGS the titles to the leased acres of land involved in the potash deposits,[70] even though they had already been agreed to as part of "in lieu" lands. These were the State lands which had been set aside by the U.S. government during statehood to support public schools through revenues from land leases instead of using federal tax revenues. At the mine site, construction was well underway when the leases were denied, and the shaft for the new mine had just reached the bottom. A royalty of three percent of the value of the potash produced at TGS was to go into the permanent State school fund. Estimates of revenue, when TGS was in full production in 1964, was for $290,000 a year. Eventually, the royalty would increase to five percent, with the federal government getting ten percent for administration of the leases, on the basis that they were originally federal in character.[71]

By February of 1963, when questioned about the leases by those in Utah, Udall claimed there was a legal question of Utah's acquisition of land on the Cane Creek property. Governor Clyde and others made the request for the federal government to live up to its promises. U.S. Senator Moss from Utah, who was Udall's biggest backer on the proposed Canyonlands National Park, did, however, take the matter to Attorney General Robert Kennedy and President Kennedy to get the matter resolved. Meeting with them at the White House, the Attorney General cited that the law favored Utah in the land swap, according to the Utah Enabling Act of 1894.

Udall granted some parcels of land, about 1,000 acres of the 7,000 applied for, and put a "freeze" on the remaining. After more wrangling by Senator Moss, Udall finally lifted the "freeze" and made the additional transfer of land to Utah.

What Udall's motivations were in the matter were not entirely clear. Some felt it was partisan politics. The State's senior U.S. Senator, Wallace Bennett (Republican), called him out on his shenanigans, claiming he had created an opportunity to "grandstand a political play in which the administration would be adamant against the State, but would eventually yield to its favorite Democratic senator."[72] The rich potash lands in the Cane Creek area twice appeared lost, but were saved for the State mainly by the lone Democratic member of the Utah Congressional delegation, Senator Frank E. Moss.[73] While Senator Moss was supportive of Udall's Canyonlands legislation, he also supported TGS acquiring the needed leases.

For others, especially those in the area of Moab, they believed Udall was using the leases as a way to get even for the election not going his way[74] and against those not supporting his proposal of Canyonlands National Park. The local paper, the *Times-Independent* reported, "One can only think, when looking back over the situation, of the trip Interior Secretary Udall made to Utah before the election. He said in effect, that if Utahns didn't vote the way he thought they should, they might regret it in the future."[75]

Whatever the reason, it created a bigger wedge between those involved in Utah, especially the Governor and the Secretary of the Interior. The land TGS expected to obtain leases on, to develop their potash mine, lay sandwiched between the proposed Canyonlands National Park[76] to the southwest, Dead Horse Point State Park to the west, and Arches National Monument to the northeast. During this period of time, there was also talk of making Arches National Monument into a national park,[77] although it was spoken about more cautiously so as not to "seriously impair" the Canyonlands legislation.[78]

Each side waged a bitter battle over the park's size and use. Udall's original proposed size for the park was whittled down from what he had originally intended.[79] For the "scenic masterpiece," he wanted a single-purpose national park. Governor Clyde and his side wanted less land for the park so the mineral rich land would not be tied up. His side also wanted a multi-use park for hunting and grazing. In late July 1963, after long, bitter wrangling, the two sides eventually compromised on the size and use. The legislation was proposed, which passed in committee, but wouldn't be voted on until the U.S. Congress reconvened again in 1964.

Now, with Secretary Udall's latest dispatch concerning the explosion, TGS was back in the crosshairs of the U.S. Interior Department. The Secretary's condemnation and disparaging remarks against TGS and the State of Utah seemed to many a continuation of past political fighting. To others, it felt like a way for the federal government to gain more power in the mining industry. For the states that had lax mine safety laws and did little to protect the miners, the intrusion would be a way to legislate laws to create legal consistency. But in Utah, many felt the State already had strict mining laws, and this was just another overreach by the federal government.

The afternoon sun beat down as nineteen-year-old Herve Roy, the son of Rene Roy, walked down towards the giant Headframe. Friends of his parents picked him up at the Grand Junction Airport in Colorado. They drove the two hours to Moab and dropped him off at the mine site. Herve had worked at Cane Creek with his father until two weeks ago when he left to go back home to Canada. When the family first heard about the explosion and that Rene was one of the men trapped, Herve flew back[80] to Moab.

Herve's father, Rene, moved his family to Ontario, Canada, initially to work in an Elliot Lake Mine and later to work at North Bay. In the early 1960's, he went to work for Harrison International sinking a shaft for IMC (also known as International Minerals and Chemical Corporation), a potash mine in Esterhazy, Saskatchewan, Canada. He was part of a handpicked team to start Harrison International's next construction job in Moab, working as a Shift Walker, sinking the shaft, and developing the potash mine for TGS.[81]

Herve had left school and started working with his father at the age of fifteen. He was still working at the Esterhazy project when his father left to begin the new project in Moab. The first of April, the work was finished in Esterhazy and Herve followed his father to Moab, where he was hired to work underground as a Shuttle Car Operator on his father's shift.

Rene's wife, Jessie,[82] and their five other children remained in North Bay, while Rene and Jessie wrote to each other almost every day. Missing his family, Rene arranged for them to spend the summer with him and Herve in Utah. At the end of a fun-filled summer, filled with trips to the Moab community swimming pool, Colorado River parks, and time spent with other miners and their families, Jessie and the children returned to Canada for the school year. Rene also sent Herve back this time to Canada as well.

Herve wasn't happy about it and couldn't understand why his father was sending him home. Jessie and the three younger children were flying home with their mother, and the three oldest would make the journey by car. With Herve at the wheel of their 1961 Pontiac Parisienne, and accompanied by Jim, Helene, and their dog, Tammy, they headed back to Canada.

It was on the 19th of August, Rene had said his final goodbyes to Jessie and his children as he dropped them off at the airport in Grand Junction, Colorado, to travel home. He gave them kisses and the big French hug he was known for, and with his broad smile, he waved goodbye. The plan was to put aside enough money to join his family back in Canada. Until then, he would move back out to the man camp where he would be closer to work.[83]

While Jessie flew home with the three younger children, the three older kids started their long journey. Herve told the other two to stop bawling after they said their goodbyes to their dad. More than halfway home, in Dubuque, Iowa, the car broke down, and the older kids had to wait for parts for several days. The trip home should have taken two to three days, but instead took nearly a week.[84]

When they finally made it to North Bay, they were only there for several days when Jessie got a telephone call from a neighbor, who said she was listening to the radio and heard about the mine explosion in Moab. She wanted to know if Jessie had heard about it and was concerned it was Rene's shift. Jessie hadn't heard a thing, nor had anyone contacted her.[85]

Jessie immediately started calling people and was only able to connect with a family friend back in Moab. He told her the explosion happened on Rene's shift the night before, and they didn't know how bad it was just yet. Jessie was devastated over the news and was having a difficult time getting any information, so she decided to send Herve back to Utah so he could keep her informed about what was going on.[86]

In the early morning hours, Herve flew from North Bay to the Toronto Airport. While waiting for his next flight to Grand Junction, Colorado, news reporters found out his father was one of the trapped men at the Cane Creek Mine explosion and that Herve was on his way back to Moab. Distraught and tired, he told the reporters that he didn't know a whole lot, but they were impertinent and relentlessly kept trying to get more information. Finally, the airline personnel could see Herve didn't want to talk to them so they moved him into a room where the press couldn't hassle him until he could board his flight.[87]

By the time Herve arrived in Grand Junction, family friends had picked him up at the airport, and they were on their way to Moab. News over the radio told of two miners who were rescued from the mine and taken to the hospital, giving hope that others would be found alive.[88]

The Canadians were intensely immersed in the tragedy and wanted any news they could get. Many of Harrison International's people from Canada were very close, since they worked together and moved from job to job together throughout the years. They were an especially close-knit group; some had worked together for years, and their families were also close. Many were even related to each other.

Dropped off at the mine site, Herve stood next to the hoist house across from the Headframe and watched what was going on with the rescue. Once Harrison International's men discovered Herve was there, they extended good wishes for his father and filled Herve in on the rescue operation. He was confused when he saw the men who worked on his father's shift. That was when he learned that his father, Rene, a Shift Walker, had traded that day with Bert Trenfield.[89]

And Trenfield had taken the place of Henry Laviolette for the week; Laviolette was the normal Shift Walker (Shift Foreman) over this crew of men. Herve also discovered his father had bought a new car before he went to work the day before and that it was out in the parking lot.[90]

Reporters seemed to be everywhere and heard that Herve was the son of one of the trapped men. They too wanted to speak with him, but TGS workers wouldn't let them and kept them away. Herve hung around most of the afternoon, waiting to hear any word of his father's fate. It was getting late in the afternoon, and he decided to leave to call his mother, so Mr. Henderson came to pick him up. Hungry and tired, he needed to get a good night's rest. The Harrison International guys assured him they would let him know if anything happened.[91]

It was just after 6:00 p.m.[92] when the next rescue team in the rotation headed down the shaft. They almost reached the bottom when they lost communications[93] again with the workers at the shaft collar and were brought back to the surface. The walkie-talkie radios used earlier with only spotty success had been brought back into service, but now they failed again.

"We had to bring them back up. It's cost us more time,"[94] an official at the collar lamented.

Rescue workers had tried everything to remedy the situation. They had wrapped the walkie-talkies in cellophane and even communications experts from Hill Air Force Base, north of Salt Lake City, were brought in to help. Still, nothing seemed to work because of the water.[95]

The frustrating breakdown in communications stalled further rescue attempts, while officials quickly decided that the best way to overcome the water knocking out the communications was to set up a phone and bell system at the bottom of the mine. As Harrison

International's team were getting ready to set up the communications system, Bud Pilling, another Harrison International's man, was first sent down to Fire Boss the mine. A Fire Boss' job is to test for gases before miners can enter a mine to work.

There was still plenty of hazards lurking down in the mine, deadly carbon monoxide gas contaminating the air and, of course, the crowning concern was an underground "waterfall"[96] in the shaft. But the hazard Pilling was testing for was explosive gases such as the presence of methane at the bottom. He found none and deemed the mine safe for Harrison International's men to rig the communications system. The team strung cables for the phone line and wire-triggered bells[97] between the top and bottom of the mine shaft to install the system. They toiled and spent two hours[98] trying to set up the simple communications lines that used the prearranged Bell Signal "language"[99] commonly used by miners in shaft mines.

As the mechanical failures and communications breakdowns added to their frustrations,[100] rescuers could not even guess when they might reach the five, let alone the other fifteen men.[101] Just over twenty-four hours since the explosion, there was still no voice contact with the five men down in the mine who survived the initial blast. But some of the rescuers didn't seem too alarmed about them.[102]

"We believe the air is probably good where the men are so we aren't too worried about them. We believe they're still behind the barricade they built to keep out the gas which saved their lives," one official said while other rescue workers were beginning to express new fears about their safety.[103]

The company never announced the identity of the five survivors although there were rumors of who they were, and no one speculated on the other fifteen men, but there seemed to be no sign of them either. However, there were some persistent whispers of other men who were dead. Whether it came from Hanna and McKinney or rescue team members, no one knew for sure.

There was some talk among officials and rescuers who believed the barricade probably saved the lives of Hanna, McKinney, and their five companions' lives. They even attributed the safety training and knowledge of building barricades to several of the men who had worked as coal miners.

Once the communications system was ready, it removed one major monkey-wrench.[104] The communications problems were somewhat resolved, and under the circumstances, this was the best they could do. While rescuers are not supposed to break a cardinal rule of mine rescue work by moving away from their source of air without communications, the Bell Signal was devised to tie the rescuers, once they got into the mine, to the surface.[105] The spotty communications in the shaft remained a problem.

Texas Gulf Sulphur's Company President, Claude Stephens, and his wife flew back to New York City where Stephens meet at his office with reporters wanting a statement. Stephens voiced his concerns and gave an update on the current situation back in Moab.

"We are heartened contact has been established with one group, and the first men were brought safely to the surface," he told reporters, assembled at his office.[106] "Our only concern is for the men and their families. Twenty-four of the original crew are employees working for Harrison International, and one man is a Texas Gulf employee," he said. He expressed gratitude, "to our friends and neighbors in the mining industry in Utah and nearby states who came forward so generously to assist in the rescue operation.[107] Everything that can be done by our company and Harrison International is being done and will continue to be done," he said.[108]

When asked about Harrison International, he told how they "hold the contract for sinking the main shaft and for the underground construction work," adding, "Their firm is widely experienced in underground development, and they have sunk more than 500 mine shafts with more than fifty over 3,000 feet deep."[109]

The Utah explosion was not the first tragedy to plague the firm during the year. The company's ocean tanker, the *Marine Sulphur Queen*," was transporting liquid Sulphur in the Gulf of Mexico with a crew of thirty-nine men when it disappeared on February 2, 1963, and the case was still unsolved. Suspicions as to its fate ranged from a rumor that Cubans had seized it as a hostage ship to a theory the ship broke up in heavy seas and sank. There was even a possibility the fumes released from the ship's cargo could have set off an explosion. They found a few pieces of debris off the Florida Keys, life preservers with the firm's name stenciled on them, and a floating piece of lumber with the ship's name.[110] Some surmised that the missing ship was connected to the Bermuda triangle.

Texas Gulf Sulphur was also taking a hit on the New York Stock Exchange. Before the closing bell, the exchange had one of its most vigorous rallies of the year. However, the company was a casualty, losing in heavy trading on bad news of the explosion at its potash mine.[111]

When asked about the mining operations, President Stephens said they "have not yet started mining. The construction of the mine is now in its final building phase, and mining ore was expected to begin in the next few weeks." Stephens also shared how the construction of the new plant has been under way since early 1961, with surface facilities completed.

"The potash deposits in the Cane Creek area are believed to be the largest and richest in the nation," Mr. Stephens said. He explained how the mine was projected to have an annual production rate of 550,000 tons, which was expected to be reached by mid-1964. The company had once hoped to obtain[112] the potash by now and to be in limited production for the next month, which was to go to the farm fertilizer trade. They were hoping to corner the market before two other potash mines in California began production.

Just as the news conference wrapped up, Stephens announced he "will fly to Moab and be there tomorrow"[113] and join Dr. Charles F. Fogarty, Senior Vice President of TGS, who is already at the scene. For a company starting out on such a positive note with so much promise and hope for many, a tragedy of this magnitude was devastating.

Chapter 15

"Canary in the Coal Mine" Moment

The rescuers were impatient. They wanted to get to the barricade and the five men reported alive as fast as they could, but the rescue operation was going painfully slow. Continually their efforts were plagued by gas, water, debris and mechanical troubles.[1] But the rescuers continued undaunted as one problem after another came and was fixed or overcome.

Once Harrison International's men had the phone and bell lines installed in the mine, teams finally had a somewhat reliable means to communicate with the surface. Now, all they needed to do was to get a team into the mine and down the East Drift to the barricade.

By the time dusk fell, a U.S. Steel Team was preparing their rescue gear to make the next descent. They shrugged themselves into their oxygen apparatuses and boarded the bucket. The team of four rescuers dangled inside getting last-minute instructions and making final checks of rescue gear. They were nearly ready to travel down the deep shaft in another effort to get to the five survivors.

Slowly, the bucket started down. This time the men were confident they would be able to reach the barricade.

As the bucket neared the bottom of the shaft, Dell Judd, one of the team members, had difficulties with his oxygen supply and became ill. The rescue team had to turn back and at 8:55 p.m.[2] surfaced. Judd's air pack had completely failed. By the time they hauled him to the surface, he was gasping for air.[3]

The flood-lit scene around the Headframe looked almost unreal as rescuers waited for their turn to travel down the shaft, bathed in cascading water. Nearby three ambulances sat with their rear doors open into the night, silently waiting for the men who might never come. Fifty rescuers waited their turn as they sat on the ground, on benches or on the back-end of open vehicles. Some talked, others stared blankly ahead waiting until they got their call to again go deep into the mine and probe for the victims.[4]

The descent into the shaft, with the water pouring down, was slow and agonizing. One rescuer called it "hell down there,"[5] while other rescuers echoed the same disdain. Talking about the men continuing the search, one official put it this way: "These men are tired as hell, and they're scared as hell."[6] Others looked on as workers helped the next team squirm into their rescue gear and then trudge over to the shaft collar to board the bucket. A Kaiser Steel Team was next to descend the shaft as 'Johnny Smoke' stepped into the bucket with three of his teammates. They were ready to endure another trip down the shaft with a flood of water pouring down on them.

Overcoming frustrating mechanical failures to the hoist and endless communications problems, officials were making yet another attempt to get rescuers into the mine. The team's mission was the same as before: get into the mine and get to the barricade made from treated collapsible vent cloth.

The bucket slowly descended, heading to the bottom. At the shaft station, it appeared the bucket would sit down on top of the long conveyor arm of the feeder-breaker. But to the terror of the men inside, as it landed it started to tip as the hoisting cable kept moving downward scaring the hell out of the men inside. The frightened men hung on, knowing if it went to one side or the other they could be dumped into the sump area below the station to a certain death.

But as the bucket hit the feeder-breaker's conveyor arm, the bucket started to roll to one side. It laid down completely on the arm of the feeder-breaker. Awkwardly, with rain pouring down on them, the men crawled and stepped over the top of each other as they cautiously stepped out onto the feeder-breaker. Carefully watching through the limited vision of their masks, they stayed in the middle of the arm of the 20-ton feeder-breaker, shoved and tightly wedged out over the shaft. The men were mindful that each side dropped off into the sump below. Guardedly, with only the light on their hard hats, they crossed and climbed down onto the shaft station. It was hard to see much in the intermittent areas of smoke, and it was equally terrifying as the team scooted across the small cement ledge to the east side of the shaft station. It was here that several of the rescuers nearly stepped on bodies. There were four on this side of the shaft station. The Map Man made a notation on his map of each of the bodies.

It was the first time a team was able to get down into the mine. Still settling down from the terrifying landing and crossing the ledge, the rescuers took inventory of their surroundings. They noticed there was a very large hook with a ring attached to the bottom of the bucket. It had hit the arm, and that's what caused the bucket to tip over as it laid down on the feeder-breaker. They were still not sure what was holding up this huge piece of equipment from plunging down into the sump; they just knew it was wedged tight. As the water beat and trickled down the shaft, it appeared to be filling up the sump area.

While there was little external evidence on the surface of the carnage caused by the explosion, the inside of the shaft had its share of destruction. But the rescuers now began to see the biggest scale of carnage underground. Around the station, there was utter devastation. It appeared the explosion came from the west side which would explain why the feeder-breaker was shoved out into the shaft from that side. Everything was charred, and death was everywhere.

After taking gas tests and checking their own and each other's breathing apparatuses, the men prepared their gear to start a probe of the mine. With multiple hooks tied into a rope linkline, they each fastened one of its hooks onto a metal ring attached to each of their mine belts. The four rescuers were now linked together in a single file formation and were now ready to explore the mine.[7] (Using a linkline is standard procedure for rescue teams while exploring a mine.)

After communicating with the surface on the phone line installed by Harrison International's men, the Captain gave the signal. Following the chain of command, the Co-Captain repeated the signal, and the men slowly headed single file towards the top of 1 South drift, the top section that made up part of the East Drift. Tools dangling from some of their mine belts clanged as they walked. The team took it slowly as they advanced to keep from overheating, which was always a huge concern while "under oxygen." With high temperatures in the mine, they had to be even more vigilant.

Going a short distance, they took a short rest and took gas tests. The barricade was located ahead, still over a half-mile away. Advancing again, they traveled several hundred feet when they ran into torn up vent tubing. Uncoiled, scattered or stacked up all over the drift, they had to move the vent tubing or crawl over it, which was difficult wearing a rescue apparatus. They continued down the hot, smoky drift, stopping to rest and test for gases as they went. The team encountered deadly levels of carbon monoxide gas[8] throughout the drift, in some areas the concentrations were higher than others.

As the men moved through the thick smoke, their cap-lamps dimly lit the way. They soon came to the three-way junction of 3U.

Here, the team came upon the unsettling scene of "three dead men." One was laying off to the side, and it looked like two had been holding the large vent pipe open to get some air."[9] They thought this must be the three men Hanna and McKinney told officials about, but they weren't sure. The survivor's stories were a bit different and somewhat confusing.

This location was as far as the team went before they were compelled to retreat when some of the men's oxygen supply started to run low.[10] Reluctantly, the men turned back towards the shaft station so they would have enough oxygen to get out of the mine. While on the way, Harry Krebs[11] "passed out" when his oxygen tank and mask malfunctioned temporarily.[12] His team members were able to get the apparatus working again, and Krebs was quickly brought around.[13] Instead of going back over the cement ledge to get to the other side, the men took the No. 1 crosscut. On their way, they passed a couple more bodies and made a note of them.

At the station, the team figured they had traveled just over halfway down the East Drift before they had to turn back. With their oxygen supplies dwindling,[14] they barely had enough to get back to the surface. Disappointed they had to abandon their attempt to reach the barricade, the team felt they hadn't accomplished much as they boarded the bucket. As it ascended, thirty-year-old 'Johnny Smoke' thought to himself, "if they would stop and clean this place up they could get into a drift and explore it quickly; in no time, they could cover the whole mine."

Back on the surface at 9:40 p.m.,[15] the tired, grimy rescuers climbed out of the wet bucket. Officials soon discovered the four-man team had covered a "substantial part" of the mine as they pushed forward to locate the barricade. Unable to reach it, the team instead brought out devastating news. They reported finding eight bodies scattered near the shaft and down the East Drift.[16]

The identities of the men found dead, if known, were not disclosed[17] by officials, and they presumed that the eight included the three dead reported earlier by Hanna and McKinney. It left the fate of fifteen men still unaccounted for;[18] the five in the barricade and the location of the other ten men was still unknown.[19] The team also reported the water level was rising rapidly in the sump area. It had not yet backed up into the drifts, nonetheless, it concerned officials.

Still, the biggest obstacle for rescuers was the oxygen supply. Teams were now able to get into the mine, but they quickly realized they couldn't carry enough oxygen to get down the shaft and still cover the full distance to the barricades.[20] As rescuers struggled toward the barricade, their limited air supply crippled their progress. It was the same limited air problems rescue teams experienced while working in the shaft. This last team was at least able to get down into the mine and make some progress in probing the East Drift, but the news they brought out was disturbing. Eight men were now known to be dead.

Earlier in the evening, around 9:00 p.m., Bob von Storch, the General Superintendent at Columbia-Geneva mines, who was coordinating his team's activities with the Command Center, went looking for Guy Hersh. He had a special assignment for him. He was to go "under oxygen" and take the small length of rubber hose von Storch had with him down into the mine and put a patch on the line that Hanna and McKinney had worked on, but had been unable to complete, lacking nearly eighteen inches to get them connected.[21]

Now that teams were able to get down into the mine, officials wanted to get someone in there quickly to make the patch on the line, hoping the air would get to the barricade for the five survivors reported to be alive. Alex Mondlak, the U.S. Steel's Columbia-Geneva safety man, who was a young trainee, quickly helped Hersh shrug into his rescue gear and then helped him to get the oxygen hoses and everything connected. Mr. von Storch walked back over and told Hersh that if he wasn't feeling right about it, not to go. But

Disaster at Cane Creek

Hersh said he'd be okay. They chose a young kid from Harrison International's men to go down with him. Rescuers never go alone. If they get monoxide built up in their breathing apparatus, they push a lever to blow it out; if something like this happens, they might need someone to help. That's just one reason a rescuer should never go by himself.[22]

The two-man team descended into the shaft just after the previous team surfaced. Once they got near the bottom, about the last ninety feet, the bucket slowed down. Crews had cleared some of the debris and repaired a couple of sections to the large metal vent line, so some air was getting down into the mine. But along this area, the line was still blowing water all over the place from the air pressing out of the damaged and torn sections. Since some air made it down into the mine, the gas near the bottom of the shaft wasn't as concentrated. The bucket came down on the west side and sat on the top of the conveyor arm of the big feeder-breaker blown out into the shaft. This 20-ton piece of machinery with steel track wheels was resting on a three-inch thick bolt sticking out from the shaft and was wedged tight on its bent mount.[23]

The first thing Hersh and the kid tried to figure out was how they were going to get out of the bucket; that's when they found steps on the side. With their face masks limiting their vision, each of the men carefully climbed out of the bucket and down onto the feeder-breaker, then to the ground of the shaft station. The Harrison International kid had a Chemox self-generating oxygen breathing apparatus that was effective at filtering the air he was breathing, but it was only good for about forty-five minutes. It was eerie as each of the men looked around with the lights on their hard hats to get a sense of where they were. Everything was covered with gray dust with a bit of red dust mixed in. The red dust had apparently come back down the shaft from the surface during the time the mine was trying to equalize the air pressure immediately after the explosion. The mine was charred, and everything was torn to pieces.[24]

Over on the other side of the shaft, up under the front end of the feeder-breaker on the east side, they could clearly see a dead body that had been blown there by the blast. It looked like it was about ready to slide the rest of the way over the edge of the shaft, down into the sump but the feet and arms were hung up. The body was out on the edge of the shaft station where water was running and dripping down from above. The water had washed the dust off, and the two rescuers could clearly see the face of the dead miner. His face was burnt and had turned dark, and was puffy especially around the eyes. Other bodies were lying under the dust—all were decomposing. It was a horrible sight. Smoke still shrouded much of the area but had cleared out in some places.[25]

It was very unsettling for the young Harrison International kid. Hersh was able to get him settled down and convinced him to stay put so he could get the air line fixed. Since the previous team had found eight bodies, Hersh decided to leave the kid near the shaft station where Harrison International's crews had set up the phone. The body was under the feeder-breaker, out of the kid's line of sight. Knowing he would be okay, Hersh left the kid and headed towards the East Drift. He was not going far, just around the corner from the shaft station, barely out of view, to make a patch to the air line.[26]

As Hersh came upon the two sections of air line, he found a wrench lying on the ground.[27] It was Hanna's crescent wrench left there earlier. Hanna told others they lacked about eighteen inches, but Hersh saw that it was closer to about a foot, and the ninety pounds of air coming from the one end made it difficult to get the two ends connected.

Hersh was finally able to get the hose connected to one end with a coupling. When he tried to hook up the other end, the line broke the first coupling off. He worked on the line for a while and found that if he let it leak air instead of fastening it tight, the hose would stay connected. After making the patch, Hersh signaled by rapping on the line several times, hoping to get a response back from the five men behind the barricade, but there was no reply.[28]

Making sure the connection would hold, Hersh headed back to the shaft station. It was now around 10:00 p.m., about thirty hours since the explosion, and there was no way to know if any of the air in the compressed air line was making it back to the barricade over a half-mile away. He could only hope it was getting to the men, and they were still alive.

Hersh made it back to where he left the kid, and they both crawled back into the bucket and headed out of the mine. On the way up, Hersh started to feel really sick. After the bucket had surfaced, he ran through the men and out of the Headframe about thirty feet thinking he was going to throw-up. Walking it off, the workers eventually got Hersh's gear off and put him on a gurney. Still feeling pretty sick, the doctor attending to him said he wasn't to go back under oxygen.[29]

Some of the survivors in the barricade were getting the jitters and talked about walking out again. It had been a long thirty-hour wait, and they were discouraged rescuers had not made it to them. While they talked one of the men heard a noise. Coming from the broken air hose, they discovered air was coming through the line.[30]

The hiss of air was the most welcome sound the men had heard since they entered the mine. They had been getting a little "dopey" from the lack of oxygen until the fresh air arrived. The temperature started to go down and spirits soared.[31] It seemed that before they started getting more air through the compressed air line, breathing was getting a bit labored.[32]

The air also meant rescuers were probably on their way. It was a huge morale boost. Being resourceful, together the men improvised personal air hoses.[33] They had enough fittings to connect a water line header securely to the air line, giving each of them a personal air supply.[34]

The water line header was once used to service five machines. The men worked to attach the header to the end of the compressed air line, attaching the five hoses that hooked to it. Each man now had a line of his own and could lie on the ground with fresh air blowing through his hose that he could breathe.[35] By using ingenuity, the air coming through each hose was like a very gentle breeze blowing through a soda straw, but it made a real difference.[36]

The only problem was that the air was saturated with the stench of oil. So 'Blackie' said he preferred to breathe what was in the drift. It wasn't long before he was laying on the ground breathing through his tube like the other four.[37]

At least they were safe for now as the men went back to waiting. The air coming through the line made a world of difference, both in breathing and morale.[38] The heat was exhausting, and each man was extremely hungry.

In the darkness, they longed for life, for light, for freedom from the hot, hellish confines of their dark tomb that held them captive beneath the earth. Their worst fears weighted on their mind as hope continually waned. The dread, terror and anguish for some of them were as thick as the blinding smoke that filled the mine. In their private moments when the lights were off, the suffocating darkness toyed with their minds. While they languished between two worlds, the thoughts came like lurking smoke, and the deadly gases were spreading and seeping deep into their consciousness. The question came: what would be their fate? Much like the words of English writer William Wordsworth, "Thoughts that do often lie too deep for tears."[39]

Whenever someone shuffled and turned a light on to get a drink, it was a reprieve from the darkness and the haunting images that inflicted their minds. For now, in the unbearable heat, each man resolved to stay behind the barricade and wait for rescuers. While there was always some talk of leaving the barricade, patience was wearing thin.[40]

Disaster at Cane Creek

After officials met with family members in the lab building to inform them about the bodies that were found, Frank Tippie made a formal announcement at a press conference held at 10:00 p.m.[41] at the glass-walled administration building, 300 yards from the mine shaft. He first talked about the rescue efforts by the exhausted rescuers and their concentrated efforts in the East Drift, where five survivors were reportedly alive.

"It's not known the exact spot of the explosion," Tippie said. "It is assumed a blast detonated undetected methane gas."[42]

After a momentary pause, Tippie said rescuers were still unable to reach the five. "Earlier in the night, teams were only able to travel about 1,500 feet into the East Drift before being forced back by a lack of oxygen."[43] He continued while speaking in a strained voice, "In covering the area, rescuers have observed eight bodies."[44] The gravity of the moment hit everyone who heard.

Tippie told how the four-man team found three bodies at the mouth of the East Drift near the shaft station. Another body was 100 feet away near a turn leading to the West Drift, and a fourth body was around 200 feet from the shaft in a cross-drift on the west side. Three more bodies were 1,500 feet down the East Drift,[45] the ones reported by the two rescued miners.[46] Tippie said rescuers did not reach the barricades which were believed to be a 1,000 feet further down the drift.[47] The heat and dwindling oxygen supply forced them to retreat. The bodies weren't identified, Mr. Tippie said, and none would be brought to the surface until the living, if any, were rescued. There was little hope in Tippie's comments, and when asked how the situation looked, Tippie replied, "When you find eight bodies, it doesn't look good."[48]

Tippie also talked about the patch made to the air line Hanna and McKinney worked on, but rescuers were not confident the five men were getting compressed air through the pipes going into their barricade.[49] He also said the water pouring into the shaft posed no serious problem, but it was now making it difficult to lower the hoist; so, one of the next steps in the rescue operation would be to get the water pumps operating.

Tippie also mentioned rescuers were making an extra effort to plan another expedition into the mine. "They hope to put a shuttle car into the drift. The shuttle car," Mr. Tippie said, "will enable rescuers to move with more speed as each man's oxygen is limited and the equipment weighs thirty pounds."[50]

Tippie talked about how the four-man team tried desperately to reach the five miners and returned to the surface to report seeing the bodies of the eight men.[51] The fate of the remaining ten miners remained unknown. There was "a slim possibility these ten would be found alive," Casper Nelson, Utah State Mine Commissioner, offered grudgingly.

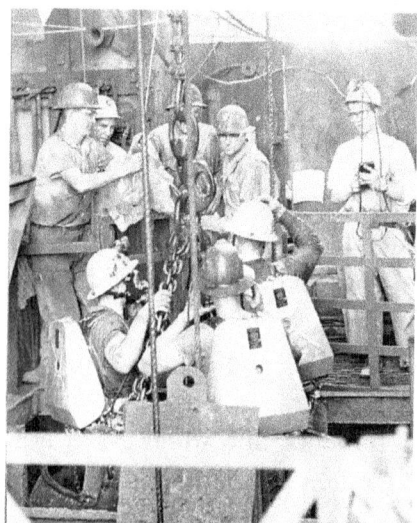 

1. Another rescue team surfaces, soak and wet from the water pouring in the shaft. (*Times-Independent*) 2. Casper Nelson, a member of the Utah Industrial Commission, uses a map of the mine to explain the location of eight men known to be dead. (*Salt Lake Tribune*)

"It's reasonable to assume," Nelson said, "that the ten men were at work in the West Drift." Five were known to have been members of a dynamite crew near the working Face of the West Drift (2 South). Three others were assigned to work near the vertical shaft, and two electricians were believed to have been working in an east-west crosscut near the West Drift.[52]

"Since it's believed the methane gas explosion was triggered by the dynamite blast in the West Drift, it's logical to assume the West Drift and its occupants suffered the whole force from the blast," Nelson said.

"Unless they had some kind of cover...," he offered a bleak chance the other men might be alive. Nelson also said several of the eight men died of carbon monoxide poisoning.[53]

He also commented on the small compressed air line in the East Drift that workmen believe they had repaired.

"The compressed air line is normally used to operate power tools in the drilling operation, but in emergency situations, the released compressed air can furnish trapped men a breathing supply," Nelson said.[54]

In the mining industry, a mine "disaster" is defined as one in which five or more fatalities occur, while those with less than five fatalities get classified as "incidents." With eight men now known to be dead, the Cane Creek explosion just officially became classified as a mine "disaster." With the prospects for the other ten not good, it threatened to increase the total number dead in the Cane Creek Mine disaster.

At the start of the 20th Century, mine disasters were appallingly common. The mining industry in 1907 experienced eighteen coal mine disasters, plus two more in metal/nonmetal mines. (The U.S government categorizes mining into two main groups; coal and metal/nonmetal with sub-groups listed under metal/nonmetal mines). It was the worst year in mining history. Mine accidents have declined dramatically in number and severity over the decades due to research, new and better technology, and preventive safety programs. Today, mine accidents resulting in five or more deaths are not as common. However, preventing recurrence of disasters like those of the past decades remains a top priority in the mining industry, requiring constant vigilance by management, labor, and government.[55]

Facing another night of not knowing, family members from as far away as Uvalde, Texas, and North Bay, Ontario, Canada, and from as close as a Moab trailer court, kept an agonizing vigil.[56]

Some were at the Moab hospital. Some gathered at the Texas Gulf Sulphur (TGS) Potash Mine. Most of them sat quietly, hope battling despair in their hearts. They were the anxious wives and relatives of the men trapped deep under the red-earthed Colorado Plateau.[57]

For two families, there was joy when the two survivors were pulled alive from the deep mine. For the rest, only an agonizing wait with the knowledge that at least eight men are now known to be dead. Which eight? Maybe some of the families knew. The company officials and the rescue crews were not saying whose bodies they found.[58]

Dorothy LeBlanc waited quietly in the hospital lobby. She had only been in Moab for a week. She and her husband, Emile, and their three small children came here to start a new life. But for her husband, the sky fell in on his fifth day at work. For others, it happened after careers as long as two decades.[59]

"Why don't you go home," a nurse quietly asked Dorothy. She smiled and whispered, "Oh, it's all right, I don't mind waiting at all,"[60] she said with a quiet dignity. Close by was her friend, Alice Barber.

Thirty-years-old Emile LaBlanc was a native of Inverness, Nova Scotia. In 1954, while living in Boston, Massachusetts, Emile and

Dorothy were married, and that same year, they moved to Windsor, Ontario, Canada. He and his pretty wife, Dorothy, lived in Windsor for three years until a work shortage forced them to move to Elliott Lake, Ontario. Emile had just completed a welding course in Windsor with a friend and planned to use their experience to find a job. When a job came open only one welder was needed, so Emile stepped aside for his friend and took a job working in the Milliken Uranium Mine, where he remained until last month when he discovered that the mine might close down. He contacted 'Paddy' Harrison, a friend he had met in Elliott Lake, who was president of the family company, Harrison International. He learned they were working on a project at the Moab mine and 'Paddy' assured him of a job.[61]

The LeBlancs sold their furniture and began preparing for the trip west. With their three small children in tow, six-year-old Joey and two small baby girls, Ann, nineteen months, and Geralyn, eight months, they left Elliott Lake. Their plans included "last stops" at Uncle Pat LeBlanc's farm near Huntsville. Then they stayed at the home of Victor Kendziora in Windsor, who was a childhood friend from Inverness. The well-liked couple was able to visit with many of their old friends while they stayed in town. They talked of someday returning to Windsor to make it their home. After a four day stay, the LeBlancs left Windsor on August 13th and arrived in Moab six days later. They were supposed to leave on the 12th, but a rear wheel bearing went in Emile's car, and they were forced to stay over for an extra day. With his blue eyes flashing and his happy-go-lucky smile, Emile's last words to his friends were, "Well, we got off to a poor start, but it's sure to be a good finish."[62]

Now, all of the LeBlanc's family and friends back in Canada were following the news of the explosion and praying for Emile. Meanwhile, his mother who lived in Eastern Canada, was on her way to Moab.

Violet June, a thirty-four-year-old mother of six children, was among the other wives keeping an agonizing vigil at the hospital. She knew there were seven survivors. She had been told by Blake Hanna (after he had been rescued and brought to the hospital) that her husband, Bob June, was one of the survivors still in the barricade. No one waiting there with her knew the names[63] of the other men.

Everyone was trying to find out what they could, or at least verify, what they heard as the rumors flew. And so it went, around the room, around the grounds, and around town.[64]

The dark-eyed expectant mother, Mollie McKinney, was happy as she checked on her burly husband, Paul, during the evening who was now safe in the Moab hospital.[65]

"I've got to go home and rest," she said. "I haven't slept all last night and today." Mollie was expecting their first child before Christmas.

Hanna was visiting with his young son, Danny, and other family members. Talking a bit about his ordeal, he started to describe some of the events. Visiting hours were ending soon, so family members started to make their goodbyes to leave.

Wayne Hanna walked out of Hanna's hospital room and headed towards the lobby when a reporter asked him about his brother. Wayne said he was doing well and had talked a bit about his ordeal. Wayne recounted what he could remember.

In the hospital lobby, the UPI reporter Robert Flick was leaning against the wall writing notes. The curious, hardworking reporter from California was trying to get additional information but to no avail. An image of toughness behind his gruff demeanor, Flick was known by his colleagues for being unfailingly kind and generous and was sensitive to the tragic plight of the families.[66] Empathetically, he watched as an older woman, sitting upright, turned to a woman half her age and asked; "Do you have anybody in the mine?"

"My husband," came the reply.

The older woman was one of the lucky ones. Blake Hanna, her son, was one of the two men rescued.[67]

Hanna's attractive, blond wife, Myrna Hanna, also felt extreme joy, yet it was tempered with empathy and compassion for the other families still waiting to hear about their loved ones.[68]

"I'm happy my husband is safe," Myrna quietly said while speaking with another reporter. "I feel so sorry for the rest," she said as she glanced about the hospital lobby as other family members sat quietly, hoping.[69]

"You can't give up hope," she added.

With her was their seven-year-old son, Danny. The Hanna's three other children (a son and two daughters) were at home, unaware of how close they came to losing their dad.[70]

Myrna Hanna at the hospital visiting her husband with their son, Danny Hanna. (*Salt Lake Tribune*)

"They're home playing with the cat," Danny, the blond, crew-cut boy said. Myrna said her husband was "just fine, his eyes hurt, but he is fine." She then turned to speak with her family members in the hospital lobby before they took Danny home after his visit with his dad.[71]

Hanna was having difficulty resting. He was apprehensive and worried about the other five men. He couldn't understand what was taking rescue crews so long to get to the barricade. He constantly asked for any updates from the mine site. But no one at the hospital knew anything. The doctor decided Hanna needed something to settle him down that would help him sleep.[72]

After a long, eventful day, Dr. Jay Munsey felt it was time to put both men to bed, sedating them so they could get some sleep. When asked how they were doing, the doctor said their "condition was excellent given their ordeal. They were very thirsty, hungry and really played out," he said. "But they won't be in the hospital more than twenty-four hours."[73]

Reporters were everywhere trying to get a story. Most of the reporters were sensitive to the situation and were, for the most part, considerate. Some were not. There were a few reported incidents of just how intrusive and insensitive some of them could be, first at the mine, then at the hospital and even at the homes of some of the families. Reporters went as far as trying to take pictures of families inside their homes through the windows or whenever they came or left. Some reporters shoved microphones at people and demanded answers to their questions while taking pictures. A few times, the local police were called, and the reporters were removed from the family's private property.[74] The reporters seemed to be lurking everywhere and even eavesdropped on conversations. They jotted down scraps of information as they talked and asked questions with anyone who would speak with them. For a few, their insistent behavior bordered on obnoxious and distasteful.[75]

To insure Hanna wasn't bothered by the reporters, Myrna went without rest, sitting by her husband's bed or outside his hospital room door throughout the night[76] instead of going home with her family.

"No visitors. He's been through enough," she would say. Or, "He's gone through a terrible ordeal. His eyes hurt and he needs to rest," as reporters sought access.[77]

The hospital atmosphere was quiet, but expectant. And although it was late, staff members were ready for when the other men trapped in the blast were rescued and brought to the hospital for needed medical care. Many of the hospital staff would have gone home by 8:00 p.m., but some stayed on duty voluntarily as long as the need existed.[78]

Under the glow of a waxing moon, James Westfield and Anthony Moschetti parked the car and made their way down to the Headframe where the rescue operation was in full swing. Moschetti had picked Westfield up at the Denver Airport earlier in the evening after Westfield had flown from Pennsylvania where he had been assisting with the Sheppton Mine Rescue. Both men drove to Moab arriving at the Cane Creek Mine site at 11:00 p.m.[79] As soon as reporters knew Westfield was on the property, they wasted no time for a chance to speak with the notable fifty-nine-year-old native Utahn. The ranking official from the U.S. Bureau of Mines was known as a miner's miner—a very likable people-type person.[80]

As Assistant Director in charge of Health and Safety at the U.S. Bureau of Mines, disasters were a big part of Westfield's work. He had been in charge of investigating every major mining disaster in the United States during the past decade[81] and many others since he first joined the Bureau at the district level in 1928.[82] The ex-Utahn made disasters his business, and whenever he arrived at the scene of a mining accident, he didn't just investigate, he worked.

Westfield got his first taste of a mine tragedy when he was twenty-years-old.[83] On March 8, 1924, a massive coal mine explosion at Utah Fuel Company's Castle Gate Mine #2 killed 171 miners. One rescuer also lost his life when his nose clip was accidentally knocked off causing him to inhale deadly gas, which brought the total dead to 172.[84] Westfield's father, James William Westfield, was on the Sunnyside mine rescue team[85] and with other teams from the surrounding areas, rescuers worked under extremely dangerous conditions for days as the rescue quickly turned into a recovery operation. All the men who went to work that day perished.

"I personally knew many of them," Westfield recalled. Just a year later, young Westfield went to work at the Castle Gate Mine and worked his way through college earning a degree at the University of Utah as a mining Engineer.[86]

The white-haired, bespectacled man who wore khaki trousers and shirt on the job, knew well the misery of miners' families when accidents strike.[87]

His grandfather, John Henry Westfeldt [sic], was killed in the coal mine explosion in Nanaimo, British Columbia, Canada on May 3, 1887. In all, 150 miners were killed, including one rescuer. It was the worst mine disaster in the history of British Columbia and the second worst in Canada's history.[88]

John Westfeldt was only forty-three-years-old when he died in the Nanaimo Disaster, and left behind six small children under the age of nine. The second to the oldest of his children was James William Westfeldt, who was only eight-years-old at the time. James' mother soon remarried. Not able to get along with his stepfather, he left home as soon as he was old enough and made his way from Nanaimo on the beautiful Vancouver Island in British Columbia to the wild, badlands of Utah,[89] and in the process, he adopted a different spelling of his last name.

Not long after, in 1899, "the Sunnyside mines were opened by Daniel Harrington and James Westfield, and 1,200 men soon were at work."[90] Shortly afterward, the mines were acquired by Utah Fuel Company and for fifty years, they operated the coal mines in Sunnyside, ultimately selling their interest to Kaiser Steel Corporation in 1949.

James or 'Jim,'[91] as he was called, married Nellie Henderson and made their home in the coal mining camp at Sunnyside. They had two sons, James Westfield, born on January 28, 1904, and Delone Westfield, born December 10, 1906. Delon died eight months later of cholera on August 22, 1907. James grew up in Sunnyside and graduated from Carbon High School in 1923.

"There are no better people in the world than mining people," Westfield told reporters. "Somewhere in their makeup, they seem to have something extra that gives them the strength to meet things like this,"[92] he said under the glare of the floodlights around the Headframe.

Westfield said he always enjoyed returning to his native Utah, but added, "I never like to come home to something like this." The Bureau's Assistant Director added that "Mining is one occupation that has plenty of inherent dangers. But most accidents in mines result from human failure."[93]

While this is so true, "there are those who are vitally interested in safety, but...there are far too many who are not interested in the extent that they should be."[94]

Westfield and Moschetti made their way to the conference room inside TGS's mining/engineering office building to the makeshift Command Center and were briefed on the current progress of the rescue operation. During the evening, Westfield also learned of several previous events at the mine that were never reported to the Bureau that should have been. The first was the gas ignition that happened the previous month. On July 31st, four men were burned while roof bolting. And the other event was back in December of last year when crews encountered crude oil while sinking the shaft. Neither TGS nor Harrison International notified the Bureau, although they did notify the Utah State Industrial Commission of the gas incident.[95]

Both companies defended their position, saying the law did not require them to notify the U.S. Bureau of Mines. The Utah State Industrial Commission investigated and made their recommendations. The company increased their examinations for combustible gas, and a "No Smoking" rule was put into effect underground. Permissible flame safety lamps were also carried by Harrison International's Shift Walkers and other Supervisors after the ignition. And tests for combustible gases were made by personnel during and after drilling blast holes. They started doing this before the July 31st ignition, when a representative of the U. S. Geological Survey made the recommendation of drilling holes 10 to 14 feet in depth ahead of the Face to release gas from the strata, which gave indications gas was there; so, they followed this recommendation.[96] The two events not reported to the U.S. Bureau of Mines may have been the "canary in the coal mine" moments; two warnings, yet the mine remained classified as a non-gassy mine.

An internationally famous geologist from Salt Lake City, Glen M. Rudy, came to the scene of the rescue operation Tuesday night.[97] He had prospected for natural gas and oil in the Paradox Region for the last forty years and was often a frequent visitor to Moab while operating properties in the area of the Cane Creek Mine.

Robert Bernick, the Business Editor for the *Salt Lake Tribune*, was able to speak with Rudy. He told Bernick he believed the explosion was, "Undoubtedly caused by petroleum gas. The longer East Drift (3U), had already crossed through the area of the clastic break No.

4, three weeks previous, without incident." Evidently, Rudy must not have been aware that it was "not" without incident. Four men had sustained burns when gas was released and ignited when their drift crossed the clastic break, also described as an "ancient silt river bed formation."[98]

Rudy did reason that the shorter drift, 2 South, may have been about to cross through the same formation when the explosion happened the night before.

"The drilling in the past has picked up shows of oil, and there is gas in the area," Rudy told Bernick. He related other shows of natural gas with "clastic break No.4" in the Cane Creek structure. The oil and gas were the same as when the first Wildcat Oil Well was drilled and found oil and gas in the late 1920's.[99] That oil well, at a depth of 2,028 feet, quickly exhausted the deposit. A clastic break in the Paradox salt section was described as a relatively thin "break" or "discontinuity" in the salt section in which oil or gas may accumulate in small pockets. These pockets could be in a high-pressure state and, if disturbed by a blast, etc., would emit gas with a "rush."

Rudy estimated the location of the old No. 1 Wildcat Oil Well was about a half-mile from the area of the longer of the two drifts. "This well was cemented and had no relationship to any escape of natural gas in any of the two drifts, if this were the case on Tuesday afternoon when the blast occurred," Rudy said.

"It would only take a few hundred, perhaps a few thousand, cubic feet of natural gas to cause a very serious explosion within the confined area of the mining Face at the end of the drift," Ruby surmised. "The presence of gases in salt sections is not unknown in the West and is a controllable situation with the exercise of caution and judgment on the part of the miners working in the area. I know from discussions with Harrison International's people, they took the utmost precaution and avoided shooting (dynamite in the Face) in the presence of the natural gas."

"Considerable advance drilling and testing for natural gas were carried out as a regular program," he said, adding that, "no one could know at this time what did happen."[100]

Rumors persisted of water collecting in the shaft's sump area and was rapidly rising and threatening to overflow into the drifts. It was disconcerting for family members worried about how the water might affect any survivors that rescue teams were trying to get to in the mine. Although it was another pressing problem for the rescue operation, Tippie tried to reassure everyone claiming the water was, in fact, not backing up into the drifts.

June Crawford, the company spokesman, echoed the same sentiments, saying the water hampered work in the shaft, but the drifts were comparatively dry.[101]

"It's like working in a heavy rain," Crawford said describing the water.[102] And he described how some workers estimated about forty gallons of water a minute[103] was pouring down the shaft. Rescuers often described that it was worse than a cloudburst, or like a hard rain.

The water drops fell sometimes great distances, before making contact and then ricocheting and bouncing, and then falling some more. It flowed around the different surfaces, collecting and pooling before plunging again on its downward descent. While the pelting rain continued to cascade down the concrete shaft, a virtual echo chamber, the drumming sound was intensified with every drop.

From the beginning of the rescue operation, the water created so many problems. Working in the shaft was miserable for rescuers, soaking them to the skin. The water made it difficult to see even with the light from their cap-lamps. The men even had a hard time reading their wristwatches. Before the holes were drilled in the bottom of the buckets the collecting water would generally be knee deep or even at times, waist deep by the time the buckets surfaced.[104]

About 11:30 p.m.,[105] a crew was sent to the pump station at the 1,330-foot level[106] to repair the water pumps. Officials were hoping to stop the flow of water cascading down the shaft, or at the very least, lessen the amount. The heavy runoff water was from natural seepage from groundwater that continually delayed and hampered workers.[107] The pumps that normally carried the groundwater from the shaft area[108] were damaged from the force of the explosion that ripped through the mine.

At 600-foot intervals down the shaft, collecting rings around the perimeter caught the water, and then it was pumped out of the mine. The explosion badly damaged or smashed the pumps, baffles, and large collector rings.[109] And the power to the pumps was turned off for fear of causing a secondary explosion from electrical shorts or the electrocution of rescuers.[110]

The water pumps were repaired shortly before midnight.[111] And crews were confident it was now safe to run the pumps, although the water was still pouring down the shaft because of the extensive damages to the collecting rings.[112] Some of the rings could be picking up water and pumping it out, but it probably wouldn't be enough to stop the water completely. It was just after midnight when electricians started the compressors on the surface that supplied power to the pumps[113] to begin the removal of the water.[114] Officials were hopeful that crews would have better and safer working conditions,[115] and it would eliminate the growing concern of water filling the sump area and overflowing into the drifts.

Part Four

Chapter 16

Back to "Plan A"

After several failed attempts to reach the barricade, officials made an extra effort to plan another rescue expedition. This time, they were taking a different course of action that would conserve on the rescuers' two-hour oxygen supply. The plan would make it possible for the team to go further into the mine, down the longer East Drift where the five trapped men were located. Around midnight, Kaiser Steel Rescuer, Fred Tatton, made a phone call to the hospital hoping to speak with Hanna to get more detailed information that would help with the planning.[1]

Tatton and Hanna knew each other and Hanna was more than willing to help. Tatton wanted to learn more about the men in the barricade: their conditions, the location, and the materials used to construct the barriers. Hanna went through the events that happened after the explosion, explaining how the men took a shuttle car to the top of the incline near the raise area. And how later, hours before they were rescued, he and McKinney took another shuttle car up the incline to check on the three men before walking the rest of the way to the shaft station.[2]

Tatton felt his talk with Hanna was helpful. Since time was of the essence, the plan centered on reaching the top of the incline and from there, the teams would take one of the shuttle cars to travel the rest of the way to the barricade. Then they would use it to come back as far as they could to the shaft station. A six-man crew was handpicked: Fred Tatton, William 'Bill' Shumway from the Kaiser Steel Team, 'Paddy' Harrison and two other Harrison International workers (because of their knowledge of the mine), along with Wiley Brooks, the Texas Gulf Sulphur's General Mine Foreman and rescuer. Brooks was chosen because he knew how to drive a Torkar (the diesel-powered shuttle car). At the planning meeting, the men calculated the distances and hoped this plan would buy them some much-needed time.³

'Paddy' Harrison, the President of Harrison International, had traveled to the Cane Creek Mine site from Toronto, Canada, not long after hearing about the explosion. The short, stocky, sixty-something Irishman was a seasoned miner and was now assisting with the rescue. Each rescuer donned their rescue gear. Ready, with their apparatuses on their backs, the team stepped into the bucket for the half-mile descent into the mine.

Without warning, TGS officials pulled Wiley Brooks out of the bucket at the last minute and off the team. At the company's headquarters, administrators got wind of the plan and quickly objected. Many of the officials who were manning the Command Center were strong-willed and knowledgeable mining men who had risen to the top of their profession. At times, these men found themselves at odds with each other. Critical decisions had to be made, and there were different points of view on how best to proceed. The views of some, at times, got pitted against opposing views, especially when such strong-minded men were part of the equation.

This unexpected decision left the rest of the rescue team in the bucket still ready and willing to go, but pulling one of the team members at the last minute threw the whole plan into disarray. It caused tempers to flare with a whole lot of arguing among the rescue officials as Peperakis and others defended the plan. The team was caught between opposing views and they weren't sure what to do. Everything had been planned. Finally, a decision was made for the team to go ahead with their plan and the bucket was sent down, minus one team member.⁴

1. Rescuer walking towards the entrance of the Headframe as his team prepares to descend the mine shaft. (*Deseret News*) 2. Removing breathing gear, Armond Roy (left) is assisted by a rescue worker after an hour in the mine shaft. (*Salt Lake Tribune*) 3. Steve Hatsis (right), state coal mine inspector directing the rescue operation, speaks with Wiley Brooks, TGS Engineer. (*Times-Independent*)

Once tempers settled down, General Manager, Frank Tippie, eventually announced to reporters that a crew started down the shaft at 12:55 a.m. and they planned to work through the East Drift in a diesel-powered vehicle. He said the five-man rescue team could bring the five possible survivors to the surface, "regardless of whether they are found dead or alive."[5]

The bucket slowly moved downward in the shaft. So much effort had gone into planning. Now, the team had lost one of its primary rescuers, along with his expertise. As a result, the team was not as prepared as planned. No one else knew how to run a Torkar (the diesel-powered shuttle car), and the plan centered on it to get the team further down the drift while using less oxygen. As the different officials of the companies and the agencies argued bitterly back and forth, the whole operation seemed to descend into chaos. The decision to take Wiley Brooks off the team made no sense at all, as the team tried to shake off feelings of discouragement as the bucket descended into the dark, wet mine.[6]

Communications with the surface were still dicey. Wrapped in cellophane, the walkie-talkie was still spotty because of the water. For many of the rescuers, it wasn't being in the shaft, being in the bucket, or losing contact with the surface, that gave the teams their worst fits. It was the water. It was always a terrible experience to go through the water as it poured in on them, was spewed at them from the high-pressured air or pounded down as it fell. Through his mask, it felt like a deluge and at times, Tatton thought he was going to drown. The bucket still had a considerable distance to go before they reached the bottom. At least the water wasn't collecting in the bucket any longer because of the holes drilled in the bottom.[7]

Once the bucket landed on top of the feeder-breaker, the terrified men climbed out and crossed over and onto the solid ground. On the way down the shaft, Tatton's oxygen apparatus started acting up. 'Paddy' Harrison and the other two young Harrison International guys were not experienced rescuers; they had been trained the first morning after the explosion to directly help clear debris out of the shaft. Tatton had one of the young guys switch apparatuses with him. They kept their face masks on as they changed gear. Tatton gave the young man instructions to stay right at the bottom of the shaft where the air was good, and a phone was nearby if needed. The team then crossed over the small cement ledge to the east side of the shaft station.[8]

It was a terrifying experience. Their apparatuses were cumbersome, and their face masks had limited visibility, creating blind spots. In the hot, humid and smoky environment, Shumway was particularly frightened and shaken by this scary undertaking. Being extremely careful as he crossed, he was terrified he might slip and fall into the sump area below.[9]

Once on the other side, the team hooked up their linkline, did checks of the apparatuses and took gas tests. Collecting themselves, they started towards the East Drift.[10] One of the first things the team saw were two bodies close to each other. They had heard there were four or five bodies around the shaft station, but spent no time identifying or even tagging the victims. Instead, they bypassed them and pressed on in the direction of their strongest hope: the five men believed to be alive behind a barricade more than half-mile at the end of the East Drift.[11]

Many times, rescue teams would tag the bodies they come across and document the information on their maps. With limited oxygen, the team's primary mission and concerns at the moment were to get to the barricade and the miners who may be running out of time. Once all the missing men were accounted for, and those still alive were rescued, then the bodies would be respectfully recovered and taken out of the mine.

As the team headed down the East Drift, they eventually ran into the areas where the vent line was blown apart. They climbed over the uncurled sections or moved them out of their way, just as the previous team had done. They soon came to the end of 1 South drift where it veers to the right and connects to the three-way intersection of the raise area and the top of 3U Drift.[12]

Near the corner of this intersection is where they found the three dead miners. Two were kneeling side-by-side on the ground with their heads in between an opened section of the metal vent line. They were on their haunches but slumped over, as if they had fallen to one side, one was practically lying partially on top of the other. It was apparent the men thought they could get air in the vent line. There was one other body lying on the ground, off to the side of the first two, near a shuttle car. Hanna had told Tatton there were three men in the vent line; one of them had crawled inside of the line. The team checked, but found no body inside of the vent line.[13]

The team continued and came to the second shuttle car, but they didn't know how to run it, so no one tried to start the engine. It was the shuttle car they planned to take down the drift. They continued down the incline, but didn't get far when the heat became unbearable. It was a sweltering 130 degrees, and the men started to struggle. They were sweating so badly that two of them wanted to remove their face masks so they could breathe. The team was also beginning to run low on oxygen. They stopped to rest and see if they could get cooled down. Tatton took some gas readings and found the carbon monoxide was so heavily concentrated, one squeeze of the meter turned the smoke tube almost black.[14]

Not able to get cooled down, the men soon felt like they were drowning in their own sweat. As the two rescuers struggled terribly, fighting their face masks, Tatton and 'Paddy' Harrison begged them not to remove their masks because of the gases. It would be deadly. The team immediately turned around as they encouraged the two men to hang on until they made it back to the shaft station.[15]

Tatton was totally perplexed. After taking the gas reading, he could not conceive of how Hanna and McKinney were able to go through such a large concentration of gas and still be alive.

The rescue team finally made it back to the shaft station and the other team member they had left behind. Taking their face masks off, the men soon started to feel much better. They donned their air packs again, which were beginning to run very low. They crossed over the feeder-breaker and climbed back into the bucket to travel to the surface, which was about a thirty-minute ride from the bottom of the mine to the shaft collar.[16]

Anxious officials and workers crowded around the bucket as the team carried little hope[17] for the five survivors. It had been another failed attempt to reach the barricade. The team reported their experiences as they traveled down the East Drift at their debriefing. Even though they were unable to reach the trapped men before they were forced to retreat by the extreme heat,[18] they felt they came within a few hundred yards of the barricade.[19]

At the debriefing, officials learned what Tatton's team had gone through and almost immediately made the decision to go back to "Plan A." Officials no longer wanted to waste any more time trying to make a run for the barricade. Once the current team surfaced, they would begin clearing out the debris and repair the vent line down the shaft to establish a fresh air base at the bottom.[20] Teams would no longer have to waste an hour of their oxygen supply going down and then back up the shaft. They would now have the time needed to reach the barricade. For some, it was an agonizing decision as James Westfield encouraged everyone that they needed to go slow.

In the darkness, the floodlit scene around the Headframe looked almost unreal as rescue teams waited their turn to travel down the deep shaft. The family center, set up in the lab building, had an equally surreal surrounding. The sparkling white industrial laboratory building was equipped with all the usual paraphernalia such as

Bunsen burners, odd-shaped flasks, and high wooden stools. Cots were set up in the small aisles between the laboratory tables.[21] A somber mood prevailed in the shadowy night, but no one got much sleep. At times, some of the relatives would walk quickly towards the Headframe, take a look at rescue activities, and then walk back to the comforting atmosphere and companionship in the laboratory.[22]

As each rescue team surfaced from the void, they'd report to rescue officials, who then quickly walked the path over the red pebbly ground to the laboratory, a hundred yards away, to give the latest news to anxious relatives.[23]

At times, the despair was clearly palpable as the families watched the hours tick slowly by, waiting for any word. They were sheltered and suspended in time, much like their desert surroundings which stretched back into an ancient past with its "fusion of the vast and the intimate." The land had features of both breathtaking hugeness and yet gave "a feeling of being enclosed, surrounded, and sheltered."[24]

"They are extremely tense not knowing," said Reverend Howard Mason, the minister[25] from the Episcopal Church of St. Francis in Moab.[26] He was on hand to give comfort to the relatives.

"When they found eight bodies, the anxiety deepened noticeably," he said, "especially since the dead were not identified."[27]

Since twenty-four of the twenty-five men involved in the tragedy were employed by a contract company, Harrison International, the Texas Gulf Sulphur (TGS) wives, helping at the family center, didn't know most of the other wives and families. During the time spent together in the surreal setting of the lab building, the TGS wives grew to know intimately, to love, and to admire the grieving women and their families who proved to be a constant source of inspiration and renewal of spirit.[28]

One wife, a complete stranger to Moab, said, "I have talked with a bishop. I feel much better now, and I'm ready for whatever happens."[29]

One sobbing wife was visibly quieted when a priest spoke to her in low and compassionate tones.

A seventy-two-year-old mother said, "My son won't die. He has six little children who depend on him."[30] Past the point of exhaustion, both physically and spiritually, these heavily burdened wives were admired for their own acts of caring. A lovely, young wife with three close relatives involved in the accident asked Kay Tippie, "Won't you take this cot and lie down? You must be terribly tired."[31] It was Margo Christensen who asked, she was six months pregnant.

During the long hours of waiting even into the wee morning hours, Kay Tippie never left the mine site. With the help of other TGS wives and the girl scouts, they were there to serve the needs of the waiting families at such a difficult and trying time.[32]

They witnessed the two wonderful, young Canadian mothers, Dorothy LeBlanc and Alice Barber, emanate a positive glow of faith and courage after an illustrated talk on the problems involved in the rescue work. The families leaned on their beliefs and faith, not on the certainty of an outcome, but rather on the courage to face a world of uncertainty. One young, attractive wife went up to one of the company officials, smiled and said shyly, "Thank you so much for taking the time to explain it to us."[33]

The TGS wives grieved with their new-found friends, heartbroken over their suffering during the long, painful hours.[34] They witnessed, throughout the days and into the nights, the tremendous serenity of spirit, courage, and understanding displayed by these women and their families. Kay lamented, "It's unfortunate, in their search for the sensational, the metropolitan press has missed a truly inspirational story while covering the mine tragedy."[35]

Water poured down as the bucket neared the bottom. George Ferguson, from the Kaiser Steel Team, signaled with the walkie-talkie for the Hoistman to stop. On this trip, he was asked to team up with two U.S. Steel Team members—one designated the Captain, the other the Co-Captain.

'Bob' von Storch, General Superintendent at U.S. Steel (left), watches the next team as they descend into the deep shaft. (*Daily Sentinel*)

At the bottom of the shaft, the bucket came to a stop, and Ferguson climbed out onto the feeder-breaker; the other two followed close behind, as each of them made their way down onto the solid ground of the shaft station.

The previous team reported coming across eight bodies around the shaft station and down the East Drift. This team was assigned to explore these areas using a linkline and to mark any bodies they came across on the mine map. "Just locate the bodies...do not bring them up," were the orders they were given. With the report of eight bodies found by Tatton's team, the Command Center wanted verification and a more accurate account of bodies.

In the smoky darkness, death was all around as the eerie sounds from the water poured and pelted down, pounding on metal and echoing throughout the shaft chamber. Nerves were on edge. The men had heard stories recounted by the former rescue team members who had discovered the bodies in the depths of the blackened mine. They were stories of bodies burned and mangled after being blown about the shaft area from the force of the explosion. Some miners had been blown out of their work boots, others had their clothes burned off or had their mine belts blown up under their arms. A few bodies were out in the open; others had been blown into crannies and covered with dust or debris or shoved up under metal workings.

The deterioration and decay of the bodies were unimaginable. They had laid there for over 33 hours in the hot, 130-degree temperature. They were so bloated their skin began to split. Many of the rescuers were veterans of war or had been involved in other mine disasters and had prior experience with the grizzly work of attending to bodies. Some had not.

The team set up their linkline before heading to the east side. Getting started, one body caught the men's attention. It was laying out in the open not far from the shaft on the west side. Investigating closer, the men recognized that it was Clell Johnson, Harrison International's Master Electrician.

Clell had lived in Sunnyside for years before coming to Moab. He had worked with many of the men on the rescue teams from Carbon County or at least, had dealings with them in the community. The body was in bad shape and was swollen from the heat. It had dark hair with a square hairline and what appeared to be an old injury to one hand. The rescuers knew Clell had the tip of his finger cut off from a previous mining accident while working in Sunnyside. It added to their belief that the body was Clell Johnson. Ferguson even felt it was Clell; he had driven a school bus with him for years.

This location was as far as the team went. The men never made it over to the east side of the shaft where there were reports of a group of bodies. The disturbing discovery of finding Clell's body caused some panic among the two U.S. Steel rescuers. The Captain made the decision they were going to take the body out of the mine. Ferguson tried to communicate through his mask of what they were supposed to be doing. But the team Captain wouldn't listen.

The men managed to get the body into the wet bucket and laid it awkwardly across the inside the best they could. Only now, there wasn't enough room for everyone. The Captain let Ferguson know they had to leave him and would be back to get him. Convinced Ferguson's air supply was adequate, the Captain thought Ferguson would be okay since they hadn't been "under oxygen" very long.

Ferguson again tried to protest, but the Captain took the walkie-talkie from him and got into the bucket. Ferguson watched in disbelief as the Captain gave the signal for the Hoistman to take them up. The water poured down as the bucket slowly moved up and out of sight.

Ferguson couldn't understand how other mine rescuers, trained in proper mine rescue procedures, could come to such a decision. In his mind, this was not the way his team, the Kaiser Teams, would conduct themselves. They would never violate such a basic mine rescue rule. Teams were trained that orders and procedures were to be followed. They go after the living before they recover the bodies of the dead. And they should never leave a team member alone. This was clearly a case of team endangerment. Alone, all Ferguson could do was sit and wait until someone came back for him. He hoped the time would pass quickly. In the miserable moist heat, hard feelings started to grip him. The only thing Ferguson wanted was to get out of this hell hole, as the water poured down the shaft into the sump area close to where he sat.

As the night wore on, nurses in white uniforms[36] and white hard hats paced a section of ground on the other side of the rope. They spoke to each other and to rescuers who were wrapped in blankets, sitting and resting. At one time during the long hours, there were six nurses, but as time dwindled away, so did the nurses. Ultimately, there were only four.

The eerie sound of the crank[37] pierced the night air, signaling the return of a bucket from the mine's depths. The area around the shaft collar erupted into a flurry of activity when workers discovered the team brought a body out of the mine. No one was prepared to deal with a body or knew where they should take it until identified.

The most disturbing part of the situation was that the Captain of the team had left one of the team members down in the mine. Alone. Frank Markosek, a Kaiser Steel rescuer, raised hell with the U.S. Steel rescuers for leaving Ferguson at the bottom of the shaft as the whole operation erupted into a frenzy.[38]

Meanwhile, rescue workers strung a large, gray blanket to block the view of nearby family members as they removed the body[39] from the bucket. There were heart-breaking expressions on the faces of the wives, relatives, and friends who watched the shaft area from behind ropes blocking the immediate vicinity. To them, the gray blanket was a signal of death. All eyes studied the wrapped body, as workers carefully and quickly carried it to a waiting hearse.

Who was it? No name was given.

Reliable reports quickly spread that this first body brought out was too badly disfigured for immediate identification, and no one disclosed the nature of the disfigurement.[40] It was brought out of the mine only four and a half-hours after[41] officials made the announcement that eight men caught in the explosion were found dead. Now, one was brought to the surface, leaving seven others known to be dead in the mine. Undoubtedly, there were others.

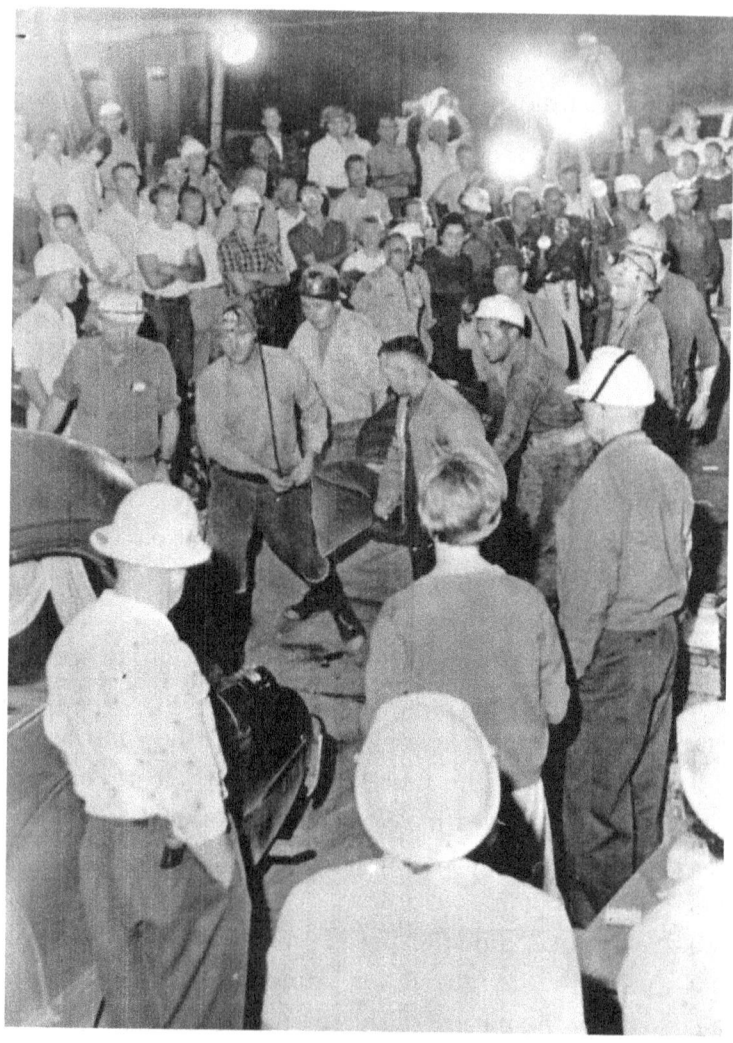

The body that was brought out of the mine during the night was taken to a waiting ambulance while the waiting crowd watched. (*Deseret News*)

After Frank Markosek[42] heard that Ferguson was left alone down in the mine, he quickly donned an apparatus as fast as he could and grabbed another rescuer from the backup team to go with him.

They boarded a bucket to go after Ferguson. There was no way of knowing of Ferguson's condition until they reached him.

The bucket arrived at the shaft station, and the two rescuers pulled Ferguson into the bucket and signaled the Hoistman to get them out of there as fast as they could travel. Up the bucket went, through the jumbled mess of cables and mangled pipes, as the water poured down on them. Ferguson was suffering from anxiety and was nearly out of oxygen. Sitting in the bottom of the bucket on the wood block, water splashed on him, and Ferguson felt a wave of relief settle over him. It wasn't long before the bucket neared the collar.

One of the first things Ferguson did after he arrived on the surface was to find John Peperakis, the Superintendent at the Kaiser Steel Mine. Ferguson let him know he wouldn't ever go down again with anyone from a U.S. Steel team. "We train with our men. They train with theirs. They must teach differently than we do."

Peperakis wanted to know what happened. Ferguson let him know that the "U.S. Steel men panicked when we got down there. They left me alone and brought a body up with them," Ferguson said and added that he would go any place with his team, but never a U.S. Steel Team. This whole incident of leaving Ferguson in the mine and bringing a body out created a huge controversy, causing a fair amount of turmoil and consternation.

It was about 3:30 a.m. in the morning when another bucket descended into the shaft as the watchers went silently back to their lonely posts. It had rained earlier as groups of wives, children, and parents of the miners stood around shifting weight from one tired foot to another. Four members of one family sat huddled together on the wet red dirt, glancing apprehensively at the shaft area. There were no tears, only intense and tired faces as the night dragged on.[43]

Some of the women slept, their faces resting on their elbows, closed fists over their bloodshot eyes. Others slept with heads leaning against large mounds of dirt. One woman, whose husband was one of the trapped miners, shed no tears at all but released her anguish by angry outbursts at newsmen, officials, miners, and her relatives.[44]

"My husband is down there! I don't know if I'll ever see him again," she cried fiercely loud. "I doubt it," she added in the same tone. "But if I do, he'll never work for this chicken outfit again!" she shouted. She learned of the tragedy through a service station operator. "I was never notified by the company," she said. Her eyes shone brightly in the night lights, flashing her anger and fear for all to see. Families were exhausted. They hardly slept and were desperate for any news of their loved ones.[45]

Arrangements were still being made for a place to take the one body for identification and the others, when they would eventually be brought out. Within the hour, an announcement came over the loudspeaker near the Headframe.[46]

"The Moab Community Baptist Church[47] will be the temporary morgue," announced Reverend Vernon Kendall. There were anguished shouts of, "Oh no, oh no," from several women present. Kendall urged relatives to stay away from the mine shaft.[48]

"All families of the miners, please go to the lab. We will notify you there of any identification." Slowly, they left, including the angry woman, her son, daughter and their little dog.[49] Despite company efforts to keep family members confined[50] to the laboratory building, there was a need to be as close to the rescue efforts as they could get.

After all the setbacks of teams not being able to get to the barricade, officials held a big meeting at the Command Center.[51] Tensions flared and words flew. Officials were grappling with tough decisions,

Disaster at Cane Creek

which had consequences for life and death. They held opposing views on how best to proceed. Peperakis also shared his views about a team leaving one of the rescuers down in the bottom of the mine, alone. On top of that, they also brought a body up before they were instructed to do so. They should have never done that before rescue teams reached the men thought to still be alive behind a barricade.

In the end, Peperakis would take charge and would direct and coordinate the activities of all the rescue teams. The two U.S. Steel rescuers and their supervisor were sent home for their apparent violation of basic mine rescue rules. Their actions caused real concern among the other rescuers, as they talked about it among themselves.[52]

Some of the other rescuers felt the U.S. Steel rescuers were motivated to bring the body out of the mine to get recognition. There was always a fair amount of competition among mine rescue teams. Perhaps, it is fostered in part by the yearly mine rescue competitions held locally, regionally and nationally. The competitions were designed to prepare teams and hone skills in the event they were actually called to a rescue operation.

Rescuers were also, by nature, highly competitive. They were men who were not only courageous, competent and bold, but they were also high achievers. They were leaders among men. There's no denying that these very traits earned mine rescuers the title of, "A Special Breed." They were men willing to put their lives on the line for fellow miners.

The meeting helped to clear the air, and everyone came to an agreement for the next course of action. Westfield was of the opinion the fresh air base should be their main focus after all the failed attempts to reach the barricade. The others agreed.[53]

The decision had already been made to go back and establish a fresh air base at the bottom of the shaft, providing rescuers enough oxygen to travel the distance to the barricade. Previously, they had wasted vital time going up and down the shaft "under oxygen," with little air to advance down the drift. It would take additional time to establish the fresh air base, but that's what they had been working on in the first place, before rescuers brought out Hanna and McKinney.[54]

Going back to "Plan A," teams would have the oxygen supply needed to get to the five men in the barricade. They could even flood the whole mine with oxygen so teams would not need an apparatus at all. Either way, establishing a fresh air base was basic mine rescue protocol.[55]

Chapter 17

Utter Turmoil of Waiting

In the wee morning hours, rescue officials announced changes to their strategy.[1] They called a temporary halt in the search for the five survivors. The order came following hours of joy, frustration, heartbreak, and despair. Two men emerged alive. Eight bodies were found. One body was brought to the surface. There was repeated failed rescue attempts[2] to get to the barricade. After their initial success in rescuing two survivors, rescuers were frustrated by breakdowns in communications, gas, water, debris and mechanical trouble.[3] During the night, hope noticeably dimmed after the bodies were found. The exhausted, grimy rescue workers had pushed the search effort since the explosion Tuesday evening.[4]

At 4:00 a.m., Commissioner Casper Nelson, who was coordinating the rescue operation, and June Crawford, a spokesman for Texas Gulf Sulphur, announced the shutdown.

The two officials told reporters that attempts to reach the five survivors had been temporarily suspended, and they were going back to the "original plan," which was to establish a fresh air base at the bottom of the mine shaft. After that, rescue workers would make trips into the long mine drifts. He pointed out again that rescue workers used about half their oxygen supply going up and down the shaft.[5]

Nelson explained that as the Rescue Teams pressed on into the East Drift, they were met with frustration after frustration. The crews could not[6] get far enough down the drift to reach the group.

In the excitement of having rescued the two trapped men and having brought them to the surface, they had abandoned their first plan of establishing a fresh air base. Hope and enthusiasm had run high, and rescue crews felt they could make a run for the barricade. Unfortunately, this had been met with repeated failed attempts, forcing officials to re-impose their "original plan."[7]

For the rescue teams to journey into the mine, it was a half-hour each way or sixty minutes for a round trip. Rescue workers who took the plunge and breathed from bottled oxygen could not work more than thirty-five minutes at the bottom without becoming exhausted and being forced to surface for fresh air. That is why the five men behind a barricade had to wait for the tedious construction of an "air base" in the bottom of the mine shaft before rescuers could go about the business of getting to them and getting them out.[8] But it was soon sadly learned that a trip that consumed so much of their oxygen supply—going and coming—didn't leave enough air for the "doing."[9]

"We are not abandoning hope,"[10] Commissioner Nelson stressed.

"We have been unsuccessful in attempts to reach the five men believed to be alive. We plan to go back to our "original plan" of establishing a fresh air base at the bottom of the shaft from which we can work," he said.

"The work to establish a fresh air base in the badly battered shaft may take twenty-four hours—at a minimum, twelve hours. During this time, rescuers will not go into the drifts," Nelson explained. Other workmen speculated, however, that the refitting of damaged sections in the large vent line could take as little as six hours, which would allow a quicker resumption of the search for the other men.[11]

Crews needed to repair or replace five, twenty to forty-foot sections[12] of the main vent tubing. They used plastic replacement tubing[13] in the shaft at the 1,200-foot level, and repaired and replaced several other sections in areas deeper in the shaft which had been damaged by the fiery explosion.

Nelson said that once the fresh air base at the bottom of the mine shaft was established, the tempo of the rescue work would quicken. Besides the problem of limited oxygen supplies, another significant hindrance to the work were the two buckets—they could only be operated one at a time.[14]

Nelson indicated that once they had the vent line repaired, air could be pumped into the bottom of the mine, and the teams would then be able to ride up and down the shaft without drawing upon their oxygen supplies. Until crews establish the fresh air base, no efforts will be made to remove the bodies or survivors. An exception to this, of course, would be a dramatic appearance near the drift entrance of any live miners,[15] such as occurred when Hanna and McKinney reached safety.

Nelson said that during the night, a two-man team (Guy Hersh and a young Harrison International Rescuer) had restored the high-pressure compressed air line leading to the five barricaded miners. Nelson said they were sent down to put a patch on the compressed air line Hanna and McKinney attempted to repair on their way out of the East Drift (3U).

"We're guessing the air is going back to the five," he said. "Rescuers had been instructed to tap on the line, but they did not receive a response.[16]

"We hope those men are getting some air through the line," Nelson said.[17] (In contrast to Nelson's viewpoint, Guy Hersh and other rescuers doubted the line was pushing compressed air to the five men behind the barricade.)[18]

Nelson believed the explosion occurred in the 2,500-foot long West Drift.[19] Methane gas could have caused the blast, which caused a violent disturbance at the surface. He also emphasized the cause has not been definitely determined. He said all indications were that the explosion occurred from a methane gas pocket set off by a dynamite explosion.[20] (Workers drill a small, deep hole and test it for gas; then, if it is gas free, they insert the dynamite charge and fire it.) Observers speculated a charged hole was tested and found free of gas, but a large pocket of gas behind the hole exploded, causing the fiery blast which ripped through the mine.[21]

Nelson informed the reporters that crews had already started repairing the main vent line in the shaft, after which they would resume efforts to rescue the miners trapped for two days a half-mile below ground.[22] The rescue crews were still battling extreme heat, deadly poisonous gas, and damaged air vents blowing and spraying groundwater. It was reported that the water hampered work in the shaft, but the drifts were comparatively dry.[23]

"We should have followed this program twenty-four hours ago," Commissioner Nelson said. Addressing the reason they did not do this originally, he stated, "Two men went through that and came out alive." Adding, "If they can come out, we could go in."[24]

There was also heightened concern for the five men in the barricade when rescue teams deep in the mine first spotted five more bodies; officials said they might be the men whom Hanna and McKinney reported were still alive when they made their way to the shaft station.[25] No one knew for sure.

At 5:00 a.m., rescue officials reluctantly announced, to family members assembled in the lab building, the suspension of rescue efforts for twelve to twenty-four hours while they repaired the vent lines.[26] They talked about the complications rescue teams had run into throughout the night and explained how they were going back to the "original plan" of establishing a fresh air base at the bottom of the shaft. Anxiety was high over the amount of time it would take to accomplish the repairs. Time was something the men in the mine

Disaster at Cane Creek

didn't have. It was already a race against time—a race many felt that the men were losing.

The families had spent another long, exhausting night, and this latest news of another delay was devastating. One wife found the generosity of spirit to say, "I feel sorry for the men who have to make these decisions. I wouldn't want to trade places with them."[27] Dozens of wives and family members kept the long, painful vigil at the mine site during the rescue operation; they were determined not to leave until they knew the fate of their loved one.[28] Others came and went during the long, exhausting hours.

Emotions ran high as families continued to watch and wait. When word came late Wednesday morning of voices heard in the mine, everyone rushed to the Headframe to be near the rescue effort. They were anxious with hope. After the first two survivors had been brought from the shaft and brought word that, "at least five more are alive," spirits soared.[29] The disappointment over a delay was crushing for those fearing the worse and who were barely able to hold on much longer.

"My husband has worked in the mines most of his life," said a gray-haired woman. "He knew it was coming. He knew it, but he wouldn't get out of the mine before it was too late." Even as she spoke, she anxiously strained to see a crew leaving the bucket at the mouth of the mine. The wives all shared a common bond as they continued to wait and hope.[30]

Jesse Fox's family had all gathered at the mine site. Along with his wife, Alice, and two daughters, Linda, fifteen, and Peggy, eleven, were his two brothers, Nelson and Kenneth, and his sister, Georgia, from Salt Lake City. His sister, Caroline, came from California. Through the long hours of waiting, they relied on each other and drew strength from their faith. His family was comforted by the fact that Jesse was a fighter. He served in the U.S. Army during World War II and had experienced some very fierce fighting and had nearly lost his life.

It had been eighteen years since the end of World War II, and ten years since the end of the Korean War. Nearly half of the twenty-five men caught in the explosion were U.S. or Canadian military veterans, much like many of the men on the rescue teams. Other families hung on to the hope and faith their loved one would prevail, knowing they had lived through hard times during the war years and were tough from their military training.

During the night, while still asleep, nurses moved Hanna and McKinney into the same room in preparation for the eventual arrival of the other five survivors. They were expected at the hospital at any time. But by the time Hanna awoke early the next morning,[31] there was still no sign of them. It was the first thing he inquired about, but each response brought the same reply. "No, they're not out yet." Hanna couldn't understand why.

He became irritable and upset over no news. And his eyes hurt, (the right eye worse than the other). McKinney, now awake, also couldn't understand. They fully expected the men to be there when they woke. How could they not be? They had told rescuers how to get to them.[32]

All morning, they repeated the general inquiry to anyone who might know something, "Have they got to them yet?"

Throughout the morning hospital routine, medications were given, eyes irrigated, bandages changed, breakfast served, and sponge baths given. With fresh gowns and bedding, both seemed to be doing well and were reported in "good" condition.[33] Both were eating well and talked with relatives and friends beginning to arrive at the hospital. They were feeling so good, in fact, that both men even discussed returning to the Cane Creek Mine to help advise rescue crews seeking to reach the five trapped men.[34] But once they heard officials delayed the rescue, in order to establish a fresh air base at the bottom, each grew more troubled and became increasingly upset and agitated by the news.

That was "something we told them they should have done a long time ago," Hanna said.[35]

"I never would have gotten into that bucket if I'd thought they weren't going to go back right then and get the other five," McKinney said.[36]

Things became worse once both men heard of dead miners found by teams, as both bitterly criticized the mine rescue effort. Both grew visibly upset and increasingly alarmed.

The trapped men were running out of time. The heat in the sweltering mine was exhausting; they could have run out of the water by now, and the air was never really good. Besides, rescuers questioned whether air from the patched line was even getting to the barricade. The worse thought was of the men coming out of the barricade. They could run into a pocket of deadly gas which shifted like sand and lurked throughout the mine. Because of that, no one even knew how Hanna and McKinney had made it through the toxic environment and lived.

From the time of the explosion, Hanna and McKinney had been on a terrifying emotional ride, and it appeared it wasn't slowing down anytime soon. Anxiously, they fretted and stewed over the welfare of their buddies, and wanted them rescued as soon as possible.

With the rising sun, the daylight took some of the edges off the drama.[37] Around the Headframe, a slight breeze through the canyon country kept the dirt blowing, covering workers and watchers with red-hued dust.

The start of the third day of the rescue operation, teams were as busy as ever, continually rotating and taking their turn while working on repairs to the vent line down the shaft. Men, scattered throughout the yard, were having a bite to eat with their morning coffee while some chatted in groups.

Nearby, an object of hope stood side-by-side with a symbol of grief—a black ambulance parked next to a gray, curtained hearse. An hour earlier, an oxygen-hungry rescue team surfaced and brought out more bad news. They added two more victims to the list, making it ten known dead.[38] Officials blamed carbon monoxide for some of the miners' deaths.[39] Another official speculated that the latest victims may have been men who left the barricade last night and died on their way toward the shaft.[40]

Teams endured a long, disappointing night. By morning, it was apparent there was dissent over authority and procedure, primarily over the decision to delay rescue exploration. Some blamed the delay on state mine officials. Others sniped at the coal miners from Sunnyside.

At one point during the rescue, a truckload of brattice cloth and timbers was brought to the mine site. Officials were set to have rescue teams build a partition down the length of the shaft. Rescue teams generally took the fresh air with them as they advanced by building temporary stoppings out of timber frames, which were generally built with 2 x 4's and covered with a brattice cloth. The plan proved to be too difficult, and the idea quickly fizzled out.

One Harrison International miner, a hard rock mining veteran, lamented that "these guys are used to coal mines. They don't operate underground like we do. And if things get a little gassy, they get out." There were even indications during the rescue of men present (mostly Harrison International workers) willing to risk everything, including their lives, to reach the five survivors. They said they would go—with or without air packs. The fact that at least two survivors without air packs came out of the mine lent authority to the opinion of the hard rock miners who clamored to get into the mine.[41]

In spite of objections, the operation proceeded at its own pace, with only oxygen-equipped rescue workers allowed to work in the shaft—three or four at a time. Utah State Mine Inspector, Steve

Hatsis lamented, "We don't know what's down there, and we're going as fast as we can."

The criticism was taken up far and wide. U.S. Secretary of State, Stewart Udall, had commented the night before that safety measures were not up to standard in some places in the mining industry. He claimed that the U.S. Bureau of Mines inspectors should have been in charge.

A TGS lawyer fired back, saying U.S. Bureau of Mines inspectors, by contract agreement, had been in on the Moab operation ever since it started, or at least, they should have been. Many believed there was blame to be laid for the accident. As one miner said, "The Utah State Industrial Commission will try to pin it on Harrison International or Texas Gulf Sulphur. Harrison International will accuse the Utah State Industrial Commission and Texas Gulf Sulphur. Texas Gulf Sulphur will put the responsibility on the Utah State Industrial Commission and Harrison International.[42]

During the morning, Hanna's older brother, Harold, who worked at Cane Creek, was also critical of the rescue operation and blamed mine officials for failure to reach the five men.[43]

"Blake told me yesterday where those guys were and sent me to tell them how to get them out. It would have meant taking chances, but we could have done it. But they wouldn't let us. Now it's too late. Those guys couldn't have made it through the night without air," Harold told reporters. "Blake walked out from behind the barricades without a mask after being down there more than nineteen hours. Why in hell couldn't men with air packs go the same distance and get the guys behind the barricades?"

Harold answered his own question: "Because they wouldn't let them."[44]

Hanna's father, Jack, was there with Harold and chimed in on the conversation. "Blake carried a flame safety lamp from the barricade to the bottom of the shaft. Using it to detect deadly methane gas, it would glow red, or it went out in its presence."

Jack Hanna, the father of survivor, Blake Hanna, draws a map for the rescue workers at the mine site.

"He said it turned red a couple of times," Jack said, "But he kept coming anyway." He said his son thought the blast occurred at the Face of the West Drift, with its force going out of the drift and up the shaft.[45] Hanna even drew a map for his father to take to rescuers that showed the location of the barricade.

A small whiff of smoke from the Camel cigarette Jack was smoking swirled slowly through the air, as he shifted it to his other hand to show the map, pointing out two right-angle turns in the long drift that had spared the group from the full force of the blast. As was his habit, he pointed out the right-angles of the drifts with the middle finger of his hand because he lost most of his index finger in a mining accident.

All morning long, as rescue crews worked in the shaft, the talk on the surface was about the delay. Rescue officials were unfazed by the criticism and continued with the task at hand.

All morning long, both Hanna and McKinney were more and more visibly upset that the other men were not yet safe at the hospital. When they heard officials had suspended the rescue operation, both men wanted to leave their hospital bed[46] and go to the mine site to help. They just couldn't understand what was going on and what those running the rescue operation were doing.

It was around 9:00 a.m. when Hanna heard officials wouldn't listen to his father and brother who had taken out information from him personally to help with the rescue. Upset, he and McKinney grew more anxious. They knew they could get to the barricade or, at least, help the teams do so. They knew the mine, inside and out. They had built it and were used to breathing in a bad atmosphere such as black powder smoke whenever the Face was blasted.

They also knew the other five men were going through a torturous hell trapped in the mine. Hanna and McKinney had no doubts they could get to the men and get them out with no problems—that's if they were still alive, which was their biggest concern. Struggling all morning and battling extreme emotions, they simply became more agitated the more they heard or didn't hear. Hanna couldn't take it any longer. He couldn't lay there anymore.

About 10:00 a.m.,[47] as Dr. Munsey was at the hospital making his rounds, he heard from the nurses and saw their notations in the patient records of just how upset both men were. They were worried sick about the other five men. Hanna demanded the doctor release him. Hanna, clad in a bathrobe, was ready and determined to walk out of the hospital.[48] Dr. Munsey agreed to let them leave for a few hours.[49] He made Myrna promise she would bring Blake back to the hospital if he had any problems.[50]

"We know where those guys are, let's go get 'em," Hanna said to McKinney, as the two men, dressed in hospital robes, were driven from the Moab hospital by Myrna Hanna in a private auto.[51] Each was taken home to dress into street clothes.

Dressed in a tee-shirt and slacks, Hanna was ready to leave. Feeling just a bit self-conscious, he grabbed his cowboy hat and put it on his balding head on the way out the door.

Separately, both men headed to the mine site. Hanna was driven by his wife, while McKinney's brother drove him.[52] Down the winding river road to the mine site, both were confident they could help and believed they could get to their buddies.

While the loss of the three men right after the explosion deeply troubled Hanna, he felt there would be no way he could handle the loss of the other five men. There was no way of knowing how long the men could hold out.

Hanna also struggled with, what was for him, a moral dilemma. For the men who were already known to be dead, and with a high probability there were others, he struggled with the question, who would speak for them? The loss of any life was haunting. For him, he believed someone needed to be the voice for the men who lost their lives, as well as for their wives and children. Someone needed to address the safety problems at Cane Creek. It was more a "lack of a safety program." Something like this should never happen to another family.[53]

Hanna knew he had to speak out. His mother begged him not to say anything. It could jeopardize his own family's livelihood. He could be blacklisted, making it difficult to get work anywhere in the state. Myrna, on the other hand, when alone with Blake, told him to do what he felt was right. She would live in a shack if that was to be the consequence for caring about the other men and their families.[54]

Time passed slowly for the families standing vigil at the mine site. Disgruntled, they complained mostly about the dangerous conditions in the mine.[55] Even before the explosion erupted, some had worried something like this might happen. Fingers immediately pointed at Texas Gulf Sulphur and Harrison International. Whenever fatal events happen, companies are closely scrutinized. Problems come to light for all to see, especially in the aftermath during investigations that can spawn liable suits.

"My brother didn't like the work or the conditions in the mine, but the pay was so good he couldn't quit," said Eldred Johnson, the brother of Clell Johnson. "He brought home anywhere from $1,000 to $1,250 a month. That means a lot to a family man," he said. Eldred, a coal miner himself, said he made about $600 a month, "just about standard pay." Clell, on the other hand, did far better working in the potash mine. He'd complain about the rough conditions, but the pay was too good."[56]

The potash miners were getting paid top dollar, at a time when the minimum wage was $1.15.[57] Starting pay for these men was $3.33, plus time and a half for overtime—and the men at Cane Creek worked seven days a week.[58] Even though they were compensated well, it was grueling and exhausting work.

"They made up in pay what they didn't do in safety precautions," said William June, the father of missing miner, Bob June.[59] William and his wife came to Moab early Wednesday, after learning their son was one of the entombed miners. They, and two other sons, Donald and Ted, were among the crowd of anxious watchers near the mine entrance waiting for word from below.[60]

Before the explosion, those working at the Cane Creek Mine had their share of "canary in the coal mine" moments. This metaphoric saying originated from days when miners used the caged canaries in mines as an advanced warning for methane and carbon monoxide gases. The birds, more sensitive to lower levels of gases, would stop singing and pass out or die as a warning to miners. Many times, the birds recovered when taken to the better air. The term is now used to describe a warning that should have been heeded.

It seemed that from the moment Harrison International started work at Cane Creek, one thing after another plagued their efforts. Aside from the difficulties with the water their crews encountered in the shaft that made work conditions miserable, there were fatalities, injuries, many close calls, and warnings.

It was a primary concern when Harrison International's men encountered ground problems while sinking the shaft. The company had never encountered the type of conditions as bad as it was at Cane Creek. Most of the miners and even the bosses spoke about how the unstable ground was so bad it made work conditions extremely unsafe. When crews dynamited, instead of the blasted area being twenty feet out, as intended, it would be thirty feet or more, too wide for the shaft.[61]

October 16, 1961, one man was killed when he was hit on the shoulder by a six-inch pipe. It fell forty feet down the shaft after it slipped from a clamp.[62]

On November 8, 1962, two men were killed by a rock burst in the shaft, a result of the stressed and unstable ground. Although rock bursts in mining were mostly unavoidable, the two men were standing in an area away from wire screening that might have protected them.[63] They were drilling when the "air burst," caused by rock tension, threw several fragments of rock into the shaft. The burst occurred just to one side of the heavy wire mesh, placed near the bottom and on one side of the shaft. Ironically, it had been put there to prevent such a possibility. A few pieces of 50-pound rock were involved in the burst. Also injured in the rock fall was Vern Palaski, who suffered a skull fracture and cuts, Guetan Blanehard and Henry Levigne, the Shift Walker, both of whom had minor injuries.

Just three days later, on November 11, 1962, there was another close call that could have ended in more fatalities. Ten men were working on the bottom of the shaft when a bucket was overwound and was pulled into the sheave wheel, putting too much strain on the cable. The cable broke and dropped the huge bucket to the bottom of the shaft, followed by an explosive noise and a cloud of dust. It landed on the top deck of the Galloway Stage,[64] just above where men were working. No one was injured, but it was a very close call, and the mishap temporarily shut down the shaft, while workmen repaired the damage.[65]

In December of 1962, crews ran into significant quantities of crude oil, about eighty feet above the shaft station level as they neared the final depth zone. Mine officials saw it as just another delay as crews worked to contain and seal[66] the oil; but even more concerning, everyone knew it was an indication there was also methane gas in the mine. After containing the oil with foam, crews put up a couple of curtains, one on each end of the station level to keep the gas out. It was an incredibly dangerous situation that was never reported[67] to the U.S. Bureau of Mines.

On June 25, 1963, one man was electrocuted while standing in a wet area and handling an electrical cable without insulated gloves. He died.[68]

Although Cane Creek was classified as a non-gassy mine, ample evidence emerged that it should have been reclassified as gassy. Had they done so, better safety precautions would have been required to deal with the hazards of gas in the mine, and would have ensured the safety of the miners. To geologist and other mine operators, it was common knowledge that there was a long history of gas problems in mining operations in the Moab area.[69] There had been ample warnings that indicated the presence of gas. During the sinking of the shaft, one worker described how he would throw a match down after lighting a cigarette, and it would go "woof" from ignited gas that was lingering near the ground.[70]

At times, gas was released while drilling the Face. Under pressure, it would blow water out of the holes. Several times when the drill hit a pocket of gas, the pressure was so intense, it ejected the drill steel and threw the drilling machine and driller twenty feet up the drift.[71] It happened to McKinney and 'C.C.' on two separate occasions.[72]

When excavation of the mine drifts began, it became common practice for the men never to look at the drill steel while drilling the Face because the cuttings would blow back much of the time into the miners' faces. They would stand off to the side, especially the first ten-foot steel they ran. Usually, after the first steel was drilled, the rest were not as bad. But the miners couldn't trust the process because some cuttings would still blow back sometimes hard enough to throw little rocks into their face and eyes.[73] This was more prevalent while they mined through the oil shale formation (an ancient silt river bed) that seemed to contain more pockets of gas.

The month before, on July 31st, four miners at the Cane Creek Mine were burned when a pocket of methane gas was unknowingly encountered. The crew had been drilling roof bolt holes while working in the 3U Drift. The gas ignited when one of the men lit a cigarette underground injuring four men: Johnnie Schear, Keith Schear, Robert Schrafft, and James McIntyre.[74] At that time, smoking was allowed underground; such was the case in many hard-rock mines across the country, at least those classified as non-gassy. Johnnie Schear suffered the more severe burns on his head, arms and upper torso and had remained in the hospital for the last month while McIntyre had been hospitalized for a week.[75] After the accident, Keith Schear, and the other Schear brother, Roy Schear (who also worked at the mine), quit in protest of the unsafe conditions at the mine.[76]

Disaster at Cane Creek

In spite of his concerns, after being off for several weeks, Keith had gone back to work the prior week for Harrison International. He and his wife, Lynn had planned to move and find a job elsewhere. He planned on working for about a week to get the funds they needed for the move.[77]

When the explosion happened Tuesday afternoon, the two older Schear brothers received the word that their brother, Keith, was one of the missing miners. Roy Schear was working at a Moab gas station, and Johnnie Schear was still in the hospital recovering from his previous injuries when they first got word of the explosion. Family members reported Johnnie was "deeply depressed" and helplessly awaited word of his brother from his hospital bed.[78]

Eudeene Hollinger was at the mine site with her family during the rescue operation. She remembered the gas ignition the month before when the four men were burned. Her husband, Jim, didn't come home after his shift. He had spent the whole night at the mine with others fighting the fire.[79] The muck pile burned for hours until it was finally put out. Now, he too was among the other missing men at the Cane Creek Mine.

Mostly hard rock miners, many of Harrison International's more senior supervisors from Canada had not been around gassy mines. Smoking underground was allowed in many of the hard rock mines at the time, while in coal mines it was not. But after the gas ignition incident, the Utah State Industrial Commission investigated and ordered that smoking be prohibited underground; and they had Texas Gulf Sulphur officials put up "no smoking" signs. Company officials told workers there would be no more smoking, no matches, and no smoking material underground at all. But no checks were ever made of men entering the mine for smoking materials to discourage the practice. Some of the workers personally knew men who never laid down their cigarettes and continued to smoke down in the mine.[80]

After the gas ignition at the Cane Creek Mine the previous month, the Utah State Industrial Commission had also instructed the mine to test continually for gas using flame safety lamps during each shift. But according to workers, some of the men were never instructed in the proper use or maintenance of the lamps. Supervisors never asked the men if they knew how to use the lamps properly, and supervisors never made sure anyone was trained in their use. Reportedly, a lighted permissible flame safety lamp was hung in each drift close to the Face and other places and only observed occasionally. Apparently, some men were under the impression that the casual observation of the hanging lamp was considered proper gas testing. There were even occasions when flame safety lamps were passed from one crew to another as the shifts changed, and some were not properly cleaned and serviced.[81] One worker witnessed one of Harrison International's supervisors frustratingly throw a new flame safety lamp down into the pile of rubble to be mucked out, claiming it didn't work properly. Only it did. The flame kept going out, which indicated there was a presence of gas.[82]

Historically, flame safety lamps were not always reliable and could even cause explosions. Because of this, the U.S. Bureau of Mines regulated the training and certification of miners in their proper use. Flame safety lamps were first utilized in the early part of the 19th Century. At that time, opinions varied as to the efficiency between the two kinds available. One was thought to be safer in the gaseous atmosphere, but when there was gas, it simply went out. The other safety lamp gave more light, but if there was a high influx of gas, the top became red hot, which could risk an explosion. Although there were improvements through the years, flame safety lamps still had to be used with caution by those who were knowledgeable about their function and care.[83]

Texas Gulf Sulphur claimed they increased gas checks in the mine. That's what 'Blackie' Eslick was doing in the mine at the time of the explosion. But some workers felt the usual type of gas tests were not made with regularity.[84] They felt the mine should have been checked every shift to find out what the levels were.[85]

Disaster at Cane Creek

It also seemed that there was never enough air to breathe down in the mine at any given time, and it was always hot. Miners became wringing wet with sweat while trying to get their job done and they had to drink water constantly to keep from getting heat exhaustion. Better ventilation would have made a difference in lowering the temperature, as well as improving the quality of air the men had to breathe.[86]

Ventilation was vital to keep gas out of the explosive ranges and flush it out of the mine. Shift Walker, Rene Roy, wrote a prophetic letter home to his wife, Jessie, in Canada, dated May 21, 1963, three months before the explosion. He told her how he had "passed out underground." He thought it was because of "too much heat and some gases," and he was not the only one. At the shaft station, he found a TGS engineer was laying on the ground who had passed out as well. Rene had gone to the surface for twenty minutes to rest and to get some fresh air. He was okay but didn't like what happened. So he stopped work at the Face until the air underground was improved. He also told her that they were going to put a new vent pipe from the surface down "to the working place" to get more air into the mine. "A real widow maker, as the Americans say, ha-ha," he joked. "Herve and I had a big laugh over that. I guess Herve did not understand, but he understands now dear," Rene wrote.[87]

Harrison International did attempt to increase the volume of air into the mine to dilute any gases to keep it out of explosive ranges and to flush any gas out of the mine. The new vent pipe Rene talked about was a second vent line installed down the side of the shaft. They also used booster fans in the line to get the air to move and circulate better. Ventilation was probably one of the biggest problems they had at Cane Creek. Along with TGS's Ventilation Engineer, the Cane Creek crews worked diligently to fix the problem. But some were not convinced the problems were fixed.

In the weeks leading up to the explosion, Paul McKinney tested the amount of the air coming out of the vent line down by the Face using an Anemometer. He got a reading of 1,500 volumes of air or CFM (cubic feet per minute). Ironically, each of the shuttle cars had 1,700 CFM stamped on their Approval Plate, indicating how much air was required to run each one. Those shuttle cars were also diesel-powered and non-permissible in gassy mines. Consequently, it was always smoky during the mucking process because of the poor ventilation.[88] When the miners had four or five shuttle cars in the Face cleaning out the muck, the conditions were deplorable for the men.

There had been several other close calls while sinking the shaft. In one incident, one crew was working in a bucket part way down the shaft. They were cutting loose a big power cable when the clamps holding it on the surface failed. The whole cable fell down the shaft and nearly wiped out the men in the bucket on its way down.

In another incident, about a month and a half before the explosion, some of the eight cables attached to the Galloway Stage rotted and rusted through. With the weight of accumulated muck and salt, it plunged into the sump about thirty feet. No one was in the shaft at the time, so no one was hurt, although Bert Trenfield, the Mine Superintendent for Harrison International, was at the station when it happened. It took crews two weeks to cut through the miles of metal cables with cutting torches, then bundle them together and haul them to the surface. Crews restrung hoisting cables to the Galloway Stage, but it was still down in the sump at the time of the explosion.[89]

Overall, there was a total of seven fatal accidents during TGS's three mammoth projects (railroad spur and tunnel; the construction of the surface facility; and the shaft and mine development) while in various phases of the construction.[90] Four of seven fatalities happened in the shaft and development of the mine. Those four men were killed in three different accidents that had nothing to do with any gas problems.

Many of Harrison International's men knew the mine was dangerous, even the bosses talked about the gas and other concerning problems.[91] Yet, many of the Canadians had never actually worked where they had to deal with methane gas.

Disaster at Cane Creek

Lamar Rushton, a Lead Miner, had been employed at the mine from the start of the shaft sinking. He had found a new job and was to leave Cane Creek right after they reached the potash ore bed. He was waiting for that event, so he could receive the bonus pay.[92]

Rene Roy sent his son, Herve, two weeks before the explosion, back home because of the dangers and was working to put away some extra money so he could also join his family back in Canada.[93]

It was the same for Hanna. He had had the same type of discussion with his wife and thought about finding new employment as soon as they saved enough funds to leave.[94]

McKinney personally called the Utah State Industrial Commission on three different occasions about three to four weeks before the explosion. He hoped to get them to come to Moab to check the ventilation since it was very obvious the miners didn't have enough ventilation. To McKinney's knowledge, the state mine inspector never showed up once, let alone on the three different times he had called the State. He never once heard back from them.[95]

Chuck Byrge wrote two letters to the State, also requesting them to come and investigate. He, too, never heard back from them.[96]

When the gas ignition happened at the mine three weeks earlier in the East Drift (3U), that's when many of the men became even more concerned.[97]

This fire incident was never reported to the U.S. Bureau of Mines, nor was the discovery of crude oil that Harrison International encountered while sinking the shaft. The State was informed, but TGS claimed they didn't need to notify the Bureau. Also, many of the men felt safety training was virtually nonexistent. With the unsafe work conditions at Cane Creek, many of the miners were of the opinion that the mining laws were lax and that no one was doing anything about it.[98]

Secretary Udall had claimed in his previous dispatch that he stated he wanted to strengthen the enforcement powers of the U.S. Bureau of Mines at metal/nonmetal mines such as the potash mine worked by Texas Gulf Sulphur. This would give the Bureau the type of regulatory authority now exercised by the federal government over coal mining in the United States on inspection, safety, and the like.[99]

Business Editor, Robert W. Bernick, at the *Salt Lake Tribune*, did some digging and discovered some troubling information about who had regulatory authority regarding the development of the Cane Creek potash development from the beginning.[100] A native of Iowa, Robert Bernick grew up in Missouri and graduated from the highly-regarded University of Missouri School of Journalism. After a stint as a gunner in an Army Air Force bomber in World War II, he started work for the Associated Press (AP) and later served with the United Press International (UPI). Bernick ended up in Salt Lake City in 1948 and soon joined the staff of the old *Salt Lake Telegram*, where he eventually became the paper's first business editor. When the *Telegram* was bought out by *Deseret News* in 1952, he joined the *Salt Lake Tribune*, where his probing reporting set a whole new style of covering business news. His column, "Up and Down the Street," was widely read in the business community and was considered an authoritative voice on commerce and industry.[101]

Bernick was able to uncover that the U.S. Bureau of Mines already had regulatory authority over the development of the Cane Creek potash property. When Secretary Udall personally signed leases with Texas Gulf Sulphur the conditions of those leases were that the operator would comply with the "Code of Federal Regulations, Title 30—Mineral Resources. Chapter II, Part 231" (30 CFR, Part 231), was a ten-page pamphlet on safety and other regulations, published by the United States Geological Survey (USGS) of the Department of Interior. These mining and safety regulations applied to all lands of the United States and most Indian tribal lands and were enforced by the U.S. Geological Survey and the U.S. Bureau of Mines.[102]

The most troubling part was that the U.S. Bureau of Mines was specifically assigned the responsibility of making inspections.

In collaboration, the USGS was specifically assigned the responsibilities of "making reports on conditions of the leased property and manner of operations, then provide recommendations for safeguarding lives, the health of employees and protection of the property."

The regulations also stated that "Where there is evidence of "flammable gas," the properties will be operated under the same regulations as coal mines under federal safety supervision in the United States." In other words, not only was the Cane Creek property supposed to be inspected by the U.S. Bureau of Mines and the USGS but, in addition, if found to be gassy, it should have been reclassified and operated under the same class of laws as coal mines, which were more stringent.[103] "Instructions and Notices are to be issued" in safety matters by the district mining supervisor, the regulation pamphlet continued, "and the mining supervisor has the authority to halt operations temporarily where he feels unsafe conditions prevailed."[104]

The regulations were broad and all-inclusive, and required operators to supply maps, plans, programs of operations and other essential data. In fact, the pamphlet listed other miscellaneous regulations that were required, on pain of having the lease canceled the loss of their investment.[105]

For many who were waiting for word of their loved one trapped in the mine, this was a bombshell. Obviously, there were others who had failed the miners and perhaps, had the U.S. Bureau of Mines been inspecting the mine all along, it might have been able to prevent the disaster.[106] There was even talk that Secretary Udall had not yet assigned the U.S. Bureau of Mines the right in any order,[107] which would have given them regulatory authority, in spite of them having made only one inspection on November 28-29, 1961, when the shaft was at a depth of 840 feet.[108]

By 10:00 a.m., Thursday morning, rescue operation had been going on forty-two hours from the time of the explosion. The one body that had been brought to the surface earlier at 3:00 a.m., during the night, had still not been identified.[109]

"Do you have any names?"

That solemn question was asked over and over, again and again, yesterday and today, by the families of the trapped miners as the rumors continued to fly.[110]

Hanna had earlier told his family members and a few others the names of the five men still alive behind the barricade: Chuck Byrge, Tom Trueman, 'C.C.' Clark, Bob June and 'Blackie' Eslick. He had also given the names to Texas Gulf Sulphur officials,[111] but for whatever reason, the company did not officially announce the names of the men. Rumors spread and were always rampant, making it difficult to know what to believe.

Herve Roy made it out to the mine site early in the morning and soon learned officials had delayed the rescue operation during the night. Rescue crews were working hard to establish the fresh air base at the bottom of the shaft.

The night before, Herve called his mother, Jessie, in Ontario, to let her know what was happening. He told her about his father trading shifts, and about the new car. Jessie knew nothing about her husband's car purchase, but expressed her surprised that Rene didn't get an Olds.[112]

The vehicle Rene traded in was an older model Oldsmobile, painted black and yellow. Rene thought it looked great, but his son, Herve, thought it looked awful, but didn't have the heart to say anything to his dad. Rene's new Impala was so much better.

Mrs. Hamilton in Moab had been calling and keeping Jessie Roy informed of the rescue, and Jessie was also able to hear hourly broadcasts in Ontario about the mine disaster.[113] Jessie felt Herve needed to take the new car back to the dealership to see if they would take it back. The manager of the dealership would not be in until noon, and they told Herve that he could meet with him at that time. Throughout the morning, Herve heard the talk at the mine site. He heard about upset rescue workers who wanted to get into the mine and about family members' stories regarding the safety issues at Cane Creek. Rene had sent Herve home not long after the gas ignition that burned the four miners. At first, Herve was upset with his father, but he gradually came to realize it was done to protect him. His father planned to be right behind him in the move to Ontario. Rene was going to save what money he could and follow since he did not like the things happening at the mine.[114]

Just after eleven, Herve decided it was probably time to leave to get back to Moab before noon. Some of Harrison International's guys said they would let him know if anything was going on at the mine, so he could still get back out to the site. Rescue crews were still busy with work in the shaft and most believed they wouldn't be finished until the late afternoon.

At the dryhouse (change house), where miners dress and keep their change of clothes, young Herve found his father's basket among the many hoisted to the ceiling. It was surreal to see all the baskets, knowing some of them belonged to the men trapped down in the mine. The baskets had their street clothes just the way they left them the day before. His father's basket was next to the one he had used when he worked at Cane Creek a couple of weeks earlier. Herve unlatched the chain, threaded over a pulley wheel, and lowered his father's wire basket from the top of the ceiling. Inside, he found the keys to his father's new 4-door Chevy Impala nestled in his clothes.[115]

At the parking lot, Herve unlocked the door to the new, sleek brown vehicle. It still had that new car smell. As he started the engine, he noticed it only had twenty-three miles on the odometer. Slowly, Herve drove out of the parking area and decided he had enough time to stop by the man camp before heading to Moab. He let himself into his father's bunkhouse but stayed only a short period. It was lonely seeing all his dad's belongings. Herve tried not to think about what was going on with the rescue. He just wanted to believe his dad would make it. Rene was a tough guy. He could make it through this, Herve reassured himself.[116]

Herve went to Moab and met with the manager of the car dealership, who said he would take the vehicle back, but he would have to deduct $3,000 for depreciation. Herve couldn't believe it. Stunned, he left to call his mom. It didn't take long before family friends found someone who would buy the car at the same price Rene had paid. Herve headed back to the mine site, worried he might have missed something.[117]

In the sweltering desert heat, tables near the rescue operation[118] stood covered with white paper. Behind them, volunteers from the Women's Auxiliary and the American Institute of Mining Engineers served a home-cooked lunch to the rescuers and officials.

Women volunteers from Moab greeted the tired rescuers with encouraging smiles and words. Groups of miners dotted the scene, each compared notes on the rescue operation while eating their lunch. Some returned for more of the stew from the large kettle.[119]

Their meals finished, rescuers turned their sweaty, dirt-stained faces toward the shaft. While those on the surface had eaten, the trapped men below in the mine had gone days without food. Weary rescuers waited their turn to work in the deep shaft while camp cots were scattered over the area near the Headframe. Some were utilized by exhausted rescuers, while other cots stood ready for the rescuers in the event there was another long and grueling night.

Disaster at Cane Creek

1. Guy Hersh left, John 'Curly' Westbrook (right) and other rescuers get some chow. (*Daily Sentinel*) 2. Johnny Schmidt gets some much needed shut eye. (*Times-Independent*) 3. Nurses from Carbon County Hospital wait out the long night. (*Daily Sentinel*) 4. Utah Industrial Commissioner, Casper Nelson, steals a nap. (*Daily Sentinel*) 5. Supplies and a row of litters are lined up near the entrance to the mine shaft. (*Daily Sentinel*)

341

Dramatically, Hanna and McKinney appeared back at the mine site shortly before noon.[120] After leaving the hospital, they were determined, if allowed, to re-enter the mine to search for their five companions they left behind.[121] The press caught wind that they were there and requested to meet with them.

McKinney went directly to the Headframe and told officials he would talk to the media later—that's if he had anything to say after watching the rescue operation. Inside the administrative office building, Hanna was led by company officials, with his wife by his side, to a roomful of reporters.[122]

Hanna had his cowboy hat on while sunglasses covered his eyes. One eye was bandaged with gauze. The hallway and press room were completely packed with people, news reporters, mine rescue workers, and officials. It was chaotic, and no one seemed to be in control of the place. With excitement and much scurrying about, reporters quickly set up cameras to take still photos and video footage, each vying to get the best angle in a near feeding frenzy.[123]

Texas Gulf Sulphur people were again put in an awkward position. Officially, Harrison International was still in control of the mine and was somewhat over the mine rescue operation, as they worked closely with the state officials. Harrison kept information close to their chest, making it difficult for TGS to get much from them.[124]

Hanna, an independent thinker and a maverick, had no problems speaking his mind; no doubt something he had probably inherited from his father, Jack Hanna. It was said of Jack Hanna that he was a fair man, and was respected by many because one always knew where they stood with him. Both had a tendency to be hard-minded, which inspired the family term, "hard-headed Hanna."

Disaster at Cane Creek

1. Blake Hanna is led by his wife, Myrna into TGS's Administrative Office Building for a press conference after returning to the mine site. (*Times-Independent*) 2. Hanna answers questions by the press. (*Daily Sentinel*) 3. Rescue Officials sit as everyone listens to what Hanna had to say. (*Times-Independent*)

Hanna sat at a table at the front of the room ready to vent his pent-up frustration and suppressed anger over events that had brought him to this point. He felt he owed it to the wives and families who were in the depths of agony, still waiting for news of their loved one.

And he owed it to the men he worked with—the ones he knew could still be alive, and the ones he knew were dead—to be their voice in an attempt to try and right a horrible, devastating wrong.

Hanna started by saying: "I figured the mine rescue operation is going too slow, so I came out here to see if I could help. I believe whoever is running the show is not doing any good. Paul and I worked three hours repairing the air line in the heat down there and almost got it linked up," he said.[125] It was quiet as all eyes were fixed on Hanna as he spoke.

"We got out of there without masks," he said. "As a matter of fact, we worked in there for three hours, replacing five long sections of high-pressure air line, and we still got out."[126]

"If Paul and I could live through it, by God, I don't see why they can't do it with equipment," he said. "Why can't they go down there now?" he rhetorically asked while reporters and officials listened.[127]

Asked if there was a chance the five trapped men would be rescued, Hanna said: "If they get there now, right now, and get them out."[128]

"A lot of time has been wasted," Hanna said. "They ought to have them out by now."[129]

The subject quickly changed when the reporters threw out other questions. When asked about mine safety, Hanna said, "I think the state is responsible for not inspecting and not enforcing state laws." He then claimed he had never seen a state inspector in the mine in the eighteen months he worked there.

"There hasn't been a state inspector into that mine," Hanna said. "I've never seen one."[130]

Criticizing the safety practices, he said, "There are no safety precautions.[131] No safety program down there at all."[132] He added that safety rules had been broken, and safety procedures were not followed before the explosion.[133]

Hanna said some of Harrison International's people didn't even know how to use a flame safety lamp. "The state never instructed them on how to use 'em.'[134]

When asked about an investigation, he said, "I'll be glad to testify before any investigating board they set up." Then added that Texas Gulf "did its best" but that "the state is responsible."[135]

The safety record of the company was brought up by reporters, turning the conversation to those records. According to the records, four deaths occurred at the mine during the construction period before Tuesday's blast. In addition, a non-fatal accident occurred, which involved an ignition of methane gas on July 31st. Two men were severely burned, and two others suffered minor burns.[136]

Pete Correy, TGS's Safety Engineer, said the company inspected the mine daily for gas, roof conditions and ventilation. "Every supervisor has been checked 100 percent in how to make these tests," Correy said[137] as he defended TGS's safety training procedures to a room overflowing with reporters.

"There were just no safety practices" Hanna snapped. He added, however, that "in the past three weeks the situation has improved."[138]

Texas Gulf Sulphur officials ended the ten-minute news conference, clearly distraught over the allegations and innuendos against their company. And rescue officials took offense over criticism of the rescue operation. Tempers were wearing thin, and everyone was weary and exhausted. Emotions ran deep as grief and anger bubbled near the surface.

Utah State Senator, Frank C. Memmott, also present at the news conference, followed the Hannas' out of the building. Hanna stopped to talk with another person, as Memmott approached Myrna standing near their car. He wanted to ask her some questions when one of the company officials told him he couldn't talk to her; they were on company property. Memmott shot back, and said that he would speak to whomever he "damn well pleased."[139]

Senator Memmott, (D), from Carbon County, a member of the Utah Senate Committee on Safety and Mining, arrived at the mine site the night before. A thirty-six-year-old Mining Engineer and a fifteen-year veteran of underground mining,[140] he had experience in mines in Utah, Pennsylvania, Kentucky and West Virginia.[141] Memmott said he came to the scene because of his concern for four close friends, who were among the men who are trapped, and to make an official inquiry into safety measures at the mine.[142]

He later told reporters he first learned of the nonfatal, July 31st, methane gas ignition at the mine the previous night for the first time. Memmott also said he intended to talk with as many miners as he could about safety procedures. He added that "anytime safety is involved, it's a matter of state concern."[143]

Commissioner Nelson, who had been at the scene of the disaster, was not immediately available[144] for comment on the remarks made by Hanna. Later, however, he defended the state's actions. Prodded by reporters on the safety record of the mine, Nelson claimed the operation met both state and federal requirements and then added, "You don't quit mining because methane is encountered." He even speculated that methane was the cause of the explosion, assuming it had been apparently triggered when a routine dynamite blast opened a pocket of natural gas.[145]

Chief Engineer, June Crawford, the spokesman for TGS, was also asked for a statement. He offered an angry defense of his firm, saying safety standards at the operation were of the highest order. "This company has a conscience," he said. "Our safety standards are higher than required by law."[146]

State metal-nonmetal mine inspector, John W. Holmes, said the mine had been inspected "about every two months since the shaft was started in 1961. The last inspection by a state personnel 'to his knowledge' was in July," Holmes said. "There had never been any serious violations noted during those inspections," he added.[147]

"Around a mine, there are always a few minor infractions from time to time," Holmes said. "But we have found none of a serious nature here." He noted that his office had ordered safety doors installed at the top of the shaft during the early stages of construction. The doors were kept closed when it was not in use.[148]

Also advised of Hanna's remarks, State Coal Mine Inspector, Steve Hatsis, said a state mine inspector was assigned to the property, and, although he personally had not been in the mine before the explosion, he had heard of nothing improper.[149] And, he said, rescue operations in the mine were being carried out in such a way to keep "risks" at a minimum. He did admit that "during the rescue operation, several risks had been taken Wednesday when it was thought rescuers could reach the five trapped miners without replenishing their oxygen."[150]

Part Five

Chapter 18

Charges Hit the Fan

After the press conference, company officials took Hanna to the scene of the rescue operation near the Headframe.¹ McKinney was already there watching. All around the yard, people were standing or sitting in the intense heat, and still, they waited as the rescue operation moved at a slow, steady pace.

Sharp criticism had arisen when officials suspended rescue operations, while they worked to repair the vent line and establish the fresh air base at the bottom. Most of the day, workers spent making the necessary repairs, but the time lag caused discontent and discouragement to grow among rescue workers and some of the family members.

More than anything, Hanna and McKinney wanted to get into the mine and get to the five men.

"Things are not as bad down there as they let on," McKinney said to one of the rescue workers. "I'm ready to go down. Right now."²

Rescue and company officials refused to let the two men re-enter the mine but were able to question them to help orient their search efforts.³ They hustled them into a steel shed where they kept them from communicating with newsmen.⁴

"There are five men down there who are depending on us,"[5] Hanna said, trying to convince officials to let them into the mine. But their requests were repeatedly refused.

There were reports that the temperature in the mine was a blistering 132 degrees or more. The heat was a big fear among relatives and doctors at the scene;[6] it could cause death-dealing dehydration. There had also been rumors some of the men might have left the barricade and died from the carbon monoxide.

Neither Hanna nor McKinney were too optimistic about the men they left behind. The plan was that the men would remain at the barricade for another twelve hours, and then start walking out toward the shaft.[7]

"If they followed the plan, they should have started for the shaft about 9:00 or 10:00 p.m. last night," said McKinney.[8] Company officials and rescue workers, however, refused to let the two men go into the mine, partly because of their ordeal.[9]

Throughout the early afternoon, rescuers continued to work hard to establish the fresh air base. Officials soon discovered the rescuers had trimmed about three hours off the estimated starting time for renewed rescue efforts underground. The air line work was progressing faster than planned and some estimated a search of the mine could begin around 3:00 p.m. [10]

By early afternoon, Utah Governor, George D. Clyde, told reporters in Salt Lake City that he was following developments at the mine site through continual contact with Utah State Industrial Commission Chairman, Otto Wiesley and Miles P. Romney, Utah Mining Association Manager.

"I'm satisfied everything humanly possible is being done to rescue those men still in the mine," he said. Turning to Utah's safety regulations for mining, "We're keeping up-to-date. Our safety record in Utah is good," he said.

"I understand the Cane Creek Mine was operating within standard procedures for safety." Recalling his mining days, he said, "It isn't always easy to know exactly where potential danger points are. Holes and new openings were then, and I'm sure now, are tested for any evidence of escaping gas."[11]

Governor Clyde also ordered a complete investigation by the Utah State Industrial Commission of the Cane Creek Mine disaster. The Governor said he wants all available information gathered and calmly analyzed, "so this kind of tragedy can be prevented in the future."

With all the talk and accusations of lax safety measures and lack of inspections at the Cane Creek Mine, the Utah State Industrial Commission made a file available[12] for examination by early afternoon at the State Capitol in Salt Lake City. The fat folder disclosed that from the time the shaft work started, ten previous state safety inspections had been conducted at Texas Gulf Sulphur's Cane Creek Mine. John W. Holmes made the inspections and filed his reports with the Commission.

It showed Holmes, who was an expert on shafts and blasting,[13] made out periodic safety inspection reports on the mine work starting May 24, 1961. Findings with subsequent dates showed Holmes paid ten more official visits to the mine, up to July 30, 1963. In addition, a Utah Industrial Commission office statement stated that Holmes and Casper A. Nelson had both been at the Cane Creek Mine earlier in the month, on August 7th. However, there was no written record of this in the Commission office.[14]

The inspections attested to by Holmes indicated he made seven standard visits and three investigations of fatal accidents. The total calls, listed in sequence, show the inspector at the mine once every three months during a twenty-nine-month period.[15]

"With the exception of one, none of his recommendations for improving safety showed up with any regularity. It indicated that the company, Harrison International, usually complied with the recommendation immediately," said a member of the Utah State Industrial Commission staff.[16]

Holmes' primary recommendation, made on a number of occasions, was to clear the decks of the Galloway Stage. He suggested they take better precautions to keep these decks, which were attached to the shaft wall, clear of tools and debris, so they would not fall on workers below. On the last inspection, after the shaft had been completed, February 28, 1963, Holmes wrote: "George Smith, Project Engineer for Harrison International, and his staff should be commended for the competent manner in which the shaft work has been done." Earlier, after the August 13, 1962, inspection, Holmes reported, "Shaft found exceptionally clean and orderly with safeguards in place."[17]

In his most recent official report, July 30, 1963, Holmes had recommended that "No smoking" be permitted underground and to keep a U.S. Bureau of Mines approved flame safety lamp at each working Face during the hours men are on shift. "Each working place must be tested for gas after blasting. If gas is found, the area must be cleared before other work is done."

Dates of all Cane Creek Mine inspections reported by the Utah State Industrial Commission were: May 24, 1961; August 15, 1961; October 18, 1961 (fatal); March 1, 1962; August 13, 1962; November 8, 1962 (2-fatal); February 29, 1963; May 14, 1963; June 25, 1963 (fatal); July 30, 1963; August 7, 1963 (no written account).[18]

Concerning the four fatalities, the Utah State Industrial Commission records show shaft work started in early 1961, and the first death occurred October 16, 1961. The last recorded death was June 25, 1963.[19]

Three of the inspections were made in connection with the fatal accidents. The dates and names of the four men[20] who lost their lives while working at the Cane Creek Mine were:

William G. Rusby, October 18, 1961, Moab, killed when a six-inch pipe slipped from a clamp and fell forty feet down the shaft, striking him on the head.

T.A. Tolson and Real Langlois, November 8, 1962, both of Moab, killed in a shaft rock burst in the shaft.

Ely O. LeMaster, June 25, 1963, Moab, electrocuted while standing in a wet area and handling an electrical cable without insulated gloves.

Other men had been injured, some seriously. Omitting the inspections that had been made for the accidents, the Commission inspected the mine eight times in two and a half years, with one of those not formally recorded.

Casper A. Nelson said Harrison International officials had "been most cooperative" in meeting and accepting recommendations by the mine safety inspector. "We have conferred many times by telephone from Moab on mine conditions and state regulations. "Our inspections are comparable to those in other states, and our regulations are probably better," he said.[21]

Nelson said there is no set schedule for mine inspections. "They are made as our personnel felt they were needed. Naturally, they try to make them often enough to determine mine conditions are safe," he added.[22]

When officials first made the announcement that they were going back to the original plan, it was 4:00 a.m. in the early morning hours. Some thought it would take twelve to twenty-four hours to establish a fresh air base at the bottom of the shaft and to pump oxygen into the mine. While officials were unsure just how long it would take, nonetheless, they went to work repairing the ventilation system.

Severed in five places,[23] ripped and smashed flat in others from the explosion, the large vent line running down the shaft had to be repaired before they could pump air down into the mine and the drifts to force the deadly gases out.[24] The damaged sections were hauled to the surface, and replacement segments were taken down the shaft to splice into the line.

That part of the job was finished about 3:00 p.m., nearly twelve hours since the time they went back to the "original plan." Finally, the switches were thrown[25] to start the fans. Their click was a sound of hope, and a sound of life as the giant fans started whirling.[26] Life-giving air swept down the deep shaft, flooding the mine and forcing out the deadly gases, lurking like phantoms, unseen but lethal. How long this part of the job would take, no one knew for sure as rescuers waited patiently around the Headframe.

Unlike the early part of the operation, once the work was finished, rescuers would no longer need their limited supply of oxygen in the heavy breathing apparatuses strapped to their backs. Nor would they have to feel the rubber masks gripping their faces, as they frequently wiped the dust and water from the lenses in front of their eyes to see.

Before, when rescuers climbed into buckets to start the thirty-minute journey into the depths, they could work, at most, only thirty minutes without being torn by exhaustion and forced to surface for fresh air because their gauges on the bottled air tanks read almost empty.

Louie Villegos (bottom) and 'Johnny Smoke' Palacios pass the time with other rescuers resting on cots against a wall. (*Deseret News*) 2. The rescue operation is painfully slow. Rescue crews talk in low tones, drink coffee, or just sit and stare as they await their turns to descend a half-mile into the earth to search. Rescuers (from left to right) Harry Krebs, Don Larsen, and Newel Crawford, (*Salt Lake Tribune*) 3. Waiting rescuers' faces reflect strain from the long vigil (seated far left is Paul Clark). (*Daily Sentinel*)

It was slow, painful and often discouraging work. The frenzied repair of the air artery was over, and now the fans were forcing the lifeblood of the rescue operation—air—into the chasm. Scientists say it's a complex arrangement of gases, but to the men above the shaft and the men entombed below, air means only one thing: Life.[27]

It was anyone's guess on how long it would take to clear the gases out of the mine. Teams continually went below to make gas checks and to make other needed preparations for the fresh air base at the bottom of the shaft. Other rescuers waited in the shade and rested.

Throughout the early afternoon in the scorching desert sun, Hanna and McKinney hung around and watched the rescue operation as teams made repairs to the large ventilation line. The closest they were allowed to get was near the paramedics, a short distance from the Headframe.

Both men's previous requests to go down into the mine had always been the same response: "No way!" Hanna and McKinney knew, if allowed, they could get to the men if still alive. That was their biggest fear—that they were no longer alive.

Everyone was weary and worn down after nearly two full days at the mine site. Rescuers had heard about Hanna and McKinney's criticism of the rescue, and a few were put off by it. The rescuers had worked hard.[28] Still, most understood the ordeal the two men had been through and their concern for the men they left behind.

Harrison International's guys would come up to chat with both men and exchange stories. They were also filled in with events that happened before they were rescued. Hanna was also able to talk to the rescuers he knew from Carbon County, many whom he worked with while at Kaiser Steel.[29] The rescuers were just as curious about what the two survivors had been through as the reporters were who wanted their story.

As the afternoon slowly wore on, Hanna eventually decided to leave with his wife around 4:30 p.m. to check himself back into the hospital.[30] He was exhausted, and his eyes were hurting, especially the right one that sustained the most damage. McKinney felt he would be okay if he stayed at the mine. His brother would take him back to the hospital if he needed.

Late in the afternoon, just before 5:00 p.m., rescue workers scurried about getting ready for another descent. Only this time, as team members got into the bucket, their oxygen apparatuses were on their backs, but they weren't wearing their masks.

Teams finally had the fresh air base set up at the bottom and fans had been running for several hours forcing air down into the mine. With tests taken periodically on the quality of the air in the mine, finally, the go-ahead was given.

Two handpicked rescue teams[31] started down the shaft one bucket at a time for what they called "a now-or-never search."[32] They were headed towards the five men behind a barricade in the furthest reaches of the mine. James Westfield was in the first bucket of rescuers when it started down at 5:00 p.m.[33]

Once in the mine, the rescuers didn't wait for the next bucket of rescuers to arrive. They immediately headed out towards the East Drift, taking gas readings along the way with their oxygen supply on their backs ready for use if needed. The rescuers were hopeful but apprehensive, not knowing what they would find. Already, ten men were known dead.[34] What if it was too late and the delays cost the five men their lives? No one wanted to think about that possibility as the men trudged down the silent drift.

Chapter 19

Behind the Barricade?

The five survivors were lying on the ground, dozing or half awake. Several had been imagining they saw lights and heard the distant clank of metal for a while, but didn't pay much attention to them.

'C.C.' heard a noise![1] Looking up, he saw some lights up the drift by the barricade curtain. He told the others, "Well, I see more lights coming, and I think they're real this time."[2]

"Here they come!" barked somebody.[3]

"They're here," another one shouted.[4]

Then they heard someone yell out, "How many of you are there?" came a voice from up the drift.[5] It was Robert von Storch[6] who asked. He was one of the first three rescuers to reach the barricade. The other two rescuers were James Westfield[7] and Henry Levigne (known as 'Little Henry' by Harrison International's men). It was 5:30 at the time they reached the barricade.[8]

"FIVE," chorused the men. After the men had hollered their happy reply, they started to make joyful sounds, whistling, shouting and laughing. And whoops of glee rang out as the two parties heard each other.[9]

Normally, none of the men slept very soundly, but the others had woken 'Blackie' when they yelled. 'Blackie' tried to shout but his throat was too dry, so he put his fingers in his mouth and parched lips and whistled as loud as he could four times. It's hard to tell who shouted the loudest, the rescue team or the five trapped miners. And it wasn't difficult to know who was saying, "Let's get out of here!"[10]

The survivors did not see their rescuers until they came through the last of the three curtains[11] and down to the camp area. The rescuers were a wonderful sight[12] as everyone started talking at once.[13]

"'Little Henry,' if you weren't so ugly, I'd kiss you," 'C.C.' told Henry Levigne[14] as the others laughed. The remaining four rescue team members caught up with the first three as the excited men hopped around trying to get dressed. The rescuers helped the men find their clothes and handed them pants and boots. The rear of Byrge's pants was torn out. A rescuer told him not to be concerned since they had blankets on the surface they would put around him.

During their confinement, the miners used only one cap-lamp at a time so they would have light as long as possible. They had only one light left when rescuers reached them.[15] The rescuers were also quite impressed by the three curtains hung by the men. It was evident that the barricade they constructed saved their lives.

The rescuers found each of the five men in surprisingly good condition.[16] Once dressed, they headed out as the men passed through each of the barricade curtains. The happy miners walked up the drift chattering, singing, shouting, back-slapping, and whistling.[17]

They had to slow down several times to let the seven rescuers catch up with them. They were in a hurry all right to get out of there.[18] It had been a long shift.[19] Too long!

As they neared the top of the incline, rescuers told them not to look as they stood in front of the three dead men who broke open the vent line. The smell of death was horrible, and a couple of them looked back and immediately wished they hadn't. It was devastating knowing the three could have lived had they stayed with the other men.

Disaster at Cane Creek

Solemnly, the men walked towards the shaft station. It soon became quite clear to them that they were in "a damn safe place." From where they were, they had no idea of the damage done until they passed by the devastation and destruction. Someone mentioned to the men the fan pipe was blown out and equipment destroyed and moved. Sure enough, a 300-pound fan was moved 100 feet from where it used to sit. Huge pieces of machinery were destroyed, and metal was twisted and snarled. It was hard to see how anyone got out alive.[20]

One rescuer rushed ahead of the others to use the telephone to officially notify the surface that there were five men alive and they were on their way up the drift. As soon as the survivors and the other rescuers arrived at the shaft station, they found the second rescue team waiting there for them. The mood was jubilant as the rescuers prepared to hoist the survivors out of the mine.

It would have been a great evening of fun at an ice cream party planned that night for Cane Creek Miners, their families and company officials. They were to celebrate reaching the potash ore bed. Instead, many of the families were at the mine site[21] waiting to hear about the fate of their loved ones during a long, agonizing wait.

In the gathering crowd, Martha Milton, the daughter of missing miner Kenneth Milton, was standing next to her boyfriend, Mike Dowd. A prominent TV news anchor sauntered towards the young couple with his microphone in hand and his cameraman and crew in tow. "So, do you really think your father is going to come out of this alive?" he brazenly asked as he thrust the microphone towards Martha. Stunned by his apparent lack of empathy and sensitivity, Martha didn't know what to say. Mike, on the other hand, came to her immediate defense and laid into the brash anchor and ran him off along with his TV news crew.[22]

One wife sat outside the ring of spectators gathered near the Headframe area and wept quietly. Then, like the wind, word spread through the waiting crowd: "Five men have been reached, and they are alive."[23] Many burst into tears of joy.[24] There was a relief knowing rescuers had finally reached the barricade and the five survivors.

It had been a long day of frustrating delays in the rescue effort. Hope had dwindled throughout the day as the flag at the top of the Headframe was now flying at half-mast for the known dead. After the mine had been flooded with air and the rescue effort had resumed, hope was rekindled again.[25]

It was 6:15 p.m.[26] when the spokesman, June Crawford, received word from deep inside the mine. He emotionally announced, "Five survivors have been found in the East Drift. The men are walking out of the drift."[27] Already, the air was thick with anticipation.

Disaster at Cane Creek

Flag flying at haft-mast at the top of the mine's headframe for the miners known to be dead.

Chapter 20

Search of the Entire Mine

At 6:30 p.m., the five survivors, along with some of their rescuers, reached the surface[1] after an agonizing trip[2] in two buckets from the depths of the shaft. The survivors were greeted by a huge roar from a crowd of 200 people who had gathered to watch the rescue operation proceed.[3]

It had taken ninety minutes, from the time the rescuers went down until the survivors were brought to the surface.[4] The men had survived nearly fifty hours underground,[5] barricaded deep in a drift a half-mile from the shaft station.

As the five men climbed from the bucket in which they had been hoisted, a bevy of relatives, friends, miners, and newsmen moved closer to catch a look at the men who made it. As the men emerged from the Headframe, one woman shrieked with glee. She almost fell from her perch, but bystanders supported her.[6]

Four of the five were smiling, grimy but in good condition.[7] Stripped to the waist, they were quickly wrapped in blankets[8] and walked under their own power. Then one of the survivors stumbled. He laughed[9] as workers caught him and helped him towards an ambulance.

Disaster at Cane Creek

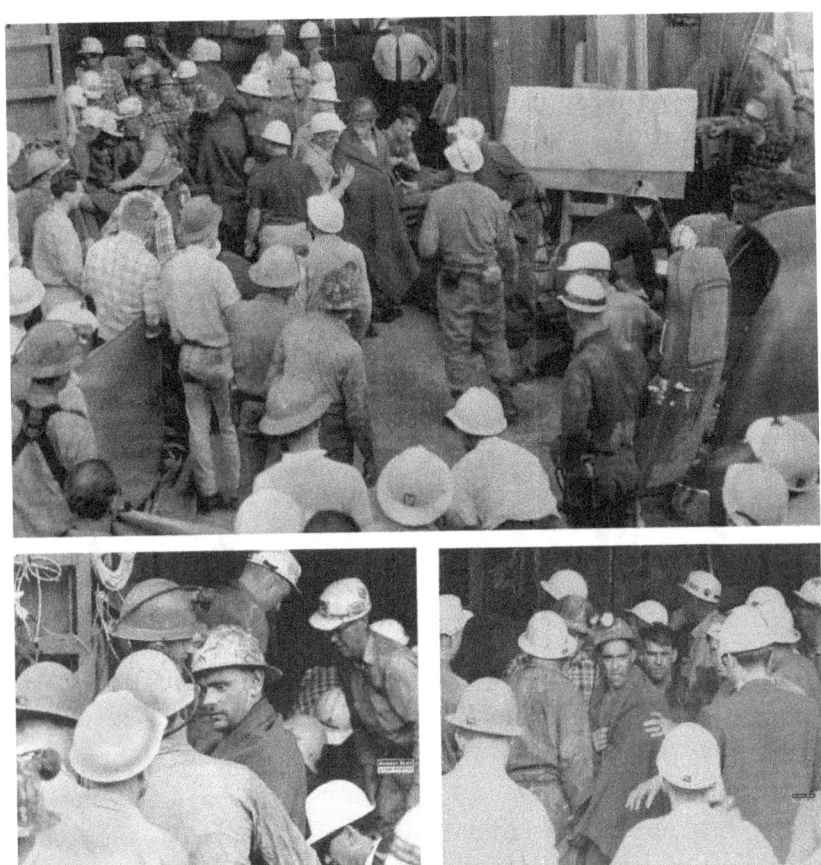

1. Survivors are brought up from the bottom of the shaft and appeared to be in good shape and taken by the ambulance to the hospital where they will be greeted by loved ones who had kept the long vigil at the mine's entrance. (*AP Wirephoto*) 2. Tom Trueman talks with rescuers. The red-headed miner came from Northern Ireland in 1961. (*Deseret News*). 3. Wrapped in a blanket, 'C.C.' Clark is guided through the crowd to an ambulance. (*Deseret News*)

Spokesman, June Crawford picked up the portable electric microphone and triumphantly announced, "These five men are in good condition. Their names are June, Clark, Trueman, Byrge, and

Eslick."[10] The five men smiled wanly and waved. Exhaustion pulled at their faces.[11]

The names, broadcast over the public address system, were difficult to understand. The women in the crowd, mostly wives, and mothers, stood with their hands at their throats or over their mouths—sisters in a sorority of women. Most of the women waited and strained to hear a name not broadcast.[12]

Some of the relatives and friends who stood vigil smiled as the names were announced. From others came muffled sobs and anxious glances toward the shaft.[13]

A son broke through the line of spectators and ran to the side of his father. Tears streamed down his face. Another youth just turned his head.[14]

One of the men was Violet June's husband, 'Bob.' Violet waited expressionlessly on a small clay dune, beside her were other wives. She had heard from Hanna that her husband was one of the five alive in the barricade, yet it had been nearly thirty hours since he had left them, and anything could have happened. When June's name was read, the other wives standing nearby hugged her. Violet hadn't always been so hopeful and admitted there were times she felt her husband wouldn't be one of the survivors.[15] A young doctor spotted Violet in the crowd, patted her arm and winked, saying, "He's fine."[16]

As workers put June into an ambulance, Violet tried to catch her husband's eye through the ambulance window. They swapped tired smiles.[17] At the same time, June's mother, who was standing in the crowd, fainted and she was taken to the hospital as well.

One slight, plain woman in her late twenties, stood stunned after all the names were read, her husband's name obviously not among those mentioned.

"They say he still has a good chance," she said several times to the ones around her. But there was no conviction in her voice.[18]

Paul McKinney was at the top of the shaft to greet his buddies,[19] overjoyed and relieved they were doing okay. Hanna, who had left earlier, was back at the hospital and planned to meet up with them there.[20]

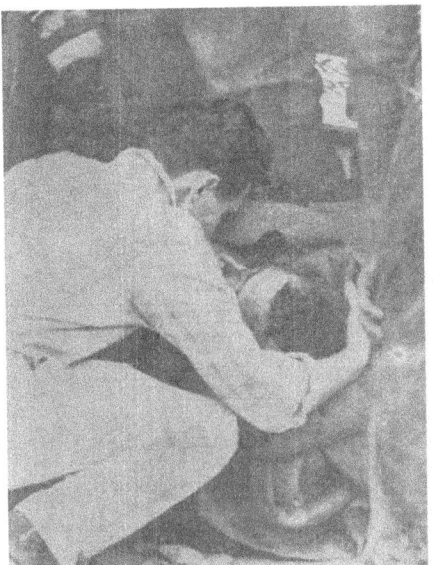
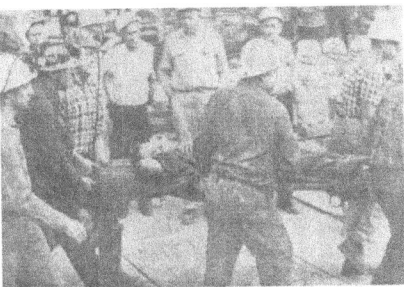

1. A young man races to the side of one of the survivors and embraces him. (*Salt Lake Tribune*) 2. & 3. Each of the survivors are carried to waiting ambulances. (*Deseret News*)

McKinney wasn't able to talk to any of them since they were immediately put into waiting ambulances and whisked to the hospital. Relatives of the rescued men jumped in cars and headed to the hospital[21] where they would be able to hug their husbands.[22] McKinney, with his brother driving, also followed the ambulances[23] to the hospital. The survivors were in an ambulance and two hearses, which had been converted for ambulance duty.

Meanwhile, relatives of the men still missing continued to mill around near the Headframe.[24] Some with folded arms walked to high places so they could watch. And wait.[25]

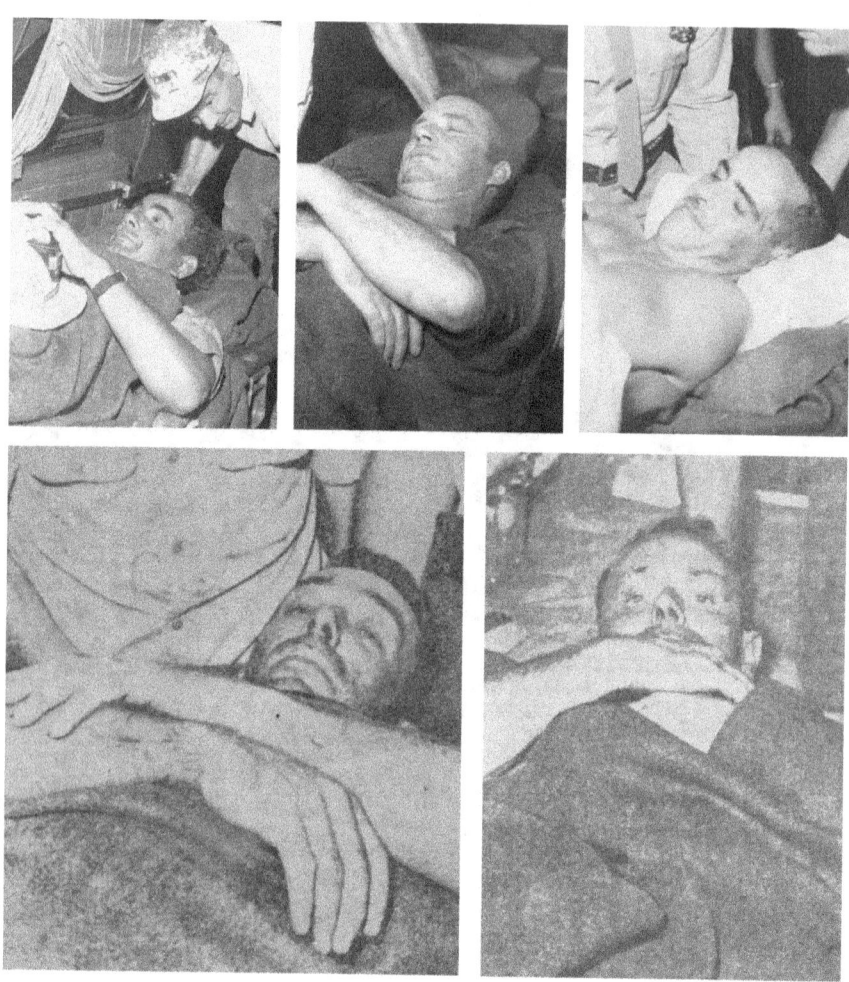

'Blackie' Eslick, Chuck Byrge, 'C.C.' Clark, 'Bob' June and Tom Trueman are loaded into ambulances to take to the hospital in Moab. (*Deseret News*)

Disaster at Cane Creek

The joy and the sadness of the moment were overpowering. The rescue of the five men and their identification was announced to a waiting crowd that brought cheers and tears of relief for some. For others, it was a portend of doom. Since 11:55 a.m. the day before, when Hanna and McKinney were rescued and told of five companions still alive, it had been rumored, but never officially expressed, that the rest of the miners were dead.[26]

At 6:25 p.m., the halls and lobby of the I.W. Allen Memorial Hospital were nearly empty. Five minutes later, they were almost full as the parking lot outside filled up. Word came from the Cane Creek Mine of the five men who had been rescued and were on their way to the hospital by ambulance.[27] The grounds outside the hospital bustled with anticipation.

Adeline Clark, wife of 'C.C.' Clark, with her mother, her sister and her brother-in-law from Wyoming, walked from her trailer home across the street from the hospital to await the arrival of the survivors, unaware 'C.C.' was among the five.

Eyes red from crying, Adeline, a devout Jehovah Witness, said, "We've just come from a twenty-minute prayer session at home. Here it comes," she said while beginning to cry upon hearing an ambulance.

"Don't collapse now. It's almost over," Adeline's mother said.

Ropes again kept waiting relatives and friends back, as ambulances screamed to a halt at the emergency entrance of the hospital, as sirens cut through the air.[28]

Some of the families of the rescued men were notified and taken in a back way to another lobby deep inside the building.[29]

After the ambulances had discharged their passengers, a mad rush started for the hospital lobby. Passes were issued to the remaining survivors' wives, and they were admitted to their husbands' bedside.

"He looks good. Dirty, but good," said Vivian Eslick after seeing her husband. "I'm going to take him home and tonight I'll call him Mr. Eslick," she said while talking to two friends waiting outside the hospital.

"I didn't get much of a chance to talk to him. There's so much confusion. But he told me he knew he'd get out. I'm supposed to keep an eye on him tonight, and if something goes wrong, I'm to bring him back," Vivian added. Sixteen-year-old Bill Eslick broke down and cried when he got word of his father's rescue.

"I've seen him, and he's fine...in good shape," a man yelled to friends outside the hospital door. He gave no indication as to which of the rescued men he had seen.

Belva Smith, the sister of Chuck Byrge's wife, Colleen, said, "We never gave up hope. We knew he was alive when Blake Hanna told us he was with Chuck down there. It was just a matter of time."[30]

A feeling of joy engulfed the hospital for most, but not the Lawrence Davidson family. They were sitting together on a couch, waiting to hear.[31] Nearby, a family friend, Alice Oliver, kept asking bystanders and newsmen, "Have you heard anything? Please tell me." No one knew what to tell her. She drifted off and wasn't around when they read off the names of the five survivors. Davidson was not among the names.[32] Other waiting families also did not hear the names of their loved ones.

Some of those family members lingered as the word got around the rescuers were still searching the mine for other survivors as they mustered one last bit of hope for a miracle that others would still be found alive.

In the warmth of the evening sun, under a waxing moon that was visible high in the sky, relatives stood gathered near the Headframe waiting for word from rescuers below. Swallowed up in the immensity of time and space and completely engulfed by the moment, the wives and families breathlessly waited. All around, the beautiful red landscape engulfed them on all sides. With no escape and daunting shadows cast in an unforgiving, ancient land—it was both haunting and magical at the same time. Uneasiness drifted on the sweltering breeze and threatened to leave the soul parched and broken.

The press was everywhere interviewing family members who would speak with them. All the major television networks carried the story, giving evening and nightly updates. Walter Cronkite of CBS News and several other anchors had arrived at the mine site earlier in the day to cover the rescue operation.

The wives all shared a common bond, having kept the long vigil all the many hours. Soon, they would finally know. Some tried to stay confident, hoping against hope their husbands would come out of the mine alive.

Everyone knew the mine's East Drift had suffered the least amount of damage from the blast and was now cleared of all the survivors. That left the West Drift to explore where the explosion most likely occurred. Everyone clung to the hope that other men had been able to barricade and had also survived.

The rescue of the five survivors brought new faith to those on the surface, but it was still tempered by the fact that some of the men were already known to be dead. This caused an unsettling despair among family members, an unspoken question. Who did these men belong to? No one knew.

"Why don't they hurry?" cried one woman.

Tess Johnson was surrounded by her family members praying that Clell would be one of the survivors.

Irene Christensen stood near the other women and patiently waited for word of her husband and son.

"They'll get out," she said. With that, she reached over and squeezed the arm of Harriette Rowley,[33] the wife of missing miner, Fred Rowley.

1. Tess Johnson, the wife of Clell Johnson, is comforted by her father and brother. (*Deseret News*) 2. A photographer snaps photos. (*Deseret News*)

"Some of the lucky ones are going to make it—I have hope,"[34] Irene said.

Perhaps the most confident were brothers, Duane and Melvin Rushton, waiting for word of their brother, Lamar Rushton.

"He's a pretty tough old boy," said Melvin Rushton. "He missed getting killed two other times. He'll get out of there if he has to dig his way out."[35]

In one incident, Lamar Ruston nearly lost his life when he first started working at Cane Creek. He and his friend, Willie, were getting to work each day by boating down the Colorado River. They were thrown out of the boat when they hit a sandbar, and the boat capsized. Both men nearly drown[36] because of strong undercurrents in the river.

Throughout this ordeal, the small community of Moab hadn't slept, nor had it given up hope. After the explosion, the first wave of horror swept through the small town. The first reaction was stunned disbelief, then depression followed, mingled with hope. That hope flickered and ebbed with each new report as everyone kept up the battle. Grand County Sheriff, John Stocks, caught only snatches of sleep Wednesday night.[37]

"I feel terrible, terrible. I know most of those fellows personally. There's so little anyone can do, and so many who want to help, but so few can," he said. "We'll have to wait. That's all. Wait."[38]

"There's still hope. There's still hope," Mayor Norman Boyd said. He had received calls offering aid from the time of the first report of the tragedy.

"I didn't know how many friends a town like Moab had," he said. He also explained how the townspeople were trying desperately to remain calm in the face of the disaster.[39]

"We know we can't help physically, and the experts are doing all that's humanly possible, so our job is to keep hoping. And praying. We are praying very hard, very hard."[40]

As soon as the five survivors were safely on the surface, rescue workers announced they were doing an immediate search in the West Drift (2 South), where many believed the explosion had taken place. Rescuers had not ventured into that drift until now,[41] and they hoped other men might have barricaded themselves and survived.

But what teams found were other bodies and destruction from the explosion strewn in their path. There was a section of uncoiled vent line they had to climb over, and stuff was blown and littered everywhere. At the West Face, rescuers found a tragic scene, three men dead behind a partially-built barricade. Overcome by smoke, before they could finish building the barricade, they died of carbon monoxide poisoning soon after the blast.

Kymberly Mele

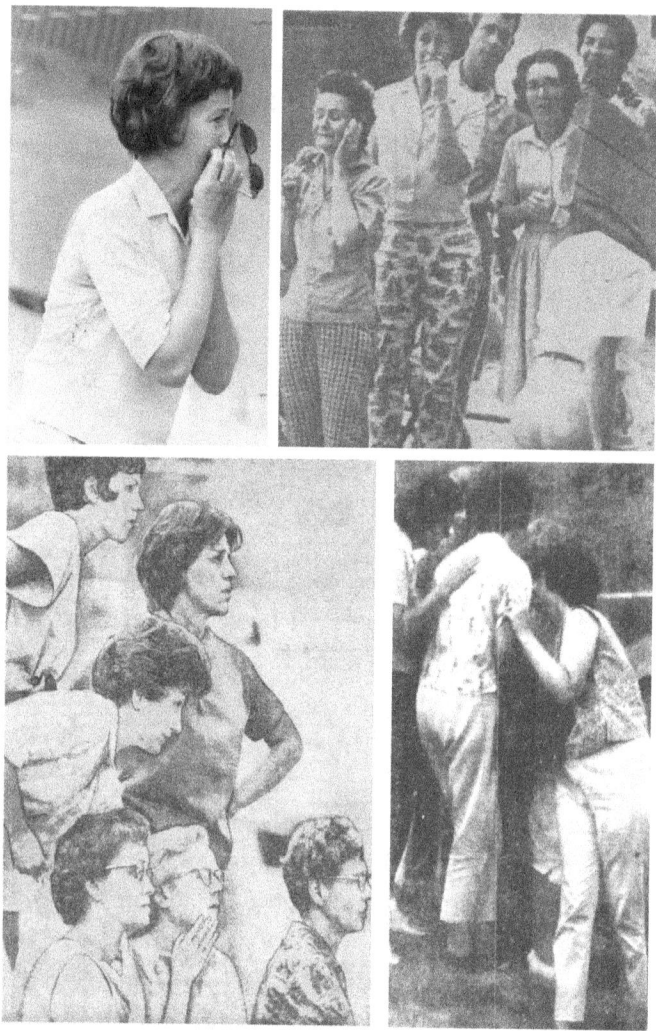

1. Barbara Waters reacts with intense emotion at the instant she sees rescued miners emerge from the shaft. Her brother-in-law, Chuck Byrge was among the five rescued. (*Deseret News*). 2. Irene Christensen, front left, and Harriette Rowley, front right and other miners' relatives mirror emotions which overflowed at mine rescue site. (*Deseret News*) 3. Other faces of those who kept the vigil near the mine shaft. Their faces are tense, full of anxiety as the await word from below about fate of miners. (*Salt Lake Tribune*) 4. Wives and family members comfort each other. (*AP Telephoto*)

After searching the entire mine, rescuers could still not find one of the missing miners. Other teams dropped down into the mine to help search and begin the recovery of bodies. With apparatuses on their backs if they should need them, 'Johnny Smoke' from the Kaiser Steel Team was told, as soon as his team got to the bottom, about the missing miner they couldn't find. Everyone kept searching as the Kaiser Steel Team went down the West Drift to search, passing all the destruction along the way.

There, they found the three dead men behind a partial barricade, built seventy-five feet out from the 2 South Face.[42] Going back behind the curtain to check the area, the rescuers ran into a pocket of carbon monoxide. One of the team members started to pass out, but he was quickly revived.

Some of the team members began the work of recovering the bodies and preparing them for the trip out of the mine. Rescue officials were also down in the mine. They went throughout the mine, doing a preliminary examination. They found the destruction concentrated mostly around the shaft station and in the shop. There, the forces from the blast scattered and destroyed everything in its path.

Part of the way down the West Drift, rescuers found sections of severely damaged vent line and a powder magazine. The explosion had blown sticks of dynamite, along with a bunch of blasting caps,[43] down the drift and scattered them for two or three hundred feet. It became evident the explosion did not happen in the West Drift. Nor was it caused by dynamite blowing up or touching off a pocket of methane gas at the Face. Instead, it appeared to have come from the shop. Inside the shop that looped around, with two entrances, there was one spot swept clean with stuff scattered in both directions. It was at this spot that the explosion had emanated from inside the shop. It was the same place Byrge saw the flame safety lamp hanging earlier. The one that had a flame burning up through the gaze, leaving soot on the Back.[44]

Chapter 21

Final Announcement

The sun began its descent in the west as a long, dark shadow, cast by the massive Headframe, covered the ground on the east side. Shadows slowly engulfed the canyon and edged up the cliffs on the east side of the river. Herve Roy sat on a stack of wood, watching the rescue operations through the large opening on the south side the Headframe. Henry Levigne, a Shift Walker, and one of Harrison International's rescuers made his way over to Herve. It was difficult, but he informed Herve that his father, Rene, was dead. He told him how he had seen his body; it was in bad shape, but he could tell it was him.[1]

Levigne, one of the first three rescuers to get to the barricade, decided to stay in the mine to help search the other parts of the mine. Herve listened, but in the back of his mind, he didn't want to believe him. Herve wasn't buying it as he continued to watch rescuers inside the Headframe. Levigne finally left.[2]

By 7:50 p.m., as the sun set[3] on the jagged edges of the dark red sandstone cliffs to the west, a report came. More missing miners were on their way up from the bottom of the mine.

For a brief moment, new hopes stirred for the wives and family members. They knew rescuers were still searching the mine. But this time, there was a subtle difference in the surface preparations for these men. The stretchers laid out near the Headframe had no pillows on them. No doctors or nurses were present as there had been when the five rescued men came up earlier. And the workers at the shaft entrance prepared to receive the delivery from the bottom. They went about their tasks woodenly, with some obvious distaste for the job ahead.[4]

A bucket surfaced at 8:00 p.m., with four bodies. Sixteen minutes later, two more bodies were brought up. All were in body bags. Workers wrapped each in a blanket, carried them to stretchers, and put them in waiting hearses or ambulances.[5]

The wait was torture. Finally, Irene Christensen's brother, LeGrande Prichard, put on his hard hat and walked down among the rescue workers to see what he could find out. He was from Carbon County, so he knew many of the rescuers. He came back to where Irene was sitting close to Margo and her sister. He stood around and stood around waiting for an official to come and talk with the women. They never did, so he finally told them what he heard. The rest of the men were dead.[6]

Irene was stunned. Her husband and young son were not among the living.[7] Her first thoughts quickly turned to Margo, pregnant with her and 'Myrley's first child. With hearts broken, the tears flowed freely as family members sweetly comforted one another.[8]

After rescue teams underground had finished searching the entire mine, they called the surface to give the news as the anxious crowd waited.[9]

The sun had already set, night came, and complete darkness enveloped the whole mine site. It was 8:19 p.m.[10] when June Crawford, Texas Gulf Sulphur's spokesman, hesitantly raised the microphone.

"For all of you on the firing line...it's all over." Pausing, he slowly added, "There are no more survivors."

Eighteen men had perished in the blast. A deep and profound stillness settled around the Headframe. All confidence was gone[11]—dashed in an instance.

During the terse announcement, silence pervaded the site, as the atmosphere of hope vanished and expectancy melted into a sorrowful letdown[12] of despair. The dreaded words came too soon as Crawford's announcement[13] meant rescue teams had found no other men alive.[14] Everyone was stunned, not quite realizing the meaning yet. For some, the grief could be seen on their faces with a blank look in their eyes. Many quietly took the news, while some appeared to have expected it.[15]

One woman buried her face in an already tear-soaked handkerchief and cried over and over, "Oh, my God. Oh, my God!" It was heart-wrenching to hear the anguished sobs. A young boy walked from the flood lit area into the darkness, kicking stones from the loose red dirt, trying to hold back the tears. They burst anyway. Unashamed, he walked back into the lighted area sobbing.[16]

An elderly man and woman sat at the edge of the darkness, staring nowhere in particular, holding onto their small dog they called Mitzie.[17] They stroked the dog lovingly. The animal sensed the tragedy and laid back its ears while searching both their faces.[18]

One woman standing near newsmen shouted.

"No more survivors? No more survivors? That's a hell of a brutal way to learn it."[19] Then she turned and shouted angrily at mine officials on the scene, accusing them of the death of her husband.[20]

For Herve Roy, there was no escape. The announcement brought the bitter reality crashing in on him. He didn't want to believe it, but now it must be true. He needed to let his mother know if she hadn't already heard. He thought about how his family would take the news. All the memories swelled below the surface—all the years working with his father, who taught him to be a man, a working man. Here in Moab, his family spent one last glorious summer together.[21] He sat silently on the stack of wood, motionless.

The tears flowed as Harriette Rowley, and the ones around her, cried. She had her five children to raise. It was a daunting thought, seeing them through the loss of their father.

Dorothy LeBlanc and Alice Barber, the young Canadian wives who had waited patiently at the hospital and then later, waited at the mine site during the ordeal, knew now that their husbands, Emile LeBlanc and Wesley Barber, were not among the rescued.[22] After the announcement, Dorothy received a shot from a doctor, as did other wives after they were told their husbands were dead. A priest and a minister were nearby to give moral support when the sedatives were administered.[23]

Dorothy's mother-in-law, Noeline LeBlanc, was en route to Moab, traveling from Goose Bay, Newfoundland-Labrador, Canada. Noeline LeBlanc had no way of knowing that her son, Emile, was one of the eighteen men who died in the explosion. Tragically, her husband, Hubert, still at home in Goose Bay, passed away just after learning about his son's death.[24] Noeline was later stopped by the Royal Canadian Mounted Police in Halifax, Canada (nearly 1,200 miles away from her home). They let her know that her husband died of a massive heart attack. (He, too, had been a lifelong miner in Newfoundland-Labrador, Canada.) Noeline turned around and went back home. It would be hours before Dorothy would hear about her father-in-law passing away.[25]

One young teenage girl buried her face into the chest of her grandfather as she cried. Her brother, with his hands in his pockets, turned his head away as the tears flowed down his face as he leaned against a pickup truck.

A kerchief tied around her head, Tess Johnson, the wife of Clell Johnson was escorted by her father and brother toward the car where her children were waiting. When they saw their mother, they knew she had received word that their father was dead. They all broke out weeping, and one of the sisters, Carolyn, was especially inconsolable. Her anguished cries were uncontrollable. Someone brought a doctor to their car. He had been nearby administering shots to family members and was able to give Carolyn a shot through the car window which helped her to calm down.[26]

For the brothers of Lamar Rushton,[27] the news was staggering as they thought about Lamar's wife, Lorraine, who was at home with their three young children. The brothers had been confident to the end, and now the end had come.[28]

The vigil of waiting was now over. There was nothing else to do. For relatives of the victims, the evening ended in weary grief.[29] The majority of the crowd left the mine area quickly, driving the twenty miles to Moab through a dark, silent canyon at a slow, procession-like speed.[30]

As a crowd gathered outside the hospital, they stood in small groups. Some talked quietly. All watched the road the ambulances had traveled.

Donna Bobo, the wife of Robert Bobo, couldn't come to the hospital. The miner's sister, Joyce Bobo, was there in her place. Donna had been under heavy sedation for two days. "When we heard the miners were coming out, we called the doctor. He said to give her more sedatives so she would go to sleep," the sister explained. Robert Bobo also was not among the five rescued men.[31]

When word finally reached the hospital of the final announcement—again, all hope was gone. For those whose loved ones were safe, it was a time of happiness. For the rest, there was nothing. With overwhelming sorrow, the crowd soon quietly left.

One woman sobbed openly, as she was tenderly led away. It appeared her husband was not among the living. A member of her family guided her gently through the crowd and into a car.[32]

Recovery teams joined rescue teams in the mine, who were still searching for one missing body. Top officials were still underground doing a preliminary exam of the mine as crews began the gruesome task of bagging bodies and taking them to the shaft station for transport out of the mine.

Disaster at Cane Creek

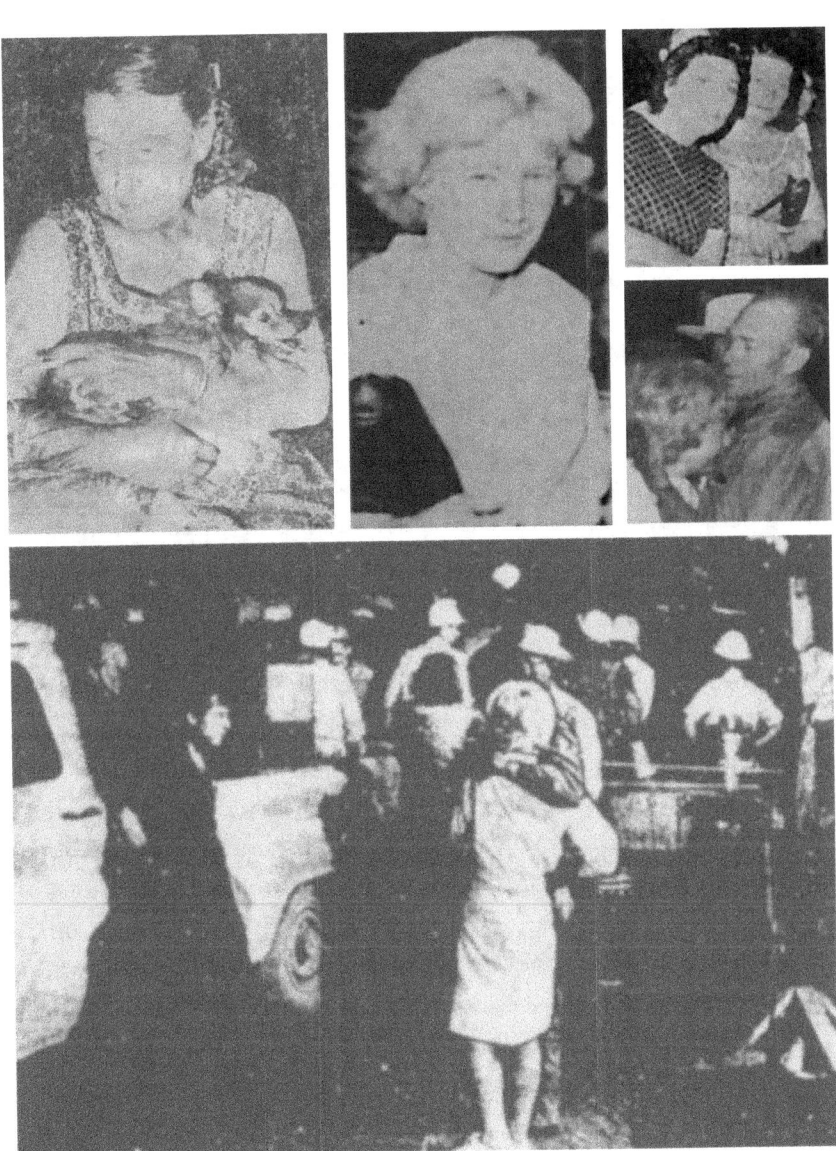

1. The mother of John Tinall who was killed in the mine explosion holds her dog Mitzie. (*Denver Post*) 2. Relative of one of the miners break into tears. (*Daily Sentinel*) 3. Two relatives await word of the miners. (*UPI Telephoto*) 4. A young woman is consoled by a relative and the young boy against the truck is also in tears as final word is received on victims of mine blast disaster. (*Salt Lake Tribune*)

George Ferguson and 'Blondie' Peterson from the Kaiser Steel Team thought they had it made when two big guys who worked for Harrison International were assigned to help them recover bodies. 'Blondie,' sizing them up, looked at Ferguson and said, "Well, now we got us some pretty good help."

When their team reached the bottom, and Harrison International's two guys saw the first body, they were overwhelmed by the gruesome sight and the smell. They wanted nothing to do with it and quickly headed out of the mine.[33] The smell of death was heavy. The conditions of burnt and mutilated bodies can be unsettling even for the strongest of men.

One coal miner aptly described his experiences after the devastating Scofield, Utah Mine Disaster in 1900 that killed 200 men. He told a reporter he had just shipped his partner, who he came west with, back to his home in Colorado for burial. He said, "When that last act was completed, I threw up the hunt for the victims for fear that I would become mentally unbalanced. It was an experience that I would not care to go through again, even if death was the penalty for the refusal to do so."[34]

At Scofield, ten from one family alone (including two brothers-in-law) perished. One living member of that family, who had been through the entire war of the rebellion in Scotland, lamented, "My God, it is awful. No tongue or pen can describe the horror of the situation down there...there are pitiful sights and cases that would stir the hearts of the most callous."[35]

While recovery work is demanding and exhausting physically, it is also draining emotionally and not for the faint of heart. Mine explosions, in general, can cause significant devastation within the small confines of a mine. They especially wreak havoc on the bodies of miners caught in their destructive force, burning many miners beyond recognition. The fiery forces have been known to rip or burn clothes right off bodies, blow men right out of their mine boots, throw them about, and mangle and mutilate their bodies in the process. Miners have been found with only their mine belts left on, forced up underneath their arms. Bodies, even those not burned, are often left in an inhospitable environment of a damaged mine—some for days during the ensuing rescue operation. The bodies would sustain further damages, rapidly decomposing and swelling beyond recognition.

Ferguson and 'Blondie' were assigned to recover seven bodies from the West Drift (2 South). Other Recovery Teams were assigned to the other ten bodies: the three bodies down the East Drift (3U), two other bodies near the No. 1 Crosscut, and five bodies near the shaft station on the east side. The explosion, like a bulldozer, pushed and shoved debris and muck into every nook and cranny,[36] making it difficult to find several bodies buried beneath the rubble. Those bodies were ultimately discovered by rescuers from the concentration of odor, as those bodies were hidden from view. Most of the victims were killed outright from the explosion, but six died of smoke inhalation. All of the bodies were badly decomposed, their condition exasperated by exposure for days to high heat in the mine. All were severely swollen.

The Recovery Teams brought body bags with them into the mine and sent down wood and metal stretchers to bring the bodies out. The recovery crews also documented all the pertinent information while bagging the bodies.

Ferguson and 'Blondie' started near the top of the West Drift where two bodies were located. Bagging each one, Ferguson and 'Blondie' secured them to the metal stretchers and took them, one at a time, to the shaft station for transport to the surface by other recovery crew members. Forty minutes after the final announcement, two more bodies were sent to the surface. About thirty minutes later, three additional bodies were hauled to the top.

Nearly halfway down the West Drift, Ferguson and 'Blondie' climbed over the damaged vent line to get to the next bodies. After preparing two bodies at that location, they started taking one of them to the shaft station, when other rescue workers came down the drift and cleared the way for them.

Back and forth George and 'Blondie' went, carrying each of the remaining bodies as other workers meet them halfway. Soon, the workers began taking the stretchers the rest of the way to the shaft. An hour after the last three bodies were sent to the surface, another body was sent up, then twelve minutes later, another.

At one point, Ferguson and 'Blondie' ran out of body bags and scrounged collapsible vent tubing large enough for each body. Most of the tubing was damaged and ripped by the explosion, with ragged and shredded edges, making it difficult to find pieces large enough to use.[37] They eventually found what they needed. Gently rolling each body into the material, they twisted the copper wire they had with them around the ends to secure them.[38]

The men threw lime down on the ground where they found each body. Simultaneously, they updated the information on the mine map. This information would prove useful in identifying the bodies and would be used for an investigation that would come later. The two rescuers soon finished bagging the last three victims found near the West Face and started transporting the bodies up the drift, one at a time to the shaft station. It took them about an hour and a half to recover the seven bodies and bring them to the shaft station.[39]

The rescuers had sympathy for the fallen men and now empathized with the families who were now left to carry a heavy burden. There is little that prepares rescue teams for what they will encounter. Recovering bodies can be an extremely grim task, but it's of vital importance for spouses and family members so they can bury their loved ones. For rescue workers or survivors who experience stress from the horrors and devastation after a mine explosion, their experiences can lead to depression and inevitably to Post Traumatic Stress Disorder (PTSD).

Moments after the five survivors entered the I. W. Allen Hospital, a team of doctors and nurses started extensive examinations. Grimy and smiling, the five were in good condition, and there was little need of treatment. They were able to cleanup, have something to eat and be reunited with their families. The grime of two days and two nights in the mine clung to their skin, and the irritating smoke reddened each man's eyes.[40] They also heard, not long after they were rescued, how Hanna and McKinney put the air line together, but lacked a small section that rescuers patched hours later.

Their reunion with their wives and family members was emotional. Each man knew how close they had come to losing their lives. Reporters and photographers were also given special access to the men as they shared some aspects of their stories.

They were asked if any of them would go back to the mine. Some smiled and looked down when the question was asked.[41] Not 'Blackie' Eslick.

"Sure, I'm ready to go back to mining."[42] Mining was in his family and his blood. The other four, 'C.C.,' Byrge, June, and Trueman, lay in hospital beds nearby.

"Brother, does that air taste good!" 'Blackie' sighed as he drew another great breath of fresh air and wrapped his arms around his sobbing wife. "I don't think I've ever felt quite so good. We never gave up hope," 'Blackie' said. "We knew it was a matter of time."[43] But it wasn't as simple as he first let on.

"We were nearly hysterical at one point," he said. "But fortunately, it passed. He said the flow of air through the air line "was a great morale booster for all of us behind the barricade."[44]

"He apologized to his wife and daughter, "I'm sorry you all had to go through such an ordeal."

Trudy, his twenty-year-old daughter, laughed and said, "Dad, you look about like you do when you come home from hunting."[45]

Violet June sat on the edge of her husband's bed as a tear trickled down her cheek. She said nothing, but the look on her face told the story. When 'Bob' June was asked if he would go back to mining, he had his answer ready. "I've been in the mines for sixteen years. I guess I'm too old to quit now."[46] Through the years, he had worked at the Climax Mine in Leadville, Colorado and for a while in Paonia, Colorado.[47]

"When the explosion came, I was drilling a hole down through the bottom of our drift to a storage area below. The blast was probably from the other drift where I was normally assigned to work. But on Tuesday, they needed some special drilling only I could do. The blast knocked us down. When I picked myself up, I got over the hole and I looked down. I couldn't see anything, but I heard the terrible screaming. I heard this man screaming for a long, long time, but there was no way we could get to him. He started screaming right after the explosion. It was pathetic, but there was nothing we could do," he said, reliving the worst moments of his experience. "It was pitch black. I don't know who it was, but after a while, the screaming stopped. I got separated from the guy I was working with—I think he must be dead. The smoke was real bad, and we barely lived through it. After we had built our barricade, there wasn't much to do but wait. We laid there and sweat.[48] We figured we had enough air for another day and we got temperature readings a couple of hours after the blast. Boy, it was hot down there. After a while, it got so you didn't notice the heat as much."[49] He paused for a moment as he looked at his wife.

"It was sure black. We kept our lights out to save the batteries. Most of the time, I hoped rescuers would come. But there were times I wasn't so sure. When they did come..." his voice trailed off, "Boy, were we glad to get out of there,"[50] June said with a grin.

"One of our biggest worries were those two guys, Hanna and McKinney. I was sure glad to see them,"[51] he said, then he took a sip of coffee.

"My wife, I know, gave up hope about noon today when they still hadn't reached us. She was sure I was dead and didn't think she'd ever see me again,"[52] June added as he glanced at his wife.

'C.C.' Clark lay quietly on his bed while his wife and friends watched over him. At the side of the bed sat Hanna, while McKinney stood next to him.

"I've never been so glad to see anyone as I was these guys,"[53] Hanna said, referring to the final five survivors. The rescued men had family and friends all around them when McKinney arrived at the hospital. The men all talked a bit about the rescue and the way Hanna and McKinney put the air line together, but with all the commotion and the emotional reunions, there was little conversation. McKinney needed to know his buddies were at the hospital and were okay. Exhausted himself, he was going home to get some much-needed sleep. He had no desire to check himself back into the hospital.[54]

Slowly, 'C.C.' began to tell about his ordeal. "It was hot down there. We drank up five gallons of water in about thirty minutes, then we started drinking water out of the line we used for drilling. It was river water, but it tasted pretty good,"[55] he said.

When asked about the rescuers, he said, "The first time I actually realized the rescuers were coming was when I looked up and saw a light about fifty yards away.[56] We never gave up hope. We were just beginning to wonder what was holding them up. They should have been there sooner. It was real rough. I was tired and hungry but now I know I can eat and sleep. It felt pretty good to get outside and get a clean breath of air."[57]

Asked how he would describe his feelings, he said, "I'm not sure I can. But it's good to be here, and I feel pretty good." The Clarks were planning to leave the next day for "a few days" of vacation.[58]

Chuck Byrge was sitting up in his bed as he talked about his ordeal. Nearby, his wife, Colleen, was sipping on orange juice and talked quietly to several visitors.[59]

Byrge had different thoughts than 'Blackie' about going back to work at the mine. "I'm not going back down there. I've lived through three explosions, and I guess I've about used up my luck. I'm not going back."[60]

Byrge was one of the coal miners credited with building the barricade that saved the men's lives. Because of his previous experience, he was a knowledgeable and confident force in the effort, while the rest of the group helped, each doing their part. After the explosion, Byrge said there was quite a bit of dust, and the men could see the gas creeping toward them.[61] He told how they made three barricades out of the tubing used for ventilation, each one farther back down the drift from the main shaft.[62] He then credited the two men who came out earlier with saving the lives of the five left behind.[63]

"We got some air out of the high-pressure line about thirty hours after the explosion," Byrge said. "It helped a lot."[64]

"I don't think we could have ever made it if it hadn't been for Hanna and McKinney.[65] They left us and went up the drift to see if they could find anyone else.[66] When they found the three dead, they decided if the carbon monoxide got those guys, it would eventually get us. They decided their only chance was to try and get out,"[67] Byrge said. "They went towards the shaft and en route, they repaired the air line enough to get us some air.[68] I'm thankful they fixed it. I don't think there was ever enough air down there, but at least, there was enough to keep us alive."[69]

More visitors came into the room. Among them were six small children. They shyly scrambled up on Byrge's bed and gave their father a big hug around his neck and kissed him. The littlest ones looked curiously at the reporters and photographers taking their pictures, not really understanding all the commotion going on around his dad, a dad that adored each one of them. It was emotional to see the love he had for those little ones and just how blessed their little family was tonight.

Hanna checked on Tom Trueman to see how he was doing. Several friends were talking with Trueman as he sipped a cup of coffee. The only bachelor of the group, he was sharing some of his experiences with them.

"It seemed like quite a while," he said, "But I knew we would get out. Just a matter of time," he said. "After we got the barricade set up so we could keep the smoke and carbon monoxide out, there wasn't much to do but drink water and sweat. Then drink more water and sweat more. It was pretty hot," he said as he continued. "After a while, we had to watch the water. We only had a ten-gallon can that was not even half-way full. Our biggest worry was for the two who left, Hanna and McKinney. We knew the drift was probably full of carbon monoxide,"[70] Trueman said.

He then propped himself up on one elbow in the hospital bed, turned to Hanna, who was nearby, and said, "You may have got us only a little air with that patch job on the line, but boy it was enough."

"It was the best we could do, Tom,"[71] Hanna replied.

Trueman said the only thing the trapped miners could do was wait for the rescue teams they were certain would come.

Several of the five men, Trueman included, credited the establishment of an oxygen source through the compressed air line with saving their lives.[72] It was "just at the time we all began to feel hazy," Trueman said. "That is when we started getting fresh air."[73]

To many observers, the five survivors owed their lives to the first two, as well as their own makeshift barricades that kept out the deadly gases while they awaited rescue. In spite of the joy the men felt, there was still a prevailing sadness that overshadowed the moment.

1. Grant Eslick with his wife, Vivian. (*Deseret News*) 2. 'Chuck' Byrge with his wife, Colleen (back row) and their six children. (*Times-Independent*) 3. 'Bob' June with his wife, Violet. (*Salt Lake Tribune*) 4. 'C.C.' Clark with his wife, Adeline. (*Salt Lake Tribune*) 5. Tom Trueman. (*Salt Lake Tribune*)

Many recognized the last five survivors owed their lives to the first two survivors and "their own makeshift barricades" that kept out deadly gases while they awaited rescue.[74] While some disaster stories have a hero, according to the press, the Moab mine blast had many. Chuck Byrge and his firsthand knowledge of barricades, along with the training of the other miners contributed to their ability to build the barrier, which aided in their survival.

Many observers, rescuers and reporters alike, lauded Hanna and McKinney as heroes for two highly significant actions they took after they left the barricade the morning after the explosion. After they had worked their way to the shaft, the pair worked three hours to replace about a hundred feet of the compressed air line blown out by the explosion. Lacking about a foot, they found they couldn't link the two ends of the line with the material they had, which provided fresh air to the men they left behind in the barricade. As a result of Hanna and McKinney's relaying this information, the rescue operation centered on that area[75] and a rescuer went down "under oxygen" and joined the two ends of the compressed air line.[76] The duo also brought out the word to rescuers of five other miners. It was the first inkling of encouragement anyone had from the bottom of the mine that more men were alive.

"I don't think we could have made it if it hadn't been for Blake Hanna and Paul McKinney. I'm thankful they fixed the air line," Tom Trueman said. "I don't think there was ever enough air down there, but at least there was enough to keep us alive," he said.[77] "It undoubtedly saved our lives."

Rescuers also felt that the effort it took to repair the air line by the two miners, Hanna and McKinney, showed they were greatly concerned for the welfare of the "other five" men. Their survival added a small, cheerful note to the devastating mine tragedy.[78]

Blackie was also credited with holding things together and discouraged the others from leaving the barricade during difficult times after Hanna and McKinney left. As an experienced miner, his knowledge and steady presence served the other men as they waited to be rescued. Trueman, in particular, who had never worked in a mine before, seemed to have depended on 'Blackie's' experience and wisdom.

"This guy, 'Blackie,' was great. Anytime somebody got a little anxious, 'Blackie' had the right thing to say," Trueman said.

Chapter 22

Tombstone and Moon Lilies

The buckets that plunged a half-mile to bring up the survivors now brought up only death and grief.[1] There were few relatives still at the mine site, most had already left for their homes—with all hope gone.[2] By midnight, the crowd of bystanders had vanished, except for a handful of family members and a few miners,[3] while the last remaining bodies were loaded for transport to town. The gruesome task of bringing the bodies out of the mine took four hours.

Since one body was still unaccounted for, officials decided to continue the search the next day. With pockets of gas still lurking throughout the drifts, they needed to flush the mine with more air to make it safer to continue the search. Workers were assigned to come back the next morning to search.

While there had been criticism directed at officials the last two days, there was a lot of praise for the rescuers who carried out the grueling search and recovery work.[4] One rescue worker, Lloyd Miller, a miner from Dragerton, Utah, snorted to a reporter who questioned him about rescue work.

"If I had been down there, I'd want someone coming after me," Miller said. While preparing to come to Moab after the explosion, his wife asked him if he had to do it. "Of course, I have to do it! All

Disaster at Cane Creek

of us have to do it," Miller told her. All miners know the dangers of the mine, but they have confidence other miners would come to their rescue were they in the same situation. Mine rescue work has become an intuition born out of many devastating mining tragedies.

Recovering bodies is one of the hardest parts of any rescue operation, not just because of the gruesome nature of the job, but also because of the sorrow—knowing a fellow miner would not be going back to his family. The inherent dangers of being a miner are always in the back of every miner's mind. Times such as these were always a vivid reminder of just how dangerous and devastating it could be to be a miner.

It was a night of triumph and tragedy, first with the dramatic rescue of five survivors after forty-nine hours, then with the discovery and recovery of the bodies.[5] Exhausted, rescuers from Carbon County packed up their rescue gear and belongings to start the long drive home. Seven men were rescued, yet there was still a sense of letdown, despair, and grief for the men who died in the explosion. It was especially felt by Harrison International's men. Many went home and broke down in agonizing tears over the loss and devastation. Some even swore they would never work at that mine again.

The rescue operation lasted nearly three days, yet, to those who were there, it felt as though it lasted days longer. Rescuers had now gone home to pick up their lives where they left off and to try and get back to a sense of normalcy. They had to burn their clothes because of the smell of death. Some were issued new boots[6] and mine belts by their companies because, unlike the hard rock miners at Cane Creek who wore rubber boots, their leather boots had curled up, and their mine belts were ruined by the salt water in the shaft.[7]

Exhausted, it would take rescuers a week to recover and regain their strength. The stress, the lack of sleep, and having worked "under oxygen" had taken its toll. One thing for sure—the mine rescuers at Cane Creek demonstrated courage and tenacity. Time after time, a mine rescuers' professionalism, bravery, and determination stood as a testimony throughout the historical record of their invaluable contributions to the mining industry.

The Cane Creek Potash Mine was shut down during the wee morning hours, and the heavy metal doors over the shaft were closed.[8] The mine was sealed on orders of state and federal officials as the stage was set for a joint State-Federal investigation starting Monday—Labor Day. The investigation could take weeks to complete and would temporarily throw some fifty miners out of work.[9]

A rescue worker, Gene Weaver, closes the diamond plate steel shaft doors of the ill-fated potash mine. (*UPI Telephoto*)

In the silent darkness, the greenish glow from the lights around the top of the Headframe cast an eerie aura around the giant cement structure as a flag at the top was blowin' in the wind at half-mast.

Disaster at Cane Creek

This tall, majestic cement structure once stood watch, like a sentinel and a beacon of hope and promise at the new Cane Creek Mine-mill complex. In the empty silence, with all hope gone, it now looked more like a massive tombstone,[10] a tragic symbol of death and despair. The Headframe marked the very spot where eighteen men died, and it seemed to broadcast its sad story far and wide. The sense of utter loss was palpable as it lingered on the desert breeze, whispering a mournful sound.

Once the steel doors over the shaft had closed, everyone prepared to go home as a somber mood gripped the site. The focus now turned to the families and burying the dead.

Now what? It was a question asked, but not quickly answered, by the families who were now left behind to pick up the pieces. Lives had been changed in a flash. And now, like a foggy dream with no awakening, it seemed to have no end. There was only a nagging question by wives and children, "What are we going to do now?" Time, for them, would now be reconciled differently: "Their life before, and their life after." For now, it was time to mourn. Eventually, there would be time to rebuild (to the degree they could) and to try to obtain a sense of normalcy.

The tears would never actually cease. They would be brought on from deep, empty longings. If only. If only to see their smile one more time. To hear their voice or joyous laughter. To feel their caring touch or a reassuring hug. They would miss all the simple things, those precious joys of love and life, too many times taken for granted.

Now courage had to be summoned, and children had to be attended to and raised. Children who would be raised without their father. A father who would be missing from family gatherings, holidays, baptisms, graduations, weddings or, in the case of a few, even the birth of the three unborn children. Always, there would be a persistent gnawing feeling of someone missing, as longings would continue to prevail. For young ones, perhaps a secret fantasy and hope that their father just had amnesia somewhere, and

395

he would regain his memory and come home.[11] Anything to make sense of it all.

The families, especially the children, were now left behind to mourn the unspeakable loss. They were, in all actuality, a monument to their deceased fathers. They were the true, living monuments dedicated to the remembrance of the men, the fathers who died that fateful day. The children would carry their stories, engraved forever on their hearts and souls. They would carry the stories that would forever continue to live on through the lives of their children and grandchildren, and beyond. They would carry the mannerisms inherited from their fathers—that same smile and laugh, the sideways glance or gesture, that same stance, gait, or voice inflection. They would carry the same eyes or the same personality traits. And, most importantly, they would carry the same dogged determination to take care of their families the same way the eighteen hard-working men, husbands and fathers did at Cane Creek. These brave men had etched out a living for their families, leaving a sacred legacy of love behind.[12]

Life makes no promises. Meandering like the Colorado River lives are carved out like canyons through time as each soul is carried to a final destination, in the same way as "all rivers flow to the sea." (Ecclesiastes 1:7)

The makeshift hearses,[13] converted station wagons, and ambulances moved slowly through the early morning darkness, carrying the mangled bodies of the victims. Starting the journey where the road ends, twenty miles from the mine site to Moab, these same vehicles, only hours before, had carried the five joyful survivors to the hospital. The bodies[14] of the dead miners now made their presence felt in an unnatural hush that enveloped the mine site and the small grieving community.

Disaster at Cane Creek

The small, sad entourage made its way through the night, traveling slowly up the river road amid the shadows of the river canyon. All around, everything was shrouded in darkness. As the procession of bodies passed by, the moon lilies, which blossom at night and grow wild in clusters along the banks of the Colorado River were in full bloom. The moon spread a silver glow on their open flowers. They appeared to be paying their respects, conveying their expression of sympathy and sadness. They were the Sacred Datura plant, commonly known as the moon lily or moon flower. While lilies normally represent life, ironically, this particular lily is extremely poisonous and can cause death. These bush type plants with their multiple blooms, offered up beautiful fragrant, clusters of flower bouquets all along the river. It was as though the lilies, also a symbol of death and the afterlife, were offering up a small token of condolences as their profuse white blooms stood in contrast to the dark shadows of grief and bereavement.

A silent waxing moon[15] floated in the western sky, tenderly casting quiet moonbeams of mournful light. Overburdened and hunched over[16] with sorrow, it watched the small procession follow the route back the way the men came only days before, full of life and laughter on their way to work "at the roads end." Now, the men traveled on a glorious, infinite journey to that place that lies beyond the "end of the road."

The silent town of Moab never noticed as the vehicles slowly passed through in the middle of the night. The Skyline Transport Company's garage,[17] several miles southeast of town, now served as a makeshift morgue. The long, high metal building made of corrugated steel was a truck repair shop.

When the first body was brought out of the mine the night before, it was announced that a temporary morgue would be at the Community Baptist Church[18] in Moab. But as more bodies were found, disfigured beyond recognition and in bad shape, the decision was quickly made to use the truck repair shop for the grim task of identifying the bodies.

Two brothers of one of the victims, Melvin and Duane Rushton, were waiting as the procession arrived at the garage. They grimly stood outside, waiting until workers carried all the bodies in—their brother Lamar was among them. But Lamar wouldn't be identified for several days. Still, the brothers waited, out of respect for him and the other men.

Reverently, the workers quietly removed the covered corpses from the vehicles. They lay as evidence of a horrible tragedy on stretchers in two long rows on the cement floor of the garage as workers packed dry ice[19] around each one. Seventeen of the eighteen men now lay silent, their burned and broken bodies shrouded under green canvas covers.[20]

Echoing the same sentiment as officials at the mine, Sheriff Stocks, who knew most of the victims personally, said visual identification would be impossible in most cases. There was a possibility he would ask the FBI to aid in the identification.[21] Only one body was identifiable. The aftermath of the disaster was beyond belief, as everyone struggled to come to terms with the devastation and the loss of so many good and beloved men.

Aftermath

Chapter 23

Blowin' in the Wind

Early the next morning, repercussions of the Cane Creek explosion were felt in Carbon County when coal miners, who belonged to the United Mine Workers of America (UMWA), staged a "walk-off" in a spirit of solidarity with Moab miners. At two Carbon County coal mines near Hiawatha and Kenilworth, more than 100 coal miners walked off the job,[1] protesting current state safety inspection practices[2] and that the state only had one coal mine inspector, when two were needed.[3]

The Texas Gulf Sulphur Potash Mine-mill complex stood strangely quiet as James Westfield and several TGS employees he had enlisted, were back at the mine site by 9:00 a.m. to look for the missing miner. The water was still pouring down the shaft, but the gnawing sense of urgency and dread was now gone.

After doing gas tests and starting their search, it didn't take long before they found the body of the last victim down in the sump area below the shaft station where the water was collecting. With no way to get to it until the water was pumped out[4] the men worked on other pre-investigation documentation. They started a list of each piece of mining equipment, its location, and its condition. They also worked on a sketch map of the body locations, identified from the

401

lime thrown down where each body was found in the mine by the recovery teams.[5] Lime powder was used to suppress the odor of decomposition that had permeated the ground, but the smell was still unsufferable.

Westfield and the men also noted all the destruction that was extensive in the shop and around the shaft station. Throughout the West Drift, there was ample evidence the blast came from the shop and not the Face. While at the West Face, they ran into a volatile mixture of explosive gases.[6]

The men worked to improve the air lines and increase the compressed airflow into both drifts. They directed more air into the West Drift to dilute and flush the gases out of the mine until crews could restore the ventilation system.[7]

Just before leaving the mine around 5:00 p.m., the crew located a hand belonging to one of the victims which was taken to the temporary morgue in Moab.

After Westfield and his crew had surfaced from the mine late in the day, he spoke with the handful of reporters. The federal official indicated a collection of gas could have been the cause of the explosion,[8] but he wanted to start the state and federal probe he said, with "no preconceived ideas."

Westfield also reported that the body of the last victim has not been removed from the mine.

"It is lodged in a pool of water at the base of the shaft, and there is no way to pump out the water at this time.[9] We will be back tomorrow to try and get it out," he said.

Morris Worley, the young Texas Gulf Sulphur (TGS) Engineer who was down in the mine helping Westfield with the pre-investigation, brought up the surveyor's theodolite atop its tripod to show Bill Smith. It had been stored underground just before Worley and Smith left the mine moments before the explosion happened Tuesday afternoon. The glass on the theodolite was melted around it from the intense heat of the blast. Bill was shaken when he saw it and swore he would never go down into a mine ever again.[10]

The morning sun slowly crossed the sky as Sheriff Stocks stood at the door of the makeshift morgue southeast of Moab, almost as an honor guard[11] for the seventeen men inside; the place for the eighteenth still vacant.

"None of the families will see the bodies until identification is positive," Sheriff Stocks told reporters.

"Most of the men have children. Some have a lot of them," he said. "What are the women going to do now?" he lamented. "Lots of relatives have been around trying to identify the bodies. We have some tentative identification, but only one can really be positive," he added.

Jessie Tinall, the wife of the victim, John Tinall, was told her husband's body was too badly charred to identify. She turned to a sheriff's deputy and commented bitterly: "Maybe next time they will put dog tags on them." Then she burst into tears.[12] Harrison International did not use the brass tag-in/tag-out system widely used in the mining industry. Unlike coal mines, they were not required to. In the event of a disaster, the brass tags could endure an explosion or fire, and identification numbers engraved on them could help to identify bodies. A second brass tag with the miner's number was placed on a board on the surface before entering the mine and was used as a means for company officials to know who was in the mine at any given time.

Tensions were high as the identification process started on the Cane Creek victims. Grieving family members, still reeling from the shock of learning their loved one was dead, were now going through the exhaustive process of planning for funerals. A grim task,[13] the identification of the bodies was slow and proceeded throughout the day. By 3:00 p.m., only two had been tentatively identified.[14] It was clear the assistance from the FBI was needed.

The victims killed at Cane Creek were listed. They are Wesley Barber, Robert Bobo, Myrlen H. Christensen Jr., Myrlen H. Christensen Sr., Lawrence Davidson, Jess Fox, James N. Hollinger, William Huzil, Clell Johnson, Jess Kassler, Emile LeBlanc, Kenneth Milton, Fred Rowley, Rene Roy, Lamar Rushton, Keith Schear, Pete Sviscsu, and John Tinall.[15]

Meanwhile, the seven survivors of the explosion were reported to be rapidly recovering[16] from their exhausting experience. The heat, the unspoken fear, the hours of anxious waiting were just memories for the men pulled alive from the depths of the Cane Creek Mine. But in a way, the nightmares had just begun. Each of the seven survivors was painfully aware of and grieving the eighteen other men—their buddies, partners, and friends who entered the mine with them on Tuesday afternoon, but did not come out alive. The seven spent Friday with families and friends, as reporters called on them at their homes throughout the day. Each had his memories.[17] What was it like to live—or exist—for two days, 3,000 feet under the earth? Each survivor would explain in their own words, words they might have thought during the tortuous hours they might never have had a chance to utter.[18]

The men spent much of the time resting and trying to recover, with no celebrations, only gratitude for being alive.[19] Hanna and Trueman, the two who stayed in the hospital overnight, were released to go home Friday morning.

During the day, some of the survivors took the time to visit some of the relatives of the dead, to pay their respects to their former friends and colleagues.[20] Soon enough, each would deal with survivors' guilt and ask the questions: Why me? Why did I live? In varying degrees, it was something they would deal with the rest of their lives. It would show up in nightmares, turmoil and attempts to cope with Post Traumatic Stress Disorder, (PTSD). In 1963, there was no such thing as counseling for rescue workers or survivors, as they dealt with the horrors they experienced inside the mine. Now, in the mining industry, the importance of counseling is better understood and many times its offered to survivors and those involved in mine rescue and recovery work.[21]

Of the seven men who survived, all, with the possible exception of Tom Trueman,[22] went back to work in various underground mines. Five retired from the mines, and one retired as a federal mine inspector.

For now, each of the men spent time with their families and friends. They also spent time telling and retelling their stories. Some observers said the stories got better[23] with each telling, as the men slowly gave more details about their harrowing ordeal.

It was on Wednesday, twelve hours after the explosion trapped the twenty-five men, that a state official said it would be "a miracle" if anyone survived.[24] By Thursday evening, seven men in total had been brought out of the mine alive. Their survival was credited to an old dull pocket knife to cut the curtains, a decision to go back instead of forward, and the personal courage of two men named Hanna and McKinney. These were only a few of the events of the drama that played itself out for the men more than a half-mile underground (the distance of two stacked Empire State buildings).

What happened 3,000 feet underground? How did the "miracle" come about? Everyone wanted to know as newspaper reporters, and TV crews made visits to each of the survivors' homes, eager to get their stories and take pictures.

Grant 'Blackie' Eslick was standing outside his home[25] in Spanish Valley, south of Moab.

"I feel good today," he said, "but kind of like I've got a hangover without a headache,"[26] he told a reporter who dropped by to get his story. There were others.

"When you're involved with something like this, you really find out you've got friends, and mine really proved themselves. Everyone has been great," he said. "While I was in there, I kept telling myself, 'I've got to get out. I've got too many jobs to do around the house.'" He glanced towards his wife who was standing nearby. "How would Vivian get along without me? I've been putting a new furnace room under the house," he said, pointing to an excavation on the northeast corner of his home, "and I sure wanted to get it finished."[27]

Once inside, 'Blackie' sat on the arm of a couch in the living room of his suburban home, and welcomed well-wishing friends throughout the day who dropped by to say hello. To one friend who brought him a fancy wrapped bottle of bourbon with a red rose on top, he quipped, "I'm glad this is Four Roses and not a bouquet."[28]

Several reporters met with 'Blackie' during the day, and with each one, he told his story, adding more or different details or elaborating a bit more as he shared his experiences. 'Blackie' told how he was in the mine the day of the explosion with a new piece of equipment that probably saved his life.[29]

"I was playing around with a new temperature gauge that day," he said. "I had stayed in the East Drift just trying it out. Ordinarily, I would have gone back to the shaft by that time."[30]

The reporter asked how he felt after he was rescued.

"As we walked along," 'Blackie' said, "I remembered what I wished I could do all during the long, hot wait in the mine. All I wanted to do was get under a hot shower and scrub with soap, then turn it on cold and stay until I was good and ready to get out.[31] That's exactly what I did when we reached the hospital. But I'm still brushing my teeth to try to get sand and the muddy water taste out of my mouth. Even the beautiful ham Vivian had waiting at home tasted like muddy water. The hotcakes were better this morning. She's improving,"[32] he said with a grin.

When asked about the claims that safety precautions were lax in the mine, 'Blackie' said, "This kind of talk comes up every time you have a thing like this." He paused then added, "I really don't want to get into that."[33]

'Blackie' was asked about his future plans and if he would go back to the mine.

"What are my plans?" 'Blackie' asked in a surprised tone. "Well, my father and grandfather both were miners, so I grew up with it. It's my livelihood.[34] We're a mining family. And once a miner, always a miner," he said.[35] 'Blackie' was raised in Muller, Idaho, in the hard rock mining district near Coeur d'Alene, Idaho.

"Why, I guess I'll go back out there tomorrow,[36] or as soon as they open back up. I want to spend the rest of my life in Moab, and that's as long of a mining job as I can see. Besides, I've mined since I was a kid, over thirty years down under."[37]

Charles Byrge, known by the others as 'Chuck,' sat in the living room of his home with his family and some friends.[38]

The reporter asked what he was thinking about while trapped in the mine.

"Well, I kept thinking about how cool the air blowing out of that air conditioner is," he laughed as he pointed across the living room.

"I don't know why I'm so tired," Byrge said. I haven't done anything but sit and sweat down in that hole for forty-nine hours. But, man it was hot down there," he said.[39]

"The old heat was really building up, and we were drinking cruddy water and sweating it out as fast as we put it in." He explained they only had a small amount of drinking water, and they soon were drinking river water pumped into the mine for use with drilling equipment.

"I was too nervous to sleep last night," he said. "I was up at daylight waking everyone else up."

He picked up his son, Rodney, age two, just as the little one leaned over to give his father a kiss.

"Isn't he a great little guy?" Byrge asked.[40] It was obvious he adored his family, as his little ones surrounded him. They were the ones Byrge was so proud of and often talked about at work.

Byrge continued telling his story, sharing much of the same information he had the night before.

"I was sure glad to see the rescuers. It was great to see them."[41]

Robert June[42] and his wife, Violet, lived in a small subdivision south of Moab, with five of their six children. Their oldest daughter, who was married, lived in Scott City, Kansas. The other children were[43] Patsy, sixteen; Robert Jr., fifteen; Linda Kay, eleven; Deborah Lee, ten; and Sandra Lorene, 18 months.

June began work for Harrison International in July the previous year.[44]

"I feel pretty good today."[45] He held his smallest child, eighteen-month-old Sandra, "our pride and joy," he said as he spoke.

Normally, I would have been in that other drift where the explosion was. That's where I was assigned. But on Tuesday, they needed some special drilling that only I could do.

"I heard this man screaming for a long time, but we couldn't get to him. He started screaming right after the explosion. The smoke was real bad, and we barely lived through it," he said.

June was asked[46] how he spent hours waiting for a rescue party.

"After we built our barrier against the gas, there wasn't much to do but wait. We kept our light out to save the batteries. It was sure black.[47] And I laid there and sweat," June said.

"Somewhere down there we lost about eight hours.[48] I thought we kept pretty good track of the time, but when we were coming out, we couldn't decide what time of day it was. I thought it would be dark, and one of the guys thought it would be daytime. It was evening when we finally got out."[49]

Hesitating for a moment, he continued. "The blast probably was from the other drift. It knocked all of us down. It was hot and smoky. When I picked myself up, I got over the hole, and I looked down. I couldn't see anything, but I heard this terrible screaming," he said.

"There was nothing we could do. Nothing. It was pitch black. After a while, the screaming stopped. I don't know who was screaming."

When June was brought to the surface with the other four survivors late Thursday evening, his mother collapsed from stress and was taken to the hospital for treatment of shock. They kept her overnight and released her to return home early the next morning.[50]

"We're so thankful and so sorry for the families who were less fortunate," June's sister said.[51] The sorrow for the men who died and their families was deeply felt by the men who survived.

One of the first two miners out of the shaft, Donald 'Blake' Hanna, sat on the couch in his downtown Moab home Friday morning as he patiently listened while his four young children chattered in his ear.[52]

It was just after 10:00 a.m. when he returned home from the hospital to find a house full of reporters waiting to interview him. Walter Cronkite, an anchor of the CBS Evening News, was there, along with other reporters and photographers. As soon as Hanna came through the front door, photographers positioned him on the couch with his family around him.

"...and I got 100 on this paper too," said seven-year-old Danny, as he waved a school paper in front of his father's face.[53] Joe, age four, leaned back against his mother, as two-year-old Becky sat on the floor looking up at her father and five-year-old Kim sat next to him on the couch.

Blake Hanna speaks to his daughter, Kim, as other family members look on; Danny, (back row), Myrna, his wife; son Joe, and daughter, Becky. (*Times-Independent*)

Hanna's eyes, damaged and irritated by smoke and gases from his ordeal in the mine, were still covered with gauze bandages.

"I feel good," Hanna said, "but the sun still hurts my eyes. I'll take these bandages off when it gets dark. My eyes will be okay in a couple of days,"[54] he said.

The children were inquisitive. For the younger three children, this was the first time they had seen their father since the explosion, and they hadn't been told much about his ordeal.

His daughter Kim, who would turn six in two days, was alarmed by the bandages on her father's eyes and finally had the courage, in front of a packed room of reporters, to ask him if he was going to be okay. Everyone looked in her direction, or at Hanna, as he looked her way and assured her he would be fine. A photographer quickly snapped a photo. There was a brief pause, then reporters continued with their barrage of questions, as Hanna patiently answered while sharing his experiences.

Thomas Trueman was living at Harrison International's man camp set up for the miners near the mine site.[55] Reporters drove there to speak with him.[56] The single, thirty-seven-years-old with carrot red hair, was a veteran of the British Air Force and a native of Northern Ireland.[57] Trueman stayed one night in the hospital and spent the next day drinking beer with his friends, trying to decide whether to go back into the mine again. He had no relatives in the area; his parents currently lived in Belfast, Ireland.[58] "But I have lots of friends," he said.[59]

Trueman lived in Toronto, Ontario, Canada when he was employed by Harrison International and came to work at Cane Creek eighteen months ago.[60]

"It was my first time underground," he said, "although I have been working around mines for five years." He had worked as a heavy equipment operator in an open pit mining operation in Canada for five years and was a foreman on two projects.[61]

"I don't intend to go back down in the mine," he declared. "I've been told by the company that I'll be given work on the surface. This is my idea for the future.[62] The surface work will include handling heavy equipment. I think I'll like that, and there will be plenty to do for some time even after the mine is completed."[63]

"I'll have a lot of time to think about whether I'll go back down. What happened was a freak," he said.[64]

He was asked what the trapped men did while they waited.

"We took turns sleeping," Trueman said. "We would sleep for a few minutes at a time. The rest of the time we would talk and wait, I guess. At first, we also wondered if the three others made it to safety."[65]

"I was never afraid while I was down there," he said. "We were all sure it was just a matter of time." He spoke in a calm voice with an Irish accent.[66]

"We knew we had to keep calm. I guess we all said a little prayer and put our trust in God.[67] It happened about twenty minutes after a dynamite blast and must have been deep in the West Drift."[68]

"The worst time for me came when we ran down the drift to the shaft and ran into that heavy smoke. We knew then we couldn't get out right away. We knew the gas was there and that it was moving.[69] It was heavy gas, creeping along the floor. For four or five hours, we built a barricade to try to stop the gas. We knew it was deadly. We built the barricade out of pieces of collapsible vent line and wood, then packed the bottom with salt.[70] Then all we could do was hope the gas would be kept out. We moved further down into the drift to get away from the gas.[71] It was hot. We, my companions and myself, drank water, and we sweated. And we worried."[72] He paused as he reflected back on his experiences.

"We used only one miner's lamp at a time so we would have light as long as possible. We still had one light when we were rescued. About twelve hours after the explosion, Hanna and McKinney left, and then we had another worry: Did they make it?[73] And we worried about the guys coming to get us."[74] Trueman took a drink of his beer and continued.

"About thirty hours after the explosion, somebody up there repaired the high-pressure air line, and we began to get a little new air. Not much, but it was enough,[75] and we knew the worst was over.[76] We still had to sit, sweat and drink water. Some of us heard the rescuers coming about ten minutes before they arrived. We heard the clank of metal and knew they were on the way. When I saw them, it was the greatest thing I have ever seen in my life,"[77] he said with a huge smile.

"I thought all along that they would come and get us out. But I guess it was 'Blackie' who kinda kept us calm. He kept telling us to stay behind the barricade and that everything would be all right."[78]

He paused for a moment, then continued. "But the happiest news we got was that our two buddies had made it out all right.[79] Hanna and McKinney saved our lives, I guess. They fixed that air line and kept us with just enough air,[80] and that undoubtedly saved our lives."[81]

Trueman answered other questions and then went back to entertaining his friends as the reporters left, heading back to town to get their story in before deadlines.

Charles 'C.C.' Clark, twenty-seven, was a nice-looking father of four, with close-cropped dark hair and a slender build. He was born in Springdale, Arkansas and when he was about a year old, his family moved to Snow Lake, Arkansas where they were "sharecroppers." There were six sisters and one brother in the family, and 'C.C.' was the youngest. The family moved several times, first to Alameda, California about 1942, back to Snow Lake in 1947, then back to Springdale in 1950.[82]

'C.C.' graduated from high school in 1953, and soon after, went with a friend to Newcastle, Wyoming, where he got a job in the oil field as a "roughneck" and driller.[83] Moving around on oil rigs, he met Adeline Koch in Sheridan, Wyoming and they were married in 1955. She was raised in a large family, with two brothers and seven sisters, on a farm in Ranchester, Wyoming, where they grew sugar beets.[84] After marriage, 'C.C.' continued oil drilling and moved his family to Monticello, Utah in 1960.[85]

Two years ago, in 1961, 'C.C.' went to work for Harrison International at the Cane Creek Mine. The shaft was about 200-feet deep at the time, and he worked as a diamond driller and did grouting around the shaft.[86] He worked fifty-six hours a week for $3.23 an hour, or about $750 a month. The Clarks, who were Jehovah's Witnesses, lived in an $8,000 trailer with three bedrooms, living room, bath, and kitchen, in a trailer park in northwest Moab.[87]

While at the hospital the night before, the medical staff first wanted 'C.C.' to stay overnight but soon allowed him to go home. After taking a shower and dressing in street clothes, he went home to a nice reunion with local friends and family, plus some relatives from Wyoming.[88]

One reporter from a Salt Lake TV station came to the house the next morning for an interview with 'C.C.'.[89] Then another reporter came later, as he and his family were preparing to leave on their trip that afternoon.

'C.C.,' with his wife nearby, stood quietly, leaning on a table in the kitchen as the reporter asked how he would describe his feelings.[90]

"I'm not sure I can. But it's good to be here, and I feel pretty good."[91] He went through the events, telling the story of his experiences as they unfolded.

"The concussion caused a painful pressure in my ears," 'C.C.' said. "I was hit by a blast of hot air, then the air seemed to be sucked back to the main shaft." He told how the crew headed towards the shaft station only to run into smoke, forcing them to turn back toward the end of the drift. With an old pocket knife 'C.C.' kept in his pocket, they cut sections from the collapsible ventilation line and hung them from the roof of the drift. Then he told how three of the men didn't stay with the rest.[92]

"Hanna went back and tried to get them to come with us," 'C.C.' said. "He knew there was better air at the Face. But they said they were staying."[93]

"We put up three barricades, one about several hundred feet from the Face, then two more 200 feet back," 'C.C.' said, "That kept the smoke away, and we had enough air."[94] He shared other experiences behind the barricade and then spoke of the decision Hanna and McKinney made to leave. When nothing further was heard from them, the five men began to fear the worst. They lay quietly on the floor, their boots off, and fanned themselves with their shirts against the heat.

"We thought the shaft was blocked, and that we weren't going to be rescued. We had no way of knowing what was being done to get us out."[95] He talked about Wednesday night when air began gushing out of the compressed air line signaling help was on the way. He also told about his experience when they were finally rescued.

His wife, Adeline, said she had given up hope for him; but that was before Hanna and McKinney brought the news he was alive. Asked if he was going back down in the mine, 'C.C.' said he hadn't decided. But his wife had a different opinion: "I don't want him to go down there again because every time he'd leave for work, I'd be constantly worrying until he was back home. I don't care what else he does. The amount of money he makes doesn't matter to me."[96]

Later that day, the Clarks left for a convention in Los Angeles, going to the Grand Canyon on the way. The Clarks planned to be gone for two weeks, and were hoping by that time, things would settle down a little in Moab.[97]

Stopping in Flagstaff, Arizona, 'C.C.' went to buy a newspaper. The guy in the shop wanted to explain all the details of the mine explosion and the rescue to 'C.C.' While the man wasn't too accurate, 'C.C.' listened politely anyway.[98]

The other survivors also had similar experiences throughout the years. Some people thought they knew the story, but for whatever reason, had elements of it that were wrong. Rumors grew out of the events as they happened, and wrong information made it into print. The retelling and elaborating through the years also added to some of the misconceptions.

———◆———

Paul McKinney[99] stood in front of the makeshift morgue at the trucking garage on the outskirts of Moab. A quiet, thoughtful young man, he had little to say, but the look in his eyes told his story. "I came down to see if I could help, but it looks like there is nothing I can do here," he said. One could tell he was torn up over the death of his friends.[100]

His wife was expecting their first child in December, and he said he was grateful he was alive. He was still bitter about early attempts to rescue the five men he and Hanna had left behind in the barricade. But he added, "I guess the important thing there is we got them out alive."[101]

McKinney's doctor talked to him about doing some surgery on his backside later that week to cut out the damaged area so it would heal better. The acid burns on his side[102] (caused by the leaky battery to his cap-lamp) covered a considerable sized area.[103] Once the doctor cut out the burned area, and he was sewn back up, McKinney would be laid up for a while as he recovered.[104]

———◆———

In the hot afternoon sun, a young man stood silently on the oil-soaked earth[105] outside the Skyline Transport garage. His head was bent forward, and the blank look on his face said nothing.

Paul McKinney at the trucking garage. (*Salt Lake Tribune*)

"My brother is in there," he said to no one in particular. "It's not easy for mom to understand, and his wife is pretty broken up," he said. "But I guess it's hard for a lot of other people too."[106]

A small knot of people stood outside the building talking in low voices. "The worst part is over, I guess," said another man. "The waiting was hell. Not knowing, but hoping. When the word finally came, it was a shock, but I guess we expected the worst all along,"[107] he continued.

"Somehow the kids and I will go on," one woman commented. "We had talked about it—an accident—before. We've lived with the possibility since we were married. But he loved his work, and I couldn't make him give it up. Somehow we'll go on."[108]

Herve Roy went by the garage with Mr. Hamilton. The smell of death was strong in the hot afternoon air. Herve came to identify his father's remains but decided against it when he was told the bodies were in really bad shape, and it would be too difficult to know for sure. However, he was able to give information to the Sheriff about his father for the death certificate.[109] He also verified arrangements were being made to have his father's remains sent home to North Bay, Ontario. Rene Roy was going home for good. Home to his final resting place.

Herve went back to the Hamilton's home to pack his suitcase to catch a flight home from Grand Junction, Colorado to Canada. In the car and ready to leave, Mr. Hamilton backed his car out of the driveway. Herve's eyes fixed on the brand new, shiny brown Impala parked in the driveway. It was the car his father had bought just hours before he was killed, and now was being sold. It was the last memory of Moab Herve had—his dad's new car.[110]

The events of the past few days would change Herve's life forever. Out of necessity, he would become the man of the family, with all that entailed. In the years to come, Herve would see to the needs of his mother and siblings, both financially and in other ways. He would also become the father figure to the younger children and especially Nelsen, his two-year-old brother, who would hardly have any memories of his father. It was such a tall order for a young nineteen-year-old son, barely entering manhood.

The Cane Creek Mine site was situated in one of the most beautiful and rugged places on earth, amid sheer sandstone cliffs of vivid colored hues of violet, brown, rust, and reds. It was an ancient place carved out through time by the water and the blowing wind that echoed through the canyons of the mighty Colorado River as it "washed the mountains to the sea."

The song, "Blowin' in the Wind," befittingly represented the struggle of young Herve Roy and his coming of age. It represented not only Herve's story on so many levels, but it also spoke to the other stories at Cane Creek—stories of all the children and the heartbreaking times they would go through and the questions they would ultimately ask. The poetic lyrics spoke of "How many roads must a man walk down before they call him a man?" Or, "How many years must a mountain exist, before it is washed to the sea?" And, "How many deaths will it take 'til he knows, that too many people have died?" With the refrain repeating throughout: "The answer, my friend, is blowin' in the wind."[111]

Like the canyons and sheer cliffs, the tragedy at Cane Creek and its profound loss, would echo through the generations forever, and the question would be asked, "Why?" Rhetorically, this very beautiful and expressive song, 'Blowin' in the Wind,'[112] asks, and in a small way, even answers, all those hard questions. "The answer, my friend, is blowin' in the wind."[113] While the song poses a series of rhetorical questions, the refrain, "The answer, my friend, is blowin' in the wind," is described as impenetrably ambiguous. Either the answer is obvious and right in front of you, or the answer is as intangible as the wind."[114]

———

By Friday afternoon, Utah Governor, George D. Clyde, ordered a complete and full-scale investigation on the causes and reasons for the mysterious blast, which ripped through the potash mine. At a press conference in Salt Lake City, he said the investigation would be conducted by the U.S. Bureau of Mines and by the Utah State Industrial Commission,[115] and he promised the report would be made public. "We are taking this action so this kind of tragedy can be prevented in the future," he said.

At about the same time, Robert Bernick, the Business Editor of the *Salt Lake Tribune* was still pursuing the truth concerning the mine leases and who had jurisdiction over the Cane Creek Mine. On Friday, Bernick interviewed Ernest Blessing, the Regional Supervisor for the U.S. Geological Survey (USGS), at his office in Salt Lake City. Blessing told Bernick that his agency had made some inspections and approved nine development plans and mining methods and that he had found "no evidence of management laxity regarding gas exposure at the Cane Creek Mine."[116]

Concerning the terms of the lease agreements, Blessing confirmed that "the USGS had concurrent jurisdiction as to safety at this property." He acknowledged that most of the potash property leased by Texas Gulf Sulphur was in the federal public domain. This gave the USGS the power and the authority under the lease agreement to shut down the property at any time if they found "conditions to be unsafe for miners or in any way involving harm to federal property," meaning the potash deposit.[117]

Blessing indicated the number of times the USGS visited the mine was about once a month, maybe not quite that often since they only had "six engineers in a five-state district, examining 1,000 properties." And he said that both the USGS Engineers and the U.S. Bureau of Mines people visited the property on occasion of accidents. Blessing did say that the Bureau did one inspection on June 12th and the report received at Salt Lake City from that investigation did not indicate conditions at the property were unsafe.

Blessing said that under regulations, the U.S. Bureau of Mines was assigned the responsibility to inspect for safety conditions and their procedures have been to work closely with state mine inspectors from the Utah State Industrial Commission.

Blessing stressed the USGS and the Bureau were empowered to make an investigation because of the very terms of the lease between the federal government and the Texas Gulf Sulphur Company.[118] Blessing then confirmed that the Bureau had possessed the right all along to go into the mine and make inspections, but added that he didn't think the Secretary of Interior had actually assigned them this right in any order.[119]

It was an interesting admission, especially in light of Udall's previous press release concerning the Cane Creek Mine explosion and his sponsored legislation designed to obtain this power. Blessing explained that neither agency had a role in inspecting metal mines on patented or unpatented metal mining claims or elsewhere in the United States. Potash was not regarded as a metal under the minerals leasing acts. Neither was trona (soda ash). And these leases, Blessing said, "derive from the federal government, so it is our responsibility to see regulations are observed."

Blessing also confirmed that both the U.S. government and the contractor, Harrison International, were certainly aware of the gas hazards. "Gas was not uncommon in these situations," Blessing said. He believed the lease agreement and regulations of the USGS dictated the Cane Creek Mine should be operated under "coal mine conditions" because of the known presence of gas and how it was operated.

Some of the miners who worked at Cane Creek had felt that TGS did not want the mine classified as a "gassy mine."[120] The company had already invested heavily in non-permissible mining equipment. There was also a perception that some of Harrison International's bosses had no real experience with gassy mines and therefore, had no real understanding of just how destructive even a small amount of gas could be in the small confines of a mine.[121]

While the *Salt Lake Tribune* was still investigating and trying to flush out the jurisdictional question over the Cane Creek Potash Mine, matters became even more confused when one high Interior Department official in Washington compared the mine to an aircraft carrier still under construction. He explained that "the carrier doesn't actually come under the Navy until the finished product is turned over by the shipbuilders. Thus, the Moab mine, since technically not yet in operation, was still in the custody of the shaft-sinking firm, which wasn't responsible to Interior Department agencies."[122]

The Director of Information, an assistant to Interior Secretary Udall, made the comparison after he had conferred with other top federal officials.[123] He quoted them as saying the department would not have authority over the mine until the jurisdiction of Harrison International, Inc., the shaft-sinking firm, ceased and the mining company, Texas Gulf Sulphur, assumes control. He cited Public Law 8730 as the basis for this opinion.[124]

This line of thinking seemed to echo an earlier statement by Frank Tippie when he said, "The property is not yet a mine."[125] If this were the case, it then begged the question: who was responsible until it was a mine? The state?

Yet, Ernest Blessing, of the USGS, had already acknowledged that the USGS and the U.S. Bureau of Mines were already empowered to make investigations because of the very terms of the leases between the federal government and the TGS Company.[126] As everyone talked in circles, it was still not clear who had jurisdiction over the mine. Possibly only a court could sort out and settle the matter.

———

Shattered and in deep mourning, Moab was a town with seventeen new widows,[127] with three of them expecting babies. There were nearly sixty children, most of whom were still dependent, while a few were older or married. The families were sharing their grief in seclusion with their immediate needs provided for by other family members, friends, and neighbors.

Father John Rasbach, the Roman Catholic priest in Moab, said a joint Requiem Mass[128] for the Catholics involved would be held if the families wished. Meanwhile, Moab residents, no longer in a state of hopeful suspense, turned to the provision of primary needs and launched a fundraising campaign to assist the bereaved families.

Tom Stocks, the president of Moab Junior Chamber of Commerce (Jaycees), was assisted by Keith Brewer, Ronald Reedy, and Betty Jacobs, the secretary of the Moab Chamber of Commerce, in their efforts to organize the fund drive on Friday night. In the small mining town of 6,000, volunteers from fifty-four civic and church organizations in Moab went door-to-door with fruit jars to collect money.[129] Leaders of the drive said citizens were "responding wonderfully,"[130] as hearts were touched by what the families were going through.

Tom Stocks said he had received calls from other Jaycee units in the state offering to help. He said the money could be sent to the "Potash Fund," care of the Moab National Bank, and it would be used to tide the families over in their period of crisis.[131]

"At the Chamber of Commerce office," said Secretary Betty Jacobs, "we've had calls from everyone wanting to help. Some don't have money to give, so they've offered food, babysitting—things like that."[132]

Richard Reynolds of Texas Gulf Sulphur, Robert Restana of Harrison International, and Robert Blagg, a banker, began to organize the disbursal program. Captain and Mrs. Charles A. Dooley, sent from the Salt Lake office by the Salvation Army, offered their help to local ministers to determine the needs of the stricken families as those more fortunate sought to provide stop-gap income until insurance arrangements could take over. The goal of the fund drive was a minimum of $5,000 for the immediate cash needs of families of the dead miners. Mrs. Jacobs assured callers to her office that this amount would soon be reached, as she waited on checks from business establishments to arrive.

She said that on Saturday morning $135 was collected in thirty minutes. "No, make that $185," she said. "The women's golf association just tossed in $50."[133]

"This whole town is in a state of shock," said Karleen Uphold, whose husband was an auto mechanic. "I didn't know any of the miners, but I'm putting in $10."[134]

Bitterness against the companies remained, but the relatives of the victims were thankful for the help[135] offered by the community fund-raising drive and other kindnesses shown to them.

Nate Harrison, president of Harrison International (no relation to 'Paddy' Harrison), also said the insurance company representatives were working around the clock so families could receive benefit payments within a week so they wouldn't have to wait the normal three or four weeks.[136]

Chapter 24

Million to One Combination

Early Saturday morning, the body of the eighteenth victim was still in the mine, with no indication when[1] it would be recovered. Crews worked throughout the day to increase the amount of air pumped into the mine to flush out the carbon monoxide and methane gases found the day before. Because of complications in clearing the West Drift of the high levels of explosive gases, the mine was still too dangerous to enter.[2] It forced a one-day delay in the investigation,[3] forcing officials to start the investigation on Tuesday instead of Monday,[4] exactly one week from the day of the explosion.[5] An official said an agreement had been reached with the U.S. Bureau of Mines to postpone the investigation to permit the needed repairs to the mine's ventilation system.[6] The setback would also give workmen more time to clear more debris and make the mine safer for investigators.[7]

As crews worked on the ventilation system and cleared debris, others were busy with the water pump system. They needed to clear as much water from the sump as possible.[8]

Meanwhile, reports kept circulating that experts were theorizing Tuesday's blast was possibly touched off in a "million to one combination." While the actual cause of the explosion had not been determined, one person in authority said it might have resulted from a dynamite blast at 4:20 p.m. in the West Drift. Presumably, this released methane gas had drifted to the shop area near the main shaft. It was believed that a spark of undetermined origin ignited the disastrous explosion.[9]

At the request of Sheriff Stocks, two FBI identification experts were sent[10] from Washington D.C. to Moab, to help identify the victims. Dental charts, fingerprints and other information such as descriptions of height, build, clothing, and identifying marks such as tattoos or scars, were gathered to help match the names with the bodies. Identification of men is easier than of women and children, the FBI said, because most American men are fingerprinted when entering military service.

The FBI's disaster squads, two from Washington, three from the SLC office, arrived early in the morning.[11] They went immediately to the truck repair shop on the outskirts of Moab. The team of five men[12] came with some fingerprint samples taken from the victims' military and other records in Washington.

The FBI identification specialists went to work, and before long they had identified more than half[13] of the seventeen charred corpses. Harry Snow, Grand County District Attorney,[14] assisted with the identifications while Sheriff Stocks helped to gather additional information on the death certificates. The Turner Funeral Home in Moab said doctors had not yet filled in the cause of death, while Texas Gulf Sulphur officials said it appeared some of the victims were killed instantly by the blast and that others died later of carbon monoxide poisoning.[15] Once identified, the bodies were dressed and placed in coffins that were sealed, while the grieving families[16] went about the work of preparing for funerals.

The FBI specialists used a new fingerprint technique[17] on some of the victims too badly burned to get regular fingerprints. After soaking the fingers to hydrate the skin, they cut just the skin around the finger about an inch from the end. The skin was then turned inside out by rolling it off the finger and onto the gloved finger of the specialist, who then inked and printed it as usual. The underside of the skin had ridges and was printed in this manner; the resulting impression was a reverse fingerprint. A photograph of the inner ridge detail was made, and the negative was printed and used to give an "as is" photograph to make the proper fingerprint comparison.[18]

The FBI identification team was professional and took the time to be painstakingly thorough. They gathered clues from other places. FBI agents went to Margo Christensen's apartment to collect something with her husband's fingerprints on it to use for comparison.[19]

Eudeene Hollinger was asked to write a description of her husband and what he might have been wearing to identify him. She told them everything she could think of or remember.[20] Eudeene's father-in-law, Joe Hollinger, wanted to see the body of his son. He had to see for himself that it was 'Jimmy.' Officials refused his request because of the bad shape of the bodies.

"I will see my son," he demanded.

"You can't," they said.

"You watch me," Joe forcefully replied.

Officials finally backed down and allowed him access. In that tragic moment, Joe Hollinger was able to tell that the body was, in fact, his son's.[21]

By Saturday afternoon, the identifications were expected to take several more hours[22] as Sheriff Stocks reported all but three[23] of the victims were identified "and we should be finished soon. It looks like we'll be able to identify all the victims," he said. "It's been a slow, painstaking operation."[24] Once the bodies were identified, they were turned over to their families, and separate arrangements were made[25] for each. Shipment of bodies to other towns for funerals began as preparations for four funerals in Moab were planned.

Before the FBI team arrived, there were many rumors, and some believed they would not be able to identify all of the bodies. It was hard for family members, and some were rightfully concerned they might not receive the right body.

Eldridge Johnson requested to identify his brother, Clell. Clell was identified by the three long and wide scars on his back from surgery after a previous mining accident. The body was partially burned, but Eldridge was certain it was Clell. When leaving, one of the other wives told Eldridge, "at least you know who you are getting."[26]

The first body brought out of the mine, which had caused so much controversy, who rescuers initially thought was Clell Johnson, turned out to be Kenneth Milton. Milton also had dark hair with a square hairline. The rescuers picked up his body on the west side of the shaft, not far from the shuttle car he took to the shaft area to charge the battery.

At the mine site, it had taken two days to recover[27] the last body. It was around 6:30 p.m. when workers transported it to the temporary morgue for identification. Badly damaged, some believed it had been the nearest to the center of the mysterious explosion.[28]

It was early in the evening when Jack Kassler, owner of the Moab Hotel, who also worked at the Cane Creek Mine, was asked by officials to identify the last body, thought to be his brother, Jesse Kassler. Once Jack identified his brother, their sister, who was in Moab from Corpus Christi, Texas, called her husband in Texas to let him know Jesse was "definitely identified[29] among the dead miners."

Friday morning, Westfield had taken several TGS employees with him into the mine to search for the missing body. After finding it down in the sump the day before, they were not able to get to it until more water was pumped out of the mine. The men also ran into large amounts of gas down in the West Drift and had to pump more air to flush it out before they could do anymore work. Besides searching for the last body, they were also doing other work to get the mine ready for the state and federal investigation that would begin the next week. They were clearing out some of the debris so the mine would be safer for the investigators.

Officials make arrangements with families and funeral homes to send the bodies to different locations for burial. In the U.S., four men would be buried in Moab, six others would be sent to different towns in Utah, and one was going to Nevada, one to Texas, one to Arizona and one to Colorado. Four of the victims, all from different towns in Canada, would be returned to their country.[30]

After the last body was recovered and the grim task of identifying the victims was completed, Utah Governor, George D. Clyde, issued a blistering statement. He lashed out at the earlier press release (made only twenty-four hours after the explosion) by Secretary of Interior, Stewart Udall. In that release, Udall used the Cane Creek Potash Mine disaster as an example in his charge of "lax safety practices in some segments of the mining industry."[31] The governor took issue with Udall's statements, and he felt the facts available at the time did not warrant the conclusions which implied blame.[32] The strained relationship between the governor and secretary was already contentious after several years of battling over the terms of the new proposed Canyonlands National Park near Moab, and the initial denial of leases promised to TGS.

The governor told reporters, "That statement gave the definite impression that management was responsible for failure to take even 'preliminary safety precautions' and for 'laxness' in the enforcement of such meager safety precautions. It greatly disturbs me this impression should be left with the grief-torn relatives of the dead and with the general public." The governor also defended the safety programs at the mine and the actions of state inspectors since the time that mine construction started nearly three years ago.[33]

Governor Clyde said the Industrial Commission records "fully document compliance with the state mine inspector's orders and his recommendations, as well as the actions that were taken by TGS and Harrison International to initiate their own programs."[34]

Governor Clyde had ordered a state investigation the day before and said it "would document the safety programs and practices of all parties concerned and would determine the cause"[35] of the explosion. He expected that it would show conscientious efforts and good faith of the state and operating parties in safety practices.[36] He also expressed hope Secretary Udall would see fit to correct the "unfortunate impression created" by his statement when the full facts were presented.[37]

"I feel we should await completion of a thorough and competent investigation before attempting to draw conclusions or fix blame in this tragic occurrence," the governor concluded.[38]

Moab, Utah
Robert Wayne 'Bob' Bobo
Saturday - August 31, 1963

The body of Robert Bobo was released early Saturday afternoon to his family after he was positively identified. His funeral, the first to be held, was at 4:00 p.m. on Saturday afternoon. The service was at The Church of Jesus Christ of Latter-day Saints (Mormon)-Moab Ward Chapel, with Mormon Bishop Henry S. Florence Jr. officiating.[39] Bobo was laid to rest at the Sunset Memorial Gardens Cemetery, southeast of town, where the blue-gray slopes of the La Sal Mountains loomed large in the background, and beautifully contrasted against the red rock landscape.

Stoically, the family gathered around the grave. Present were his pregnant widow, twenty-eight-year-old Donna Bobo, and his two young children, Daniel Wayne 'Bo', nine and Peggy Jean, six. His mother, Faye Bobo Iker,[40] and his step-father, Leonard R. Iker, both from Fritch, Texas and his two brothers, Jack Lemoine Bobo, of Moab, and Thomas Denny Iker, of Fritch, stood nearby.[41] Other family members and friends were there as all paid their last respects.

Disaster at Cane Creek

The eighteen Cane Creek Mine explosion victims. (*Deseret News and Family Photos*)

Robert Bobo was born on August 29, 1930, in Seminole, Oklahoma, to Wayne Theodore Bobo[42] and Faye Ollie Dendy Bobo. He spent his childhood in Ada, Oklahoma. He married Donna Gail Wigley on December 15, 1952, in Nena, Arkansas.[43] Robert and Donna moved their small family to Moab in 1962, from Border, Texas and resided at the Shady Rest Trailer Park.

Robert Bobo was known as 'Bob' by many and was also called Bobo by those who worked with him at the Cane Creek Mine, where he worked as a miner and the Skip Loader on the east side of the shaft. Bobo was a diabetic since childhood and was insulin dependent. He had a great smile and was loved by everyone in spite of the fact that he loved to pick and tease. Extremely mechanically inclined, Bobo could fix anything. He was only thirty-three-years-old at the time of his death.

Moab, Utah
Lawrence Ira Davidson
Sunday - September 1, 1963

Funeral services were conducted at 1:30 p.m., on a beautiful Sunday afternoon, September 1st, at the Turner Funeral Home in Moab for Lawrence Ira 'Dave' Davidson. Reverend Vernon Kendall of the Moab Community Baptist Church conducted the services. Lawrence was laid to rest in the warm afternoon sun at the Sunset Memorial Cemetery in Moab.[44] Forty-five-years-old, Lawrence was born February 18, 1918, in Washington, Iowa to Samuel Ira Davidson and Hazel Inez Beanblossom Davidson.

Davidson, commonly known as 'Junior,' was a veteran of World War II. He served in the U.S. Army from 1942 to 1945, and obtained the rank of a Technical Sergeant in his unit, while serving in the Army's Detachment Engineering Section in the Alaska Department.[45]

Lawrence married Opal Joyce Darnell on March 21, 1946, at Leadville, Colorado.[46] He was survived by his wife and three daughters, Jean, sixteen; Jane, twelve; and Margaret 'Marnie,' two and a-halfff, all of Moab. He was also survived by his parents, both of Harrison, Arkansas, and his two sisters, Alice Oliver, of Kansas City, Missouri, and Phillis Hancock, of Joplin, Missouri.[47]

Spring Glen, Utah
Fred Daniel Rowley
Sunday - September 1, 1963

About the same time that Lawrence Davidson was laid to rest in Moab, funeral services for Fred Daniel Rowley were held just north of Price, Utah, at 2:00 p.m. at The Church of Jesus Christ of Latterdayayay Saints (Mormon)-Spring Glen Ward Chapel.[48] Afterward, he was interred at the Spring Glen Cemetery.[49]

Fred was born November 24, 1921, in Spring Glen, Utah to David Smith Rowley and Sarah Noyes Rowley. He grew up in Spring Glen with seven brothers and sisters.

Fred joined the U.S. Army Air Force (USAAF) after graduating from high school in 1939 and served stateside. He was first stationed at Moffett Field in California at the Army's Western Flying Training Command, the headquarters for pilot and aircrew flight training west of the Rocky Mountains. While there, he graduated as a pilot and was also able to attend classes at Stanford University. He was transferred to Oklahoma and, then in 1943, he was sent to Alexandria Air Force Base in Alexandria, Louisiana. During World War II, the USAAF established airfields in the Alexandria area for training pilots and aircrews of fighters and bomber airplanes, where Fred flew the iconic Boeing B-17 Flying Fortress. Fred served in the military for five years and five months. He was discharged in August, 1945 from the Army Air Force, once the war was over.[50]

While in Alexandria, Louisiana, he met and married Harriette Adelaide Campbell, on December 31, 1944. Their marriage was later solemnized in the Bountiful Utah Temple. The couple settled in Fred's hometown of Spring Glen, Utah. Fred and Harriet were blessed with five children.[51] The children were Marye, eighteen; Paula, sixteen; April, fourteen; Debra, nine and Fred, Jr. 'Freddie,' six.

Fred worked as a Lead Miner for Harrison International and was forty-one-years-old at the time of his death. His wife, Harriet, and their children moved to Moab at the beginning of the summer, but now the summer was over and so was the life they had known before with the death of Fred.

Moab, Utah & Uvalde, Texas
Jesse Clinton Kassler
Sunday - September 1, 1963

That same afternoon, at the First Baptist Church of Moab, a memorial funeral service was held for Jesse Clinton Kassler at 3:00 p.m., with Reverend Leland Goodman, officiating. Afterward, Jesse's body was shipped to Uvalde, Texas, the southern limit of the Texas Hill Country, where there was a service before interment. He was laid to rest at the City of Uvalde Cemetery.[52]

Born September 25, 1924, in Ascertain, Texas to George Wesley Kassler and Betty Ann Kassler, Jesse spent his childhood in the small town of Uvalde, Texas. He attended Sundeen High School in Corpus Christi, Texas.[53]

Jesse served his country for eleven years in the U.S. Air Force and was a veteran of World War II. He was enlisted from 1942 to 1945. In 1943, he was an Army Air Corps B-17 crewman gunner and fought Air Offensive in Europe. He fought at Normandy and was credited with 85 missions overseas. He survived a crash landing in Europe and was awarded the Purple Heart, the Distinguished Flying Cross, as well as other decorations. He attained the rank of Technical Sergeant and was a top mechanic on the jets. In September 1945, while stationed in Lakeland Florida, Jesse left the Air Force. After two and half years, he re-enlisted in 1948 and was stationed in Albany, Georgia. He served until after the Korean War and retired from the Air Force in October 1953.[54]

Jesse married Mildred 'Millie' L. Wilson on May 2, 1945, in Lakeland, Florida. The couple had three children, David Allen, seventeen, a Grand County High School star athlete; Thomas Clinton, fourteen; and Douglas Byron, five.

The Kasslers lived in Moab for the past three years at the Walnut Lane Trailer Court, and Jesse worked for Harrison International as the Skip Loader on the west side of the shaft. He went by the nickname, 'Tex.' He was thirty-eight-years-old when he died. Jesse was survived by his wife and children, his father, George Wesley Kassler, of Sequim, Texas; his mother, Betty Ann Bingham, of Uvalde, Texas; a brother, Jack W. Kassler, of Moab; and three sisters: Mrs. Carl B. Smith of Corpus Christie, Texas, Mrs. Bobbie June Bingham of Uvalde, Texas, and Mrs. Marian Elaine Kolfelt of Arches City, Texas.[55]

Moab, Utah - Bluffdale, Utah
Lamar Charles Rushton
Monday - September 2, 1963

On Monday afternoon at 1:00 p.m., a memorial service was held for Lamar Charles Rushton at The Church of Jesus Christ of Latter-day Saints (Mormon)-Ward Chapel in Moab. Mormon Bishop Harry E. Snow (also Grand County District Attorney) conducted the services. Interment was to be in Bluffdale, Utah Cemetery, in Salt Lake County, on Wednesday.[56]

Lamar was born May 23, 1929, in Murray, Utah to Edward Lewis Rushton and Grace Olsen Rushton. He was the third child of six children consisting of three sons and three daughters. He grew up in Murray, Utah which is located in the heart of the Salt Lake Valley.

Lamar married Lois 'Lorraine' Brown on February 28, 1947, in Tooele, Utah, and their marriage was solemnized in the Mormon Salt Lake Temple on June 28, 1963, two months before his death. The Rushton's had three children, Maurine, fourteen; Bonnie, thirteen; and Randy LaNell, who was nine.

Lamar, or 'Rush' as he was known, worked as a Lead Miner for Harrison International and was thirty-four-years-old at the time of his death. The Rushtons had lived in Moab for the past eight years, residing at 160 South Highway.

Two weeks before his death, Lamar had a premonition, while at his grandmother's funeral, that something was going to happen. And during the rescue operation, Lorraine had a dream that Lamar came to her and said he had to go; he couldn't breathe anymore.[57] Lamar was survived by his wife, children and his parents of Taylorsville, Utah; two brothers and three sisters: Melvin E. Rushton, Taylorsville, Utah; Duane L. Rushton, Kearns, Utah; Mrs. Afton Rushton King, Kearns, Utah; Mrs. Elaine Rushton Williams, Kearns, Utah; and Miss Dolores Rushton, Taylorsville, Utah.

Moab, Utah
Harry 'Kenneth' Milton
Monday - September 2, 1963

Also on Monday afternoon, at 1:30 p.m., funeral services were held for Harry 'Kenneth' Milton at the First Baptist Church of Moab. Services were conducted by Reverend Leland Goodman. Many family members and friends gathered as Kenneth was laid to rest in the

Sunset Memorial Cemetery in Moab, where the majestic view of the La Sal Mountains dominated the tranquil scene.

Kenneth Milton was born March 31, 1920, at Pecks Mill, West Virginia, to Harry E. Milton and Elizabeth Milton.[58] His father died when he was young, and he had to quit school while still a teenager to support his mother, and brother and sisters. In the hollows of West Virginia, the highest paying (and sometimes the only) job available was in the coal mines. He did not have a lot of formal education, but continued to learn and was smart and well read. Kenneth never had any illusions about the dangers of underground mining and refused to let any of his sons become miners.

Kenneth entered the service in 1944, and served in the U.S. Navy as a Seabee, in the Construction Battalion (CB) in the Pacific Islands, during World War II. He received his training at the Davisville Naval CB Center in Rhode Island. He fought and saw fierce fighting with the Marines in the Battle of Guam, as well as combat on other islands in the Pacific.[59] After Guam had been recaptured, it was turned into a base for Allied operations. Five large airfields were built by the Navy Seabees to carry out the strategic bombing campaign against the Japanese Home Islands, using the Boeing B-29 Superfortresses.[60] The Seabees often operated under fire and were frequently forced to take part in the fighting to defend themselves and their construction projects. Kenneth saw many friends killed in the horrors of war, but never spoke about his experiences. Instead of the war making him bitter, he appreciated life, and it made him love friends and family more.

Kenneth married Ina Joyce McClellan Moore on May 1, 1946, at Lorado, West Virginia.[61] Ida had four children she was raising on her own: James, Charlie, Frank and Nancy Moore. Kenneth took them into his home and his heart to raise as his own. Two other children were eventually added to the family, Martha and Harry Kenneth, Jr., who they called 'Buz.' Milton served as a Deacon in the Lorado Methodist Church for many years, until moving to Moab, Utah.

Kenneth had quit his mining job where he was an underground boss and left West Virginia in 1962 when he could see that the mining industry was changing. He felt that the owners were trying to break the unions, and although he could not be a union member as a boss, he feared that safety at the mine would be compromised if the unions were dissolved. It was a hard decision for him and Ina since they were related to most of the people in Lorado.

He first went to work at a potash mine near Carlsbad, New Mexico, and then heard about Moab and traveled to Utah. He picked peaches for the first few days until hired on at the potash mine. Kenneth loved everything about Moab: the mountains, the rocks, the fishing, the hunting, and the people. He felt he had truly found a new home.

Kenneth worked as the Torkar-shuttle car operator for Harrison International on Hanna's crew on the east side. He was forty-three-years-old at the time of his death. Brokenhearted, all the men he rode to work with on that last day were there at his funeral. Three of them survived the explosion: Matt Rauhala, who was injured on the surface, and Chuck Byrge and Blake Hanna, who were underground. Also in attendance were Armond Roy, who was on Harrison International's mine rescue team, and his brother, Roland Roy, who helped with the rescue operation on the surface.

Kenneth was survived by his wife, Ina, and children: James Moore, U.S. Armed Forces, Germany; Charles Gary Moore of Huntington, West Virginia; Franklin Joe Moore of Arlington, Virginia; Mrs. Nancy Moore Clay of Mann, West Virginia; Martha, sixteen; and Harry Kenneth, Jr, ten. He was also survived by one sister, Mrs. Cecil Milton Adkins of West Virginia.[62]

Spring Glen, Utah
Myrlen Howard Christen, Sr.
Monday - September 2, 1963

Tragically, joint funeral services were held on Monday afternoon in Price, Utah, at 2:00 p.m. for Myrlen Howard Christensen, Sr. and his young son, and namesake, Myrlen Howard Christensen, Jr., at The Church of Jesus Christ of Latter-day Saints (Mormon)-North Carbon Stake House.[63] The deaths of both father and son were overwhelming for family members and friends, as both were laid to rest next to each other in the Price City Cemetery.

Myrlen, Sr. was born November 3, 1918, in the small community of Cleveland, Utah in Emery County, to Howard Marinus Christensen and Sarah Emma Minchey Christensen.[64] He attended high school in nearby Huntington where he was active in athletics and elected senior class president.[65]

Myrlen, Sr. married Irene Prichard March 15, 1941, in Cleveland, Utah. They had five children, three boys and two girls. 'Myrley,' Jr. was their oldest, Diane Christensen Valdez (who was married with one little boy and was pregnant with her second child) was their oldest daughter. The other Christensen children were Gail, sixteen; Lorraine, fifteen; and Rodney, fourteen.[66]

Myrlen, Sr. went to work in the nearby coal mines after graduating from high school. He worked in and around mines for twenty-five years and was a Lead Mechanic for Harrison International underground. He was forty-four-years-old at the time of his death. Myrlen, Sr. discouraged his sons from working in the mines, but that fateful day, his oldest son, 'Myrley,' was touring the new mine and was consequently killed in the explosion.[67]

"It's an age-old story of father and son miners," said a longtime friend after the discovery of the bodies. "Many of them worked in the mines because it was the only source of employment (in the area) and the only work they could do."[68]

After the heartbreak of burying her husband and son, Irene eventually remarried to Neldon Lemon, and they settled in Moab, Utah. Irene vowed she would never go down the Potash Road ever again, and she stayed true to her vow.[69]

At the time of the 50th Year Commemoration of the Cane Creek Mine Disaster on August 27, 2013, Irene came to the program at the Moab Library but refused to attend the family gathering at the mine site. It was hosted by Rick York, the General Manager of Intrepid Potash, Inc. (the current owners of the potash mine). There were just too many painful memories. Irene passed away a year later with her family near her side.

Price, Utah
Myrlen Howard Christensen, Jr.
Monday - September 2, 1963

Myrlen Howard Christensen, Jr., or 'Myrley' as he was called, was the oldest of Myrlen Howard Christensen and Irene Prichard Christensen's five children. Laid to rest alongside his father, 'Myrley' was born October 23, 1941, in Price, Utah, in Carbon County. He graduated from Carbon High School in Price, and after graduation, he enlisted in the U.S. Navy. He served three years as a Seabee, the construction branch of the Navy during peacetime. He was stationed at Camp Pendleton, San Diego, California while in boot camp and then sent to Kodiak, Alaska, and then to Hawaii. He liked Alaska the most because of the salmon fishing. He liked to watch the bears as they also fished for the salmon.[70]

After 'Myrley' had been discharged from the Navy, he married Margo Grange in Huntington, Utah on February 2, 1962. He worked for the Sun Advocate newspaper in Price as a printer.[71] In March, the new couple moved to Moab after he was hired to work for Harrison International at the Cane Creek Potash Mine.

'Myrley' worked as a surface mechanic and was over the large air compressors on the surface.[72] He was twenty-one-years-old at the time of his death, the youngest to die in the Cane Creek Mine explosion. He left a young wife who was six-months pregnant with their first child.

Pioche, Nevada
James Nesbitt Hollinger
Monday - September 2, 1963

Also on Monday, funeral services were held for James 'Jim' Nesbitt in the small town of Pioche, Nevada, a very old remote silver mining community north of Mesquite, Nevada near the Utah border. He was buried at the Hollinger-Hammond-Lytle Cemetery, east of Pioche.[73]

Jim, as he was known, was born on May 24, 1930, in Pioche to Joseph Hollinger and Blanche Thelma Drake Hollinger and was the oldest of four boys.[74] His brothers were Joseph Roger, Elwood D. (who only lived for two years) and Keith Ronald Hollinger.[75] Jim grew up in Pioche, and after high school, he served four years in the U.S. Navy during the Korean War as a Seabee. He obtained the rank of Construction Driver Petty Officer 3rd Class, which was equivalent to a Corporal in the U.S. Army.[76]

He married Melba 'Eudeene' Bishop, August 30, 1952, and became the stepfather of her son, Bill 'Billy' Cook, who was twelve. They had two other children: Dava Lee, who had passed away in 1960, and Madge, six. They moved from Pioche in 1956 and had lived in Moab the past six years at the Hayes Trailer Court. At the time of Jim's death, he was thirty-three-years-old and worked as a miner for Harrison International.[77] His parents, Joe and Blanche Hollinger, and brother, Keith, lived in Moab, while his brother, Joseph, came from Gallup, New Mexico to be with the family. Eudeene's parents, from Pioche, Nevada, were also present at the rescue operation and were there to also help with funeral arrangements.

Sheppton, Pennsylvania
Monday - September 2, 1963

As the Cane Creek mine disaster ended in the loss of life, so too did the Sheppton Rescue back east in Pennsylvania. Pennsylvania mine rescue officials finally decided to call off the rescue for the third coal miner still missing, fifty-two-year-old Louis Bova. It had been nearly a week since the other two coal miners, David Fellin and Henry Throne, were rescued on August 27th. They had last heard from Bova on August 20th while both were still trapped in a small chamber before they were rescued.[78] Continuing the search, rescue workers had drilled fifteen futile holes[79] on the west side, where Bova was thought to be located. They even dropped food and water, with a strobe light and a recording, down one of the drill holes to attract him to that area, in case he had been roaming around in the mine. Workers then put extremely sensitive listening devices down to record any sounds or any movements down in the mine. There was nothing, only the sound of pebbles falling.

Sadly, rescue officials abandoned any hope of finding Bova alive in the mine, where he had been buried along with the two other men (Fellin and Throne) in a thundering cave-in nearly three weeks earlier.[80]

"It's all over now, as far as the rescue is concerned," said Pennsylvania's Deputy Secretary of Mines.

Fellin and Throne were still in the hospital and planned on going home the next day. Fellin said through a spokesman that they were grieved by the failure to find "our buddy."[81]

Family, friends and the small coal mining communities around Sheppton were disheartened over the suspension of the rescue operation. Eventually, a tombstone was placed at the mine site with a small fence around it to mark the burial place of Louis Bova, where his wife, infant son, and other family members and friends could visit as they grieved his loss.

Chapter 25

Charges and Counterchanges

As the week began, officials and experts from around the country descended on the mine site to get ready for the week-long investigation at the Cane Creek Potash Mine. Already, half of the bodies had been buried, and the remaining nine miners' funerals were scheduled during the remainder of the week when the investigation would be underway. Many wanted answers to how this disaster could have happened.

Harrison International and Texas Gulf Sulphur (TGS) each purchased large advertisements in the *Times-Independent* to give their sincerest condolences to the families affected and to reassure citizens of the future of the mine.[1] They also jointly and separately expressed their appreciation for the great help rendered by innumerable individuals and organizations in Moab and elsewhere during the past week.[2]

"Our plans for operation of the Cane Creek Mine as the safest and most modern potash producing facility in the world remain unchanged," part of the Texas Gulf Sulphur ad stated.[3]

Disaster at Cane Creek

In Moab, families of several of the victims had already left town, mainly those from Canada. Others made arrangements to sell trailer homes and wind up personal affairs before leaving. The Grand County sheriff's office reported that all the bodies had either been buried or had been sent to their hometowns for burial. The last three were scheduled to arrive at their destinations Wednesday morning.[4]

The fund drive, sponsored by Jaycees and Moab Chamber of Commerce, to raise money to help families was nearing its goal. Chamber Secretary, Betty Jacobs, reported that by late Tuesday, $4,090 had been received. She further added that some of the funds collected had already been distributed to the families.[5]

The Chamber received responses from several other states and as far away as London, England. A letter was received from a Dr. W.D. MacDiarmid, of the University College Hospital Medical School, at the University of London, asking for details on how assistance could be sent to the families. Dr. MacDiarmid wrote that he had visited Moab recently, and was especially moved by the plight. He said he and his fellow workers wished to express their sympathy and asked where they could send a check.[6]

A telegram was also received from Fred Wortham, Jr., the *News Herald Editor*, at Border, Texas, asking for information. He said that people in his town wished to conduct a drive to help. Mr. Wortham said the parents of one of the victims had a business in Border, undoubtedly the parents of Robert Bobo, who was buried Saturday in Moab.[7] Reports indicated that Mrs. Bobo was still in Moab, but was making plans to return to her home in Border, Texas.[8]

Chamber and Jaycee members said that the families already assisted by the fund had voiced their appreciation to the people of Moab, who came to their aid in so many ways.[9] People were deeply touched by the events at Cane Creek and took the time to reach out and convey their heartfelt emotions to those affected. Empathy has always been one of the noblest traits of humanity. Sympathy cards and well wishes were sent to the victim's families and survivors from all over the world.

It was reported that on Wednesday evening, the owner of the Grand Vu Drive-In, Bob Ossana, was turning the facilities over to the Jaycees for a special show with proceeds designated for the disaster fund. Universal International Film Company donated the movie, *Joe Butterfly*, in cinemascope-color, starring Audie Murphy and Kennan Wynn, to the cause. There were to be two showings starting at 7:30; tickets were, as usual, 75 cents and 25 cents. Buck Archer was heading the show arrangements.[10]

By Wednesday evening, it was reported that the disaster fund had netted a total of $4,245.46 to date, but fund raisers were still working towards the goal set at $5,000. The bulk of the funds had been raised in the door-to-door canvass the previous Friday evening, conducted by the organization members and businessmen who generously contributed. Several more checks were received from other outside sources.

Throughout the drive, the disbursement committee had worked hard to take care of the immediate emergency needs of the families and would continue to do so with the remaining funds to be distributed as each families' needs indicated.[11]

Meanwhile, emergency insurance compensation checks, sent to meet immediate financial needs, were distributed on Thursday, September 5th, to assist families of the victims until complete insurance adjustments could be made. The emergency payments were arranged by Travelers Insurance Company and the Utah State Industrial Commission. Nathanial Harrison, partner and chairman of the Harrison International Company, said, "The initial payments averaged about $200, varying with the number of dependents."[12]

The co-sponsored disaster fund-raising drive by the Chamber and the Jaycees was inching near its $5,000 goal, said Secretary Betty Jacobs. Scores of donations and letters were received from a wide area of the country. A $200 check was received that day, bringing the total to approximately $4,400, Mrs. Jacobs said. She added that "most of the families of the eighteen men who came here from other areas of the United States and Canada had left for their homes. I believe there are only five or six families left in Moab."[13]

By evening on the fifth, the total amount of contributions for the fund drive neared the $4,700 mark. "Distribution of the money to the explosion victims' families would be made Monday," Mrs. Jacobs said.[14]

Contributions continually came in from all over the world to assist the families of the disaster victims. By October 10th, over $5,000 had been collected, and each victim's family had been given a base amount of $100, with other additional needs being handled out of the fund as well. One contribution that was added to the fund came from Charles A. Boynton, president of the Gray Line in Salt Lake City. He had received the contribution from a former miner, Joseph B. Roberts and said that Roberts had been ill and could not send aid before this time. He accordingly forwarded the contribution to the Jaycees.[15]

For one of the mine victims, Pete Sviscsu, who had no survivors, the base amount of $100 was set aside for him and placed in a permanent disaster fund by the Jaycees. They hoped it would increase and be on hand for any other disasters that might occur in Moab.[16]

Moab, Utah
Peter Sviscsu
Tuesday - September 3, 1963

On Tuesday morning, at 10:00 a.m.,[17] a graveside funeral was conducted by Father John Rasbach from the St. Pius X Catholic Church for Pete Sviscsu, at the Moab Sunset Memorial Cemetery. There were a few friends present, but unlike the other men's funerals, where teary-eyed family members were present, grieving the loss of their loved one, Pete Sviscsu died mostly alone. Pete was the only victim who was not married. Emigrating from Europe, he had not seen his family since World War II and did not know if they were dead or alive. Officials tried to locate his family to notify them of his death, but they were unsuccessful. Just knowing the circumstances surrounding Sviscsu's life and death were heartbreaking. Surviving the explosion, he was one of the three men who chose not to go to the barricade and consequently died when he could have lived. The men he worked with, and a few other friends, were as close as Pete would get to a family. Born June 13, 1921, the forty-two-year-old had been laid to rest alongside Kenneth Milton,[18] who was buried the day before.

Several days after Sviscsu's funeral, a situation came up that had Grand County officials checking their law books for an answer. Sviscsu, a native of Czechoslovakia, apparently had no family.[19] He lived in one of the bunkhouses at Harrison International's man camp near the mine site.[20] The officials determined that at least part of his personal effects, which included a 1953 automobile and other personal items, should be sold. Along with any death compensation that was to be paid out to him, they had discovered that all should be donated to a charity, which they decided would be the state school system.

A few of Sviscsu's friends told officials that they understood his parents had been taken as political prisoners[21] during the war and were thought to be dead. Some thought he might have been from Yugoslavia, while others said Czechoslovak. Some thought that he had a brother whom he had not seen or heard from since he was in Europe after World War II.[22] While another thought his mother and sister were still alive back in his home country.

According to Sviscsu, he had told several fellow workers that he had been taken captive by the Red Army after the war while a young man and put into the Russian Gulag, their system of slave labor camps. Later, after he had been released from the Gulag, he emigrated to the West.[23]

The county officials found that, as a rule, the Social Security benefits were to be paid to the victims' families, but in cases where there was no widow or family, a lump sum payment should be made to the person taking care of burial expenses.[24] Unfortunately, in the wake of trying to determine what to do with Sviscsu's belongings and any money that was part of his estate, no one made sure that Peter Sviscsu had a headstone to mark his grave and unknowingly condemned him to obscurity. Not done intentionally, it was simply an oversight since the headstone was a matter that generally families took care of after the burial. But since he had no family in the states, his headstone was overlooked.

Through research during the writing of this book, a passenger list was found that appears to be a record of Peter Sviscsu's immigration to the West. It listed a Petro Sviscsu, age 30, who boarded passage on the ship Montcalm, of the Cunard Line, sailing (about) May 16, 1951, from London to Montreal, Canada. It listed Petro Sviscsu as a citizen of Ukraine, with his last permanent residence in the United Kingdom.[25] The surname spelling on Sviscsu's death certificate is the same as that on the passenger list, but had the name Petro as his first name. The passenger list also did not have a date of birth but listed Petro as thirty-years-old. This fits with the age Sviscsu would have been in 1951, using the year he was born (1921) that was on his death certificate.[26]

Sviscsu had told fellow workers at Cane Creek that after he was set free from the Gulag's mining prison camp he was first held in, he was taken to another part of Russia to learn their agricultural system, which at that time, would have been Stalin's collectivization farms. Ukraine could very well be where Sviscsu was taken as it was an important agricultural area that had been known as "the breadbasket of Russia." After a while, Sviscsu was then set free.[27]

After obtaining a copy of Sviscsu's handwritten U.S. Social Security application, he had listed Selvus [sic], Czechoslovakia as his place of birth. This small town was located in the small, historic region of Subcarpathia Ruthenia (also known as Transcarpathia) that was located on the western slopes of the Carpathian Mountains. At the end of the 11th century, this region came under Hungarian rule. The town of Selvus [sic] was renamed throughout the many years in different languages and with different spellings (like Szevljus, Sevluš, Sevliush, or Nagyszolos, (or Nagyszöllös, the Hungarian name), but the meaning mostly remained the same. It meant "grape." In the 13th Century, the area had become an important wine district and was inhabited by winemakers of the royal court who helped make the town and the rest of the province an important wine district.[28]

At the end of the 17th century, this region was annexed by Austria (the Austro-Hungarian Empire) and was considered a frontier boarder region. After World War I, in 1919, Subcarpathia Ruthenia became an independent territory and was awarded to the Republic of Czechoslovakia.[29] This new republic was created when territorial boundaries were redrawn from the remnants of the defeated Austro-Hungarian Empire as part of the Treaty of Versailles, and it incorporated four "lands" (or regions): Bohemia, Moravia-Silesia, and the autonomous regions of Slovakia and Subcarpathia Ruthenia.[30] Pete Sviscsu was born in 1921, several years after the creation of the new Czechoslovakian Republic.

During WWII, after Hitler invaded Czechoslovakia, in March 1939, Subcarpathia Ruthenia was reclaimed by Hungary who was fighting on the side of Nazi Germany. By 1944, thousands of Jews from the area had been forcibly moved to the town of Sevluš. A brick factory became a Jewish ghetto where many families lived together in the same room, purposely done to cause suffering and disease. Between May 20 and June 3, 1944, the Jews at Sevluš/Nagyszöllös were deported by train in three transports to Auschwitz concentration camp in southern Poland, where most were exterminated during the Holocaust.³¹ But first, they suffered greatly at the hands of their Hungarian captors. They were robbed of their worldly belongings and suffered unimaginable indignities well before the Jews were handed over to the Germans on their journey to Auschwitz.³²

The Subcarpathia Ruthenia (also known as Transcarpathia) was held by the Nazi forces until October 24, 1944, when the Red Army fought their way east and overthrew the Germans and Hungarians, and captured the town of Sevluš.³³ At this time, the inhabitants of this town counted 13,331 people of mixed origins.³⁴

Germany finally surrendered on May 8, 1945, ending World War II. While allies in Western Europe were celebrating V-E Day (Victory in Europe) for Eastern Europe, the end of the war was not a liberation, but the beginning of another tyranny.³⁵ It was at this time that Soviet leader Joseph Stalin had hundreds of thousands of civilians rounded up and taken as prisoners from the Eastern European countries to the Soviet Union as prisoners to work in the Gulag³⁶ System of slave labor camps. Sviscsu was in his early twenties when he was picked up and taken to Russia or Siberia.

Figures released by Soviet historians in 1989, supposedly compiled by the Gulag administration itself, showed that a total of 10 million people were sent to the camps in the period between 1934 to 1947. The true figures remain unknown.³⁷ From Sviscsu's hometown, about 4,000 people were deported from the male civilian population and taken into the Soviet Union, with seventy percent of the deportees perishing in captivity.³⁸

Millions of prisoners were sent to the Gulags (labor work camps) in Siberia to extract the coal, gold, and other minerals with picks and shovels to industrialize and build up the Soviet Union. While not "extermination camps," life in the Gulags was unrelentingly brutal. The Soviet Gulag was a massive system of slave labor, and it is estimated that only about a third of those in the system survived.³⁹

In the late 1920's, Stalin's Gulag System underwent an enormous expansion. By 1936, the Gulag held a total of 5,000,000 prisoners, a number that was probably equaled or exceeded every subsequent year until Stalin died in 1953. Persons sent to the Gulag included rich or resistant peasants arrested during collectivization. Also included were purged Communist Party members and military officers, German and other Axis prisoners of war, and members of ethnic groups suspected of disloyalty (German, Hungarians, even those who had names that sounded German or Hungarian). Other persons sent to the Gulag were captured Soviet soldiers and citizens taken from war torn areas as prisoners and used as slave laborers by the Germans,[40] suspected saboteurs, traitors, dissident intellectuals, ordinary criminals, and many utterly innocent people who were hapless victims of Stalin's purges.[41] In these camps, prisoners were also kept isolated and were not permitted to communicate with the outside world.

According to Sviscsu, he was taken to a mining camp where he said it was so cold that, at times, the miners lived underground in the mine. It's possible the camp he was held in was in Siberia or in the extreme north of Greater Russia (both regions have lands within the Arctic Circle boundaries) where life in the Gulag camps was extremely brutal.

At its height, the Gulag consisted of many hundreds of camps scattered across the Soviet Union, with the average camp holding 2,000–10,000 prisoners. Prisoners felled timber, labored on general construction projects (such as the building of canals and railroads), or worked in mines. Most prisoners labored under the threat of starvation or execution if they refused. It is estimated that the combination of very long working hours, harsh climates, poor working conditions, inadequate food, lack of warm clothing, or lack of medical care and summary executions were the reasons large percentages of the Gulag's total prisoner population were killed off each year. Western scholarly estimates of the total number of deaths in the Gulag in the period from 1918 to 1956 range from 15 to 30 million.[42]

Prisoners in these camps were required to meet work quotas, and if they were not met, their food rations were reduced. This put many of the prisoners on a downward spiral, and many succumbed to disease and eventual death. Sviscsu said he was later taken from the mining camp to another part of Russia where he was taught their agricultural system, which, most likely, would have been Stalin's collectivization farming system. Then one day the Russians just turned him loose, and Sviscsu immigrated to the West. It's not known where or how long Sviscsu was held as a prisoner.[43]

Not long after WW II ended, the Subcarpathia Ruthenia region of Czechoslovakia was taken over by the Soviet Union. Boundaries were redrawn, and Stalin officially made this small region a part of Ukraine. The town of Sevluš was granted city status in 1946; it was renamed and is currently known as Vynohradiv, Zakarpattia Oblast (county), of Ukraine.[44] The new name of the city, Vynohradiv, also means "grape."

After Pete or Petro Sviscsu emigrated from Ukraine to England and then to Montreal, Canada in 1951, nine years later, he came to the United States to work. His Social Security application listed the name and date of Sviscsu's employer in Grants, New Mexico. Dated December 16, 1960, it appears that Sviscsu went to work at a uranium mine, owned by the Kermac Nuclear Fuels Corporation[45] before he eventually went to work at the Cane Creek Potash Mine in Moab where he lost his life.

Through further research, additional information was obtained about Pete Sviscsu and his life back in his hometown of Sevlus/Vynohradiv, where he was born.[46] Pete's baptism records were located in the archive of the Greek Catholic Church, of the town's historic Church of Ascension in Sevlus. The record was written in Hungarian, and it verified that Pete Sviscsu was indeed, Petro Sviscsu (or Петро Свищу in Cyrillic alphabet). It also showed that he was named after his father, Petro Sviscsu (Петро Свищу). His mother's name was Maria Kocan (Марія Коцан). The church record indicated that he was born on June 12, 1921, and was baptized on June 19, 1921. The record, written in Hungarian, appears to be quite typical of that region and era. The Hungarian origin of Pete's last name indicated the family were most likely ethnic Hungarians and were Ruthenes/Ukrainians, a distinct ethnic group found in that area.[47] The Greek Catholic Church (also known as the Ukrainian Greek Catholic Church) was at that time distinct from the Roman Catholic Church and the Greek or Russian Orthodox Churches.[48]

Through additional research, Pete's family was found, and through one of his nieces named Mariya, more information was obtained. It appears that there were quite a few of Pete's relatives still living in Sevlus/Vynohradiv, although his parents and siblings have since passed away. Pete had four brothers and two sisters. He was the second oldest child in the Sviscsu family, the oldest was a sister. The family was well off and owned some land. They had a small vineyard where the children grew up helping with farm work and doing chores.[49]

Reportedly, Pete was the only one in the family who fought in WWII on the Soviet's side[50] and it's likely he had no other choice. "In order to reduce mobilizing the base of the Ukrainian Insurgent Army (UIA), the Soviets issued the order to mobilize men aged from 15 to 50 from "liberated" territory to the Soviet Army. Many of those "volunteers" were immediately thrown into the war, so they could pay for their "guilt" with blood."[51]

Pete's family survived the war okay, without any major losses. But the situation of Pete's parents being political prisoners appears to be incorrect. According to information obtained by his niece, Mariya, Pete's parents were never deported and lived in Sevlus/Vynohradiv until the end of their lives.[52] It is impossible to know the circumstances after the war, which led to Pete Sviscsu being picked up by the Red Army and taken to a Gulag camp in the Soviet Union. Apparently, there were some 10,000 ethnic Hungarians from the Transcarpathia region alone who were displaced to work camps after WWII.[53]

In the Hungarian territory occupied by the Red Army, armed men gathered people from the streets and took them away with the excuse of the removal of ruins. The expression "malenkaia rabota" or "malenki robot" (a little work) was used to justify their actions and to offer reassurance. It indicated the need for the work of the civilians, though for a short time only. It was a ruse to keep the local populations from rebelling, as they incarcerated and transported thousands of able-bodied men to work prisons. Today, the expression, perceived as "malenki robot" by the Hungarians, evokes memories of deportation to the Soviet Union and forced labour [sic].[54]

The last time Pete had been seen in Sevlus was around 1945, or just after Maria's (his older sister) wedding. At first, no one in his family knew what happened to him and diligently searched for him. Unsuccessful and after not receiving any news from him, relatives worried but did not know where else to look.[55]

In the ship's passenger list, when Pete emigrated west, the address in the UK where Pete stayed before leaving for Canada was in Coventry. There was a big Displaced Persons (DP) camp in Coventry, where many Ukrainians ended up after WWII before immigrating to the U.S. or Canada. According to his niece, Pete had once said that one day he would like to go to Canada.[56] Unfortunately, his parents and siblings had all passed away and therefore, never learned the whereabouts of their son or brother.

There is no way of knowing why Pete never made contact with his family after immigrating to the west. Many Gulag prisoners, when released, were threatened never to talk about their time while imprisoned or they would be returned. Many were even treated badly or ostracized in their communities when they did return home. One example stands out of how released prisoners were threatened upon their release. In 1948, Alexander Dolgun, (a U.S. citizen) was working as a file clerk at the U.S. Embassy in Moscow when he was taken into custody by the Soviets. He was falsely accused of espionage against the Soviet Union and endured nearly eight years of confinement in the Russian Gulag system. Suffering, at times, brutal torture to extract a confession, Dolgun was released in 1956, and then returned to Moscow. Under his release conditions, he was not allowed to contact American authorities.[57] With a very caustic atmosphere within Stalin's Soviet Union, it is also possible Pete was fearful of bringing harm to his family if he went back to his hometown or if he made contact with his family.

After enduring the horrors of war as a young man, subjected to incarceration by a dictatorial regimen under extremely brutal conditions in an unforgiving land far from his home and witnessing many evil atrocities perpetrated by his captors, Pete Sviscsu died a horrendous death at Cane Creek. He died an agonizing death by asphyxiation, all alone, a half a world away from his family and loved ones and forgotten in an unmarked grave. In spite of all the indignities he endured throughout his life, he was described by the men he worked with as pleasant but serious, and a damn hard worker.

Orangeville, Utah
Jesse Eliot Fox
Tuesday - September 3, 1963

Funeral services for Jesse Eliot Fox were held at The Church of Jesus Christ of Latter-day Saints (Mormon)-Orangeville Ward Chapel at 10:00 a.m.,[58] the same time as Pete Sviscsu's service in Moab. Mormon Bishop Blaine Tuttle conducted the service. A chorus furnished the musical numbers, and Jesse was eulogized with several talks. He was laid to rest at the Orangeville City Cemetery with full military honors. The military escort and service at the cemetery were performed by the American Legion Post 39.[59]

Jesse Fox was born July 28, 1911, to George Eliot Fox and Luella Jane Christensen Fox in Orangeville, Utah, where he was raised. He was the oldest of six children, five who lived to adulthood.[60]

Jesse served his country in the U.S. Army during World War II, under General Patton, from early 1942 until August 1945. He fought in six battle conflicts and was wounded in one.⁶¹ Jesse was with the troops that made the invasion of Africa, November 8, 1942, and was among the first to land on the beach when they invaded Sicily. He was also with Patton's Army when they invaded Italy. It was there that he was wounded. In the months between November 1943 and the fall of Rome on June 5, 1944, the 36th Division saw some of the heaviest fighting in the Italian campaign. When Jesse was released from the Army in 1945, he had received the rank of Staff Sergeant.

Jesse married Alice Dee Bailey November 30, 1945, in Salt Lake City, Utah and they had two daughters: Linda, fifteen and Peggy, eleven. He was a loving father and devoted husband. He loved to hunt and fish. He loved music and could sing a nice tune, but was extremely shy, so he only sang occasionally for the family. Jesse had a great sense of humor and loved to tease. He worked as a Mechanic for Harrison International and was fifty-two-years-old at the time of his death.⁶²

Dragerton, Utah
Clell Johnson
Tuesday - September 3, 1963

In the small coal town of Dragerton, Utah, near Sunnyside, a funeral service was held for Clell Johnson at The Church of Jesus Christ of Latter-day Saints (Mormon)-Dragerton Ward Chapel at 1:00 p.m.⁶³ He was then laid to rest in the Price City Cemetery, twenty-seven miles away.

Clell was born March 16, 1918, in Huntington, Utah to Joseph Buriah Johnson and Alice Allen Johnson. He married Tess Lake,⁶⁴ April 20, 1940, in Huntington, Utah. They had four children, two sons and two married daughters: Ned Johnson, nineteen; Kirt Johnson, sixteen; Dianne Johnson Zacherson; and Carolyn Johnson Arroyo, of Salt Lake City. Clell was also the uncle of Margo Christensen, widow of Myrlen Christensen, Jr.[65] Clell was forty-four-years-old at the time of his death.

Clell worked extremely hard, sometimes working two or three jobs to have the finer things in life he liked, such as new cars. He had a reputation for being able to fix just about anything. He loved to hunt, mostly in Huntington Canyon, near his hometown.

Ned Johnson, the oldest of Clell's four children, was serving in the military in Europe. He first heard of the explosion when his uncle, Berdell Lake, called him. With no money to get home, the Red Cross made arrangements to get him back to the states. He left London in the middle of the night and was unable to land in New York because of bad weather. The plane was rerouted to another airport, making it difficult for Ned to find a direct flight to Salt Lake City. After two days of traveling, he finally made it to Utah and arrived just before his father's funeral.[66]

Tess later married Howard Peirce, March 19, 1966. He also preceded her in death. Tess passed away February 11, 2004, and was buried next to Clell in the Price City Cemetery.

Dove Creek, Colorado
Floyd 'Keith' Schear
Tuesday - September 3, 1963

Also on Tuesday, funeral services were held for Keith Schear at the Assembly of God Church in Dove Creek, Colorado, a small farming community in the southwestern part of the state. Reverend Nick Resovich officiated. Keith was laid to rest at the Dove Creek Cemetery, located at the top of a hill with a beautiful view of the surrounding country side. He was twenty-two-years-old at the time he was killed at the Cane Creek Mine.[67]

Keith was born March 20, 1941, in Pleasant View, Colorado to Glen R. Schear and Zelpha Faye Thompson Schear. He was raised in Dove Creek, with four brothers and three sisters, fifth of the eight

Disaster at Cane Creek

children. Keith's mother died of cancer when he was fourteen years old, and his oldest brother had just turned twenty. His father, Glen Schear, was devastated by his wife's death and overwhelmed with the care of the younger children. A close-knit family, the older siblings, cared and watched out for the younger ones. Zelda, the oldest sister, was in high school when her mother passed away; shortly after that, she married. She and her new husband were many times able to be there to see to the needs of the younger children.

Keith married Mary 'Lynn' Mir on January 30, 1961, in Monticello, Utah.[68] They came to Moab from Dove Creek, Colorado. Keith started work at the Cane Creek Mine, where two of his brothers worked. They lived in Moab for three months before the explosion happened. Their young son, Garry Lee, was eighteen months old at the time.

Besides his mother, Zelpha, Keith was preceded in death by an infant son, Roy Dale Schear, who was born in 1962 and lived only a day after birth. Keith was laid to rest next to his infant son and not far from where his mother was buried in the Dove Creek Cemetery.

Keith was survived by his wife, Lynn; his small son, Garry; his father, Glen; and his brothers: Johnnie Wayne (Carolyn) Schear and Raymond G. (Nadine) Schear of Moab; Delbert Ray and Elden Kay of Dove Creek; and sisters: Betty Schear Gaines, of Bluff, Utah; Zelda Schear Bucher, and Carol Schear, both of Dove Creek.[69]

Lynn Schear later married Dale Howard Tingley and lived in Durango, Colorado with Gary Lee, and eventually had other children.

———

Cottonwood, Arizona
John Bowman Tinall
Tuesday - September 3, 1963

Funeral services were held for John Bowman Tinall, thirty-eight-years-old, at Cottonwood, Yavapai County, Arizona,[70] an Old West settlement town located in the scenic Verde Valley region, not far from Sedona. The lone bugle's soft, mournful sound of "Taps" played slowly and drifted away on the air, as John was laid to rest in the military section of the Cottonwood Cemetery.[71] All his family, children and friends were there to pay their last respects.

John was born on July 14, 1925, in Globe, Gila County, Arizona to Peter Bowman Tinall and Bertha Mae McBride Tinall.[72] John was raised with three sisters and two brothers: Katherine, Fred, Anna, Geneva, and Charles.[73]

John's father passed away at the beginning of 1943 when John was seventeen-years-old. Later that year, after John turned eighteen, he joined the military. He served in the U.S. Navy Reserves during World War II, between 1943 and 1946 aboard the U.S.S. Hermitage[74] as a Seaman 1st Class.[75] A troop transport, the Hermitage was an Italian luxury liner before it was commissioned in 1942 for U.S. Navy service. It made many perilous crossings of the Atlantic and Pacific Oceans taking troops to and from the different theaters of operations during the war.[76]

John married Pauline Viletta Ray on April 23, 1946, in Flagstaff, Arizona. They had five children and later divorced. Their children's names and their ages at the time of the explosion were John 'Paul,' sixteen; Peter 'Pete' Milton, fourteen; Myrtle 'Jane,'[77] twelve; and Kathryn Jeanne 'Kathy,' who was born in 1952, but passed away eleven months later of bronchial pneumonia.[78] Three years after Kathryn's death, Pauline gave birth to another son, Robert Phil Tinall, who was eight[79] at the time of the explosion. After the divorce, Pauline and their children stayed in Cottonwood, Arizona and John left the area to seek work. He had married Jessie Jane Perry Jacobson and had become the stepfather to Jessie's four children, Edward M. Jacobson, nineteen; Glade W. Jacobson, seventeen; Judy Jacobson, sixteen; and Leonard Jacobson, fourteen.[80]

Yorkton, Saskatchewan, Canada
William 'Bill' Huzil
Thursday - September 5, 1963

On a mildly warm day, on September 5, 1963, William 'Bill' Huzil was laid to rest at the pine-tree-filled Yorkton City Cemetery, on the town's southern edge of the small Canadian farming community.[81]

When Bill Huzil perished in the mine that fateful day, he left behind Mary, his wife of twenty-years, a son Richard, seventeen; and three daughters Rose Marie, fourteen; Audrey, eleven; and Janice, six.[82] They were all heartbroken when they heard the news that he did not survive the explosion. In a sad twist of fate, Bill was working the shift that day for another miner from Canada. He was forty-one at the time of his death.

William Huzil was born on December 11, 1920, in Sylvan,[83] a small settlement in Northern Manitoba, Canada and he was called Bill by most everyone.[84] He married his wife, Mary, on April 12, 1943, in Sudbury, Ontario, Canada.

In December of 1943, Bill entered the Royal Canadian Army and proudly served his country in Europe during World War II. While he served in Europe, his expectant wife returned home to Saskatchewan to be close to her family. She gave birth to their son in 1944. Bill was finally discharged from his duties in May of 1946[85] and returned home to his family in Saskatchewan.

Bill worked as a coal dock attendant for Canadian Pacific Railways. It had become increasingly more difficult to secure full-time employment, so he decided to return to Ontario with his family and to the mining industry. Over the next few years, he moved his family several times while working at various mines. His mining experience grew, and so did his family. Three daughters were born in Ontario. The family's last Ontario move was to Elliott Lake, where Bill worked for Rio Algom Ltd., at the Stanleigh Uranium Mine, which would produce millions of tons of ore.[86]

461

Once again, Bill returned to Saskatchewan, where he obtained work with Harrison International at International Mines and Chemical (IMC) in Esterhazy, sinking the first shaft for their massive potash mine.[87] The family lived there for two years, and the children attended school in Esterhazy.[88] Locally, Bill was well known and liked.

After the completion of the IMC shaft in 1962, the final move was to Yorkton, Saskatchewan, about an hour northwest of Esterhazy. After which, Bill was on the advanced team to work for Harrison International at the Cane Creek Potash Mine[89] near Moab, where he worked as a Lead Miner over one of the crews at the mine.

Elliot Lake, Ontario, Canada
Joseph "Emile" LeBlanc
Thursday - September 5, 1963

Funeral services were held in Elliot Lake, Ontario, at 8:30 a.m., for Joseph 'Emile' LeBlanc, at the Janisse Brothers Funeral Home and then the Holy Name of Mary Roman Catholic Church at 9:00 a.m. After which, Emile was laid to rest at the St. Alphonsus Cemetery. The week before, his father, Heubert LeBlanc, was laid to rest in Halifax, Newfoundland. Heubert passed away after hearing his son, Emile, was killed in the Moab mine explosion.

Emile Leblanc was thirty-two at the time of his death. He was born October 15, 1930, in Inverness, Cape Breton Island, Nova Scotia, Canada to Heubert and Noeline LeBlanc.

Emile had always worked as a miner. After he met Dorothy Frances McLean from Inverness, he worked in a mine in northern Quebec to save money to marry her. After they had married, they lived in Boston, Massachusetts then moved to Windsor, Ontario in 1954. In 1957, they had their first child, Joseph William. They

Disaster at Cane Creek

next moved to Elliot Lake, Ontario, where Emile worked in a uranium mine. While there, two daughters were born, Anne Elise and Geralyn Noeline.

An avid outdoors man, Emile enjoyed hunting and fishing and had a motorcycle he loved to ride. He was a talented musician and loved playing the accordion. The Leblanc's had a good life together, and Emile was a devoted husband and loving father. Always happy-go-lucky and fun to be around, he loved to spend time with family and friends.

In 1963, when all the mines in Elliot Lake closed, Emile packed up his family and what little material goods he could fit in a small trailer, and headed off to the United States to mine potash. They journeyed for many days from the cool northern woodlands of Canada to the hot desert of Moab. Emile settled his family into their unknown surroundings and began work. It was only four days later when tragedy struck, and Emile did not return home from work.

Thirty-year-old Dorothy and her children, Joseph, 'Joey,' six; Anne, two; and Geralyn, one, were alone, with no family or friends to help with the grief and burden from the terrible news that Emile had died at the mine, along with seventeen other men. The community of Moab rallied together to help provide whatever comfort they could to Dorothy and the other families.

Dorothy's brother came from Boston to Moab to be with her and the children for the short time before they left to go home to Canada to bury Emile. The Texas Gulf Sulphur wives from the mine site came to Dorothy's home and packed up the family's clothes and belongings. Someone gave her a check for $300.00, which was money that had been collected from the townspeople. The store where they had recently purchased a washer and TV came to their home, took the items back and refunded their money. The LeBlanc's had amazing friends in Windsor, Ontario. One friend, Joseph 'Joe' McPhee[90] went to Moab to drive Dorothy's car back to Canada. First,

463

a mechanic in town overhauled it at no cost. And arrangements were made by someone in Moab for Dorothy and the children to fly to Salt Lake City to catch a flight to Windsor, Ontario, Canada.

Dorothy felt the people of Moab were excellent to her during such a difficult time and she was very grateful for their kindnesses.[91] Her brother, William 'Bill' McLean, wrote a heartfelt letter to the editor expressing the family's thankfulness, which was published in the Moab newspaper, the *Times-Independent*.[92]

In it, he asked if the letter could be printed to thank the people of Moab. He expressed appreciation for the kindness and hospitality they showed his sister in her hour of grief and desperation.

"Everyone outdid themselves trying to be sympathetic and helpful. We have often heard here in New England how kind and generous the people in the west are and in this disaster, you have certainly lived up to your reputation," McLean wrote.[93]

Dorothy started dating a family friend, Joe McPhee in 1965, and they married in 1966. Joe helped Dorothy raise her three young children, and they added two more daughters to the family, Lisa and Veronica. Dorothy passed away on July 28, 2015, at the age of 82 and was surrounded by her loving family.[94]

North Bay, Ontario, Canada
Joseph "Rene" Roy
Thursday - September 5, 1963

On Thursday, forty-year-old, Rene Roy was laid to rest in North Bay, Ontario, Canada with family and friends there to pay their final respects.

A French Canadian, Rene was born November 10, 1922, in rural northern Quebec. He had eight siblings and came from a family with very little means, so he and his brothers left school early to work to help the family.

During WWII, Rene served with the First Canadian Army forces in Belgium, a scene of major fighting. The Canadian soldiers were tasked with clearing coastal areas and opening the English Channel ports for supplies vital to the Allied advance in the north of France. They were also tasked with the capture of the launching sites of German rockets, hoping to put an end to attacks on southern England. They also played a leading role in opening the Scheldt estuary (tidal river), gateway to the Belgian port of Antwerp. (Access to this port was essential to maintain supply lines to the Allied armies as they continued their push towards Germany to defeat Hitler's forces and free Western Europe from four years of Nazi occupation.) In their efforts, the Canadian forces sustained substantial casualties.[95]

Rene met Jessie Cruickshank from Aberdeen while he was on leave in Scotland and they eventually married. After the war, their first born, Herve, traveled with his mother, a war-bride, across the Atlantic and made Rouyn, Quebec, Canada their home with Rene.[96]

It had been a long wait for Jessie Roy and her children for that dreaded phone call to finally come, after the last five survivors were rescued. For twelve-year-old Helene, Rene's oldest daughter, the memories were hazy; she remembered something about her hitting their minister with the newspaper. She was sitting on the porch with her youngest brother, Nelson, on her knee when a news reporter walked over and asked him how old he was. He proudly held up two little chubby fingers. When the reporter asked for her mom, Helene remembered going inside to get her. The house was full, especially once Rene's mother and the other families came from Quebec for Rene's funeral. There was a mass of people, yet Helene still felt so alone.[97]

Then the unbelievable happened. The funeral had to be postponed. Rene's coffin went missing en route from Utah. They found that it had been held up in Chicago, so they rescheduled the funeral that would have been on Wednesday at 2:00 p.m., for the following day.

Finally, the coffin arrived and, with it, the day of the funeral services and the final goodbyes. On Thursday, September 5th, the Martyn Funeral Chapel in North Bay[98] was packed with flowers and people, as many in line waited outside. Rene's daughter, Helene, was nauseous from the scent of the flowers as she watched family and friends shuffle through, giving their condolences and well wishes. The casket, chosen by Harrison International's people, was ornate, with bronze, brass, and sleek wood. Helene knew this was not what her mom would have chosen.[99]

Before the family was notified of Rene's death, her mother had a dream about him. In the dream, Rene told her not to make a fuss—just place him in an orange crate and toss him over the fence. It sounded like her dad and his funny sense of humor. Besides, their home was on Terrace Lawn Drive, and out of the living room window, part of the Terrace Lawn Cemetery could be seen.[100]

While at the cemetery, Helene watched as her Mamere,[101] (grandmother) Rene's mother, fell to her knees. She could not let him go. Through tears, Helene watched and remembered thinking that her heart could only break so many times. Not true.[102]

Rene left behind his wife, Jessie, and his six children: Herve, nineteen; James, sixteen; Helene, twelve; Marlene, eight; Joanne, seven; and Nelson, two.

Herve was now the man of the house, and he knew that he had to hold it together and be strong for the others. After the funeral, he came home and went downstairs to his bedroom. As he got to the bottom of the steps, he had to pass by the bar his father had built to entertain family and friends. Referred to as "the life of the party," Rene was known for hosting many visitors and for having great parties where all were welcome with a huge smile and a big French hug. Rene had been so proud of that bar.[103]

It was there at the bar that Herve saw Rene sitting. He spoke and told Herve, "Come on son, come and have a drink with me, eh!" For a brief moment, Herve saw and heard his father, and then he was gone. That was it. That was when it all hit. Herve finally broke down.

His heart was badly broken, and he was missing the father whom he had been so close to.[104]

Growing up without a father was difficult, especially for the younger children. Jessie was enormously brave and wore the role of both parents extremely well. She passed in 2006 and had the blessing of having her children, grandchildren, and great-grandchildren close by.[105]

Ottawa, Ontario - Killaloe, Ontario, Canada
Wesley Joseph Barber
Thursday & Saturday - September 5 & 7, 1963

The body of Wesley Joseph Barber, thirty-six, was sent first to the Kelly Funeral Home in Ottawa, Ontario, Canada, for services at 10:00 a.m. His body was next sent to Killaloe, Ontario, two hours west of Ottawa for another service at the Zummach Funeral Home. The funeral was on Saturday at St. Andrews Church for a Requiem High Mass at 10:00 a.m. and then the interment was in the parish cemetery.[106]

Wesley left behind his wife, Alice Richer Barber, two young daughters, Louise, five, and Linda, two, and two sisters from Ottawa, Ontario, Canada.[107] He was thirty-six at the time of his death at Cane Creek.

Wesley Barber was born September 27, 1927, to Lloyd and Elizabeth Holly Barber in Pembroke, Ontario, Canada, near the town of Killaloe. He was born small and slightly premature and was not expected to survive. Money was scarce, but hopes and prayers were plenty. With his mother's strong determination to keep her baby alive, he survived. While growing up, mischief came easily to him. Wesley loved to pull pranks, and he quickly figured out, much to the chagrin of his sisters, that being the only boy in the family had its perks. He was spoiled and could get away with almost anything. He loved cars and he loved driving fast.[108]

Settling down and having a family was the last thing on his mind, but the tragic death of his father was a major turning point for him.

He took a job in the mines and worked at several of them, including one in the Yukon. While spending time with his mother in Ottawa, Ontario, in 1954, he met Alice, the love of his life. A long courtship was out of the question, as a new job was waiting for him. Not long after they met, Wesley and Alice were married, and they left together for New Brunswick.[109]

Elliot Lake, Ontario, was booming in the late 50's, so they packed their Chevy and the trailer and the family headed there and stayed for several years. Eventually, things started slowing down in Elliot Lake, so when the opportunity came to work and provide a better life for his family in Moab, he didn't hesitate. Once again, the Chevy and the trailer were packed, and the family headed west. Wesley loved going to work and being with the guys, but the highlight of his day had always been coming home to "his girls." Wesley had only worked at the Cane Creek Mine for about six weeks and had brought Alice and the girls with him when he came to Moab.[110]

Alice and her girls were devastated when they learned Wesley did not survive the explosion. For her, the kindness and generosity of the community and the people of Moab would always remain clear in their hearts. They were fed and cared for, so they could grieve. Their bills were paid, their bags packed, and their plane tickets bought. A small private plane flew into Moab and whisked them off to Salt Lake City, so they could catch their flights back to Canada.[111]

The first day of the official investigation was postponed a day because of gases still lurking in the mine. So by Tuesday, a week to the day since the devastating explosion, after gases underground had been cleared, investigative teams descended into the depths of the blast-shattered Cane Creek Potash Mine.

The official Utah State and a federally ordered investigation were scheduled on September 3rd through the 6th. The probers represented six agencies and companies: besides those at the U.S. Bureau of Mines, the Utah State Industrial Commission, and the U.S. Geological Survey, they also included Officials and Engineers of Texas Gulf Sulphur Company, Harrison International, and agents from the Travelers Insurance Company, which had the insurance coverage on the contract.[112] Others who participated included engineers, geologists and other specialists from the Bureau.

James Westfield (right) meets with the press before the investigation begins. Also pictured from left to right are TGS President, Claude Stephens, TGS Senior Vice President, C.F. Fogarty Jr. and Utah Industrial Commissioner, Casper A. Nelson. (*Salt Lake Tribune*)

Their job was to do an in-depth probe into the cause of the mine explosion as they covered all parts of the mine in their search for clues. The teams sifted through the piles of dust and debris stacked all around the shaft station and in the shop. They combed through the dirty, grimy remains of twisted metal and other scattered mining material. The destruction around the shaft area was extensive with wreckage everywhere.

In the shop area, everything was scattered and thrown from one end to the other. Thrown about were parts of an electric welder, a fire extinguisher, tools, a switch panel and five five-gallon cans of diesel fuel. They also found thrown about a cutting torch, three large acetylene gas cylinders, and an oxygen cylinder. A broken flame safety lamp[113] was on the ground with scattered pieces of it nearby. Oil covered both ribs[114] near the middle of the shop. At that spot, there was clear evidence the explosion's force emanated out, hurling everything in its path in both directions.

The Bureau had the remains of a flame safety lamp, found in the shop, flown to Pittsburgh, Pennsylvania for metallurgical testing at the U.S. Bureau of Mines laboratories to determine if the lamp had been overheated.[115] Several other items were also sent for testing.

By the next day, investigators returned to the mine to make a more thorough check of the blast damage to the machinery and equipment. They also conferred with each other and meet with miners who escaped the explosion. One top investigator was even heard to say that the "pages of the disaster story are beginning to fall into place."[116]

On the third day of the investigation, the board began work at 9:00 a.m., and spent the day interviewing survivors and others who might have information about the cause of the tragedy.[117] The first miner questioned before the board expressed criticism of safety procedures at the mine. Johnnie Wayne Schear testified about the earlier fire and also the explosion that killed his brother, Keith Schear.[118]

Johnnie had returned home from the hospital on Friday, just two days before his brother was laid to rest. Hospitalized with severe burns after the July 31st fire, he was still wearing scars from second and third-degree burns he had received on his face, arms, hands, back, chest and legs.[119] Johnnie told investigators, "In my opinion, the mine was an unfit place to work. Safety rules were not enforced."[120]

He was then asked to tell his story of the fire and the events of the day he had been injured so severely. He paused for a moment as he prepared to talk about his horrible experience.

"I was drilling rock bolt holes at 10:55 p.m. when I stopped to rest and light a cigarette. It blew up in my face, and I thought my butane cigarette lighter exploded. I was knocked off the loading machine, and when I looked up, I saw fire shooting out of one of the drill holes like a torch. That is why I am sure it was methane. I started hollering for help. My hair was on fire. Some guys came back and put it out and took me out of the mine."

Johnny said smoking was not prohibited until his cigarette ignited a pocket of methane gas that day, injuring himself and three other men.[121]

Harrison International's mine spokesman admitted that smoking was not prohibited in the mine until after the first explosion, noting that the Utah State Industrial Commission had not ordered a ban on cigarette smoking at that time.[122]

Johnnie next claimed the July 31st ignition and the subsequent injuries of the four miners had never been made known to the public. The spokesman noted this but said the radio station, KURA in Moab, broadcast news of that incident the same evening, including word of the injuries. KURA officials confirmed this was correct, although the broadcast indicated injuries were "not too serious." The spokesman also said that the local Moab newspaper, the *Times-Independent*, did not inquire about the accident and was, therefore, not informed. Editor Sam Taylor said July 31st was a Wednesday, and they had already gone to press.[123]

Johnnie told how blasting powder and primers were consistently transported together in buckets and shuttle cars, as well as stored together underground, which is a violation of mine rules. The mine spokesman fired back and said transportation and storage of powder and primer together were definitely prohibited, saying, "We doubt very much whether this rule was ever violated, because of the danger involved with the men working in the area."[124]

There was one previous incident that stood out because of the potentially deadly consequences. A bucket had been loaded with blasting powder and primers with a hand full of men going down with it; one man rode in the bucket, while the others were on the rim. Going down fairly fast, the Hoistman slammed the brake. The bucket came to an abrupt stop, throwing the men on the rim down into the bucket onto the other miner, who then had an instant panic attack over the whole situation.[125]

Johnnie further claimed that he was one of the five miners who walked off the job in protest against "poor ventilation" a month and a half before the July 31st gas ignition. The men returned to the job after an additional fan was installed but "in my opinion, the air supply was still inadequate for the amount of diesel smoke in the mine," Johnnie said. "It was always smoky because ventilation was really poor. If we had had adequate ventilation, it would have carried the methane gas to the mine's surface, preventing the first explosion," he continued. The spokesman's response to this charge was that Harrison International installed a fan in the area of the mine where the air was reportedly "moving slowly."[126]

Johnnie next told how high voltage wires were allowed to hang low to the ground, presenting a deadly hazard to workmen and equipment. Again, the spokesman denied this charge saying, "Such an occurrence as low-hanging electrical lines would be almost impossible because qualified electricians were on duty every shift to take care of such eventualities."[127]

Another unsafe charge Johnnie made was about the number of men who rode the bucket at one time. As many as eighteen men at a time rode the mine's bucket lifts, even though mine rules limited the capacity to six. But according to the spokesman, it is physically impossible for eighteen men to ride one bucket. "Mr. Schear's statement does not fit with the facts," he said. Then added that Mr. Schear's charges were false.[128]

Johnnie's charges were, in fact, true. While sinking the shaft, many times, as the bucket came up from the bottom through the three levels of the Galloway decking, men would jump inside, stand, sit on the rim, or even be on top of the crosshead (that sits just above the bucket) and ride it to the top.[129]

"This is the first time we have heard these complaints, and we suggest Mr. Schear direct them to the proper authorities," the spokesman concluded. Ironically, Johnnie was directing his complaints to the proper authorities.[130] Harrison International officials 'Paddy' Harrison, his brother, Norman Harrison, and their Chief Engineer, George E. Smith, all denied Schear's claims.[131]

Johnnie further charged that a mine official once told his brother, Keith, to re-enter the mine, although his miner's flame safety lamp indicated a dangerous level of methane gas. It had been the first day Keith returned to work after the gas ignition when he was using the flame safety lamp to check for methane gas. The flame climbed to the "third ring" (lines painted on the circular glass of the lamp surrounding the flame), indicating a dangerous level of methane gas. Keith left the shaft immediately as he had been instructed to do by prior officials. He then met a mine official who adjusted the lamp to show a non-dangerous level and instructed him to go back to the mine, which he did. Johnnie then gave investigators the name of this official.[132]

Harrison International's spokesman immediately denied Johnnie's claims. He said procedure demands that as soon as safety lamps indicate a high gas reading, men are directed to make more significant tests with proper instruments. Such a situation as Mr. Schear described, therefore, would not have been allowed.[133]

After a short break for lunch, the investigating board continued interviewing others throughout the rest of the day.[134] Blake Hanna testified next and told how he and Fred Rowley were given flame safety lamps to use, yet no one asked either man if they knew how to use them or if they had been certified. In this instance, both men had been certified, but there were other men who had not been. He tried to explain this and give examples, but it seemed they didn't want to know the details and had him simply answer "yes" or "no" to their questions. After the gas ignition, permissible flame safety lamps were carried by each of Harrison International's three Shift Walkers, and other Supervisors while TGS personnel did tests for combustible gases during and after drilling blast holes.[135] Most of the men were not certified, and many didn't know how to use the lamps properly or how to service them.

During questioning, Hanna became frustrated over their dismissive attitude. He was eventually deemed a "hostile" witness and was only allowed to answer the investigator's questions with "yes" or "no" answers, which allowed the investigators to ask leading questions. Hanna felt they did not want to hear the whole truth.[136] Everyone knew a wrongful death suit would probably be filed by the families of the men who were killed, and it would most likely be against the very agencies and companies who were conducting the investigation.

Questioning other employees from both companies revealed that following the July 31st ignition, additional flame safety lamps were issued, but some of the men were not properly instructed in the use of these lamps.[137] It corroborated both Johnnie and Hanna's statements.

The testimony revealed a lighted permissible flame safety lamp was hung in each drift close to the Face and was occasionally observed. Some of the men believed the casual observing of the hanging lamp was considered proper gas testing. It was also common practice to keep a lighted flame safety lamp in the shop, suspended from the roof, for testing gas. Officials could not determine whose responsibility it was to use the lamp, and apparently, there was a misconception that the lighted lamp would indicate the presence of gas, by just keeping it suspended in the area with the flame burning. They learned there were occasions when the lamp was left hanging from one shift to another without being taken to the surface for refueling, cleaning, and checking. This was the case on the day of the explosion.[138]

One TGS employee said he tested for combustible gases in the shop area during the day shift about 3:00 p.m., on the day of the explosion, but had used a permissible methane tester, and found no gas.[139] These tests were made only at heights reached by the man standing on the ground. It was possible combustible gas had accumulated in the high spot in the shop, which would have made it nearly impossible to detect.[140] The shop was at an elevation slightly higher than the surrounding area, and the Back had been taken down to provide room for a steel beam, which was used to support a chain block. The height in this critical area was about eleven feet from floor to Back. This high place extended for several feet along the shop drift and created a natural cavity for collection of gases.[141]

Investigators also did an inspection of the company's paperwork and found that the necessary types of gas tests were not made with regularity.[142] The "Shift Summary" reports also showed that TGS personnel tested for combustible gas using permissible electric methane testers and permissible flame safety lamps. During the period between August 7th and August 26th, they found gas in amounts ranging from 0.1 to 5.0 percent at various locations.[143] These gas readings were after the earlier gas ignition and should have been more evidence that the mine was gassy.

There was also testimony that Harrison International's men had set up the electric welder at the outby (mining term relating to nearness to the shaft) entrance to the shop to charge batteries. It was done by connecting battery cables to the machine and using a lower amp. Some thought that a spark from the battery cables could have set off the methane gas when Kenneth Milton put his shuttle car's battery on charge. The mine report indicated there was no evidence of this or that the acetylene cylinders were involved in the explosion after soot scrapings were sent to the lab for testing.[144]

There was also testimony by some workers who had witnessed other men smoking underground, even after the "No Smoking" signs had been put up and a ban on smoking underground had been issued. Investigators had found numerous cigarette butts, empty cigarette packages, a book of matches, and other empty matchbooks in areas that had been driven after the July 31st ignition, which suggested that some miners had indeed continued smoking underground after the ban. Before the July 31st incident, smoking was practiced freely in the mine and was allowed in many hard rock mines. Following the ignition, smoking in the mine was prohibited. And although they posted the "No Smoking" signs, mine officials never searched the miners to see if they were carrying smoking materials into the mine.[145]

On the final day of the investigation, officials spent the day matching fact with fact that had been uncovered in the probe and they were also evaluating a variety of additional evidence and testimony.

Later in the day, the week-long investigation was terminated without a determination of a cause.

Officials investigating the mine explosion released a three-agency joint statement that said that while the investigation was virtually complete,[146] results of laboratory analysis from the U.S. Bureau of Mines laboratory at Pittsburgh, Pennsylvania[147] were still pending. These items included a flame safety lamp, dust and soot particles, and other items officials declined to identify.

The investigators said they could not determine the immediate cause of the explosion with certainty and that each agency involved in the investigation would continue to analyze the information and data collected before preparing its final report. While they believed the underground shop area was the center of the explosion, a number of possible ignition sources were still being investigated and evaluated.[148]

Investigation officials still hedged on designating a specific cause. The investigation was not complete, emphasized James Westfield. Samples of mine dirt, a flame safety lamp, and other equipment were still being analyzed. Westfield felt these items may contain the vital clue to tip the scales for one of the several possible causes unearthed from the dark shaft and mine by investigators. He also refused to enumerate the possible causes of the blast.[149]

"They cannot agree that it was methane gas," Westfield said. "They cannot now agree that it was any one thing." He also declined to identify just what equipment was being analyzed but indicated that this information may hold the investigation's missing link[150]

He was asked when the full story would be available.

"My boss expected a report on the day before yesterday," Westfield said. "We will have it as quickly as possible."[151] Reportedly, the final report was expected in two to four weeks.[152]

By mid-afternoon, officials turned the mine over to the contractor for recovery work to begin, which could take several weeks to complete. Harrison had made arrangements to provide above-ground work for most of the men to keep the highly-trained crews together until mining could begin again.[153] They had been put to work at odd jobs on the surface at their same rate of pay until operation resumed. This work would continue until the recovery of the mine was complete, and they could return to the normal work of developing the mine.[154]

While the investigation showed very little damage to the mine's structure, all air vent lines would need to be pulled out and replaced; all hoisting cables and damaged communications and other electrical installations had to be checked and most likely replaced.[154] Damaged equipment that could not be salvaged and debris would be hauled out of the half-mile deep shaft, and new equipment would be taken down. Development work at the mine would halt until after the release of the mine report. The report would establish certain requirements before the mine was cleared and development could begin again.

While permission was granted to resume work, it was only for recovery work. Before further development work and actual mining operations could resume once again, the Utah State Industrial Commission would issue further safety orders and procedures.[156]

The recovery of the mine after a disaster is another equally important element of the rescue operation, after the bleak task of recovering any bodies. While most mining operations after a disaster were recoverable, some had been damaged beyond repair and were completely shut down and abandoned. When this happened, it threw all their employees immediately out of work and robs companies of their investments. Recovering a mine takes time, additional sums of money, and hard work to get it operating again. The lost revenue, while going through this process, can be staggering. Many companies struggle for years; some make it, while other eventually succumb and shut down completely. Besides the incalculable costs of the loss of human life, companies are usually sued for wrongful deaths that can run into the millions. It proves that if people value their own life and the lives of others and the sources of income to sustain their families, safety certainly pays.

Most of Harrison's original employees were kept on the payroll, and a ventilation project was expected to get underway in the shaft. And since the number of men who can work in the shaft was limited, above-ground work was provided for the rest.

Until the completion of the mine recovery work, and the mine was put back into operation, it was impossible to determine the monetary damages incurred by the explosion.[157] Disasters (and the shutdowns they entailed) caused so much damage, threw breadwinners out of work, and were costly both in dollars and cents. So safety pays—quite literally.[158]

Chapter 26

Wheels of Justice?

During the investigation, Commissioner Nelson had pointed out that a report, as such, would not be forthcoming from the Commission.[1] He claimed that "This will not be like the detailed report issued by the U.S. Bureau of Mines. Our responsibility is toward Texas Gulf Sulphur and Harrison International. They already know the results of the probe because they had representatives on the investigation team." The Utah State Industrial Commission would instead issue a summary of investigation findings, along with a series of orders and directives for further operation of the mine.[2]

"It will be a matter of us telling them, from here on, do this," Nelson explained.[3]

On September 12, 1963, the Utah State Industrial Commission issued their safety directives in a letter sent to Harrison International. Addressed to Norman Harrison, the project manager, it said "the known cause of the explosion in the potash mine has not yet been determined with certainty. However, sufficient information has been obtained to warrant reaffirmation of previous recommendations and issuance of additional safety orders for your guidance prior to and during the cleanup and development work."[4]

Essentially, the orders reaffirmed the issue of no smoking and no smoking material underground. It listed ventilation requirements in the mine using air splits and the proper use of auxiliary fans. It also listed the minimum amount of fresh air that had to be delivered to each working Face while taking into consideration the requirements for the safe operation of diesel equipment.

The use of explosives was also addressed as was the testing for gas by a flame safety lamp by a person who was certified. Also, reaffirmed was the practice of the dispersing any gas found through proper ventilation before any blasting could take place.

Nelson also said that further orders or recommendations may be forthcoming following tests[5] by the U.S. Bureau of Mines technicians.

October 4, 1963
Mine Report Released

Friday, October 4th, the U.S. Bureau of Mines issued the long-awaited mine report on the investigation of the explosion,[6] which confirmed many earlier guesses about the blast. The report described in great detail evidence of repeated negligence and apathy in nearly every phase of the operation.[7] It contained twenty-nine recommendations "to prevent a similar disaster." Heading the list was the "positive ventilation of all underground workings." Ample ventilation would be required to carry away combustible gas mixtures before they accumulated and mixed into explosive ranges. It called for constant testing of the mine atmosphere to detect any unusually large gas emissions by those who were trained and certified.

One key recommendation was that the Cane Creek Mine "should be operated as a gassy mine." The lengthy report confirmed the fact that the underground explosion was the result of an ignition of combustible gas, mostly methane, and they found that acetylene gas was not a contributing factor. Reportedly, on August 27th, an explosive mixture of combustible gas was liberated after they blasted the Face of the West Drift (2 South). The gas was then carried by the return air current and directed by a fan into the underground shop area where it exploded.[8]

The report that came was technically correct but somehow had an inadequate conclusion. On page twenty-seven, it explained that the explosion was the result of the explosive mixture of gases which was ignited by "electrical arcs or sparks, open flame, or heated metal surfaces."[9]

Carefully documented, the physical and chemical conditions that made the explosion possible left little doubt about what had happened. But the answer to what had ignited the gas was left to the reader to conclude on their own. The report showed that before the blast, there was no lack of "handwriting on the wall" and that the danger signs were ignored by state and federal mine inspectors, Texas Gulf Sulphur Company (the mine owners), Harrison International (the mine builders), and the men who worked underground.[10] The U.S. Bureau of Mines had made only one regular inspection of the mine in three years. That inspection was on November 28-29, 1961, when the shaft was at a depth of 840 feet.[11] Utah mine inspectors went into the mine more often, but were lax enough to allow the work to continue despite safety rule violations, according to the report. Both Utah state and federal mine agencies apparently were satisfied to let the mine development go on under "non-gassy" rules and the use of non-permissible mine equipment, despite the known facts.[12]

Gas had been emitted during the blast hole drilling with sufficient pressure to eject the drill with force and push the drill and operator back twenty feet from the Face. Also, gas had occasionally been released from fractures encountered in the strata during mining operations. So, the mine was gassy—not as gassy as a coal mine perhaps—but gassy.

The investigation team found evidence of other unallowable practices. These included handling of explosives and blasting methods. None of them led to tragedy, but the air circulation and gas test negligence did.[13]

Recommendations were made to install a suitable dividing partition in the shaft to aid in ventilation. An additional recommendation was made for a second shaft to be sunk to the underground mine as soon as possible. It would provide sufficient airways and a second escape way.[14] Positive ventilation of all underground workings was also recommended, with a minimum of 40,000 cubic feet of air a minute provided at each working Face, to properly dilute unexpected gas releases and give adequate ventilation for diesel shuttle cars. Underground shops were to be ventilated with a separate split of air.

Preshift examinations (by certified persons) were to be made of the entire mine. Key men were to have, at all times, safety lamps or gas testers in their possession. Gas tests were to be made immediately before and after blasting, and near all operating electrical equipment. Examinations for gas in workings were to be made often enough to detect gas before it built to dangerous proportions. If combustible gases in the mine exceeded one percent, no shots were to be fired, nor cars operated. The report also noted that some of the men using flame safety lamps in the mine had not been adequately trained in their use as gas testing instruments.

The report called for strict enforcement of the no-smoking rule, including a procedure to search men for smoking materials before they went underground. It called for extreme care in the handling of electrical and diesel equipment and the use of miner identification.

The findings on the broken flame safety lamp found in the shop during the investigation were the most disappointing. The position of the wick, the lack of normal combustion deposit on the gauzes, and the amount of gauze rust suggested that this lamp was not in use or burning just before the explosion.[15] Findings showed that the wick had been turned down, and therefore, could not have supported a flame, nor could one be established with the igniter. The report concluded that the flame would have been extinguished when the wick was turned down to the position in which it was found. Fuel was available, but there was no evidence of charring, which would have been expected had the fuel been exhausted in burning. The conclusions suggested the safety lamp had been abandoned and left in the mine and that the safety lamp maintenance program was poor.

Some of the men took issue with the flame safety lamp findings. They felt it was the lamp Byrge had seen in the shop and felt it was likely on fire at the time of the explosion because it still had fuel. And there were several alternative reasons to explain the position of the wick. It was not known how many hands the lamp passed through before it was sent to Pittsburgh for testing. The findings also did not support the experiences that the miners had with flame safety lamps.[16] The lighted lamps were generally hung from the miners' belts, ready for use. The heat from the flame could sometimes get hot, and when felt by the miners, it would cause them to turn the wick down—sometimes several times throughout the day. When the wicks were turned down in this manner, the men had to turn the wicks back up before they could light the lamp the next time.

Not long after Harrison International's men returned to work at the mine, Chuck Byrge asked Matt Rauhala (now a Lead Miner on the ventilation project) to take him down into the mine. After getting permission, the first place Byrge needed to see was the shop area. There, towards the middle of the shop, where he saw the lamp hanging, the floor had been wiped clean in both directions. It was the exact spot of the explosion. And just above it, soot from the flame covered the roof. For many, there was no mistake, the flame from the lamp had set off the gases that fateful day.[17]

Many of the men believed that the flame safety lamp was the "open flame" the report listed as one of the possible ignition sources. They believed the lamp that was tested was the lamp Byrge had seen, with a flame burning up through the gauze, in the shop that day. The Grand Junction, Colorado newspaper, the *Daily Sentinel,* even managed to report the facts as seen by Byrge: "a lighted safety lamp was burning in the shop area at the time. A spark or flame ignited the gas..."[18]

There were other theories of what set off the methane gas. Some believed it was the flame of a cutting torch or the electrical arch from battery cables. Others believed a cigarette touched off a pool of oil. In truth, was it possible there was no way of really knowing for sure?

In spite of the objective, impersonal phrasing of the report, it also told of the heroism and violence and how the eighteen men died, and how seven survived. It documented the heroism of two trapped miners. It told how Hanna left the barricade to advise three men to go to the safety of the barricade, but he was unsuccessful in his attempt, and that it left him in "poor physical condition." It told that the three men remained and died there. It told Hanna and McKinney's story and how they left the barricade and how they eventually worked to repair the damaged compressed air line for the men they left behind. It also reported how once rescued, the two miners let rescuers topside know that five others were alive in the mine.[19]

The released mine report described the location of the mine victims. Not using names, it only indicated the men's occupations. However, most of the names could be deduced from Appendix G in the report that has the miners' information, which included their occupation. Since several had "miner" as their occupation, all but a few of the names could be determined by the locations described in the report. (Although, several of the locations were identified by several of the survivors.) The survivors also filled in some of the needed information of who was working where in the mine at the time of the explosion.

Below, the names are given in parentheses after the location description from the report and are numbered accordingly to the area on the map. The report states:

"There was no way to determine the actions or movements of the 2 South crew members after they fired the blast in the 2 South Face at 4:20 p.m. Location of the Face equipment and examination of the shot Face indicated that no work had been done at the Face after the blast." (The numbers correspond to Figure 26-3 Cane Creek Mine Map—Victim Locations)

1. "Following the explosion, some of the 2 South crew members erected a barricade about 75 feet outby the West Face of 2 South (West Drift); this barricade erected from the ripped-open flexible tubing was not airtight. Three victims who had died of asphyxiation were found by the recovery teams in the barricade. One of the three victims found in the 2 South barricade was the employee who had been heard screaming at the bottom of the raise—1U North—shortly after the explosion. Footsteps in the settled dust showed that the man traveled from 2 South Drift into 1U North and back to 2 South Drift."[20] (Lead Miner-Fred D. Rowley, 41, and Miner-Unknown were the two men who started the barricade. See note below. Miner-John B. Tinall, 38, was believed by to be the victim screaming at the bottom of the raise area. His footprints lead to the barricade in the West Drift where the other two miners were trying to build a barricade. All three were overtaken by smoke and died of smoke inhalation.)

2. "The bodies of two other members of the 2 South crew were found 725 feet from the Face of 2 South. They had been killed by violence."[21] (Miner-Unknown; and Miner-Unknown. See note below.)

   "Whether men were actually in or working within the shop area could not be determined definitely."

3. "Bodies of two men were found at the inby junction of 2 South Right and 2 South Left. These two men were the Master Mechanic and a Mechanic who normally worked on the surface, but had traveled underground with a part for the inoperative loading machine under repair."[22] (Master Mechanic-Lawrence I. Davidson, 45 and Surface Mechanic's Helper-Myrlen H. Christensen, Jr., 21.)

4. "Bodies of two additional men were found at the outby junction of 2 South Right and 2 South Left; these were the bodies of the Shift Walker and a Shuttle-car Operator. (Shift Walker -Joseph Rene Roy, 40, and Miner, Torkar Operator in the West Drift-Keith Shear, 22.)
5. "The body of a Shuttle-car Operator from 3U Drift was found on the west side of the shaft station. He had traveled to the station with his shuttle car to charge the car batteries." (Torkar Operator [from the East Drift]-Kenneth Milton, 43.)

   "The body in the shaft sump area was that of the Skip Loader on the west side.[23] (Skip Loader-Jesse C. Kassler, 38.)

   "The four bodies found on the east side of the shaft station were those of two underground shop Mechanics, an underground Electrician, and a Miner."[24] (Lead Mechanic-Myrlen H. Christensen, Sr., 44; Mechanic-Jesse E. Fox, 52; Electrician-Clell Johnson, 44; and Miner/Skip Loader on the East Side-Robert W. Bobo, 33.)[25]
6. The three men who opened the vent line at the top of the East Drift (3U) who refused to go to the barricade with Hanna and died at this location of smoke inhalation.[26] (Lead Miner-Lamar C. Rushton, 35; Miner-Wesley J. Barber, 35; and Miner-Peter Sviscsu, 42.)[27]

Note: Three of the victims, Miner-James N. Hollinger, 33; Miner-Emile J. LeBlanc, 32; and Lead Miner-William 'Bill' Huzil, 41, are not listed above and are the "Unknown" men. Their exact location could not be deduced from the information in the mine report or by interviews. Although their approximate locations have been narrowed down: one of the men was the third "miner" behind the partially built barricade near the West Face (2 South), the other two were found 725 feet from the West Face (2 South).

Disaster at Cane Creek

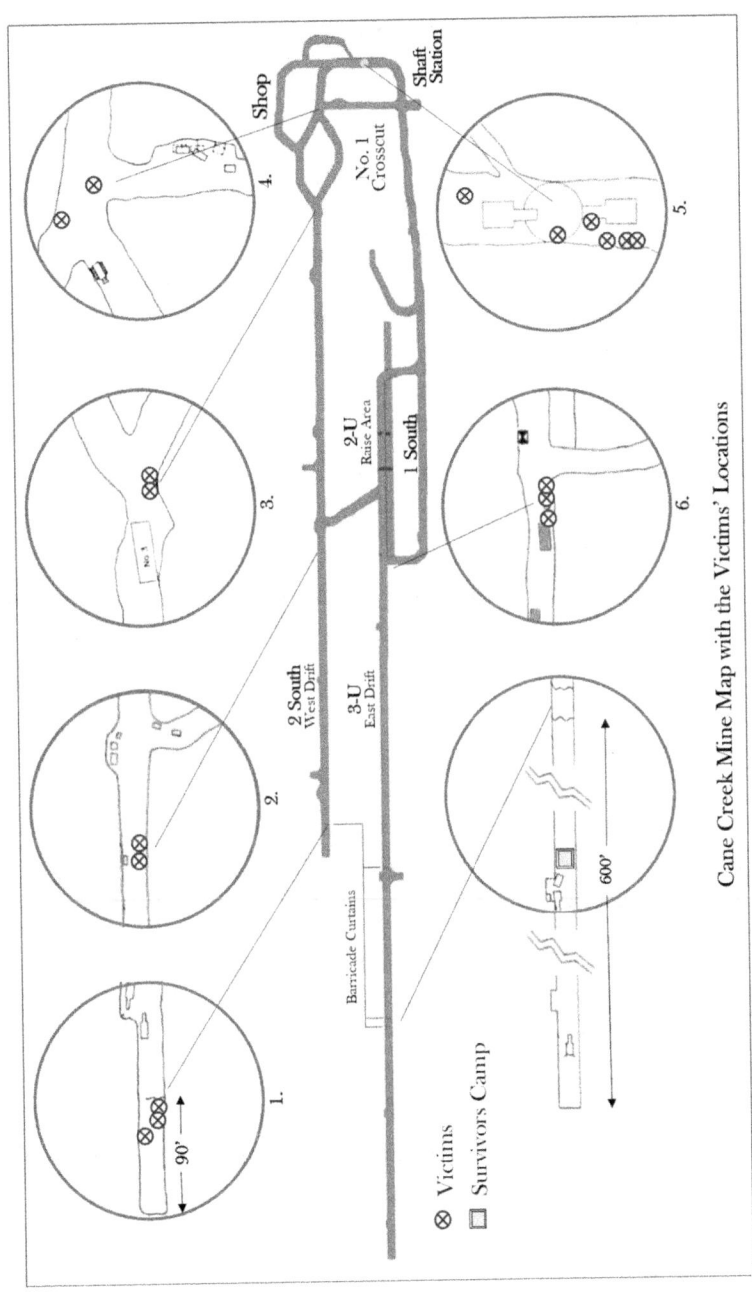

Paul McKinney went back to work at the Cane Creek Mine after being off for twenty-nine days recuperating after surgery from acid burns on his backside. Harrison International had him working as a Bottom Lander to receive materials into the mine and to send items out. Crews were still busy doing recovery work.[28]

At noon time, McKinney called for a bucket so he and six other men could go to the surface to eat their lunch. He had called two or three times before a bucket was finally sent down. Ivan James was the Hoistman on shift. There were no bells installed in the mine at the time, so McKinney called on the phone pager system where everyone could hear what was said over it. James finally sent down a bucket. It was the one on the east side of the shaft that had the loose guide cable from the explosion. It still hadn't been fixed, which was a worry for McKinney. The bucket could easily go up and into the sheave wheel and potentially bust the bucket cable, sending it plummeting down the shaft. (It had happened before, even though the bucket was empty at the time. Men were working below, but were on the bottom level of the Galloway Stage when it hit. Several of the men were banged up from the close call.)

The six men got into the bucket, some of them sitting on the rim. For some reason, McKinney felt this wasn't good and told them to get down inside the bucket. Using the phone, he asked James to give him thirty seconds, so he could get into the bucket and then they could be hoisted to the surface. McKinney hopped into the bucket and, after a short wait, the bucket started going up fairly fast, as it normally did. Halfway up the shaft, Armond Roy, now the new Walking Boss, was with Ray Green, an Electrician, working on some wires in the shaft. Green shorted a cross-hair on the bell wire, and it rang once, which was the signal to stop. James heard this and instantly slammed the lever to the stop position which threw the men down into the bottom of the bucket. Had any of them been sitting on the rim, the force could have thrown them off and possibly down the shaft. Not knowing what to do next, and instead of finding out what happened, James then hoisted the bucket back up the shaft. In an instant, it was racing towards the top, throwing the men down inside the bucket yet again.

By the time the bucket reached the surface, McKinney, madder than hell, caught up with James and let him know. Then he found Armond Roy up near the Harrison dryhouse and let him have it as well. McKinney wanted to know what the hell they were thinking. They knew to let the Hoistman know when they were working in the shaft and not to hoist anyone until they were finished. McKinney was so angry he felt like throwing Armond down the shaft; but instead, he quit his job right then and there—right in the middle of the shift and got out of that place as fast as he could. He had never quit a job like that before—in the middle of a shift—and it was something he never did again. But to do something so asinine that could have cost someone their life was unforgivable, especially considering what everyone had gone through the month before because of the explosion.[29]

At the end of October, the new Potash Road (State Route 279) between Moab and the potash mine was given national attention when it won "special mention" amidst 300 entries for the annual Scenic Highway Award, bestowed by *Parade* magazine.[30] Although constructed to service mainly the Cane Creek Potash Mine-mill complex, the road quickly became popular with tourists. This Colorado River canyon highway passes by dinosaur footprints and Indian petroglyphs. Jeep trails lead to Canyonlands National Park, Shafer Trail, and Dead Horse Point State Park through Long Canyon. The highway also passes by three natural arches.

Work at the mine on the concrete curtain wall began October 21st, as part of the ventilation project. Rising from the bottom of the deep shaft, the curtain would divide it into two separate shafts.

As part of the ventilation structure, adequate, positive air would be pumped down one side and directed throughout the mine with return air coming out of the other side of the shaft, and then channeled away at the top. It would facilitate the installation of two 24-ton ore skips and utilize the massive permanent hoisting equipment already installed at the top of the Headframe. The construction of the dividing wall was already part of the original design, but now it was in keeping with recommendations to make the mine safe. These recommendations had been issued by the agencies after the investigation of the tragedy.[31]

By the first part of November, Harrison International had reduced its workforce at the mine by thirty-three men due to continued delays in the operation.[32] For some of the personnel let go, especially some of the survivors, it felt more like TGS was trying to get rid of them.

Chuck Byrge was laid off and believed that TGS didn't want people like him around talking about the disaster, especially to the new hires. He and Bob June, as well as Paul McKinney, found work in mines in Nevada. Byrge would eventually end up finding work back in Carbon County at one of the coal mines where he would retire. He passed away on December 7, 2009, at the age 76 in Price, Utah. At the time of his death, the Byrges had six children, sixteen grandchildren, twenty-seven great-grandchildren, and one great-great-grandchild.[33] He was surrounded by his family and all his little ones.

Bob June eventually ended up in Wyoming, working at a mine just outside of Casper.

Paul McKinney found work at the Nevada test site and lived in Henderson, Nevada. He retired and now lives between two homes, one in Nevada and one in Fruita, Colorado, with his second wife, Pat McKinney. He feels deeply about mine safety and hopes others will learn from the experiences they suffered at Cane Creek.

'C.C.' Clark was laid off by Harrison International but was offered a job with them if he would relocate, which he declined. He asked about a job with TGS and was told they would likely hire him, but it would be awhile before they would need him. 'C.C.' went back to work on an oil rig until he was hired on permanently back at the TGS potash mine in September 1964. He retired from the potash mine which was owned by a Canadian potash company at that time,[34] the Potash Corporation of Saskatchewan (PCS). 'C.C.' had worked from early summer, 1961, to August 1, 1996, a total of thirty-five years at the Cane Creek Mine. The Clarks raised their family in Moab. His wife, Adeline, passed away at the end of 2016, and 'C.C.' still lives in Moab, surrounded by his family and the beautiful red rock country.

Grant 'Blackie' Eslick worked for TGS for eleven years, then moved to Tucson, Arizona where he worked for Hecla Mining Company for eleven years before he died after a short illness. Born July 3, 1915, in Boulder, Colorado, he died on March 26, 1976, in Tucson, Arizona at the age of 61 and was buried in Mullen, Idaho.

Blake Hanna was laid off at Cane Creek. TGS had wanted him gone for speaking out against the company. Norman Harrison asked him to go to work in Colorado at one of their other projects and told Hanna that he knew he had had some bad luck. Hanna told Norman, after working for him and surviving, that he was one of the luckiest men alive. Hanna found work at one of the potash mines near Carlsbad, New Mexico, where he relocated his family. After about a year, while still working at the potash mine, the Hannas bought a home in nearby Artesia, thirty miles north of Carlsbad, where they raised their children, and added a fifth child to the family, a son they named Trent. In 1973, they moved back to Price, Utah, having been gone from Utah for about ten years. Hanna worked at the Deer Creek Coal Mine for several years before becoming a federal mine inspector with the Mine Safety and Health Administration (MSHA). He took a position as a metal/nonmetal MSHA inspector in Nevada and moved his family to Reno. The next year a position opened in Carbon County, Utah and the Hannas moved back to

Price. As an MSHA inspector, Hanna worked hard to see that other families would not have to go through the trauma that many had experienced at the Cane Creek Mine. He worked for MSHA until his retirement in 1999. He and his wife, Myrna lived in Price, Utah until their deaths. Hanna died August 10, 2017, surrounded by family. Twelve days later, Myrna died, also surrounded by family. Both died at home, the way they wanted, and were buried at Price City Cemetery.

Chapter 27

Life Goes On

Moab, Utah
Friday - November 22, 1963

In Moab, the dawn of November 22nd broke sunny and bright, though the temperature had fallen to just below freezing the night before. The desert sun quickly removed the chill from the air, and by noon, the thermometer read in the 50's. It was a typical fall, shirt-sleeve weather in the canyon country. The town bustled with activity. With the weekend rapidly approaching, Moabites were planning their Friday evening.[1]

At the Cane Creek Mine site, Harrison International's reduced work crews were busy pouring concrete for the curtain wall in the shaft. Improvements to the ventilation system had to be made before the crews could continue to develop the mine. It was estimated to take several more months before the wall would be completed.[2]

'Paddy' Harrison had been in Moab since the rescue operation. He took part in the investigation and supervised the recovery of the mine along with his brother, Norman Harrison. After the deadly explosion, crews worked to clean up the debris, all the tangled metal, miles of wire and cables and destroyed vent line. It all was brought to the surface and discarded. Then it was all replaced with new.

493

Now that the mine was recovered and the dividing wall was going in, 'Paddy' felt confident enough to leave the Cane Creek project in the hands of his brother, Norman. He booked a flight for the upcoming Tuesday evening, November 26th, on Frontier Airlines out of Moab. The Irish Canadian was traveling home to Toronto, Canada to spend the Thanksgiving holiday on Thursday with his family.[3]

Martha Milton, the daughter of Kenneth Milton who was killed at Cane Creek, buried herself in school activities. As a senior at Grand County High School, she very much missed her father from her life and activities. Just the previous month, the pretty blond had been chosen Homecoming Queen. Martha and her attendants were announced at the annual Letterman's Banquet. Dressed in formal gowns, they rode in a convertible in the parade. Then the royal entourage was presented during halftime of the football game.[4] While the grief was still new, Martha stayed busy with other activities in school. She was made co-editor of the high school's yearbook[5] and was chosen for Girls State.[6] At the beginning of the month, the new high school[7] was completed, and students and faculty had moved into the new building. The senior class would be the first to graduate from the new Grand County High School.

Moab's high school basketball team, the Red Devils, after a week of drills and the first scrimmage, was ready for the open of their 1963-64 cage season against Emery High School. The following evening (Saturday), before the home folks, they were to play their first home game. The tall, lanky six-foot-six, Dave Kassler, a senior, was one of the team's starters.[8] It had been barely three months since his father, Jesse Kassler, was killed in the explosion. Dave particularly felt the absence of his father and his family. After the funeral, his mother and two brothers moved back to Florida. Dave stayed in Moab to graduate from high school, during which time he lived with the Engstrom family.[9]

As life continued forward, feelings were still very tender for the families who had experienced the devastating loss of a loved one at

Cane Creek and grieved their absences in their lives and activities. Just over a total of sixty children were growing up and experiencing life without their fathers, missing them each day and grieving in their own way at every milestone, important event, and holiday. It was as though a thick, dark cloud still hung over the families and community.

For the past two weeks, the talk about town was mostly about the filming of Warner Brothers' movie, *Cheyenne Autumn*. For Dave, it brought back memories of when his father and Uncle Jack worked as carpenters on the set for the movie, *The Comancheros*, starring John Wayne. Dave's middle brother, Tom, was able to get a picture with the 'Duke,' who even signed his hat. After filming had wrapped up, his dad and uncle had poached two mule deer and cooked them in the ground for a cast party. Everyone had sat around drinking draft beer with John Wayne, Stewart Whitman and the rest of the crew.[10]

For others in Moab, the past two weeks had been a great distraction as the legendary Director John Ford,[11] now sixty-nine and his stock company were back in town. Basically shy, and intensely private, Ford, was still wearing the same hat he had worn for the past twenty years.[12]

Ford had already filmed a number of movies in the Moab and Monument Valley area and had long been a favorite of Moabites. It was his love of the majestic red rock scenery that put Moab on Hollywood's map.[13] Ford had made frequent use of location shooting and long shots, in which his characters were framed against a vast, harsh and rugged natural terrain, making his Western films legendary.

Moab was typically chosen for films, not only for its versatile scenery and unlimited views of the dramatic red rock background (for which the area is noted) but also for the Colorado River, its green valleys, arid spots and snow-capped mountains. All these features fit with the new film he was shooting, *Cheyenne Autumn*, which was being filmed in Technicolor, a new technology. The recent snow storm, which covered the La Sal Mountains, was welcomed by the photographers, as was the wind storm, which blew the day they filmed at Fisher Point, dramatically whipping scarfs and banners as the cavalry rode up the mountainside.[14]

Since this wasn't Director Ford's first trip to the Moab area, he indicated that it wouldn't be the last. Not only was the scenery around Moab spectacular, but Ford was grateful "to be able to escape modern installations such as telephone wires, traffic, and airplanes since jet trails play havoc with western sky scenes in a movie."[15]

After shooting scenes in Monument Valley earlier in the month, Ford's company moved to Moab for another thirteen days of filming and stayed in various motels.[16] The film featured a star-studded cast,[17] along with about 300[18] supporting cast and crew. Although John Wayne was not part of the cast, his son, Patrick Wayne, played a West Point lieutenant in the film.[19]

Having the movie crews and stars in town gave the community some levity and helped to change the solemn atmosphere. For two weeks, when the moon came up, the stars in Moab were out. Unhampered by small town night life, they were found in almost every night spot in the city. They played pool, bowled, and made most of the cafes their gathering spots.[20]

Several locations around Moab were used for movie scenes, but on this morning, Ford, his Stock Company, and extras were shooting at the movie-made Indian village, which was northeast of Moab and near George White's Ranch.[21] They were filming the climactic scene of the movie, *Cheyenne Autumn*, with the long shot of Little Wolf shooting Red Shirt.

At that exact same moment in time, "the New Frontier" of the 1960's was coming to an end with the assassination of President John F. Kennedy[22] in Dallas, Texas. The news was too unbelievable. The first reports that the president had been shot, first filtered out of Dallas through the local radio and TV stations. At the ranch, the news would not reach Ford and company until a short time later.

Disaster at Cane Creek

From the time John F. Kennedy announced his candidacy for president of the United States, won the election, and served three short years of his term, another parallel story, also tragic in scope, unfolded in the "frontier lands" of the West. The announcement of the new Texas Gulf Sulphur Potash Mine-mill complex and the evaluation work coincided with JFK's election campaign. The construction phase of the Cane Creek project had begun just as JFK was inaugurated as president. Three months after the tragic death of eighteen miners in the Cane Creek Mine explosion, came the devastating death of the President of the United States.

At the ranch, Director John Ford was not getting the performance that he wanted from one of his stars. It was the last part of the scene, and both characters, Little Wolf and Red Shirt, were to fight to the death for a woman they both loved. When the smoke cleared, Red Shirt lay dead. Dolores Del Rio, who portrayed Red Shirt's mother, fell to her knees and was supposed to weep uncontrollably for her fallen son. But for the camera, the tears would just not flow the way Ford expected them. Take after take was shot, but Ford was dissatisfied with each one. He was determined to get it right, even if he had to stay there all day.[23]

It was high noon in canyon country, and Dolores Del Rio was still struggling to cry properly for John Ford's camera. At that same moment, millions of Americans were just starting to learn the president had been shot, among them, were stunned residents of Moab. News reached the set of *"Cheyenne Autumn"* by way of a local man who had been hired as a movie extra. A transistor radio broadcast the details, as this real-life drama unfolded to an audience who specialized in make-believe. Members of the cast and crew dissolved into tears, but John Ford was not yet ready to release them. Ford forced Dolores Del Rio to recite her lines one last time. This time, the tears flowed freely. "Cut. Print," said Ford grimly. Her performance was perfect, but it didn't require acting. Dolores Del Rio's grief for the fallen President was recorded forever on film.[24]

On TV, CBS News broke into the regular daytime programming of the soap opera, "As the World Turns" and Walter Cronkite reported the shooting of the president. Just three months earlier, Cronkite had been in Moab covering the mine rescue operation.

"Here is a bulletin from CBS News. In Dallas, Texas, three shots were fired at President Kennedy's motorcade in downtown Dallas. The first reports say that President Kennedy has been seriously wounded....," Cronkite solemnly reported. The nation waited breathlessly for more news of the president's condition. Following the newscasts announcing the shooting, groups of Moab residents huddled around radios and TV's in homes and in the downtown area, tensely hoping for encouraging words from the Dallas hospital where the President had been taken.[25]

A short time later, Cronkite reported what no one wanted to hear, "From Dallas Texas, the flash apparently official, President Kennedy died at 1:00 p.m., CST some 38 minutes ago."

On the Warner Brothers' movie set, Director John Ford called a wrap and dismissed his cast, and the group returned to Moab.[26] Distraught, Ford spent the rest of the day in his motel room. Later, someone from the cast figured out that when Lee Harvey Oswald shot the President, it was at the same time that Little Wolf (actor Ricardo Montalban) shot Red Shirt (actor Sal Mineo) on the set of *Cheyenne Autumn*.[27] As it did all over the world, the announcement of the President's death left in its wake a stunned and shocked city, which was still trying to move past the grief the last three months because of the Cane Creek Mine disaster. Heavy dark clouds of despair gripped the community once again. A period of quiet, respectful inactivity settled over Moab after the tragic assassination.[28]

Openly sobbing, some of the school children left their lunches untouched. People went through robotic motions in downtown cafes and businesses, seemingly just to get through the day. All social events throughout Moab were canceled, and throughout the weekend, the crepe-draped, flag-lined streets of the city were virtually deserted. Only vital business operations continued.[29]

A Requiem High Mass was celebrated in Moab at St. Pius X Catholic Church Friday evening, with Father John Rasbach officiating. He honored the fallen president, the first Catholic of Irish descent to hold the office of the President of the United States. Throughout the long weekend, special church services were held at various other churches in Moab, who conducted memorials to the President. Some of the denominations opened their doors to the public for meditation and prayer. On Sunday, church services around the valley were dedicated to the deceased President, with periods of silent prayer and special memorial words and music. At the Church of Christ, a special patriotic song service and prayer were offered, with J.G. Pinkerton presiding over the music.[30]

On Saturday morning, the day after Kennedy's death, Director John Ford, who ardently admired the president, donned his World War II fatigue jacket, assembled his cast and crew, and held a memorial ceremony in which taps was sounded, and a flag lowered to half-mast, a purely Fordian gesture. Filming activities ended, and everyone made plans to return to Hollywood the next day. In time, it would be impossible to ignore the analogous nature of the death of "the New Frontier" and the death of the Ford Western. Because of his failing health, *Cheyenne Autumn* would be the last Western movie John Ford would make.[31]

American flags draped with black banners flew throughout Moab's business and residential districts during Monday's national day of mourning for the late President John F. Kennedy. All the schools were dismissed to allow students and faculty members to attend services, pay their respects to the late President, and to observe the televised funeral services in the nation's capital. Heads of leading nations all over the world gathered to pay their respects to America's deceased president, and Moab residents withdrew to the seclusion of their homes to witness this tremendous display of respect for the late

President Kennedy.[32] For so many, the shooting in Dallas was forever etched into their mind and the national psyche.

For three days, Moab looked like every other town and city in America, bound together by a common loss. Americans viewed painful images on mostly black and white TV sets of President Kennedy's funeral. Coming so soon after the Cane Creek Mine explosion, it was particularly poignant for those in Moab to see another widow, and her fatherless children, dealing with such a horrendous death. After going through their own heartbreaking tragedy, it reignited and triggered the pain of their own recent loss. The grief and the sympathy Moabites and family members felt for the fallen president ran especially deep.

As the world watched the funeral proceedings and wept, unforgettable images were broadcast. The body of the murdered president lay in state at the Capitol rotunda. Jacqueline Kennedy draped in black, and hand-in-hand with her daughter, Caroline, knelt and kissed her husband's casket, which was draped in an American flag. The Army squad, with their white cotton gloves, brought the casket out of the Capitol and placed the president's remains on a horse-drawn caisson, as family members and world leaders walked behind to St. Matthew Cathedral. Hundreds of thousands of Americans lined the streets to view the funeral procession and pay their final respects. The spirited, riderless horse, Black Jack, trailed the procession, stirrups fitted with boots, symbolically pointed backward, and with a sword, which hung from his empty saddle.[33]

Jacqueline Kennedy, in stoic grandeur, stood behind her children, Caroline, and John-John (nicknamed by the press). The adorable three-year-old son, "dressed in shorts with a matching overcoat, cuter than all four of its buttons," gave a final salute to his father.[34]

Muffled drums swept melancholy waves over the hushed throng.[35]

Tum—Tum—Tum R-o-o-o-o-o-o-o-ll.

Tum—Tum—Tum R-o-o-o-o-o-o-o-ll.[36]

Disaster at Cane Creek

The drums beat as the caisson delivered the young president's body to Arlington National Cemetery. The horse-drawn ride was accompanied by a military escort. Once inside the cemetery, they rolled past endless lines of white headstones reverently marking the military dead. The sad stillness was interrupted only by the steady clack of the hoofs and the slow creak of the caisson wheels.[37] After the ceremony, the flag atop the casket was carefully folded by the military honor guard, and then the tri-colored triangle was presented to Jacqueline Kennedy. Through the black veil, the grief could be seen on her face and the blank look in her eyes. The coffin was sprinkled with holy water before Mrs. Kennedy touched a flame to a gas jet, igniting the eternal flame. As the nation and the world said their final goodbyes to the fallen president, it was an unspeakably sad day.[38]

The young, virile Jack and his radiant wife, Jacqueline, embodied the American dream and the hopes of a nation. He was to lead the nation to a bright future and the world to a united front. All were brought to an untimely end when President Kennedy was shot and killed.[39] Both tragic stories, the Cane Creek Mine explosion and the death of the President, coincided and intersected in time and were encapsulated in the early sixties, spanning those iconic moments in history.

Three days after President Kennedy's funeral, Thanksgiving Day came and a broken nation still grieved the death of their young president. Families across the country gathered to celebrate and give thanks for all the blessings in their lives. The Cane Creek families went through the motions and grappled with their daily grief, each in their own way. It would be the first holiday and family gathering where the absence of their loved one would be especially felt.

Margo, the young wife of Myrlie Christensen, had moved back to Huntington, Utah after the explosion to be near her family. While the family members were gathering, and preparing for their family's Thanksgiving dinner, Margo went into labor. She was rushed to the Price Memorial Hospital, twenty-two miles away. Later that evening, Margo gave birth to a beautiful baby girl she named Alisa Jo Christensen. Born on the day to acknowledge blessings, this special baby girl had her father's curly red hair[40] and was a tiny memorial and sweet remembrance of the life of her young father. Little Alisa was also a blessing in the life of her grandmother, Irene Christensen, who was still trying to come to terms with the loss of both her husband, Myrlen and her first-born child, Myrlie.

It soon became apparent to Margo's mother that it was too difficult for Margo to see the other new mothers at the hospital with their husbands and their newborn babies. At such a deeply emotional and tender time as the birth of a child, Margo's emotions of joy and grief were magnified. That's when Margo's mother took her and the baby home early from the hospital and attended to them.

With the support of her and Myrlie's family, Margo was able to get through the hard times as both families grieved together. Margo's sister-in-law, Myrlie's younger sister, also gave birth to a baby girl. Both young mothers had each other as they struggled through this time of loss in their lives.

As time passed, Margo remarried in 1965 to LaNae Jones, also from Huntington, who helped raise Alisa Jo and was a wonderful father.[41] The couple eventually added a son, Nick Jones, to their family and raised their children in the small, close-knit mining community of Huntington, Utah.

―――――

By early spring, a time of rebirth and renewal, more blessings came out of the tragedy at Cane Creek. After moving back to Texas to be near family, Donna Bobo gave birth to a beautiful baby boy, on March 3, 1964. Born in Borge, Texas, Donna named her newborn son, Robert Leonard Bobo, after his father and his grandfather; Leonard Iker.[42] Donna, her two young children, Daniel and Peggy, and other family members welcomed the special newborn into their family.

Robby, as he was called, would grow up to look just like his father. A living memory, he was a son who would never know his father and would miss all the things sons share and learn.

Donna would eventually marry Robert Wright, and they added another son to the family, Terry Lee Wright. Donna passed away at her home in the Rock Hill Community of Panola County, Texas, on September 29, 2009.[43] She was seventy-five-years-old.

Nine days after the birth of Robby Bobo, on March 12, 1964, Martha Milton married her high school sweetheart, Mike Dowd, who had always been there for her through the hard times after losing her father. The church wedding was held at the Southern Baptist Church in Moab. Martha was dressed in a beautiful white brocade gown with pink accessories and carried a sweetheart bouquet of red roses.[44] It was a beautiful ceremony. The only thing missing was the bride's father to give her away.

Five days after Martha Milton's wedding, on March 17, 1964, Eudeene Hollinger, who was also two months pregnant at the time of the explosion, gave birth to a daughter, Jamie Lynn Hollinger.[45] She was given the female version of her father's name of James, this beautiful baby girl was also a blessing in the lives of her family who were still reeling from the cruel blow from the loss of 'Jimmy.'

After Jimmy's death at Cane Creek, Eudeene stayed in Moab and went about the tasks of raising her three young children, 'Billy,'

Madge and now little Jamie. Eudeene would eventually remarry and she and her husband, Roy Weeks, added another son, Barry Jay Weeks, to the family. A beloved mother, Eudeene raised her family in Moab and lived there until her death, May 25, 2008.[46]

Like the glorious rays of light that penetrate the smallest opening of the darkest clouds, the births of the three beautiful babies were, for those Cane Creek families, an enduring blessing left behind. For Martha Milton, her wedding would be the first. More would come. While life goes on, other life events and holidays would come and go. But each would be marked by the same empty space for the one who was missing—their fathers.

A year after the Cane Creek Mine explosion, on March 6, 1964, the widows of ten of the men killed filed wrongful death lawsuits in the U.S. District Court for Utah, seeking damages of 4.75 million dollars. On June 17, 1964, Harrison International, Inc. was named as a third-party defendant.[47] By December 3, 1964, additional lawsuits were filed by more widows. Eventually, all seventeen widows[48] combined suits and asked for damages totaling eight and one-quarter million dollars ($8,250,000). Each family was seeking about five hundred thousand dollars ($500,000) in damages. The complaint contended that the miners were killed August 27, 1963, due to the negligence of Texas Gulf Sulphur Company and the United States of America; both were named as co-defendants. Instead of naming a particular government agency, like the U.S. Bureau of Mines, the wives' attorneys named the United States of America, so blame couldn't be passed to another agency.

The complaints, identical in allegations, supported the damage claims, which stated that all the explosion victims were employees of Harrison International, Inc., "a business invitee in the potash mine leased from the defendant, the United States of America and constructed, controlled and operated by the defendant, Texas Gulf Sulphur."[49]

However, just hours before the suit was scheduled, and those involved had gathered at the courthouse for the trial on November 29, 1965, the judge instead announced that a settlement had been reached. U.S District Judge Willis W. Ritter announced that Texas Gulf attorneys agreed to a settlement of $1,312,000 to be distributed among the seventeen widows and their dependent children.[50]

Some of the survivors and others called as witnesses in the case were sitting in court when the suit was dismissed and the settlement announced. Of the 1.3 million dollar settlement,[51] a third of it would go to the five attorney's representing the widows.[52] The remainder would be parceled out to the seventeen widows, using a formula set up that used such factors as the number of children, victim's ages, and their projected wages.[53]

Many felt the settlement should have been substantially more, but the attorneys for the widows didn't feel they had a strong case. Wives, already struggling to raise families without a primary breadwinner, felt that dragging the suit out in court for possibly years, with no guarantee of winning, would not serve their families' needs.[54] Since the Canadian families were not U.S. citizens, they were not entitled to U.S. Social Security payments and had been especially affected by the loss of their previous income in the two years since the explosion. The settlement was a much-needed blessing for those families.

In 1966, the Federal Metal and Nonmetallic Mine Safety Act was passed. It was the first federal statute that regulated non-coal mines. The Act formally proclaimed the new standards, many of which were advisory, and for inspections and investigations; however, its enforcement authority was still minimal.[55]

Three years later, the Federal Coal Mine Health and Safety Act of 1969 was passed. Generally referred to as the Coal Act, it was more comprehensive and more stringent than any previous federal legislation governing the mining industry.[56] The Act of 1969 was the precursor of the Federal Mine Safety and Health Act of 1977, the legislation which currently governs MSHA's activities for all mines. This act required that all contract company personnel, who do work for mining companies, take the 40-hour MSHA training that all mining personnel take each year.

Assistant Director of U.S. Bureau of Mines, James Westfield, was instrumental in the writing, and the eventual passage and implementation of the Mine Safety Act of 1969. He had retired the year before its passage in 1968, but was recalled five months later to head the Bureau's investigation of the Farmington Coal Mine disaster at the Consol No. 9 mine in West Virginia, which claimed seventy-eight lives on November 20, 1968. The Coal Act, as it was called, was not a cure-all as a number of disasters occurred after its passage, leading to criticism from the public and within the mining industry. After the Act's passage, it suffered from criticism when the loss of life in mines went up the next year, from 209 miners killed in 1969 to 255 miners killed in 1970.[57] Politics played a part as those in the federal agencies grappled with the implementation of the Act, while taking the heat.

Two years after the passage of the 1969 Coal Act, in March of 1971, Westfield was forced out as the Health and Safety Assistant at the Bureau, but was offered a new position as acting special assistant for mine investigations and rescue at the same salary previously earned. The changes came amid reports of coal industry complaints that Westfield had been "too tough" in enforcing the Coal Mine Health and Safety Act. Many of his colleagues and others in the industry disagreed with these reports and felt he was being scapegoated. Because Westfield was widely admired in the industry by the Bureau's men in the field, his dismissal caused a great deal of surprise even though he was over the mandatory age for retirement. The Bureau immediately went into damage-control over their decision. A miner's miner, Westfield commanded a great deal of respect in the mining industry because of his extensive mining background. He was acknowledged to be one of the country's top authorities on mine disaster prevention. His dismissal happened simultaneously with the Bureau being blamed for the shabby and shoddy performance in failing to enforce the new Coal Act.[58]

"They finally got rid of the only guy in the Bureau who knew about Mining Engineering," commented one high-ranking Bureau man. An irony in the Westfield situation was that mine safety critics on Capitol Hill and in the reform wing of the United Mine Workers had charged that the Bureau was too lax and too lenient in enforcing the safety law.[59]

At the age of sixty-seven, Westfield had been with the Bureau for forty-three years and had been kept in service beyond the normal retirement age of sixty-five on a year-to-year basis from the time he came back.[60] Over the past two decades, Westfield had been involved in virtually every mine disaster investigation conducted by the Bureau of Mines.[61] He and his closest colleagues were known as intellectuals and were responsible for writing thousands of reports and safety training circulars. They are even credited with introducing new mining terminology that caught on in the industry and is widely used today, such as outby and inby.

Westfield moved back to Carbon County Utah and worked as a consultant to numerous government and mining agencies throughout the United States. He became a member of the Carbon Country Club and a member of the Price Elks Lodge. On October 12, 1976, while in Tacoma, Washington where his daughter lived, Westfield passed away in the hospital after a short illness at the age of seventy-two. He was buried in the Price City Cemetery, not far from his hometown of Sunnyside, Utah, where he was raised. James Westfield was survived by his wife Mary, his son, James D. Westfield, of Sandwich, Massachusetts, his daughter, Joan Marie Sikonia of Tacoma, Washington, his mother, Nellie of Lone Beach, California and three grandchildren.[62]

For a number of years, the Rocky Mountain Coal Mine Rescue Association, who is over the mine rescue competition in Price, Utah, awarded a "James Westfield Traveling Trophy" to the first place mine rescue team during their awards banquet. A fitting honor in remembrance of the many contributions James Westfield made during his long, distinguished career within the mining industry.[63]

In the aftermath of the Cane Creek tragedy, the companies, employees, community and families, all trudged forward picking up the pieces. At the mine site, the concrete curtain wall, which divided the shaft, was in by December 26, 1963, and proved beneficial in ventilating the mine. Made of pre-stressed concrete, each segment of the wall was thirty inches high. The ends were grouted in on each side after placement. Crews topped 100 feet in one day during the installation job.[64] The curtain wall made two shafts of one and permitted the installation of permanent ventilating equipment. Fabrication and placement of the equipment got underway and involved both surface and underground work.[65]

Employment at the potash complex showed that TGS surpassed Harrison International, who had approximately sixty men, while TGS raised its work force to eighty.[66]

On April 19, 1964, Harrison International's crews broke into the ore body, and by August 7th, a milestone was reached underground when the two entries from the shaft (East Drift and West Drift) were joined using crosscuts. On the first day of September, a year after the explosion, TGS officials accepted the mine from Harrison International. Forty months earlier, the complex was only a six-foot hole in the ground and a metal shack.[67]

Five months later, on September 12, 1964, legislation creating the Canyonlands National Park was signed into law by President Lyndon Johnson. Moab was, as the city's new slogan indicated, the

Disaster at Cane Creek

Heart of Canyonlands National Park. Tourists throughout the nation were already following its lure to see the spectacular red wonderland. Using other parks as a guide, they predicted that within ten years, they would have a million visitors a year. It would have surprised no one if the number was reached in Canyonlands before the ten-year-goal.[68] More definite than the estimated visitor count was the undisputed fact that these visitors would pass through Moab. Moab's geographical location would play into the hands of its future. For the town, centered between the northern and southern entrances of Canyonlands, the lion's share of the tourists would no doubt choose it as headquarters for their park tours.[69]

Originally, Arches National Monument, just north of Moab, was created on April 12, 1929, and it was designated as a national park on November 12, 1971.[70] An extremely popular tourist destination, Delicate Arch became its iconic symbol and is recognized worldwide. Others travel to Moab for recreational adventures ranging from river rafting on the Colorado River, Slick Rock Bike Riding, the annual Jeep Safari, rock climbing, hiking and many other adventure activities.

Moab is now not only a major tourist town, but it has also continued to be a popular movie- making location. Through the years, the red rock backdrops have continued to be popular and featured in the many movies, commercials and music videos shot in the area.

On January 13, 1965, at 11:15 on a Wednesday morning, President Claude O. Stephens of TGS Company triggered the automatic loading devices at the company's mine-mill complex and the first load of potash cascaded into a railroad car. It was the culmination for Texas Gulf Sulphur of a $40 million plus potash project,[71] four years of research, exploration development, delays, devastation, and recovery.

The new Utah Governor, Calvin Rampton, joined with company officials, local civic leaders and representatives of Utah's news media in touring the surface facilities of the complex. Newly elected State Senator Sam Taylor (the local newspaper editor), and Representative

E.J. Mayhew interrupted a busy legislative session to join the governor for the flight from the state capital to Moab for the event.[72]

Representing the Moab areas were Moab Mayor, Norman Boyd, and County Commission Chairman, Ralph J. Miller. Also at the ceremony was another major industrial personage, Gus B. Aydelott, the president of Denver & Rio Grande Western Railway. The D&RGW Railroad would carry the first carload and the thousands that would follow, over the new thirty-five-mile rail spur joining "Potash, Utah, U.S.A,"[73] (the name of the mine's rail terminal) with the main line at Crescent Junction.[74]

The governor exhibited as much curiosity about the ultramodern mill as the dozens of newsmen who quizzed TGS personnel about the plant and the growing potash industry. On hand to answer the many questions, in addition to President Stephens, were Dr. C. F. Fogarty, Executive Vice President of TGS, and Frank Tippie, General Manager of the complex, along with other supervisory personnel of the mine and mill. Dr. Fogarty, before his elevation to Executive Vice President, had personal supervision of the potash diversification project. Tippie had been Project Manager of TGS since the initiation of research and exploration before 1961.[75]

The group of newsmen and officials toured the surface facilities for one and a half hours following a 9:30 meeting. The tour, by vehicle and foot, ended at the landing-out station near the Colorado River. As the tour proceeded, there, before appreciative eyes and cameras, the potash that was being mined and milled, traveled to the final stage and then, with only the push of a button, was loaded into a rail car. The visitors were then entertained at an informal luncheon at the Desert Inn after returning to Moab.[76]

Ore extraction that began in 1965 used the conventional "room and pillar" mining techniques, and they cut some 340 miles of mine workings. For TGS, plagued with problems from the start, the conventional mining proved to be increasingly difficult. The mine still contained explosive methane. It was hot and, instead of being level and flat, the ore layer was distorted in undulating sections.[77] Because of the problems associated with underground mining, management started to discuss the possibility of conversion to solution mining. Extensive research produced a full report in August 1969, which convinced management that solution mining was, in fact, a practical and economic plan. The board of directors approved the project in July 1970 and launched the unique program.[78] The facility was converted to solution mining between 1970 and 1972. By abandoning conventional mining processes, they prepared the mine for the project. They drilled wells down into the mine from the surface and constructed 420 acres of solar evaporation ponds.[79]

By this time, an underground area of more than 500 acres had been intensively mined in a four-square-mile region, centered under the crest of the anticline with approximately 150 miles of passageways.[80] The plan was to flood the mine deliberately with Colorado River water through a series of injection wells. A brine would dissolve the potash and, after the average residence time in the mine (about a year), recovery wells would return the brine to the surface. Potash extraction from the brine would be through an evaporation and chemical refining process[81] using the solar evaporation ponds.

All aspects of this design were implemented. With the experience of sinking the 22-foot diameter shaft behind them, it came as no great surprise that the company planners gave little attention to groundwater.[82] The initial flooding of the mine was not accomplished by the use of Colorado River water[83] as planned. Instead, water under artesian conditions was encountered. Injection well No. 7 was spudded on the crest of Cane Creek Anticline on December 27, 1970. The target depth was 3,016 feet down to the roof of the underlying mine.[84] At a depth of 600 feet, they encountered uncontrollable quantities of brine water under artesian conditions. Immediately, massive attempts were undertaken to seal off the unwanted water, even as the decision was made to continue drilling.

Nearing the roof in injection Well 7, and with the weight of the water and mud in the hole, the roof of the mine collapsed, and water began flooding down the uncased well into the mine. Not able to plug the hole, the mine was unexpectedly filling with groundwater. The flow rate was unknown and out of control. If all had gone as planned, in the spring of 1971, this volume of water would have been injected from the Colorado River into the mine through several wells over a four-month period. Instead, the brine-filled fractures above the mine did the identical job through a single one-foot diameter hole in two weeks.[85] Along the crest of the Cane Creek Anticline, it hosts a productive brine-filled water aquifer, which was the source of the water.[86]

In 1972, Texas Gulf Sulphur became known as Texasgulf, Incorporated. Moab Salt, Inc. was formed in January 1988 as a joint-venture between Texasgulf, Inc., and the Carey Salt Company to market salt, while Texasgulf continued to market the potash. Texasgulf bought out Carey Salt in January 1990 to become sole owner once again. Texasgulf was sold to the Potash Corporation of Saskatchewan (PCS) in April 1995. PCS sold their operation to Intrepid Potash - Moab, LLC in Denver in February 2000. Intrepid Potash is currently the owners of the mine.[87]

The solar evaporation ponds, with colors of vivid blues, yellow and white (created from chemicals used in the evaporation process), contrast against the brilliant red desert that surrounds the ponds. Some view the ponds as mesmerizing, while others see them as scars on the beautiful red rock landscape. If scars, it might well suggest that they are the scars from that tragic event on August 27, 1963, when the Cane Creek Mine exploded, and eighteen men died. It was a fateful day in the expansive, wild frontier land of haunting beauty. A land that refused to be tamed.

This remarkable place, in the heart of the beautiful red rock canyon country, is where so many go to be renewed and to find their heart and soul. But, here in this place, is a memory of shattered hearts and sadness that echoes through the canyons of this wild broken terrain.

Chapter 28

Epilogue:
"Safety, the Responsibility of All"

In 1963, according to figures from the U.S. Bureau of Mines, the loss of eighteen lives in the Cane Creek tragedy tied at that time, as the 30th worst mining disaster. It was also the fourth time a Utah mine disaster appeared on the "principal disaster" list. The other Utah disasters were all coal mine explosions in Carbon County: May 1, 1900, Scofield, 200 died; March 8, 1924, Castle Gate, 171 died, and May 9, 1945, Sunnyside, 23 miners died.[1]

An ancient occupation, mining has always had considerable risks. Not long after the nation's worst mine disaster that happened on December 6, 1907, at Monongah, West Virginia, where 361 miners died,[2] the U.S. Bureau of Mines was organized. Through the efforts of the Bureau to educate and train the mining workforces, fatalities rates had dropped exponentially throughout the last century. The work of subsequent safety and regulatory agencies that replaced the U.S. Bureau of Mines, such as the Mining Enforcement and Safety Administration (MESA) and lastly, the Mine Safety and Health Administration (MSHA), have worked diligently to improve the safety of the nation's mines. Subsequent safety legislation was passed through the years to help address safety issues.

Mining may seem very dangerous to people on the outside, and understandably, they might question why anyone would want to work as a miner. For the miner, the dangers are often minimized because of their training. Training has always been, and will continue to be, a vital factor in improving safety in the mining industry. Other dangerous occupations also carry risks, much like mining, such as construction laborers, truck drivers, deep sea fishermen, and lumberjacks. For mining participants, mining may be seen as a casual activity because they are familiar with the dangers and know they can take appropriate action when danger occurs.[3] In much the same way, it's possible for the average person to take part, quite casually, in a very hazardous activity such as driving their car, despite the high statistical chances of being killed or injured. The driver's assurance arises from the confidence that he or she has knowledge of the dangers and of the rules and procedures necessary to avert mishap. The driver also assumes that other drivers share the same rules and act by them.[4]

On October 5, 1963, one article appeared[5] in the *Deseret News and Salt Lake Telegram*, titled, "To Make Mining Safer." At the time, the Cane Creek Mine report had just been released, this article was particularly poignant in pointing out why safety is so important. It stated:

> Even at best, mines are dangerous places in which to work. And after an accident as destructive as an explosion has occurred in one of them, it is difficult to ascertain all the facts. Yet, some facts are clear and the U.S. Bureau of Mines report yesterday on the August 27th explosion in a Moab potash mine it was obvious that certain procedures at the mine left much to be desired.
>
> In essence, the Bureau's inspectors found non-permissible equipment at the mine, inadequate training of the miners both as rescue teams and in use of flame safety lamps

as gas testing instruments, and evidence of smoking inside the mine in violation of "No Smoking" signs and despite the known presence of gas from previous incidents. Like most accidents, evidently, no single factor was to blame. Rather, it was a combination of several circumstances.

As the report says: "The disaster was caused by the ignition of combustible gas in the shop area by "electric arcs or sparks, open flame, or heated metal surfaces." The gas was liberated from blasting in the West Face of 2 South Drift and was carried by return air toward the shop. The fan, operated openly in the shop area, drew some of the gas-laden return air from 2 South into the open shop and then recirculated it."

Conceivably if any one of these various factors had been absent, the explosion that cost eighteen lives might never have occurred. But even if the blast were triggered by, say, an electric arc it would still be no excuse for smoking in a "gassy" mine. Nor would it condone the operation of nonpermissible equipment. Mine safety requires attention to many details, not to just a few of them, but to all of them. Such attention is the responsibility not of any one particular group or person involved; it is the responsibility of all.

For the company's part, though safety procedures can be expensive, accidents are even more expensive. Safety pays in dollars and cents as well as in lives saved.

For the workers' part, it just isn't practical to have an inspector standing over a worker all the time. Even if it were, what worker would really want that? Some self-enforcement of safety procedures is essential. After all, it's to a man's own benefit when he calls a fellow worker to task for violating a safety regulation since his own safety is involved as well as that of the other fellow miners.

The investigation was conducted not for the purpose of finding a scapegoat or for pinning the blame on someone.

Rather, it was to make sure that what happened in the Moab mine disaster doesn't happen again. It's in this spirit that the report was produced by this investigation and the comments growing out of it should be viewed.[6]

"Safe Production" should always be the standard in all industries, not just mining. It has always been vitally important that top company officials, management, and supervisors, show and not just tell that they are committed to a safety model and demonstrate that they are invested in the health and safety of each one of their employees first and foremost.

With "Safety is a Value" adopted within each company, employees can have confidence that their employers are invested in their wellbeing. For the employee, it takes leadership and courage to call out peers who violate safety laws and regulations in any industry. Not to do so shows complacency and reckless disregard for their own lives and the lives of others. It also shows a level of selfishness, incompetence, and immaturity not to think of the consequences and how they could affect the lives of so many others.

In 1963, Utah State Mine Inspector, Victor G. Pett, was convinced that "practically 99 percent of all accidents were preventable. The only real type of accident is when a person gets hit by lightning," he said. Pett, who headed a committee that drafted the revised safety regulations at that time for the State of Utah, added that "Lots of times people are not smart enough to see in advance that their actions can trigger an accident."[7]

Most industrial laws, as well as societal laws, are written in someone's blood, someone who was loved and valued by others. So, it behooves everyone to commit to a higher standard of safety in all areas of life and to work together to create a "safety culture" so families can be spared the devastation of losing someone they love.

Mining has always been a hazardous occupation and the more rules and procedures that are disregarded, the higher the odds of an accident. The responsibility tends to be passed to the men who go underground. If an accident is preventable, they are the ones who have to prevent it.[8]

While Cane Creek is a story forgotten by most—except those who lived it, it is the hope of the survivors, and the families of the men killed, that in telling their story of the devastation and loss, it will inspire those who read it. The hope is that all will commit to, and take personal responsibility for, living a safety-conscious life at work, at home, at play and in all endeavors of life. The rewards for doing so are incalculable; the consequences for not doing so could prove to be terribly devastating. It's a chance where the potential costs are too high to risk.

The trauma, grief and broken lives because of the loss of a loved one can be generational. Rene Roy's oldest daughter, Helene, said it best, "Life continues and sometimes the pain lives in the marriages and births of our children and their children with the absence of dad."[9]

Appendix A

Mine Rescue and Recovery Team Members

U.S. BUREAU OF MINES:
James Westfield, Assistant Director of Health and Safety for the U.S. Bureau of Mines, Washington, D.C.

UTAH STATE INDUSTRIAL COMMISSION:
Steve Hatsis, Coal Inspector, Price, Utah

KAISER STEEL CORPORATION SUNNYSIDE MINES:
John Peperakis, Superintendent, Sunnyside, Utah
Tom R. McCourt, Team Trainer, Sunnyside, Utah
Fred Tatton, Sunnyside, Utah
Frank Markosek, Team Captain, Sunnyside, Utah
George 'Red' Ferguson, Communications Man, Sunnyside, Utah
Louis Villegos, Sunnyside, Utah
Lloyd Jaramillo, Sunnyside, Utah
John Schmidt, Sunnyside, Utah
John 'Johnny Smoke' Palacios, Sunnyside, Utah
James Harvey, Dragerton, Utah
Howard E. Kissell, Sunnyside, Utah

Wallace 'Wallie' Christman, Sunnyside, Utah
Caratat B. 'Oly' Olson, Sunnyside, Utah
Clive 'Blondie' Peterson, Sunnyside, Utah
Bruno Dalla Corte, Sunnyside, Utah
*Newell Crawford,
Walter Jones, Dragerton, Utah
Newell Kofford, Sunnyside, Utah
Harry Krebs, Sunnyside, Utah
Don Larsen, Sunnyside, Utah
M. Donald Ross, Sunnyside, Utah
Clair E. Self, Sunnyside, Utah
William 'Bill' Shumway, Sunnyside, Utah
Nick Tallerico, Sunnyside, Utah
Floyd Tucker, Sunnyside, Utah
John 'Curly' Westbrook, Sunnyside, Utah

COLUMBIA-GENEVA STEEL DIVISION, UNITED STATES STEEL CORPORATION, COLUMBIA, AND GENEVA (HORSE CANYON) MINES:
Robert M. 'Bob' von Storch, General Superintendent, Dragerton, Utah
Guy Hersh, Dragerton, Utah
Lloyd Miller, Dragerton, Utah
Willie Poglajen, Columbia, Utah
Bert Frandsen, Dragerton, Utah
Dell Judd, Dragerton, Utah
Paul Clark, Dragerton, Utah
J.D. Gray, Dragerton, Utah
Paul W. Butler, Dragerton, Utah
Med Allred, Dragerton, Utah
Hugh Belging, Dragerton, Utah
Lyle Burdick, Mine Inspector, Dragerton, Utah
James Cassano, Dragerton, Utah
Henry Collette, Dragerton, Utah
George Dunham, Columbia, Utah

*Leroy M. 'Tom' Hersh, Dragerton, Utah
Robert 'Bob' Kilcrease, Dragerton, Utah
Kenneth "Kenny" Litster, Dragerton, Utah
Alex Mondlak, Safety Manager, Dragerton, Utah
Emery C. Olsen, Dragerton, Utah
Oscar Pagette, Columbia, Utah
Ted Self, Price, Utah
'Frosty' Alden Dudley Swasey, Dragerton, Utah
Kenneth 'Kenny' Walters, Dragerton, Utah
William 'Bill' Ward, Dragerton, Utah
R.E. Yourston, Dragerton, Utah

TEXAS GULF SULPHUR COMPANY CANE CREEK MINE:
Wiley Brooks, General Mine Foreman, Moab, Utah
Morris Worley, Engineer, Moab, Utah
Bob Mashaw, Engineer, Moab, Utah

HARRISON INTERNATIONAL, INC.:
*Patrick 'Paddy' Harrison, President of Harrison International, Toronto, Ontario
Norman Harrison, Project Manager, Moab, Utah
*Albert 'Bert' Trenfield, Mine Superintendent, Moab, Utah
Henry 'Big Henry' Laviolette, Shift Walker, Moab, Utah
Henry 'Little Henry' Levigne, Shift Walker, Moab, Utah
Armond Roy, Moab, Utah
George McCloud, Moab, Utah
Bud Pilling, Moab, Utah
*Benny Cable, Moab, Utah
* Robert Rediger, Moab, Utah
Lorenzo Boren, Moab, Utah
Ronald Cressler, Moab, Utah
E. Jessome Moab, Utah
Ray Long, Moab, Utah

Vernon Martin, Moab, Utah
L.H.Thomas, Moab, Utah
*Gene Weaver, Moab, Utah
Robert Zimmerman, Moab, Utah

Note: Apparently, Standard Metals Company, a mining company in the Moab area offered assistance and assembled rescue crews ready to assist. They were under the direction of W.R. 'Bill' McCormick, president of the company.[1] It is not known if or in what capacity they assisted with the rescue operation, and no names were listed in the Mine Report along with the other rescue teams and their members.

*(Rescuers and Rescue Workers not listed in the Cane Creek Mine Report but their participation was verified through interviews with the author or were named in newspaper articles or photo captions.)

Selected Bibliography

BOOKS:

Abbey, Edward and David Petersen. *Postcards from Ed: Dispatches and Salvos from an American Iconoclast.* Minneapolis: Milkweed Press, 2006.

Agnew, Jeremy. *The Old West in Fact and Film: History Versus Hollywood.* Jefferson, NC, and London: McFarland & Company, Inc., 2012.

Associated Press. *The Torch Is Passed: The Associated Press Story of the Death of a President* New York: Western Printing & Lithographing Co., 1963.

Bodmer, Rudolph John, et. *The Book of Wonders and the Wonders Produced by Man.* Edited by Inc. Bureau of Industrial Education Washington D.C.: Presbrey Syndicate, Inc., 1918.

Bogdanovich, Peter. *Who the Hell's in It: Conversations with Hollywood's Legendary Actors* New York: Ballantine Book, 2004.

Davis, Ronald L. *John Ford: Hollywood's Old Master.* Norman, OK, and London: University of Oklahoma Press, 1995

Eyman, Scott. *Print the Legend: The Life and Times of John Ford.* New York: Simon & Schuster, 1999.

Firmage, Richard A. *A History of Grand County.* Utah Centennial County History Series. Salt Lake City: Utah State Historical Society, 1996.

Fischer, Heinz Dietrich and Erika J. Fisher, *Complete Biographical Encyclopedia of Pulitzer Prize Winners 1917-2000*. Germany: K.G. Saur Munchen, 2002.

Fish, Lydia. *The Folklore of the Coal Miners of the Northeast of England*. Vol. 2, Norwood, PA: Norwood Editions, 1975.

Gallagher, Tag. *John Ford: The Man and His Films*. Berkeley, Los Angeles: University of California Press, 1986.

Goodman, James A. *Two Weeks under, the Sheppton Mine Disaster/Miracle*. Bloomburg: Coal Hole, 2003.

Gyorgy, Dupka, ed. *Genocide, the Tragedy of the Hungarians of Transcarpathia*. Budapest: Intermix Editions, 1993.

Hafen, LeRoy R., and Ann W. Hafen. *Old Spanish Trail, Sante Fe to Los Angeles*. Lincoln and London: University of Nebraska Press, 1993.

Hoffmann, E.T.A. *The Mines of Falun, Fantasy and Horror Classics*. Fantasy and Horror Classics. British Library: Read Books Ltd., 2012.

Katz, Jay, Alexander Capron and Eleanor Swift Glass. *Experimentation with Human Beings: The Authority of the Investigator, Subject, Professions and State in the Human Experimentation Process*. Hartford: Connecticut Printers, Inc., 1972.

Kelly, Charles. *The Outlaw Trail: A History of Butch Cassidy and His Wild Bunch*. Lincoln: University of Nebraska Press, 1996.

Lucas, Rex A. *Men in Crisis, a Study of a Mine Disaster*. New York and London: Basic Books, 1969.

McBride, Joseph. *Searching for John Ford*. Jackson: University Press of Mississippi, 2001. 2011.

Oliver, Thomas., M.D., F.R.C.P. *Diseases of Occupation, from the Legislative, Social, and Medical Points of View*. London: Methuen & CO., 1908.

Onofrio, Jan. *Texas Biographical Dictionary*. 3rd ed. New York: Somerset Publishers, Inc., 1996.

Polisenska, Milada. *Czechoslovak Diplomacy and the Gulag, 1945-1953*. English Translation ed. New York: Central European University Press, 2015.

Powell, Allan Kent. *The Next Time We Strike*. Logan: Utah State University Press, 1985.

Ringholz, Raye. *Uranium Frenzy: Saga of the Nuclear West*. Logan: Utah State University Press, 2002.

Rolt, L. T. C. *George and Robert Stephenson: The Railway Revolution*. London: Longmans, 1960.

Sando, J. Ronnie. *The Famous Sheppton Mine Rescue*. Baltimore: Publish America, 2006.

Stanton, Bette L. *"Where God Put the West," Movie Making in the Desert*. Moab: Four Corners Publications, 1994.

Stegner, Wallace Earle, et al. *Wilderness at the Edge: A Citizen Proposal to Protect Utah's Canyons and Deserts* Layton, UT: Gibbs M. Smith, 1990.

Tanner, Faun McConkie. *The Far Country: A Regional History of Moab and La Sal, Utah*. Salt Lake City: Olympus Publishing Company, 1976.

Trimble, Stephen, ed. *Blessed by Light, Visions of the Colorado Plateau*. Layton, Utah: Gibbs M. Smith, 1986.

Whitley, Colleen, ed. and Philip F. Notarianni. *From the Ground up, the History of Mining in Utah*. Logan: Utah State University Press, 2006.

Wordsworth, William and Norah Neilson Gray. *Ode, Intimations of Immortality from Recollections of Early Childhood*. London: J.M. Dent, 1913.

Zoellner, Tom. *Uranium: War, Energy, and the Rock That Shaped the World*. New York: Viking, 2009.

GOVERNMENT DOCUMENTS AND PUBLICATIONS:

"Social Security Card Application for Pete Sviscsu." U.S. Social Security Administration, 1961.

"Underground Mine Disaster Survival and Rescue: An Evaluation of Research Accomplishments and Needs." In *Report of the Committee on Underground Mine Disaster Survival and Rescue, Commission on Sociotechnical Systems*, 17. Washington D.C.: National Research Council, 1981.

Jambrek, Peter, ed. "Crimes Committed by Totalitarian Regimes." Brussels: Slovenian Presidency of the Council of the European Union, 2008.

Kennedy, John F. "Public Papers of the Presidents of the United States: John F. Kennedy, 1963." Best Books on Corporation, 2013.

Paul, James W., and H. M. Wolflin. *Rescue and Recovery Operations in Mines after Fires and Explosions*. Washington D.C.: U.S. Bureau of Mines, 1916.

Rachunis, William, Arthur A. Sinicrope, F. Wilscon, and James A. Moore. *Final Report of Collapse of Slope Pillar Accident and Rescue of Two of the Three Entombed Men, Oneida No. 2 Slope, Fellin Mining Company, Oneida, Schuylkill County, Pennsylvania, August 13, 1963*. Wilkes-Barre: U.S. Bureau of Mines, 1963.

Westfield, James, Lester D. Knill and Anthony C. Moschetti. *Final Report of Major Mine-Explosion Disaster, Cane Creek Mine, Potash Division, TGS Company, Grand County, Utah (Mine Development under Contract with Harrison International, Incorporated), August 27, 1963*. Lakewood, CO: U.S. Bureau of Mines, 1963.

JOURNALS, PERIODICALS, AND NEWSLETTERS:

Crampton, C. Gregory. "Utah's Spanish Trail." *Utah Historical Quarterly* 47, no. 4 (Fall 1979): 369.

Fraser, Marianne. "Warm Winters and White Rabbits: Folklore of Welsh and English Coal Miners." *Utah Historical Quarterly* 51, no. 3 (Summer 1983): 236-58.

Harrington, Daniel. "Coal Mining at Sunnyside, Utah." 227-35: Colorado School of Mines Bulletin 1, 1901.

Huntoon, Peter W. "Incredible Tale of Texasgulf Well 7 and Fracture Permeability, Paradox Basin, Utah." *Ground Water; National Ground Water Association* 24, no. 5 (September 1986): 644.

Kowalski-Trakofler, Kathleen M., and Charles Vaught. "Psycho-Social Issues in Mine Emergencies: The Impact." *Minerals* (June 11, 2012).

Jackson, Daniel. "Solution Mining Pumps New Life into Cane Creek Potash Mine." *Engineering and Mining Journal (E&MJ)* (July 1973): 59-69.

Rakes, Paul H. "Acceptable Casualties: Power, Culture, and History in the West Virginia Coalfields, 1900-1945." (2002): 44.

Rushton, Mrs. Duane. "Sincere Thanks." *The Trooper Newsletter* Volume III (October 1963 1963).

Smith, Thomas G. "John Kennedy, Stewart Udall, and New Frontier Conservation." *Pacific Historical Review* 64, no. 3 (August 1995): 329-262.

Smith, Thomas G. "The Canyonlands National Park Controversy, 1961-64." *Utah Historical Quarterly* 59, no. 3 (Summer 1991): 216.

Salmon, Rusty, "Samuel John Taylor." *Eastern Utah Human History Library* (July 25, 2003): 31.

Worley, Morris T., P.E. "The Cane Creek Mine Disaster: Personal Observations." *Mining History Journal* 16 (2009): 5-9.

MAGAZINE ARTICLES:

"Builder Harry Morrison, to Tame Rivers and Move Mountains, the Earth Mover." *TIME*, May 3, 1954, 86-93.

Caudill, Donna. "The King of Longwall." *American Longwall Magazine*, May 2007.

Gold, Mick. "Life & Life Only: Dylan at 60." *Judas! Magazine*, April 2002, 43.

Gonzales, Arturo F., Jr. "Cave-In! Drama Deep in the Earth." *Popular Science Magazine*, December 1963, 204, 06, 44, 45, 46.

Petty, Patricia Curtis. "Construction and Philosophy." *Mines Magazine*, September 1980, 11.

Sanda, Art. "Dan Baker: Cattle Ranching Can't Keep Dan Baker out of the Coal Mines." *Coal People Magazine*, May 2009, 22.

MANUALS, BULLETINS, PAMPHLETS, AND CIRCULARS:

"Handbook of Training in Mine Rescue and Recovery Operations." edited by Inspection Branch of the Ontario Department of Mines. Canada, 1964.

Grove, G.W. "Loss of Life among Wearers of Oxygen Breathing Apparatus." *U.S. Bureau of Mines Information Circular 7279* (April 1944).

Maize, E.R. and J.V. Berry. "A Plan for Training Mine Officials in Rescue Organization and Disaster Prevention." *United States Bureau of Mines Information Circular (IC) No. 7353* (June 1946).

Phillips, Margie. "Cane Creek Mine Solution Mining Project, Moab Potash Operations, Texasgulf, Inc.". *Four Corners Geological Society, Canyonlands Country, Eighth Field Conference, AAPG Datapages, Inc. Archives* (1975): 261-62.

MISCELLANEOUS:

"Civil Court Docket, United States District Court. District of Utah, Location #8nn 89-23, Case #C48-64." edited by United States Courthouse Office of the Clerk. Salt Lake City, UT: National Archives Center, 1964.

Harrison, Patrick. "Cage and Operating Mechanism for shaft Shovels." U.S. Patent 2587844-A. 1952.

I.W. Allen Memorial Hospital. "Donald Blake Hanna, Patient Records." 1963.

McDonald, Mary Ann. "UK, Outward Passenger Lists, 1890-1960: *Ancestry.Com.*"

Acknowledgments

When I first started working on the book in 1996, I was able to interview some of the survivors, family members, and mine rescuers. Just as my research and writing was taking off, it all abruptly stopped with the death of my daughter in 1998 from a tragic car wreck. For about five years, it was difficult to think, let alone write. They say writers write from their experiences. Experiencing the horrible grief of losing a child, I believe, informed my writing and my understanding of what the families went through at Cane Creek. Eventually, I was able to get back to work on this massive project. Although, at times, parts of the book would trigger my own grief and chase me away again. Back and forth it went. As the years passed, many of the people connected to this story, I discovered, had passed away. This created a sense of urgency to get the book finished. So, in 2014, I quit my full-time job to work on the book and completed the first draft of the manuscript at the end of 2016.

There are so many that I owe a huge debt of gratitude for the help and support given me throughout the years. To my regret, there are some who have passed away.

First, I would like to thank the many individuals and families directly affected by this disaster who shared their firsthand accounts of this story. They have been an inspiration throughout. Special thanks to the survivors: Donald Blake Hanna (my father); Paul McKinney; Charles 'C.C.' Clark; and Charles 'Chuck' Byrge, who allowed me to interview them. And the surface survivor: Matt Rauhala.

Special thanks to the mine rescue team members I was able to interview: Fred Tatton, 'Johnnie Smoke' Palacios, Louie Villegos, Guy Hersh, George Ferguson, Walter 'Wallie' Christman, Paul Butler and Bud Pilling.

Thanks to the TGS personnel: Ed Ziolkowski; Morris Worley (who also allowed me to use his published article, *"Remembrance of the Cane Creek Mine Disaster"*); and J.G. Pinkerton for their interviews.

Also, thanks to Charles 'Chuck' McClellan, Harrison International's Hoistmen, and Harry Snow, the Grand County District Attorney in 1963, for their stories.

I am also indebted to the wives I was able to personally interview, speak to on the phone or communicate with electronically: Myrna Hanna (my mother); Irene Christensen Lemon; Margo Christensen Jones; Opal Davidson; Eudeene Hollinger Weeks; Tess Johnson; Violate June; Dorothy LeBlanc McPhee; and Lorraine Rushton. They are amazingly strong women and inspiring role models.

Many of the children who were old enough to remember this terrible event also shared their accounts, while some of the younger children at the time shared newspaper clippings, photos and other pertinent family stories and information. Thanks to all of them. During those discouraging times when I was drowning in research and trying to organize all the data into a readable story, the children and their mothers were a vital source of inspiration who constantly encouraged me to finish this massive project. I am grateful for the many friendships I have forged with many of them throughout the years. Their fathers would be proud of them. Thanks to: Peggy Bobo, Linda Barber, Alisa Christensen Alleman, Bill Eslick, Audrey Huzil Clayton, Marnie Davidson Melo, Linda Fox Hansen, Madge Hollinger Rodman, Ned and Kirt Johnson, Dianne Johnson Zachreson, Carolyn Johnson Arroyo, Patricia June Meilleur, David Kassler, Geralyn LeBlanc, Martha Milton Dowd, Herve Roy, Helene Roy McGruthers, Marlene Roy, Bonnie Rushton Wolverton and John 'Paul' Tinall.

Thanks to other family members and friends who have made contributions: Mike Dowd, Ivan McKinney, Rita Kassler, William Sikonia (James Westfield's son-in-law), Dwayne "Pat" Hand, Lyra Hollinger, Myriam Laviolette Macleod-Allard, Nadine Schear, Zelda Schear Bucher, Carolyn Schear, Sheila Rauhala Shumway and Cynthia Tinall. Thanks to all the many others who have helped and contributed in so many countless ways throughout the years. There are too many to name, and I'm sure I may have inadvertently left someone out. You know who you are. Thank you.

I would like to thank Rick York, General Manager, Utah - Division of Intrepid Potash, Inc. (current owners of the Cane Creek Potash Mine). At the beginning of this project, Rick was incredibly generous to loan many binders filled with newspaper accounts, development photographs and slides that the company had collected since the time TGS first started the Cane Creek Mine-mill Complex, through the mine explosion and investigation. This material was one of the main sources of research for the book. Mr. York also sponsored a family gathering at the mine site during the 50th Year Commemoration of the Cane Creek Mine Disaster in August of 2013. A year later, at his direction, some of his employees erected the Cane Creek Memorial at the edge of the company's property near the main entrance to the mining facility.

Next, I would like to thank Sam Taylor, the owner/editor of the *Times-Independent,* Moab's weekly newspaper. Now deceased, Mr. Taylor graciously allowed me to interview him and loaned me a file of photographs. Also, special thanks to Dorothy Anderson, one of Mr. Taylor's longtime employees at the newspaper, who is also my dear great aunt for all her help. I would also like to thank the primary source newspapers (which make up the bulk of the articles used) and for their permission to use their articles and photos. Also, the other publications I used under the "fair use" terms. Many of the journalist, named and unnamed, left firsthand accounts of the Cane Creek story in the written pages of their newspaper articles. I have religiously sourced each article used in the book to acknowledge and give credit for the contributions made by so many journalists. New Journalism[1] was a popular writing style used in the 60's and 70's. This style adhered to the rigid organizational journalism style of the older writing form, but it reads more like fiction. Because of this style, scattered throughout the newspaper accounts covering the Cane Creek Mine disaster, are scene-by-scene accounts, a record of dialogue, third-person point of view and other incidental and descriptive details with additional details that helped round out characters. These elements, indicative of the New Journalism style, were viewed at that time as unconventional. This style combined journalistic research and used techniques borrowed from fiction writing in reporting about real-life events, while portraying them as vividly as possible. It is as reliable as any reporting that sought the larger truth by compiling verifiable facts. While not all of the newspaper accounts were a hundred percent accurate, for the most part, the journalists did a superb job documenting this dramatic story. Ninety-nine percent of the dialogue used in the book came from the newspaper accounts the remaining one percent came from interviews.

Thanks to those at General Chemical Trona Mine (now Tata Chemicals) near Green River, Wyoming for their support when I first started research on the book; David Graham, the Safety Director and General Chemical's Mine Rescue Teams (the Black Team and Blue Team) for allowing me to tag along during their training and ask lots of questions. And thanks to my husband, Greg Mele, who was at that time, General Chemical's Safety Coordinator and Mine Rescue Trainer. The many mine rescue competitions across the country that I was able to attend with him when his teams were competing were very informative and helpful in understanding so much.

I would like to thank my friends and family who were a source of encouragement, who read through the manuscript or gave valuable feedback. They are my sister, Becky Hanna Timothy; my brother, Trent Hanna; my daughter-in-law, Rose Mele; my sons, Tyson, Rory, Levi and Damon; my daughter, Michon; and my dear friends, Marradee Alexander and Bea Overton. Also, a special thanks to Sam Hadlock, Graphic Designer, for the cover design.

I would also like to thank my very dear friend and my editor, Tamela Lewis (Santa Fe, New Mexico). She has been my best friend since junior high school in Artesia, New Mexico. We did everything together: walked to school, hung out, were sophomore cheerleaders, etc. I am so proud of her business accomplishments and her tenacity to obtain a Masters Degree from Harvard, graduating with a 4.0. It has been so much fun working with her on this book.

Last, but certainly not least, I would like to thank my dear husband, Greg, for his love and support throughout the years while working on this project. Greg's in—depth knowledge of mining, mine rescue and safety were invaluable, not only while writing, but in doing the initial edits after the manuscript was finished. During the last several years, when I went deep into that "writer's cave" where I could completely block out life and totally zone, Greg was there to pick up the slack. He has been amazing.

About the Author

Author, Kymberly Mele

Kymberly Mele is a wife, mother of six children, and grandmother of fourteen grandchildren. She was born a coal miner's daughter in Price, Utah (located in Carbon County, the coal mining area of the state). Her father, Donald Blake Hanna, is one of the survivors of the Cane Creek Mine disaster.

Kymberly attended three different high schools as her father moved around, as he transitioned from miner to federal mine inspector during those years in the mining industry (Artesia High School, Artesia, New Mexico; Carbon High School, Price Utah; and Earl Wooster High School, Reno Nevada, where she graduated in 1976). She attended Brigham Young University for a short time before marrying her husband, Greg Mele, who she has been married to him for forty-one years.

Kymberly is the president of her company, Mele Enterprises, and is a member of the Utah League of Writers. She has been a freelance writer, has done graphic arts work, produced and published newsletters for several companies and for International Society of Mine Safety Professionals. She has also written articles for Joseph A. Holmes Safety Association's The Bulletin (a prominent mining magazine). Mele has also been a public speaker for youth groups and was a speaker at the 1996 National Mine Rescue Competition (Metal and Nonmetal) sponsored by the Mine Safety and Health Administration (MSHA) in Las Vegas, as well as the Carbon County Mine Rescue Competition in Price, Utah that same year.

Kymberly has been associated with mining through her husband's career. Greg started work in the mining industry at the age of eighteen before they were married. Through the years, he advanced through the ranks while working in different mining positions and also did mine rescue work. He eventually rose to the corporate level in mining and, at one point during those years, he started work on the safety side of the industry and became a Certified Mine Safety Professional (CMSP). Greg currently works as the Safety Director for Bronco Utah Operations in Ferron, Utah—a new coal mine that recently opened. Just before moving back to Carbon County in early 2017, Greg worked as the Vice President of Environmental, Health, and Safety at BHI, Inc., in Vernal, Utah. BHI is a contracting company that does work for mining, oil, and gas, and a host of others industries, across the United States. Greg also has a safety consulting business, Mele Safety Services, where Kymberly and their son, Rory Mele, have active roles.

Endnotes

Part One
Chapter 1

1. Arturo F. Gonzales, Jr., "CAVE-IN! Drama Deep in the Earth," *Popular Science*, December 1963, 206.
2. Dom Antonelli, Bill McLaughlin and Vince Citro, "Throne and Fellin Safe, Rescuers Now Seek Bova," *Hazleton Standard-Speaker*, August 27, 1963, Early Edition.
3. UPI, "Trapped Pair Never Lost Good Spirits," *Deseret News*, August 27, 1963.
4. Ibid.
5. William Rachunis, Arthur A. Sinicrope, Harrison F. Wilscon, and James A. Moore. *Final Report of Collapse of Slope Pillar Accident and Rescue of Two of the Three Entombed Men, Oneida No. 2 Slope, Fellin Mining Company, Oneida, Schuylkill County, Pennsylvania, August 13, 1963*. Wilkes-Barre: U.S. Bureau of Mines, 1963, 2.
6. Dom Antonelli, Joe Maggio, Bill McLaughlin and Vince Citro, "Fellin and Throne Safe, Rescuers Now Seek Bova," *Hazleton Standard-Speaker*, August 27, 1963, Final Edition.
7. Rachunis et al., *Final Report of Fellin Mining Company*, 17.
8. "Fellin, Throne Believe Bova Is Alive; Drillers Expect to Reach Lou's Location Today," *Hazleton Standard-Speaker*, August 28, 1963, Early Edition.

9   Dom Antonelli, Bill McLaughlin and Vince Citro, "Throne, Fellin Rescued," *Hazleton Standard-Speaker*, August 27, 1963, Early Edition.
10 Antonelli et al., "Throne and Fellin Safe," August 27, 1963, Final Edition.
11 Gonzales, "CAVE-IN!" 206.
12 Rachunis et al., *Final Report of Fellin Mining Company*, 17.
13 Antonelli et al., "Throne, Fellin Rescued," August 27, 1963, Early Edition.
14 "Fellin, Throne Believe," August 28, 1963, Early Edition.
15 Gonzales, "CAVE-IN!" 44.
16 Antonelli et al., "Fellin and Throne Safe," August 27, 1963, Final Edition.
17 David Fellin, AP, "David Fellin's Story: 'We Could See Beautiful Marble Steps'," *Hazleton Standard-Speaker*, August 29, 1963, Early Edition.
18 Antonelli et al., "Throne, Fellin Rescued," August 27, 1963, Early Edition.
19 Ibid.
20 Fellin, AP, "David Fellin's Story," August 29, 1963, Early Edition.
21 Rachunis et al., *Final Report of Fellin Mining Company*, 18.
22 Fellin, AP, "David Fellin's Story," August 29, 1963, Early Edition.
23 UPI, "Trapped Pair Never," August 27, 1963.
24 Rachunis et al., *Final Report of Fellin Mining Company*, 18.
25 Antonelli et al., "Throne, Fellin Rescued," August 27, 1963, Early Edition.
26 Rachunis et al., *Final Report of Fellin Mining Company*, 1.
27 Gonzales, "CAVE-IN!" 44.
28 Ibid, 44. Sheppton-pop. 1,100; Oneida-pop. 500.
29 J. Ronnie Sando, *The Famous Sheppton Mine Rescue* (Baltimore: Publish America, 2006), 11.
30 Ibid, 12.
31 Rachunis et al., *Final Report of Fellin Mining Company*, 2.
32 James A. Goodman, *Two Weeks Under, the Sheppton Mine Disaster/Miracle* (Bloomburg: Coal Hole, 2003), 11.
33 Gonzales, "CAVE-IN!" 46.
34 Dom Antonelli, "Rescue Operations Halted at Sheppton Mine Disaster," *Hazleton Standard-Speaker*, August 14, 1963, Early Edition.
35 Ibid.

36   Gonzales, "CAVE-IN!" 45.
37   Ibid.
38   Rachunis et al., *Final Report of Fellin Mining Company*, 17. Gordon Smith was the top mining official.
39   Sando, *Famous Sheppton Mine Rescue*, 16.
40   Ed Conrad, "50 Years Later: A Look Back at the Sheppton Mine Disaster," *Hazleton Standard-Speaker*, August 13, 2013. (accessed on October 27, 2015), http://standardspeaker.com/news/mine-cave-in-50-years-ago-would-grab-world-s-attention-1.1535236
41   Rachunis et al., *Final Report of Fellin Mining Company*, 12.
42   Ibid, 13.
43   Gonzales, "CAVE-IN!" 46
44   Goodman, *Two Weeks Under*, 49.
45   Sando, *Famous Sheppton Mine Rescue*, 17. The drill was a big electric Bucyrus-Erie 50-R from the Sullivan Trail Coal Company of West Pittston, PA; owned by Lewis Pagnotti, Sr., and operated by his drill crews who worked on the rescue team, 14 and 18. This drill stood 11 stories high with its massive derrick in the air, 17.
46   Gonzales, "CAVE-IN!" 204
47   "Navy Plane Due Here Today with Radio Gear," *Hazleton Standard-Speaker*, August 21, 1963, Final Edition. Westfield flew from Washington D.C. to Sheppton on August 19, 1963, arriving at the mine site at 3:00 p.m.
48   "Fellin, Throne Believe," August 28, 1963, Early Edition.
49   Rachunis et al., *Final Report of Fellin Mining Company*, 18.
50   Charles Catherman, "Hank Throne Breaks Down in Tears at Press Conference," *Hazleton Standard-Speaker*, August 28, 1963, Early Edition.
51   Tom Zoellner, *Uranium: War, Energy, and the Rock That Shaped the World* (New York: Viking, 2009), 133.
52   Richard A. Firmage, *A History of Grand County, Utah Centennial County History Series* (Salt Lake City: Utah State Historical Society, 1996), 327.
53   Raye Ringholz, *Uranium Frenzy: Saga of the Nuclear West* (Logan: Utah State University Press, 2002).

54 "Charles Steen—Uranium King of San Juan," *San Juan Record,* May 6, 2009, (accessed February 28, 2016), http://www.sjrnews.com/view/full_story/6746859/article-Charles-Steen?instance=series_giants_sanjuan

55 Ronald L. Davis, *John Ford: Hollywood's Old Master* (Norman: University of Oklahoma Press, 1995), 234.

56 Scott Eyman, *Print the Legend: The Life and Times of John Ford* (New York: Simon & Schuster, 1999), 343.

57 Zoellner, *Uranium: War, Energy,* 133.

58 Bette L. Stanton, *""Where God Put the West," Movie Making in the Desert,"* (Moab, Utah: Four Corners Publications, 1994), 1.

59 Joseph McBride, *Searching for John Ford* (Jackson: University Press of Mississippi, 2011), 656.

60 Frank Jensen, "Moab Movie Town," *Salt Lake Tribune,* November 26, 1961, Sec. Z.

61 Stanton, *"Where God Put the West,"* 1.

62 Ibid.

63 Maxine Newell, "Four Hundred Moabites Take Roles in George Stevens Production Here," *Times-Independent,* May 23, 1963. J.G. Pinkerton and Herve Roy are other known potash employees who were extras. J.G. Pinkerton, Interview by author, Stamford, CT, January 28, 1995, also in photo in the article listed above. Herve Roy, Telephone interview by author, April 14, 2014. See also "Movies Filmed in the Moab Area," *discovermoab.com* (accessed September 3, 2015), http://www.discovermoab.com/movie.htm or "Movies Filmed in Moab," *moabadventurecenter.com* (accessed September 3, 2015), http://www.moabadventurecenter.com/areainfo/moab-movies/

64 Jeremy Agnew, *The Old West in Fact and Film: History Versus Hollywood* (Jefferson, North Carolina, and London: McFarland & Company, Inc., 2012), 91-92.

65 "Warner Brothers Ready Filming for Moab Area in October," *Times-Independent,* August 29, 1963. The stars were Spencer Tracy, James Stewart, Richard Widmark, Karl Malden and others.

66 Ibid.

67   LeRoy R. Hafen and Ann W. Hafen, *Old Spanish Trail, Santa Fe to Los Angeles* (Lincoln and London: University of Nebraska Press, 1993), 348-349. See also C. Gregory Crampton, "Utah's Spanish Trail," *Utah Historical Quarterly*, vol. 47, no. 4 (Fall 1979): 361-383. http://utah.ptfs.com/awweb/awarchive?type=file&item=34978 Orville C. Pratt's journal, dated September 16th 1848, he writes about crossing the Grand River (now called the Colorado River) and describes how it, "falls into a deep canion [sic] about 600 yards below the crossing." This location is upstream from "the Portal" where the river enters into the canyon. There may be several other locations from Courthouse Wash to "the Portal," where one of three islands may have been used, making the distance to cross shorter.

68   Jeffrey D. Nichols, "The Spanish Trail Cut a Roundabout Path through Utah," *History Blazer*, June 1995, historytogo.utah.gov (accessed May 4, 2014), http://historytogo.utah.gov/utah_chapters/trappers,_traders,_and_explorers/thespanishtrailcutapaththroughutah.html See also Crampton, "Utah's Spanish Trail," *Utah Historical Quarterly* (Fall 1979): 369. A steep wall of red rock 1,500 feet high flanks the valley on the southwest, but the opposite wall is much lower, permitting views of the laccolithic peaks of the La Sal Mountains towering over 12,000 feet on the southeastern skyline some fifteen miles distant. The level valley floor is about two miles wide; it lays in a northwesterly direction. See also Faun McConkie Tanner, *The Far Country: A Regional History of Moab and La Sal, Utah* (Salt Lake City: Olympus, 1976), 34. The Colorado River emerges from an eastern canyon of steep cliffs and curves around the top end of Moab Valley (also called Spanish Valley or Grand Valley) and disappears through "The Portal" as it flows in a southwesterly direction on its way towards the Grand Canyon.

69   Ibid.

70   Robert D. Mullins and Paul Swenson, "Injured Worker Thanks 'Lull'," *Deseret News*, August 28, 1963.

71   James Westfield, Lester D. Knill and Anthony C. Moschetti, *Final Report of Major Mine-Explosion Disaster, Cane Creek Mine, Potash Division, Texas Gulf Sulphur Company, Grand County, Utah (Mine Development under Contract with*

Harrison International, Incorporated), August 27, 1963, (Lakewood, CO: U.S. Bureau of Mines, 1963), 3.

72 Morris Worley, Interview by author, Carlsbad, NM, October 2, 2016.

73 CKA, Canadian Slang and English Words, (accessed September 9, 2015), http://www.canadaka.net/content/page/124-canadian-slang—english-words A spoken interjection to ascertain the comprehension, continued interest, agreement, etc., of the person or persons addressed ("That was a good game last night, eh?"). Also used instead of "huh?" or "what?" meaning "please repeat or say again."

74 "Drive toward Ore Body Shows Good Progress," *Times-Independent,* June 6, 1963.

75 1960s Flashback, "1963 Economy/Prices," (accessed August 16, 2012), http://www.1960sflashback.com/1963/economy.asp

76 Matt Rauhala, Interview by author, East Carbon, UT, August 15, 1995.

77 Ibid.

78 Charles Byrge, Interview by author, Price, Utah, November 23, 1994.

79 Robert W. Bernick, "Sulphur Firm Signs for Potash Work," *Salt Lake Tribune,* April 7, 1961, Sec. C.

Chapter 2

1 Wallace Earle Stegner, ed., W*ilderness at the Edge: A Citizen Proposal to Protect Utah's Canyons and Deserts* (Layton, Utah: Gibbs M. Smith, 1990), 97. Originally named the "Colorado Plateaus" by explorer John Wesley Powell, the "Plateau" is in fact a huge basin ringed by highlands and filled with plateaus. Sprawling across southeastern Utah, Northern Arizona, northwestern New Mexico, and western Colorado; the Colorado Plateau province covers a land area of 130,000 square miles.

2 Ibid, 274.

3 Ibid, 97-104.

4 Stephen Trimble, ed., *Blessed by Light, Visions of the Colorado Plateau* (Layton, UT; Gibbs M. Smith, 1986), Introduction.

5 Stegner, ed., *Wilderness at the Edge, 100.*

6   "Potash 'Find' Brewing Utah Boom, Multimillion Dollar Mine, Mill," *Salt Lake Tribune*, April 28, 1960.

7   Jan Onofrio, *Texas Biographical Dictionary*, 3rd ed. (New York: Somerset), 1996, 52. In 1947 Murchison founded the Delhi Oil Corporation, and after several years merged with the Taylor Refining Company, and the new Delhi-Taylor Oil Corporation developed into a multimillion-dollar wholly-integrated oil company. Murchison served as president and chairman of the board for the new company until 1964, when assets were sold to Tenneco.

8   "Milestones Mark TGS Development," *Times-Independent*, January 14, 1965.

9   Ibid.

10 "Texas-Gulf Plans Three Wells on Cane Creek Acreage," *Times-Independent*, December 26, 1957.

11 "Three Tests Drilling Ahead on Big Flat West of Moab," *Times-Independent*, May 8, 1958.

12 Sandy Perlic, "Seeing Red: Canyonlands, the Calm of the Canyonlands," *DesertUSA.com* (accessed January 26, 2016), http://www.desertusa.com/desert-utah/exploring-canyonlands.html Butch Cassidy began using the Roost in the 1880s to hide cattle that he rustled with Mike Cassidy. Legend has it that he became a full-time outlaw in 1884, adopting the name Butch Cassidy in honor of his mentor. Robbers' Roost was one of several hideouts along what became known as the Outlaw Trail.

13 Jeffrey D. Nichols, "Robbers' Roost in Utah's "Outback" was a Haven for Outlaws," The History Blazer, August 1995, *historytogo.utah.gov* (accessed January 27, 2016), http://historytogo.utah.gov/utah_chapters/pioneers_and_cowboys/robbersroostwasahavenforoutlaws.html Over the years the Robber's Roost refuge gained a reputation as being impregnable as stories about its defenses contributed to its legend. See also Sandy Perlic, "Seeing Red: Canyonlands, The Calm of the Canyonlands," *DesertUSA.com* (accessed January 26, 2016), http://www.desertusa.com/desert-utah/exploring-canyonlands.html As the *Denver News* reported on March 4, 1898. "This strip of country is rugged and broken and almost impregnable by a stranger, and abounds in caves, deep gorges, and strongholds

from which it is impossible to dislodge the outlaws who have trails unknown to any except themselves."

14   Charles Kelly, *The Outlaw Trail: A History of Butch Cassidy and His Wild Bunch* (Lincoln and London: University of Nebraska Press, 1996), 152.

15   "Robbers Roost, Outlaw Legend," *Climb-Utah.com* (accessed March 6, 2016), http://www.climb-utah.com/Roost/rrhistory.htm One of Cassidy and his gang's most spectacular robbery was in 1897, when they stole the $8,800 payroll from the Pleasant Valley Coal Company in Castle Gate, Utah, then hiding out in the impregnable canyons of the Robbers Roost. The Castle Gate robbery was the gang's one and only major holdup in Utah. On April 21st, 1897 the train from Salt Lake City entered Castle Gate coal mining camp carrying the payroll for the Pleasant Valley Coal Company. Men carrying the money were making their way through town towards the company office when they were robbed of the $8,800 they were carrying. Cassidy and the gang fled to Robbers Roost, cutting telegraph wires along the trail to prevent the news of the robbery from spreading to lawmen along their escape route.

16   Tanner, *The Far Country*, 297-298. John Shafer described it as, "only a rather bad stock trail."

17   "New Location in Lisbon Announced by Pure Oil," *Times-Independent*, June 22, 1960. See also "Three Tests Drilling," May 8, 1958.

18   "Murphy Corp. Adds to Big Flat Oil Play with New Discovery," *Times-Independent*, June 8, 1960.

19   "Three Tests Drilling," May 8, 1958.

20   "New Location in Lisbon," June 22, 1960.

21   "State Road Commission Meets in Moab, Reviews New Route," *Times-Independent*, May 25 1960, 1. Talks began May 20, 1960.

22   "Dead Horse Point Road Will Go Down River When Built," *Times-Independent*, October 20, 1960, 1. See also "Dead Horse Point State Park," *Discovermoab.com* (accessed August 18, 2013), http://www.discovermoab.com/stateparks.htm Dead Horse Point State Park was founded in 1959, and the new visitor center built in 1963. See also "Moab, Utah: Two National Parks - One Destination," *Discovermoab.com* (accessed August 18, 2013), http://www.discovermoab.com/index.htm

23 "Gulf Sulphur Completes Latest of Six Drill Holes," *Times-Independent,* July 20, 1960.
24 "Drilling Slows on Potash Land as Evaluation Continues," *Times-Independent,* August 17, 1960.
25 "Groups Join State in Urging Quick Withdrawal of Area Potash Lands," *Times-Independent,* August 11, 1960.
26 Ibid.
27 Ibid. Governor George D. Clyde, the State Land Board, the State Industrial Commission, the Salt Lake City and Moab Chambers of Commerce, the Grand County Commission, the city of Moab, the Utah Mining Assn., Utah Manufacturers Assn., Utah Manufacturers Assn., and U.S. Geological Survey favored the potash development.
28 "Senators Reply to Request on Potash Land Withdrawal," *Times-Independent,* August 18, 1960.
29 Washington Bureau, "Seaton Bans Oil, Gas Wells in Utah's Potash Fields," *Salt Lake Tribune,* August 31, 1960.
30 "Dead Horse Point Road Will Go Down River When Built," *Times-Independent,* October 20, 1960.
31 "Dead Horse Point Is State Park after Friday Ceremonies," *Times-Independent,* December 17, 1959.
32 "Dead Horse Point Awaits Visitors," *Times-Independent,* April 25, 1963.
33 "News Comes via Wire after Nov. 2 Meet," *Times-Independent,* November 3, 1960.
34 "Potash 'Find' Brewing," April 28, 1960.
35 "Business Cycle Expansions and Contractions," *Internet Archive Wayback Machine* (accessed October 31, 2015), https://web.archive.org/web/20080925210636/http://www.nber.org/cycles.html This recession lasted for 10 months, beginning in April 1960 and ending in February 1961.
36 "Grand County Location Probable, Says TGS," *Times-Independent,* November 17, 1960.
37 Sam Taylor, Interview by author, Moab, UT, August 17, 1995.
38 "Dr. Fogarty Is to Head Moab Project," *Times-Independent,* February 2, 1961.
39 "Texas Gulf Names General Manager, Superintendent of Potash Division," *Times-Independent,* January 24, 1963.

40 Elcous History, "U.S. History, 1950-1975," *Tripod.com* (accessed October 31, 2015), http://elcoushistory.tripod.com/economics1960.html
41 "Blast Marks Start on TGS Shaft at Cane Creek," *Times-Independent,* March 2, 1961.
42 "Plant Site Excavation Marks Progress at Cane Creek," *Times-Independent,* July 20, 1961.
43 "Contractors Set to Begin Work," *Times-Independent,* March 30, 1961.
44 "Potash Company Prepares for Closing of River Access Road," *Times-Independent,* April 6, 1961.
45 Ibid.
46 "Bulletin, Work Stops Again at TGS Site," *Times-Independent,* May 25, 1961.
47 "Difficult Road Bed," *Times-Independent,* June 15, 1961 (Caption).
48 "Excavation for Potash Mill Begins at Cane Creek Site," *Times-Independent,* June 29, 1961.
48 C. Graham and V. Evans, "The evolution of shaft sinking systems (Part 4), Shaft sinking from 1900 to 1940: start of the Modern Era, History of Mining," *CIM Magazine, Canadian Institute of Mining, Metallurgy and Petroleum,* February 2008 (accessed April 15, 2015), http://www.cim.org/en/Publications-and-Technical-Resources/Publications/CIM-Magazine/February-2008/history/history-of-mining.aspx
49 Ibid.
50 C. Graham and V. Evans, "The evolution of shaft sinking systems (Part 5), Shaft sinking from 1940 to 1970: The Golden Age," *CIM Magazine, Canadian Institute of Mining, Metallurgy and Petroleum,* March/April 2008 (accessed April 15, 2015), http://www.cim.org/en/Publications-and-Technical-Resources/Publications/CIM-Magazine/March-April-2008/history/history-of-mining.aspx
51 Graham, Shaft Sinking Systems (PART 4).
52 Bernick, "Sulphur Firm Signs," April 7, 1961, Sec. C.
53 Graham, Shaft Sinking Systems (PART 5).
54 Patricia Curtis Petty, "Construction and Philosophy," *Mines Magazine,* Vol. 70, No. 7, September 1980, 11, http://minesmagazine.com/wp-content/

archives/Mines_Mag.v70.n7.pdf Harrison International, Inc., a subsidiary of Patrick Harrison & Co., was part of the Harrison Group of companies.

55 "Shaft Contractor Begins Work, Will Complete Job in 17 Months," *Times-Independent,* June 29, 1961.
56 "Walkout Ends after 36-Hour Shut-Down," *Times-Independent,* May 18, 1961.
57 Ibid.
58 Herve Roy, Telephone interview by author, April 14, 2014.
59 Charles "C.C." Clark, Email correspondence with author, March 25, 2016.
60 "Shaft Contractor Begins," June 29, 1961.
61 "T.G.S. Mine-Mill Site Flurry of Activity," *Times-Independent,* October 5, 1961.
62 Patrick Harrison. 1952. Cage and Operating Mechanism for Shaft Shovels. U.S. Patent 2587844-A, Filed May 19, 1949, and issued March 4, 1952.
63 "Plant Site Excavation," July 20, 1961.
64 Firmage, *History of Grand County,* 338.
65 "Railroad Completion Seen in 200 Days," *Times-Independent,* October 5, 1961.
66 "Contractors Set to Begin," March 30, 1961.
67 Robert W. Bernick, "D&RG to Build 30-Mile Spur for Potash Mine in S. Utah," *Salt Lake Tribune,* July 16, 1961, Sec. C.
68 "Potash Rail Spur Was Mammoth Project," *Times-Independent,* July 18, 1963.
69 "Morrison-Knudsen to Build Rail Line," *Times-Independent,* July 27, 1961.
70 "Builder Harry Morrison, to Tame Rivers and Move Mountains, the Earth Mover," *TIME,* May 3, 1954, 86-93.
71 "Ceremonies Mark Rail," August 17, 1961.
72 Wikipedia contributors, "Morrison-Knudsen," *Wikipedia, The Free Encyclopedia* (accessed on November 2, 2014), https://en.wikipedia.org/wiki/Morrison-Knudsen One of the most significant milestones in the growth of Morrison-Knudsen Company was, construction of the Hoover (Boulder) Dam, contracted in 1931. The magnitude of the job led to the 1932 incorporation of Morrison-Knudsen Company, Inc. The project was massive, drawing on 5,000 workers. It called for 4.5 million yards of concrete (enough to pave a four-lane highway from Seattle to Miami, according to company sources)

and reached a height of 726 feet upon completion. The dam was completed in 1935, two years ahead of schedule. See also Funding Universe, "Morrison Knudsen Corporation History," *Fundinguniverse.com* (accessed October 12, 2015), http://www.fundinguniverse.com/company-histories/morrison-knudsen-corporation-history/ See Morrison Knudsen Corporation "About MK," (accessed September 24, 2014), http://morrison-knudsen.com/sample-page/ Documentary video of the History of Morrison Knudsen at the bottom of the page.

73 "Ceremonies Mark Rail Start," *Times-Independent,* August 17, 1961.

74 "New Access Road Joined near Potash Properties," *Times-Independent,* September 7, 1961. This dirt road descends from the mesa down 2,200-feet in just over 7 miles to the river canyon below. The upper end of this route, Pucker Pass, apply named, is a very narrow section as the road snakes its way down a 19-percent grade with deep ravines. See also "T.G.S. Mine-Mill Site Flurry of Activity," *Times-Independent,* October 5, 1961.

75 "TGS Projects Progress on Schedule; Employment Continues to Rise," *Times-Independent,* June 7, 1962.

76 "Railroad Completion Seen," October 5, 1961. Material removed during the tunnel construction was used to establish grade for a 3,500 foot passing track.

77 Ibid.

78 "Contractor Finishes Big Rail Cut," *Times-Independent,* July 26, 1962.

79 Ibid.

80 "Crews Break through on Rail Spur Tunnel Friday," *Times-Independent,* June 28, 1962.

81 "Contractor Finishes Big," July 26, 1962.

82 "Morrison-Knudsen to Build," July 27, 1961.

83 "Potash Rail Spur," July 18, 1963.

84 "Strike Ends at Potash Plant," *Times-Independent,* May 31, 1962.

85 Ibid.

86 Ibid.

87   Ibid. See also "TGS Projects Progress on Schedule; Employment Continues to Rise," *Times-Independent,* June 7, 1962.
88   "TGS Projects Progress," June 7, 1962.
89   "Shaft Water No Problem, Harrison Manager States," *Times-Independent,* December 14, 1961.
90   "Harrison Moving Ahead on Potash Shaft near Moab," *Times-Independent,* January 11, 1962.
91   "Water Slows Potash Shaft Progress as Other Contracts Forge Ahead," *Times-Independent,* February 1, 1962.
92   Ed Ziolkowski, Telephone interview by author, October 20, 2016.
93   Paul McKinney, Telephone conversation with author, January 12, 2015.
94   "TGS Projects Progress," June 7, 1962.
95   "Work Forges Ahead on Potash Project," *Times-Independent,* July 19, 1962.
96   "Harrison Moving Ahead," January 11, 1962.
97   Donald Blake Hanna, Interview by author, Vernal, UT, April 24, 2015.
98   Grant V. Messerly, "Rescue Workers Sum Up: It's Hell," *Salt Lake Tribune,* August 29, 1963.
99   Westfield, Knill and Moschetti, *Final Report of Cane Creek* Mine, 6.
100 Herve Roy, Telephone interview by author, April 14, 2014.
101 "Construction Ends at Potash Site as Contractor Completes Work," *Times-Independent,* January 24, 1963.
102 Don C. Woodward, "Production Nears on Utah Potash-Target Date Set for July," *Deseret News,* February 25, 1963, Sec. B, (Photo Caption).
103 "Drive toward Ore," June 6, 1963.
104 "Potash Operation in Final Phase, TGS President Tells Analysts," *Times-Independent,* July 4, 1963.
105 Don Robinson, "Oil Activity Highlights Area News This Week, Potash," *Times-Independent,* July 4, 1963.
106 Edward Abbey and David Petersen, *Postcards from Ed: Dispatches and Salvos from an American Iconoclast* (Minneapolis: Milkweed Press, 2006), 175.
107 Stegner, ed., *Wilderness at the Edge,* 98.

108 UPI, "Mine Had Been Scheduled for Operation Soon," *Daily Herald*, August 28, 1963.
109 "T.G.S. Mine-Mill Site," October 5, 1961.
110 John Wesley Powell, "Canyons of the Colorado" (1895), The Project Gutenberg EBook, *gutenberg.org* (accessed August 4, 2016), http://www.gutenberg.org/files/8082/8082-h/8082-h.htm

Chapter 3

1 "Mining Lights and Hats-Electric Lamps," *The National Museum of American History* (accessed April 27, 2015), http://americanhistory.si.edu/collections/object-groups/mining-lights-and-hats?ogmt_page=miners-electric-lamps
2 Morris Worley, Interview by author, Carlsbad, NM, October 2, 2016. MSA Intercom System.
3 Herve Roy, Telephone interview by author, April 14, 2014.
4 Helene Roy McGruthers, Email correspondence with author, April 6, 2015.
5 Westfield, Knill and Moschetti, *Final Report of Cane Creek Mine*, 2.
6 "Shaft Contractor Begins," June 29, 1961.
7 Paul McKinney, Interview by Pat McKinney, Armargosa Valley, NV, July 21, 1996.
8 Herve Roy, Telephone interview by author, April 14, 2014.
9 MCG Marketplace, "1963 Chevrolet Impala," (accessed April 27, 2015), http://myclassicgarage.com/marketplace/knowledge_base/1963-chevrolet-impala
10 Passageways are not referred to as tunnels in mining. They are typically called "drifts" in metal/nonmetal mines and "entries" in coal mines.
11 Donald Blake Hanna, Interview by author, Price, UT, November 24, 1994.
12 Matt Rauhala, Interview by author, East Carbon, UT, August 15, 1995.
13 Paul McKinney, Interview by Pat McKinney, Armargosa Valley, NV, July 21, 1996.
14 Donald Blake Hanna, Interview by author, Price, UT, November 24, 1994.
15 Paul McKinney, Interview by Pat McKinney, Armargosa Valley, NV, July 21, 1996.
16 Donald Blake Hanna, Interview by author, Price, UT, November 24, 1994.

17 Paul McKinney, Interview by Pat McKinney, Armargosa Valley, NV, July 21, 1996.
18 Paul McKinney, Telephone interview by author, June 16, 2015.
19 Westfield, Knill and Moschetti, *Final Report of Cane Creek Mine*, 3.
20 Paul McKinney, Interview by Pat McKinney, Armargosa Valley, NV, July 21, 1996.
21 Paul McKinney, Interview by Pat McKinney, Armargosa Valley, NV, July 21, 1996.
22 Harrison International, "Harrison at Esterhazy, Saskatchewan, Canada-IMC Potash Mine," *HarrisonInternational.blogspot.com* (accessed August 15, 2013), http://harrisoninternational.blogspot.com/2015/05/esterhazy-sask-canada-imc-potash-mine.html
23 Westfield, Knill and Moschetti, *Final Report of Cane Creek Mine*, Appendix E. See also Matt Rauhala, Interview by author, East Carbon, UT, August 15, 1995.
24 Matt Rauhala, Interview by author, East Carbon, UT, August 15, 1995.
25 Ned Johnson, Telephone interview by author, February 23, 2015.
26 Ibid.
27 Ibid.
28 Matt Rauhala, Interview by author, East Carbon, UT, August 15, 1995.
29 Robert Mullins and Paul Swenson, "Celebration Planned, but Fate Intercedes," *Deseret News*, August 29, 1963.
30 Dianne Johnson Zacherson, Telephone interview by author, July 12, 2016.
31 Mullins and Swenson, "Celebration Planned, but," August 29, 1963.
32 Westfield, Knill and Moschetti, *Final Report of Cane Creek Mine*, 3.
33 Rudolph John Bodmer, et, Bureau of Industrial Education, Inc., *The Book of Wonders and the Wonders Produced by Man* (Washington D.C.: Presbrey Syndicate, Inc., 1918), 263.
34 Heading Out, "Tech Talk: Manually Mining Coal Underground," *The Oil Drum*, May 9, 2010 (accessed May 29, 2015), http://www.theoildrum.com/node/6416
35 Westfield, Knill and Moschetti, *Final Report of Cane Creek Mine*, 16.
36 Ibid, 16 and 11.

37 Ibid, 16.
38 Grant V. Messerly, "Saved Miners Tell Ordeal of Survival," *Salt Lake Tribune*, August 31, 1963.
39 Maxine Newell, "Moab Miner Relates Ordeal Trapped under Ground," *Times-Independent*, September 5, 1963.
40 Ibid, 12.
41 Grant Eslick, AP, "Safe; Sure, I'll go Back, Says One," *Ogden Standard-Examiner*, August 30, 1963.
42 Westfield, Knill and Moschetti, *Final Report of Cane Creek Mine*, 16.
43 Ibid, 16. See also Appendix H.
44 "Missing and Rescued Involve Many Friends and Relatives in Moab Area," *Times-Independent*, August 29, 1963.
45 Morris T. Worley, P.E., "The Cane Creek Mine Disaster: Personal Observations," *Mining History Journal 16* (2009), 6.
46 Paul McKinney, Interview by Pat McKinney, Armargosa Valley, NV, July 21, 1996.
47 Charles Byrge, Interview by author, Price, UT, November 23, 1994.
48 Ibid.
49 Donald Blake Hanna, Interview by author, Price, UT, November 24, 1994.
50 Charles Byrge, Interview by author, Price, UT, November 23, 1994.
51 Outby - A mining term relative to position, meaning farther from the Face, opposite to inby. It is loosely used at times by miners to signify the surface.
52 Ibid.
53 Ibid.
54 Ibid.
55 Westfield, Knill and Moschetti, *Final Report of Cane Creek Mine*, 8.
56 Charles Byrge, Interview by author, Price, UT, November 23, 1994.
57 Ibid.
58 Westfield, Knill and Moschetti, *Final Report of Cane Creek Mine*, 15.
59 Mullins and Swenson, "Celebration Planned, but," August 29, 1963.
60 Ibid, Appendix D.
61 Westfield, Knill and Moschetti, *Final Report of Cane Creek Mine*, Appendix D.
62 Ibid, 16.

63 Donald Blake Hanna, Telephone conversation with author, July 12, 2014.
64 Westfield, Knill and Moschetti, *Final Report of Cane Creek Mine*, 16. Also called a 'shooting battery' or 'blasting ram.'
65 Morris Worley, interview by author, Carlsbad, NM, October 2, 2016.
66 Morris, "The Cane Creek Mine Disaster," 5.
67 Ed Ziolkowski, Telephone interview by author, October 20, 2016.
68 Morris, "The Cane Creek Mine Disaster," 5.
69 Ed Ziolkowski, Telephone interview by author, October 20, 2016.
70 Morris, "The Cane Creek Mine Disaster," 5.
71 Morris Worley, interview by author, Carlsbad, NM, October 2, 2016.
72 Westfield, Knill and Moschetti, *Final Report of Cane Creek Mine*, 20.
73 Paul McKinney, Interview by Pat McKinney, Armargosa Valley, NV, July 21, 1996.
74 Westfield, Knill and Moschetti, *Final Report of Cane Creek Mine*, 16.
75 Donald Blake Hanna, Interview by author, Price, UT, November 24, 1994.
76 Mullins and Swenson, "Injured Worker Thanks," August 28, 1963.
77 Matt Rauhala, Interview by author, East Carbon, UT, August 15, 1995.
78 Mullins and Swenson, "Injured Worker Thanks," August 28, 1963.
79 Dianne Johnson Zacherson, Telephone interview by author, July 12, 2016.
80 Reid G. Miller, AP, "Smiling Survivors Okay after Ordeal in Mine," *Ogden Standard-Examiner*, August 30, 1963. Also see Morris Worley, Interview by author, Carlsbad, NM, October 2, 2016.
81 Mullins and Swenson, "Injured Worker Thanks," August 28, 1963.
82 Morris, "The Cane Creek Mine Disaster," 5.
83 Matt Rauhala, Interview by author, East Carbon, UT, August 15, 1995.
84 Ibid.
85 Morris, "The Cane Creek Mine Disaster," 5.
86 Ibid.
87 Westfield, Knill and Moschetti, *Final Report of Cane Creek Mine*, 1.

Chapter 4

1 "Survivors Relate Ordeal of Blast," *Salt Lake Tribune*, August 29, 1963.
2 Donald Blake Hanna, Interview by author, Price, UT, November 24, 1994.

3   Paul McKinney, Interview by Pat McKinney, Armargosa Valley, NV, July 21, 1996.
4   Newell, "Moab Miner Relates," September 5, 1963.
5   Charles "C.C." Clark, Interview by author, Moab, UT, August 18, 1995.
6   Paul McKinney, Interview by Pat McKinney, Armargosa Valley, NV, July 21, 1996.
7   Charles "C.C." Clark, Interview by author, Moab, UT, August 18, 1995.
8   Newell, "Moab Miner Relates," September 5, 1963.
9   Charles "C.C." Clark, Interview by author, Moab, UT, August 18, 1995.
10 Ibid.
11 Charles Byrge, Interview by author, Price, UT, November 23, 1994.
12 Ibid.
13 Ibid.
14 Morris, "The Cane Creek Mine Disaster," 5.
15 Matt Rauhala, UPI, "Says Survivor: 'Blast Knocked Me through the Wall'," *Ogden Standard-Examiner*, August 28, 1963.
16 Morris, "The Cane Creek Mine Disaster," 5.
17 Mullins and Swenson, "Injured Worker Thanks," August 28, 1963.
18 Matt Rauhala, Interview by author, East Carbon, UT, August 15, 1995.
19 Rauhala, UPI, "Says Survivor: 'Blast Knocked,'" August 28, 1963.
20 Matt Rauhala, Interview by author, East Carbon, UT, August 15, 1995.
21 Ibid.
22 Morris, "The Cane Creek Mine Disaster," 5.
23 Ed Ziolkowski, Telephone interview by author, October, 19, 1995.
24 Ed Ziolkowski, Telephone interview by author, October 20, 2016.
25 Morris, "The Cane Creek Mine Disaster," 5.
26 Matt Rauhala, Interview by author, East Carbon, UT, August 15, 1995.
27 Mullins and Swenson, "Injured Worker Thanks," August 28, 1963.
28 Rauhala, UPI, "Says Survivor: 'Blast Knocked,'" August 28, 1963.
29 Dianne Johnson Zacherson, Telephone interview by author, July 12, 2016.
30 Morris, "The Cane Creek Mine Disaster," 5.
31 Westfield, Knill and Moschetti, *Final Report of Cane Creek Mine*, 17.

32 Robert June, AP, "'I Heard This Man Screaming...'" *Daily Sentinel*, August 30, 1963.
33 Donald Blake Hanna, Interview by author, Price, UT, November 24, 1994.
34 Paul McKinney, Interview by Pat McKinney, Armargosa Valley, NV, July 21, 1996.
35 Ibid.
36 Ibid.
37 Donald Blake Hanna, Interview by author, Price, UT, November 24, 1994.
38 Ibid.
39 Westfield, Knill and Moschetti, *Final Report of Cane Creek Mine*, Appendix H. No. 3 Crosscut.
40 Charles "C.C." Clark, Interview by author, Moab, UT, August 18, 1995.
41 Donald Blake Hanna, Interview by author, Price, UT, November 24, 1994.
42 Charles "C.C." Clark, Interview by author, Moab, UT, August 18, 1995.
43 Paul McKinney, Interview by Pat McKinney, Armargosa Valley, NV, July 21, 1996.
44 Westfield, Knill and Moschetti, *Final Report of Cane Creek Mine*, 17.
45 Paul McKinney, Interview by Pat McKinney, Armargosa Valley, NV, July 21, 1996.
46 Ibid.
47 Ibid.
48 Charles "C.C." Clark, Interview by author, Moab, UT, August 18, 1995.
49 Westfield, Knill and Moschetti, *Final Report of Cane Creek Mine*, 17.
50 Newell, "Moab Miner Relates," September 5, 1963.
51 Ibid.
52 "Berserk Worker Saved Despite Self," *Deseret News*, May 10, 1945.

Chapter 5

1 Charles "C.C." Clark, Interview by author, Moab, UT, August 18, 1995.
2 Westfield, Knill and Moschetti, *Final Report of Cane Creek Mine*, 17.
3 Ibid, 17. Also called flexible vent tubing.
4 Charles "C.C." Clark, Interview by author, Moab, UT, August 18, 1995.

5   Westfield, Knill and Moschetti, *Final Report of Cane Creek Mine*, 18.
6   Donald Blake Hanna, Interview by author, Price, UT, November 24, 1994.
7   Westfield, Knill and Moschetti, *Final Report of Cane Creek Mine*, 18.
8   Donald Blake Hanna, Interview by author, Price, UT, November 24, 1994.
9   Ibid.
10 Charles "C.C." Clark, Interview by author, Moab, UT, August 18, 1995.
11 Paul McKinney, Interview by Pat McKinney, Armargosa Valley, NV, July 21, 1996. Blackie reported it took about an hour and a half to build the barricades. Paul calculated from the time of the explosion and the last curtain was hung. 'Blackie most likely included the time the men worked on the curtains to make them more air tight after they were hung.
12 Eslick, AP, "Safe; Sure, I'll," August 30, 1963.
13 Morris, "The Cane Creek Mine Disaster," 5.
14 Matt Rauhala, Interview by author, East Carbon, UT, August 15, 1995.
15 Ibid.
16 Ibid.
17 Ibid.
18 Morris, "The Cane Creek Mine Disaster," 6.
19 Norman Harrison was the brother of Paddy Harrison.
20 Morris, "The Cane Creek Mine Disaster," 6.
21 Ibid. See also Westfield, Knill and Moschetti, *Final Report of Cane Creek Mine*, 13. Texas Gulf had a mine rescue station set up for when they would officially take over the mine and begin mining the potash ore. At that time they would have the manpower to staff several mine rescue teams but for now the equipment they had on hand included: 6 McCaa self-contained 2-hour breathing apparatus and spare parts; Electrically driven oxygen pump; 6 Chemox self-generating oxygen breathing apparatus; One permissible mine rescue communication system; 1,000 foot life line; 6 permissible flame safety lamps; 48 self-rescuers and 10 first-aid kits.
22 Morris Worley, interview by author, Carlsbad, NM, October 2, 2016.
23 *Handbook of Training in Mine Rescue and Recovery Operations* (Inspection Branch of the Ontario Department of Mines, 1964), Acknowledgement.
24 Donald Blake Hanna, Interview by author, Price, UT, November 24, 1994.

25 Ibid.
26 Westfield, Knill and Moschetti, *Final Report of Cane Creek Mine*, 18.
27 Donald Blake Hanna, Interview by author, Price, UT, November 24, 1994.
28 Ibid.
29 Ibid.

Chapter 6

1   Morris, "The Cane Creek Mine Disaster," 6.
2   Newton-le-Willows-History, "Parkside Part 2- Newton-le-Willows," *YouTube.com* (accessed January 11, 2009), https://www.youtube.com/watch?v=X0nEWdFnqbQ&index=2&list=PLc2KSZYzGd-GzFzVK_AQ6CBnS94XuLroO For an example of crossheads and guide ropes, see video at 2:20 minutes.
3   Morris Worley, interview by author, Carlsbad, NM, October 2, 2016.
4   Westfield, Knill and Moschetti, *Final Report of Cane Creek Mine*, 21.
5   Morris, "The Cane Creek Mine Disaster," 6.
6   Robert W. Bernick, "'Petroleum Gas Blast Cause,' Famous S.L. Geologist Says; Tragedy Despite Utmost Precaution," *Salt Lake Tribune*, August 29, 1963.
7   Westfield, Knill and Moschetti, *Final Report of Cane Creek Mine*, 21.
8   Morris, "The Cane Creek Mine Disaster," 6.
9   Ibid.
10 Matt Rauhala, Interview by author, East Carbon, UT, August 15, 1995.
11 Mullins and Swenson, "Injured Worker Thanks," August 28, 1963.
12 Matt Rauhala, Interview by author, East Carbon, UT, August 15, 1995.
13 Sheila Rauhala Shumway, Telephone interview by author, June 24, 2016.
14 Ibid.
15 Ibid.
16 Sheila Rauhala Shumway, Telephone interview by author, June 24, 2016.
17 Westfield, Knill and Moschetti, *Final Report of Cane Creek Mine*, 18.
18 Charles Byrge, Interview by author, Price, UT, November 23, 1994.
19 Eslick, AP, "Safe; Sure, I'll," August 30, 1963.
20 Westfield, Knill and Moschetti, *Final Report of Cane Creek Mine*, 18.

21 Paul McKinney, Interview by Pat McKinney, Armargosa Valley, NV, July 21, 1996.
22 Charles Byrge, Interview by author, Price, UT, November 23, 1994. Byrge was one of the men June had drawn a cartoon on his hard hat.
23 Newell, "Moab Miner Relates," September 5, 1963.
24 AP, "What's Life Like in Trap under Ground 2 Days? Survivors Tell Reaction," *Salt Lake Tribune*, August 30, 1963.
25 Paul McKinney, Interview by Pat McKinney, Armargosa Valley, NV, July 21, 1996.
26 Charles "C.C." Clark, Interview by author, Moab, UT, August 18, 1995.
27 "It Was Smoky Dark, Last Survivors Say—Grateful Five," *Deseret News*, August 30, 1963.
28 Rex A. Lucas, *Men in Crisis, a Study of a Mine Disaster* (New York and London: Basic Books, 1966), 6-7.
29 Ibid, 11.
30 Paul McKinney, Interview by Pat McKinney, Armargosa Valley, NV, July 21, 1996.
31 Some newspaper accounts have Yugoslavia as Sviscsu's native country. Other accounts and his death certificate had Czechoslovakia.
32 Charles Byrge, Interview by author, Price, UT, November 23, 1994.
33 Ibid.
34 "It Was Smoky Dark," August 30, 1963.
35 James Bapis, UPI, "Moab Tragedy Toll: 18 Dead; 7 Safe, Probe Ordered Of Mine Blast," *Daily Herald*, August 30, 1963.
36 Grant V. Messerly, "Saved Miners Relive Anxiety, After Two Days in Tomb," *Salt Lake Tribune*, August 31, 1963.
37 Morris, "The Cane Creek Mine Disaster," 6.
38 Morris Worley, interview by author, Carlsbad, NM, October 2, 2016.
39 Don Robinson, "Night at Potash Filled with Tension," *Times-Independent*, August 29, 1963.
40 J.G. Pinkerton, Telephone interview by author, Stamford, CT, January 28, 1995.
41 Ibid.

42   Ibid.
43   Ibid.
44   "Now to Find the Cause," *Salt Lake Tribune,* August 31, 1963.
45   "Utah Mining Bears Scars of Disasters," *Ogden Standard Examiner,* December 18, 1963, Sec. C. The Sunnyside mine explosion occurred two days before the end of World War II in Europe. Ignition of "black damp," a mixture of coal dust that needed only a spark to set it off was the cause of the explosion. The blast occurred 45 minutes before the end of the shift, killing 23 men and injuring seven others. At the time of the explosion, the Sunnyside No. 1 mine was owned by Utah Fuel Company, who later sold its interest to Kaiser Steel Corporation in 1949.
46   Don Reed, UPI, "Scofield Ranks as Utah's Worst Mine Disaster," *Daily Herald,* August 28, 1963.
47   Grant Messerly and Jim G. Baldwin, "Tragic Scene: West of Moab," *Salt Lake Tribune,* August 28, 1963.
48   Westfield, Knill and Moschetti, *Final Report of Cane Creek Mine,* 14.
49   Dom Antonelli and Jerry Gallagher, "Food Sent through Pipe; Plan Drilling Rescue Hole," *Hazleton Standard-Speaker,* August 19, 1963, Final Edition.
50   United States Department of Labor, "The History of Mine Rescue, A Journey Through Time..." *Mine Safety and Health Administration-MSHA* (accessed December 12, 2013), http://www.msha.gov/TRAINING/LIBRARY/historyofminerescue/page2.asp
51   ""The History of Mine Rescue," A Journey through Time, Deadliest Decade in U.S. Underground Coal Mines," *Mine Safety and Health Administration - MSHA* (accessed January 12, 2015), http://arlweb.msha.gov/training/library/historyofminerescue/page2.asp
52   Lucas, *Men in Crisis,* 13.
53   Ibid, 35.
54   Ibid, 40.
55   E.R. Maize and J.V. Berry, "A Plan for Training Mine Officials in Rescue Organization and Disaster Prevention," *United States Bureau of Mines Information Circular (IC) No. 7353,* June 1946, http://babel.hathitrust.org/cgi/pt?id=mdp.39015074127930;view=1up;seq=1

56   Westfield, Knill and Moschetti, *Final Report of Cane Creek Mine*, 21.

57   Bernick, "'Petroleum Gas Blast," August 29, 1963. Rescue teams from Standard Metals Company were under the direction of W.R. 'Bill' McCormick, Standard president at Moab.

58   Matt Rauhala, Interview by author, East Carbon, UT, August 15, 1995.

59   Messerly and Baldwin, "Tragic Scene: West," August 28, 1963.

60   Matt Rauhala, Interview by author, East Carbon, UT, August 15, 1995.

61   Ibid.

62   Ibid.

63   Messerly and Baldwin, "Tragic Scene: West," August 28, 1963.

64   AP, "Gas Dims Hopes for 25 Entombed by Mine Explosion-Deep Utah Potash Tunnels Blocked by Violent Blast," *Lincoln Evening Journal and Nebraska State Journal*, August 28, 1963.

65   "Medical Aid Stands by for Miners," *Deseret News*, August 28, 1963.

66   AP, "Gas Dims Hopes," August 28, 1963.

67   "Medical Aid Stands," August 28, 1963.

Chapter 7

1   "Disaster Strikes, Reporters Jump," *Deseret News*, August 28, 1963.

2   Joe Bauman, "Dogged Pursuit of Story Paid Off, News Reporter Won the Pulitzer 44 Years Ago," *Deseret News (SLC, UT)*, July 4, 2006 (accessed April 26, 2016), http://www.deseretnews.com/article/640192066/Dogged-pursuit-of-story-paid-off.html?pg=all

3   "Disaster Strikes, Reporters Jump," August 28, 1963.

4   Ibid. DeMar Teuscher, staff writer, and Ray G. Jones, photographer flew to the area by chartered plane. Reed Madsen, news Bureau Chief from Richfield, also flew to Moab to set up the News' mobile telephoto transmitter. Rewrite men were Joseph Lundstrom and Paul Swenson.

5   Ibid.

6   Heinz Dietrich Fischer and Erika J. Fischer, *Complete Biographical Encyclopedia of Pulitzer Prize Winners 1917-2000* (Germany: K.G. Saur Munchen, 2002), 173.

7   Ibid.

8   Joe Bauman, "Dogged Pursuit of Story Paid Off, News Reporter Won the Pulitzer 44 Years Ago," *Deseret News (SLC, UT)*, July 4, 2006 (accessed April 26, 2016), http://www.deseretnews.com/article/640192066/Dogged-pursuit-of-story-paid-off.html?pg=all

9   Ibid.

10   "Tragedy—Talented Team Moves in," *Salt Lake Tribune*, August 29, 1963.

11   Ibid. The other reporters were Jim G. Baldwin, Robert H. Woody and the staff artist was Dick Miller.

12   Westfield, Knill and Moschetti, *Final Report of Cane Creek Mine*, 21.

13   "Blast Rocks Potash; Hopes Rise for Men," *Times-Independent*, August 29, 1963.

14   Westfield, Knill and Moschetti, *Final Report of Cane Creek Mine*, 21.

15   "Blast Rocks Potash," August 29, 1963.

16   Bernick, "'Petroleum Gas Blast," August 29, 1963.

17   Paul McKinney, Interview by Pat McKinney, Armargosa Valley, NV, July 21, 1996.

18   Charles Byrge, Interview by author, Price, UT, November 23, 1994.

19   Paul McKinney, Interview by Pat McKinney, Armargosa Valley, NV, July 21, 1996.

20   Westfield, Knill and Moschetti, *Final Report of Cane Creek Mine*, 6.

Chapter 8

1   Messerly and Baldwin, "Tragic Scene: West," August 28, 1963.

2   Morris, "The Cane Creek Mine Disaster," 6.

3   Messerly and Baldwin, "Tragic Scene: West," August 28, 1963.

4   Robert Mullins, Steve Hale and Joseph Lundstrom, "Lack of Air Slows Mine Rescue Work," *Deseret News*, August 29, 1963.

5   Robinson, "Night at Potash Filled," August 29, 1963.

6   Ibid.

7   "Sunrise Sunset Calendar," http://www.sunrisesunset.com/calendar.asp Moab, Utah, August 1963; Sunset: about 7:59 p.m.; dark about half an hour later. 8:29 p.m.

8   Robinson, "Night at Potash Filled," August 29, 1963.
9   Ibid.
10 Ibid.
11 "Utah Publishers Enjoy Convention in Moab during Last Week-end," *Times-Independent*, August 29, 1963.
12 Bill Eslick, Telephone interview by author, April 3, 2015.
13 Ibid.
14 Opal Davidson, Interview by author, Green River, WY, June 9, 1996.
15 AP, "Ill-Fated Shift Change Put One Miner in Shaft," *Ogden Standard-Examiner*, August 28, 1963.
16 "Fate Traps Father in Mine Disaster," *Daily Sentinel*, August 28, 1963.
17 AP, "Report from Miner's Wife—'Yes, He's Down There'," *Salt Lake Tribune*, August 28, 1963.
18 Eudeene Hollinger, Interview by author, Moab, UT, August 17, 1995.
19 "Blast Traps Utah Miners," *Rocket-Miner*, August 28, 1963.
20 Messerly and Baldwin, "Tragic Scene: West," August 28, 1963.
21 AP, "Explosion in Utah Potash Mine Traps 16 Construction Workers," *Hazleton Standard-Speaker*, August 28, 1963.
22 Louis Villegos, Telephone interview by author, August 23, 2010.
23 Robinson, "Night at Potash Filled," August 29, 1963.
24 Westfield, Knill and Moschetti, *Final Report of Cane Creek Mine*, 21.
25 Robinson, "Night at Potash Filled," August 29, 1963.
26 "Blast Rocks Potash," August 29, 1963.
27 Westfield, Knill and Moschetti, *Final Report of Cane Creek Mine*, 21.
28 Reed, UPI, "Scofield Ranks as Utah's," August 28, 1963.
29 Robinson, "Night at Potash Filled," August 29, 1963.
30 George Ferguson, Interview by author. East Carbon, UT, August 15. 1995.
31 Louis Villegos, Telephone interview by author, January 24, 2009.
32 Lucas, *Men in Crisis*, 21.
33 Ibid, 22.
34 Ibid, 20.
35 Ibid, 19.
36 'Johnny Smoke' Palacios, Telephone interview by author, May 6, 2015.

37 Ibid.
38 Donna Caudill, "The King of Longwall," *American Longwall*, May 2007.
39 "Death: John Peperakis (Obituary)," *Deseret News*, January 24, 1993, (Accessed November 1, 2015), http://www.deseretnews.com/article/271238/DEATH—JOHN-PEPERAKIS.html?pg=all
40 Art Sanda, "Dan Baker: Cattle Ranching Can't Keep Him out of the Coal Mines," *Coal People Magazine*, May 2009, 22, http://coalpeople.com/old_coal-people/2009_May_Issue/files/cpm_may09.pdf
41 "Death: John Peperakis (Obituary)," *DN*, January 24, 1993.
42 Sanda, "Dan Baker: Cattle Ranching," May 2009.
43 Charles "C.C." Clark, Interview by author, Moab, UT, August 18, 1995.
44 Ibid.
45 Newell, "Moab Miner Relates," September 5, 1963.
46 Paul McKinney, Interview by Pat McKinney, Armargosa Valley, NV, July 21, 1996.
47 Newell, "Moab Miner Relates," September 5, 1963.
48 Paul McKinney, Interview by Pat McKinney, Armargosa Valley, NV, July 21, 1996.
49 UPI "Waited, Drank Water, Sweated, Survivors Say," *Ogden Standard-Examiner*, August 30, 1963.
50 George Ferguson, Interview by author, East Carbon, UT, August 15, 1995.
51 "Blast Rocks Potash," August 29, 1963.
52 George Ferguson, Interview by author, East Carbon, UT, August 15, 1995.
53 Ibid.
54 Westfield, Knill and Moschetti, *Final Report of Cane Creek Mine*, 21.
55 Ibid, 21.
56 Messerly and Sorensen, "2 Saved, 5 Believed," August 29, 1963.
57 Mullins, et al., "Lack of Air Slows," August 29, 1963.
58 'Johnny Smoke' Palacios, Telephone interview by author, May 6, 2015.
59 George Ferguson, Interview by author, East Carbon, UT, August 15, 1995.
60 Ibid.
61 Westfield, Knill and Moschetti, *Final Report of Cane Creek Mine*, 21.
62 'Johnny Smoke' Palacios, Telephone interview by author, May 6, 2015.

63 Grant V. Messerly and George A. Sorensen, "Still Puzzle: Fate of 10," *Salt Lake Tribune,* August 28, 1963.

64 George Ferguson, Interview by author, East Carbon, UT, August 15, 1995.

Part Two
Chapter 9

1 Donald Blake Hanna, Interview by author, Price, UT, November 24, 1994.
2 Westfield, Knill and Moschetti, *Final Report of Cane Creek Mine,* 18.
3 Ibid.
4 Paul McKinney, Interview by Pat McKinney, Armargosa Valley, NV, July 21, 1996.
5 Westfield, Knill and Moschetti, *Final Report of Cane Creek Mine,* 18.
6 Morris, "The Cane Creek Mine Disaster," 6.
7 Robinson, "Night at Potash Filled," August 29, 1963.
8 Guy Hersh, Interview by author, East Carbon, UT, August 15, 1995.
9 Ibid. Guy Hersh thought Kenneth Walters and possibly J.D. Gray were on this team but he couldn't remember who the other team members were. The #1 teams from Columbia and Horse Canyon Mines arrived at Cane Creek first and other teams were put on alert and followed later during the night or the next day.
10 Ibid.
11 Messerly and Sorensen, "Still Puzzle: Fate," August 28, 1963.
12 Guy Hersh, Interview by author, East Carbon, UT, August 15, 1995.
13 Messerly and Baldwin, "Tragic Scene: West," August 28, 1963.
14 "Sentinel Team at Mine Scene," *Daily Sentinel,* August 28, 1963.
15 Robinson, "Night at Potash Filled," August 29, 1963.
16 Ibid.
17 Ibid.
18 E.T.A. Hoffmann, *The Mines of Falun, Fantasy and Horror Classics* (British Library: Read Books Ltd., 2012), 930.
19 Ibid.
20 Robinson, "Night at Potash Filled," August 29, 1963.
21 Ibid.
22 Ibid.

23 Robinson, "Night at Potash Filled," August 29, 1963.
24 J.G. Pinkerton, Telephone interview by author, Stamford, CT, January 28, 1995.
25 Guy Hersh, Interview by author, East Carbon, UT, August 15, 1995.
26 Guy Hersh, Interview by author, East Carbon, UT, August 15, 1995.
27 Guy Hersh, Interview by author, East Carbon, UT, August 15, 1995.
28 Ibid.
29 Ibid.
30 Ibid.
31 'Johnny Smoke' Palacios, Telephone interview by author, May 6, 2015. Howard Kissell was one of the other team members thought to be in the stranded bucket with James Harvey (Captain). No one could remember who the other two team members were.
32 Guy Hersh, Interview by author, East Carbon, UT, August 15, 1995.
33 Ibid.
34 'Johnny Smoke' Palacios, Telephone interview by author, May 6, 2015.
35 Ibid.
36 "Superintendent Named for Geneva Coal Mines, Quarries," *Daily Herald*, December 2, 1954.
37 Mine Disasters in the United States, "Rescuer Deaths during Recovery Operations," *United States Mine Rescue Association* (accessed January 6, 2016), http://usminedisasters.com/rescuer_deaths.htm
38 George Ferguson, Interview by author, East Carbon, UT, August 15, 1995.
39 G.W. Grove, "Loss of Life among Wearers of Oxygen Breathing Apparatus," *U.S. Bureau of Mines*, I.C. 7279, April 1944 (accessed January 6, 2016), http://miningquiz.com/pdf/Mine_Rescue/IC_7279_Loss_of_life_among_wearers_of_oxygen_breathing_apparatus.pdf
40 George Ferguson, Interview by author, East Carbon, UT, August 15, 1995.
41 AP, "Poison Gas Hinders Attempts of Rescuers," *Brandon Sun,* August 28, 1963.
42 AP, "Fear for 25 in Utah Mine, Moab Stunned," *Kansas City Times,* August 28, 1963.
43 AP, "16 Feared Dead in Mine Disaster, Utah Area Rocked," *Troy Record,* August 28, 1963.

44 Carolyn Johnson Arroyo, Telephone interview by author, February 18, 2015.
45 "Quiet Question: 'Any Chance?'" *Deseret News,* August 28, 1963.
46 Ibid.
47 Paul McKinney, Interview by Pat McKinney, Armargosa Valley, NV, July 21, 1996.
48 Ibid.
49 Charles Clark, Email correspondence with author, March 30, 2016.
50 Bill Eslick, Telephone interview by author, April 3, 2015.
51 Newell, "Moab Miner Relates," September 5, 1963.
52 Find a Grave contributors, "Steve Hatsis," *findagrave.com* (accessed November 1, 2015), http://www.findagrave.com/cgi-bin/fg.cgi?page=gr&GRid=63454387 Birth: November 23, 1913; Death: June 9, 1989.
53 AP, "Poison Gas Hinders," August 28, 1963.
54 Leonard Larsen, "Utah Rescue Team Must Overcome Tremendous Obstacles," *Denver Post,* August 28, 1963.
55 Ibid.
56 Jack Kisling, "Two Rescued from Shaft in Moab Mine Disaster," *Daily Sentinel,* August 28, 1963.
57 Messerly and Baldwin, "Tragic Scene: West," August 28, 1963.
58 Larsen, "Utah Rescue Team," August 28, 1963.
59 Kisling, "Two Rescued from Shaft," August 28, 1963.
60 'Johnny Smoke' Palacios, Telephone interview by author, May 6, 2015.
61 Westfield, Knill and Moschetti, *Final Report of Cane Creek Mine,* 22.
62 Larsen, "Utah Rescue Team," August 28, 1963.
63 AP, "Poison Gas Hinders," August 28, 1963.
64 Kisling, "Two Rescued from Shaft," August 28, 1963.

Chapter 10

1 Westfield, Knill and Moschetti, *Final Report of Cane Creek Mine,* Table 1: (August 28, 1963-5:45 a.m.), Carbon Dioxide-0.27 percent, Oxygen-20.44 percent, Carbon Monoxide- 0.04 percent, Total Hydro-carbons-0.29 and Nitrogen-78.96 percent.

Disaster at Cane Creek

2   AP, "Poison Gas Hinders," August 28, 1963.

3   Westfield, Knill and Moschetti, *Final Report of Cane Creek Mine*, Table 1: (August 28, 1963-12:45 a.m.), Carbon Dioxide-0.11 percent, Oxygen-20.86 percent, Carbon Monoxide- 0.01 percent, Total Hydro-carbons-0.07 and Nitrogen-79.20 percent.

4   Donald Blake Hanna, Interview by author, Price, UT, November 24, 1994.

5   Messerly and Sorensen, "Still Puzzle: Fate," August 28, 1963.

6   Messerly and Baldwin, "Tragic Scene: West," August 28, 1963.

7   Westfield, Knill and Moschetti, *Final Report of Cane Creek Mine*, 19.

8   Myrna Hanna, Interview by author, Price, UT, November 23, 1994.

9   Donald Blake Hanna, Interview by author, Price, UT, November 24, 1994.

10   "Disaster Strikes, Reporters Jump," August 28, 1963. Their staff writer was DeMar Teuscher, and photographer, Ray G. Jones. Reed Madsen, the paper's News Bureau Chief and rewrite men, Joseph Lundstrom and Paul Swenson.

11   "Disaster Strikes, Reporters Jump," August 28, 1963.

12   M. DeMar Teuscher, "Deceptive Air of Calm Covers Disaster Scene," *Deseret News*, August 28, 1963.

13   "2 Post Staffers at Moab Scene," *Denver Post*, August 29, 1963. Their reporter was Leonard Larsen and photographer Cloyd Teter.

14   "The Mail Box," *Country Mail*, September 11, 1963. KWSL received one direct telephone report from a Daily Sentinel staff member, however, during the next forty-eight hours of continuous coverage by John McKean, sixty-three direct reports were aired from the scene on a twenty-four hour basis. His job would earn him the plaudits of thousands of listeners, the Mutual Broadcasting System, and other national news gathering agencies. In the coverage of this disaster, some thought no local radio station kept pace with John McKean's reports.

15   R. Greg Nokes, "Grieving Relatives Complain of Unsafe Mine Conditions," *Ogden Standard-Examiner*, August 30, 1963.

16   Mullins and Swenson, "Celebration Planned, but," August 29, 1963.

17   Ibid.

18   Ibid.

19   Donald Blake Hanna, Interview by author, Price, UT, November 24, 1994.

20 Paul McKinney, Interview by Pat McKinney, Armargosa Valley, NV, July 21, 1996.
21 Ibid.
22 Robert D. Mullins, Steve Hale, Reed Madsen, and David E. Jirovec, "50-Hour Wait: Here's Account," *Deseret News*, August 30, 1963.
23 Ibid.
24 Ibid.
25 Charles Byrge, Interview by author, Price, UT, November 23, 1994.
26 Newell, "Moab Miner Relates," September 5, 1963.
27 Paul McKinney, Interview by Pat McKinney, Armargosa Valley, NV, July 21, 1996.
28 Donald Blake Hanna, Interview by author, Price, UT, November 24, 1994.
29 "Rynios in Moab at Time of Mine Disaster," *Rocket-Miner*, September 4, 1963. Mrs. Ray Rynios, who is from Rock Springs, WY, was one of the volunteers who helped serve meals to the rescuers.
30 AP, "7 Survive, 3 Dead in Utah Mine Disaster; More Alive in Shaft? Survivors Deep in Shaft in Shattering Explosion," *Ogden Standard-Examiner*, August 28, 1963.
31 Messerly, "Rescue Workers Sum," August 29, 1963.
32 AP, "7 Survive, 3 Dead," August 28, 1963.
33 Ibid.
34 Larsen, "Utah Rescue Team," August 28, 1963.
35 Kisling, "Two Rescued from Shaft," August 28, 1963.
36 Ibid.
37 James Bapis and Duston Harvey; UPI, "Potash Mine Explosion Traps Workers 3000 Feet below the Surface," *Daily Herald*, August 28, 1963.
38 Steve Hale, Robert D. Mullins and Joseph Lundstrom, "First Miners Rescued from Moab Explosion," *Deseret News*, August 28, 1963.
39 Bapis and Harvey; UPI, "Potash Mine Explosion Traps," August 28, 1963.
40 "8 Dead in Utah Mine; Fate of 15 Unknown," *New York Times*, August 29, 1963.
41 Kisling, "Two Rescued from Shaft," August 28, 1963.
42 Bapis and Harvey; UPI, "Potash Mine Explosion Traps," August 28, 1963.

43 AP, "7 Survive, 3 Dead," August 28, 1963.
44 AP, "Poison Gas Hinders," August 28, 1963.
45 Kisling, "Two Rescued from Shaft," August 28, 1963.
46 "'It Takes a Lot of Nerve' to Carry out Rescue Plans," *Deseret News*, August 28, 1963.
47 Messerly and Sorensen, "Still Puzzle: Fate," August 28, 1963.
48 Paul McKinney, Interview by Pat McKinney, Armargosa Valley, NV, July 21, 1996.
49 Ibid.
50 Donald Blake Hanna, Interview by author, Price, UT, November 24, 1994.
51 Paul McKinney, Interview by Pat McKinney, Armargosa Valley, NV, July 21, 1996.
52 Ibid.
53 Donald Blake Hanna, Interview by author, Price, UT, November 24, 1994.
54 Donald Blake Hanna, Telephone conversation with author, January 24, 2016.
55 Paul McKinney, Interview by Pat McKinney, Armargosa Valley, NV, July 21, 1996.
56 Donald Blake Hanna, Interview by author, Price, UT, November 24, 1994.
57 Thomas Oliver, M.D., F.R.C.P., *Diseases of Occupation, From the Legislative, Social, and Medical Points of View* (London: Methuen & CO., 1908), 403.
58 Dr. D. Rao, "Muscular Changes, Rigor Mortis," *Dr. Dinesh Rao's Forensic Pathology*, (accessed January 14, 2016), http://www.forensicpathologyonline.com/e-book/post-mortem-changes/muscular-changes
59 James M. Corrigary, "The Great Disaster at Avondale Colliery, Part I," and "The Great Disaster at Avondale Colliery, Part II," homasgenweb.com (accessed June 23, 2015), http://www.thomasgenweb.com/avondale_report.html See also "The Great Disaster at Avondale Colliery, September 6, 1869." *MSHA. com*, Letter from J.W. Paul, Chief of Coal Mining Investigations. To W.J. Updyke, Marshall, Texas. September 25, 1922, 12-13 (accessed June 23, 2015), http://www.msha.gov/District/Dist_01/Reports/Avondale/page12.htm and http://www.msha.gov/District/Dist_01/Reports/Avondale/page13.htm
60 Bill Carey, "Doomed Miners Take Time to Write Poignant Farewells," *Tennessee Magazine*, October 2011, 22-23.

61   C.E. Smith, "All Hope Is Gone, 425 Are Dead, Most Appalling Disaster in the History of Coal Mines, Cause of Explosion May Never Be Known," *Fairmont Times*, December 7, 1907, West Virginia Archives and History (accessed: Tuesday, June 23, 2015), http://www.wvculture.org/history/disasters/monongah04.html

62   Paul H. Rakes, "Acceptable Casualties: Power, Culture, and History in the West Virginia Coalfields, 1900-1945," *Dissertation Paper at West Virginia University*, 2002, 44 (accessed June 23, 2015), http://www.ibrarian.net/navon/paper/Acceptable_Casualties__Power__Culture__and_Histor.pdf?paperid=18081974

Chapter 11

1   Robert W. Flick, UPI, "Hope Rises, Sink as Relatives Maintain Vigil Outside Disaster-Ridden Moab Mine," *Daily Herald*, August 29, 1963.
2   Messerly and Sorensen, "Still Puzzle: Fate," August 28, 1963.
3   AP, "7 Survive, 3 Dead," August 28, 1963.
4   Messerly and Baldwin, "Tragic Scene: West," August 28, 1963.
5   "'It Takes a Lot," August 28, 1963.
6   Paul McKinney, Interview by Pat McKinney, Armargosa Valley, NV, July 21, 1996.
7   Donald Blake Hanna, Interview by author, Price, UT, November 24, 1994.
8   Westfield, Knill and Moschetti, *Final Report of Cane Creek Mine*, Appendix H.
9   Donald Blake Hanna, Interview by author, Price, UT, November 24, 1994.
10 Paul McKinney, Interview by Pat McKinney, Armargosa Valley, NV, July 21, 1996.
11 Donald Blake Hanna, Interview by author, Price, UT, November 24, 1994.
12 Jack Kisling, "Moab Rescue Delayed; Death List Mounting," *Daily Sentinel*, August 29, 1963.
13 Ibid.
14 Westfield, Knill and Moschetti, *Final Report of Cane Creek Mine*, 3.
15 Ibid.
16 Paul McKinney, Interview by Pat McKinney, Armargosa Valley, NV, July 21, 1996.

17 Donald Blake Hanna, Interview by author, Price, UT, November 24, 1994.
18 Ibid.
19 Paul McKinney, Interview by Pat McKinney, Armargosa Valley, NV, July 21, 1996.
20 Donald Blake Hanna, Interview by author, Price, UT, November 24, 1994.
21 Paul McKinney, Interview by Pat McKinney, Armargosa Valley, NV, July 21, 1996.
22 Westfield, Knill and Moschetti, *Final Report of Cane Creek Mine*, 12.
23 Paul McKinney, Interview by Pat McKinney, Armargosa Valley, NV, July 21, 1996.
24 Mullins and Swenson, "Injured Worker Thanks," August 28, 1963.
25 Anjan Chakraborty, "Blowin' in the Wind," *youtube.com* (accessed February 12, 2011), https://www.youtube.com/watch?v=cuAl5cMTJ7A
26 Canal de anblog21, "Bob Dylan and Joan Baez 1963 March on Washington," *YouTube.com* (February 12, 2016), https://www.youtube.com/watch?v=WLwHnNybADo
27 Michael Tomasky, "Bob Dylan, Joan Baez & More Music at 1963's March on Washington," August 27, 2013, *TheDailyBeast.com*, (accessed March 12, 2015), http://www.thedailybeast.com/articles/2013/08/27/bob-dylan-joan-baez-more-music-at-1963-s-march-on-washington.html
28 Sheila Rauhala Shumway, Telephone interview by author, June 24, 2016.
29 Mullins and Swenson, "Injured Worker Thanks," August 28, 1963.
30 Ibid.
31 James Bapis and Duston Harvey, UPI, "25 Trapped in Utah Mine Explosion, Rescue Workers See Possibility of Some Survivors," *Tipton Daily Tribune*, August 28, 1963.
32 Rauhala, UPI, "Says Survivor: 'Blast Knocked,'" August 28, 1963.
33 Ibid.
34 Ibid.
35 Mullins and Swenson, "Injured Worker Thanks," August 28, 1963. Paul Swenson was the other writer.
36 "Son's Picture: Proof of Pride, Anxiety," *Deseret News*, August 29, 1963.
37 Ibid.

38   Ibid.
39   Irene Christensen Lemon, Interview by author, Moab, UT, August 17, 1995.
40   "Son's Picture: Proof," August 29, 1963.
41   Ibid.
42   Steve Hale, "Waiting, Tears Etch Faces," *Deseret News*, August 29, 1963.
43   Irene Christensen Lemon, Interview by author, Moab, UT, August 17, 1995.
44   Ibid.
45   Ibid.
46   Ibid.
47   Ibid.
48   Mullins and Swenson, "Celebration Planned, but," August 29, 1963.
49   "Son's Picture: Proof," August 29, 1963.
50   Irene Christensen Lemon, Interview by author, Moab, UT, August 17, 1995.
51   Ibid.
52   "Son's Picture: Proof," August 29, 1963.
53   Ibid.
54   Irene Christensen Lemon, Interview by author, Moab, UT, August 17, 1995.
55   J.G. Pinkerton, Telephone interview by author, Stamford, CT, January 28, 1995.
56   Bapis and Harvey, UPI, "25 Trapped in Utah," August 28, 1963.
57   Messerly and Baldwin, "Tragic Scene: West," August 28, 1963.
58   Kisling, "Two Rescued from Shaft," August 28, 1963.
59   Ibid.
60   Hale, et al., "First Miners Rescued," August 28, 1963.
61   Messerly and Baldwin, "Tragic Scene: West," August 28, 1963.
62   "No Official Label yet but Gas Gets Blame," *Deseret News*, August 29, 1963.
63   Grant V. Messerly, "Two Moab Miners Blast Safety, Rescue Methods," *Salt Lake Tribune*, August 30, 1963.
64   'Johnny Smoke' Palacios, Email communications with author, February 6, 2016.
65   "Men's Faces Write Vivid Moab Story," *Daily Sentinel*, August 29, 1963.
66   Westfield, Knill and Moschetti, *Final Report of Cane Creek Mine*, Appendix F.
67   "Men's Faces Write," August 29, 1963.

68 "Early Printing May Confuse Today's Readers," *Times-Independent*, August 29, 1963.
69 Sam Taylor, Interview by author, Moab, UT, August 17, 1995.
70 Firmage, *History of Grand County*, 325.
71 AP, "Rescuers Find Much Debris, Intense Heat," *San Bernardino Daily Sun*, August 28, 1963.
80 UPI, "Mine Had Been Scheduled," August 28, 1963.
81 AP, "Rescuers Find Much Debris," August 28, 1963.
82 Firmage, *History of Grand County*, 325.
83 "T-I Editor Appointed to State Senate," *Times-Independent*, April 12, 1962.
84 "Steen Drops Senate Seat-Announces Move to Nevada," *Times-Independent*, March 16, 1961.
85 Sam Taylor, "The Way Sam Remembers It, Sept. 20, 2007," *Times-Independent*, September 20, 2007. November 1963 elections. Sam Taylor was elected to two terms as a member of the State Senate, he decided not to run for a third term but was later appointed as a member of the State Transportation Commission where he served for 21 years. See also Rusty Salmon, "Samuel John Taylor," *Eastern Utah Human History Library*, July 25, 2003, at Moab, Utah, 31. (Accessed August 29, 2015), http://centralpt.com/upload/345/2882_taylor,%20sam.pdf
86 Firmage, *History of Grand County*, 337.
87 Jeff Richards, "Charlie Steen's Uranium Discovery-July 6, 1952," *MoabHappenings.com* (accessed May 4, 2014), http://www.moabhappenings.com/Archives/pioneer0307.htm
88 Firmage, *History of Grand County*, 326-327.
89 Philip Lindstrom, "Letters to the Editor," *Times-Independent*, March 23, 1961.
90 Firmage, *History of Grand County*, 337.
91 "How Many Trailers in Moab? Recent City Survey Tells," *Times-Independent*, January 5, 1961.
92 Myrna Hanna, Interview by author, Price, UT, November 23, 1994.
93 UPI, "Moab Stunned by Tragedy," *Daily Herald*, August 28, 1963.
94 Ibid.

95 Sam Taylor, Interview by author, Moab, UT, August 17, 1995.
96 Ibid.
97 Donald Blake Hanna, Interview by author, Price, UT, November 24, 1994.
98 Ibid.
99 Paul McKinney, Interview by Pat McKinney, Armargosa Valley, NV, July 21, 1996.
100 Donald Blake Hanna, Interview by author, Price, UT, November 24, 1994.
101 Paul McKinney, Interview by Pat McKinney, Armargosa Valley, NV, July 21, 1996.
102 Ibid.
103 Ibid.
104 Donald Blake Hanna, Interview by author, Price, UT, November 24, 1994.
105 Paul McKinney, Interview by Pat McKinney, Armargosa Valley, NV, July 21, 1996.
106 Donald Blake Hanna, Interview by author, Price, UT, November 24, 1994.
107 Bapis and Harvey; UPI, "Potash Mine Explosion Traps," August 28, 1963.
108 Robert W. Bernick, "Here're Facts on Site of Explosion, 30 Million Dollar Mine," *Salt Lake Tribune*, August 28, 1963.
109 Bapis and Harvey; UPI, "Potash Mine Explosion Traps," August 28, 1963.
110 "Rescue Crews Fight Debris," *Salt Lake Tribune*, August 28, 1963.
111 AP, "7 Survive, 3 Dead," August 28, 1963.
112 Ibid.
113 "Rescue Crews Fight," August 28, 1963.
114 Messerly and Baldwin, "Tragic Scene: West," August 28, 1963.
115 Bapis and Harvey; UPI, "Potash Mine Explosion Traps," August 28, 1963.
116 AP, "3 Miners Rescued after Utah Blast; Others Still Sought," *Greeley Daily Tribune*, August 28, 1963.
117 Messerly and Baldwin, "Tragic Scene: West," August 28, 1963.
118 AP, "7 Survive, 3 Dead," August 28, 1963.
119 Ibid.
120 Ibid.
121 J.G. Pinkerton, Telephone interview by author, Stamford, CT, January 28, 1995.

122 Ibid.
123 AP, "16 Buried in Utah Mine," *Evening Times*, (Sayre, PA), August 28, 1963.
124 AP, "Fiery Blast Traps 16 in Depths of Utah Mine," *Long Beach Independent*, August 28, 1963.
125 Audrey Huzil Clayton, Email correspondence by author, May 28, 2015.
126 Ibid.
127 Ibid.
128 Emile's death certificate has 1276 Harrison, Windsor, Ontario, Canada.
129 Myriam Laviolette Macleod-Allard, Telephone interview by author, June 3, 2016. Henry Laviolette's daughter.
130 Kay Tippie, "Letters to Editor," *Times-Independent*, September 5, 1963.
131 Mrs. Duane Rushton, "Sincere Thanks," *The Trooper Newsletter,* Volume III NO.2, Utah Girl Scout Council, Salt Lake City, Utah, October 1963. List of Cadette Girl Scouts of Troop #110: Terry Drake, Carrie Leonard and Virginia Tippie.
132 Ibid. List of Senior Girl Scouts of Troop #110: Vana Johnson, Rena Lindstrom, Dodie Poole and Sandy Bacha.
133 Ibid. (Letter printed in *The Trooper* Newsletter thanking Moab's Girl Scout Troop #110, Kay Tippie, a leader, and the girls who helped make the families comfortable during such trying times. Letter was from Mrs. Duane Rushton, sister-in-law of Lamar Rushton who died at Cane Creek.)
134 "Son's Picture: Proof," August 29, 1963.
135 Kisling, "Two Rescued from Shaft," August 28, 1963.
136 Tippie, "Letters to Editor," September 5, 1963.
137 "Rescue Crews Work in 'Rain'," *Deseret News*, August 28, 1963.
138 "Son's Picture: Proof," August 29, 1963.
139 "Rescue Crews Work," August 28, 1963.
140 "Son's Picture: Proof," August 29, 1963.
141 "Rescue Crews Work," August 28, 1963.
142 Irene Christensen Lemon, Interview by author, Moab, UT, August 17, 1995.
143 Lyra Hollinger, Electronic message to author, February 28, 2017.
144 Eudeene Hollinger, Interview by author, Moab, UT, August 17, 1995.
145 Myrna Hanna, Interview by author, Price, UT, November 23, 1994.

146 Ibid.
147 Dorothy Anderson, Telephone conversation with author, February 24, 2015.
148 Myrna Hanna, Interview by author, Price, UT, November 23, 1994.
149 Ibid.
150 Ibid.
151 Lydia Fish, *The Folklore of the Coal Miners of the Northeast of England*, 2 vols. (Norwood, Pa: Norwood Editions, 1975), 115.
152 Marianne Fraser, "Warm Winters and White Rabbits: Folklore of Welsh and English Coal Miners," *Utah Historical Quarterly*, vol. 51, no. 3 (Summer 1983): 248-249. http://digitallibrary.utah.gov/awweb/awarchive?type=file&item=35433
153 Ibid, 255.
154 Ibid, 256.
155 Myrna Hanna, Interview by author, Price, UT, November 23, 1994.
156 "Rescue Crews Work," August 28, 1963.
157 Larsen, "Utah Rescue Team," August 28, 1963.
158 Ibid.
159 Westfield, Knill and Moschetti, *Final Report of Cane Creek Mine*, Appendix F.
160 "Blast Rocks Potash," August 29, 1963.
161 Messerly, "Rescue Workers Sum," August 29, 1963.
162 Ibid.
163 "Rescue Crews Fight," August 28, 1963.
164 AP, "7 Survive, 3 Dead," August 28, 1963.
165 Messerly and Sorensen, "Still Puzzle: Fate," August 28, 1963.
166 Messerly, "Rescue Workers Sum," August 29, 1963.
167 "Rescue Crews Fight," August 28, 1963.
168 Messerly and Sorensen, "Still Puzzle: Fate," August 28, 1963.
169 Messerly, "Rescue Workers Sum," August 29, 1963.
170 "Rescue Crews Work," August 28, 1963.
171 Messerly and Sorensen, "Still Puzzle: Fate," August 28, 1963.
172 Messerly, "Rescue Workers Sum," August 29, 1963.
173 "Rescue Crews Work," August 28, 1963.
174 Guy Hersh, Interview by author, East Carbon, UT, August 15, 1995.

175 "Blast Rocks Potash," August 29, 1963.
176 James Bapis, UPI, "15 Men Still Unaccounted for in Moab Mine Blast, 8 Known Dead; Only 2 Rescued," *Daily Herald*, August 29, 1963.
177 Larsen, "Utah Rescue Team," August 28, 1963.
178 "Rescue Crews Work," August 28, 1963.

Chapter 12

1 Donald Blake Hanna, Interview by author, Price, UT, November 24, 1994.
2 Ibid.
3 Paul McKinney, Interview by Pat McKinney, Armargosa Valley, NV, July 21, 1996.
4 Ibid.
5 Donald Blake Hanna, Interview by author, Vernal, UT, April 24, 2015.
6 Donald Blake Hanna, Interview by author, Price, UT, November 24, 1994.
7 Paul McKinney, Interview by Pat McKinney, Armargosa Valley, NV, July 21, 1996.
8 Donald Blake Hanna, Interview by author, Price, UT, November 24, 1994.
9 Paul McKinney, Interview by Pat McKinney, Armargosa Valley, NV, July 21, 1996.
10 Ibid.
11 Donald Blake Hanna, Interview by author, Price, UT, November 24, 1994.
12 Paul McKinney, Interview by Pat McKinney, Armargosa Valley, NV, July 21, 1996.
13 Donald Blake Hanna, Interview by author, Price, UT, November 24, 1994.
14 Paul McKinney, Interview by Pat McKinney, Armargosa Valley, NV, July 21, 1996.
15 Donald Blake Hanna, Interview by author, Price, UT, November 24, 1994.
16 "Rescue Crews Work," August 28, 1963.
17 Ibid.
18 Leonard Larsen, "7 Others Contacted by Voice," *Denver Post*, August 29, 1963.
19 Ibid.

20   "Rescue Crews Work," August 28, 1963.
21   Leonard Larsen, "Wrong Choice Proves Fatal to 3 in Mine," *Denver Post*, August 29, 1963.
22   "Rescue Crews Work," August 28, 1963.
23   Larsen, "7 Others Contacted," August 29, 1963.
24   AP, "Salt Lake City, Utah (Bulletin)." *Hazleton Standard-Speaker*, August 28, 1963.
25   Ibid.
26   UPI, "Moab Stunned by," August 28, 1963.
27   "Men's Faces Write," August 29, 1963.
28   Ibid.
29   Ibid.
30   Carolyn Habbeshaw, "No School for Child—and Dad Fine Too," *Salt Lake Tribune*, August 29, 1963.
31   "Medical Aid Stands," August 28, 1963.
32   Ibid.
33   UPI, "Mine Disaster Saddens Clyde," *Ogden Standard Examiner*, August 29, 1963.
34   Orthopedic Surgeon, Dr. Robert W. Carson was the head of the Flying Physicians Association of Utah.
35   Carolyn Habbeshaw, "Utah Flying Doctors Alerted for Moab Emergency Duty," *Salt Lake Tribune*, August 29, 1963.
36   "Additional Blood Flown to Moab," *Salt Lake Tribune*, August 29, 1963.
37   Habbeshaw, "No School for Child," August 29, 1963.
38   Ibid.
39   Donald Blake Hanna, Interview by author, Price, UT, November 24, 1994.
40   Paul McKinney, Interview by Pat McKinney, Armargosa Valley, NV, July 21, 1996.
41   Grant V. Messerly and George A. Sorensen, "2 Saved, 5 Believed Alive in Mine," *Salt Lake Tribune*, August 29, 1963.
42   Paul McKinney, Interview by Pat McKinney, Armargosa Valley, NV, July 21, 1996.
43   Larsen, "Wrong Choice Proves," August 29, 1963.

44	Paul McKinney, Interview by Pat McKinney, Armargosa Valley, NV, July 21, 1996.
45	Ibid.
46	Paul McKinney, Interview by Pat McKinney, Armargosa Valley, NV, July 21, 1996.
47	Messerly and Sorensen, "Still Puzzle: Fate," August 28, 1963.
48	Ibid.
49	Ibid.
50	Paul McKinney, Interview by Pat McKinney, Armargosa Valley, NV, July 21, 1996.
51	J.G. Pinkerton, Telephone interview by author, Stamford, CT, January 28, 1995.
52	Lloyd Pierson, "Moab's Concentration Camp, How the Dalton Wells C.C.C. Camp became a Living Hell for Japanese-Americans," *canyoncountryzephyr.com* (accessed May 26, 2015), http://www.canyoncountryzephyr.com/oldzephyr/feb-march2001/moabconcentrationcamp.htm See also Mary Cokenour, "World War 2 Leaves its Mark on Moab," *The Southwest Through Wide Brown Eyes*, (accessed May 26, 2015), http://www.southwestbrowneyes.com/2013/10/world-war-2-leaves-its-mark-on-moab.html At a young age, Carl had started taking photographs. The early 1940's was a sad chapter in American history when Carl, who at the time, was in high school. His family, along with other Japanese Americans, were relocated from their west coast homes during the World War II to internment camps to the interior of the country. The Iwasaki family was sent to the Heart Mountain Relocation Camp in northeastern Wyoming. There, Carl was noticed for his photography abilities, and the War Relocation Authority (WRA) hired him to document life in the internment camps. It was the beginning of what would become a distinguished photography career after the war. One of two isolation camps connected to the internment camps was located fifteen miles north of Moab, at the old Dalton Wells Civilian Conservation Corps Camp. Here, the "so-called" troublemakers were sent from the internment camps. "So-called" because they were not given due process under the law or had any rights at the time. Carl happened to visit the Dalton Wells Camp

as a young man during the war years in the course of documenting life in the internment camps. Now he was back in the Moab area again, this time, to photograph the Cane Creek rescue effort for *LIFE* magazine. Carl adjusted his telephoto lens to get ready to photo document the survivors who lived through a massive mine explosion.

53 Monroe Gallery of Photography, "May 17, 1954: Brown vs Board of Education Decided," May 15, 2011, *monroegallery.blogspot.com* (accessed May 26, 2016), http://monroegallery.blogspot.com/2011_05_01_archive.html Carl Iwasaki's assignment for *LIFE* Magazine was to photograph the Brown Sisters starting school during the time of the Brown vs. Board of Education trial. This essay ultimately was one of Iwasaki's most poignant and significant. The remarkable photograph of Linda Brown and her younger sister walking to school is one of the more iconic photographs representing the early civil rights struggles of the 1950s.

54 Ibid.
55 Ibid.

Part Three
Chapter 13

1 Donald Blake Hanna, Interview by author, Price, UT, November 24, 1994.
2 Ibid.
3 Ibid.
4 Ibid.
5 Ibid.
6 Westfield, Knill and Moschetti, *Final Report of Cane Creek Mine*, 22.
7 Larsen, "7 Others Contacted," August 29, 1963.
8 Kisling, "Two Rescued from Shaft," August 28, 1963.
9 Messerly and Sorensen, "Still Puzzle: Fate," August 28, 1963.
10 Paul McKinney, Interview by Pat McKinney, Armargosa Valley, NV, July 21, 1996.
11 Myrna Hanna, Interview by author, Price, UT, November 23, 1994.
12 Paul McKinney, Interview by Pat McKinney, Armargosa Valley, NV, July 21, 1996.

13 Lloyd McKinney, Telephone conversations with author, September 13, 2016.
14 Larsen, "7 Others Contacted," August 29, 1963.
15 Messerly and Sorensen, "Still Puzzle: Fate," August 28, 1963.
16 Myrna Hanna, Interview by author, Price, UT, November 23, 1994.
17 "8 Dead in Utah," August 29, 1963.
18 Ibid.
19 Paul McKinney, Interview by Pat McKinney, Armargosa Valley, NV, July 21, 1996.
20 Ibid.
21 AP, "3 of 25 Trapped Miners Pulled to Safety in Utah," *Tucson Daily Citizen*, August 28, 1963.
22 Robert W. Flick, UPI, "Moab Waits Word as Rumors Fly," *Ogden Standard-Examiner*, August 29, 1963.
23 Hale, "Waiting, Tears Etch," August 29, 1963.
24 Flick, UPI, "Moab Waits Word," August 29, 1963.
25 Ibid.
26 Jill Leovy, "Robert Flick Dies at 84; NBC News Producer Survived Jonestown Attack," *latimes.com* (Accessed January 12, 2017) http://www.latimes.com/local/obituaries/la-me-robert-flick-20160106-story.html An action man, Robert Flick covered far-flung stories of tragedy and specialized in tough assignments few others wanted. A consummate journalist who was curious, cynical, tough and driven. He was known for remaining "a true old-school journalist" who "told it like it is" and worried about upholding journalistic values. Joe Saltzman, a USC professor and former colleague, said Bob Flick, was "a legendary character among journalists. I'd been to USC and Columbia Journalism School, but I never learned as much there as I did from Bob Flick."
27 Flick, UPI, "Moab Waits Word," August 29, 1963.
28 Ibid.
29 Ibid.
30 Ibid.
31 Habbeshaw, "No School for Child," August 29, 1963.

32 Dorothy LeBlanc McPhee, Correspondence with author, November 10, 2014.
33 CP and AP, "But Names Didn't Show Up," *Regina Leader-Post*, August 30, 1963.
34 Hale, "Waiting, Tears Etch," August 29, 1963.
35 Ibid.
36 CP and AP, "But Names Didn't," August 30, 1963.
37 Ibid.
38 Habbeshaw, "No School for Child," August 29, 1963.
39 Ibid.
40 Hale, "Waiting, Tears Etch," August 29, 1963.
41 Ibid.
42 Ibid.
43 "3 Miners Victims of Wrong Turn," *Salt Lake Tribune*, August 28, 1963.
44 Hale, "Waiting, Tears Etch," August 29, 1963.
45 "3 Miners Victims," August 28, 1963.
46 Hale, "Waiting, Tears Etch," August 29, 1963.
47 Ibid.
48 Steve Hale, "It's Hardest to Wait-Women Stand Hospital Vigil," *Deseret News*, August 29, 1963.
49 Hale, "Waiting, Tears Etch," August 29, 1963.
50 Martha Milton Dowd, Telephone interview by author, July 12, 2016.
51 Mike Dowd, Telephone interview by author, July 12, 2016.
52 Ibid.
53 AP, "7 Survive, 3 Dead," August 28, 1963.
54 AP, "3 of 25 Trapped Miners," August 28, 1963.
55 "Kansan among Miners Trapped in Utah," *Kansas City Times*, August 29, 1963.
56 "Kansan Tells Ordeal Story, "Terrible Screaming,"" *Salina Journal*, August 30, 1963.
57 Violet June, Conversation with author, Castle Rock, WY, July 19, 1996.
58 Opal Davidson, Interview by author, Green River, WY, June 9, 1996.
59 AP, "7 Survive, 3 Dead," August 28, 1963.

60 Opal Davidson. Interview by author, Green River, WY, June 9, 1996.
61 AP, "7 Survive, 3 Dead," August 28, 1963.
62 Carolyn Schear, Telephone interview by author, December 15, 2016.
63 Ibid.
64 Hale, "It's Hardest to Wait," August 29, 1963.
65 "Survivors Relate Ordeal," August 29, 1963.
66 Hale, "Waiting, Tears Etch," August 29, 1963.
67 "Survivors Relate Ordeal," August 29, 1963.
68 "3 Miners Victims," August 28, 1963.
69 Ibid.
70 Hale, "It's Hardest to Wait," August 29, 1963.
71 I.W. Allen Memorial Hospital Patient Records, Donald Blake Hanna, August 1963. Patient authorized copy sent to author, June 26, 1998. The time is when patient was admitted to hospital.
72 Ibid.
73 AP, "7 Survive, 3 Dead," August 28, 1963.
74 Ibid.
75 M. DeMarr Teuscher, "2 Families Full of Joy; Others Wait—and Hope," *Deseret News*, August 29, 1963.
76 Myrna Hanna, Interview by author, Price, UT, November 23, 1994.
77 Teuscher, "2 Families Full of Joy," August 29, 1963.
78 Steve Hale, "Freed Miner Tells of Blast Ordeal," *Deseret News*, August 28, 1963.
79 Ibid.
80 Myrna Hanna, Interview by author, Price, UT, November 23, 1994.
81 AP, "7 Survive, 3 Dead," August 28, 1963.
82 Myrna Hanna, Interview by author, Price, UT, November 23, 1994.
83 "Survivors Relate Ordeal," August 29, 1963.
84 Flick, UPI, "Moab Waits Word," August 29, 1963.
85 Paul McKinney, Interview by Pat McKinney, Armargosa Valley, NV, July 21, 1996.
86 Ibid.
87 Teuscher, "2 Families Full of Joy," August 29, 1963.

88 Ibid.
89 Westfield, Knill and Moschetti, *Final Report of Cane Creek Mine*, 1.
90 Teuscher, "2 Families Full of Joy," August 29, 1963.
91 Bill McLaughlin, Dom Antonelli and Chuck Gloman, "Microphone, Camera Efforts to Contact Bova Fail, Continue Drilling Two Holes," *Hazleton Standard-Speaker*, August 29, 1963.
92 Kutztown University, "KU to Commemorate Anniversary of Dr. Martin Luther King's March on Washington," *2.kutztown.com* (accessed March 23, 2014), http://www2.kutztown.edu/news-and-media/news-releases/august-2013/ku-to-commemorate-anniversary-of-kings-march-on-washington.htm Dr. King was the concluding speaker of the day, and afterward, he and other top civil rights leaders rushed to meet with President Kennedy at the White House to talk about the passage of the pending civil rights legislation.
93 Peter Edson, "'Bring Food, Comfortable Shoes,' Marchers Were Told," *Hazleton Standard-Speaker*, August 27, 1963, Final Edition.
94 Larsen, "7 Others Contacted," August 29, 1963.
95 Paul McKinney, Interview by Pat McKinney, Armargosa Valley, NV, July 21, 1996.
96 Donald Blake Hanna, Interview by author, Price, UT, November 24, 1994.
97 Messerly and Sorensen, "2 Saved, 5 Believed," August 29, 1963.
98 AP, "Children Talk of Drama," *Regina Leader-Post*, August 28, 1963.
99 Ibid.
100 Carolyn Habbeshaw, "Hospital's 'Mood' Quiet, Expectant," *Salt Lake Tribune*, August 29, 1963.
101 Ibid.
102 Habbeshaw, "Hospital's 'Mood' Quiet," August 29, 1963.
103 Patricia Ann June Meilleur, Telephone interview by author, August 15, 1997.
104 Myrna Hanna, Interview by author, Price, UT, November 23, 1994.
105 "Survivors Relate Ordeal," August 29, 1963.
106 Teuscher, "2 Families Full of Joy," August 29, 1963.
107 AP, "7 Survive, 3 Dead," August 28, 1963.
108 Paul McKinney, Interview by Pat McKinney, Armargosa Valley, NV, July 21, 1996.

109 AP, "7 Survive, 3 Dead," August 28, 1963.
110 Teuscher, "2 Families Full of Joy," August 29, 1963.
111 "3 Miners Victims," August 28, 1963.
112 Teuscher, "2 Families Full of Joy," August 29, 1963.
113 Messerly and Sorensen, "Still Puzzle: Fate," August 28, 1963.
114 "Mine Rescue: 'Just Like Christmas'," *Salt Lake Tribune*, August 29, 1963.
115 "Survivors Relate Ordeal," August 29, 1963.
116 Reid G. Miller and William C. Mudgett, "Crews Hold up Rescue Attempts to Establish Fresh Air Pocket; 8 Dead Found in Mine; First Body Removed," *Ogden Standard-Examiner*, August 29, 1963.
117 "Survivors Relate Ordeal," August 29, 1963.
118 "Mine Rescue: 'Just Like," August 29, 1963.
119 "Survivors Relate Ordeal," August 29, 1963.
120 "Mine Rescue: 'Just Like," August 29, 1963.
121 Hale, "Freed Miner Tells," August 28, 1963.
122 Teuscher, "2 Families Full of Joy," August 29, 1963.
123 Hale, "Freed Miner Tells," August 28, 1963.
124 Messerly and Sorensen, "Still Puzzle: Fate," August 28, 1963.
125 "Mine Rescue: 'Just Like," August 29, 1963.
126 Hale, "Freed Miner Tells," August 28, 1963.
127 "Survivors Relate Ordeal," August 29, 1963.
128 "Mine Rescue: 'Just Like," August 29, 1963.
129 Ibid.
130 Ibid.
131 "8 Dead in Utah," August 29, 1963.
132 Ibid.
133 Fred Tatton, Interview by author. Wellington, UT, November 21, 1994.
134 Messerly and Sorensen, "2 Saved, 5 Believed," August 29, 1963.
135 Robert Mullins and Paul Swenson, "Trips Down, up Leave Little Air for Rescue," *Deseret News*, August 29, 1963.
136 Ibid.
137 Mullins and Swenson, "Trips Down, up Leave," August 29, 1963.

Chapter 14

1. "Foreman's Bravery Saves Many in Mine Blast," *Salt Lake Telegram*, May 10, 1945.
2. "Carbon Miner Honored for Heroism," *Salt Lake Telegram*, April 19, 1946.
3. "Former Workers Here among Mine Victims," *Esterhazy Miner-Journal* September 5, 1963.
4. Myriam MacLeod, Email correspondence with author, March 18, 2015. Henry Laviolette's granddaughter.
5. Messerly and Sorensen, "2 Saved, 5 Believed," August 29, 1963.
6. Ibid.
7. Ibid.
8. Paul McKinney, Interview by Pat McKinney, Armargosa Valley, NV, July 21, 1996.
9. Messerly and Sorensen, "2 Saved, 5 Believed," August 29, 1963.
10. Ibid.
11. Messerly and Sorensen, "Still Puzzle: Fate," August 28, 1963.
12. "Blast Rocks Potash," August 29, 1963.
13. AP, "7 Survive, 3 Dead," August 28, 1963.
14. Larsen, "Wrong Choice Proves," August 29, 1963.
15. R. Greg Nokes, AP, "Mine Blast Traps 25; Nine Alive, 3 Rescued," *Idaho State Journal*, August 28, 1963.
16. UPI, "Nine Out of 25 Survive Deep Mine Blast," *Corsicana Daily Sun*, August 28, 1963.
17. AP, "Nine Found Alive in Utah Potash Min," *Mt. Vernon Register-News*, August 28, 1963.
18. AP, "3 Miners Rescued; Others Are Alive," *Salina Journal*, August 28, 1963.
19. AP, "7 Survive, 3 Dead," August 28, 1963.
20. Mullins, et al., "50-Hour Wait," August 30, 1963.
21. Paul McKinney, Interview by Pat McKinney, Armargosa Valley, NV, July 21, 1996.
22. Charles "C.C." Clark, Interview by author, Moab, UT, August 18, 1995.
23. Newell, "Moab Miner Relates," September 5, 1963.
24. Ibid.

25 Ibid.
26 J.G. Pinkerton, Telephone interview by author, Stamford, CT, January 28, 1995.
27 Ibid.
28 Ibid.
29 Sam Taylor, Interview by author, Moab, UT, August 17, 1995.
30 Ibid.
31 Ibid.
32 Ibid.
33 Ibid.
34 Ibid.
35 Ibid.
36 AP, "Strict Rules Set at Mine," *Idaho State Journal*, August 28, 1963.
37 Hale, et al., "First Miners Rescued," August 28, 1963.
38 James W. Paul and H. M. Wolflin, *Rescue and Recovery Operations in Mines after Fires and Explosions* (Washington D.C.: Bureau of Mine, 1916), 19. See online version: *Hathi Trust Digital Library* (accessed on October 2, 2014), http://babel.hathitrust.org/cgi/pt?id=hvd.32044092005370;view=1up;seq=7
39 Sam Taylor, Interview by author, Moab, UT, August 17, 1995.
40 "Local Phone Company Accepts Challenge," *Times-Independent*, September 12, 1963. Jack Corbin was President, and Wally Corbin the Moab District Manager of the Midland Telephone Company.
41 Ibid.
42 Ibid.
43 Ibid.
44 Ibid. During the next few days, after Hanna and McKinney were rescued, an even greater demand on an overloaded telephone communication facility was created. With the rescue of five more survivors and the announcement that the remaining 18 men were dead, the demand for telephone service died almost as fast as it had arisen. The "Spirit of Service," that on so many occasions, came through in the time of need, again played its part in a remote area to handle an unprecedented calling load.

45 AP, "Find 8 Dead in a Mine; Bar to Rescue," *Kansas City Times*, August 29, 1963.
46 UPI, "2 Men Rescued from Utah Mine, 5 Others Alive; 3 Known Dead," *Valley Morning Star*, August 29, 1963.
47 Miller and Mudgett, "Crews Hold up Rescue," August 29, 1963.
48 AP, "Rescue Try Stalled in Utah Mine Blast," *Pottstown Mercury*, August 29, 1963.
49 Miller and Mudgett, "Crews Hold up Rescue," August 29, 1963.
50 George Ferguson, Interview by author, East Carbon, UT, August 15, 1995.
51 Miller and Mudgett, "Crews Hold up Rescue," August 29, 1963.
52 Messerly and Sorensen, "Still Puzzle: Fate," August 28, 1963.
53 UPI, "Clyde Takes Issue with Udall on Moab Mine Safety," *Sunday Herald*, September 1, 1963.
54 Ibid.
55 Jack Kisling, "Blast Blame Debate Rages," *Daily Sentinel*, August 30, 1963.
56 Michael Tomasky, "The Racist Redskins," *The New York Review*, November 10, 2011, nybooks.com (accessed February 22, 2016), http://www.nybooks.com/articles/2011/11/10/racist-redskins/
57 Webster Tarpley, "Webster Tarpley on Who Killed Kennedy (23:34), *YouTube.com* (Accessed January 13, 2017), https://www.youtube.com/watch?v=CPJKoaRXRoU&t=67s
58 Ibid.
59 Thomas G. Smith, "John Kennedy, Stewart Udall, and New Frontier Conservation," *The Pacific Historical Review*, vol. 64, No. 3, (August 1995), 335.
60 AP, "Udall Flays Mine Safety Lag, Blast Accents 'Laxness' Charge," *Salt Lake Tribune*, August 29, 1963.
61 "President Kennedy Hails Fellin, Throne," *Hazleton Standard-Speaker*, August 29, 1963, Early Edition.
62 Ibid.
63 John F. Kennedy, *"Public Papers of the Presidents of the United States: John F. Kennedy, 1963,"* Best Books on Corporation, 2013. December 8, 2013, 130-131. Letter on the 'Need for a Review of Mine Safety Regulations and

Practices.' Dated April 30, 1963. In President Kennedy's letter Secretary Udall referred to, said, "Within the past five months two major coal mine disasters have occurred, involving a total loss of 59 lives." The disasters Kennedy was referring to were the Robena No. 3 Mine disaster in Carmichael, Pennsylvania, on December 6, 1962, that killed 37 miners and the Compass No. 2 Mine disaster in Dola, West Virginia, on April 25, 1963, that killed 22 miners.

64 Commission on Sociotechnical Systems, National Research Council, "Report of the Committee on Underground Mine Disaster Survival and Rescue: An Evaluation of Research Accomplishments and Needs," 17, Washington D.C.: National Research Council, 1981. This is a study into the causes and prevention of injuries and health hazards in metal and nonmetal (non-coal) mines and was authorized by Congress in 1961, Public Law 87-300. The conclusions were largely responsible for passage of the Federal Metal and Non-metallic Mine Safety Act of 1966 (the 1966 Metal Mine Act). The 1966 Act provided for the promulgation of standards, many of which were advisory, and for inspections and investigations but gave only minimal enforcement authority.

65 Robert W. Bernick, "Udall 'Powers' Noted in Blast," *Salt Lake Tribune*, August 30, 1963.

66 UPI, "Clyde Takes Issue," September 1, 1963.

67 Thomas G. Smith, "Canyonlands National Park Controversy, 1961-64," *Utah Historical Quarterly*, vol. 59, no. 3 (Summer 1991): 218. http://utah.ptfs.com/awweb/awarchive?type=file&item=35219

68 Washington Bureau, "Moss Vows Try to Get Potash Lands," *Deseret News*, December 22, 1962, Sec. B.

69 Ibid, 235.

70 "Utah's Disappointment," *Times-Independent*, December 13, 1962.

71 Don Robinson, "Rise in Employment Due to Missile Work," *Times-Independent*, July 25, 1963.

72 Frank Hewlett, "Bennett: Udall Hits Lake Bill, Claims 'Grandstand Play'," *Salt Lake Tribune*, February 28, 1963.

73 Ibid.

74 "Utah's Disappointment," December 13, 1962.
75 Ibid.
76 Legislation creating the park was signed into law by President Lyndon Johnson on September 12, 1964.
77 Wikipedia contributors, "Arches National Park," *Wikipedia, the Free Encyclopedia* (accessed June 12, 2014), https://en.wikipedia.org/wiki/Arches_National_Park The Arches area was originally named a National Monument on April 12, 1929. It was designated as a National Park on November 12, 1971.
78 Smith, "Canyonlands National Park Controversy, 233.
79 Ibid, 236.
80 Herve Roy, Telephone interview by author, April 14, 2014.
81 Ibid.
82 "Names Listed, Firm," *DN*, August 28, 1963.
83 Herve Roy, Tape recording sent to author, April 13, 2015.
84 Helene Roy McGruthers, Email correspondence with author, April 3, 2015.
85 Ibid.
86 Herve Roy, Tape recording sent to author, April 13, 2015.
87 Ibid.
88 Herve Roy, Telephone interview by author, April 14, 2014.
89 Ibid.
90 Ibid.
91 Ibid.
92 AP, "Find 8 Dead," August 29, 1963.
93 Ibid.
94 Ibid.
95 Donald Blake Hanna, Interview by author, Price, UT, November 24, 1994.
96 Mullins and Swenson, "Trips Down, up Leave," August 29, 1963.
97 Messerly and Sorensen, "Still Puzzle: Fate," August 28, 1963.
98 AP, "Rescue Try Stalled," August 29, 1963.
99 Mullins, et al., "Lack of Air Slows," August 29, 1963.
100 "8 Dead in Utah," August 29, 1963.
101 AP, "Rescue Try Stalled," August 29, 1963.

102   Ibid.
103   AP, "Find 8 Dead," August 29, 1963.
104   Mullins and Swenson, "Trips Down, up Leave," August 29, 1963.
105   Ibid.
106   "Gulf Officials to Visit Site," *Salt Lake Tribune*, August 29, 1963.
107   "Texas Gulf President Voices Deep Concern," *Deseret News*, August 29, 1963.
108   "Gulf Officials to Visit," August 29, 1963.
109   "Texas Gulf President," August 29, 1963.
110   UPI, "Moab Blast Second for Mining Firm," *Daily Herald*, August 29, 1963.
111   Ed Morse, AP, "Hope for Avoiding Rail Strike Brings Strong Stock Rally," *Independent*, August 29, 1963, Sec. E.
112   UPI, "Potash Deposits in Moab Area Called Largest in the Country," *Daily Herald*, August 29, 1963.
113   "Texas Gulf President," August 29, 1963.

Chapter 15

1   AP, "Rescue Try Stalled," August 29, 1963.
2   Kisling, "Moab Rescue Delayed," August 29, 1963.
3   AP, "Rescue Try Stalled," August 29, 1963.
4   AP, "Lights Play on Tragic Mine Area, Seems Unreal," *Ogden Standard-Examiner*, August 29, 1963.
5   AP, "Scene at Mine," August 29, 1963.
6   Flick, UPI, "Moab Waits Word," August 29, 1963.
7   "8 Dead in Utah," August 29, 1963.
8   Messerly and Sorensen, "Still Puzzle: Fate," August 28, 1963.
9   'Johnny Smoke' Palacios, Telephone interview by author, May 6, 2015.
10   Messerly and Sorensen, "Still Puzzle: Fate," August 28, 1963.
11   'Johnny Smoke' Palacios, Telephone interview by author, May 6, 2015.
12   Mullins, et al., "Lack of Air Slows," August 29, 1963.
13   'Johnny Smoke' Palacios, Telephone interview by author, May 6, 2015.
14   George A. Sorensen, "Silent Town Grieves in Tragedy's Wake," *Salt Lake Tribune*, August 31, 1963.
15   Kisling, "Moab Rescue Delayed," August 29, 1963.

16 UPI, "Deadly Fumes Block Mine Rescue Crews—Eight Bodies Sighted," *Carlsbad Current –Argus,* August 29, 1963.
17 Messerly and Sorensen, "Still Puzzle: Fate," August 28, 1963.
18 UPI, "Deadly Fumes Block," August 29, 1963.
19 Messerly and Sorensen, "Still Puzzle: Fate," August 28, 1963.
20 Kisling, "Moab Rescue Delayed," August 29, 1963.
21 Guy Hersh, Interview by author, East Carbon, UT, August 15, 1995.
22 Ibid.
23 Ibid.
24 Ibid.
25 Ibid.
26 Ibid.
27 Robert D. Mullins, Steve Hale and Joseph Lundstrom, "Fresh Air Speeds Survival Search," *Deseret News,* August 29, 1963.
28 Guy Hersh, Interview by author, East Carbon, UT, August 15, 1995.
29 Ibid.
30 Newell, "Moab Miner Relates," September 5, 1963.
31 Mullins, et al., "50-Hour Wait," August 30, 1963.
32 Charles "C.C." Clark, Correspondence with author, February 20, 2016.
33 Newell, "Moab Miner Relates," September 5, 1963.
34 Charles "C.C." Clark, Correspondence with author, February 20, 2016.
35 Newell, "Moab Miner Relates," September 5, 1963.
36 Charles "C.C." Clark, Correspondence with author, February 20, 2016.
37 Newell, "Moab Miner Relates," September 5, 1963.
38 Charles "C.C." Clark, Correspondence with author, February 20, 2016.
39 William Wordsworth and Norah Neilson Gray, *Ode, Intimations of Immortality from Recollections of early Childhood* (London: J.M. Dent, 1913).
40 Ibid.
41 Kisling, "Moab Rescue Delayed," August 29, 1963.
42 "8 Dead in Utah," August 29, 1963.
43 "Pause in Efforts to Reach Miners—Air Pocket Needed in Rescue Attempt," *Saskatoon StarPhoenix,* August 29, 1963.
44 "Statistical Picture of Explosion is Described in Human Terms," *Deseret News,* August 29, 1963.

45   Kisling, "Moab Rescue Delayed," August 29, 1963.
46   Miller and Mudgett, "Crews Hold up Rescue," August 29, 1963.
47   Kisling, "Moab Rescue Delayed," August 29, 1963.
48   Grant V. Messerly and George A. Sorensen, "2 Safe, 8 Dead in Utah Mine; Still Puzzle: Fate of 15," *Salt Lake Tribune,* August 29, 1963.
49   Ibid.
50   Ibid.
51   Mullins, et al., "Lack of Air Slows," August 29, 1963.
52   Messerly and George A. Sorensen, "2 Safe, 8 Dead," August 29, 1963.
53   Ibid.
54   "Moab Mine Safety Record Defended by Owners, State Aide—Previous Accidents Recalled," *Denver Post,* August 30, 1963.
55   "Historical Data on Mine Disasters in the United States," *msha.gov* (accessed January 10, 2002), http://www.msha.gov/MSHAINFO/FactSheets/MSHAFCT8.HTM
56   AP, "Find 8 Dead," August 29, 1963.
57   Teuscher, "2 Families Full of Joy," August 29, 1963.
58   Ibid.
59   Flick, UPI, "Moab Waits Word," August 29, 1963.
60   Ibid.
61   Don Harris, "Mourning Victim, Miner Lived in Windsor," *Windsor Star,* August 31, 1963.
62   Ibid.
63   AP, "7 Survive, 3 Dead," August 28, 1963.
64   Flick, UPI, "Moab Waits Word," August 29, 1963.
65   Teuscher, "2 Families Full of Joy," August 29, 1963.
66   Jill Leovy, "Robert Flick Dies at 84; NBC News Producer Survived Jonestown Attack," *latimes.com* (Accessed January 12, 2017) http://www.latimes.com/local/obituaries/la-me-robert-flick-20160106-story.html
67   Flick, UPI, "Moab Waits Word," August 29, 1963.
68   Teuscher, "2 Families Full of Joy," August 29, 1963.
69   Ibid.
70   Ibid.
71   Habbeshaw, "No School for Child," August 29, 1963.

72   Hospital Patient Records, Hanna, August 1963.
73   AP, "7 Survive, 3 Dead," August 28, 1963.
74   Martha Milton Dowd, Email correspondence with author, January 5, 2009.
75   Ibid.
76   Habbeshaw, "Hospital's 'Mood' Quiet," August 29, 1963.
77   Ibid.
78   Ibid.
79   Westfield, Knill and Moschetti, *Final Report of Cane Creek Mine*, 14. Anthony C. Moschetti was the technical assistant, district headquarters office, Denver, Colorado.
80   William Sikonia, Correspondence with author, March 23, 1999. Sikonia was married to Joan Westfield, the daughter of James Westfield.
81   "Ex-Utahn Makes Disaster His Business," *Deseret News*, August 31, 1963.
82   "Utahn Named to Head Safety Group," *Deseret News*, September 26, 1950, Sec. B.
83   "Ex-Utahn Makes Disaster," August 31, 1963.
84   Allan Kent Powell, *The Next Time We Strike* (Logan: Utah State University Press, 1985), 143.
85   "Rescuers of the Castle Gate Mine Explosion," *Sun Advocate*, March 14, 1924, (accessed February 14, 2016), http://www.carbon-utgenweb.com/cgminers.html
86   "Ex-Utahn Makes Disaster," August 31, 1963.
87   Ibid.
88   "B.C.'s Worst Coal Mining Disaster," *Islander* magazine (accessed February 15, 2016), http://victoriahistory.ca/blog/2010/07/b-c-s-worst-coal-mining-disaster/ Notable articles from the Victoria Times Colonist's Islander Magazine. See also Historica Canada, "Coal Mining Disasters," *Canadian Encyclopedia* (accessed February 15, 2016), http://www.thecanadianencyclopedia.ca/en/article/coal-mining-disasters/
89   William Sikonia, Correspondence with author, March 23, 1999.
90   Daniel Harrington, 1901, Coal mining at Sunnyside, Utah: *Colorado School of Mines Bulletin 1*, 227-235. See footnote: Frank W. Osterwald, John O. Maberry, and C. Richard Dunrud, "Bedrock, Surficial, and Economic

Geology of the Sunnyside Coal-Mining District, Carbon and Emery Counties, Utah," *Geological Survey Professional Paper 1166* (Washington: United States Government Printing Office, 1981), 52. For Daniel Harrington, see: "Mining Disasters - An Exhibition, 1900 Winter Quarters No. 4 Mine Disaster Near Scofield, Utah - May 1, 1900," *MSHA.gov* (accessed February 15, 2016), http://arlweb.msha.gov/disaster/scofield/scofield17.asp [Early 1900,] Daniel Harrington, joined the Federal Bureau of Mines in 1914. He was a known associate to the elder Westfield. Harrington may have been the inspiration for the young Westfield in seeking a career with the Bureau of Mines.

91 "James Westfield (Obituary)," *Sun Advocate,* October 14, 1976.
92 "Ex-Utahn Makes Disaster," August 31, 1963.
93 Ibid.
94 Jay Katz, Alexander Capron and Eleanor Swift Glass, *Experimentation with Human Beings: The Authority of the Investigator, Subject, Professions and State in the Human Experimentation Process* (Hartford: Connecticut Printers, Inc., 1972), 155. Quote by Mr. Evans (no first name given).
95 Westfield, Knill and Moschetti, *Final Report of Cane Creek Mine,* 6.
96 Ibid.
97 Bernick, "'Petroleum Gas Blast," August 29, 1963.
98 Donald Blake Hanna, Interview by author, Price, UT, November 24, 1994.
99 Bernick, "'Petroleum Gas Blast," August 29, 1963. See also B.J. Eardley, "The Dream of Oil," *The Canyon Country Zephyr,* 1991 Archive (accessed August 20, 2014), http://www.canyoncountryzephyr.com/2014/04/01/from-the-1991-zephyr-archives-the-dream-of-oil-by-b-j-eardley/
100 Ibid.
101 Kisling, "Moab Rescue Delayed," August 29, 1963.
102 Miller and Mudgett, "Crews Hold up Rescue," August 29, 1963.
103 Messerly, "Rescue Workers Sum," August 29, 1963.
104 'Johnny Smoke' Palacios, Telephone interview by author, May 6, 2015.
105 UPI, "Deadly Fumes Block," August 29, 1963.
106 Westfield, Knill and Moschetti, *Final Report of Cane Creek Mine,* 10.
107 Mullins, et al., "Lack of Air Slows," August 29, 1963.

108 Messerly, "Rescue Workers Sum," August 29, 1963.
109 Messerly and Sorensen, "2 Saved, 5 Believed," August 29, 1963.
110 Mullins, et al., "Lack of Air Slows," August 29, 1963.
111 Ibid.
112 Ibid.
113 Westfield, Knill and Moschetti, *Final Report of Cane Creek Mine*, 12.
114 "Pause in Efforts," August 29, 1963.
115 UPI, "Deadly Fumes Block," August 29, 1963.

Part Four
Chapter 16

1 Fred Tatton, Interview by author, Wellington, UT, November 21, 1994.
2 Donald Blake Hanna, Interview by author, Price, UT, November 24, 1994.
3 Fred Tatton, Interview by author, Wellington, UT, November 21, 1994.
4 Ibid.
5 James Bapis, UPI, "5 Known Safe; 8 Bodies Found in Utah Mine," *Tipton Daily Tribune*, August 29, 1963.
6 Fred Tatton, Interview by author, Wellington, UT, November 21, 1994.
7 Ibid.
8 Donald Blake Hanna, Interview by author, Price, UT, November 24, 1994.
9 Fred Tatton, Interview by author, Wellington, UT, November 21, 1994.
10 Ibid.
11 Kisling, "Moab Rescue Delayed," August 29, 1963.
12 Fred Tatton, Interview by author, Wellington, UT, November 21, 1994.
13 Ibid.
14 Ibid.
15 Ibid.
16 Ibid.
17 Kisling, "Moab Rescue Delayed," August 29, 1963.
18 Fred Tatton, Interview by author, Wellington, UT, November 21, 1994.
19 Mullins, et al., "Lack of Air Slows," August 29, 1963.
20 Fred Tatton, Interview by author, Wellington, UT, November 21, 1994.
21 AP, "Lights Play on Tragic," August 29, 1963.

22 Ibid.
23 Ibid.
24 Stegner, ed., *Wilderness at the Edge*, 98.
25 AP, "Lights Play on Tragic," August 29, 1963.
26 "Rev. H.M. Mason Accepts Post at St. Francis," *Times-Independent,* August 10, 1961.
27 AP, "Scene at Mine Seems 'Unreal'," *North Bay Nugget,* August 29, 1963.
28 Tippie, "Letters to Editor," September 5, 1963.
29 Ibid.
30 Ibid.
31 Ibid.
32 Rushton, "Sincere Thanks," *The Trooper Newsletter.*
33 Tippie, "Letters to Editor," September 5, 1963.
34 Ibid.
35 Ibid.
36 Carolyn Habbeshaw, "Families Huddle, Fight Anxiety in Plight—Gray Blanket a Signal of Death," *Salt Lake Tribune,* August 30, 1963.
37 Ibid.
38 George Ferguson, Interview by author, East Carbon, UT, August 15. 1995.
39 Mullins, et al., "Lack of Air Slows," August 29, 1963.
40 Miller and Mudgett, "Crews Hold up Rescue," August 29, 1963.
41 "Moab Mine Safety," August 30, 1963.
42 George Ferguson, Interview by author, East Carbon, UT, August 15. 1995.
43 Habbeshaw, "Families Huddle, Fight," August 30, 1963.
44 Ibid.
45 Ibid.
46 Ibid.
47 Habbeshaw, "Families Huddle, Fight," August 30, 1963.
48 "Moab Mine Safety," August 30, 1963.
49 Habbeshaw, "Families Huddle, Fight," August 30, 1963.
50 "Moab Mine Safety," August 30, 1963.
51 Fred Tatton, Interview by author, Wellington, UT, November 21, 1994.
52 George Ferguson, Interview by author, East Carbon, UT, August 15. 1995.
53 Fred Tatton, Interview by author, Wellington, UT, November 21, 1994.

54 Ibid.
55 Ibid.

Chapter 17

1. Kisling, "Moab Rescue Delayed," August 29, 1963.
2. Leonard Larsen, "Utah Rescue Efforts Held Up," *Denver Post*, August 30, 1963.
3. Miller and Mudgett, "Crews Hold up Rescue," August 29, 1963.
4. Ibid.
5. Larsen, "Utah Rescue Efforts," August 30, 1963.
6. Mullins, et al., "Lack of Air Slows," August 29, 1963.
7. Larsen, "Utah Rescue Efforts," August 30, 1963.
8. Mullins and Swenson, "Trips Down, up Leave," August 29, 1963.
9. Ibid.
10. Miller and Mudgett, "Crews Hold up Rescue," August 29, 1963.
11. Larsen, "Utah Rescue Efforts," August 30, 1963.
12. Mullins, et al., "Lack of Air Slows," August 29, 1963.
13. Mullins and Swenson, "Trips Down, up Leave," August 29, 1963.
14. Mullins, et al., "Lack of Air Slows," August 29, 1963.
15. Ibid.
16. Miller and Mudgett, "Crews Hold up Rescue," August 29, 1963.
17. Mullins, et al., "Lack of Air Slows," August 29, 1963.
18. "Pause in Efforts," August 29, 1963.
19. UPI, "Deadly Fumes Block," August 29, 1963.
20. Mullins, et al., "Lack of Air Slows," August 29, 1963.
21. Ibid.
22. Mullins, et al., "Lack of Air Slows," August 29, 1963.
23. Kisling, "Moab Rescue Delayed," August 29, 1963.
24. Bapis, UPI, "15 Men Still Unaccounted," August 29, 1963.
25. "8 Dead in Utah," August 29, 1963.
26. Tippie, "Letters to Editor," September 5, 1963.
27. Ibid.
28. "They Waited, and Hoped against Hope," *Salt Lake Tribune*, August 31, 1963.

29 Ibid.
30 Nokes, "Grieving Relatives Complain," August 30, 1963.
31 Hospital Patient Records, Hanna, August 1963. Hanna woke at 6:24 a.m.
32 Paul McKinney, Interview by Pat McKinney, Armargosa Valley, NV, July 21, 1996.
33 Mullins, et al., "Lack of Air Slows," August 29, 1963.
34 Ibid.
35 "Rescue Efforts Dimmed," *Morning Herald*, August 30, 1963.
36 Kisling, "Blast Blame Debate Rages," August 30, 1963.
37 Habbeshaw, "Families Huddle, Fight," August 30, 1963.
38 Kisling, "Moab Rescue Delayed," August 29, 1963.
39 Miller and Mudgett, "Crews Hold up Rescue," August 29, 1963.
40 Kisling, "Moab Rescue Delayed," August 29, 1963.
41 Kisling, "Blast Blame Debate Rages," August 30, 1963.
42 Ibid.
43 Kisling, "Moab Rescue Delayed," August 29, 1963.
44 Ibid.
45 Kisling, "Two Rescued from Shaft," August 28, 1963.
46 Miller, "Smiling Survivors Okay," August 30, 1963.
47 Hospital Patient Records, Hanna, August 1963.
48 AP, "5 More Men Found Alive in Utah Mine," *The Derrick*, August 30, 1963.
49 Hospital Patient Records, Hanna, August 1963.
50 Myrna Hanna, Interview by author, Price, UT, November 23, 1994.
51 "2 Survivors Return to Aid in Rescue," *Deseret News*, August 29, 1963.
52 Paul McKinney, Interview by Pat McKinney, Armargosa Valley, NV, July 21, 1996.
53 Myrna Hanna, Interview by author, Price, UT, November 23, 1994.
54 Ibid.
55 Nokes, "Grieving Relatives Complain," August 30, 1963.
56 Ibid.
57 United State Department of Labor, "History of Changes to the Minimum Wage Law," Adapted from 1988 Report to the Congress, *dol.gov* (Accessed September 29, 2015), http://www.dol.gov/whd/minwage/coverage.htm

58 Linda Barber, Email correspondence with author, April 5, 2015. Copies of Wesley Barber's pay stubs show that he worked at the mine 5 1/2 weeks as a miner. Sent by Linda Barber, the daughter of Wesley Barber.

59 Nokes, "Grieving Relatives Complain," August 30, 1963.

60 "Final Rescue Ends Anxiety of Family," *Daily Sentinel*, August 30, 1963.

61 Herve Roy, Telephone interview by author, April 14, 2014.

62 "Mine's Pre-Blast Toll-4, Matter of Record," *Salt Lake Tribune*, August 30, 1963.

63 Ibid.

64 "Doctor Arrives at TGS Mishap as Tourist," *Times-Independent*, November 15, 1962.

65 "Accidents Claim Two Lives at Potash Project Shaft," *Times-Independent*, November 15, 1962.

66 Herve Roy, Telephone interview by author, April 14, 2014.

67 Westfield, Knill and Moschetti, *Final Report of Cane Creek Mine*, 6.

68 "Mine's Pre-Blast," August 30, 1963.

69 "No Official Label," August 29, 1963.

70 Dwayne "Pat" Hand, Email correspondence with author, June 5, 2015.

71 Westfield, Knill and Moschetti, *Final Report of Cane Creek Mine*, 7-8.

72 Paul McKinney, Interview by Pat McKinney, Armargosa Valley, NV, July 21, 1996. Also Charles Byrge, Interview by author, Price, UT, November 23, 1994.

73 Paul McKinney, Interview by Pat McKinney, Armargosa Valley, NV, July 21, 1996.

74 "Earlier Blast Unreported at Utah Mine, Data on 4-Injury Mishap Not Received, Aide Says," *Deseret News*, September 2, 1963, Sec. B.

75 Paul Swenson, "Safety Rules Ignored, Moab Miner Charges," *Deseret News*, September 5, 1963, Sec. B.

76 Mullins and Swenson, "Celebration Planned, but," August 29, 1963.

77 Zelda Schear Bucher, Telephone interview by author, December 15, 2016.

78 Mullins and Swenson, "Celebration Planned, but," August 29, 1963.

79 Eudeene Hollinger, Interview by author, Moab, UT, August 17, 1995.

80 Paul McKinney, Interview by Pat McKinney, Armargosa Valley, NV, July 21, 1996.

81 Westfield, Knill and Moschetti, *Final Report of Cane Creek Mine,* 7-8. Following the July 31 explosion, additional flame safety lamps were issued, but questioning of employees revealed some had not been properly instructed in the use of these lamps.
82 Paul McKinney, Interview by Pat McKinney, Armargosa Valley, NV, July 21, 1996.
83 L. T. C. Rolt, *George and Robert Stephenson: The Railway Revolution* (London: Longmans, 1960), 34.
84 Westfield, Knill and Moschetti, *Final Report of Cane Creek Mine,* 7.
85 Herve Roy, Telephone interview by author, April 14, 2014.
86 Paul McKinney, Interview by Pat McKinney, Armargosa Valley, NV, July 21, 1996.
87 Helene Roy McGruthers, Email correspondence with author, April 3, 2015. Copies of Rene Roy's letters were sent to author by Helene Roy McGruthers, his daughter.
88 Paul McKinney, Interview by Pat McKinney, Armargosa Valley, NV, July 21, 1996.
89 Ibid.
90 "Accidents Claim Two," November 15, 1962.
91 Herve Roy, Telephone interview by author, April 14, 2014.
92 Lorraine Rushton, Telephone conversation with author, November 15, 1995.
93 Helene Roy McGruthers, Email correspondence with author, April 3, 2015.
94 Donald Blake Hanna, Interview by author, Vernal, UT, April 25, 2015.
95 Paul McKinney, Interview by Pat McKinney, Armargosa Valley, NV, July 21, 1996.
96 Charles Byrge, Interview by author, Price, Utah, November 23, 1994.
97 Herve Roy, Telephone interview by author, April 14, 2014.
98 Paul McKinney, Interview by Pat McKinney, Armargosa Valley, NV, July 21, 1996.
99 Ibid.
100 Bernick, "Udall 'Powers' Noted," August 30, 1963.
101 "Robert W. Bernick Sr." *DeseretNews.com* (accessed October 16, 2015), http://www.deseretnews.com/article/333014/ROBERT-W-BERNICK-SR.html?pg=all

102 Bernick, "Udall 'Powers' Noted," August 30, 1963.
103 Ibid.
104 Ibid.
105 Ibid.
106 Ibid.
107 Robert W. Bernick, "'No Evidence of Laxity,' USGS Official Reports, Mine Observed Rules," *Salt Lake Tribune*, August 31, 1963.
108 Westfield, Knill and Moschetti, *Final Report of Cane Creek Mine*, 3.
109 Kisling, "Moab Rescue Delayed," August 29, 1963.
110 Flick, UPI, "Moab Waits Word," August 29, 1963.
111 Ibid.
112 Helene Roy McGruthers, Email correspondence with author, April 3, 2015.
113 "Missing and Rescued," August 29, 1963. The first name of Mrs. C.J. Hamilton is not known.
114 Herve Roy, Telephone interview by author, April 14, 2014.
115 Ibid.
116 Ibid.
117 Ibid.
118 Habbeshaw, "Families Huddle, Fight," August 30, 1963.
119 Ibid. Women volunteers listed were: Mary Unger, Mrs. R.L. Curfman, Mrs. R. F. Hollis and Mrs. H.W. Ranspot.
120 "2 Survivors Return," August 29, 1963.
121 Mullins, et al., "Fresh Air Speeds," August 29, 1963.
122 "2 Survivors Return," August 29, 1963.
123 J.G. Pinkerton, Telephone interview by author, Stamford, CT, January 28, 1995.
124 Ibid.
125 "2 Survivors Return," August 29, 1963.
126 Messerly, "Two Moab Miners," August 30, 1963.
127 "2 Survivors Return," August 29, 1963.
128 UPI, "Five More Rescued from Utah Mine," Clipping, Newspaper Unknown, August 30, 1963.
129 Messerly, "Two Moab Miners," August 30, 1963.
130 Ibid.

131 UPI, "Five More Rescued," August 30, 1963.
132 AP, "Miner Rakes Lack of Safety Plan," *Ogden Standard-Examiner*, August 29, 1963.
133 Messerly, "Two Moab Miners," August 30, 1963.
134 UPI, "Five More Rescued," August 30, 1963.
135 AP, "Miner Rakes Lack," August 29, 1963.
136 "Moab Mine Safety," August 30, 1963.
137 Ibid.
138 "One of Rescued Men Assails Mine Safety," Clipping, Newspaper Unknown, August 30, 1963.
139 Myrna Hanna, Interview by author, Price, UT, November 23, 1994.
140 UPI, "Clyde Takes Issue," September 1, 1963.
141 AP, "New Probe of Utah Mine Tragedy Slated," *Racine Sunday Bulletin*, September 1, 1963.
142 "Moab Mine Safety," August 30, 1963.
143 Ibid.
144 AP, "Miner Rakes Lack," August 29, 1963.
145 "Moab Mine Safety," August 30, 1963.
146 Ibid.
147 Messerly, "Two Moab Miners," August 30, 1963.
148 Ibid.
149 AP, "Miner Rakes Lack," August 29, 1963.
150 Messerly, "Two Moab Miners," August 30, 1963.

Part Five
Chapter 18

1 "2 Survivors Return," August 29, 1963.
2 Mullins, et al., "Fresh Air Speeds," August 29, 1963.
3 Ibid.
4 Mullins, et al., "Fresh Air Speeds," August 29, 1963.
5 "2 Survivors Return," August 29, 1963.
6 "Wives, Kin Leaned," August 31, 1963.
7 Mullins, et al., "Fresh Air Speeds," August 29, 1963.
8 Ibid

9   "Maximum Rescue Effort Saved 5 Potash Miners—Last 10 Bodies Found," *Saskatoon StarPhoenix*, August 30, 1963.
10 Kisling, "Moab Rescue Delayed," August 29, 1963.
11 "Clyde Orders Moab Mine Blast Probe," *Salt Lake Tribune*, August 30, 1963.
12 "State Safety Inspections: 10 Listed in 27 Months," *Salt Lake Tribune*, August 30, 1963.
13 UPI, "Four Miners Died Earlier at Moab," *Troy Record*, September, 2, 1863.
14 "State Safety Inspections," August 30, 1963.
15 Ibid.
16 Joseph Lundstrom, "Probes Vowed in Mine Blast," *Deseret News*, August 30, 1963.
17 "State Safety Inspections," August 30, 1963.
18 Ibid.
19 "Mine's Pre-Blast," August 30, 1963.
20 Ibid.
21 Lundstrom, "Probes Vowed in Mine," August 30, 1963.
22 Ibid.
23 "Key Rescue Step: Flood of Life-Giving Air," *Salt Lake Tribune*, August 30, 1963.
24 Sorensen, "Silent Town Grieves," August 31, 1963.
25 "Key Rescue Step," August 30, 1963.
26 Ibid.
27 Ibid.
28 George Ferguson, Interview by author, East Carbon, UT, August 15. 1995.
29 Donald Blake Hanna, Interview by author, Vernal, UT, April 25, 2015.
30 Hospital Patient Records, Hanna, August 1963. Hanna checked back into the hospital at 5:00 p.m.
31 "Maximum Rescue Effort," August 30, 1963.
32 Reid G. Miller, "Seven Survive, 18 Dead in Utah's Mine Disaster," *Daily Sentinel*, August 30, 1963.
33 Westfield, Knill and Moschetti, *Final Report of Cane Creek Mine*, 22.
34 "Maximum Rescue Effort," August 30, 1963.

Chapter 19

1. Mullins, et al., "50-Hour Wait," August 30, 1963.
2. Duston Harvey and James Bapis, UPI, "What Happened Underground… Between Moab Blast and Rescue?" *Sunday Herald,* September 1, 1963.
3. Mullins, et al., "50-Hour Wait," August 30, 1963.
4. Newell, "Moab Miner Relates," September 5, 1963.
5. Mullins, et al., "50-Hour Wait," August 30, 1963.
6. "Joyful Whoops Greet Rescuers," *Deseret News,* August 30, 1963.
7. "Ex-Utahn Makes Disaster," August 31, 1963.
8. Westfield, Knill and Moschetti, *Final Report of Cane Creek Mine,* 22.
9. "Joyful Whoops Greet," August 30, 1963.
10. Newell, "Moab Miner Relates," September 5, 1963.
11. "Joyful Whoops Greet," August 30, 1963.
12. "It Was Smoky Dark," August 30, 1963.
13. Ibid.
14. Charles "C.C." Clark, Interview by author, Moab, UT, August 18, 1995.
15. UPI, "Waited, Drank Water," August 30, 1963.
16. AP, "18 Dead 7 Saved in Mine," *Brandon Sun,* August 30, 1963.
17. Mullins, et al., "50-Hour Wait," August 30, 1963.
18. Harvey and Bapis, UPI, "What Happened Underground?" September 1, 1963.
19. Mullins, et al., "50-Hour Wait," August 30, 1963.
20. Newell, "Moab Miner Relates," September 5, 1963.
21. Nokes, "Grieving Relatives Complain," August 30, 1963.
22. Mike Dowd, Telephone interview by author, July 12, 2016.
23. "They Waited, and Hoped," August 31, 1963.
24. Nokes, "Grieving Relatives Complain," August 30, 1963.
25. "5 More Rescued in Utah Mine, but 10 Others Are Found Dead," *New York Times,* August 30, 1963.
26. Ibid.
27. Reid G. Miller, "Yorkton Resident among Moab Victims," *Regina Leader-Post,* August 30, 1963.

Chapter 20

1. George A. Sorensen and Grant V. Messerly, "Moab Scene-Joy, Sorrow," *Salt Lake Tribune*, August 30, 1963.
2. George A. Sorensen and Grant V. Messerly, "Bodies Taken from 'Trap'," *Salt Lake Tribune*, August 30, 1963.
3. Duston Harvey, "5 More Utah Miners Saved; Search Ends," *Washington Post*, August 29, 1963.
4. "Maximum Rescue Effort," August 30, 1963.
5. Sorensen and Messerly, "Bodies Taken from 'Trap'," August 30, 1963.
6. "Joyful Whoops Greet," August 30, 1963.
7. Miller, "Smiling Survivors Okay," August 30, 1963.
8. Harvey, "5 More Utah Miners," August 29, 1963.
9. "Joyful Whoops Greet," August 30, 1963.
10. Ibid.
11. Sorensen and Messerly, "Moab Scene-Joy," August 30, 1963.
12. "Joy, Grief Mingle at Mine as Last Survivors Come Out," *Daily Sentinel*, August 30, 1963.
13. Sorensen and Messerly, "Moab Scene-Joy," August 30, 1963.
14. "They Waited, and Hoped," August 31, 1963.
15. "Wives, Kin Leaned on Confidence," *Deseret News*, August 31, 1963.
16. "Joyful Whoops Greet," August 30, 1963.
17. "Wives, Kin Leaned," August 31, 1963.
18. "Joy, Grief Mingle," August 30, 1963.
19. UPI, "Five More Rescued at Mine," *Nevada State Journal*, August 30, 1963.
20. Hospital Patient Records, Hanna, August 1963. Hanna returned to the hospital at 5:00 p.m.
21. Harvey, "5 More Utah Miners," August 29, 1963.
22. "Joyful Whoops Greet," August 30, 1963.
23. Paul McKinney, Interview by Pat McKinney, Armargosa Valley, NV, July 21, 1996.
24. Harvey, "5 More Utah Miners," August 29, 1963.
25. "Joyful Whoops Greet," August 30, 1963.
26. "Joy, Grief Mingle," August 30, 1963.

27 "Hospital Scene: Joy, Sorrow Greet Survivors," *Deseret News,*, August 31, 1963.
28 Carolyn Habbeshaw, "Joy, Despair Reflect in Faces of Kin, Scenes Happy, Sad," *Salt Lake Tribune*, August 30, 1963.
29 "Hospital Scene: Joy," August 31, 1963.
30 Habbeshaw, "Joy, Despair Reflect," August 30, 1963.
31 Ibid.
32 "Hospital Scene: Joy," August 31, 1963.
33 Ibid.
34 Nokes, "Grieving Relatives Complain," August 30, 1963.
35 "Wives, Kin Leaned," August 31, 1963.
36 Bonnie Rushton Wolverton, Telephone conversation with author, November 7, 2014.
37 "Afraid to Sleep, Despair, Tense Moab Held Hope," *Salt Lake Tribune*, August 30, 1963.
38 Ibid.
39 Ibid.
40 Ibid.
41 UPI, "Five More Rescued at Mine," August 30, 1963.
42 Ibid, 19.
43 Ibid.
44 Charles Byrge, Interview by author, Price, UT, November 23, 1994.

Chapter 21

1 Herve Roy, Telephone interview by author, April 14, 2014.
2 Ibid.
3 Sorensen and Messerly, "Bodies Taken from 'Trap'," August 30, 1963.
4 "Joy, Grief Mingle," August 30, 1963.
5 Ibid.
6 Irene Christensen Lemon, Interview by author, Moab, UT, August 17, 1995.
7 Nokes, "Grieving Relatives Complain," August 30, 1963.
8 Irene Christensen Lemon, Interview by author, Moab, UT, August 17, 1995.
9 "They Waited, and Hoped," August 31, 1963.
10 Sorensen and Messerly, "Bodies Taken from 'Trap'," August 30, 1963.

11 "Wives, Kin Leaned," August 31, 1963.
12 Steve Hale and Robert D. Mullins, "Moab Mine Blast Toll: 18 Men Killed, 7 Saved—5 Survivors Rescued after 50-Hour Wait," *Deseret News*, August 30, 1963.
13 UPI, "5 More Miners Saved in Utah; 18 Lives Lost; Federal Probe Ordered," *Long Beach Independent*, August 30, 1963.
14 Sorensen and Messerly, "Bodies Taken from 'Trap,'" August 30, 1963.
15 Harvey, "5 More Utah Miners," August 29, 1963.
16 "Terse, Grim Word: '...No Survivors'," *Salt Lake Tribune*, August 30, 1963.
17 Mrs. Bertha Snyder the mother of John Tinall, with her dog, Mitzie (photo caption), *Denver Post*, August 30, 1963.
18 "Terse, Grim Word," August 30, 1963.
19 UPI, "5 More Miners Saved," August 30, 1963.
20 "Joy, Grief Mingle," August 30, 1963.
21 Herve Roy, Telephone interview by author, April 14, 2014.
22 CP and AP, "But Names Didn't," August 30, 1963.
23 Dorothy LeBlanc McPhee, Correspondence with author, November 10, 2014.
24 Harris, "Mourning Victim, Miner," August 31, 1963.
25 Dorothy LeBlanc McPhee, Correspondence with author, November 10, 2014.
26 Dianne Johnson Zacherson, Telephone interview by author, July 12, 2016.
27 "Wives, Kin Leaned," August 31, 1963.
28 Duston Harvey, UPI, "Task Begins of Identifying Bodies Of Victims in Potash Mine Blast," *Daily Herald*, August 30, 1963.
29 Nokes, "Grieving Relatives Complain," August 30, 1963.
30 "Terse, Grim Word," August 30, 1963.
31 "Hospital Scene: Joy," August 31, 1963.
32 Ibid.
33 George Ferguson, Interview by author, East Carbon, UT, August 15, 1995.
34 Kymberly Mele, ""One Spark of Time," The Winter Quarters Mine Disaster, Part II," Bulletin; The Holmes Safety Association, July 2000, 16-23. http://www.holmessafety.org/wp-content/uploads/bulletins/july00.pdf See also

Part I; May/June 2000, 16-24. http://www.holmessafety.org/wp-content/uploads/bulletins/mayjun.pdf
35 Ibid.
36 Walter 'Wallie' Christman, Telephone interview by author, August 10, 1995.
37 George Ferguson, Interview by author, East Carbon, UT, August 15, 1995.
38 Ibid.
39 Ibid.
40 Grant V. Messerly, "Never Lost Hope, Survivor Says, Knew It Was 'a Matter of Time'," *Salt Lake Tribune,* August 30, 1963.
41 Ibid.
42 Miller, "Smiling Survivors Okay," August 30, 1963.
43 Messerly, "Never Lost Hope," August 30, 1963.
44 Hale and Mullins, "Moab Mine Blast Toll," August 30, 1963.
45 Miller, "Smiling Survivors Okay," August 30, 1963.
46 Messerly, "Never Lost Hope," August 30, 1963.
47 "Final Rescue Ends," August 30, 1963.
48 June, AP, "'I Heard This Man," August 30, 1963.
49 "Final Rescue Ends," August 30, 1963.
50 June, AP, "'I Heard This Man," August 30, 1963.
51 Messerly, "Never Lost Hope," August 30, 1963.
52 June, AP, "'I Heard This Man," August 30, 1963.
53 Messerly, "Never Lost Hope," August 30, 1963.
54 Paul McKinney, Interview by Pat McKinney, Armargosa Valley, NV, July 21, 1996.
55 Messerly, "Saved Miners Tell," August 31, 1963.
51 "It Was Smoky Dark," August 30, 1963.
52 Ibid.
53 Messerly, "Saved Miners Tell," August 31, 1963.
54 Messerly, "Never Lost Hope," August 30, 1963.
55 "It Was Smoky Dark," August 30, 1963.
56 AP, "What's Life Like," August 30, 1963.
57 Ibid.

58 Ibid.
59 Messerly, "Never Lost Hope," August 30, 1963.
60 "It Was Smoky Dark," August 30, 1963.
61 AP, "What's Life Like," August 30, 1963.
62 Ibid.
63 "It Was Smoky Dark," August 30, 1963.
64 UPI, "Waited, Drank Water," August 30, 1963.
65 Messerly, "Never Lost Hope," August 30, 1963.
66 Miller, "Smiling Survivors Okay," August 30, 1963.
67 Hale and Mullins, "Moab Mine Blast Toll," August 30, 1963.
68 Ibid.
69 AP, "18 Dead 7 Saved," August 30, 1963.
70 De Van L. Shumway, "Heroism of Hanna, McKinney Credited with Saving 5 Men," *Daily Herald*, August 30, 1963.
71 "3 Survivors Credited with Saving Others," *Deseret News*, August 30, 1963.
72 UPI, "Waited, Drank Water," August 30, 1963.
73 Shumway, "Heroism of Hanna, McKinney," August 30, 1963.

Chapter 22

1 UPI, "Bodies of Dead Moved to Makeshift Morgue," *Ogden Standard-Examiner*, August 30, 1963.
2 Ibid.
3 Hale and Mullins, "Moab Mine Blast Toll," August 30, 1963.
4 "Joy, Grief Mingle," August 30, 1963.
5 Miller, "Yorkton Resident among," August 30, 1963.
6 'Johnny Smoke' Palacios, Telephone interview by author, May 13, 2015.
7 Ibid.
8 George A. Sorensen, "Moab Shaken by Disaster," *Salt Lake Tribune*, August 31, 1963.
9 William C. Mudgett, AP, "New Potash Blast Theory Advanced," *Daily Sentinel*, August 31, 1963.
10 Sorensen and Messerly, "Moab Scene-Joy," August 30, 1963.
11 Helene Roy McGruthers, Email correspondence with author, April 3, 2015.

12 Tippie, "Letters to Editor," September 5, 1963.
13 UPI, "Bodies of Dead," August 30, 1963.
14 Sorensen, "Silent Town Grieves," August 31, 1963.
15 "Moon Phase Calculator," Stardate.org (accessed January 20, 2015), https://stardate.org/nightsky/moon
16 Any moon that appears more than half lighted but less than full is called a gibbous moon. The word gibbous comes from a root word that means hump-backed.
17 "They Waited, and Hoped," August 31, 1963.
18 Habbeshaw, "Families Huddle, Fight," August 30, 1963.
19 Sorensen, "Moab Shaken by Disaster," August 31, 1963.
20 "Moab Mine Shut Down to Await Investigation," *Washington Post,* August 31, 1963.
21 "Begin Identification of 18 Mine Victims; Repair Shop Turned to Makeshift Morgue," *Daily Plainsman,* August 30, 1963.

Aftermath
Chapter 23

1 "Carbon Coal Miners Strike," *Salt Lake Tribune,* August 31, 1963. The miners were represented by Louis Dalpiaz, president of Castle Gate Local 5916, and Harold W. Jewkes, president of Kenilworth Local 5861.
2 "Earlier Blast Unreported," September 2, 1963, Sec. B.
3 UPI, "Clyde Takes Issue," September 1, 1963.
4 William C. Mudgett; AP, "Gas Said Likely Explosion Cause-in Moab Mine," *Saskatoon StarPhoenix,* August 31, 1963.
5 Morris Worley, Interview by author, Carlsbad, NM, October 2, 2016.
6 Ibid, Table 1 & 2. Table 1, Composition of Mine Air Samples Taken At the Cane Creek Mine After Explosion on August 27, 1963, and Table 2, Representative Composition of Hydrocarbon Gases Reported as Total Hydrocarbons in Table 1.
7 Westfield, Knill and Moschetti, *Final Report of Cane Creek Mine,* 7.
8 Mudgett, AP, "New Potash Blast," August 31, 1963.
9 Ibid.

10 Morris Worley, Interview by author, Carlsbad, NM, October 2, 2016. As far as Morris Worley knew, Bill Smith never went down into a mine again.
11 Nokes, "Grieving Relatives Complain," August 30, 1963.
12 Miller, "Smiling Survivors Okay," August 30, 1963.
13 UPI, "Bodies of Dead," August 30, 1963.
14 UPI, "Identification of Dead Continues after Blast," Clipping, Newspaper Unknown.
15 Sorensen, "Silent Town Grieves," August 31, 1963. See Appendix A for more information.
16 Robert D. Mullins and Steve Hale, "Clean-Up Job Snags Moab Mine Probe—Families Preparing Victims' Final Rites," *Deseret News,* September 1, 1963.
17 Messerly, "Saved Miners Tell," August 31, 1963.
18 AP, "What's Life Like," August 30, 1963.
19 Sorensen, "Silent Town Grieves," August 31, 1963.
20 Mudgett; AP, "Gas Said Likely," August 31, 1963.
21 Kathleen M. Kowalski-Trakofler and Charles Vaught, "Psycho-Social Issues in Mine Emergencies: the Impact on the Individual, the Organization and the Community," *Minerals,* June 11, 2012, 136.
22 Tom Trueman said in a printed interview he was not going back underground. There is no way to verify this since he has not been located by the author.
23 AP and UPI, "Gas Suspected in Utah Mine Blast; Probe Near," *Ogden Standard-Examiner,* August 31, 1963.
24 Harvey and Bapis, UPI, "What Happened Underground?" September 1, 1963.
25 Messerly, "Saved Miners Tell," August 31, 1963.
26 Newell, "Moab Miner Relates," September 5, 1963.
27 Ibid.
28 Ibid.
29 Messerly, "Saved Miners Tell," August 31, 1963.
30 Ibid.
31 Newell, "Moab Miner Relates," September 5, 1963.
32 Ibid.

33 R. Greg Nokes, AP, "Order Closes Potash Mine Pending Blast Investigation; Gas Drives out Rescue Crew," *Lubbock Avalanche Journal*, August 31, 1963.
34 Messerly, "Saved Miners Tell," August 31, 1963.
35 Newell, "Moab Miner Relates," September 5, 1963.
36 Messerly, "Saved Miners Tell," August 31, 1963.
37 Newell, "Moab Miner Relates," September 5, 1963.
38 Messerly, "Saved Miners Relive," August 31, 1963.
39 Nokes, AP, "Order Closes Potash," August 31, 1963.
40 Messerly, "Saved Miners Relive," August 31, 1963.
41 "It Was Smoky Dark," August 30, 1963.
42 Messerly, "Saved Miners Tell," August 31, 1963.
43 "Kansan Tells Ordeal," August 30, 1963.
44 Ibid.
45 Messerly, "Saved Miners Tell," August 31, 1963.
46 UPI, "Seven Reach Safety," Clipping, Newspaper and Date Unknown.
47 AP, "What's Life Like," August 30, 1963.
48 Messerly, "Saved Miners Tell," August 31, 1963.
49 Ibid.
50 "Final Rescue Ends," August 30, 1963.
51 Ibid.
52 Messerly, "Saved Miners Tell," August 31, 1963.
53 Ibid.
54 Ibid.
55 Messerly, "Saved Miners Tell," August 31, 1963.
56 AP and UPI, "Gas Suspected in Utah," August 31, 1963.
57 Shumway, "Heroism of Hanna, McKinney," August 30, 1963.
58 AP and UPI, "Gas Suspected in Utah," August 31, 1963.
59 Messerly, "Saved Miners Tell," August 31, 1963.
60 "'No More Mine' Says Survivor of Moab Disaster," *Daily Herald*, September 2, 1963.
61 UPI, "Rescued Worker Will Not Return to Moab Mine," Clipping, Newspaper and Date Unknown.
62 "'No More Mine'," September 2, 1963.

63 UPI, "Rescued Worker Will Not Return to Moab Mine," Clipping, Date Unknown
64 AP and UPI, "Gas Suspected in Utah," August 31, 1963.
65 UPI, "Waited, Drank Water," August 30, 1963.
66 Messerly, "Saved Miners Tell," August 31, 1963.
67 Ibid.
68 UPI, "Waited, Drank Water," August 30, 1963.
69 "It Was Smoky Dark," August 30, 1963.
70 UPI, "Waited, Drank Water," August 30, 1963.
71 AP, "What's Life Like," August 30, 1963.
72 Ibid.
73 UPI, "Waited, Drank Water," August 30, 1963.
74 "It Was Smoky Dark," August 30, 1963.
75 UPI, "Waited, Drank Water," August 30, 1963.
76 "Utah Mine Tragedy Had Two Heroes," *Times Record,* August 30, 1963.
77 UPI, "Waited, Drank Water," August 30, 1963.
78 "It Was Smoky Dark," August 30, 1963.
79 AP, "What's Life Like," August 30, 1963.
80 "It Was Smoky Dark," August 30, 1963.
81 "Utah Mine Tragedy," August 30, 1963.
82 Charles Clark, Email correspondence with author, March 30, 2016.
83 Harvey and Bapis, UPI, "What Happened Underground?" September 1, 1963.
84 Charles Clark, Email correspondence with author, March 30, 2016.
85 Ibid.
86 Ibid.
87 Harvey and Bapis, UPI, "What Happened Underground?" September 1, 1963.
88 Charles Clark, Email correspondence with author, March 24, 2016.
89 Ibid.
90 Messerly, "Saved Miners Tell," August 31, 1963.
91 Ibid.
92 Harvey and Bapis, UPI, "What Happened Underground?" September 1, 1963.

93   Ibid.
94   Ibid.
95   Ibid.
96   Ibid.
97   Charles Clark, Email correspondence with author, March 24, 2016.
98   Ibid.
99   Messerly, "Saved Miners Tell," August 31, 1963.
100 Ibid.
101 Ibid.
102 Paul McKinney, Interview by Pat McKinney, Armargosa Valley, NV, July 21, 1996.
103 Ibid. McKinney was off work for 29 day recovering after surgery. The doctor cut out the damaged area on his backside and sewed him back together. He had an insurance policy at the time and didn't know until after the fact, that had he taken off 30 days it would have paid his wages. Since he went back to work after 29 days he didn't get anything out of the policy.
104 Ibid.
105 "They Waited, and Hoped," August 31, 1963.
106 Ibid.
107 Ibid.
108 "Terse, Grim Word," August 30, 1963.
109 Herve Roy is listed as 'Informant' on Rene Roy's death certificate.
110 Ibid.
111 Mick Gold, "Life & Life Only: Dylan at 60," *Judas! Magazine*, April 2002, 43. The lyrics to *'Blowin' in the Wind'* were written in 1962 by Bob Dylan to the melody of an old Negro spiritual, *'No More Auction Block.'* "Blowin' in the Wind' follows the same feeling. It was first recorded and released early in 1963 by Peter, Paul and Mary and then a month later by Bob Dylan.
112 Posted by "Anjan Chakraborty, "Blowing in the Wind Peter Paul n Mary," *YouTube.com,* July 26, 2013 (accessed April 10, 2015), https://www.youtube.com/watch?v=cuAl5cMTJ7A
113 Brian Naylor, "'Blowin' In the Wind' Still Asks the Hard Questions," *NPR.org* (accessed April 10, 2015), http://www.npr.org/2000/10/21/1112840/

blowin-in-the-wind This song had great significance for the civil rights movement and later, the anti-war movement and also has deep meaning for life in general.

114 Gold, "Life & Life Only," *Judas! Magazine*, April 2002, 43.
115 Lundstrom, "Probes Vowed in Mine," August 30, 1963.
116 Bernick, "'No Evidence of Laxity," August 31, 1963.
117 Ibid. The terms of the potash lease executed between Texas Gulf Sulphur Company and the U.S. Department of Interior provides procedures that should be followed as found in mining operating regulations of the USGS, Part II.
118 Ibid.
119 Ibid.
120 Donald Blake Hanna, Interview by author, Price, UT, November 24, 1994.
121 Herve Roy, Telephone interview by author, April 14, 2014.
122 Frank Hewlett, "U.S. Had 'No Controls' at Mine," *Salt Lake Tribune*, August 31, 1963.
123 Marlin J. Ankeny, Director of the U.S. Bureau of Mines and John M. Kelly, Assistant Secretary for Mineral Resources.
124 Ibid.
125 Sorensen, "Silent Town Grieves," August 31, 1963.
126 Bernick, "'No Evidence of Laxity," August 31, 1963.
127 Sorensen, "Moab Shaken by Disaster," August 31, 1963.
128 AP and UPI, "Gas Suspected in Utah," August 31, 1963.
129 Ibid.
130 Mullins and Hale, "Clean-Up Job Snags," September 1, 1963.
131 George A. Sorensen, "Laxity Charges, Denials Erupt over Mine Blast—Clyde Calls for Probe, Defends State's Role," *Salt Lake Tribune*, September 1, 1963.
132 Nokes, AP, "Order Closes Potash," August 31, 1963.
133 Ibid.
134 Ibid.
135 AP and UPI, "Gas Suspected in Utah," August 31, 1963.
136 Sorensen, "Laxity Charges, Denials Erupt," September 1, 1963.

Chapter 24

1. William C. Mudgett, "Second State Probe of Mine Revealed," *Daily Sentinel*, September 1, 1963.
2. Ibid.
3. Mullins and Hale, "Clean-Up Job Snags," September 1, 1963.
4. Ibid.
5. Sorensen, "Laxity Charges, Denials Erupt," September 1, 1963.
6. Ibid.
7. AP, "2d Utah Disaster Probe Set as Miners Demand More Safety," *Indianapolis Star*, September 1, 1963.
8. Sorensen, "Laxity Charges, Denials Erupt," September 1, 1963.
9. Harvey and Bapis, UPI, "What Happened Underground?" September 1, 1963.
10. AP, "FBI Tackles Moab Job," *Salt Lake Tribune*, August 31, 1963.
11. UPI, "Safety Practice Dispute Flares over Mine Blast," Clipping, Newspaper Unknown, September 1, 1963.
12. Sorensen, "Laxity Charges, Denials Erupt," September 1, 1963.
13. Mudgett, "Second State Probe," September 1, 1963.
14. Harry Snow, Telephone interview by author, Orangeville, UT, August 2, 1995.
15. AP, "2d Utah Disaster Probe," September 1, 1963.
16. Harry Snow, Telephone interview by author, Orangeville, UT, August 2, 1995.
17. "The Science of Fingerprints, Classification and Uses, by Federal Bureau of Investigation John Edgar Hoover, Director," The Project Gutenberg EBook #19022, 141 (accessed May 24, 2010), http://www.crime-scene-investigator.net/fbiscienceoffingerprints.html
18. Harry Snow, Telephone interview by author, Orangeville, UT, August 2, 1995.
19. Irene Christensen Lemon, Interview by author, Moab, UT, August 17, 1995.
20. Eudeene Hollinger, Interview by author, Moab, UT, August 17, 1995.
21. Ibid.
22. Mullins and Hale, "Clean-Up Job Snags," September 1, 1963.

23 Mudgett, "Second State Probe," September 1, 1963.
24 UPI, "Clyde Takes Issue," September 1, 1963.
25 AP and UPI, "Gas Suspected in Utah," August 31, 1963.
26 Ned Johnson, Telephone interview by author, February 23, 2015.
27 Westfield, Knill and Moschetti, *Final Report of Cane Creek Mine*, 22.
28 "Earlier Blast Unreported," September 2, 1963, Sec. B.
29 "Ex-Resident Here among Dead Miners," *Corpus Christi Caller Times*, August 31, 1963.
30 Sorensen, "Laxity Charges, Denials Erupt," September 1, 1963.
31 "Clyde Blasts Udall for Mine Stand—Tragedy Blame?" *Salt Lake Tribune*, September 1, 1963.
32 Ibid.
33 UPI, "Safety Practice Dispute Flares over Mine Blast," September 1, 1963.
34 UPI, "In Utah: Dispute after Disaster," *New York Harold Tribune*, September 1, 1963.
35 Ibid.
36 "Clyde Blasts Udall?" September 1, 1963.
37 Sorensen, "Laxity Charges, Denials Erupt," September 1, 1963.
38 "Clyde Blasts Udall?" September 1, 1963.
39 "Services Held Today for Victims of Mine," *Deseret News,*, September 2, 1963, Sec. B.
40 Minton-Chatwell Funeral Directors, "Faye Ollie Dendy Iker," m*inton-chatwell.com* (accessed February 17, 2017), http://www.mintonchatwell.com/services.asp?page=odetail&id=16150&locid=21 Bob Bobo's mother, Donna married Leonard Iker April 10, 1939.
41 "Funeral Rites Pending for 18 Victims of Explosion at Cane Creek Mine," *Deseret News*, August 31, 1963, Sec. B.
42 Kandace Cone Brynun, "Wayne Theodore Bobo," *ancrestry.com* (accessed February 17, 2017), http://person.ancestry.com/tree/83778544/person/38484872666/facts Bobo's father passed away in 1956 in Kentucky.
43 Ibid.
44 "Funeral Rites Pending," August 31, 1963, Sec. B.

45 "Lawrence I Davidson; Utah, Veterans with Federal Service Buried in Utah, Territorial to 1966," *FamilySearch.org* (accessed November 21, 2015), https://familysearch.org/ark:/61903/3:1:S3HY-6XMQ-YWY?wc=M6PD-F9Q%3A10 2553001%2C102906901%3Fcc%3D1542862&cc=1542862
46 "Funeral Rites Pending," August 31, 1963, Sec. B.
47 Ibid.
48 "Services Held Today," September 2, 1963, Sec. B.
49 Ibid.
50 "Fred Daniel Rowley, Fred Rowley's Life Story, Page 2" *FamilySearch.org* (accessed August 6, 2016) https://familysearch.org/photos/people/6294964
51 Ibid.
52 Jesse Clinton Kassler, *findagrave.com* (accessed January 22, 2015), http://www.findagrave.com/cgi-bin/fg.cgi?page=gr&GSln=Kassler&GSiman=1&GScid=641479&GRid=146817737&
53 "Ex-Resident Here," August 31, 1963.
54 Rita Kassler, Email correspondence with author, January 5, 2009.
55 "Ex-Resident Here," August 31, 1963.
56 "Services Held Today," September 2, 1963, Sec. B.
57 Lorraine Rushton, Telephone conversation with author, November 15, 1995.
58 "Funeral Rites Pending," August 31, 1963, Sec. B.
59 Martha Milton Dowd, Email correspondence with author, January 5, 2009.
60 Frank Moore, Email correspondence with author, January 5, 2009. See also Wikipedia contributors, "Battle of Guam," *Wikipedia.com* (accessed August 6, 2016) https://en.wikipedia.org/wiki/Battle_of_Guam_(1944)
61 Ibid.
62 "Services Being Held across Nation for Eighteen Mine Blast Victims," *Times-Independent*, September 5, 1963.
63 "Services Held Today," September 2, 1963, Sec. B.
64 "Funeral Rites Pending," August 31, 1963, Sec. B.
65 UPI, "Dad, Son Die Together in Potash Mine," *Daily Herald*, August 30, 1963.
66 Irene Christensen Lemon, Interview by author, Moab, UT, August 17, 1995.
67 Ibid.

68 UPI, "Dad, Son Die," August 30, 1963.
69 Madge Hollinger Rodman, Telephone interview by author, April 17, 2015.
70 Margo Christensen Jones, Email correspondence with author, January 4, 2009.
71 Ibid.
72 Irene Christensen Lemon, Interview by author, Moab, UT, August 17, 1995.
73 "Funeral Rites Pending," August 31, 1963, Sec. B.
74 Ibid.
75 Ibid.
76 Ibid.
77 Madge Hollinger Rodman, Telephone interview by author, Moab, Utah, April 17, 2015.
78 "Searchers Drop Hopes for Rescuing Bova," *Deseret News*, September 2, 1963.
79 AP, "Fellin, Throne to Leave Hospital; Bova Given Up," *Ogden Standard-Examiner*, September 3, 1963.
80 "Searchers Drop Hopes," September 2, 1963.
81 Ibid.

Chapter 25

1 "Probe Extended in Moab," September 5, 1963, Sec. B.
2 "Potash Firm Comments," September 5, 1963.
3 "Probe Extended in Moab," September 5, 1963, Sec. B.
4 Sorensen, "Silent Town Grieves," August 31, 1963.
5 Ibid.
6 "Area Residents Contribute to Growing Disaster Fund," *Times-Independent*, September 5, 1963.
7 Sorensen, "Silent Town Grieves," August 31, 1963.
8 Ibid.
9 "Area Residents Contribute," September 5, 1963.
10 Ibid.
11 Ibid.
12 George A. Sorensen, "Mine Puzzle—'the Pieces Fall in Place', Moab Tragedy Probers Press Analysis Today," *Salt Lake Tribune*, September 6, 1963, Sec. B.

13 Ibid.
14 Sorensen, "Mine Blast Inquiry," September 6, 1963.
15 "Money Comes from Afar for Disaster Fund," *Times-Independent,* October 10, 1963.
16 Ibid.
17 "Services Held Today," September 2, 1963, Sec. B.
18 Martha Milton Dowd, Email correspondence with author, January 5, 2009.
19 George A. Sorensen, "Mine Blast Inquiry Ponders Pro, Con," *Salt Lake Tribune,* September 6, 1963.
20 Peter Sviscsu's Death Certificate has Harrison International's man camp listed as his address.
21 "Services Being Held," September 5, 1963.
22 Sorensen, "Mine Blast Inquiry," September 6, 1963.
23 Donald Blake Hanna, Interview by author, Price, UT, November 24, 1994.
24 "Miners' Survivors Due Benefit Payment," *Deseret News,* November 7, 1963.
25 UK, Outward Passenger Lists, 1890-1960: *Ancestry.com,* Copy sent to author from Mary Ann McDonald, *McDonald Genealogy,* Lyman, Wyoming, April 13, 2013. The address given in the United Kingdom was Block 8, Room 12, Binley Road, Coventry, West Midlands, United Kingdom.
26 "Peter Sviscsu, Death Certificate," 1905-1965 Utah Death Certificate Index: Utah Division of Archives and Records Service, 1963.
27 Donald Blake Hanna, Interview by author, Price, UT, November 24, 1994.
28 "Vynohradiv, Ukraine," *Encyclopedia of Jewish Life before and During the Holocaust,* (2001), 663.
29 "Vynohradiv," *Internet Encyclopedia of Ukraine* (accessed May 15, 2016), http://www.encyclopediaofukraine.com/display.asp?linkpath=pages%5CV%5CY%5CVynohradiv.htm
30 Wikipedia contributors, "First Czechoslovak Republic," *Wikipedia, the Free Encyclopedia* (Accessed May 15, 2016), https://en.wikipedia.org/wiki/First_Czechoslovak_Republic
31 "Vynohradiv, Ukraine," JewishGen Kehilalinks (accessed May 14, 2016), http://www.kehilalinks.jewishgen.org/Vynohradiv/
32 "Looting," DEGOB National Committee for Attending Deportees (accessed May 15, 2016), http://degob.org/index.php?showarticle=2030

33   "Vynohradiv," *MEMIM Encyclopedia* (accessed May 15, 2016), http://memim.com/vynohradiv.html

34   Gyorgy Dupka, et, *Genocide, the Tragedy of the Hungarians of Transcarpathia*, (Budapest: Intermix Editions, 1993).

35   Peter Jambrek, et, *Crimes Committed by Totalitarian Regimes*, (Brussels: Slovenian Presidency of the Council of the European Union, 2008), 248.

36   "Gulag" is an acronym for Glavnoe Upravlenie Ispravitel'no-trudovykh Lagerei, which translates to "main administration of corrective labor camps."

37   Editors of Encyclopedia Britannica, "Gulag," *britannica.com* (Accessed May 4, 2017), https://www.britannica.com/place/Gulag

38   "Vynohradiv," *MEMIM Encyclopedia* (accessed May 15, 2016), http://memim.com/vynohradiv.html

39   Milada Polisenska, *Czechoslovak Diplomacy and the Gulag, 1945-1953*, English Translation ed. (New York: Central European University Press, 2015), 24.

40   Soviet citizens captured during the war were sent to the Gulags once released from German prisoners because of Stalin's belief that they "were influenced by hostile ideology and needed re-education."

41   Editors of Encyclopedia Britannica, "Gulag," *britannica.com*

42   Ibid.

43   Donald Blake Hanna, Interview by author, Price, UT, November 24, 1994.

44   Polisenska, *Czechoslovak Diplomacy and the Gulag, 1945-1953*, 117.

45   "Social Security Card Application for Pete Sviscsu," U.S. Social Security Administration, 1961. Copy of original application sent to author April 26, 2016.

46   Oleh Khalimonchuk, PhD., Email correspondence with author, March 10, 2017. (Along with the help of Jaroslav Marjan, a local historian in Vynohradiv, Ukraine.) Through the help of Dr. Oleh Khalimonchuk, an Associate Professor of Biochemistry at University of Nebraska-Lincoln.(who was born in Ukraine but has long since been a U.S. citizen), he was able to make contact with Jaroslav Marjan, a local historian in Vynohradiv, Ukraine. Marjan was able to research the family and supple additional information about Pete Sviscsu and also made contact with his family still living in Sevlus/Vynohradiv.

47 Ibid.
48 The Greek Catholic Church adhere to the Byzantine Liturgy Rite, used the Julian calendar and among other distinctions, its roots are traced back to early Christianity in the Medieval Slavic state of Ruthenia. The 9th-century mission of Saints Cyril and Methodius in Great Moravia had particular importance as their work was allowed the spread of worship in the Old Church Slavonic language. After World War II, church members and especially priests were also persecuted, and many of them were sent to the Gulag or were killed. See "Liquidation of the Ukrainian Greek Catholic Church," Territory of Terror, (accessed May 15, 2016), http://www.territoryterror.org.ua/en/history/1945-1953/ugcc-liquidation/
49 Oleh Khalimonchuk, PhD., Email correspondence with author, March 10, 2017. (Along with the help of Jaroslav Marjan, a local historian in Vynohradiv, Ukraine.) Pete's niece kindly provided two pictures from the family archive: a family photo from his sister's wedding, and a portrait photo of Pete in his twenties. See the Memorial page of the blog.
50 Ibid.
51 "Ukrainian Resistance Movement," Territory of Terror, (accessed May 15, 2016), http://www.territoryterror.org.ua/en/history/1939-1945/resistance-movement/
52 Oleh Khalimonchuk, PhD., Email correspondence with author, March 10, 2017. (Along with the help of Jaroslav Marjan, a local historian in Vynohradiv, Ukraine.)
53 Ibid.
54 Tamas Stark, "Malenki Robot" - Hungarian Forced Labourers in the Soviet Union (1944-1955)," (accessed March 28, 2017), file:///C:/Users/kymme/AppData/Local/Microsoft/Windows/INetCache/IE/2MR5IT53/155_stark.pdf
    See also "Malenkij Robot in Transcarpathia," The Roman Catholic Diocese of Mukachevo (accessed May 15, 2016), http://www.munkacs-diocese.org/en/index.php?option=com_content&view=article&id=26:malenkij-robot-in-transcarpathia&catid=1:news-2010&Itemid=1
55 Ibid.

56 Ibid.
57 Wikipedia contributors, "Alexander Dolgun," *Wikipedia, the Free Encyclopedia* (accessed May 15, 2016), https://en.wikipedia.org/wiki/Alexander_Dolgun
58 "Services Held Today," September 2, 1963, Sec. B.
59 "Funeral Rites Tuesday Honor Mine Victim," *Emery County Progress*, September 5, 1963.
60 Linda Fox Hansen, Email correspondence with author, January 5, .2009.
61 Ibid.
62 Linda Fox Hansen, Email correspondence with author, January 5, .2009.
63 "Services Held Today," September 2, 1963, Sec. B.
64 Tess Johnson, Interview by author, East Carbon, UT, August 15, 1995.
65 Tess Johnson, Interview by author, East Carbon, UT, August 15, 1995.
66 Ned Johnson, Telephone interview by author, February 23, 2015.
67 "Funeral Rites Pending," August 31, 1963, Sec. B.
68 Ibid.
69 Ibid.
70 "Services Being Held," September 5, 1963.
71 John 'Paul' Tinall, Telephone conversation with author, February 20, 2017.
72 "Funeral Rites Pending," August 31, 1963, Sec. B.
73 Ibid.
74 "U.S. World War II Navy Muster Rolls, 1938-1949; John Bowman Tinall," *Ancestry.com* (accessed on August 7, 2016) http://search.ancestry.com/cgi-bin/sse.dll?_phsrc=jNh88&_phstart=successSource&usePUBJs=true&db=navymuster&so=2&pcat=ROOT_CATEGORY&gss=angs-g&new=1&rank=1&msT=1&gsfn=John%20Bowman&gsln=Tinall&msbdy=&msddy=&msidy=&msydy=&_83004003-n_xcl=f&gskw=&uidh=&ssrc=pt_t%7B%7Bmodel.treePerson.treeId%7D%7D_p%7B%7Bmodel.treePerson.personId%7D%7D
75 "Funeral Rites Pending," August 31, 1963, Sec. B.
76 Wikipedia contributors, "USS Hermitage," *Wikipedia, The Free Encyclopedia* (accessed August 7, 2016) https://en.wikipedia.org/wiki/USS_Hermitage_(AP-54)
77 Cynthia Tinall, Telephone conversation with author, February 20, 2017. Jane's married name was Cody.

78 "Kathryn Jeanne "Kathy" Tinall," findagrave.com (accessed February 17, 2017), https://www.findagrave.com/cgi-bin/fg.cgi?page=gr&GRid=174787136&ref=acom

79 Cynthia Tinall, Correspondence with author, February 20, 2017.

80 "Funeral Rites Pending," August 31, 1963, Sec. B.

81 K, "William Huzil," *findagrave.com* (accessed November 1, 2015), http://www.findagrave.com/cgi-bin/fg.cgi?page=gr&GRid=102131940. See also Donna Eckhart, "Saskatchewan Cemeteries, Yorkton City Cemetery, Section D," *rootweb.ancestry.com* (accessed November 1, 2015), http://rootsweb.ancestry.com/%7Ecansacem/yorkton/D443.jpg

82 "Services for William Huzil Will Be Held in Yorkton, Saskatchewan, Canada," *Regina Leader-Post*, September 5, 1963.

83 Canadian Press, "Funeral Held for Mine Victim," *Saskatoon StarPhoenix*, September 10, 1963.

84 Audrey Huzil Clayton, Email correspondence with author, May 28, 2015.

85 Ibid.

86 Ibid.

87 Ibid.

88 "Former Workers Here," September 5, 1963.

89 Audrey Huzil Clayton, Email correspondence with author, May 28, 2015.

90 Geralyn LeBlanc, Email correspondence with author, April 11, 2016.

91 Geralyn LeBlanc, Email correspondence with author, April 11, 2016.

92 Dorothy LeBlanc McPhee, Correspondence with author, November 10, 2014..

93 William McLean, "Letters to the Editor," *Times-Independent*, September 19, 1963.

94 Geralyn LeBlanc, Email correspondence with author, April 11, 2016. Dorothy and her children were in Moab, Utah for the 50th Commemoration of the Cane Creek explosion, August 27, 2013.

95 Veterans Affairs Canada, "Canadians in Belgium 1944," *Veterans.gc.ca* (accessed January 3, 2015), http://www.veterans.gc.ca/eng/remembrance/history/second-world-war/canada-belgium

96 Marlene Roy, Email correspondence with author, April 5, 2016.

97 Helene Roy McGruthers, Email correspondence with author, April 1, 2015.

98 Marlene Roy, Email correspondence with author, April 5, 2016.
99 Helene Roy McGruthers, Email correspondence with author, April 1, 2015.
100 Ibid.
101 Ibid, The French word for grandmother.
102 Helene Roy McGruthers, Email correspondence with author, April 1, 2015.
103 Herve Roy, Telephone interview by author, April 14, 2014.
104 Ibid.
105 Marlene Roy, Email correspondence with author, April 5, 2016.
106 "Barber, Wesley Joseph (Obituary)," *Ottawa Journal*, September 5, 1963.
107 Ibid.
108 Linda Barber, Email correspondence with author, January 5, 2009.
109 Ibid.
110 Ibid.
111 Ibid.
112 George A. Sorensen, "Probe Sifts Mine Debris, Hunts Moab Blast Clues," *Salt Lake Tribune*, September 4, 1963.
113 Ibid, 8.
114 Ibid, Appendix G.
115 Sorensen, "Silent Town Grieves," August 31, 1963.
116 Sorensen, "Mine Puzzle—'the Pieces," September 6, 1963, Sec. B.
117 AP, "Probe of Moab Mine Blast Nearing Finish," *Ogden Standard-Examiner*, September 6, 1963.
118 Sorensen, "Mine Blast Inquiry," September 6, 1963.
119 Ibid.
120 Sorensen, "Mine Blast Inquiry," September 6, 1963.
121 Swenson, "Safety Rules Ignored," September 5, 1963, Sec. B.
122 Ibid.
123 Ibid.
124 Ibid.
125 Donald Blake Hanna, Conversation with author, Price, UT, May 3, 2016.
126 Swenson, "Safety Rules Ignored," September 5, 1963, Sec. B.
127 Ibid.
128 Ibid.
129 Donald Blake Hanna, Conversation with author, Price, UT, May 3, 2016.

130 Swenson, "Safety Rules Ignored," September 5, 1963, Sec. B.
131 Sorensen, "Mine Blast Inquiry," September 6, 1963.
132 Ibid.
133 Ibid.
134 Ibid.
135 Westfield, Knill and Moschetti, *Final Report of Cane Creek Mine*, 7.
136 Donald Blake Hanna, Interview by author, Price, UT, November 24, 1994.
137 Westfield, Knill and Moschetti, *Final Report of Cane Creek Mine*, 7.
138 Ibid, 17.
139 Ibid, 16-17.
140 Ibid.
141 Ibid.
142 Ibid, 8.
143 Ibid, 7.
144 Westfield, Knill and Moschetti, *Final Report of Cane Creek Mine*, 13.
145 Ibid, 13.
146 AP, "Cause of 18-Fatality Potash Mine Blast Still Obscure, Probers Say," *Ogden Standard-Examiner*, September 7, 1963.
147 George A. Sorensen, "Blast Cause Unknown, Probe over—Moab Tragedy," *Salt Lake Tribune*, September 7, 1963.
148 AP, "Cause of 18-Fatality," September 7, 1963.
149 Paul Swenson, "Mine Probe: Explosion Still Mystery," *Deseret News*, September 7, 1963, Sec. B.
150 Ibid.
151 Ibid.
152 Ibid.
153 Sorensen, "Mine Puzzle—'the Pieces," September 6, 1963, Sec. B.
154 "Probe Extended in Moab," September 5, 1963, Sec. B.
155 Sorensen, "Blast Cause Unknown," September 7, 1963.
156 AP, "Cause of 18-Fatality," September 7, 1963.
157 "Investigation of Potash Blast Ends, Cleanup Starts," *Times-Independent*, September 12, 1963.
158 "What Went Wrong at Moab," *Deseret News*, September 2, 1963.

Chapter 26

1. Swenson, "Mine Probe: Explosion," September 7, 1963, Sec. B.
2. Ibid.
3. Ibid.
4. "Stricter Rules Ordered at Utah Potash Mine at Moab," *Daily Herald*, September 12, 1963.
5. Ibid.
6. "Mine Bureau Airs Moab Data Today," *Salt Lake Tribune*, October 4, 1963, Sec. B.
7. Jack Kisling, "The Tragedy at Cane Creek," *Daily Sentinel*, October 13, 1963.
8. Ibid.
9. Westfield, Knill and Moschetti, *Final Report of Cane Creek Mine*, 27.
10. Kisling, "The Tragedy at Cane," October 13, 1963.
11. Westfield, Knill and Moschetti, *Final Report of Cane Creek Mine*, 3.
12. Ibid.
13. Ibid.
14. Ibid.
15. Westfield, Knill and Moschetti, *Final Report of Cane Creek Mine*, 8.
16. Charles Byrge, Interview by author, Price, UT, November 23, 1994. Also Donald Blake Hanna, Interview by author, Price, UT, November 24, 1994.
17. Ibid.
18. Kisling, "The Tragedy at Cane," October 13, 1963.
19. Steve Hale, "Report Tells Story of Mine Heroism," *Deseret News*, October 4, 1963, Sec. B.
20. Westfield, Knill and Moschetti, *Final Report of Cane Creek Mine*, 19.
21. Ibid.
22. Westfield, Knill and Moschetti, *Final Report of Cane Creek Mine*, 20.
23. Ibid.
24. Ibid.
25. Donald Blake Hanna, Interview by author, Vernal, UT, April 25, 2015.
26. 18.
27. Donald Blake Hanna, Interview by author, Vernal, UT, April 25, 2015. Also Paul McKinney, Telephone conversation with author, April 23, 2016.

28 Paul McKinney, Telephone conversation with author, April 23, 2016.
29 Ibid.
30 "Road to Potash Gets National Award Mention," *Times-Independent*, October 31, 1963.
31 Don Robinson, "Major Construction Underway at Potash," *Times-Independent*, October 24, 1963.
32 "Airport Master Plans Reviewed by F.A.A.," T*imes-Independent*, October 10, 1963.
33 "Charles Byrge Obituary," *Deseret News*, December 8, 2009, http://www.legacy.com/obituaries/deseretnews/obituary.aspx?n=chuck-byrge&pid=137018998
34 Charles Clark, Email correspondence with author, May 10, 2016.

Chapter 27

1 Jim Stiles, "Moab, Utah: November 22, 1963, It Was a Quiet Day When the World Turned Upside Down," *Canyon Country Zephyr* (accessed January 24, 2014), http://www.canyoncountryzephyr.com/oldzephyr/feb-march2003/nov1963.htm
2 "Potash Mine 'Curtain' Partially Completed, *Deseret News*, December 25, 1963. See also Don Robinson, "Survey Complete, Firing Set Now for February," *Times-Independent*, January 9, 1964.
3 "Frontier Loads 100 Passengers in Moab So Far This Year," *Times-Independent*, November 28, 1963.
4 "Homecoming Event Here Friday Listed as Top School Event," *Times-Independent*, October 31, 1963.
5 "High School Journalism Students Busy," *Times-Independent*, October 17, 1963.
6 "Legion and Auxiliary Host Boys, Girls State Attenders at Banquet," *Times-Independent*, October 31, 1963.
7 "Move to New High School Planned for Monday, Nov. 5.," *Times-Independent*, October 25, 1963.
8 "Moab Opens Cage Season Saturday," *Times-Independent*, November 28, 1963.
9 Rita Kassler, Email correspondence with author, January 5, 2009. Included in email was "Memories of Moab and the explosion" by David Kassler.
10 Rita Kassler, Email correspondence with author, January 5, 2009.

11 Wikipedia contributors, "John Ford," *Wikipedia, the Free Encyclopedia* (accessed January 21, 2015), https://en.wikipedia.org/wiki/John_Ford (February 1, 1894 – August 31, 1973) John Ford was an Irish-American film director, renowned both for Western films such as *Stagecoach* (1939), *The Searchers* (1956), and *The Man Who Shot Liberty Valance* (1962), as well as adaptations of classic 20th-century American novels such as the film *The Grapes of Wrath* (1940). One of the films for which he won the award, *How Green Was My Valley*, also won Best Picture. In a career that spanned more than 50 years, Ford directed more than 140 films and he is widely regarded as one of the most important and influential film-makers of his generation. Ford's work was held in high regard by his colleagues, with Orson Welles and Ingmar Bergman among those who have named him one of the greatest directors of all time. In 1966, *7 Women*, was the last feature film directed by Ford, ending a career that spanned approximately fifty years. Some of John Ford's films earned him four Academy Awards for Best Director in 1935, 1940, 1941, and 1952, which remain a record and made him one of America's true cinematic giants.

12 Tag Gallagher, *John Ford: The Man and His Films* (Berkeley, Los Angeles: University of California Press, 1986), 382.

13 Maxine Newell, "Cheyenne Autumn Company Enjoys Week-end in Moab with Traditional Location Party," *Times-Independent*, November 21, 1963.

14 "Filming Nears Completion Here," *Times-Independent*, November 21, 1963.

15 Jim Stiles, "Moab, Utah: November 22, 1963, It Was a Quiet Day When the World Turned Upside Down," *Canyon Country Zephyr* (accessed January 24, 2014), http://www.canyoncountryzephyr.com/oldzephyr/feb-march2003/nov1963.htm

16 Davis, *John Ford: Hollywood's*, 326.

17 "Moab Plays Host to Movie Group," *Times-Independent*, November 14, 1963.

18 Ibid.

19 "Filming Nears Completion," November 21, 1963.

20 "Movie Company People Found All Over Moab," *Times-Independent*, November 21, 1963.

21 "Movie & Western Memorabilia Museum at Red Cliffs Lodge," *moabhappenings.com* (accessed June 12, 2016), http://www.moabhappenings.com/

museum.htm. George White's Ranch is now the Red Cliffs Lodge, on the banks of the Colorado River northeast of Moab.

22 McBride, *Searching for John Ford*, 656.
23 Jim Stiles, "Moab, Utah: November 22, 1963, It Was a Quiet Day When the World Turned Upside Down," *Canyon Country Zephyr* (accessed January 24, 2014), http://www.canyoncountryzephyr.com/oldzephyr/feb-march2003/nov1963.htm
24 Ibid.
25 "Moab Joins Nation in Mourning Pres. Kennedy," *Times-Independent*, November 28, 1963.
26 Ibid.
27 Peter Bogdanovich, *Who the Hell's in It: Conversations with Hollywood's Legendary Actors* (New York: Ballantine Books, 2004), 232.
28 "Moab Joins Nation," November 28, 1963.
29 Ibid.
30 Ibid.
31 McBride, *Searching for John Ford*, 656.
32 "Moab Joins Nation," November 28, 1963.
33 Associated Press, *The Torch Is Passed: The Associated Press Story of the Death of a President* (New York: Western Printing & Lithographing Co., 1964), 79.
34 Larry McShane, "The Day America Watched a Son's Final Salute to Slain Father, JFK, as Nation Buried a Beloved Leader," *New York Daily News*, November 17, 2013 (accessed January 24, 2014), http://www.nydailynews.com/news/national/jfk-funeral-article-1.1514720
35 AP, *Torch Is Passed*, 79.
36 Ibid.
37 McShane, "America Watched a Son's Final Salute."
38 "50th Anniversary, the Death of a President, the Assassination of President John F. Kennedy, November 22, 1963, Captured by the AP," *AP.org* (accessed April 28, 2016), http://www.ap.org/explore/jfk-assassination
39 Ibid.
40 Margo Christensen Jones, Email correspondence with author, January 4, 2009.

41 Margo Christensen Jones, Email correspondence with author, January 4, 2009.
42 Peggy Bobo Cone, Electronic communications with author, February 17, 2017.
43 Jimerson-Lipsey Funeral Home, "Donna Wright," jimerson-lipsey.com (accessed February 17, 2017), http://www.jimerson-lipsey.com/mobile/obituaries-details.cfm?o_id=433052&fh_id=10709
44 "Moab Couple Married Saturday in Impressive Church Rites," *Times-Independent*, March 12, 1964, 8.
45 Madge Hollinger Rodman, Telephone interview by author, Moab, Utah, April 17, 2015.
46
47 Office of the Clerk, United States Courthouse, Salt Lake City, Utah: Civil Court Docket, United States District Court, District of Utah, Location #8NN 89-23, Case #C48-64, filed 1964. U.S.; National Archives Center; District Judge Willis W. Ritter assigned the case. A *third-party defendant*: is a party brought into a lawsuit as a defendant by the original defendants.
48 Westfield, Knill and Moschetti, *Final Report of Cane Creek Mine*, Appendix D. Peter Sviscsu, one of the 18 miners killed, had no dependents.
49 "Victims' Kin File Suit in Mine Deaths," *Salt Lake Tribune*, March 7, 1964.
50 "Miners' Families Accept $1,312,000 Settlement," *Salt Lake Tribune*, November 30, 1965.
51 Inflation Calculator, *Dave Manuel.com* (accessed September 26, 2015), http://www.davemanuel.com/inflation-calculator.php?theyear=1873&amountmoney=7000000.
52 Paul McKinney, Telephone interview by author, June 23, 2015.
53 "Miners' Families Accept," November 30, 1965, 8. Note: Plaintiffs in the suit were: Opal J. Davidson and 3 children, Moab; Mrs. Ina Milton and 2 children, Moab; Mrs. Lois L. Rushton and 3 children, Lehi; Mrs. Alice Barber and 2 children, Ottawa, Ontario; Mrs. Mildred L. Kassler and 3 children, Lakeland, Florida.; Mrs. William Huzil and 4 children, Yorkton, Saskatchewan; Mrs. Mary Lynn Schear and Child, Durango, Colorado; Mrs.

Jessie Roy and 6 children, North Bay, Ontario; Mrs. Dorothy LeBlanc and 3 children, Riverside, Ontario; Mrs. Jessie Tinall, Rocklin, California; Mrs. Tess Johnson and 4 children, Price; Mrs. Eudeene Hollinger and 3 children, Moab; Mrs. Harriet A. Rowley and 5 children, Price; Mrs. Alice B. Fox and 2 children, Price; Mrs. Irene P. Christensen and 4 children, Price; Mrs. Margo G. Christensen and child, Price, and Mrs. Donna Hill, formerly Mrs. Robert Bobo, and 3 children, Wichita Falls, Texas.

54 Donald Blake Hanna, Interview by author, Vernal, UT, April 25, 2015.
55 "History of Mine Safety and Health Legislation." MSHA.gov (Accessed May 4, 2016), https://arlweb.msha.gov/mshainfo/mshainf2.htm
56 Ibid.
57 Walter Trohan, "Mine Safety Act Not a Cure-All," *Chicago Tribune,* April 28, 1971.
58 Ward Sinclair, "U.S. Bureau of Mines Fires Veteran Westfield from Job as Chief of Inspectors," *Courier-Journal,* April 2, 1971.
59 Ibid.
60 AP, "Mine Safety Expert Replaced," *The Derrick,* April 3, 1971.
61
62 "James Westfield (Obituary)," Sun Advocate, October 14, 1976.
63 Gary Christensen, telephone conversation, July 31, 2017.
64 "Milestones Mark TGS," January 14, 1965.
65 Ibid.
66 Don Robinson, "Shaft Curtainwall Completed at T.G.S.," *Times-Independent,* December 26, 1963.
67 "Milestones Mark TGS," January 14, 1965.
68 "Moab Has Weathered Many a Rugged Storm; Keeps Growing Despite Temporary Setbacks," *Times-Independent,* December 29, 1966.
69 Ibid.
70 "Arches National Park," *The National Parks: Index 2009-2011,* National Park Service, Archived from the original, June 29, 2011.
71 "TGS Begins Production of Potash; First Boxcar Loaded at Plant Site," *Times-Independent,* January 14, 1965.

72 Ibid.
73 "Morrison-Knudsen to Build," July 27, 1961.
74 "TGS Begins Production," January 14, 1965.
75 Ibid.
76 Ibid.
77 Margie Phillips, "Cane Creek Mine Solution Mining Project, Moab Potash Operations, Texasgulf, Inc.," *Four Corners Geological Society Guidebook*, 8th Field Conference, Canyonlands Country, 1975, 261–62.
78 Daniel Jackson, Jr., "Solution Mining Pumps New Life into Cane Creek Potash Mine," *Engineering Mining Journal*, July 1973, 59-69.
79 Colleen Whitley, ed. and Philip F. Notarianni, *From the Ground Up, the History of Mining in Utah* (Logan: Utah State University Press, 2006), 123.
80 Peter W. Huntoon, "Incredible Tale of Texasgulf Well 7 and Fracture Permeability, Paradox Basin, Utah," *Ground Water*, Vol. 24, No. 5, September 1986, 644. https://booksc.unblocked.video/book/10006676
81 Ibid, 646.
82 Ibid, 650.
83 Ibid, 646.
84 Ibid, 650.
85 Ibid, 651.
86 Ibid, 643.
87 Rick York, Email correspondence with author, January 17, 2017.

Chapter 28

1 "Tragedy Toll 30th Worst," *Salt Lake Tribune*, August 31, 1963.
2 Ibid.
3 Lucas, *Men in Crisis*, 16.
4 Ibid.
5 "To Make Mining Safer," *Deseret News*, October 5, 1963, 14. (Author Unknown)
6 Ibid.
7 Don Reed, UPI, "Mine Inspector Says 99% of Accidents Preventable," *Sunday Herald*, September 1, 1963.

8   Kisling, "The Tragedy at Cane," October 13, 1963.
9   Helene Roy McGruthers, Email correspondence with author, April 3, 2015.
10 Bernick, "'Petroleum Gas Blast," August 29, 1963.

www.ingramcontent.com/pod-product-compliance
Lightning Source LLC
Chambersburg PA
CBHW060357230426
43663CB00008B/1304